AF505458

PICASSO

KUNSTHAUS ZÜRICH
PABLO PICASSO
11. SEPT. – 30. OKT.
TÄGLICH GEÖFFNET 10–12 UND 2–5 UHR • MONTAGS GESCHLOSSEN

PICASSO

By Picasso
HIS FIRST MUSEUM EXHIBITION 1932

Tobia Bezzola

With contributions by Simonetta Fraquelli,
Christian Geelhaar and Michael FitzGerald

KUNSTHAUS ZÜRICH

PRESTEL
Munich · Berlin · London · New York

LENDERS

The exhibition and accompanying publications would not have been possible without the support and help of many persons within and outside the Kunsthaus Zürich. We owe a particular debt of gratitude to Claude Ruiz Picasso, Bernard Ruiz Picasso and Diane Widmaier Picasso, who have supported our project from the outset. We are also greatly obliged to the lenders, whose generosity made it possible for the exhibition to take place. We would like to make special mention of those colleagues at great institutions who have entrusted many works to us: Bernhard Mendes Bürgi and Nina Zimmer, Kunstmuseum Basel; Sir Nicholas Serota and Matthew Gale, Tate, London; Glenn D. Lowry and Cora Rosevear, The Museum of Modern Art, New York; Thomas Campbell and Gary Tinterow, The Metropolitan Museum of Art, New York; Richard Armstrong and Susan Davidson, The Solomon R. Guggenheim Museum, New York; Alfred Pacquement, Musée National d'Art Moderne, Centre Pompidou, Paris. Our sincere thanks are also due to Helly Nahmad in London for his most generous loans and to William Acquavella and Paul Gray for their invaluable assistance.

University of Michigan Museum of Art, Ann Arbor
The Baltimore Museum of Art
Museu Picasso, Barcelona
Kunstmuseum Basel
The Art Institute of Chicago
Cincinnati Art Museum
Detroit Institute of Arts
Kunstsammlung Nordrhein-Westfalen, Düsseldorf
Galérie Patrick Cramer
Museum Ludwig Köln
Ohara Museum of Art
Helly Nahmad Gallery, London
Tate, London
Los Angeles County Museum of Art
Private collection, Courtesy Fundación Almine y Bernard Ruiz-Picasso para el Arte, Madrid
Museo Thyssen-Bornemisza, Madrid
Museo Picasso, Málaga
Merzbacher Kunststiftung
Aichi Prefectural Museum of Art, Nagoya
Solomon R. Guggenheim Museum, New York
The Metropolitan Museum of Art, New York
The Morgan Library & Museum
The Museum of Modern Art, New York
The Steven and Alexandra Cohen Collection
Musée National d'Art Moderne, Centre Pompidou, Paris
Musée de l'Orangerie, Paris, Collection Jean Walter et Paul Guillaume
Philadelphia Museum of Art
Saint Louis Art Museum
Kawamura Memorial Museum of Art, Sakura
Fondation Beyeler, Riehen/Basel
Moderna Museet, Stockholm
Staatsgalerie Stuttgart
Tehran Museum of Contemporary Art
Musée Jenisch, Vevey
National Gallery of Art, Washington
Albertina, Vienna
Kunstmuseum Winterthur
Bollag Galleries, Zurich
Foundation E.G. Bührle Collection
Private collection. Courtesy Thomas Ammann Fine Art AG Zurich
museum of design zurich, poster collection

And all lenders who wish to remain anonymous

SPECIAL THANKS

We are grateful to numerous individuals for providing us with information, contacts, suggestions and support. Particular thanks go to:

Marion Ackermann
Marilynn Alsdorf
Doris Ammann
Dany Ardouin
Richard Armstrong
Sebastiano Barassi
Stephanie Barron
Graham W.J. Beal
Brent R. Benjamin
Aaron Betsky
Ernst Beyeler †
Beno Blumenstein
Doreen Bolge
Arlette Bollag and Toni Hutmacher
Wolfgang Bortlik
Emily Braun
Emmanuel Bréon
Janet F. Briner
Philippe Büttner
Aisling Byrne
Olivier Camu
Guy Cogeval
Steven and Alexandra Cohen
Caroline Collier
Alessia Contin
Patrick Cramer
James Cuno
Anne d'Harnoncourt †
Angela Denier
Casimiro Di Crescenzo
Ralph J. Dosch
Ann Dumas
Jean Edmonson
Isabelle Edwards
Christoph Eggenberger
John Elderfield
Hans Erni
Andrew Fabricant
Julia Feldman
Evelyne Ferlay
Michael Findlay
Olivier Fink
Jay M. Fisher
Manuel Fontán del Junto
Michael Foster
Georg Frei
Hanny Fries †
Martin Gasser
Adrian Glew
Lukas Gloor
Elizabeth Gorayeb
Michael Govan
Paul Gray
William M. Griswold
Charlotte Gutzwiller
Marla H. Hand
Sanford Heller
Gottfried Honegger

Cynthia Iavarone
Motoko Ikeda
Florence Isler-Gächter
Samuel Keller
Kasper König
Eberhard W. Kornfeld
Dorothy Kosinski
Nina Kronauer-Kohler
Elizabeth Kujawski
Angela Lampe
Paul Lang
Benedict Leca
Josie Lerch
Livia Leu Agosti
Ken'ichiro Makino
Elisa Maldonado
Eloise W. Martin
Caroline Mathieu
Marilyn McCully
Werner and Gabrielle Merzbacher
Sabine Münzenmaier
Masahi Nakajima
Lars Nittve
Maja Oeri
Halina Pichit
Christine Pinault
Joachim Pissarro
Jacques Plancherel
Earl A. Powell III
Mira Preisig
Christian Pudelko
Dominique Radrizzani
Sean Rainbird
Romana Revel
Bettina Richter
Joseph Rosa
Elaine Rosenberg
Jason Rosenfeld
Angela Rosengart
Katy Rothkopf
James Roundell
Almine and Bernard Ruiz Picasso
Linda Schädler
Michael Schmid
Manuel Schmit
Klaus Albrecht Schröder
Claudia Schuh
Dieter Schwarz
Anne-Marie Schweingruber-Geelhaar
Pepe Serra
Mahmood Shalooei
Guillermo Solana
Nancy Spector
Barbara Stadler
José Lebrero Stals
Chikako Takaoka
Shuji Takashina
Michael Taylor
Ann Temkin
Ladina Tschander
Sylvie Vautier
Suzanne Waldvogel-Hürzeler-Erb
Oliver Wick

CONTENTS

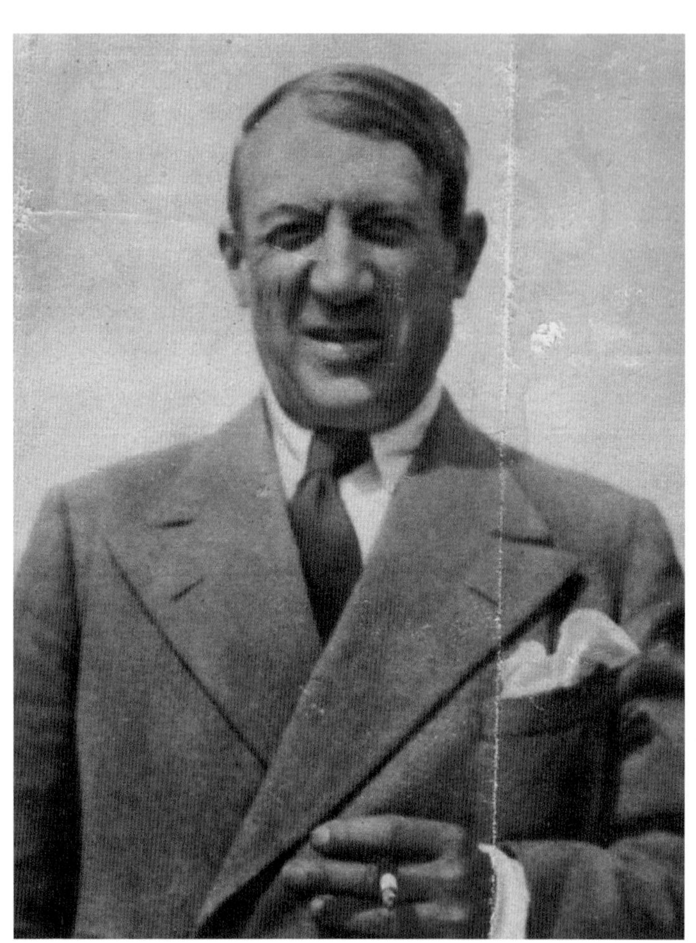

SPONSOR'S FOREWORD

Pablo Picasso is regarded by many as the most important artist of the twentieth century. His work is both multi-faceted and revolutionary.

The Picasso retrospective held in Zurich in 1932 was ground-breaking for several reasons — not least because the artist himself selected the artworks. By paying homage to this significant event in art history, the Kunsthaus Zürich emphasises, in its jubilee year, its long-standing commitment and openness towards avant-garde movements.

Thanks to the perseverance, excellent international relations and outstanding reputation of the Kunsthaus, the very first museum retrospective of this artistic genius can be shown once again in a concentrated form in the Kunsthaus Zürich. Loans from major private collections and the world's great museums make it possible for visitors to experience the myth of Picasso through his paintings.

As the long-term partner of the Kunsthaus Zürich, Credit Suisse is delighted to contribute to the staging of this remarkable exhibition and, at the same time, congratulates the Kunsthaus Zürich on its hundredth anniversary!

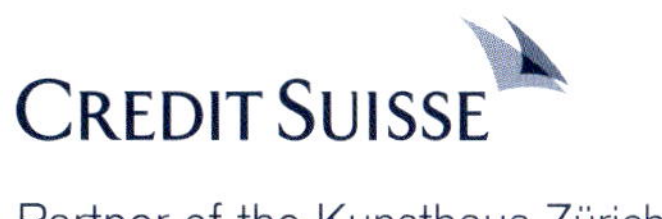

Partner of the Kunsthaus Zürich

FOREWORD

Have you ever heard of Picasso!? Today this sounds like a ridiculous question to ask. Every schoolchild knows the name, and the public, not just museum-goers, associates it with paintings by the most famous artist of the twentieth century; as if, even decades after his death, his name were synonymous with modern art itself. Our exhibition has a simple but ambitious aim: to celebrate the reunion of some of Picasso's finest works that were presented originally at the Kunsthaus Zürich, in his very first museum exhibition in 1932. This is not a nostalgic undertaking. Many of the works that some eighty years ago were received with great enthusiasm now belong to the canon of modern art and Picasso's art, perhaps more than that of any other artist of the twentieth century, has remained astonishingly modern.

The 1932 exhibition was remarkable. The entire upper floor of the Kunsthaus, which had opened in 1910 and which had been designed and extended by the architect Karl Moser in 1925, was emptied; the collection was placed in storage, and the stage was set. Two hundred and forty metres of wall space was freed, and several sections of the walls were clad in white cloth. Curtains up for an epoch-making project! The origins of the project were somewhat unusual, however. Wilhelm Wartmann, the Kunsthaus's first director, following a suggestion of the collector Emil Friedrich-Jezler, had proposed initially an exhibition of the triumvirate of modern art: Picasso, Braque and Léger. The Paris-based artist Carl Montag was to act as intermediary between Paris and Zurich, as he had already done for the Bonnard-Vuillard exhibition of 1932. This catalogue relates in detail how Wartmann and the Kunsthaus upstaged their rivals, the Museum of Modern Art in New York and the Kunsthalle Basel, by deciding to bring to Zurich an extended version of the retrospective held in the Galeries Georges Petit in Paris which was selected by Picasso and his dealers Paul Rosenberg and Georges Wildenstein.

The exhibition was due to stay open for four weeks; in the end it ran for six. Thirty-three thousand visitors came, a moderate figure by today's standards but a sensation at the time, for all those involved, not only for Wilhelm Wartmann.

Looking back at the numerous projects that have been presented at the museum over years, one could say that the Picasso exhibition was "typical of the Kunsthaus": a mixture of caution and boldness, of down-to-earth yet cosmopolitan attitudes, of discretion, of wait-and-see balanced with swift action and a marked commitment to contemporary art. Above all, the public has always embraced our endeavours enthusiastically. What more could a museum desire? This is why, on its hundredth birthday, the Kunsthaus Zürich can look to the future with optimism. One hundred years on, Moser's building remains both beautiful and functional. However, if everything goes to plan (and there are several incorrigible optimists at the Kunsthaus who believe it will), the Moser ensemble will be enhanced by more than a mere architectural extension: with the proposed new building by David Chipperfield, the Kunsthaus will take a giant leap forward, providing its collections of Impressionist, modern and contemporary art with a new state-of-the-art home.

Tobia Bezzola has organised the exhibition, and we thank him for this curatorial achievement. All the works in the current exhibition were displayed here in 1932 — with the small difference that today they belong to some of the world's great collections and, if they were to come onto the market, they would fetch dizzy prices. With the assistance of Simonetta Fraquelli, Tobia Bezzola has succeeded in reuniting some seventy masterpieces. To achieve this they have been able to rely on the support of many colleagues around the world.

In her catalogue essay Simonetta Fraquelli analyses the exhibition held at the Galeries Georges Petit in Paris in the summer of 1932. We are indebted to Michael FitzGerald, a leading Picasso scholar, for his essay that considers the Zurich retrospective in the light of Picasso's subsequent career. We would also like to thank Frau Annemarie Schweingruber-Geelhaar for her kind permission to reprint the chapter dedicated to the Zurich exhibition from the authoritative book originally published in 1993 by her prematurely deceased brother Christian Geelhaar.

We particularly thank all those private collectors and public institutions who have so generously entrusted us with their treasured works. We encountered receptive eyes and ears, and were gratified at the success met by our — by no means modest — requests for major works, even though we were surprised that the Musée Picasso in Paris was not willing to participate in our project. Nevertheless, thanks to forward planning and intense work, our purpose has been achieved. We are indebted to all our colleagues within the Kunsthaus for bringing this auspicious project to fruition. I would especially like to mention Esther Braun-Kalberer, who supported the ambitious undertaking with great efficiency and managed the complex loan transactions with the utmost calm and professionalism; she took on the task of collating the reconstruction of the documentary material for the exhibition of 1932; she edited the trilingual catalogue, and kept a good-humoured eye at all times on the myriad details that are essential to the success of such a large project. Julia Burckhardt Bild immersed herself with great commitment in scholarly research. Transport and complicated questions of insurance were in the experienced hands of Gerda Kram. And Franziska Lentzsch helped behind the scenes with many of the organisational tasks. My sincere thanks for this remarkable achievement go to them all.

Credit Suisse, partner of the Kunsthaus Zürich, has taken this jubilee exhibition under its wing, and we are most grateful to have the support of this institution for our historic project. We would like to thank the management board and all those who have worked so energetically to make the exhibition happen, especially Mira Song and Susanne Reisacher of Credit Suisse and Monique Spaeti of the Kunsthaus. The Truus and Gerrit van Riemsdijk Foundation spontaneously contributed a considerable sum, and we would like to express our delight and our thanks to the members of its Board.

Unlike in many other countries, there is no state indemnity in Switzerland for such major exhibition projects. Despite this we have been able to present numerous high value works thanks to the cooperation between the Kunsthaus and internationally renowned insurance companies. It is well known that Picasso's early works in particular are sold on the art market at extremely high prices. One hundred million dollars or more is not out of the ordinary, and if such valuable cultural treasures have to be insured for an exhibition, the sum to be paid in premiums adds up to a truly sobering figure for the organising venue. We are extremely grateful that Kuhn & Bülow GmbH, especially Sandra Aebersold, as well as the Zürich Versicherungsgesellschaft together with the Swiss Re have made an extra effort to support the project, and by increasing the sum insured have made it possible for us to show all the desired works in Zurich. The most famous exhibition at the Kunsthaus has finally turned into the most expensive — but it has been worthwhile, as even a cursory look through this catalogue will attest. We are delighted to be able to present this exhibition to all the people of Zurich and all our visitors as a birthday gift for the hundredth anniversary of the Kunsthaus!

Christoph Becker

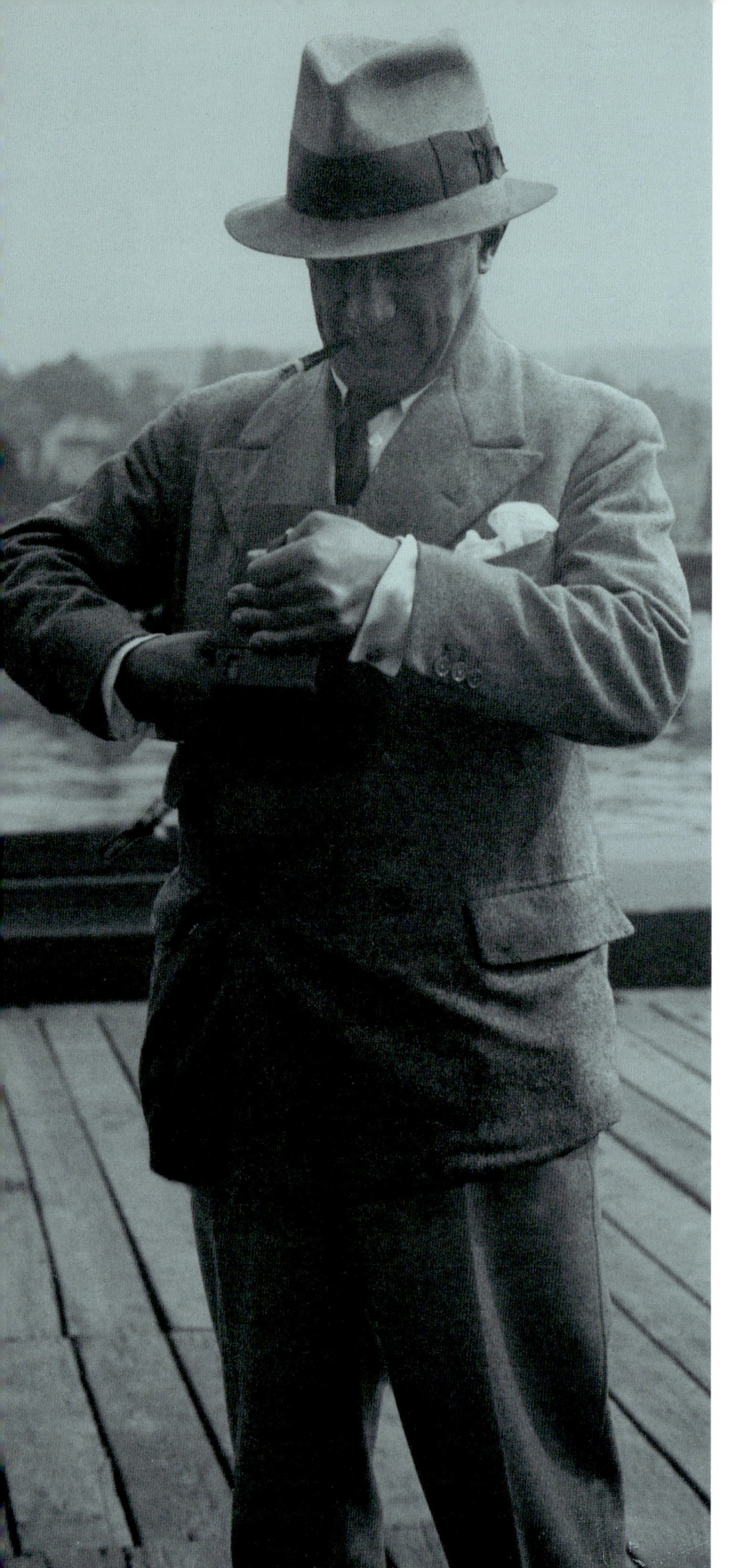

Tobia Bezzola

A RETROSPECTIVE IN RETROSPECTIVE — ABOUT THE EXHIBITION(S)

Pablo Picasso's first great retrospective in a museum took place in the Kunsthaus Zürich in autumn 1932; to mark its 100th anniversary that same institution is making the same event the subject of an exhibition. We do not wish this to be seen as a sheer gesture of self-congratulation: apart from the exhibition itself, the project also illuminates the historical circumstances that made this scoop possible. Today it is taken for granted that museum retrospectives are devoted to living artists. However, a system had first to be established in the course of the twentieth century that permitted the interests of artists, art dealers, collectors and those responsible for museums to be combined in such events. The institutional pole around which this system revolves is usually known today as a 'museum of contemporary art'. Interest in the Picasso exhibition of 1932 thus goes beyond interest in the artist himself and the history of the reception of his work. This exhibition may have been one of the very first events of a kind that today dominates the programmes of museums worldwide: a big retrospective of work by a living artist, conceived and organised by the museum in close cooperation with the artist, his dealers and his collectors.

In comparison with monographic or thematic art history, a survey of the history of exhibitions has the advantage of putting the spotlight on the web of social, political, psychological and economic pre-requisites that make it possible for an artist to have his work communicated to other artists, critics, collectors, institutions, the public and the mass media by means of public presentation.

Today it will hardly come as a shock — not only for those who are familiar with the customs of the art business — when we state here from the outset that the staging of the exhibition of 1932 was not primarily dependent on the Kunsthaus Zürich and its director Wilhelm Wartmann.[1]

◀

Picasso on Lake Zurich, 1932

On the contrary: in 1926 Wartmann had already tried to bring about a major Picasso exhibition. In doing so, however, like his colleague Wilhelm Barth, director of the Kunsthalle Basel, he had quickly come to the conclusion that such a project was entirely dependent on the plans of the artist and his main dealer, Paul Rosenberg.[2] To this day the makers of exhibitions have to be opportunists. Admittedly, for this exhibition Zurich was indebted to Wartmann and the Kunsthaus, which decisively seized the opportunity that arose in 1932; however, the real initiative throughout emanated from Picasso and the Galerie Rosenberg. And ultimately Zurich even owed its exhibition to Henri Matisse, whose first retrospective at Galeries Georges Petit in summer 1931 had aroused Picasso's ambition.[3] To surpass and trump his colleague — that was Picasso's motivation for involvement in an exhibition that consumed so much time and energy. The global depression was the second decisive factor. By the early 1930s it had practically brought the international art trade to a standstill, forcing the galleries Bernheim, Rosenberg and Wildenstein, which were actually competitors, to cooperate. This was the pre-requisite for both exhibitions, that of Matisse and that of Picasso.[4]

All those involved were aware of this from the beginning. Thanks to its constitution as a private art association, the Kunsthaus Zürich was a rare example of a museum that was able to sell works direct from its exhibitions. In January 1932 the collector Emil Friedrich-Jezler, the true initiator of the Zurich Picasso project, first wrote to the painter Carl Montag, who was to act as an agent in Paris for the Kunsthaus. Picasso himself was not mentioned in the letter. Instead it notes that the "planned exhibition is to take place with the participation of the companies P. Rosenberg and Wildenstein and of Dr Reber."[5] Friedrich knew that the prospects of immediate sales were gloomy in Zurich too, but he instructed Carl Montag how he should gain support in Paris for the plan to hold an exhibition in Zurich: "Even if the material rewards for the exhibiting companies may perhaps not take immediate effect, it should be possible to establish a solid basis of relationships and possible contacts."[6]

If surprise was expressed about why Picasso's retrospective should be presented in the Kunsthaus Zürich in 1932, then the question that arises is: where else? At that time Alfred Barr was also attempting to gain a Picasso retrospective for his New York Museum of Modern Art, which was just three years old. However, he felt the offer of taking over an exhibition conceived by the artist and dealers to be a compromising affront that was detrimental to his prestige.[7] Wilhelm Wartmann, by contrast, already had more than twenty years of experience with exhibitions of contemporary art. He had a realistic view of the situation and gave the opportunity to stage a unique exhibition, which might not recur, priority over curatorial niceties.

Few alternatives remained to Picasso and his dealers. British, Spanish and Italian museums did not exhibit and purchase contemporary art. Only in Germany would there have been suitable institutions. Indeed, Wartmann's correspondence reveals that Picasso would have been interested in a third venue:[8] "... if Berlin had been an option." However, the Nationalgalerie in Berlin was not an option in autumn 1932, in the middle of an aggressive Nazi election campaign; its director, Ludwig Justi, was removed from office in early 1933 immediately after the Nazis seized power.

It should however also be noted that in Switzerland the ground had been well prepared for Picasso. As early as 1908 Wartmann's predecessor as secretary of the Zürcher Kunstgesellschaft, Elimar Kusch, had shown works by Picasso in the Künstlerhaus (the forerunner of the Kunsthaus).[9] In 1914 a considerable solo exhibition of forty-six oil paintings, seventeen drawings and sixteen etchings was held in Gottfried Tanner's Moderne Galerie in Zurich.[10] Picasso had also already been introduced to the public in association with the exhibitions of the Moderner Bund

(1911)[11] and the Dadaists. In February 1916 Hans Arp personally brought to the Spiegelgasse the four works *Eau-forte I, II, III, IV* that were marked for the opening exhibition of the Cabaret Voltaire in the anthology *Cabaret Voltaire*. Tristan Tzara commented on Picasso's works in his review of the first Dada exhibition.[12] In 1924 the Kunsthaus Zürich made its first purchase of fourteen lithographs. And although Switzerland did not boast any Picasso collections — apart from that of Gottlieb Friedrich Reber — that could stand comparison with those of Shchukin (Moscow), Kramár (Prague), Stein, Doucet (Paris) and Quinn (New York), the works by Picasso that had found their way into about a dozen Swiss collections since approximately 1908 were nevertheless of some significance.[13]

The detailed circumstances under which the Zurich exhibition came to be held have been well documented by researchers. Thanks to the work of Geelhaar, FitzGerald, Nathan and Richardson[14] we can easily read today how it was possible to coordinate the interests of Picasso and his dealers with those of Wilhelm Wartmann. It is well known that, at the suggestion of Emil Friedrich, Wartmann had initially thought of a Picasso-Braque-Léger exhibition. On the occasion of the opening of the exhibition at Petit in Paris, however, it became clear to him that Picasso was by now in a league of his own and was no longer interested in group exhibitions. The opportunity to present a major monographic retrospective made the original project obsolete. No dark intrigues were thus necessary on the part of Picasso[15] to move Wartmann to withdraw his invitation to Braque and Léger somewhat inelegantly, with the promise of a solo exhibition later. For Picasso himself the episode in Zurich was — in addition to a chance to make a trip — above all an opportunity to see his paintings, which he personally hung in Paris in a curious, associative medley[16], in a comparatively conventional, chronological hanging. The persons responsible for this were Wartmann and Sigismund Righini, a Swiss painter who, as president of the exhibition commission at the

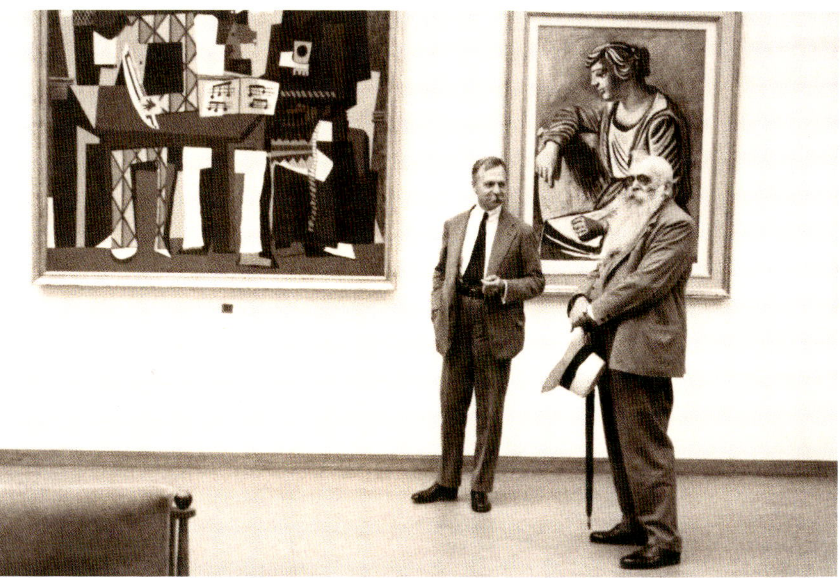

Kunsthaus, was in charge of hanging the works, as was then customary. The irony here was that the chronological hanging in Zurich was probably recognised as such only by Picasso himself and a small number of connoisseurs: almost all the reviews, including those by well-qualified critics, deplored the inaccessible, confusing and chaotic presentation without realising that the reason for this was Picasso's work itself and not the curators' decisions. For the exhibition-going public in Zurich was prepared for Picasso; they were aware of the sequence of canonical stylistic stages (the Blue and Rose Periods, Analytic and Synthetic Cubism) in his œuvre. Now they expected to find an analogous continuation of this in the work he did after the middle of the decade beginning in 1910. The fact that no such continuation exists led to great frustration. Commentators either attributed this to a hanging "according to a decorative scheme",[17] as was automatically assumed, or sought an explanation, as did the reviewer from the *Winterthurer Landbote,* following C. G. Jung's remote psychiatric diagnosis[18], in the "inner turmoil" of the artist: the "chaotic structure of the work as a whole" showed "that it is not possible to demonstrate an organic development in Picasso's vocabulary of forms."[19] In a similar way, though on a higher plane of reflection, the art historian who devoted more extensive and thorough consideration to Picasso than anyone else in connection with the Zurich exhibition, Gotthard Jedlicka, sought the spiritual roots of the "chameleon" Picasso in the thought processes of the early German Romantics and their revulsion at everything that was unambiguous, definite and conclusive.[20] It was true that the Paris and Zurich exhibitions were fragmentary: for one thing, a number of important loans were not available, even for Picasso himself; for another, it was not part of Picasso's purpose to demonstrate an organic, coherent, consistent and stringent development. Discontinuity goes deep in Picasso's work.[21] The thought experiment of a monumental complete show of all his many thousands of paintings quickly makes it clear that even such a comprehensive presentation would not be able to crystallise Picasso's development (apart from the Cubist years) into a textbook-style step-by-step progression. This was surely the decisive characteristic of the exhibitions of 1932 in Paris and Zürich. For the first time the nature of this œuvre became apparent, in which the artist applies several brushes in parallel, as it were, and in which the idea of linear progress to ever higher spheres may be of interest to the critics but not for one moment to the painter himself.

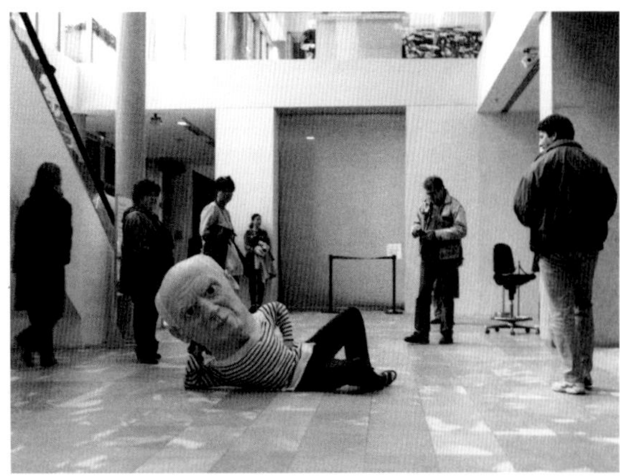

Fig. 2
Maurizio Cattelan,
Projects 65
6.11.1998 to 4.12.1998,
The Museum of Modern Art,
New York

And our exhibition too can be understood in this manner: as a fragment of a fragment, a kaleidoscope of partial reconstruction from which an image of Picasso emerges that once more emphasises clearly the detours and deviations of his work, its leaps and breaks, its self-commentaries and self-contradictions, its by turns pathos-charged and sarcastic self-image. The Picasso who emerges from this is not so distant from his bêtes noires Duchamp and Picabia, who derided him as a nineteenth-century painter and whose acolytes today ridicule him as the Mickey Mouse of modern art, who amuses tourists and begs from them.[22]

1   See article by Christian Geelhaar in this catalogue, pp. 26.
2   Christian Geelhaar, *Picasso. Wegbereiter und Förderer seines Aufstiegs 1899–1939*, Zurich 1993, p. 164.
3   See Simonetta Fraquelli's essay in this catalogue, p. 76.
4   John Richardson with the collaboration of Marilyn McCully, *A Life of Picasso, The Triumphant Years 1917–1932*, London 2007, p. 474.
5   The collector Gottlieb Friedrich Reber was in financial difficulties at that time and tried to sell his Picasso collection. On Reber's collection, cf. Dorothy Kosinski, 'G. F. Reber: Collector of Cubism', in: *The Burlington Magazine*, vol. 133, no. 1061, August 1991, pp. 519–531.
6   Letter from Emil Friedrich to Charles Montag, 29 January 1932. — Dossier Charles Montag, Swiss Institute for Art Research.

7   See Michael FitzGerald, *Making Modernism: Picasso and the Creation of the Market for Twentieth-Century Art*, New York 1995, p. 205.
8   Wilhelm Wartmann to the board of the Württembergische Kunstvereine, 1. 10. 1932. — archive of the Zürcher Kunstgesellschaft, copies of correspondence on exhibitions, vol. 53.
9   See Lukas Gloor, 'Zwischen Innovation und Investition. Picassos Sammler und Händler in der Schweiz', in: Marc Fehlmann and Toni Stooss (eds.), *Picasso und die Schweiz*, exh. cat., Kunstmuseum Bern 2001, p. 46.
10   See Geelhaar (note 2), p. 61; Gloor (note 9), p. 56.
11   See Geelhaar (note 2), p. 45 f.
12   Thanks to Raimund Meyer, Zurich, for information; cf. also: Hans Bolliger, Guido Magnaguagno and Raimund Meyer, *Dada in Zürich*, Sammlungsheft 11, Kunsthaus Zürich 1994, p. 18.
13   See Gloor (note 9).

14   Geelhaar (note 2); FitzGerald (note 7); Johannes Nathan, "... für Picasso mindestens 240 Meter ...", in: *Picasso und die Schweiz* (note 9), pp. 65–73; Richardson (note 4).
15   See Nathan (note 14).
16   See Simonetta Fraquelli's essay in this catalogue, p. 76.
17   *Neue Zürcher Zeitung*, no. 2094, 10. 11. 1932.
18   See Geelhaar (note 2), p. 38.
19   Der *Landbote Winterthur*, no. 254, 29. 10. 1932.
20   Gotthard Jedlicka, *Picasso*, lecture given at the Kunsthaus Zürich on the occasion of the Picasso exhibition, October 1932, Zurich 1934, p. 60 ff.
21   See Elizabeth Cowling, 'Introduction: A Painter without Style', in: ead., *Picasso. Style and Meaning*, London 2002, pp. 9–31.
22   Maurizio Cattelan, *Picasso Mouse*, The Museum of Modern Art, New York, 6 November to 4 December 1998.

INSTALLATION VIEWS
OF THE PICASSO EXHIBITION
AT THE KUNSTHAUS ZÜRICH 1932

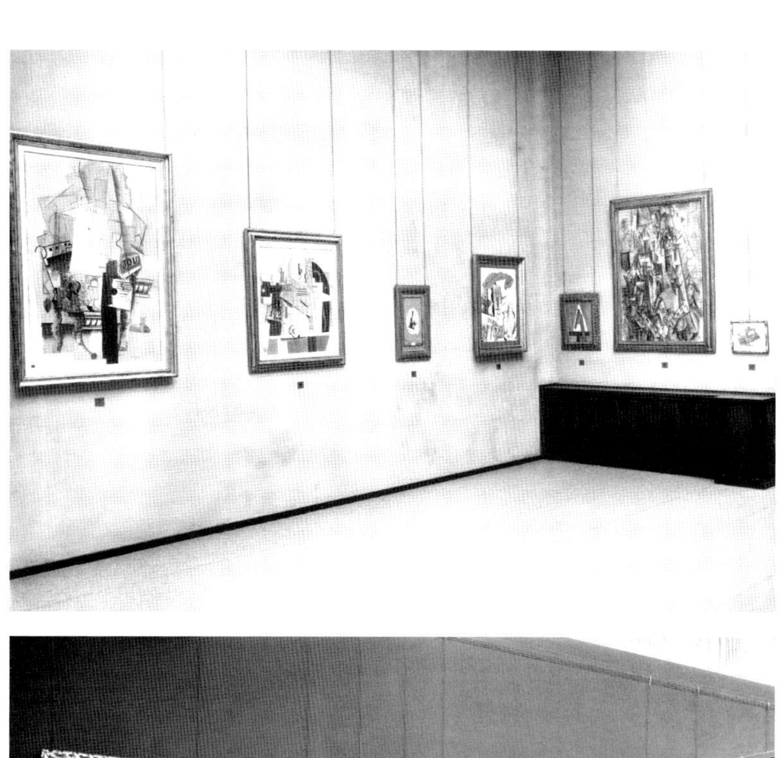

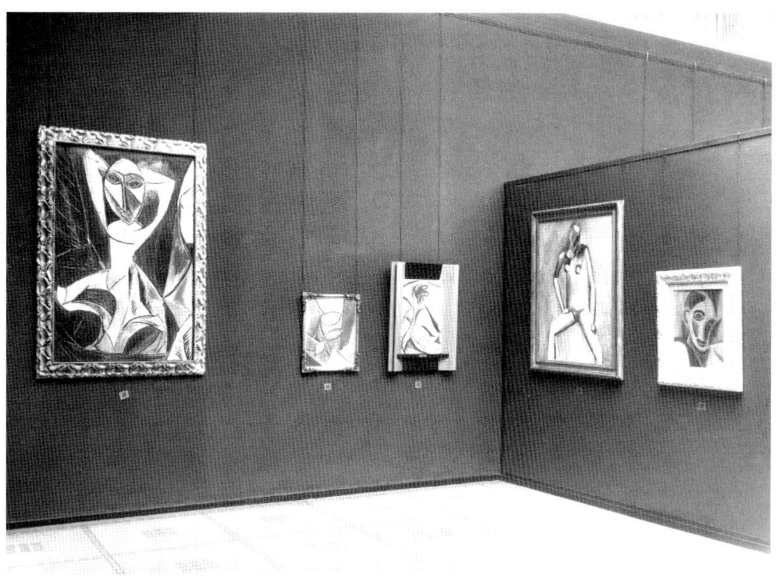

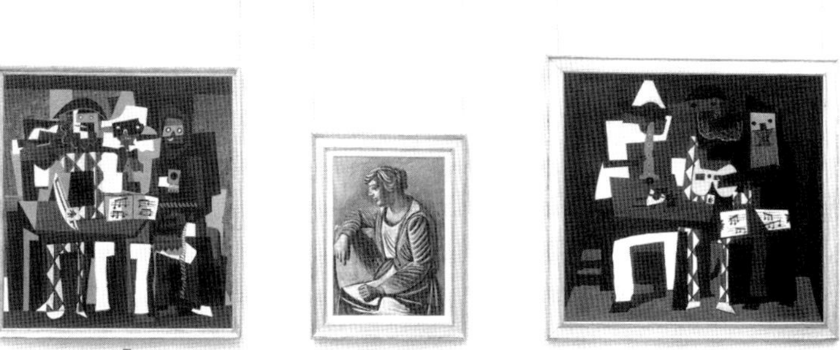

Installation views of the
Picasso exhibition at the
Kunsthaus Zürich 1932

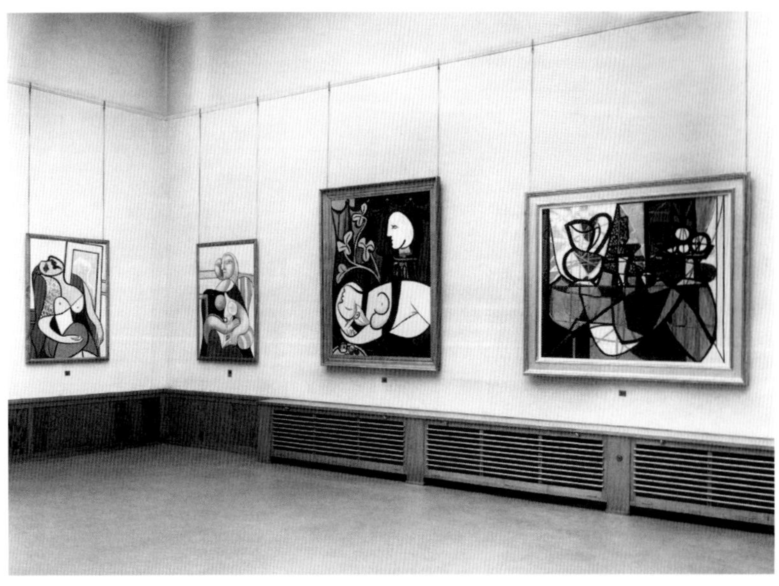

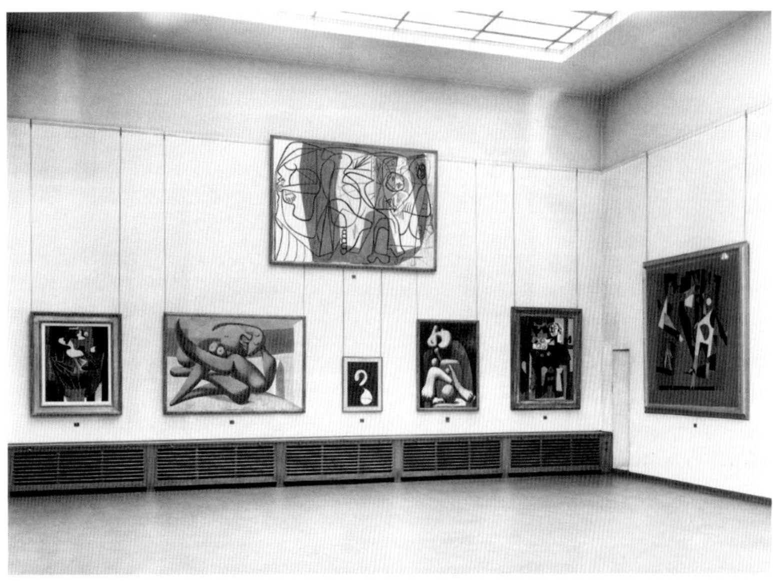

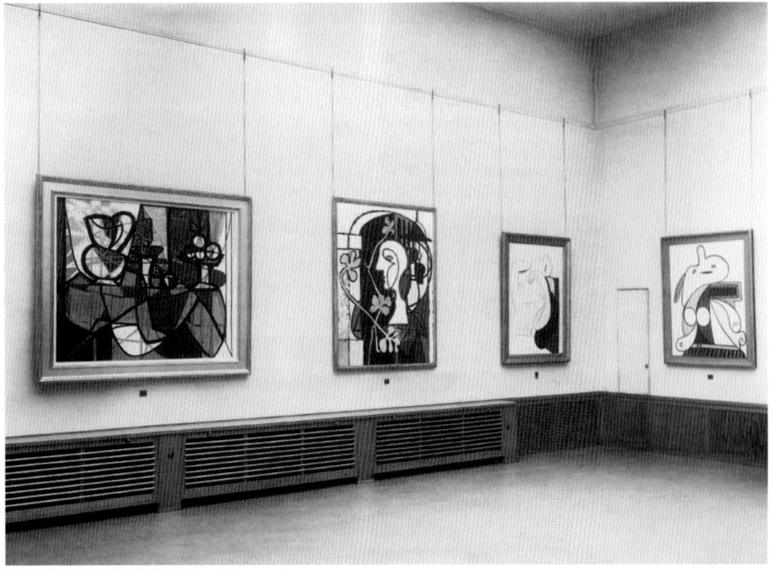

    INSTALLATION VIEWS OF THE PICASSO EXHIBITION AT THE KUNSTHAUS ZÜRICH 1932

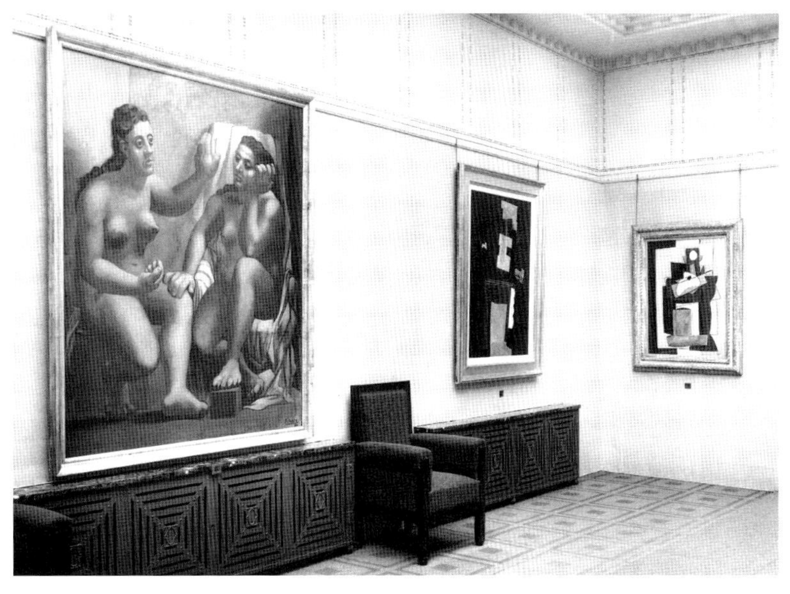

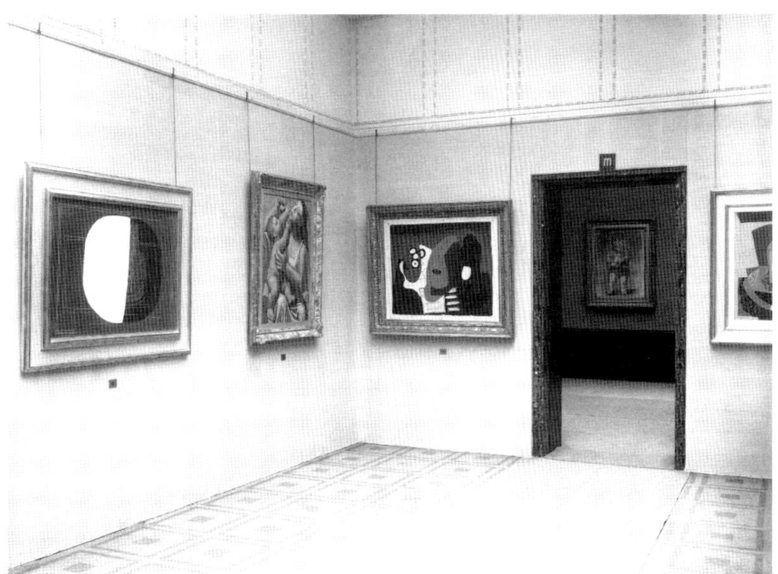

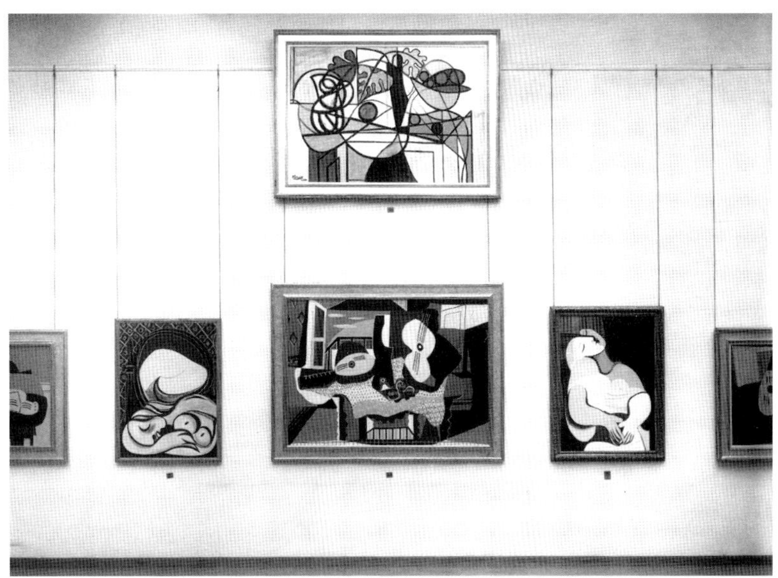

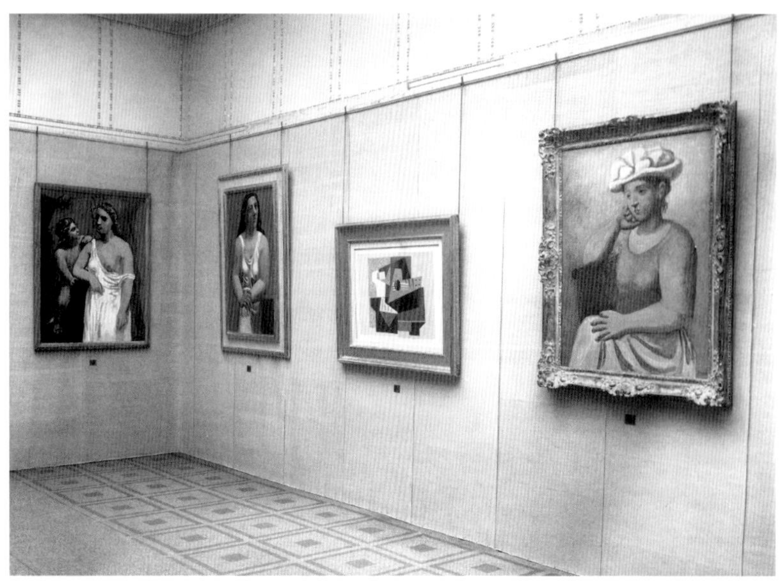

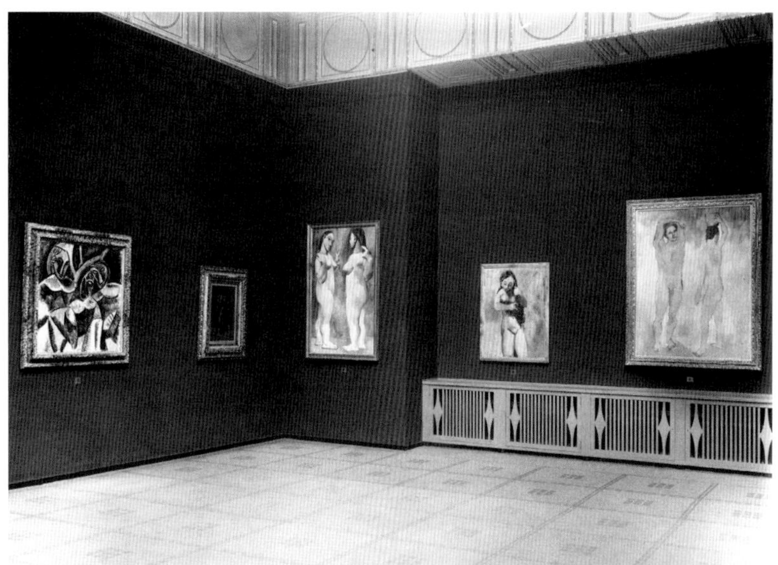

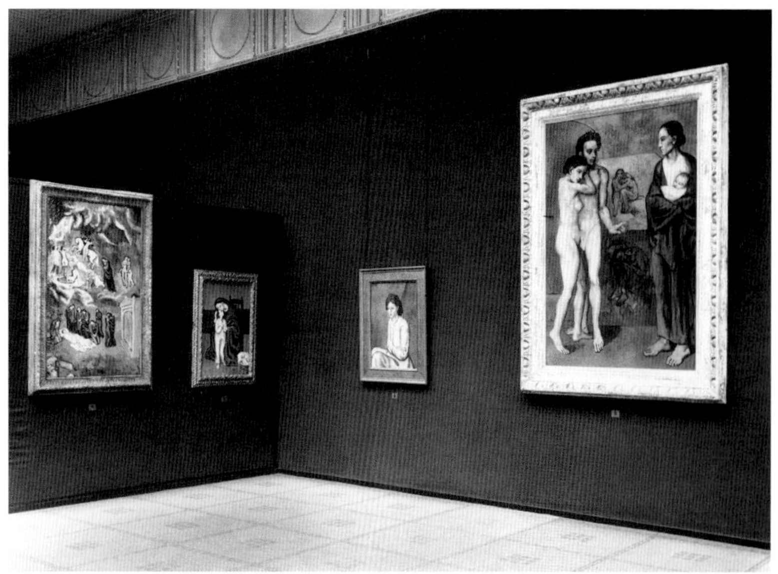

  INSTALLATION VIEWS OF THE PICASSO EXHIBITION AT THE KUNSTHAUS ZÜRICH 1932

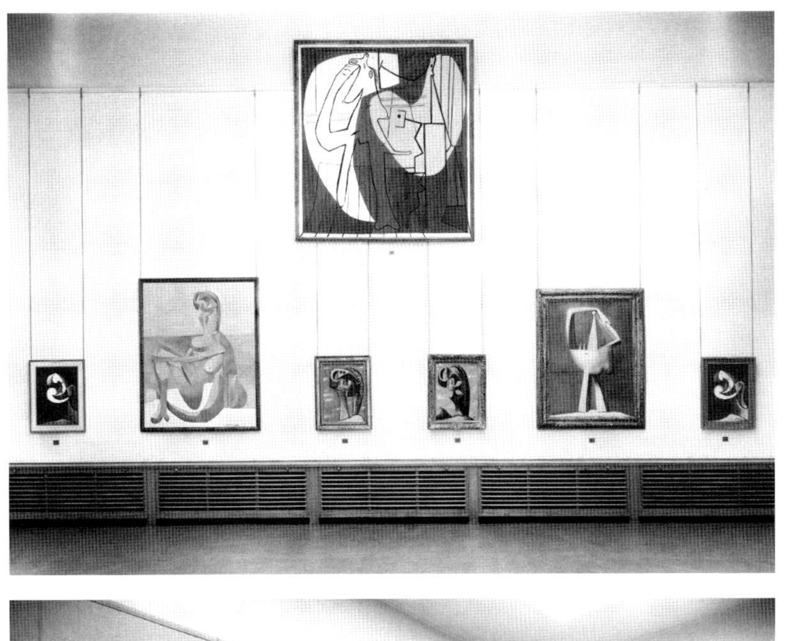

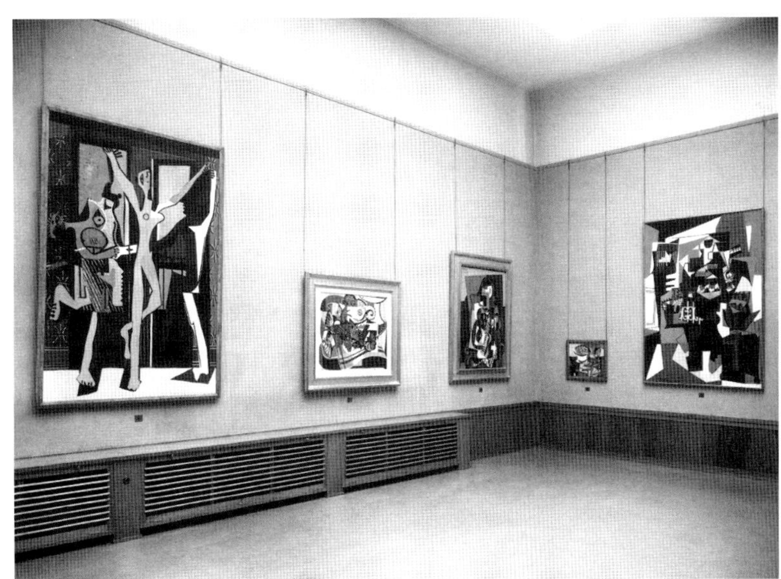

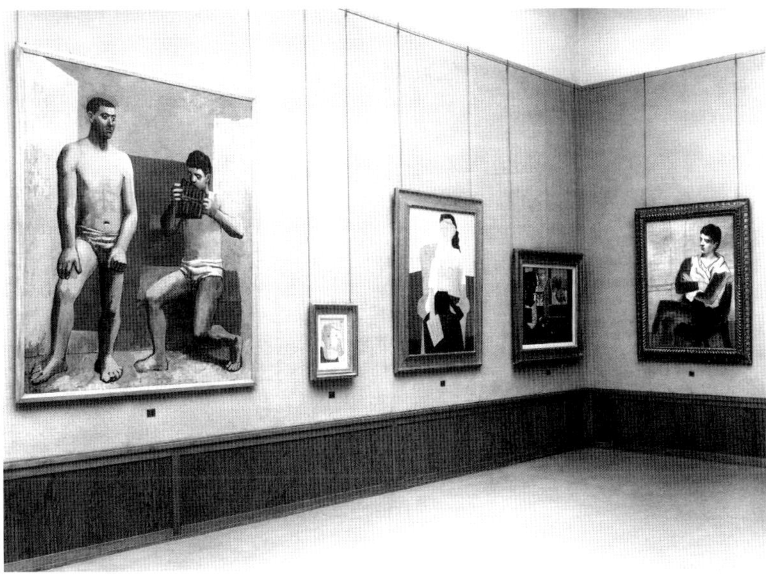

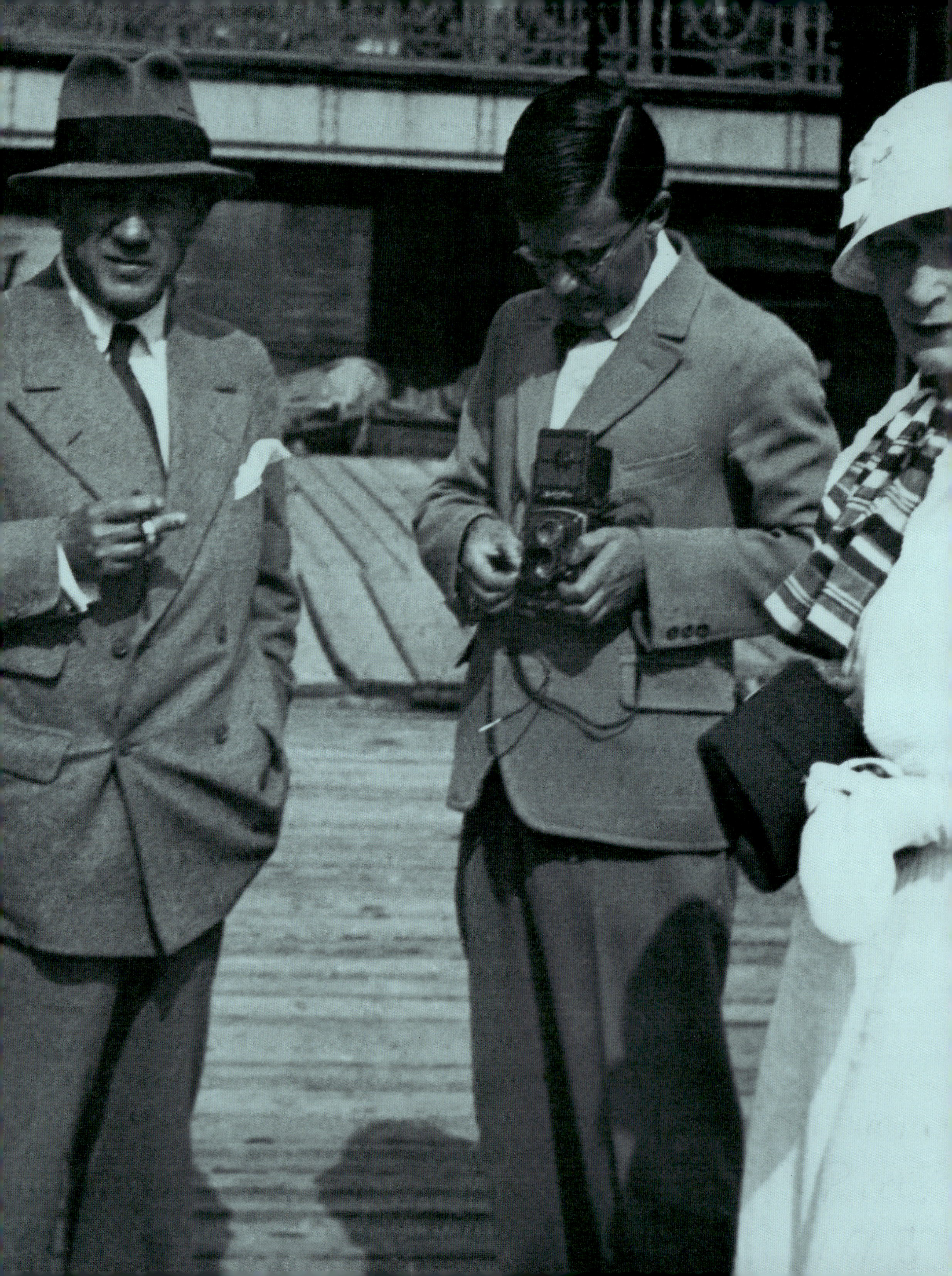

Christian Geelhaar

PICASSO.
THE FIRST ZURICH EXHIBITION

AN EXHIBITION OF PICASSO, BRAQUE AND LÉGER

At the time when Alfred H. Barr had to abandon temporarily his plans for a Picasso retrospective in New York, the Zürcher Kunstgesellschaft (Zurich Society of Arts) began to make initial preparations for a big exhibition. It was, however, not to be devoted entirely to Picasso's work; although this had been chosen as the focus of the exhibition, the intention was to complement it with groups of works by two other Cubist masters, Georges Braque and Fernand Léger. This project originated in a suggestion by the Zurich banker and collector of Cubist art Dr Emil Friedrich-Jezler (1892–1973).[1] In autumn 1931, on the occasion of a trip to Paris, the painter Carl Montag, who was also born in Winterthur, had led Friedrich-Jezler and his wife Clara "behind the scenes at Mr Paul Rosenberg's" and enabled them to take "a long look in this great art dealer's treasure store." The Friedrichs felt pleased "to be among the chosen few who had been permitted to see the recent work of Picasso, Braque and Léger shown and represented so comprehensively." Back in Zurich, in a letter of thanks written to Montag, Friedrich immediately raised the question of "whether it would be possible to hold a major exhibition of works by Picasso, Braque and Léger in Switzerland, initially in Zurich and Basel. I personally believe that great progress has been made here in recent years with regard to attitudes to modern art and that an artistic success may be regarded from the very beginning as absolutely certain. However, I also realise that such an exhibition cannot be brought about without guiding participation by P. R. Do you not, therefore, agree with me that there could be a certain attraction for you, as you have done so much to promote the understanding of art in Switzerland in the last twenty years, in taking up this matter and persuading P. R. to take a decisive part? I am sure that the idea would today be received with great delight by the Kunsthaus Zürich, and I believe I am in a position to cause

◄

Picasso, Gotthard Schuh (with Rolleiflex)
and Lucie Turel-Welti, Zurich 1932

an official invitation to participate to be sent to you by the board of the Kunstgesellschaft."[2]

Carl Montag (1880-1956) had moved to Paris in 1903 on the advice of the painter Rudolf Koller (1828-1905) in order to continue his artistic training. Paris became his adopted home. In 1913 he began to act as an agent for the works of French artists at the Moderne Galerie Zürich, which had been founded by Gottfried Tanner. In the same year he organised an exhibition of French art for the opening of the Königliches Kunstgebäude in Stuttgart. Montag became one of the most important disseminators of French art of the late nineteenth and early twentieth century in Switzerland and played a decisive part in building up many significant private collections. He was not only commissioned by the French Foreign Ministry for official missions (with a propaganda character) but also called in to organise exhibitions by several leading Swiss art institutes. In 1918 Montag gave up his own painting career but continued his work as the art teacher of Winston Churchill, whom he had met in 1915 and whose friendship he retained for the rest of his life.[3]

During this period Montag kept frequent contact to the Kunsthaus Zürich, which he helped in the organisation of the double exhibition *Pierre Bonnard, Edouard Vuillard* (29 May to 3 July 1932). He responded immediately to Dr Friedrich's suggestion and already on 22 January 1932 was able to hold out to him the prospect of participation by the art dealers Paul Rosenberg and Georges Wildenstein as well as the collector G. F. Reber.[4] Now Wilhelm Wartmann, director of the Kunsthaus, also put out feelers to Carl Montag,[5] and on 20 February 1932 Dr Adolf Jöhr, president of the Zürcher Kunstgesellschaft, officially expressed thanks for his willingness to "make his exclusive collaboration available" to the Kunsthaus "in carrying out a Picasso-Braque-Léger exhibition planned for late summer or autumn of this year." "We conceive the exhibition as one of those events whose importance and influence have attained a standing beyond Zurich and its region for the whole of Switzerland and for interested circles in neighbouring countries," the letter continued: "In this connection we are aware that collections of paintings that put on show the life's work of the three named artists, above all of Pablo Picasso, if not in numerical then in artistic terms can only be assembled with great difficulty and with the collaboration of persons who have a very close relationship to and enjoy the trust of the circles that at present hold the works of these artists. We know that you are in such a favoured position and that with your help the implementation of this great plan will certainly succeed, in so far as you are convinced of its artistic and cultural significance."[6]

The original intention was to hold the exhibition in the Kunsthaus from mid-May until late June 1932. Out of consideration for the plans of the Galeries Georges Petit for a big Picasso retrospective in early summer, which became known in Zurich at the start of February, a decision was taken to postpone it until the autumn in order to avoid a conflict of dates. This had the possible advantage of being able to take desired works by Picasso straight from the Paris exhibition. Wartmann met Carl Montag on 2 March in Paris and on the same day visited Fernand Léger, Paul Rosenberg and Josef Müller, a collector from Solothurn who was living in the French capital at that time. He was able to assure the exhibition commission on his return home that the Picasso-Braque-Léger exhibition was "achievable on a grand scale" and that 100 selected works by Picasso and fifty important works each by Braque and Léger ought to be obtainable. In the case of Picasso it would be possible to take over works loaned from America to the Georges Petit exhibition. In addition, major works by Picasso would be available for Zurich that were off-limits to the organisers of the Paris retrospective, who were rivals of the owners. All in all the show had prospects of being an event "the like of which has never taken place before in Europe."[7] On 2 April the Parisian magazine *Comoedia* published an advance notice both of the forthcoming Bonnard-Vuillard exhibition in Zurich and of the Picasso-Braque-Léger show planned for September, "which will bring together an especially significant ensemble from the work of these three painters." As far as Picasso was concerned, "a sufficiently large number of paintings" would be on display in Zurich, "in order to be able to provide as full an overview as possible of his work as a whole and his development."[8]

One question did, however, vex the organisers of the Zurich exhibition in these weeks and months: what was the Basler Kunstverein (Basel Art Association) up to? Its president, Dr Emanuel Hoffmann, had most probably heard from Dr Emil Friedrich of the plan to stage a comprehensive exhibition of Cubist artists. On 12 February 1932 he informed his commission of this plan, which was "still maturing." The commission expressed its wish to take over the exhibition, but wanted to limit it to Picasso and Braque, "with an emphasis on the work of Picasso in particular." The months of October and November were envisaged as a possible date.[9] When word reached Basel that Carl Montag was responsible for the Zurich exhibition, Wilhelm Barth, the conservator there, appealed to Montag in emotional terms on 4 April: "After a lengthy interval I am once again knocking at your door, indeed seeking refuge ... A few years ago you were so kind as to support vis-à-vis Mr Paul Rosenberg my endeavours to assemble works by Picasso for an exhibition in Basel — without success at that time, as the resistance was too powerful. I resigned myself to this then, and until now. Today I have learned that this exhibition will come about in Zurich with your help. And are you not thinking, have never thought, of Basel? Is that final? Is there nothing that can change this?"[10]

The fact that the Kunsthalle Basel was attempting to hold a Picasso exhibition and was considering taking on the Zurich show had long been known in Zurich.[11] However, as neither the conservator nor the president of the Basler Kunstverein had ever consulted their Zurich colleagues, "no intervention from Basel now" was expected on that score. It was therefore all the more surprising that on Monday, 7 April, in reaction to Wilhelm Barth's call for help, Wartmann communicated Barth's wish for involvement in the project by telegram. "If Basel would now like to join in, please write to the gentlemen there that they should get in touch with us," Wartmann wrote to Carl Montag; "perhaps an opportunity can be found that will be unfair to no-one. We urgently request, however, that you act only for the big Picasso-Braque-Léger exhibition in Zurich in your work and your negotiations with the artists, dealers and collectors. If a change were to be expected to the end that the form and idea of the exhibition were no longer exclusively an event of the Kunsthaus with unconditional priority for Zurich in artistic and moral terms, then the assistance (financial) hitherto gained from certain parties, and thus the event itself in Zurich, would be endangered. In terms of space, too, we envisage an event on a much larger scale than the Kunsthalle could devote to a Picasso exhibition."[12]

On 11 June Wilhelm Barth finally wrote to his colleagues in Zurich: "An arrangement was made on our part with Mr Charles Montag in Meudon Val Fleury, the organiser of your Picasso-Braque-Léger exhibition, that we wished to show the exhibition in Basel in a somewhat modified form after it is held in Zurich." However he had now learned that the exhibition in Zurich was not taking place in the months of August and September, as he had previously been informed, but later, in September and October. For Basel the month of November — according to tradition December was reserved for the Christmas exhibition — would, however, "not leave enough scope to take over the exhibition." Wartmann was "surprised" that Barth spoke of an "agreement" with Montag; it seemed to him "that there was a misunderstanding on the part of Basel that the Kunsthaus was seemingly regarded as no more than the fortunate recipient of an exhibition organised by you. We would be most pleased to take this role if we were thereby relieved not only of the artistic but also of the financial responsibility. So long as both risks weigh on us, however, and have been taken on by us with the intention of carrying out such an exhibition in the Zürcher Kunsthaus, I believe the Kunsthaus should call the tune, which, as the old saying has it, does go with the part of paying the piper." Nevertheless, Wartmann concluded his explanations, it was "certainly not undesirable" for Basel to take over as much as possible of the Zurich exhibition on account of the resultant sharing of costs.[13] (...)

After his return from the opening of the Picasso retrospective in Paris, Wilhelm Wartmann set about making arrangements for the rooms for his Picasso-Braque-Léger show. The whole second floor, which was usually reserved for the permanent collection, was to be made available. "On all accounts this allocation of space must make the Zurich exhibition, as far as its arrangement and the overall impression are concerned, even more beautiful and earnest than the Paris exhibition, which is in fact the only justification for holding it," he wrote to Carl Montag on 19 June. Montag was asked to outline to Picasso the extent of the display space and approach him about a drawing for the poster.[14]

In mid-July the president of the Zürcher Kunstgesellschaft sent an official letter of thanks to Picasso: the artist had accepted the invitation passed on by Carl Montag to take part in the triple exhibition, for which between 150 and 200 of his works were foreseen, and promised his personal participation by means of the loan of a considerable number of works that were in his own possession.[15] Eight days later the president was also able to thank Georges Braque for his assent to the Zurich exhibition project and for his announcement that he was engaged in putting together an ensemble of about 40 pictures.[16] Finally Carl Montag promised to attend to the group of works by Fernand Léger before his and Paul Rosenberg's departure for a summer break.[17]

At the end of July Wartmann once again travelled to Paris in order to supervise the transfer of the loaned Picassos destined for Zurich after the end of the exhibition at the Galeries Georges Petit. Only then — obviously in accordance with Picasso's wishes — was the original project of a collective Picasso-Braque-Léger showing dropped in order to devote it exclusively to the Spanish artist. Braque and Léger, who had already set aside collections of their paintings for the exhibition, were understandably "at first very displeased, but subsequently it was possible to pacify them and win them over for later special exhibitions."[18] A show of

Braque's works was to be held directly after the Picasso retrospective in November 1932 and one of Léger's the following year. Braque then, however, withdrew from holding an event in Zurich and instead displayed his works in the Kunsthalle Basel in spring 1933.[19] The solo exhibition devoted to Fernand Léger, which comprised 150 paintings, went on show in the Kunsthaus Zürich in May 1933; it had been preceded in April by an equally large memorial exhibition to Juan Gris.

THE FIRST MUSEUM EXHIBITION

The Picasso exhibition in the Kunsthaus Zürich — as already mentioned, this was the first-ever exhibition of the artist's work in a museum — was opened on the morning of Sunday, 11 September 1932, in the presence of representatives of the cantonal government, the city council of Zurich and numerous invited guests.[20] Picasso had already travelled to Zurich on 7 September for the final phase of preparations, [21] and stayed there for two days with his wife Olga and ten-year-old son Paulo. The programme laid on for the artist and his family included a boat trip on Lake Zurich and a reception with lunch in the Belvoirpark. After that, before the opening of the exhibition, the Picassos left for the Engadin valley.[22] On 17 September Picasso was at work again in Boisgeloup and began a series of ink drawings that were inspired by the depiction of the Crucifixion in Grünewald's *Isenheim Altar*. It is therefore more than likely that his return journey from Switzerland took him to France and Colmar.[23]

Some paintings — including *The Couple (The Wretched Ones)* from the collection of Bernhard Mayer, Zurich — and four sculptures could not be incorporated in the exhibition, which was arranged and installed by Sigismund Righini (1870–1937), a painter from Ticino who was president of the exhibition commission, until ten days after the opening; the four rooms on the ground floor, where about 100 drawings and the same number of etchings and lithographs were displayed, were also not opened to the public until later. Works on paper, absent from the Paris exhibition, were newly added in Zurich. Most of the ninety-eight water-colours and drawings came from commercial galleries and were for sale. However, G. F. Reber had contributed twenty-two and Dr Arthur and Hedy Hahnloser-Bühler, collectors from Winterthur, had four sheets on loan. Picasso's graphic work, from the early *La Suite des Saltimbanques* to the etchings for Balzac's *Le Chef-d'œuvre inconnu* and Ovid's *Metamorphoses,* was well represented thanks to the suggestion and collaboration of the art historian Dr Bernhard Geiser (1891–1967) from Bern, who had just completed the first volume of his catalogue of works, *Picasso. Peintre-Graveur*; it was published in early 1933 by Gutekunst & Klipstein in Bern.[24]

The number of paintings shown in Zurich was overall practically unchanged compared with the Paris exhibition. The Kunsthaus was able to take over 181 of the total of 225 pictures that had been exhibited by Georges Petit; 43 additional ones were on display in Zurich. Works from Picasso's early years, the so-called Blue Period and the Rose Period, were somewhat less well represented in Zurich than they had been in Paris due to the loss of several important loans from American and French private collections. This was compensated by a larger number of later works, as Picasso had sent ten further paintings to Zurich, thus increasing the number of works loaned by the artist to fifty-six. Thirty of these paintings were for sale, including such major works as *La flûte de Pan* and *Les trois danseuses*, which could be acquired for 500,000 and 400,000 French francs respectively. In both Paris and Zurich the most important lenders after the artist himself were the art dealer Paul Rosenberg and the collector G. F. Reber, with twenty-five and eighteen paintings respectively. As early as May the Berlin art dealer Albert Flechtheim had offered to help Wartmann in acquiring further works that were in Germany for his exhibition, as he had already done in the case of the show *Thirty Years of Pablo Picasso*, which took place in June 1931 in the Lefevre Galleries in London, and as the organiser in Paris had done. Flechtheim urged Wartmann to approach above all the Wallraf-Richartz

Museum in Cologne and the Städtisches Museum in Wuppertal-Elberfeld with requests to borrow *La famille Soler* and *Acrobate et jeune Arlequin*; however, both museums declined to help.[25] Furthermore, works from the collection of Dr Vincenz Kramár and from the Moderne Galerie in Prague, which in Flechtheim's opinion "must not be absent,"[26] were not available.

Several Swiss collectors such as Josef Müller from Solothurn, Dr Emanuel Hoffmann-Stehlin from Basel, Marcel Fleischmann from Zurich, Frau Emil Staub-Terlinden from Männedorf and the Basel banker Raoul La Roche, who lived in Paris, had made loans for the retrospective at Galeries Georges Petit. In Zurich ten further paintings were added from the art salon of Gustave and Léon Bollag in Zurich and from Swiss private collections: those of Hermann Rupf in Bern, Dr Georg Reinhart in Winterthur and Dr Emil Friedrich-Jezler and Bernhard Mayer in Zurich. It is noticeable that the Picasso paintings from the collections in Basel of Karl Im Obersteg and Rudolf Staechelin were not present. They were reserved for an exhibition entitled *Moderne Kunst aus Basler Privatbesitz* (Modern Art from Private Collections in Basel) which Wilhelm Barth was planning for October 1932 in the Kunsthalle "as a bit of competition for Zurich" to compensate the failure to take over the Picasso exhibition from Zurich: "I have a few fine Picassos in it that did not go to Zurich," he gloated.[27] (As a result of the sudden death of Dr Emanuel Hoffmann-Stehlin, president of the Basler Kunstverein, from injuries sustained in a car accident, Barth was forced to drop this project too.)[28] All in all the Zurich retrospective could claim the honour of presenting the most comprehensive view hitherto of Picasso's development and work.

The exhibition catalogue, illustrated with thirty-two plates and containing an appreciation by Wilhelm Wartmann and a full list of the exhibits, was not published until mid-October. With reference to the catalogue Bernhard Geiser had drawn Wartmann's attention to the fact that the artist "did not like to see the first name Pablo" in the title of a publication (the short version of the catalogue of the Zurich exhibition bears the title "Pablo Picasso"): "His legally binding signature in civil law is Pablo Ruiz-Picasso, but as an artist he always signs Picasso and would like always to be known in this way as an artist. I had the opportunity at that time to speak to him about this matter, and I just want to point out to you that all writers who know Picasso and have written about him, Raynal, Level, Zervos etc., have consciously omitted his first name."[29]

Many well-attended guided tours and courses were held to explain the exhibition to interested visitors, and a series of four lectures aimed to deepen public appreciation. On 6 October Max Raphael spoke on the subject of "Picasso. Einheit und Logik seiner Entwicklung" (Picasso. The Unity and Logic of his Development),[30] on 13 October Professor Hans Hildebrandt from Stuttgart on "Die Wandlung des Sehens" (The Transformation of Seeing)[31] and on 20 October Dr Hans Curjel from Berlin on "Strawinsky und Picasso" (Stravinsky and Picasso)[32]. The cycle was concluded on 27 October by a local speaker, the art historian Dr Gotthard Jedlicka, who had already written his thoughts on "Matisse und Picasso" (Matisse and Picasso) on 2 October in the *Neue Zürcher Zeitung*[33] and now spoke about "Picasso und die Malerei in Frankreich" (Picasso and Painting in France)[34]. Max Raphael gave a second lecture on 17 October 1932 in the Kunstgewerbemuseum on "Picasso als soziologisches Problem" (Picasso as a Sociological Problem), organised by the society Das neue Russland (The New Russia). In 1933 the text of this lecture was included in the publication *Marx Proudhon Picasso*.

The daily newspapers gave almost weekly reports on the growing numbers of visitors. On Sunday, 25 September 2,362 art-lovers attended the exhibition, and the total number of visitors since the opening thus exceeded 7,000. "Among the visitors from abroad, in addition to American, English and German guests Italians are now coming, too," in the words of a press release issued by the Kunsthaus.[35] On Sunday, 9 October 2,371 visitors were recorded. On 23 October the total attendance exceeded 20,000, and a week later the figure was over 28,000.

The continuing crowds amounted to a strong reason for extending the exhibition by two weeks until 13 November. Picasso transmitted his consent to Wartmann by telegram on 10 October: "AUTORISE REMETTRE FIN EXPOSITION TREIZE NOVEMBRE."[36] On 26 October the three works loaned by the Hoffmann-Stehlin collection were recalled early in order to be included from 30 October in an exhibition in the Kunsthalle Basel that the Basler Kunstverein dedicated to the memory of its deceased president.[37] To make up for this it was hoped to acquire the *Arlequin assis* of 1923 from the collection of Karl Im Obersteg, but this wish was disappointed.[38] The organisers had to make do with two still-lifes loaned by Alfred Flechtheim as substitutes: *Treffass* of 1919 and *Fish on Table* of 1922. On 28 October they also succeeded in incorporating the *Portrait of Clovis Sagot* of 1909 from the collection of G. F. Reber into the exhibition.[39]

"The Picasso exhibition in Zurich seems to have been a record-breaking event, purely in terms of visitor numbers," noted Oskar Schlemmer with amazement.[40] It had attracted a total of 34,027 visitors in nine weeks. However, this figure included only 14,078 admission fees (single admission cost 1.50 francs). 5,644 copies of the short catalogue (price: 0.50 francs) and 716 copies of the illustrated catalogue (price: 5 francs) were sold.[41] The proceeds were, however, not nearly enough to cover the costs of transport, insurance, production of the catalogues and other expenses, and it was to be expected that the excess costs would exceed the amounts available in the approved budget of the Kunsthaus by 20,000 to 30,000 francs. In early October the Zürcher Kunstgesellschaft therefore asked the city authorities to grant them a sum of between 15,000 and 20,000 francs, but on 11 November the city council approved a one-off contribution of only 10,000 francs, "debited to account number Q 74b of the approved transactions of 1932." The Kunsthaus was therefore left with a deficit of 5,000 to 7,000 francs.

The municipal subsidy for the exhibition was not undisputed. In view of the Depression and the rise in unemployment, its supporters argued that "the city has a great interest in the stimulus to the economy expected from the exhibition. As the holding of such an exhibition also provides employment for a number of auxiliary workers for a few weeks, support for the proposal is also justified from this point of view."[42] On 11 October a commentary in the social-democratic daily *Volksrecht* raised the following question: "Should the city authorities give financial support to the Picasso exhibition?", going on to reject the proposition with the argument that Picasso's art was "typically bourgeois and decadent" and represented a playful attitude to art that meant nothing to the workers; justifiably "the term 'painted psychoanalysis' was used to characterise a particular period in Picasso's art," but psychoanalysis was "a sign of the decadence of our age."[43] No less a person than the art historian and theoretician of Modernism Sigfried Giedion (1888–1968) took issue with this polemic and countered: "If the work of Picasso is characterised as bourgeois and decadent, how should the fountains and monuments of art conservation in Zurich be described? At bottom these monuments made of stone are no more than cheap plaster-casts of the past." [44]

C. G. JUNG'S DIAGNOSIS OF PICASSO

This was not the only controversy occasioned by the Picasso exhibition. On 13 November, its last day in the Kunsthaus, an essay about Picasso written by the psychologist and psychotherapist Carl Gustav Jung (1875–1961) was published in the *Neue Zürcher Zeitung*. It caused "an international furore that has not subsided to this day."[45] In the introduction Jung finds he must "almost apologise" to the reader for "intervening in the commotion about Picasso as a psychiatrist." If he expressed anything about Picasso, he did so with the explicit reservation "that he only had something to say about the psychology of his art" and restricted himself "to the psychology that underlies such artistic creativity", but left "the aesthetic problem to the scholars of art." In the chronological development of Picasso's work Jung saw "an increasing distance from the

empirical object and an increase in those elements that no longer correspond to any external experience, but stem from an 'interior' that lies
behind the consciousness which is directed to the outer world, like a
general organ of perception to which the five senses are subordinate."
Supporting his argument with observations of the drawings of his neu-
rotic and schizophrenic patients, Jung classified Picasso among the
schizophrenic group, "which produces pictures that immediately reveal
their alienation from feeling. They convey at all events no unified, harmo-
nious feeling but feelings of contradiction or even complete absence of
feeling. In purely formal terms the dominant characteristic is inner conflict, which is expressed in so-called 'fractures', i.e. a kind of psychic
fault line that runs across the picture."

In the large-format painting *Evocation* from the early Blue Period,
loaned to Zurich by Ambroise Vollard, Jung claimed to recognise "the
symbol of a nekyia, a journey to Hades, a descent into the unconscious
and a farewell from the world above." On the basis of this painting he
interpreted Picasso as a "person who turns not to the world of daylight
but fatefully into the darkness, following not the ideal of what is recognised as beautiful and good but the demonic attraction of the ugly and
evil that wells up in modern man in the manner of the Antichrist or Lucifer
and generates an apocalyptic mood, veils this bright world of day
with infernal fog, infects it with fatal dissolution and finally disintegrates
it like an earthquake zone into fragments, fault lines, remains, rubble,
scraps and anorganic units." The 'Baroque' apotheosis *Evocation*,
inspired by El Greco, is however not a representation of Picasso himself
and his own 'underworld destiny' (seen as the 'journey to hell', to Cubism),
as Jung asserts, but in reality is a metaphor for the 'resurrection' and
'ascension' of his friend Carlos Casagemas, who had committed suicide
on 17 February 1901.[46]

"A journey through the history of the soul of humankind" aims to
"restore man as a whole," taught Jung: "That is why the symbols of
experiences of madness are followed by pictures that represent the

encounter of pairs of opposites, light-dark, above-below, white-black, male-female etc." In Picasso's most recent paintings Jung thought he recognised "the motif of the union of contrasting elements with their direct opposites." A work of 1932, *Girl before a Mirror*, contained — "though cut to pieces by many fractures" — a composition of the light and the dark anima of the artist (once again, however, Picasso portrays not himself but his lover Marie-Thérèse Walter)[47]: "The garish, unambiguous, even brutal colours of the last period correspond to the tendency of the unconscious to master emotional conflicts with violence (colour = emotion)." This condition in the spiritual development of a patient is, however, "neither the end nor the goal. Picasso's 'drame intérieur' has grown to this last level before the peripeteia. With respect to the future Picasso I prefer not to attempt prophecies, as this interior adventure is a dangerous thing, which in every phase can lead to a standstill or a catastrophic detonation of opposites that are yoked together."[48]

The first to take issue with the "psychological comments of Dr C. G. Jung" was K. H. David, who feared that here "a heavy blow has been struck against modern artists in general, of a kind that could shake their precarious position in relation to society even further."[49] The lawyer and painter Hanns Welti (1894–1934), who had looked after Picasso and his family during their short stay in Zurich and reported on it several times, also protested vehemently against the psychiatrist's negative view: "Because expressions like those ventured by Dr Jung have seldom been such misunderstood, such dangerous instruments in the hands of a layman as in this case"[50]. Indeed! The perfidious joking of the editor of the *Neue Zürcher Zeitung* review section about "Paul Klee's garden of schizophrenia"[51] a few years later are not likely to have aided Klee's prospects of gaining Swiss citizenship.[52] Not only in the columns of the *Neue Zürcher Zeitung* were voices raised against Jung's 'diagnosis'. Rudolf Grossmann took a stand against it in the art magazine *Kunst und Künstler*[53], and Christian Zervos in his *Cahiers d'Art*[54]. However, the most pointed attack on the Zurich psychiatrist was made by Max Raphael; his merciless exposure of Jung's "nebulous metaphysics" culminated in the assertion of a sociological distinction: while Picasso created art "without any consideration of the public's wishes," Jung "curries favour like a philistine with the small-minded bourgeoisie who make their own monied impotence the measure of all things" and "places his name and his knowledge at their service in order to justify them."[55]

C.G. Jung concluded his observations: "As the favourable reader sees, I regard Picasso as a drama. Because I do this, I would have welcomed it if his paintings for once had been hung not on the basis of aesthetic reasons that I find dubious, as it were 'pêle-mêle', but in strict chronological order." Most art critics were in agreement with him in this wish. Georg Schmidt feared that the hanging of the works in the Kunsthaus according to decorative principles would necessarily leave most visitors with the impression of "considerable chaos." In his three-part review in the Basel *National-Zeitung* he represented Picasso's work in the chronological development of his style.[56] In the same way Hans Graber and Berthold Fenigstein also took a chronological approach in the series of articles that they devoted to the Picasso retrospective in the *Neue Zürcher Zeitung* and the *Tages-Anzeiger* respectively.[57]

THE FIRST PICTURE BOUGHT FOR ZURICH

In his first exhibition report Hans Graber noted: "Strangely, not one Swiss museum possesses a work by the Spaniard to this day. That needs to change. Perhaps Zurich will set a good example." Gustav Kahnweiler (1895–1989), the younger brother of Daniel-Henry Kahnweiler and head of Galerie Flechtheim & Kahnweiler in Frankfurt am Main, had offered paintings by Picasso to the Kunsthaus more than once since the beginning of the 1930s and even sent them for viewing.[58] In autumn 1932 several lenders also informed Wartmann that they were willing to part with one or the other work from their collection that was displayed in Zurich. Gertrude Stein, for example, who had loaned eight paintings, inquired whether the Kunsthaus would be interested in acquiring her *Girl with a Basket of Flowers*, the first picture by Picasso that she had purchased jointly with her brother Leo.[59] Wartmann appears not to have responded to this proposal. An offer that seemed to him more worthy of consideration, by contrast, was that of the Chilean art-lover and patron Eugenia Huici de Errazuriz, who announced her possible willingness to sell one of her two pictures that were exhibited in the Kunsthaus; when asked, she disclosed that she hoped to gain 150,000 French francs from the sale of the *Young Girl* of 1914 and 200,000 French francs for the large-format *Man Leaning on a Table* of 1916.[60]

In the matter of desired purchases, attention finally centred on two works dating from 1915: no. 91 of the exhibition catalogue, *Guitar on a Guéridon*, and no. 92, *Guitar and Clarinet on a Mantlepiece*. The first was owned by the artist and insured for 200,000 francs, while the latter belonged to the art dealer Georges Wildenstein and had an insured value of 250,000 French francs. However, prices like these were far beyond the range of the Kunsthaus, which was forced to admit to the two owners that, due to the reduction of municipal subsidies for the exhibition caused by the financial crisis, the sum of 150,000 French francs originally set aside for purchases had been reduced to half of that amount, which must seem "presque ridicule."[61] The letter to the artist read: "It would be more of a gift on your part to the museum and the city of Zurich than a sale . . ."[62] Wildenstein communicated through Carl Montag that he was prepared to reduce the price to 125,000 francs."[63] Picasso gave his consent by telegram: "ACCEPTE PRIX TABLEAU QUATRE VINGT ONZE CATALOGUE."[64] At this the board and collection commission decided on 22 November to purchase *Guitare on a Guéridon*. A painting by Picasso was thus represented in a Swiss museum collection for the first time. (In April 1924 the Zürcher Kunstgesellschaft had already acquired the series of etchings *La Suite des Saltimbanques* for the collection of prints and drawings.)[65] On 5 December the artist telegraphed to Wartmann: "ENVOYEZ MOI CHEQUE PARIS."[66]

The Zurich Picasso retrospective had attracted extraordinary attention. It is therefore not surprising that elsewhere, too, desires were aroused to shine in the glory reflected from the event. Several exhibition venues in Switzerland and abroad, for example the Württembergische Kunstverein Stuttgart[67] and the Kunsthalle Bern[68], inquired about the conditions for taking over the show. Wilhelm Barth, too, made a last effort at the eleventh hour to gain at least part of the Picasso exhibition for Basel. "The Picasso exhibition in Zurich was a severe blow for me," he admitted to a colleague: "Paul Rosenberg and his associate G. F. Reber can tell you how long I tried to get Picasso, even earlier!"[69] Shortly before the exhibition closed, Barth phoned G. F. Reber to inquire whether he would be prepared to pass his loans on to Basel.[70] He tasked his cousin, the painter Paul Basilius Barth (1881–1955), who was staying in Paris, to take a letter to Picasso with a similar request. On 9 November Paul Basilius reported to his cousin Willy how he had carried out his mission: "Your letter woke me up this morning; at 11 o'clock I was at Picasso's, 23 rue de la Boëtie, 4me étage au dessus de l'entresol, Ascenceur, and handed your letter to a very distinguished-looking bonne, as Monsieur Picasso would come home only pour le déjeuner. By now he will have read it and thrown it in the waste-paper basket. So you want to carry on in Basel with all this to-do? Derain is a big man, too, though not so much for the Bourgeois Suisses and for all those who know nothing about art such as the Critique d'art and the rest of the rabble. The next Turnuser and Salongs suisse[71] will be just crawling with sous-Picassos. Pauvre Génie du Mal! I was sorry not to have met the gentleman himself, but perhaps it's better that way, as our name is suspicious to him." Paul Basilius Barth ended his letter with a sigh of resignation: "What a pity I wasn't born 150 years earlier; I would have fitted in that era better than in the age of Picasso."[72] The Basler Kunsthalle never held a second Picasso exhibition, either then or later.

We would like to thank Anne-Marie Schweingruber-Geelhaar, the sister of Christian Geelhaar, for her kind permission to reprint this text, which was first published in: Christian Geelhaar, *Picasso. Wegbereiter and Förderer seines Aufstiegs 1899–1939*, Zurich 1993, pp.179–202, and is here printed in excerpts.

1 Brigit Blass and Rudolf Koella, *Eine Pioniersammlung moderner Kunst. Das Legat Clara und Emil Friedrich-Jezler im Kunstmuseum Winterthur*, Zurich 1985.
2 Letter from Dr. jur. Emil Friedrich to Carl Montag, 23 November 1931. Swiss Institute for Art Research, Zurich, SIKDok, NM, IV: Dossier 12.
3 Cf. exhibition catalogue *Carl Montag: Maler und Kunstvermittler (1880–1956)*, published by Stiftung 'Langmatt' Sidney and Jenny Brown, Baden 1992.
4 Letter from Dr. jur. Emil Friedrich to Carl Montag, 29 January 1932. cf. his letter to Montag of 13 January 1932. — SIKDok, NM, IV: Dossier 12.
5 Letter from Wilhelm Wartmann to Carl Montag, 30 January 1932. — SIKDok, NM, IV: Dossier 12.
6 Letter from Dr Adolf Jöhr and Wilhelm Wartmann to Carl Montag, 20 February 1932. — SIKDok, NM, IV: Dossier 12.
7 Minutes of the meeting of 4 March 1932. — Minutes of the exhibition commission, VII, 11 April 1929–9 August 1932, p.138. Archive of the Zürcher Kunstgesellschaft.
8 "qui réunira un ensemble particulièrement significatif de l'œuvre de ces trois peintres … un nombre de toiles suffisant pour donner une idée aussi complète que possible sur l'ensemble de son œuvre et l'évolution de son talent", 'Bonnard, Vuillard, Braque et Picasso présentés à Zurich', in: *Comoedia*, 2 April 1932. — Archives Picasso, Argus de presse.
9 Commission meeting on 12 February 1932. Minutes of the Basler Kunstverein 1927–1933, p.177. — Archive of the Basler Kunstverein in the Staatsarchiv Basel.
10 "Après un long intervalle, je viens encore une fois dans cette vie frapper à votre porte et même me jeter dans vos bras … Vous étiez assez bon, il y a quelques années, de me soutenir — en vain alors, les obstacles étant trop massifs — auprès de Mr Paul Rosenberg, dans mes tentatives d'assembler des œuvres de Picasso pour une exposition de Bâle. J'y ai renoncé, cette fois-là et jusqu'ici. Aujourd'hui, j'apprends que cette exposition se fera à Zurich, par vos bons soins. Et Bâle alors, vous n'y pensez plus, vous n'y avez pas pensé du tout? Est-ce sûr? Ne peut-on rien y changer?" Letter from Wilhelm Barth to Carl Montag, 4 April 1932. — SIKDok, NM, IV: Dossier 12.
11 Letter from Wilhelm Wartmann to Carl Montag, 10 March 1932. — SIKDok, NM, IV: Dossier 12.
12 Letter from Wilhelm Wartmann to Carl Montag, 12 April 1932. — SIKDok, NM, IV: Dossier 12.
13 Letter from Wilhelm Wartmann to Carl Montag, 14 June 1932. — SIKDok, NM, IV: Dossier 12.
14 Letter from Wilhelm Wartmann to Carl Montag, 19 June 1932. — SIK-Dok, NM, IV: Dossier 12.
15 Letter from Dr Adolf Jöhr to Picasso, 15 July 1932. — Copies of correspondence sent, vol. 53, exhibition from 22 July to 19 December 1932, p.3f. — Archive of the Zürcher Kunstgesellschaft.
16 Letter from Dr Adolf Jöhr to Georges Braque, 23 July 1932. — Copies of correspondence sent, vol. 53, exhibition from 22 July to 19 December 1932, p.5. —

17 Letter from Carl Montag to Wilhelm Wartmann, 19 July 1932. Archive of the Zürcher Kunstgesellschaft.
18 Meeting of the exhibition commission, 16 November 1932. — Minutes of the exhibition commission VIII, 15 November 1932 to 22 November 1932, p.2. — Archive of the Zürcher Kunstgesellschaft.
19 For the genesis of this exhibition cf. Windhöfel, Lutz, 'Braque und Picasso — erste Schritte ihrer Rezeption in der Schweiz', in: *Basler Magazin, Politisch-kulturelle Weekend-Beilage der Basler Zeitung*, no. 6, 10 February 1990. p.6f.
20 wti., 'Eröffnung der Picasso-Ausstellung', in: *Neue Zürcher Zeitung*, year 153, no. 1675, 12 September 1932, sheet 1.
21 Telegram to Carl Montag, 7 September 1932: *Parti ce matin Zurich Picasso*. — SIKDok, NM, IV: Dossier 12.
22 Hanns Welti, 'Picasso auf dem Zürichsee', in: *Neue Zürcher Zeitung*, year 153, no. 1693, 14 September 1932, sheet 6. — 'Pablo Picasso in Zürich', in: *Zürcher Illustrierte*, year VIII, no. 39, 23 September 1932, p.1230. — Hanns Welti, 'Picasso in Zürich', in: *Sie und Er*, no. 39, 24 September 1932, p.1021. — Doris Wild, 'Begegnung mit Picasso', in: *Neue Zürcher Zeitung*, year 153, no. 1811, 2 October 1932, sheet 3.
23 That Picasso could have visited the Unterlinden Museum in Colmar in autumn 1932 has often been doubted and only recently described as "très probablement un mythe inventé par l'historiographie locale." cf. Christian Heck, 'Entre le mythe et le modèle formel, Les Crucifixions de Grünewald et l'art du XXe siècle', in: *Corps crucifiés*, Musée Picasso exhibition catalogue, Paris 1992, p.104 and note 104.

24 Letters from Bernhard Geiser to Wilhelm Wartmann, 3 August and 1 September 1932. — Archive of the Zürcher Kunstgesellschaft.
25 Letters from Direktor Ernst Buchner, Cologne, 3 September 1932 and from Direktor Victor Dirksen, Elberfeld, 31 August 1932 to Wartmann. — Archive of the Zürcher Kunstgesellschaft.
26 Letter from Alfred Flechtheim to Wartmann, 29 July 1932. — Archive of the Zürcher Kunstgesellschaft.
27 Letter from Barth to Prof. Dr Herbert Reiners, Fribourg, 19 September 1932. — Archive of the Basler Kunstverein in the Staatsarchiv Basel. — Hans Graber notes in his review of the exhibition: "It is most regrettable that the Collection St. in Basel, which possesses several of Picasso's major works, is not represented." (H. Gr., 'Picasso im Zürcher Kunsthaus', in: *Neue Zürcher Zeitung*, year 153, no. 1743, 22 September 1932, sheet 1.)
28 cf. Christian Geelhaar, 'Bejahung der Gegenwart and Zuversicht auf die Zukunft, Zur Geschichte der Emanuel Hoffmann-Stiftung', in: *Emanuel Hoffmann-Stiftung Basel*, Basel 1991, p.10.
29 Letter from Bernhard Geiser to Wilhelm Wartmann, 13 September 1932. — Archive of the Zürcher Kunstgesellschaft.
30 Summary, 'Max Raphael über Picasso', in: *Neue Zürcher Zeitung*, year 153, no. 1855, 7 October 1932, sheet 6.
31 Summary, 'Hans Hildebrandt über Picasso', in: *Neue Zürcher Zeitung*, year 153, no. 1905, 14 October 1932, sheet 9.
32 Summary, 'Strawinsky und Picasso', in: *Neue Zürcher Zeitung*, year 153, no. 1952, 21 October 1932, sheet 6.
33 *Neue Zürcher Zeitung*, year 153, no. 1811, 2 October 1932, sheet 3.

34   Summary, 'Gotthard Jedlicka über Picasso', in: *Neue Zürcher Zeitung*, no. 2008, 29 October 1932, sheet 3. — The lecture was printed in: Gotthard Jedlicka, *Picasso*, (Oprecht & Helbling) Zurich 1934. Partial reproduction in: *Werk*, year 32, issue 4, April 1945, pp. 125–128.

35   Kunstchronik, in: *Neue Zürcher Zeitung*, year 153, no. 1795, 29 September 1932, sheet 6.

36   Archive of the Zürcher Kunstgesellschaft.

37   Letters from Maja Hoffmann-Stehlin to Wartmann, 16 and 25 October 1932. — Archive of the Zürcher Kunstgesellschaft.

38   Letters from Wartmann to Karl Im Obersteg, 26 and 28 October 1932. Copies of correspondence sent, vol. 53, exhibition from 22 July to 19 December 1932, p. 329 and p. 338.

39   Kunstchronik, in: *Neue Zürcher Zeitung*, year 153, no. 2031, 1 November 1932, sheet 7.

40   Letter to Otto Meyer-Amden, 14 December 1932. — Oskar Schlemmer, *Briefe und Tagebücher*, ed. Tut Schlemmer, Munich 1958, p. 304.

41   Meeting of the exhibition commission, 16 November 1932. — Minutes of the exhibition commission VIII, 15 November 1932 to 22 November 1939. — Archive of the Zürcher Kunstgesellschaft.

42   *Zürcher Tagblatt*, no. 238, 10 October 1932.

43   H. O., 'Soll die Stadt die Picasso-Ausstellung finanzieren helfen?', in: *Volksrecht*, year 35, no. 239, 11 October 1932.

44   S. Giedion, 'Über Picasso. Ist das Schaffen Picassos typisch bürgerlich-dekadent?', in: *Volksrecht*, year 35, no. 246, 19 October 1932.

45   Reinhold Hohl, 'Picasso, Zürich and die C. G. Jung-Konservativen', in: *Tages-Anzeiger*, year 90, no. 30, 6/7 February 1982, p. 49f.

46   cf. Theodore Reff, 'Themes of Love and Death in Picasso's Early Work', in: *Picasso in Retrospect*, Advisory editors Sir Roland Penrose and John Golding, New York 1973, pp. 11–47.

47   cf. commentary by William Rubin, in: *Picasso in the Collection of The Museum of Modern Art*, New York 1972, pp. 138–141.

48   Jung, C. G., 'Picasso', in: *Neue Zürcher Zeitung*, year 153, no. 2107, 13 November 1932, sheet 2. — Reprinted in: Jung, C. G., *Wirklichkeit der Seele*, 1934.

49   'Picasso als Patient?' in: *Neue Zürcher Zeitung*, year 153, no. 2145, 18 November 1932, sheet 3.

50   H. W., 'Picasso ein Drama', in: *Neue Zürcher Zeitung*, year 153, no. 2233, 30 November 1932, sheet 5.

51   wti. [Jakob Welti], 'Aus dem Zürcher Kunsthaus', in: *Neue Zürcher Zeitung*, year 161, no. 468, 30 March 1940, sheet 2.

52   cf.: Stefan Frey, 'Chronologische Biografie' (1933–1941), in: *Paul Klee, Das Schaffen im Todesjahr*, exhibition catalogue, Kunstmuseum Bern, 1990, p. 123. — Werckmeister, Otto Karl, *Paul Klee in Exile*, 1933–1940, exhibition catalogue, Himeji City Museum of Art, Tokyo 1985, p. 40f.

53   'C. G. Jung diagnostiziert Picasso', in: *Kunst und Künstler*, year 32, issue 1, January 1933, p. 28ff.

54   'Picasso étudié par le Dr Jung', in: *Cahiers d'art*, 7ᵉ année, 8–10, 1932, p. 352ff.

55   'C. G. Jung vergreift sich an Picasso', in: *Information*, Zurich, no. 6, December 1932, pp. 4–7. — Reprinted in: Max Raphael, *Aufbruch in die Gegenwart, Begegnungen mit der Kunst und den Künstlern des 20. Jahrhunderts*, ed. Hans-Jürgen Heinrichs, Frankfurt am Main 1989, pp. 21–27.

56   dt. [Georg Schmidt], 'Pablo Picasso, Im Zürcher Kunsthaus', I, in: *National-Zeitung*, year 90, no. 486, 18 October, p. 2f; II, no. 488, 19 October, p. 2f; III., no. 492, 21 October 1932, p. 2.

57   H. Gr. [Hans Graber], 'Picasso im Zürcher Kunsthaus', I, in: *Neue Zürcher Zeitung*, year 153, no. 1743, 22 September, sheet 1; II, no. 1811, 2 October, sheet 3; III, no. 1895, 13 October, sheet 6; IV, no. 1997, 28 October, sheet 1; V, no. 2055, 5 November, sheet 2; VI, no. 2094, 10 November 1932, sheet 7. — Berthold Fenigstein, 'Picasso im Kunsthaus', I, in: *Tages-Anzeiger*, year 40, no. 222, 21 September; II, no. 229, 29 September; III, no. 233, 4 October; IV, no. 241, 13 October 1932.

58   Letters to Wilhelm Wartmann, 16 and 26 May, 1 and 25 June 1931, and 4 January 1932. Archive of the Zürcher Kunstgesellschaft. — The offers related to works painted in 1929: *Woman in an Armchair* (92 × 60 cm) and *Woman with a Towel* (73 × 60 cm); price: 20,000 and 16,000 Swiss francs respectively.

59   Letter from Gertrude Stein to Wartmann, 16 October 1932. — Archive of the Zürcher Kunstgesellschaft.

60   Letters from Eugenia Huici Errazuriz to Wartmann, 14 and 20 October 1932. — Archive of the Zürcher Kunstgesellschaft. — *Man Leaning on a Table* was bought by Comte Etienne de Beaumont in the course of the 1930s. In 1934 the painting featured in the Picasso exhibition at the Wadsworth Atheneum in Hartford, still as a loan from the Errazuriz Collection.

61   Letter to Georges Wildenstein, 12 November 1932. — Copies of correspondence sent, vol. 53, exhibition, from 22 July to 19 December 1932, p. 384. — Archive of the Zürcher Kunstgesellschaft. — 75,000 French francs were worth approximately 10,000 Swiss francs.

62   "Ce serait plutôt un don de votre part que vous feriez au Musée et à la Ville de Zurich qu'une vente . . ." Letter to Pablo Picasso, 12 November 1932. — Copies of correspondence sent, vol. 53, exhibition, from 22 July to 19 December 1932, p. 385. — Archive of the Zürcher Kunstgesellschaft.

63   Note in file, 16 November 1932. — Archive of the Zürcher Kunstgesellschaft.

64   Telegram, 16 November 1932. — Archive of the Zürcher Kunstgesellschaft.

65   A further copy of *La Suite des Saltimbanques* came in March 1925 to the Collection of Prints and Drawings of the Öffentliche Kunstsammlung Basel; it was from the collection of Dr Paul Linder.

66   Archive of the Zürcher Kunstgesellschaft.

67   Letters of 8 September and 3 October 1932. — Archive of the Zürcher Kunstgesellschaft.

68   Letter from Max Huggler to Wartmann, 14 September 1932. — Archive of the Zürcher Kunstgesellschaft.

69   Letter to Prof. Dr. Herbert Reiners, Fribourg, 19 September 1932. — Archive of the Basler Kunstverein in the Staatsarchiv Basel.

70   Letter from G. F. Reber to Wilhelm Wartmann, 16 November 1932. — Archive of the Zürcher Kunstgesellschaft.

71   This refers to the exhibitions put on by the Schweizerischer Kunstverein, the 'Schweizerische Ausstellungen', which took place by rotation (Turnus) in several cities and the Nationale Kunstausstellungen der Schweiz, also known as 'Salon'.

72   Letter from Paul Basilius Barth to Wilhelm Barth, 9 November 1932. — Wilhelm Barth Archive in the Staatsarchiv Basel.

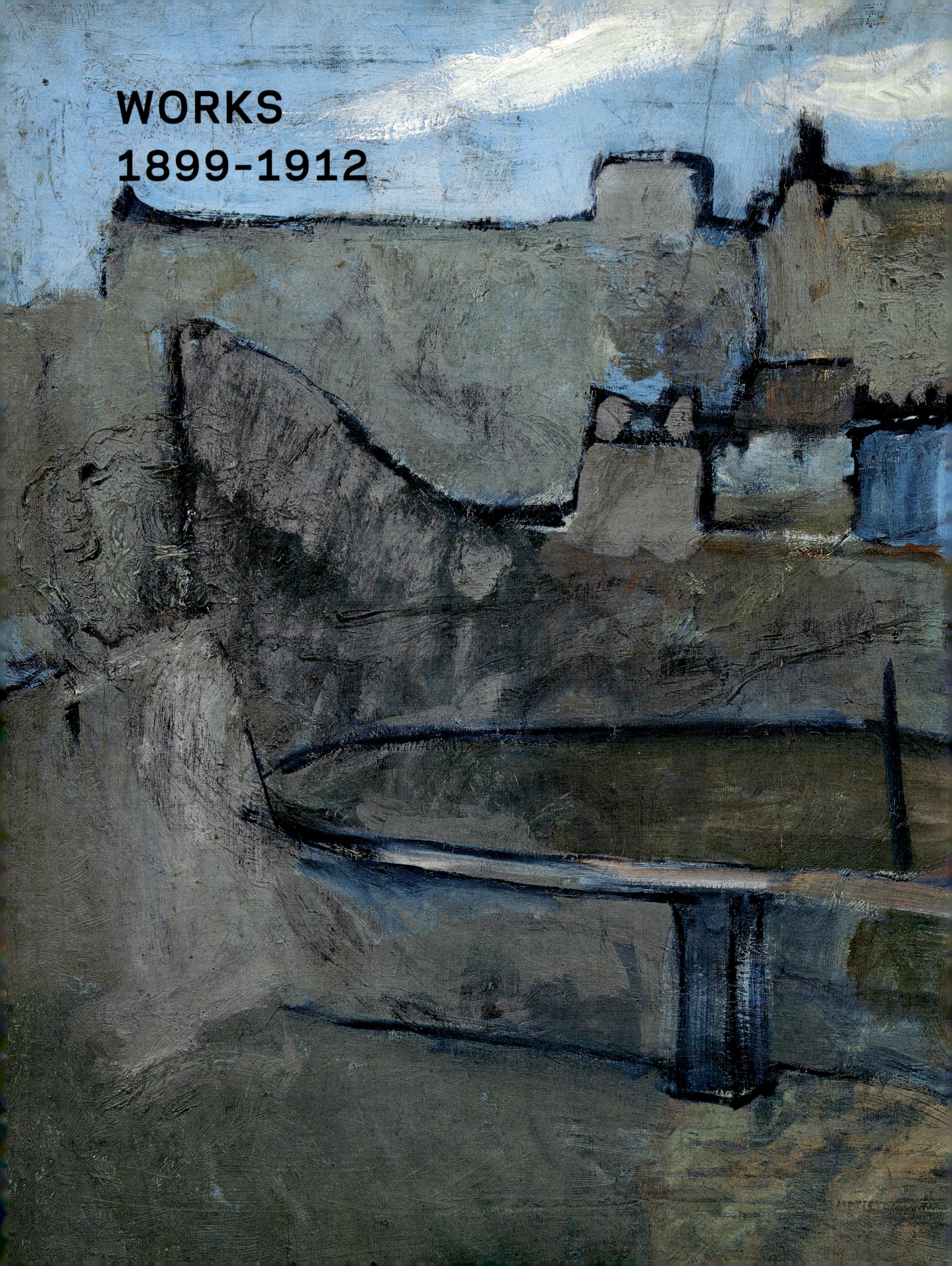

WORKS
1899-1912

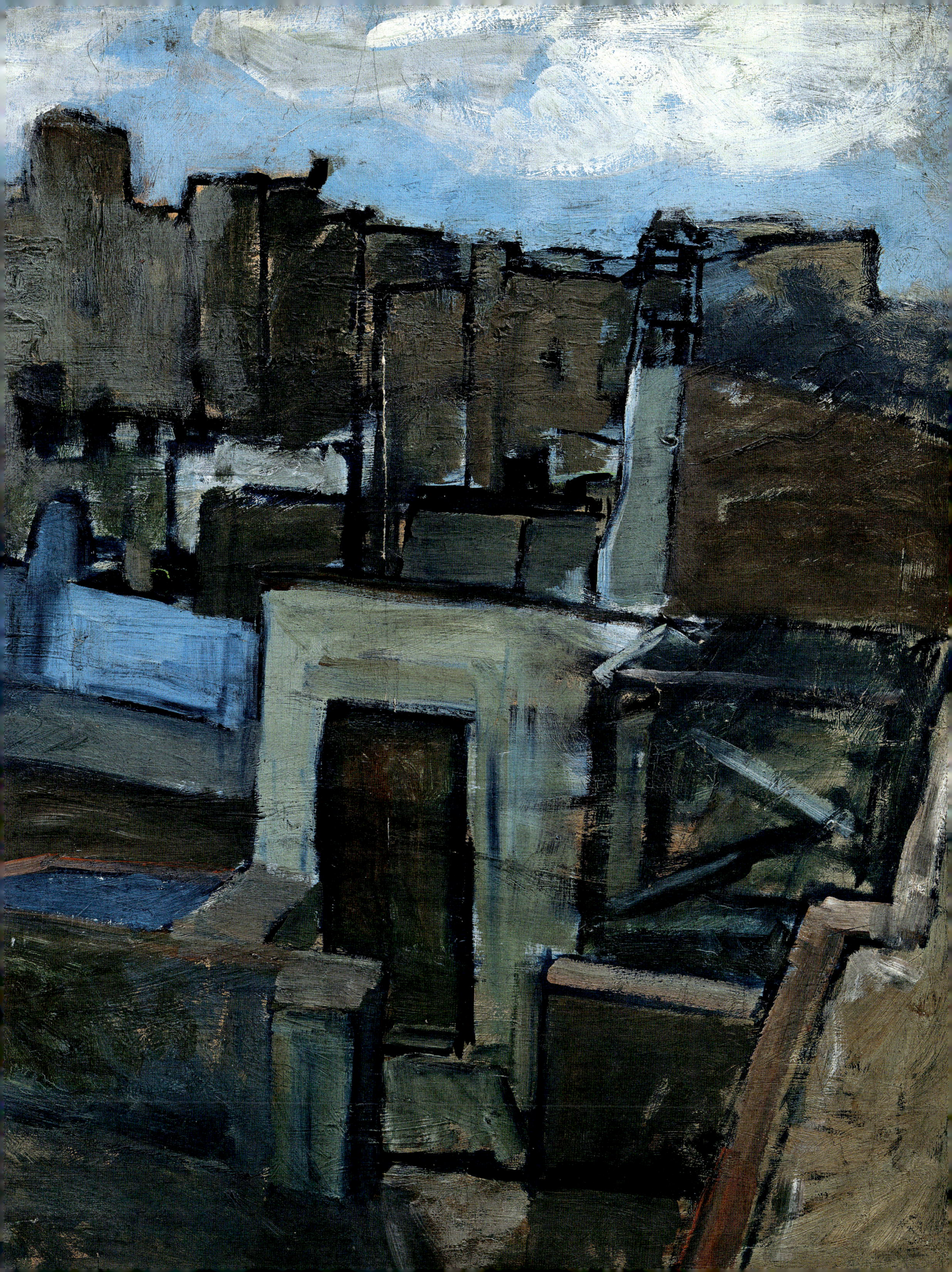

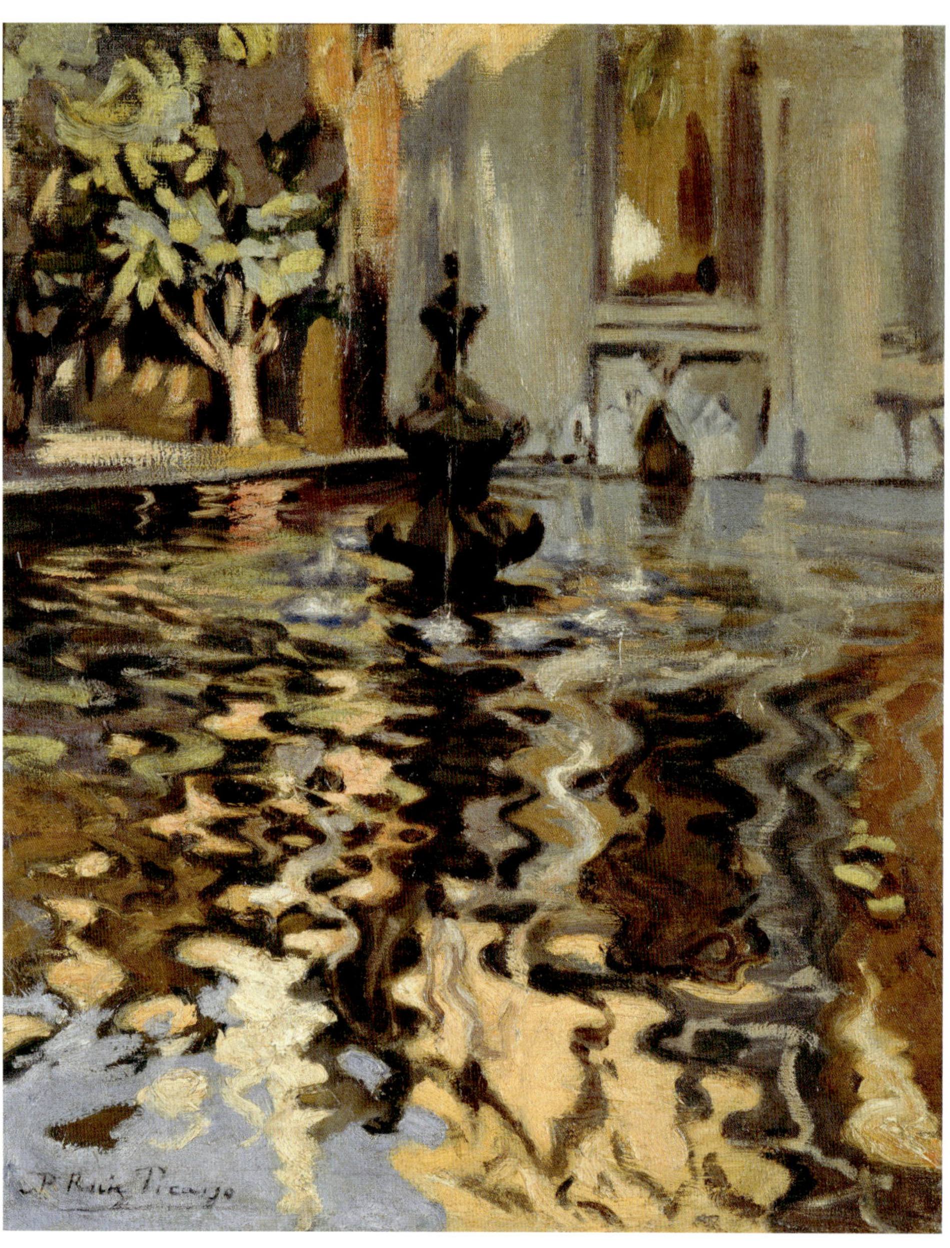

1
The Fountain, 1899
Oil on canvas
61 x 50.8 cm
Musée Jenisch, Vevey
Bequest of Alain Ollivier

previous double page
Barcelona Rooftops, 1902/03 (detail)
Oil on canvas
71 x 111 cm
Museu Picasso, Barcelona

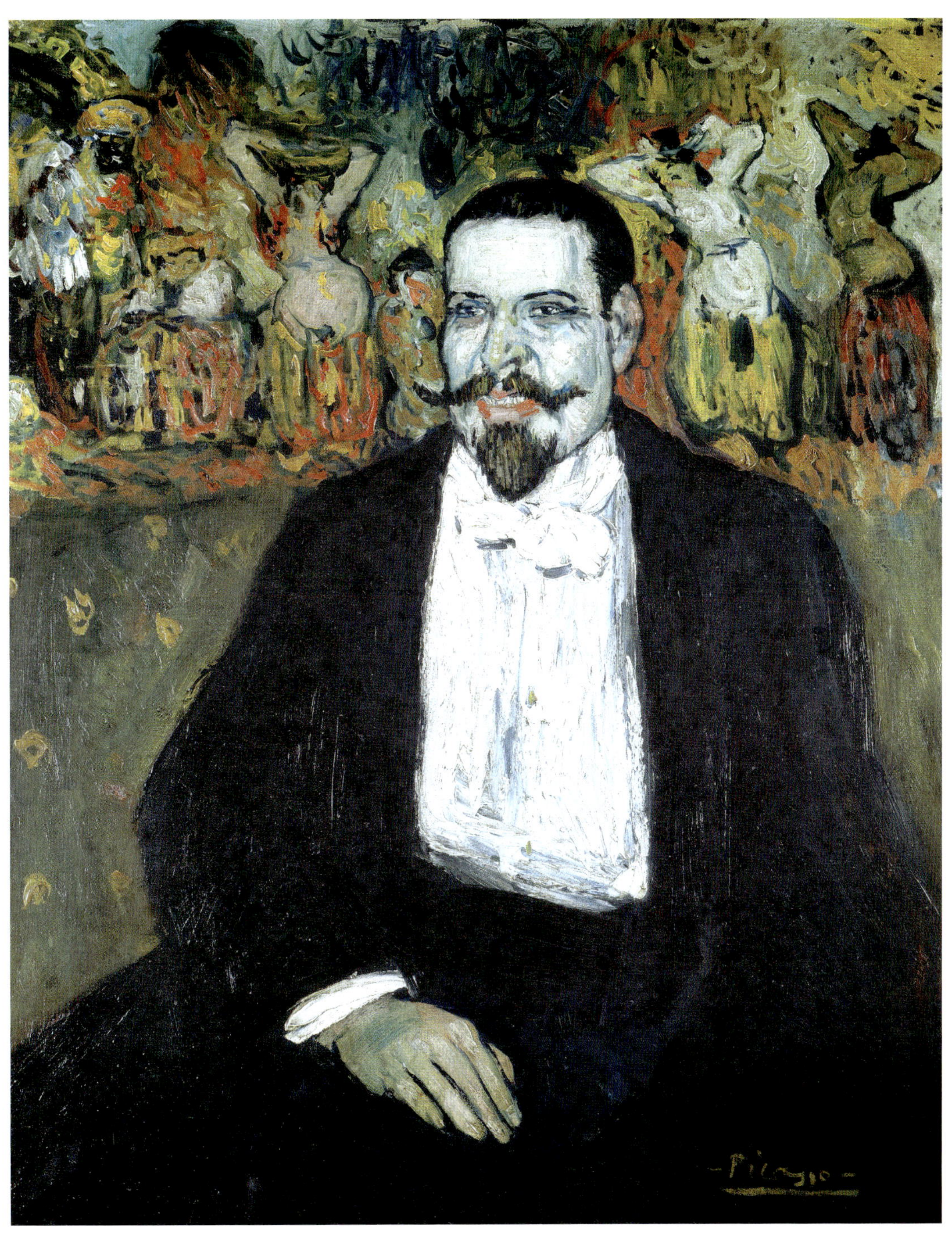

2

Portrait of Gustave Coquiot, 1901
Oil on canvas
100 x 81 cm
Centre Pompidou, Paris
Musée national d'art moderne/
Centre de création industrielle
Donated by Mme Gustave Coquiot, 1933

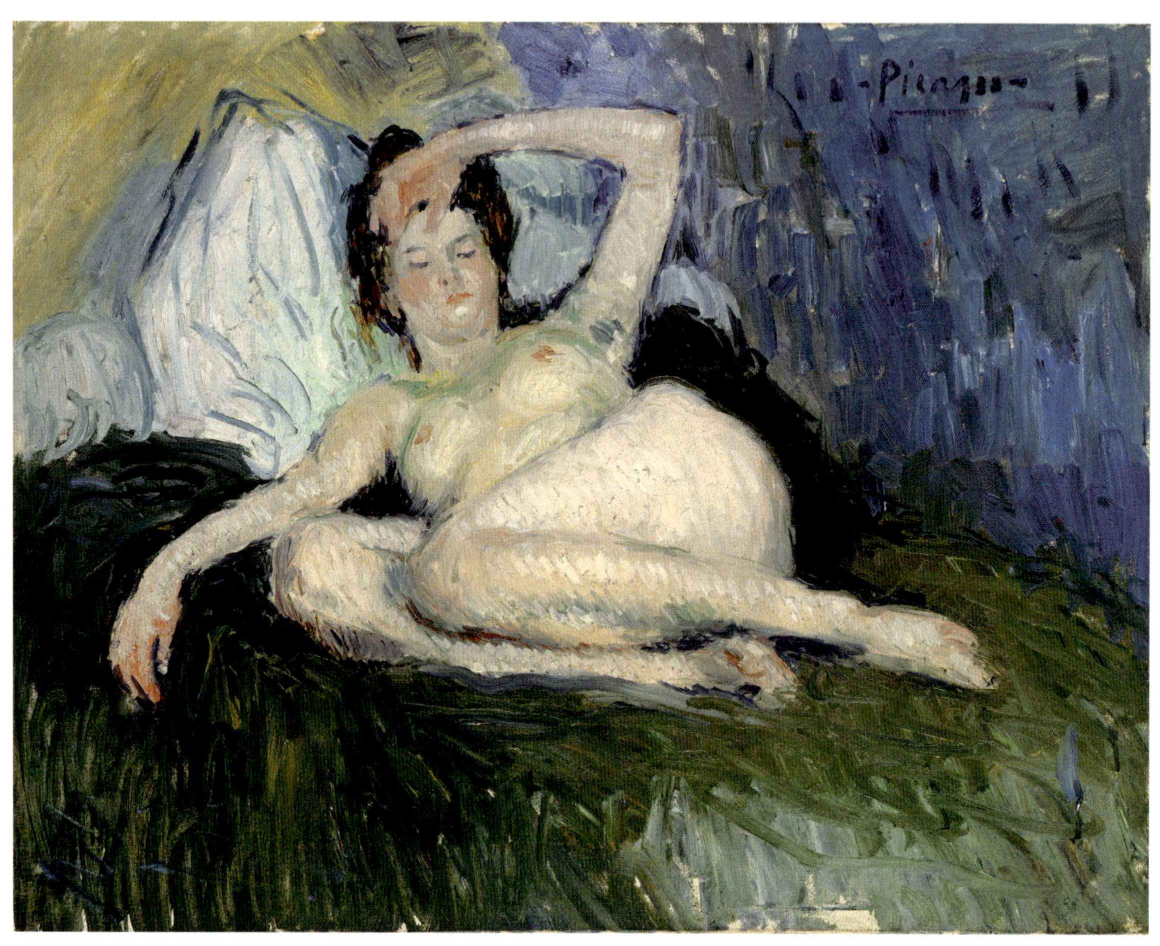

3
Jeanne, 1901
Oil on canvas
70.5 x 90 cm
Centre Pompidou, Paris,
Musée national d'art moderne/
Centre de création industrielle
Bequest of Baronne Eva Gourgaud, 1965

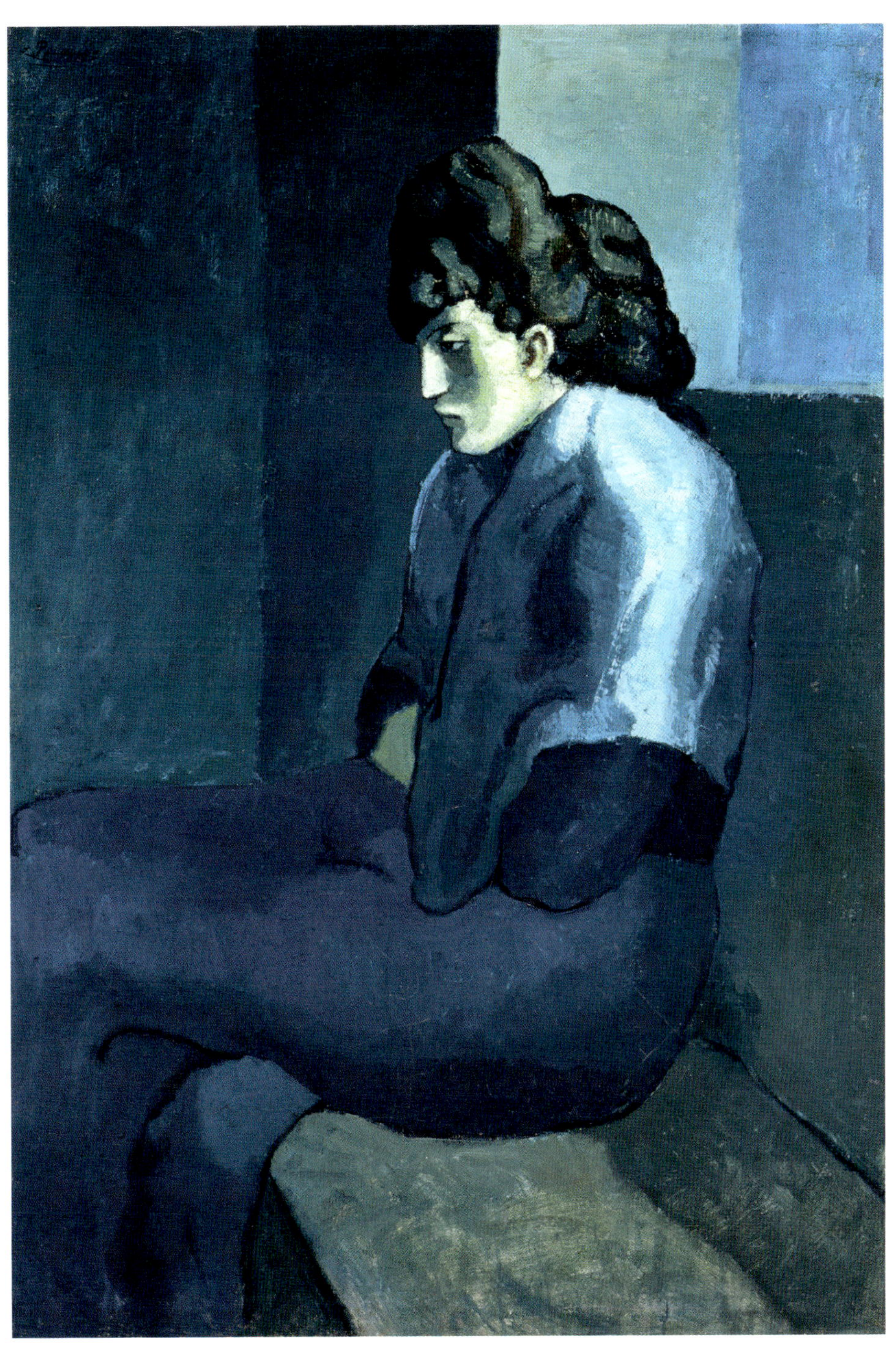

4
Melancholy Woman, 1902
Oil on canvas
100 x 69.2 cm
The Detroit Institute of Arts
Bequest of Robert H. Tannahill

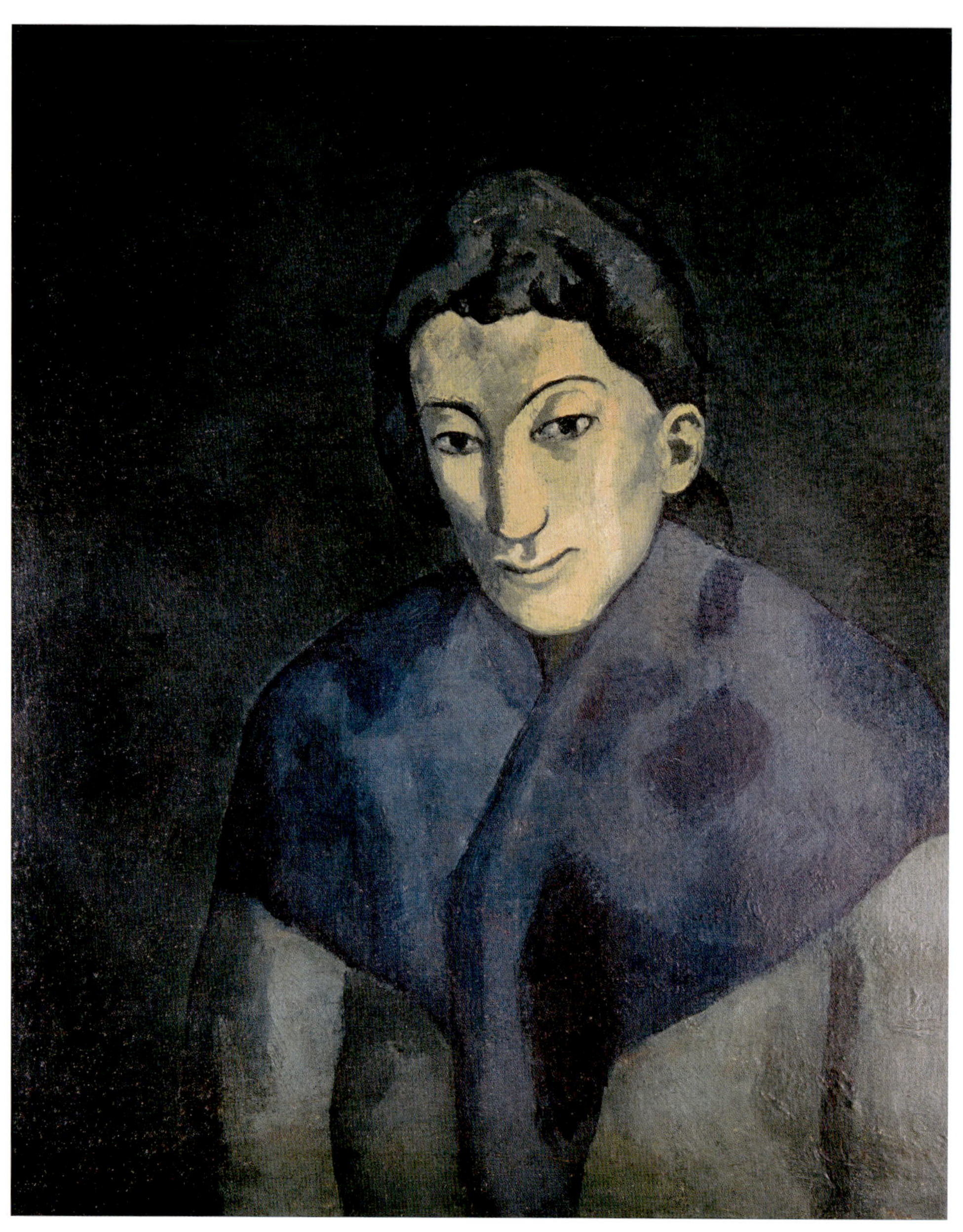

5

Woman in a Blue Shawl, 1902

Oil on canvas

60.3 x 52.4 cm

Aichi Prefectural Museum of Art, Japan

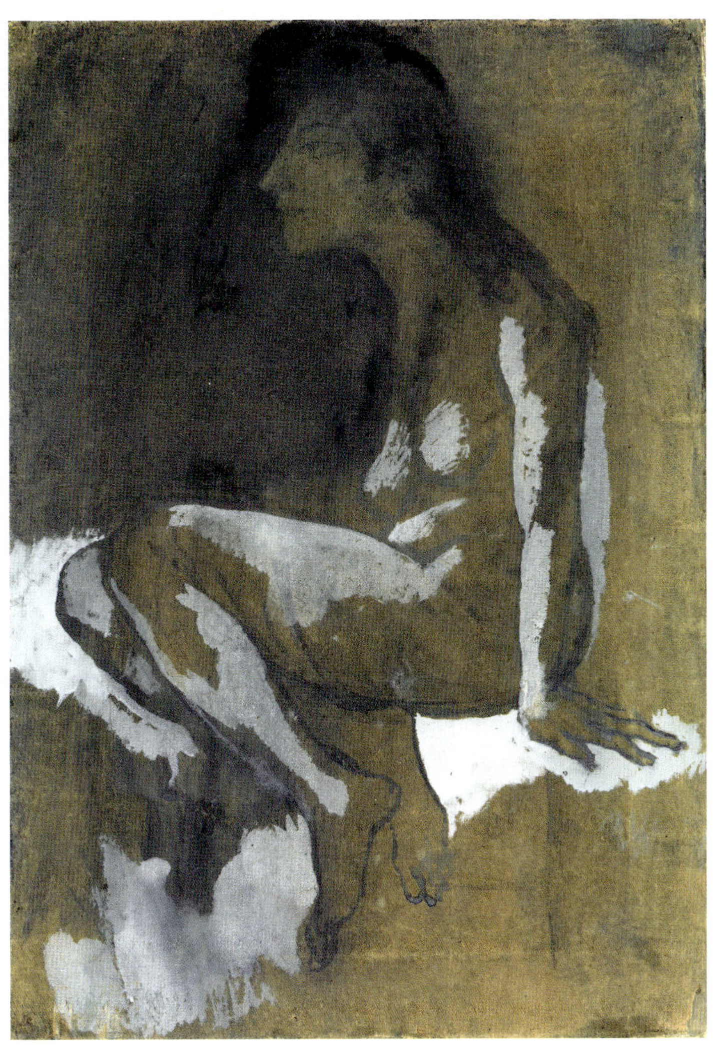

6
Crouching Woman, 1903
Gouache and watercolour on
grounded paper
55 x 38 cm
Bollag Galleries

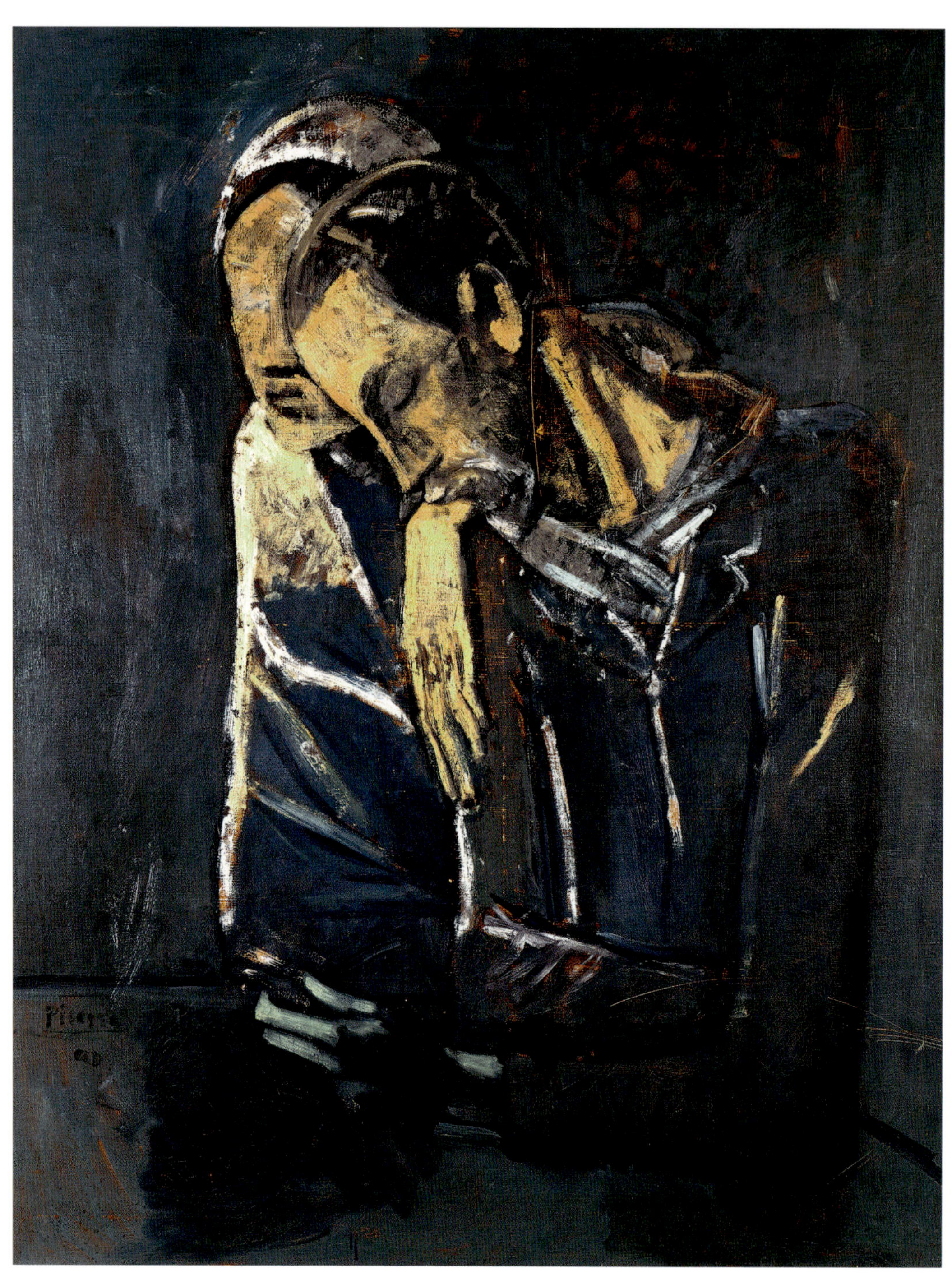

7

The Couple (The Wretched Ones), 1904
Oil on canvas
100.5 x 81.5 cm
Merzbacher Kunststiftung

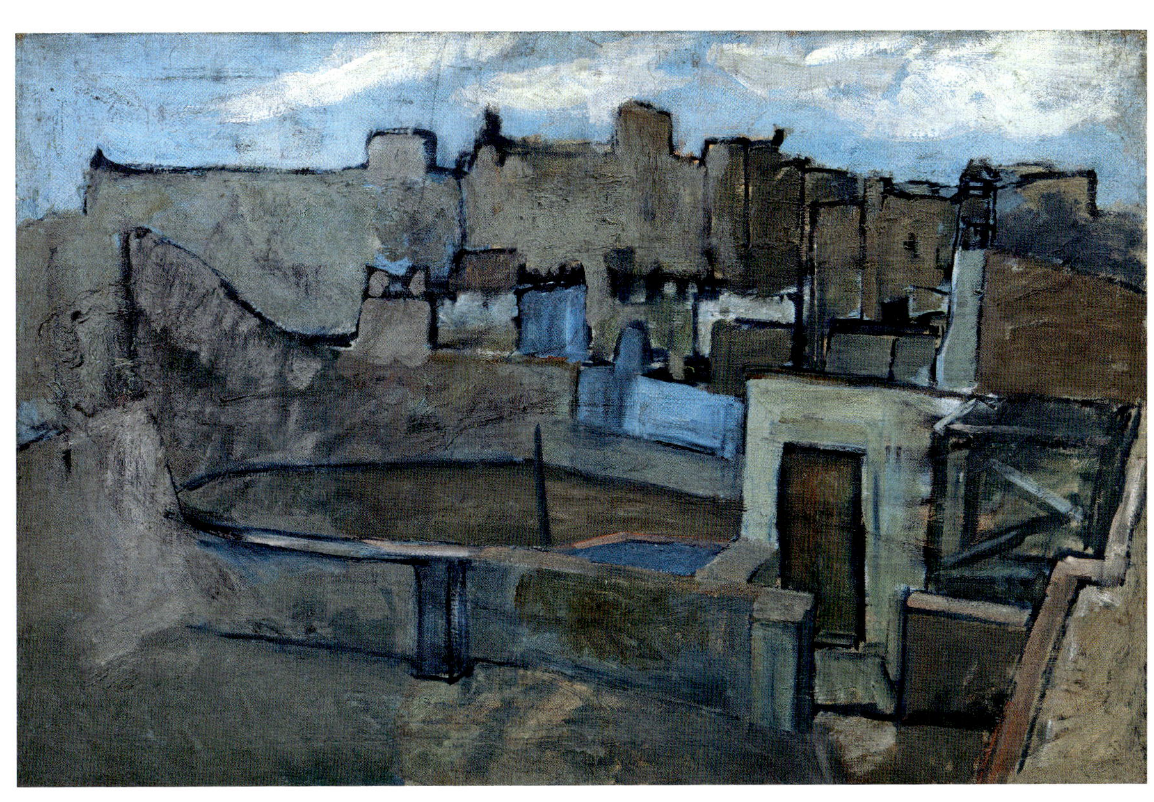

8
Barcelona Rooftops, 1902/03
Oil on canvas
71 x 111 cm
Museu Picasso, Barcelona

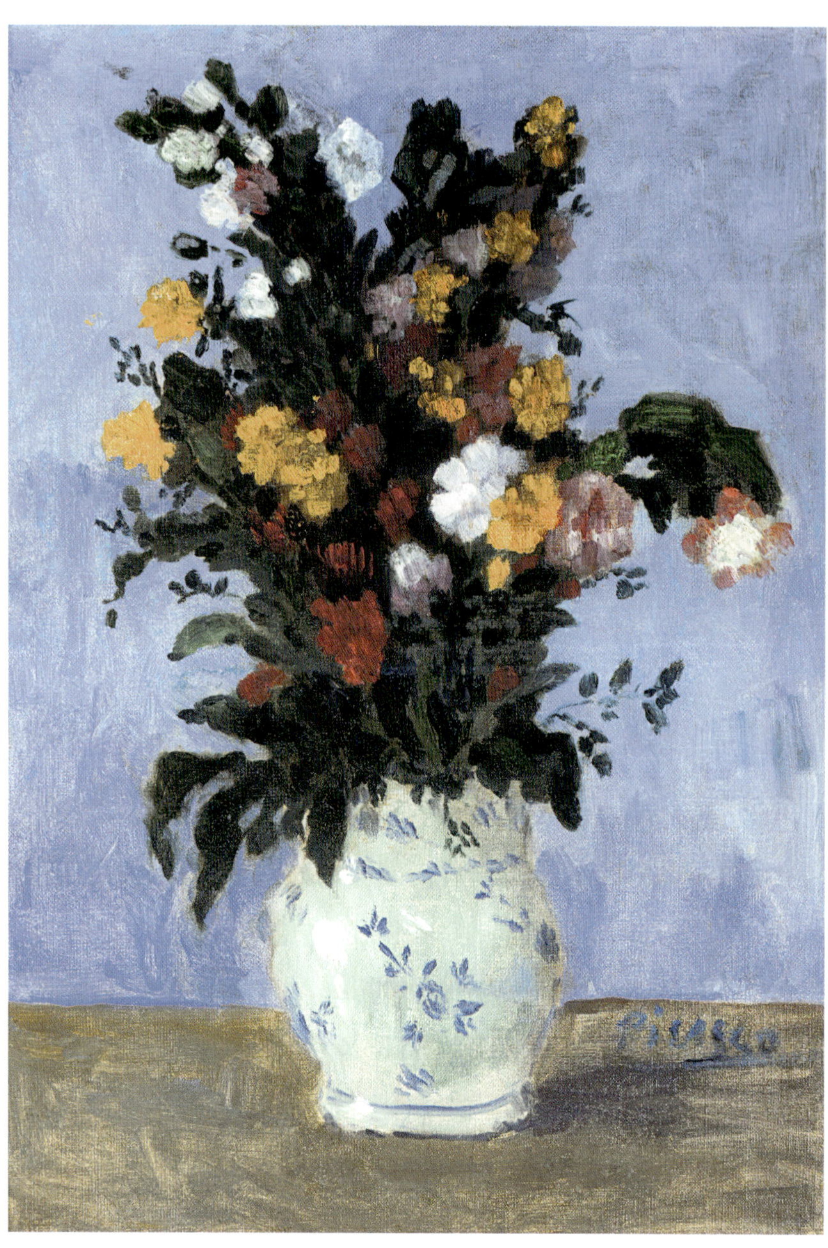

9
Vase of Flowers, 1901/04
Oil on canvas
66 x 46.5 cm
Courtesy Nahmad Collection, Switzerland

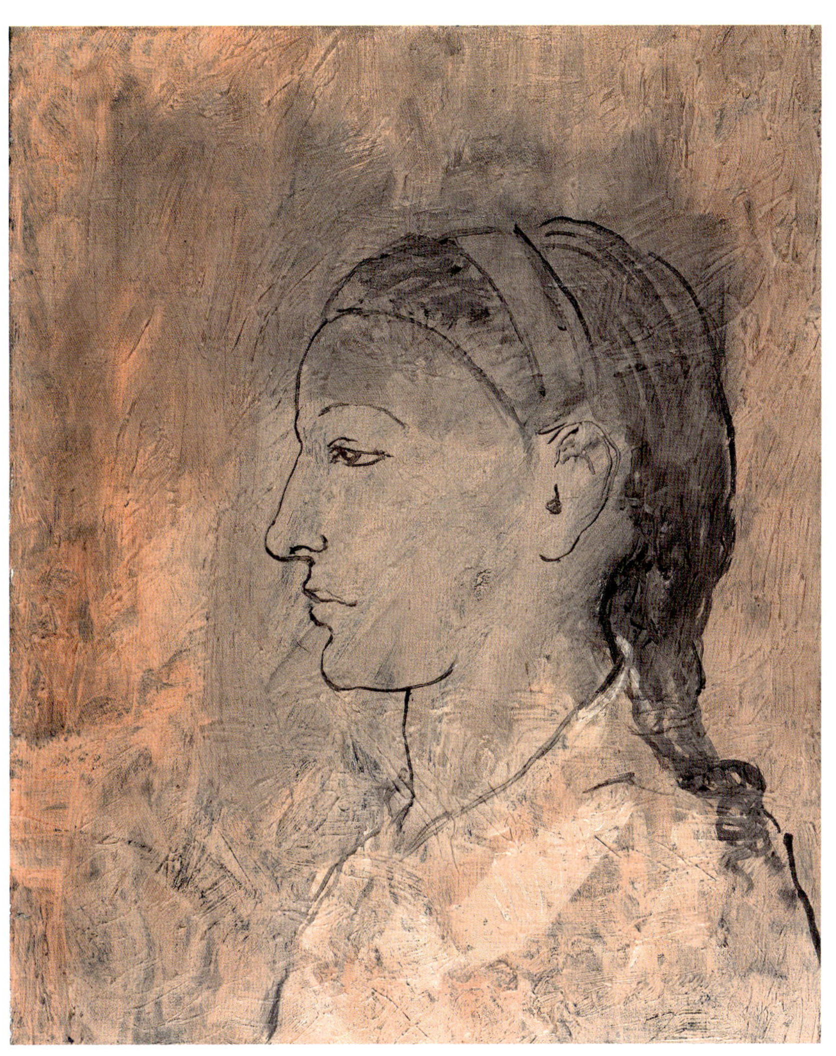

10
Portrait of Fernande Olivier, 1906
Oil on canvas
46 x 38 cm
Private collection

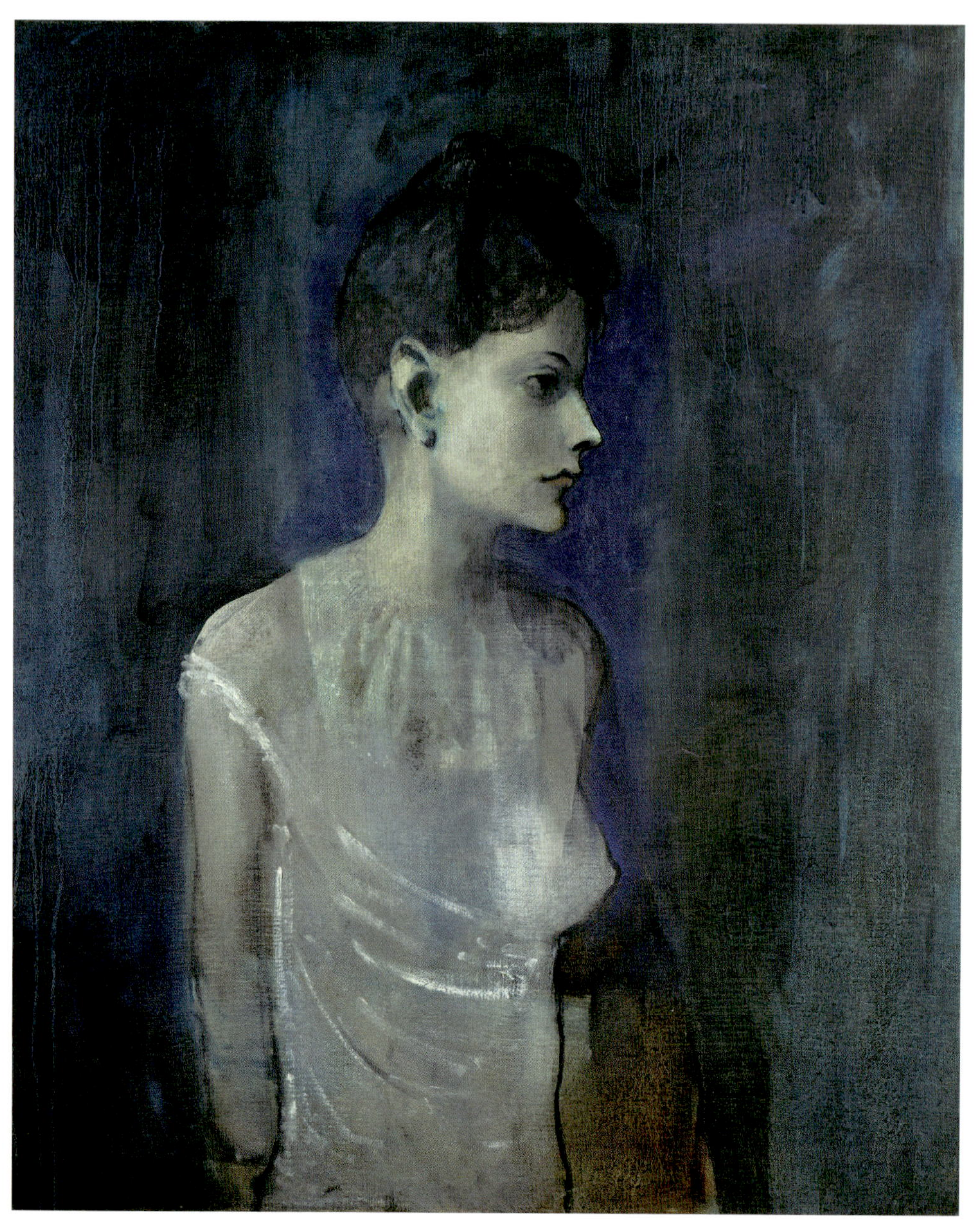

11
Girl in a Chemise, c. 1905
Oil on canvas
72.7 x 60 cm
Tate, London
Bequeathed by C. Frank Stoop, 1933

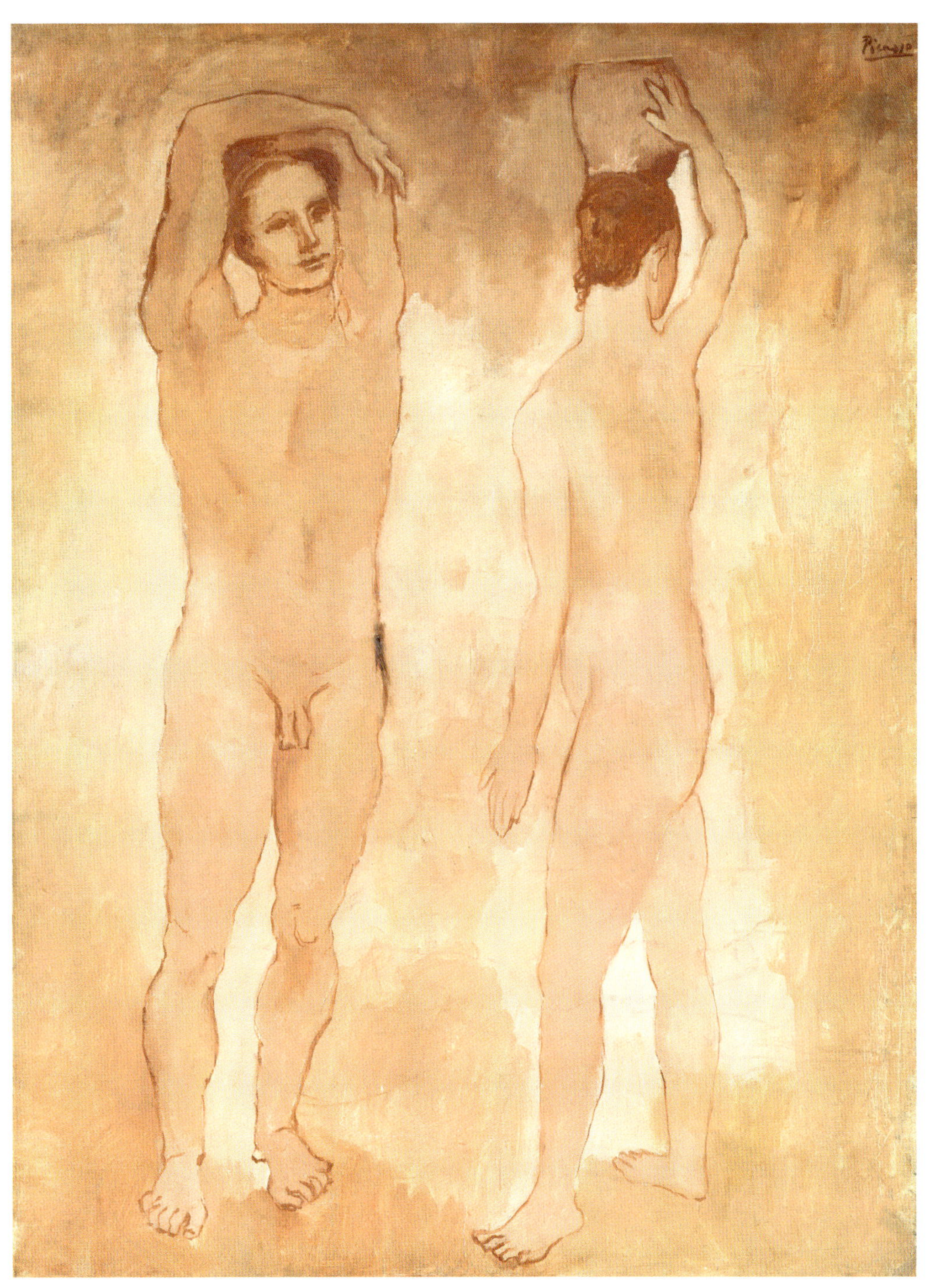

12
Adolescents, 1906
Oil on canvas
157 x 117 cm
Musée de l'Orangerie, Paris
Collection Jean Walter et
Paul Guillaume

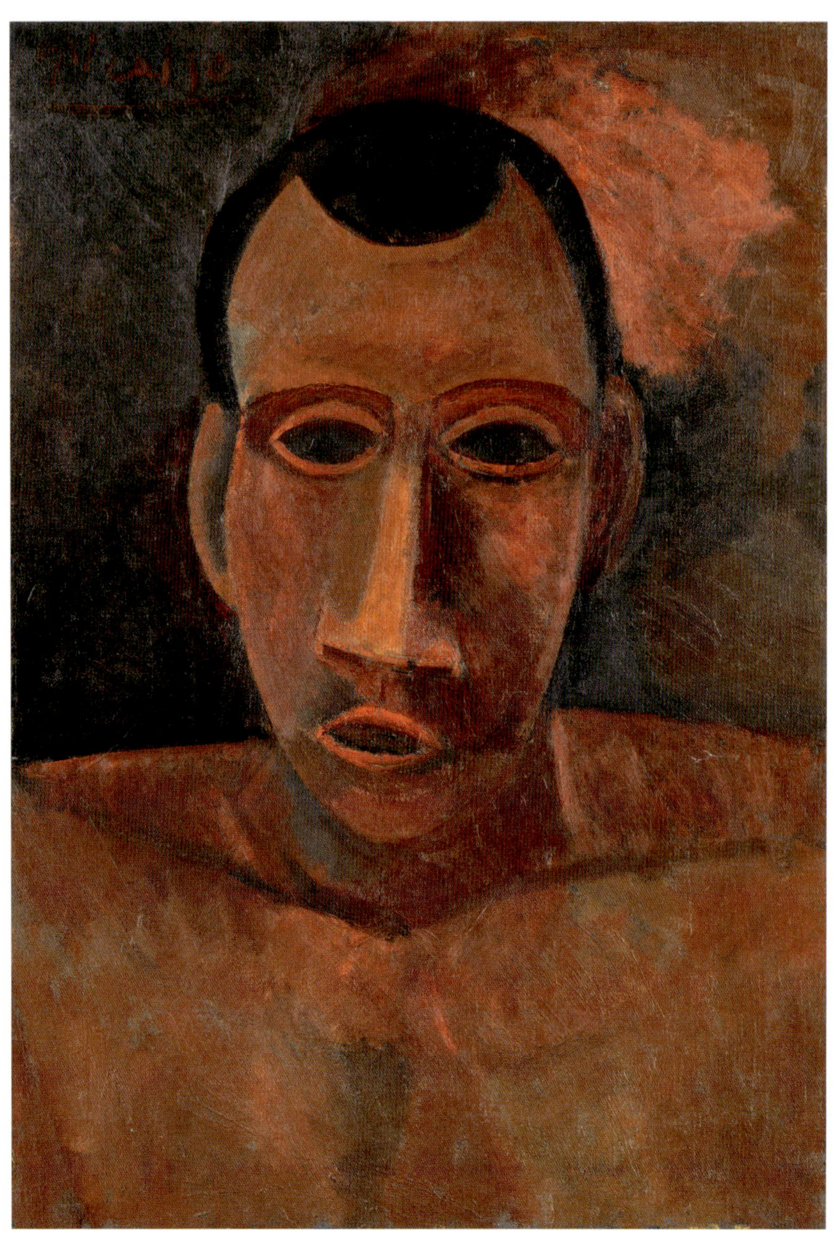

13
Bust of a Man, 1908
Oil on canvas
62.2 x 43.5 cm
The Metropolitan Museum of Art,
New York
Bequest of Florene M. Schoenborn, 1995

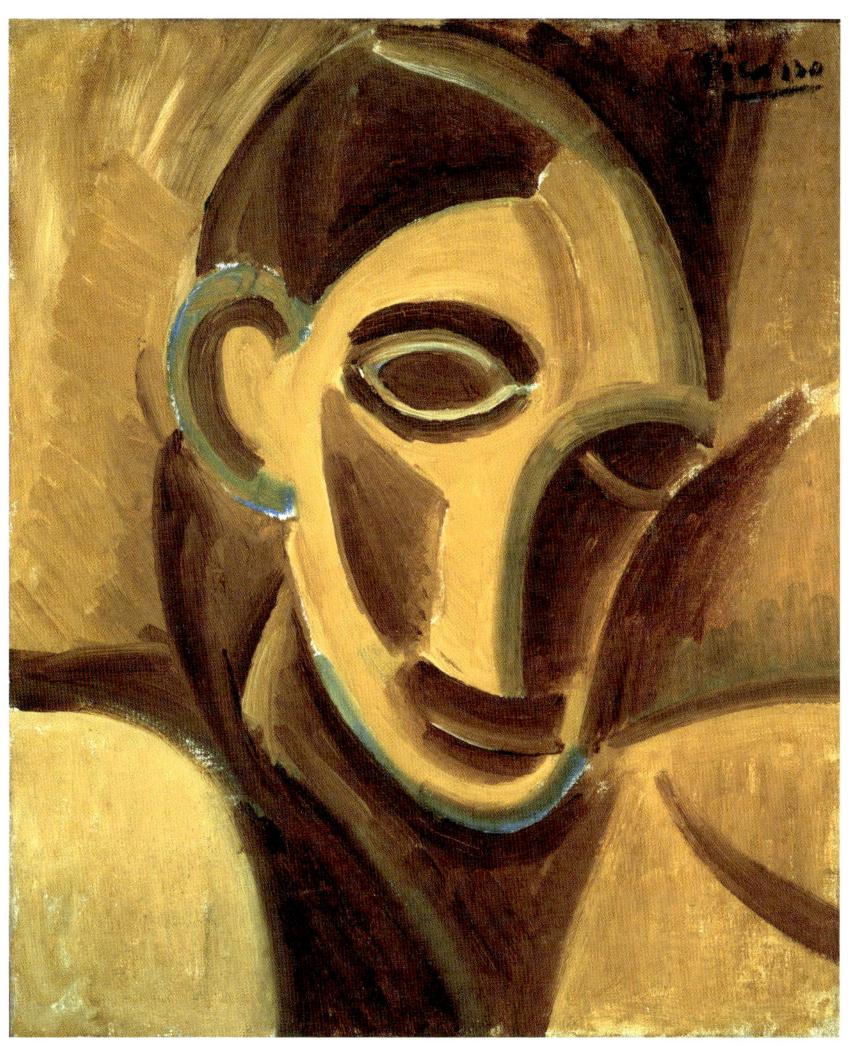

14
Woman's Head, 1907
Oil on canvas
54.5 x 46 cm
Private collection

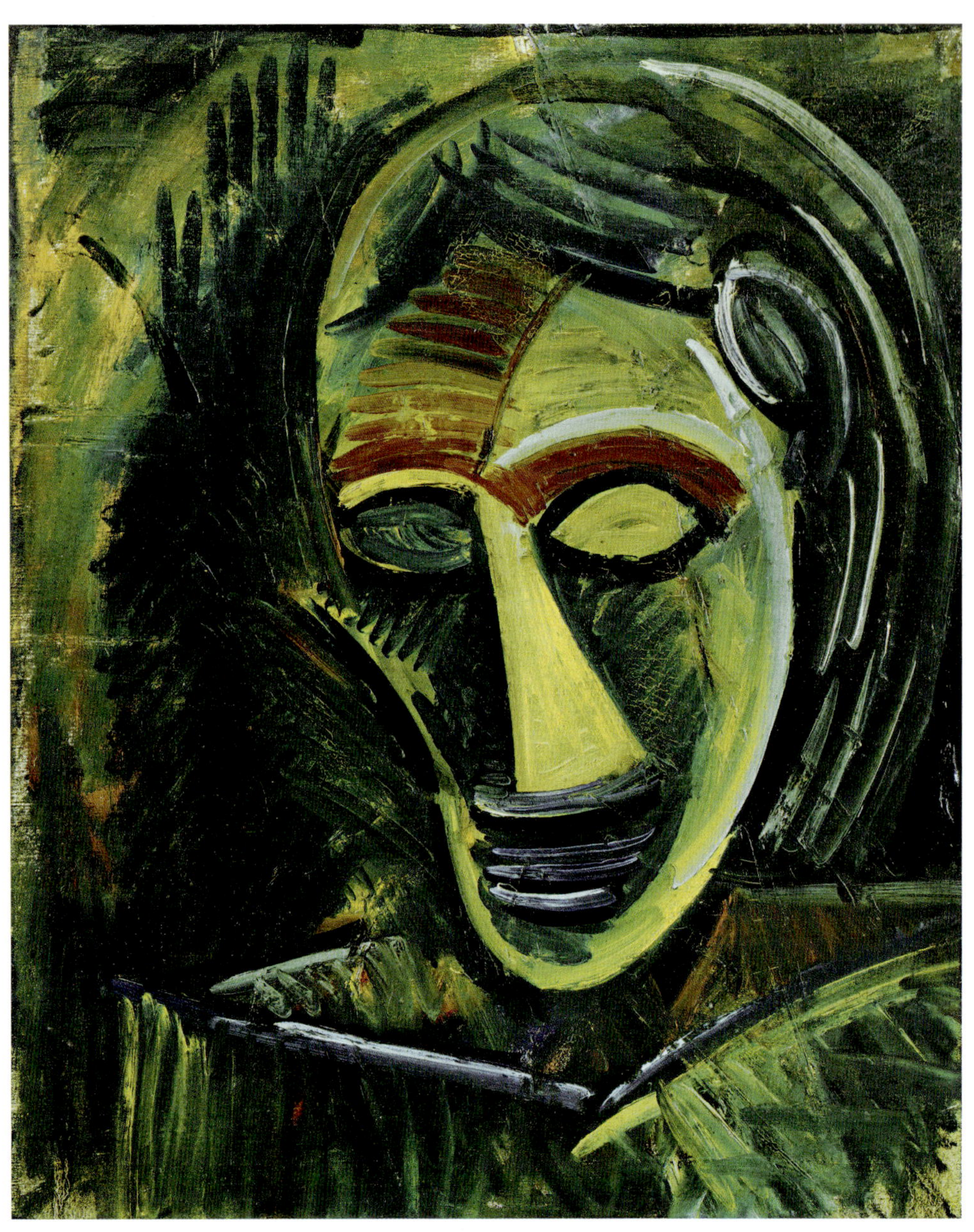

15
Woman's Head, 1908
Oil on canvas
73.6 x 60.6 cm
The Museum of Modern Art,
New York
Florene May Schoenborn Bequest, 1996

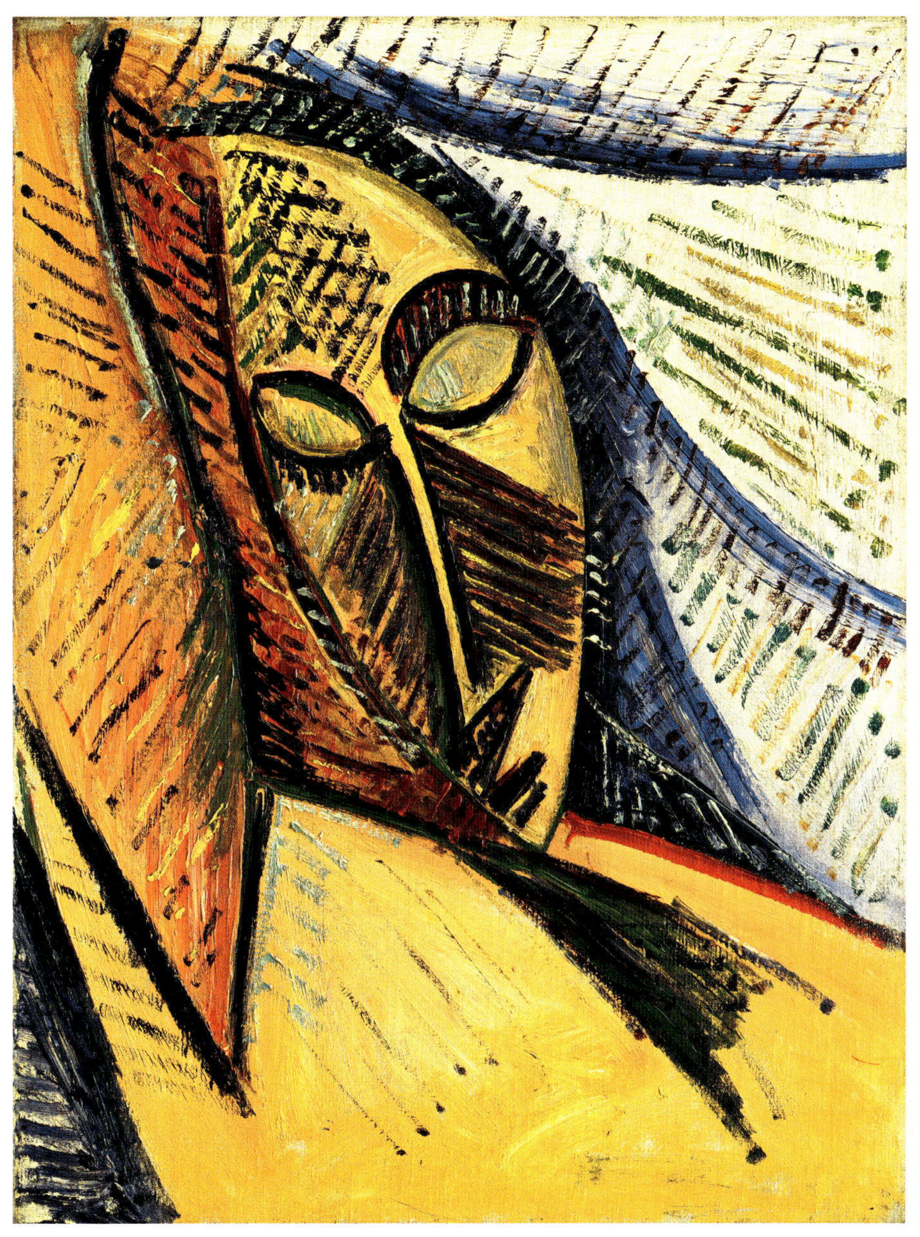

16
**Head of a Sleeping Woman
(Study for Nude with Drapery),** 1907
Oil on canvas
61.4 x 47.6 cm
The Museum of Modern Art,
New York
Estate of John Hay Whitney, 1983

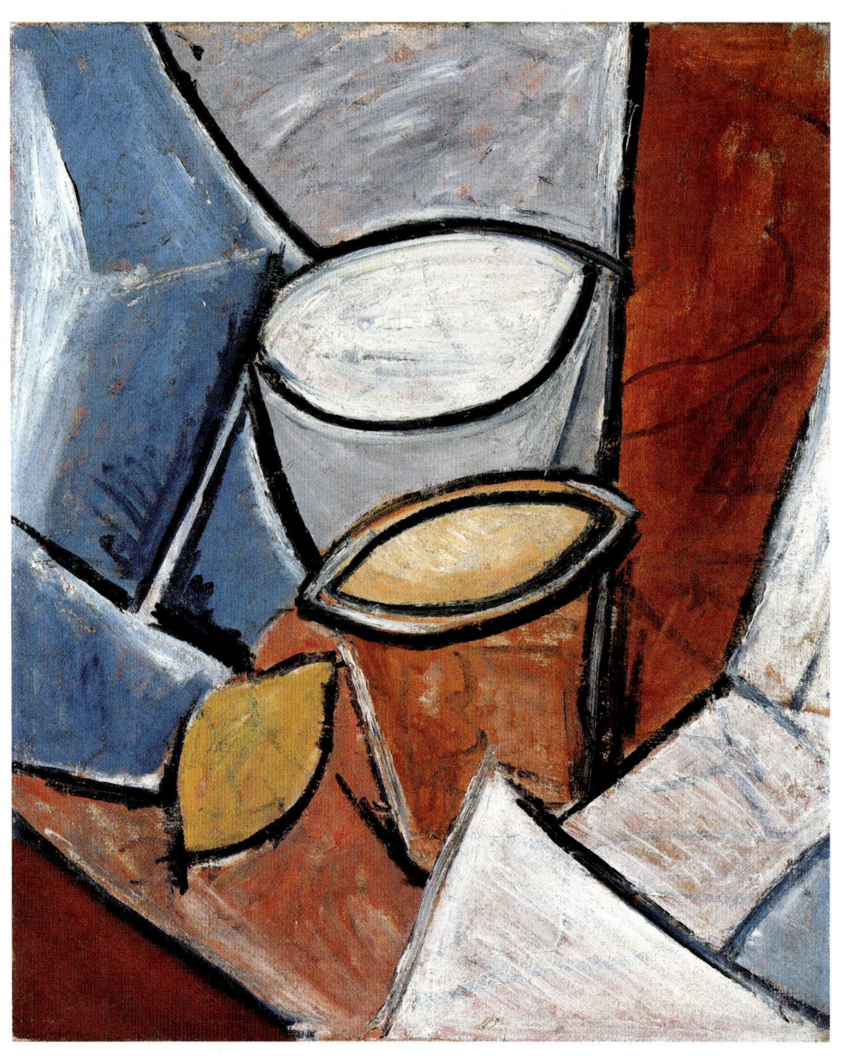

17
Jugs with Lemon, 1907
Oil on canvas
55 x 46 cm
Albertina, Vienna
Batliner Collection

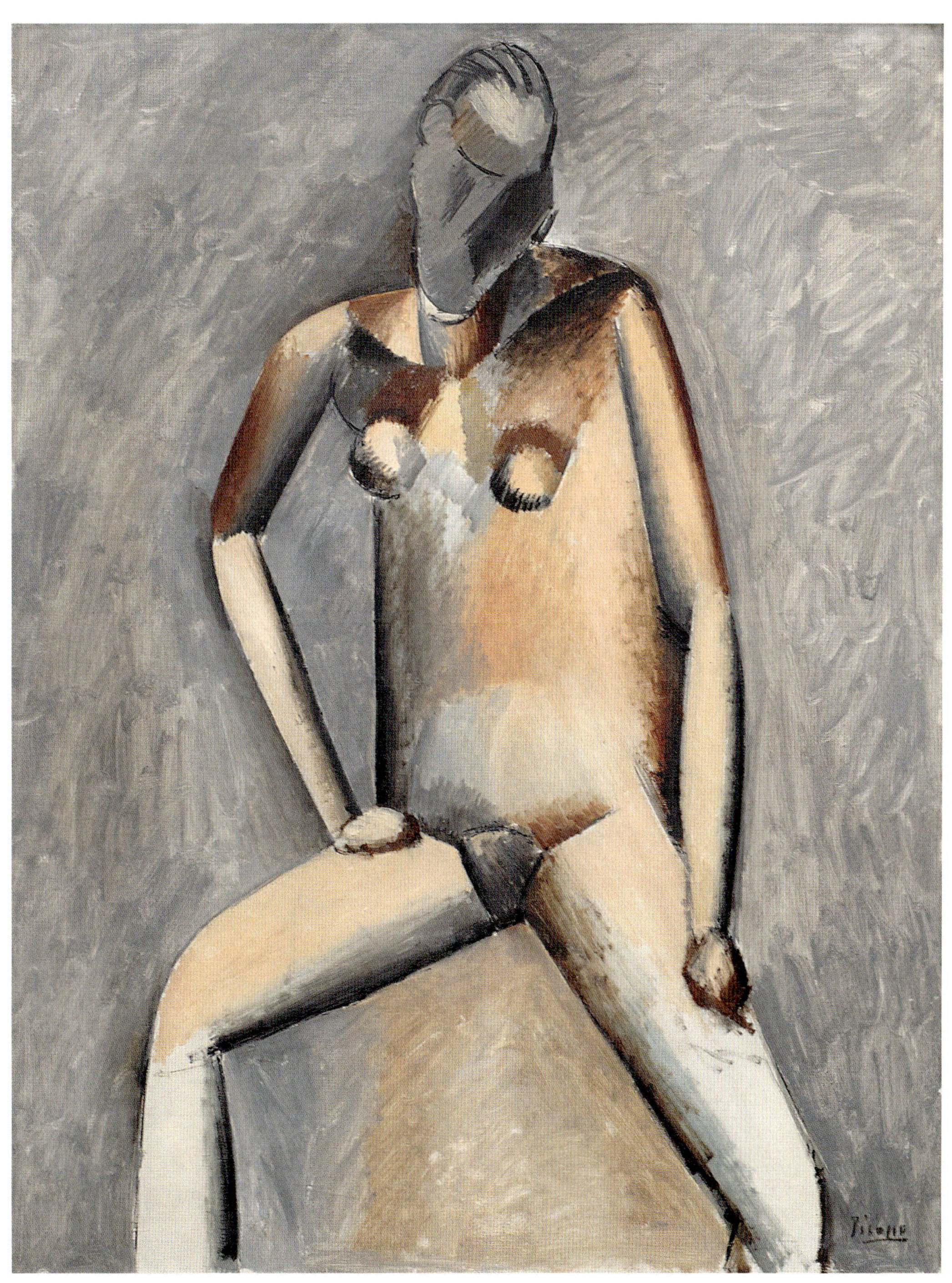

18
Seated Female Nude, 1908/09
Oil on canvas
116.5 x 89.4 cm
Philadelphia Museum of Art
The Louise and Walter Arensberg
Collection, 1950

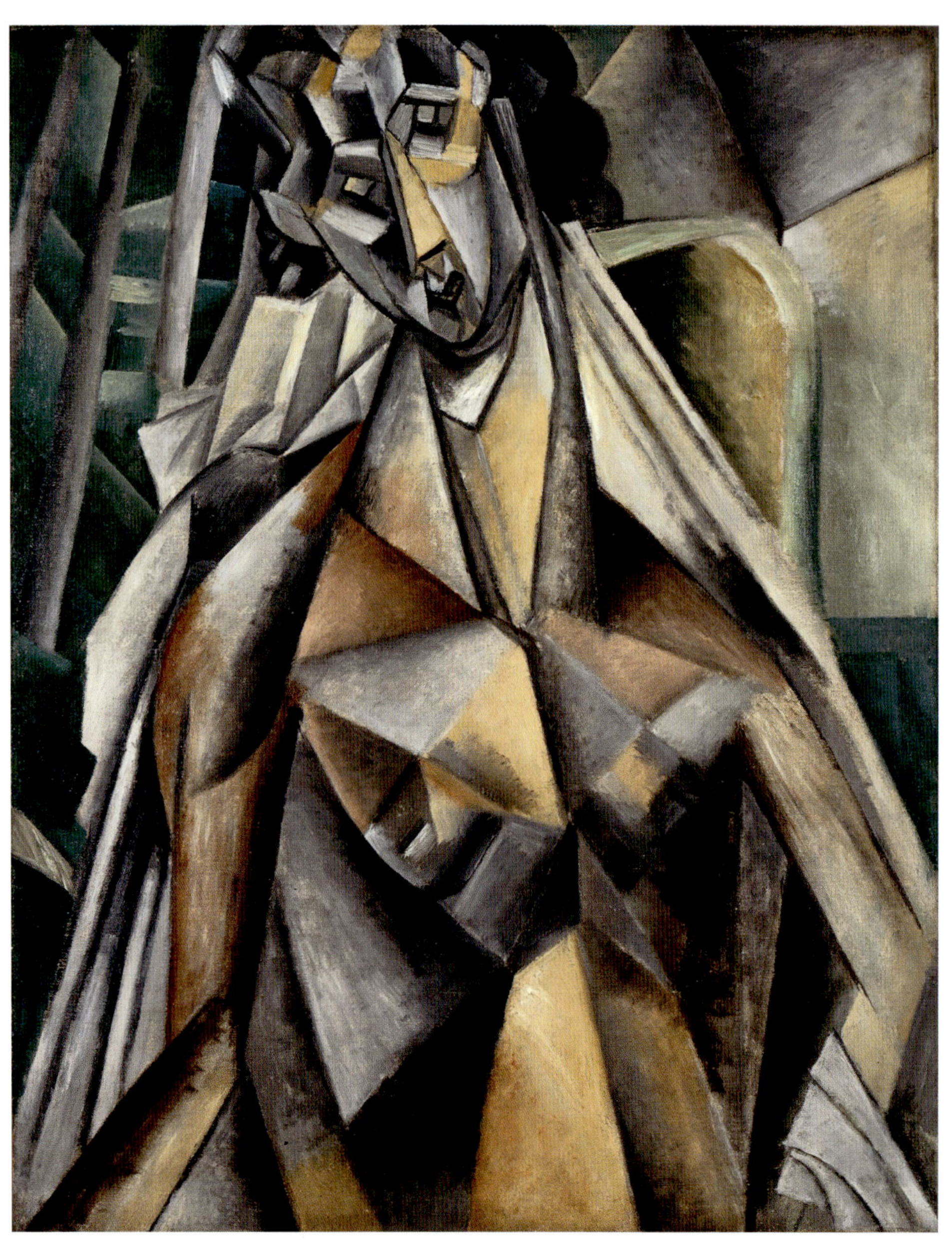

19
Nude Woman in an Armchair, 1909
Oil on canvas
93.5 x 75 cm
Private collection

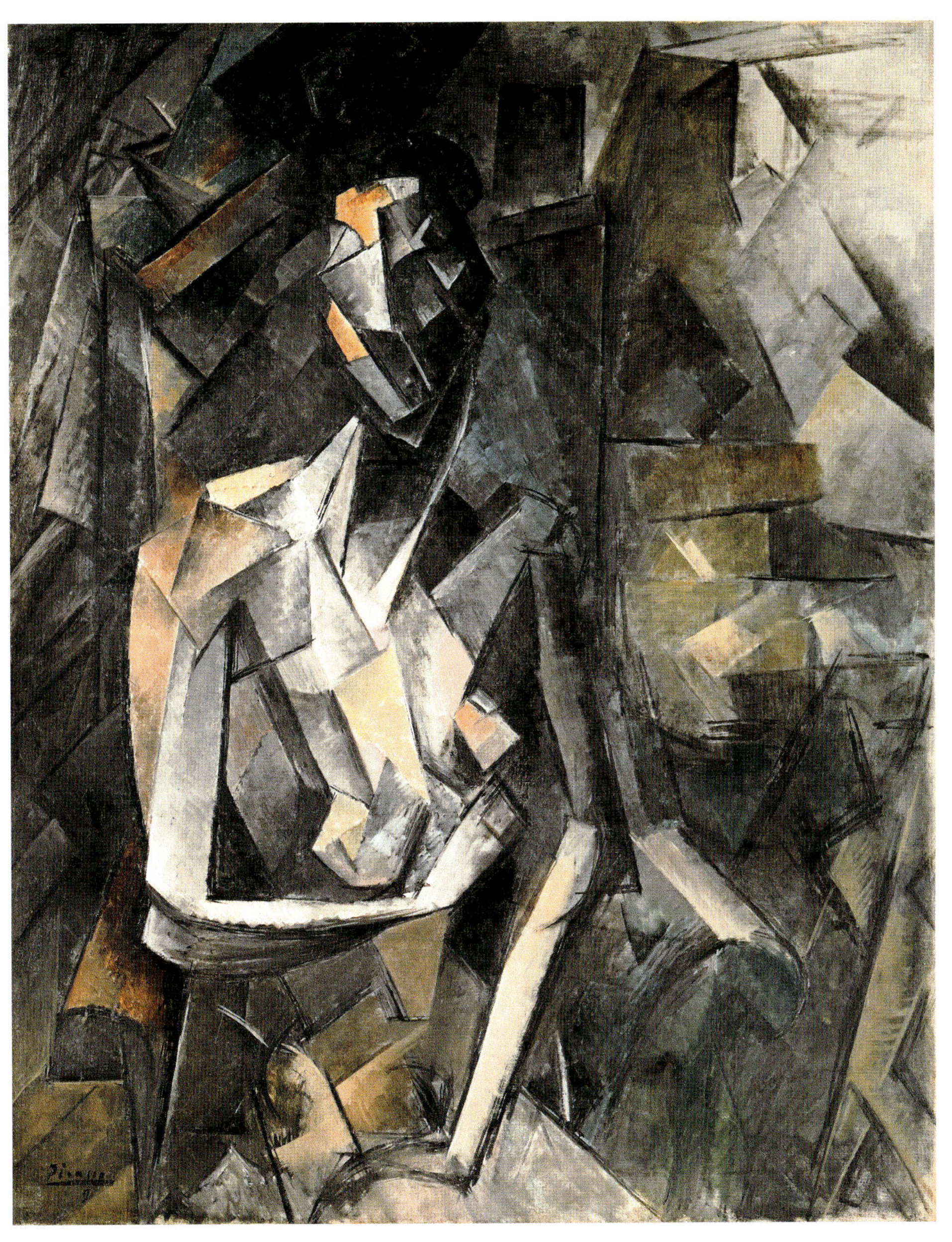

20
Seated Nude, 1909/10
Oil on canvas
92.1 x 73 cm
Tate, London, Purchased 1949

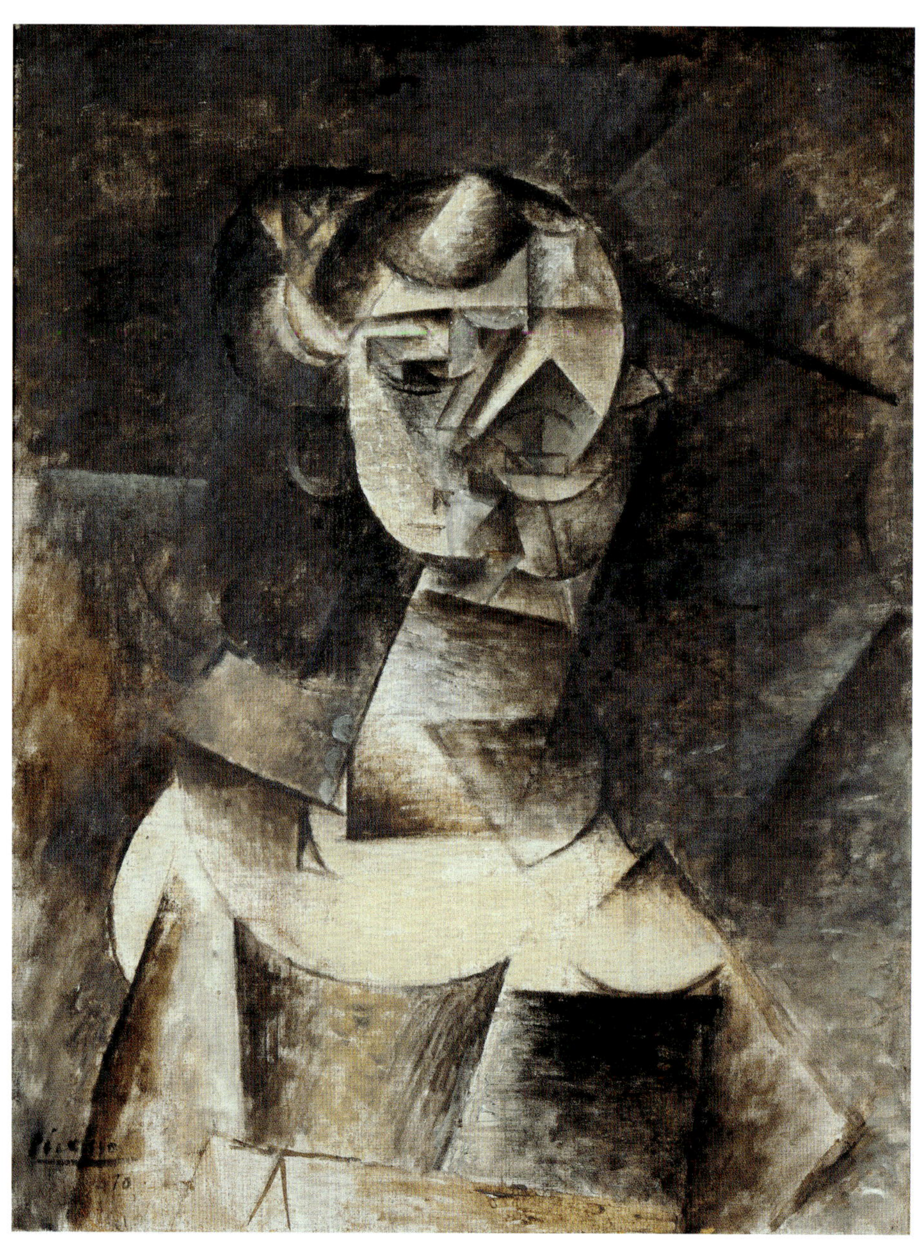

21
Mademoiselle Léonie, 1910
Oil on canvas
65 x 50 cm
Private collection

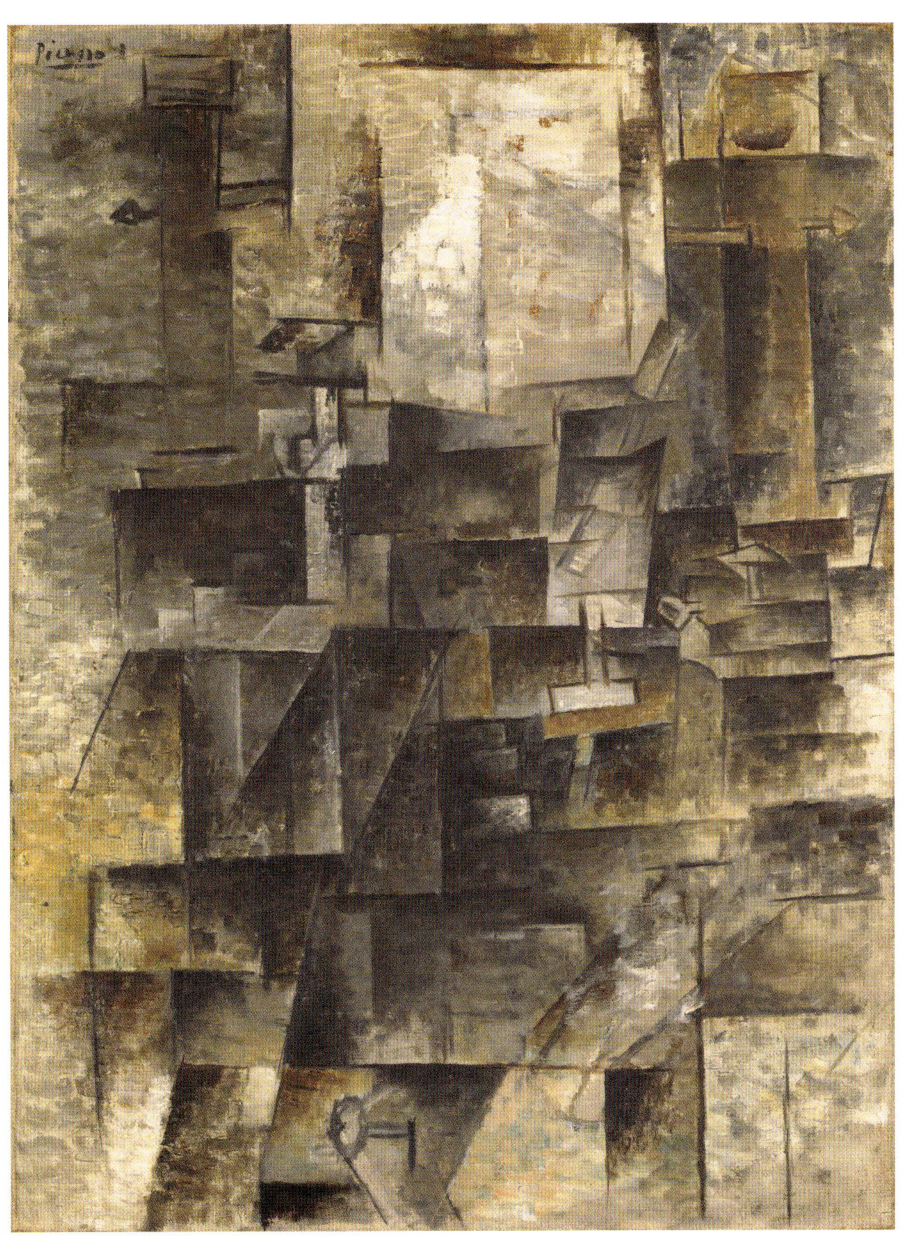

22
Dressing Table, 1910
Oil on canvas
61 x 46 cm
Private collection

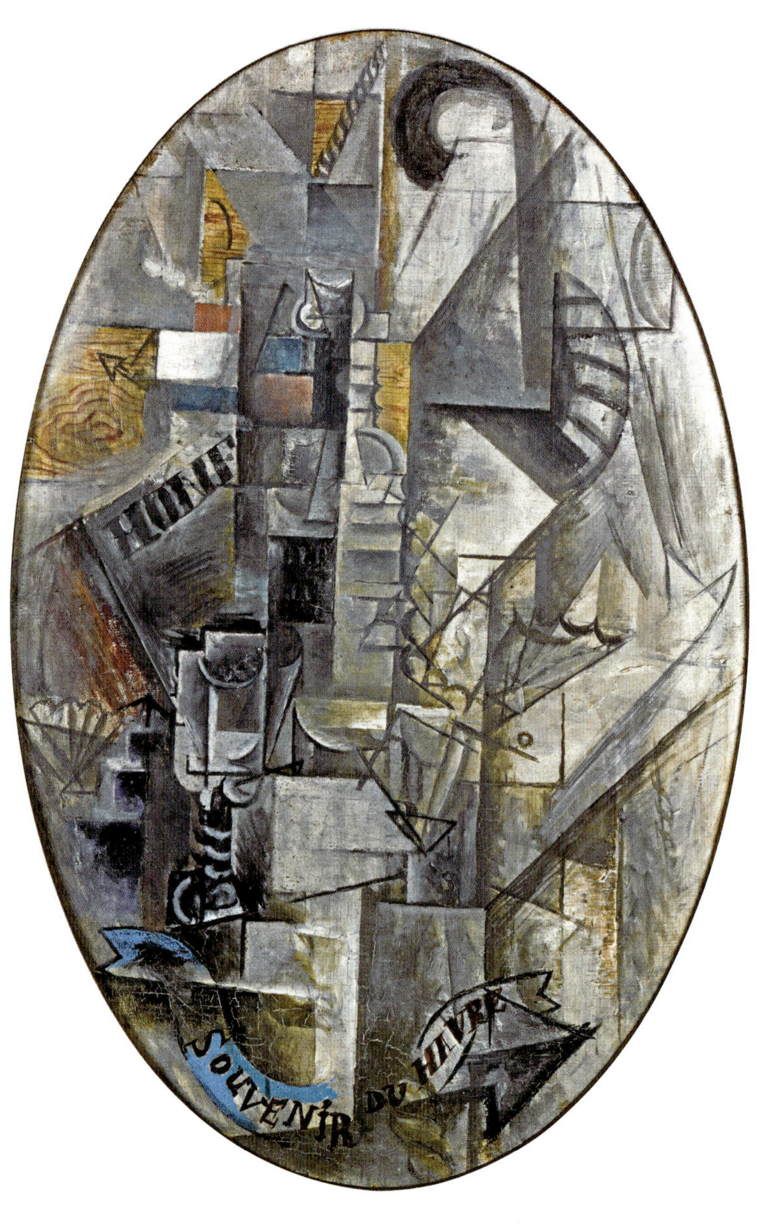

23
Souvenir du Havre, 1912
Oil and gloss paint on canvas
81 x 54 cm
Private collection
Courtesy Thomas Ammann
Fine Art AG Zurich

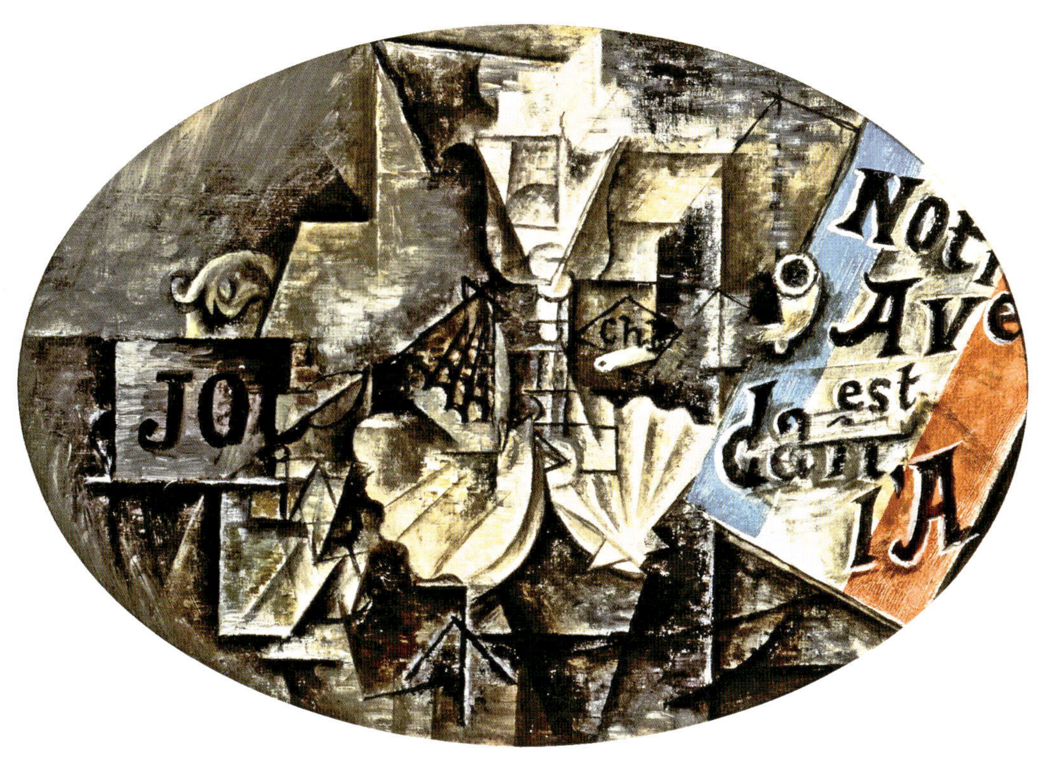

24
The Scallop Shell.
"Notre avenir est dans l'air", 1912
Oil on canvas
38 x 55 cm
Private collection

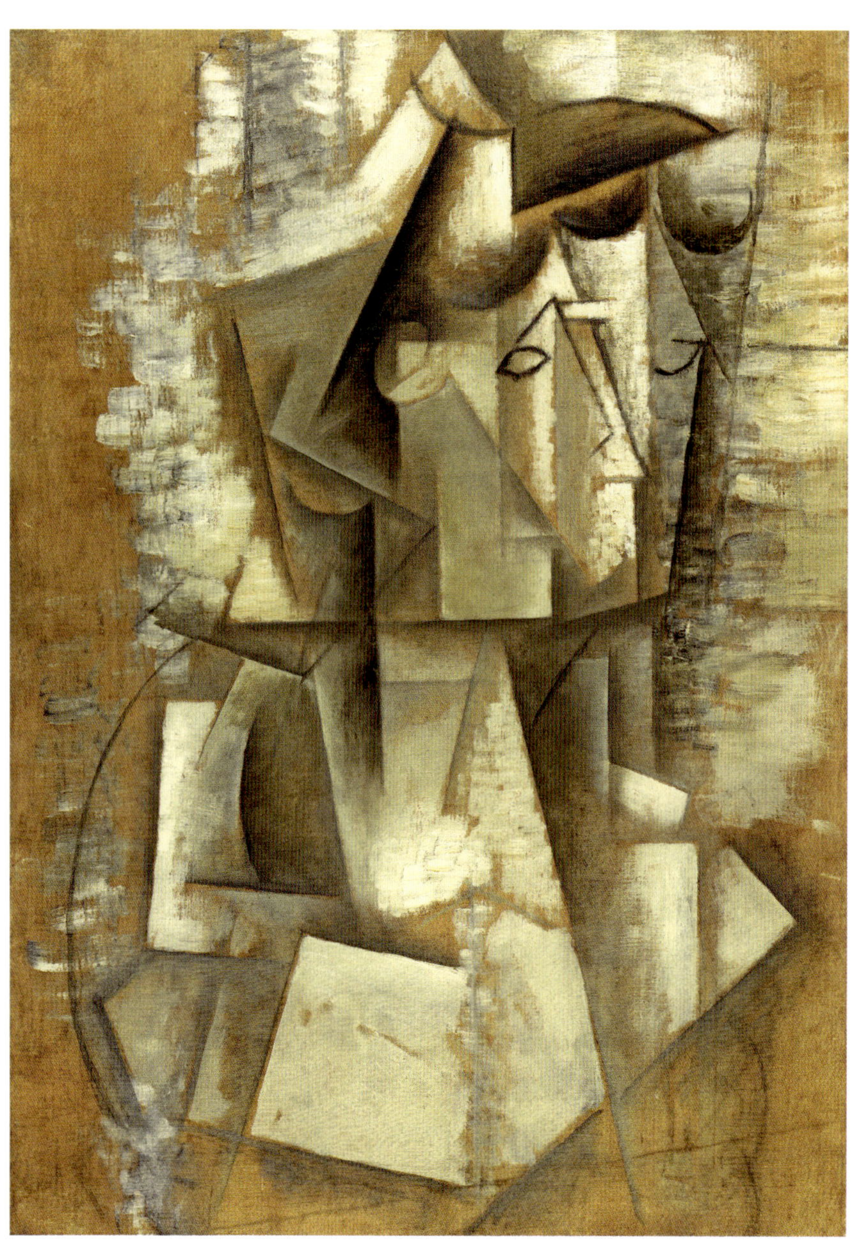

25
Girl from Arles, 1912
Oil on canvas
73 x 54 cm
Private collection
Courtesy Thomas Ammann
Fine Art AG Zurich

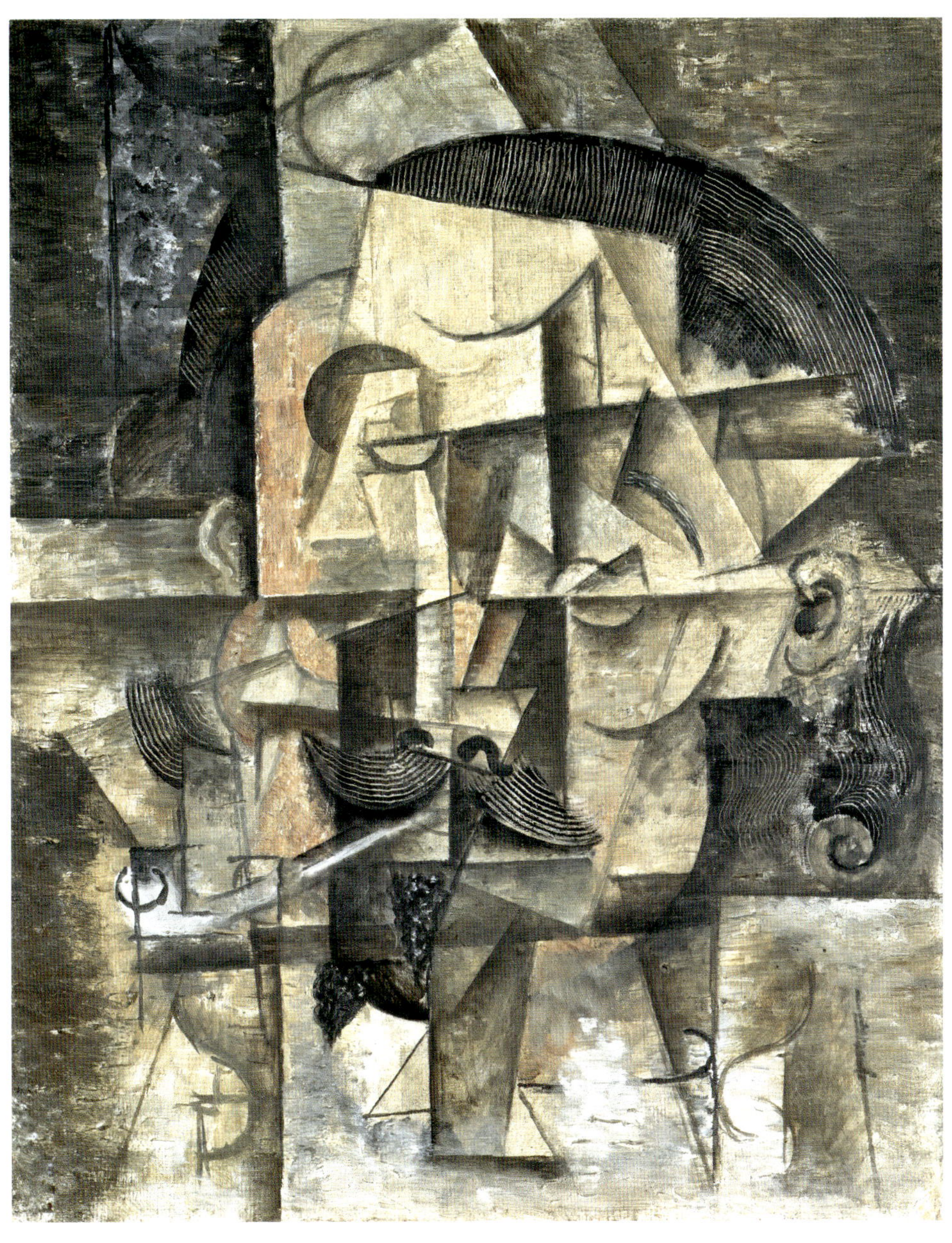

26
The Poet, 1912
Oil on canvas
60 x 48 cm
Gift of Maja Sacher-Stehlin,
deposited by the commune of
inhabitants of the canton
Basel-Stadt, 1967

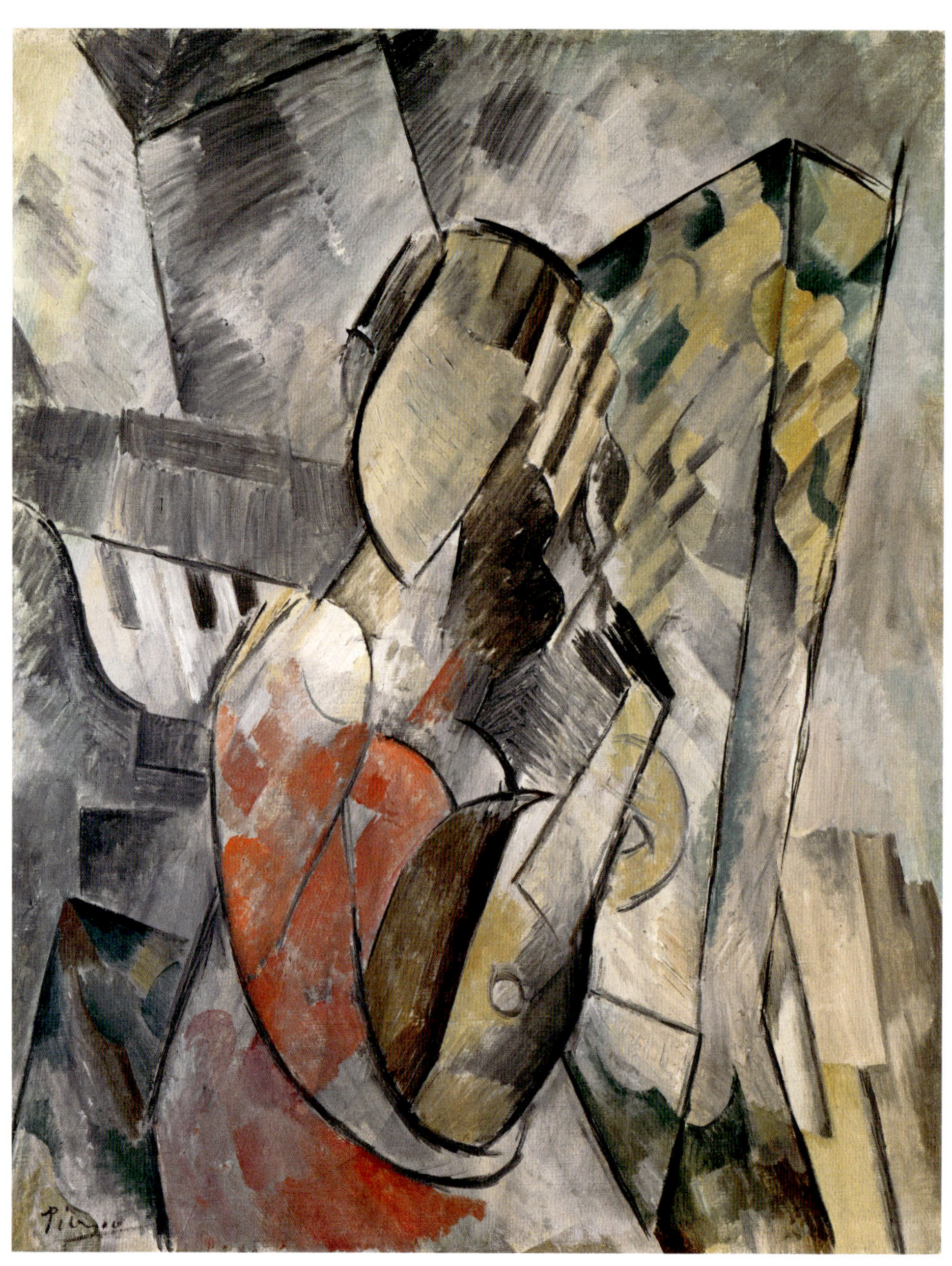

27

Woman with Mandolin, 1908
Oil on canvas
100 x 80 cm
Kunstsammlung Nordrhein-
Westfalen, Düsseldorf

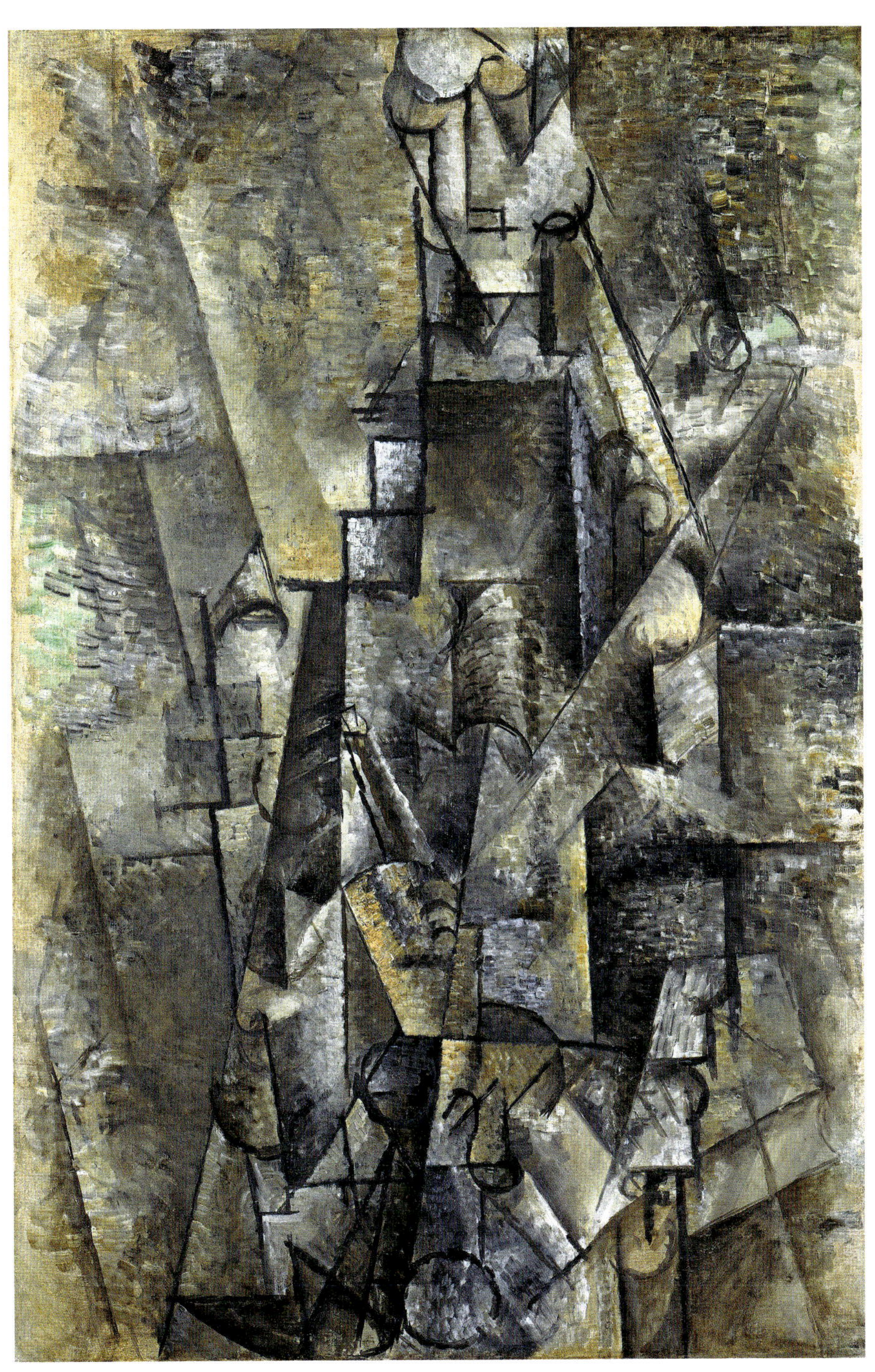

28
Man with a Clarinet, 1911/12
Oil on canvas
106 x 69 cm
Museo Thyssen-Bornemisza, Madrid

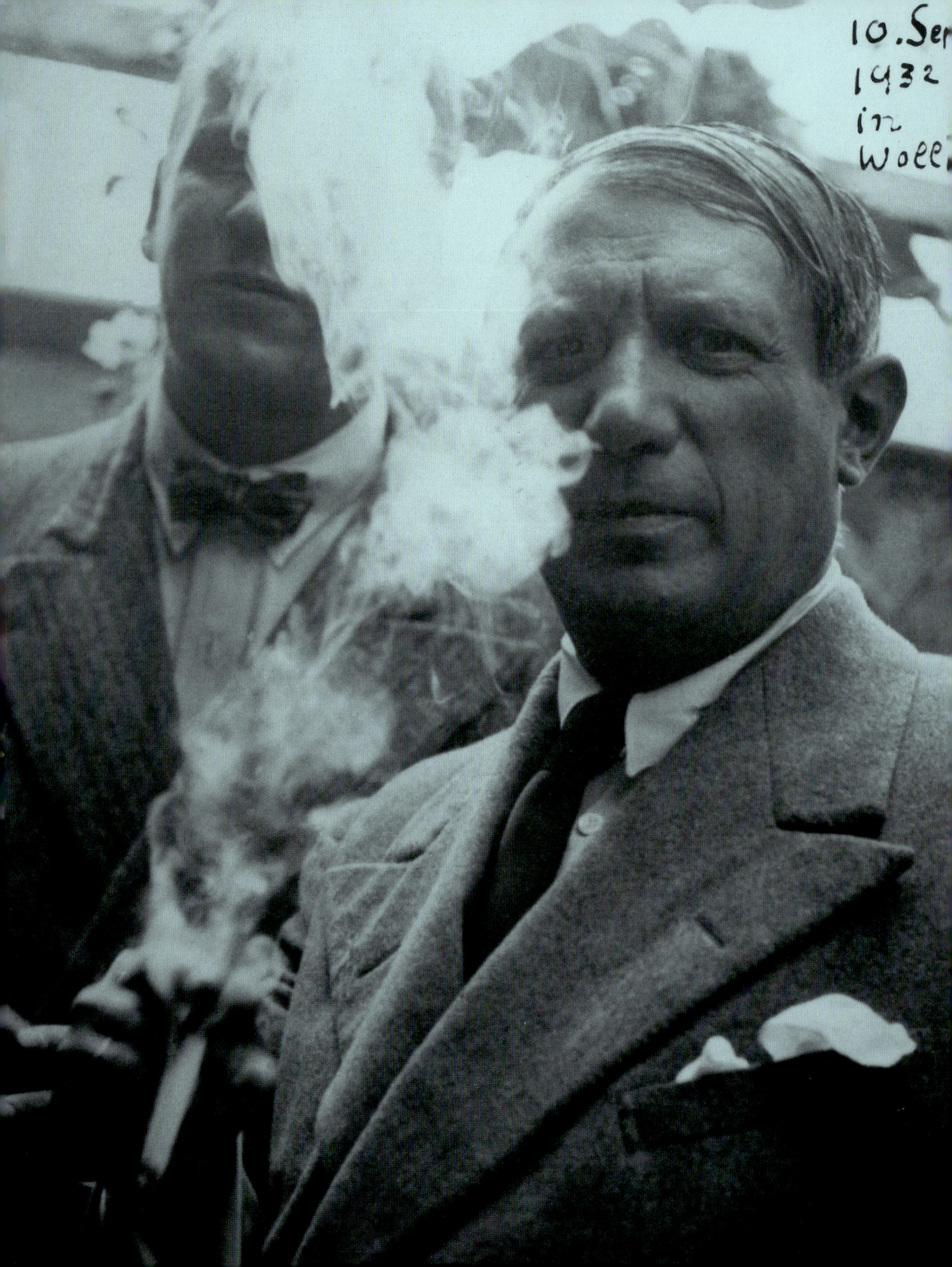

10. Sep
1932
in
Woll

Simonetta Fraquelli

PICASSO'S RETROSPECTIVE AT THE GALERIES GEORGES PETIT, PARIS 1932: A RESPONSE TO MATISSE

Picasso's six-week exhibition at the Galeries Georges Petit in Paris in the summer of 1932 (16 June to 30 July) was the first retrospective of a living artist to resemble a modern-day blockbuster. Although the show was a commercial enterprise, with many of the artworks for sale, its scope and aims were more akin to those of a museum undertaking, with Picasso himself acting as the chief curator. It celebrated, above all, the years 1931 and 1932, which many scholars consider a superlative moment in Picasso's career. The exhibition was launched with a glitzy opening on 15 June 1932, a year to the day after the same gallery had inaugurated a major show devoted to the work of Henri Matisse, Picasso's foremost artistic rival. The white-tie event attracted Paris's high society, and collectors mingled with artists, dealers and critics, all of whom pondered the staggering range of Picasso's art (fig. 2).[1] William Rees Jeffreys, one of a handful of British collectors who lent paintings to the exhibition, commented that it "was a *tour de force* of [the] creative imagination of one man".[2]

The luxurious rooms of the Georges Petit Gallery provided the ideal setting for Picasso's *tour de force*. Situated on the first floor of a *hôtel-particulier* in the Rue de Sèze in the elegant ninth *arrondissement* of Paris, not far from the Église de la Madeleine, the gallery had belonged to the 'formidable salesman' Georges Petit (1856–1920). In the last decades of the nineteenth century, Petit had amassed a substantial for-tune by representing Eugène Delacroix, Gustave Courbet, Jean-Bap-tiste Camille Corot, Jean François Millet and others.[3] By the time of his death, however, his business had faltered considerably and the gallery was made over to the dealers Josse and Gaston Bernheim-Jeune (who represented Matisse) and Etienne Bignou. Thereafter it primarily hosted

◄

Picasso and Hanns Welti,
Zurich 1932

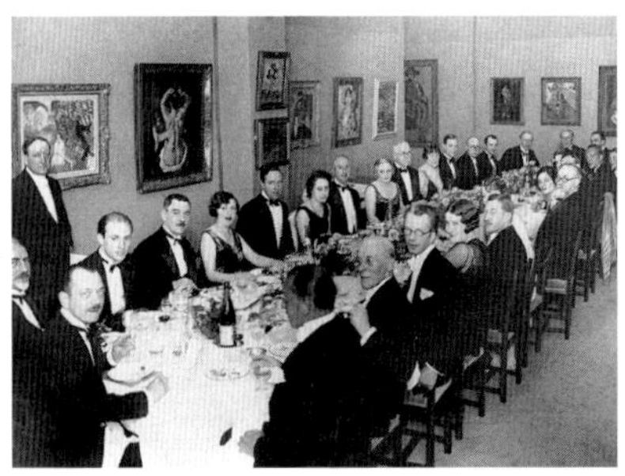

auctions. In an attempt to revive their dwindling fortunes after the stock market crash of 1929, the new owners joined forces with their main competitor, Paul Rosenberg, Picasso's dealer at the time. Together they refurbished the gallery, installing a modern lighting system, but preserving the building's nineteenth-century character, complete with fabric-lined walls in the grand exhibition hall and elaborate marble fireplaces and ornately patterned wallpapers in some of the adjoining rooms. Infused with cash from the American stockbroker and collector Chester Dale, they presented exhibitions with a contemporary orientation, including the survey *One Hundred Years of French Painting* in 1930 and the retrospective-style showings of Matisse and Picasso in 1931 and 1932 respectively.[4] The survey acknowledged the success of the gallery under Monsieur Petit while also embodying the dealers' new aim of concentrating on the work of living artists. Matisse and Picasso, both represented with three paintings, were treated as Old Masters: an accolade that may have given more pleasure to Matisse than Picasso at this time.[5]

The Matisse exhibition attracted a great deal of press coverage when it opened on 16 June 1931. It too was launched with a glittering *vernissage*, followed by a banquet in honour of the artist (fig. 1). The show, although sizeable, was considerably smaller than Picasso's a year later: it consisted of 141 paintings,[6] compared to the 225 paintings, pastels and works on paper that Picasso was to present. Its catalogue soberly announced that the event was "in aid of orphans of the arts". Moreover, the soft-back cover had none of the embossing that distinguished that of the Picasso exhibition the following year, and the entries for each work were far less detailed. Loans came from international sources, but the catalogue emphasised that the show was not intended to be retrospective. Hence, despite the presence of many important early canvases, the vast majority of the paintings dated from Matisse's

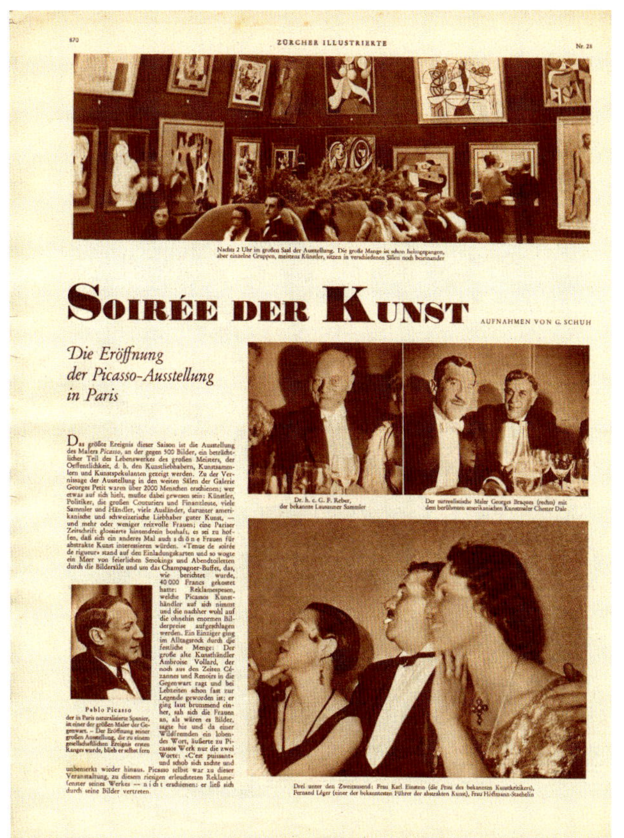

recent Nice period. The ornamental backgrounds and bright colours of his contemporary odalisques, with their suggestive eroticism, doubtless appealed to more conservative collectors, and their inclusion underlined the dealers' commercial objectives.

A critic remarked that, at the opening of his show, "Matisse refused to be lionised and slipped away early in the evening, preferring that his pictures speak for him. But Picasso, who, with Matisse, shares the distinction of being [the] leader of twentieth-century painting, was much in evidence."[7] Matisse had not even been in Paris during the preparatory stages. He had spent the preceding months in Nice, working on a large-scale mural commission for the American collector and pharmaceutical manufacturer Dr. Alfred C. Barnes. Much to the detriment of his exhibition, he paid relatively little attention to its selection and left the hanging to his dealers. Despite excellent attendance figures, the show was not received particularly well by the critics: most of all, they regretted the exclusion of important early works in favour of a large number of recent paintings from dealers' stock. Picasso, well aware of this response, was determined that a similar fate would not befall his exhibition. In fact, the Matisse show re-awakened his keen sense of professional rivalry.[8] He would mastermind the selection of his own exhibition and, most significantly, he would decide precisely how each and every artwork was to be presented.[9] Picasso was not willing to leave anything to chance. He had turned fifty on 25 October 1931, was at the height of his career and intended to retain his position as the world's most famous living artist.

Picasso's retrospective spanned his entire career, beginning in 1901 with a gouache entitled *Le Pierrot*. Every year in the three decades of his activity as an artist was represented by at least one picture. It was a remarkable achievement. Officially, nothing was for sale, but Wilhelm Wartmann, director of the Kunsthaus Zürich, noted in his copy of the catalogue prices being asked for many works (fig. 3).[10] With the effects of the Depression now clearly felt, sales were sparse. Works were also put on sale at the Kunsthaus, whence the exhibition transferred from Paris. The greater financial rewards promised by a Zurich showing may have played a major part in Picasso's choice of the Kunsthaus over the Museum of Modern Art in New York, where Alfred H. Barr Jr. was keen to present the retrospective.[11]

Picasso spent a week hanging the Paris exhibition, experimenting with various combinations before deciding on the final display. Many of the paintings were double or even triple hung and were adorned with heavy gilt frames, which created a nineteenth-century 'Salon effect'. Some critics deplored the garish décor, but Picasso evidently took great delight in the sumptuous surroundings and enjoyed the contrast with his startling new paintings.[12] Moreover, his careful study of Matisse's paintings in the gallery the year before had given him an intimate acquaintance with its spaces. The Parisian painter and critic Jacques-Émile

Blanche, privileged to see the exhibition prior to the public opening, remarked in his review: "As soon as I entered [the gallery], I bumped into Picasso. He was orchestrating the hanging, removal and re-hanging of a group of panels by a team of tired art handlers who had been accommodating his wishes for over a week."[13] Exhausted by the intensity and exhilaration of installing his work, Picasso chose not to attend the opening, preferring, as he joked to an American critic, to go to the movies instead: "I've been hooking these things on the wall for six days now and I have had enough of them," he confessed to Guy Hickok of the *Brooklyn Eagle Magazine*.[14] Georges Braque did attend. A photograph shows him sitting next to Chester Dale at the banquet and looking content. At this time he was still doubtlessly convinced that he would be included in the show when it travelled to Zurich.[15]

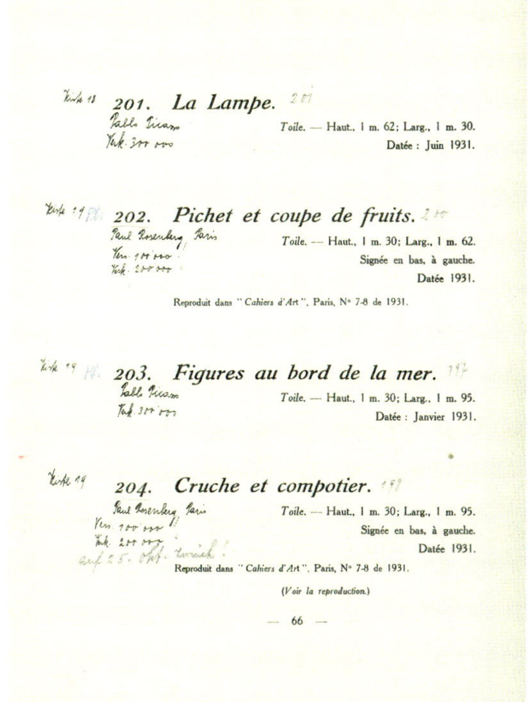

fig. 3
Galeries Georges Petit, *Exposition Picasso*, June to July 1932, exhibition catalogue, p. 66, with notes by Wilhelm Wartmann

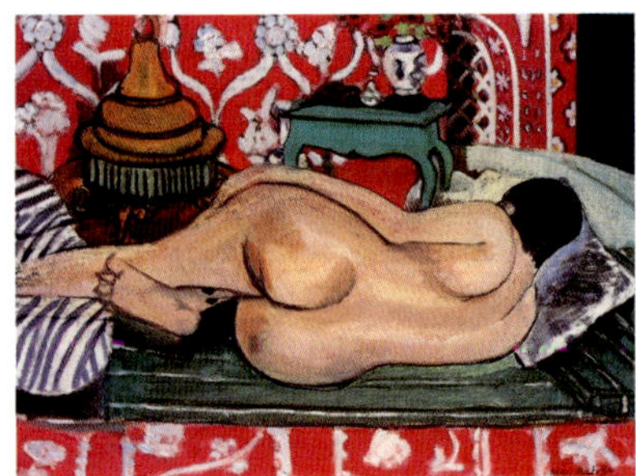

fig. 4
Henri Matisse, 1869-1954
Nu couché de dos,
summer 1927
Oil on canvas, 66 x 92 cm

In addition to many Parisian collectors, an array of people from as far afield as Berlin, New York, Amsterdam, Berlin, London, Lausanne, Krefeld, Barcelona and Arnau (Hostinné, today's Czech Republic) had lent generously to the exhibition.[16] Picasso himself provided numerous works from his personal collection. To complement the paintings, some of which had been completed in as late as April 1932, only two months before the opening, he added seven sculptures and six illustrated books. The latter included a series of etchings for Ovid's *Metamorphoses* published by Albert Skira in 1931 to mark the artist's fiftieth birthday.[17] These neoclassical prints acknowledged Picasso's debt to Matisse's fine line drawings and laid the formal foundations for the series of Marie-Thérèse Walter paintings on which he was soon to embark.

From December 1931 to April 1932, Picasso created some thirty new paintings, twenty-two of them specially for the exhibition. These staggering images, showing his young lover Marie-Thérèse Walter seated or lying down, have been referred to as "an ecstatic outpouring of painted love poetry".[18] Matisse's reclining odalisques of the same period, though received coolly by the critics, had a mesmerising effect on Picasso, spurring him to depict his new love with great panache. (fig. 4) He responded to his artistic rival with gusto, appropriating his style and subject matter in a way he had not done previously. The Marie-Thérèse paintings are the most unashamedly Matissian in his entire œuvre, prompting Bois to note that Picasso "chose to signify sensuality via a detour through Matisse's language".[19] Like his still lifes of this period, the seated figures are full of dramatic flowing lines, vibrant areas of strong colours and black contours, with mirror reflections that both draw upon and anticipate the work of the older artist. Picasso pushed Matisse's sensuality to an almost brash extreme. As Flam has said, it was as if he were telling the older artist, "Look, here's how it should be done!"[20] It is worth recalling that from 1930 to 1933 Matisse virtually abandoned easel painting, so as to concentrate on his mural commission. Picasso will clearly have been aware of this and it is as if he could not resist the temptation to take on the mantle of 'grand master' and paint for two, himself and Matisse.[21]

Picasso chose not to include any of his more recent modelled sculptures in the Petit exhibition, pieces that likewise betray the influence of Matisse, if indirectly.[22] With their curvilinear shapes and distinctive forms, these sculptures were so obviously inspired by his young lover that he may have wished to avoid recriminations from his tremendously jealous wife, Olga Khokhlova.[23] That did not prevent him from provoking her with three welded sculptures also inspired by Marie-Thérèse, although this would have been a closely guarded secret at the time: *Head of a Woman* (1929–30), made from two colanders, and both versions of *Woman in the Garden* (1930, 1931; (fig. 5; Barr no. 1).

Knowledge of how Picasso's show at the Galeries Georges Petit looked derives from the catalogue, from thirteen annotated photo-

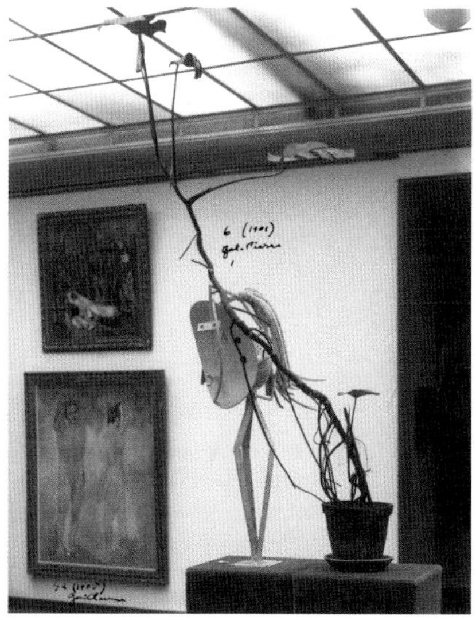

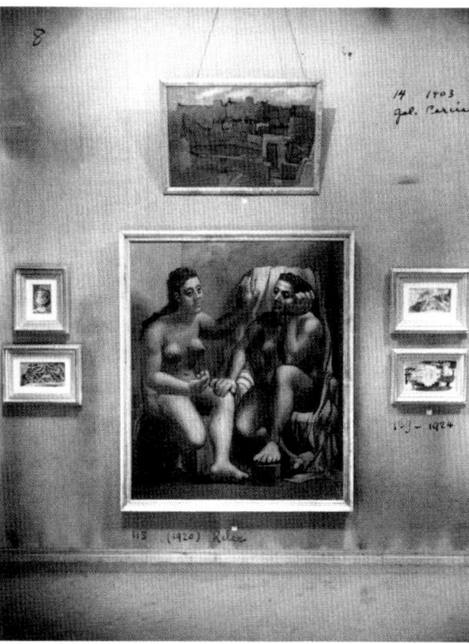

fig. 5
Barr no. 1, Galeries Georges Petit, *Exposition Picasso*, June to July 1932
Courtesy of Alfred H. Barr Jr. Archives, The Museum of Modern Art, New York

fig. 6
Barr no. 8, Galeries Georges Petit, *Exposition Picasso*, June to July 1932
Courtesy of Alfred H. Barr Jr. Archives, The Museum of Modern Art, New York

graphs in the Barr papers at the Museum of Modern Art, New York, and from a series of previously unknown installation photographs that have recently surfaced in the collection of the grandson of the Swiss collector Dr Georges Reber, one of the foremost lenders to the exhibition.[24] Some images are published here for the first time (Reber nos. 1–18).[25] Commitments in America had prevented Barr from travelling to Paris for the exhibition, but his wife Margaret Scolari Barr made the journey in his stead. She visited the Petit Gallery in the mornings and afternoons and was invited to attend the 'décrochage', at which she met Picasso, who was walking back and forth through the largest gallery "pleased and self-assured in his success".[26] It is possible that she brought the photographs back from Paris to New York. However, it is not clear exactly when all these photographs were taken or by whom, although it seems likely they were shot during the hanging, for they show several paintings resting on the floor and others leaning against the backs of chairs. They appear to record a variety of stages in the preparation of the exhibition. Barr no. 8 (fig. 6) and Reber no. 13, for instance, show the same wall dominated by *Two Women* (1920; G. P. no. 115), but the angle is different in each photograph and the Reber image includes two Blue period paintings, *Portrait of Corina Pere Romeu* (1902; G. P. no. 15), and *Celestina* (1904; G. P. no. 21), resting on the floor. The aim seems to have been a complete documentation of the works included, rather than a record of their definitive placement.[27]

At first sight, the photographs convey a somewhat haphazard impression, suggesting that the installation resembled the way Picasso kept his paintings in his studio (fig. 7). Yet, as will emerge, the display was anything but random. The images show that most paintings were double, if not triple, hung, with the lower register almost at ground level. No contemporary floor plan of the Petit Gallery has survived, so the

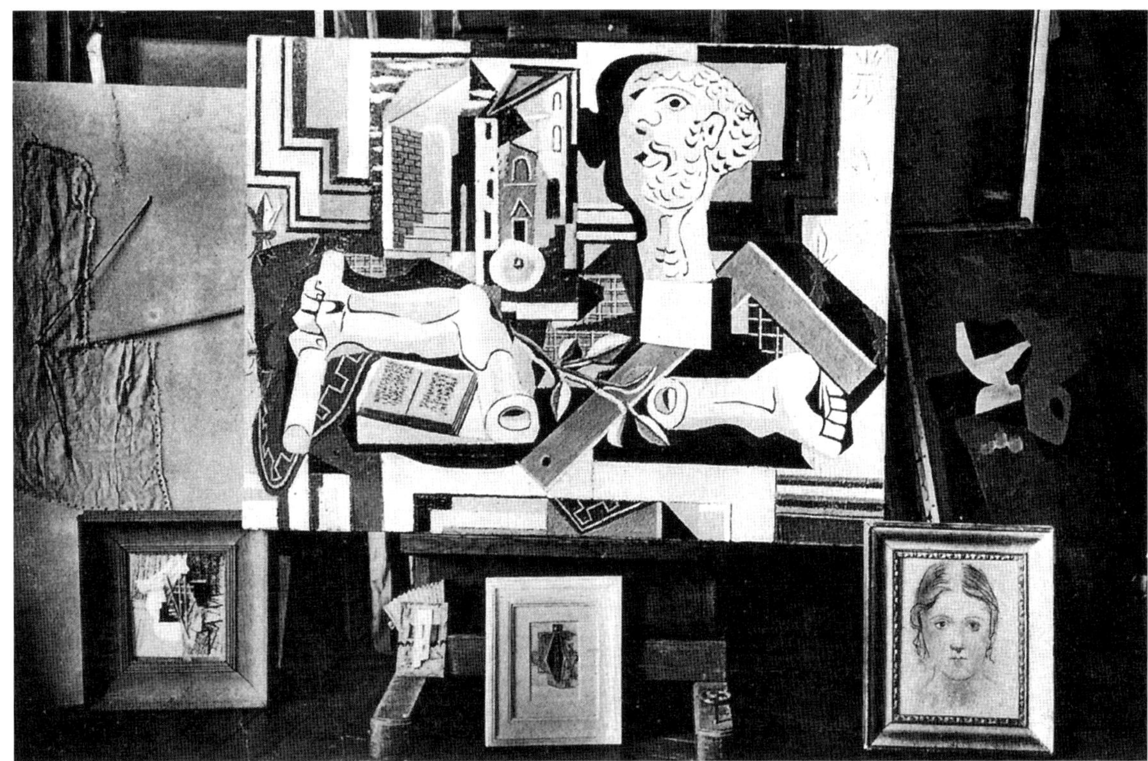

exact sequence of rooms is not known; yet the installation shots provide a reasonably clear idea of how the works were distributed between smaller, more intimate galleries and the grander halls. The photographs facilitate identification of at least five distinct spaces, each containing paintings on similar themes from different periods of Picasso's career. A comparison with photographs of the Matisse exhibition enables the Salle Godot, the Salle Carrée and the Grande Salle to be identified by name. Two further named spaces, the Salle Verte and Salle Ancienne, are known to have existed, but it is not clear which works by Picasso were shown in these possibly smaller rooms. One of them is likely to have contained only works on paper (Reber no. 4). No views including the illustrated books have so far come to light.[28]

The photographs make it evident that Picasso amended his selection during the installation process so as to emphasise certain aspects of his career. As Michael FitzGerald has pointed out, the distribution of styles or periods was neither proportional nor intended to match contemporary critical opinion: "Instead — and this is what made it unique at the time —

it suggests Picasso's personal view of his œuvre, seen through the lens of his most recent work."[29] To create a precedent for the alternative Classicism of his recently completed Marie-Thérèse paintings, and perhaps to deflect attention from their Matissian influences, Picasso chose to highlight two earlier aspects of his career: his Cubist period (represented by fifty-five paintings, dating from 1907 to 1914) and his grand still lifes of the mid-1920s (G. P. nos. 147–156). Both sets of work share a sense of purity and order. These quiescent qualities are absent from his so-called 'African' period (1906–8). That may account for the most glaring omission, at least from a present-day perspective: *Les Demoiselles d'Avignon* (1907; Museum of Modern Art, New York).[30] This acknowledged masterpiece remained in Jacques Doucet's Paris study, attached to the wall in its elaborate metal frame.[31] John Richardson has suggested that Picasso omitted the *Demoiselles* because he was keen to show his more recent works in the best possible light and feared that the scale and virtuosity of the earlier painting might overshadow them.[32] A handful of paintings from the years 1906 to 1908, including Reber's large canvas *Three Figures under a Tree* (G. P. no. 51), was interspersed

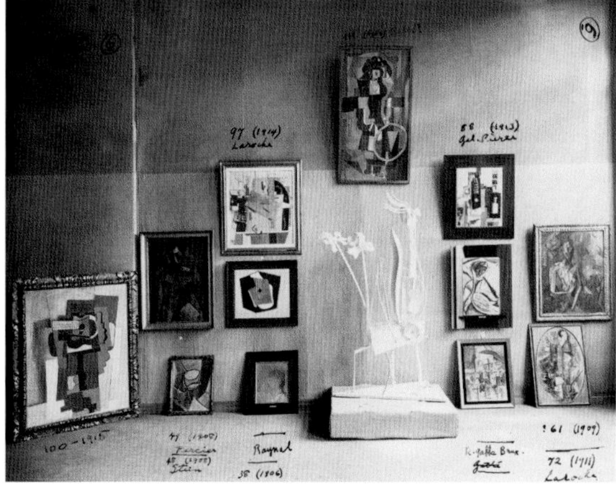

fig. 8
Barr no. 6, Galeries Georges Petit, *Exposition Picasso*, June to July 1932
Courtesy of Alfred H. Barr Jr. Archives, The Museum of Modern Art, New York

with examples of Analytical Cubism in the Salle Godot, which had lightly patterned fabric walls (fig. 8, Barr no. 6 and Reber no. 3).[33] Picasso may not have wanted the contorted anatomies of the *Demoiselles* to dominate the space, which also contained the two versions of the *Woman in a Garden* sculpture, positioned at each end of the gallery.

There were other notable omissions. Practical considerations prevented his striking Rose period painting *The Family of Saltimbanques* (1905; National Gallery of Art, Washington, D.C.), from returning to France. This large canvas had been removed from its stretcher in order to enter Chester Dale's New York apartment and Dale had no desire to risk damaging it by repeating the process.[34] Even more devastating for Picasso was the fact that none of the paintings of his acquired so judiciously by the Russian collectors Ivan Morosov and Sergei Shchukin was available, having become state property as a result of the Soviet revolution of 1918.[35] His most celebrated portrait, that of *Gertrude Stein* (1905–6; Metropolitan Museum of Art, New York) was also absent. This is a curious omission, as Stein lent six other paintings to the exhibition.[36] Picasso's rather aloof relations with the formidable American writer in the early 1930s may have induced to him to exclude this iconic image.

A small but ornate gallery — maybe the Salle Ancienne — with panelling, marble fireplaces and dark-coloured patterned wallpaper was reserved for a mixture of small- and large-scale works (Reber no. 12). The photographs show several works on chairs, on the floor and on the mantelpiece, indicating that Picasso had not yet decided where to place them. Another, as yet unidentified room contained several of Picasso's biomorphic figures and related paintings of bone-like structures from 1929–30 (fig. 9, Barr no. 2), one of which belonged to the British collector William Rees Jeffreys (G. P. no. 192). Referred to as 'Metamorphoses' in the catalogue, these challenging images were shown alongside earlier large-scale figure paintings from the artist's Blue period and neoclassi-

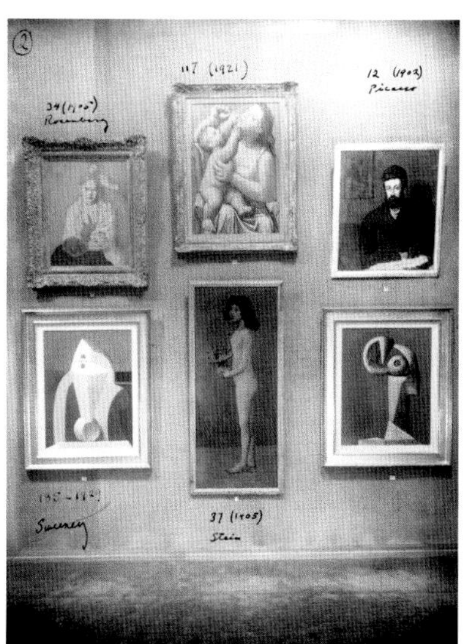

fig. 9
Barr no. 2, Galeries Georges Petit, *Exposition Picasso*, June to July, 1932
Courtesy of Alfred H. Barr Jr. Archives, The Museum of Modern Art, New York

cal figures of the early 1920s. It was an unusual arrangement, and the inclusion of the 'Metamorphoses' emphasises the fact that Picasso had complete control over the exhibition, for it is unlikely that the dealers would have considered such demanding works commercially viable.

The large Salle Carrée, featuring light coloured walls and a glass-tiled ceiling, contained exclusively figure paintings, many monumental in size, from the artist's Blue period and his neoclassical phase of the early 1920s (see fig. 5, Barr no. 1 and Reber nos. 7–11). On velvet covered pedestals in the centre of the gallery stood the sculpture *Head of a Woman* (G. P. no. 228) alongside a potted philodendron (Reber no. 8). This type of plant, which Scolari Barr states "had recently become fashionable in Paris", appears repeatedly in Picasso's welded sculptures and paintings of the early 1930s and one feels that its inclusion must have served a more than purely decorative purpose. One of the long walls in this gallery was devoted to images of his family (Reber no. 9). The famous *Portrait of Olga* (1917; G. P. no. 105) hung in the centre, directly beneath the artist's Blue period *Self-Portrait* (1901; G. P. no. 3). Four images of Paulo, their son, appeared on either side of Olga. One showed him dressed in a harlequin costume (G. P. no. 148), another two wearing a Pierrot outfit (G. P. nos. 166, 188) and the fourth, a pastel, holding a toy (G. P. no. 126). In the upper register, next to the self-portrait, were two small paintings of Paulo's head as a baby and two of Olga. Given that in many ways the exhibition paid homage to Marie-Thérèse, this 'family wall' may have been intended to appease the *haut bourgeois* expectations of the artist's status-conscious wife.[37] The exhibition marked the end of what the poet Max Jacob had called the 'époque des duchesses'; henceforth Picasso would no longer court Parisian society.

The exhibition culminated in the huge rectangular exhibition hall known as the Grande Salle. Closely hung, it featured some seventy paintings, including the lion's share of the recent Marie-Thérèse paintings and several grand mid-1920s post-Cubist still-lifes, which were double hung on a dark red fabric. Several undisputed masterpieces from other periods also hung in this gallery: *Woman in an Armchair* (1913; G. P. no. 89), *Man with a Pipe* (1915; G. P. no. 103), *Standing Figure* (1915–16; G. P. no. 101), *La Flûte de Pan* (1923; G. P. no. 138) and two versions each of *Three Musicians* (1921; G. P. nos. 119, 120) and *The Dance* (1925; G. P. no. 162). The sheer density and variety of the works must almost have overwhelmed visitors: an illustration in the *Zürcher Illustrierte* shows several of them in a central seating area looking rather bemused (see fig. 2, p. 79).

The exhibition certainly ended on a high note. Picasso's primary goal, which he surely reached, was to present his recent work as a continuation of his past achievements. His installation confirmed how consistently he drew upon his past in creating the present. Speaking to Tériade in an interview published the day before the exhibition opened to the public, he remarked: "Someone asked me how I was going to hang my exhibition. 'Badly', I replied, because an exhibition is like a picture: whether it is well 'arranged' or badly 'arranged', it comes to the same thing. What counts, is the element of continuity in [the artist's] ideas. And when this sense of continuity exists, everything ends up falling into place, just as it does in the worst of households."[38] Richardson speculates that "Picasso's disregard for chronology may have been intended to deprive the surrealists of a handle on his more recent work, and at the same time to demonstrate that he had never been indebted to their movement." André Breton's reticence about the exhibition can be seen as confirmation of this hypothesis.[39] FitzGerald quite rightly describes the hang as a work of art in itself, underlining Picasso's desire to see his œuvre as an organic whole with several recurring themes and not as a series of 'isms'.

Many critics were openly antagonistic, attacking what they perceived as Picasso's intentionally destructive approach to the figure throughout his abruptly shifting styles. His supporters naturally did their best to hype the occasion. Christian Zervos devoted a special number of *Cahiers d'art* to Picasso[40] that contained twice the number of pages he had accorded Matisse the previous year. He also marked the event by publishing the first instalment of his monumental, 32-volume catalogue raisonné of the artist's work.

Picasso's non-chronological presentation confused most members of the public, but this defiant break with the scholarly compartmentalisation of his œuvre — Blue period followed by Rose period followed by Cubism, first Analytic, then Synthetic, and so forth — had a precedent in the writings of the Catalan essayist Eugeni d'Ors, who had produced a lavish monograph on the artist in 1930.[41] This volume, while not particularly enlightening in detail, argued strongly against imposing a chronological reading on the œuvre. D'Ors, who had known Picasso in Barcelona and who claimed to be a close friend, wrote with an authoritative tone. He insisted that all the conventional reading does:

"is to confuse, by presenting the idea of a succession of changes, a versatility of experiences, an adventurous multiplicity of incidents, of at least *an evolution*, in the case of a spiritual life-story which by its nature, and in a manner which is of exceptional worth in the contemporary world, presents a character of constancy, of permanence, of higher unity in a production which in fact ought to be envisaged before our eyes as a single block: a block as massive, as solid, as enduring as — to repeat which I said at the outset — is the glory with which this production has been surrounded. ... It is the assurance that this detail of a date, of chronological order, *is of no importance.*"[42]

It has been suggested that at this time Picasso had little sympathy for D'Ors.[43] Yet his former friend's ideas may already have borne fruit in London, where the Alex Reid and Lefevre Gallery had chosen a non-chronological hang for its Picasso exhibition in 1931.[44] By choosing to abandon chronology Picasso apparently wished to coax spectators, particularly his critics, into seeing individual paintings untrammelled by the usual historical or critical prejudices. It goes almost without saying that Wartmann opted for a more conventional, chronological hang when the Paris exhibition reached the Kunsthaus Zürich.

Picasso was never again to be so intimately involved in the presentation of his work as at the exhibition in the Georges Petit Gallery. The show stands as a monument to his fierce determination to control his own reputation. It served to change the public's approach to his art and it has affected interpretations of his œuvre ever since. Effective opposition to a reading of successive styles as an 'evolving language' allowed — and allows — Picasso to emerge as an artist of many styles, not as an artist of a clearly demarcated sequence of styles. He is not seen as someone painting his way towards an inevitable goal that represents his mature style. As Brassaï was later to write:

"When I first crossed the threshold of his studio, Picasso had just turned fifty. Of course, his reputation was already established. It was in that crucial year, however, that he would begin to achieve worldwide renown. The major retrospective of his work, inaugurated on 15 June in the gilded salons of the Georges Petit Gallery — the event was the culmination of the Paris season — was a turning point in his life."[45]

The catalogue references (G. P.) in this essay refer to the exhibition catalogue *Exposition Picasso*, Galeries Georges Petit, Paris, 16.6.-30.7.1932.

1 Harold Stanley (Jim) Ede, assistant curator at the National Gallery, Millbank, London (now Tate Britain), attended the event and noted in his diary entry for 16 June 1932 that the 'Picasso party' began at 11.45 p.m. Ede, an ardent supporter of Picasso and other modernist artists, bequeathed his house and art collection in Cambridge to the University, establishing Kettle's Yard Art Gallery. I am grateful to Sebastiano Barassi, Curator of Collections at Kettle's Yard, for this information from Ede's diary.

2 William Rees Jeffreys archive, London School of Economics, diary entry for Monday, 27 June 1932: "went with Madeleine to 6 (sic) Rue de Sèze (G. Petit) and saw the Picasso exhibition. Surprised at the fine Exhibition rooms and still more at the magnificence of the Exhibition, a tour de force of creative imagination of one man. Confess that his earlier work appealed to me most - *The Woman with a Fan* - in particular. Our picture is 192 in the catalogue under the title 'Metamorphose'. The charge for admission was 5 francs and quite a large number of people attended and paid for admission. Met the Director, Mons. Etienne Bignou to whom I was introduced by Mons. Loeb (Pierre) and the Manager Keller whom I had seen previously in London. Mr Bignou said he would introduce me to Picasso. Gave me a catalogue and asked me to lend my picture to an official exhibition at Zurich which I provisionally and conditionally agreed to do."

3 See Anne Distel, *Impressionism: The First Collectors*, New York, 1990, pp. 36-7. I am grateful to Casimiro Di Crescenzo for sharing with me his knowledge of the Galeries Georges Petit at the time of the Matisse exhibition in 1931.

4 For a thorough overview of the activities of the Galeries Georges Petit and the dealers Etienne Bignou and the Bernheim-Jeune brothers, see Michael C. FitzGerald, *Making Modernism: Picasso and the Creation of the Market for Twentieth-Century Art*, New York 1995.

5 See Yve-Alain Bois, *Matisse and Picasso*, exh. cat., Kimbell Art Gallery, Fort Worth 1998, p. 246, no. 118: "Picasso too was treated as an Old Master in the exhibition. But given his 'eclecticism', highly publicised (and most often criticised) at the time, such an accolade had far less significance for him."

6 The exhibition included one sculpture (*Large Seated Nude*, 1922-9), a selection of prints and about one hundred drawings. It was one of four retrospectives of Matisse's work to be held in Berlin in 1930 and Basel and New York in 1931, yet the first in Paris since 1910.

7 Helen Appleton Read, 'Matisse accepted at last,' in: *Brooklyn Eagle Magazine*, 26-31 July 1931, repr. in *Matisse Picasso*, exh. cat., Tate, London 2002, p. 376.

8 The 'fuss' over Matisse's exhibition also prompted Picasso to arrange for two exhibitions of his work to open shortly after Matisse's: a mini-retrospective at the Galerie Percier and a smaller show at Paul Rosenberg's gallery, which included four recent paintings. See Jack Flam, *Matisse and Picasso: The Story of their Rivalry and Friendship*, Cambridge, Mass., 2003, p. 152.

9 "No doubt he made choices in collaboration with Paul Rosenberg and other dealers (as he had done since at least 1918), but the idiosyncratic selection reflects Picasso's taste". FitzGerald, 1995 (note 4), p. 201.

10 See Wilhelm Wartmann's personal copy of the Galerie Georges Petit Picasso catalogue, Archives Kunsthaus Zürich. See also Christian Geelhaar's essay in this catalogue, pp. 26.

11 For a thorough analysis of the proposed New York exhibition see, FitzGerald, 1995 (note 4), pp. 204-14.

12 John Richardson, *A Life of Picasso*, vol. 3: *The Triumphant Years*, London 2009, p. 475.

13 Jacques-Émile Blanche, 'Rétrospective Picasso,' in: *L'Art vivant*, no. 162, July 1932, p. 34.

14 Guy Hickok, 'He Keeps the Art Boys Guessing,' in: *Brooklyn Eagle Magazine*, 17 July 1932, p. 7.

15 See fig. 2, *Zürcher Illustrierte*, 'Soirée der Kunst', June 1932, no. 28, p. 870; Wartmann had intended to include both Braque and Léger in the Zurich exhibition, but, after visiting the Georges Petit show, was persuaded by Picasso to focus exclusively on his work. Braque, who had already agreed to lend Wartmann forty paintings, was understandably furious, as was Léger. See Richardson, 2009 (note 12), p. 481.

16 No French museum lent work, but this is less surprising than it may seem, since at this time the Musée de Grenoble was the only public gallery in France to own a Picasso. See Richardson, 2009 (note 12), p. 476 (*Femme Lisant*, 1920)

17 Commissioned in 1929, Picasso began the illustrations for Ovid's *Metamorphoses* in September of the following year. His *Métamorphoses* was the first book published by Albert Skira and contained thirty etchings. The idea of illustrating Ovid had come from Matisse's son Pierre.

18 Flam, 2003 (note 8), p. 155.

19 Bois, 1998 (note 5), p. 64.

20 Flam, 2003 (note 8), p. 154.

21 Isabelle Monod Fontaine, in: *Matisse Picasso*, London 2002, p. 248.

22 See Bois, 1998 (note 5), p. 58, and Flam, 2003 (note 8), p. 152: "In 1930, Picasso was working mostly in welded steel constructions, but after seeing Matisse's sculptures at the Galerie Pierre in 1930, he began to model in clay again."

23 In conversation with the author Marilyn McCully voiced her opinion that at this time Picasso, too, considered himself primarily a painter and that it was only later, after his death, that the innovative qualities of his sculpture were recognised.

24 Christian Pudelko, Reber's grandson, told Esther Braun-Kalberer (Exhibition Organiser at Kunsthaus Zürich) that the photographs had been given to his grandfather by Barr during one of the latter's visits to Switzerland. Reber lent eighteen paintings to the exhibition; only Picasso himself and Paul Rosenberg, his dealer, lent more.

25 Of these new photographs, three are copies of those in the Barr archives Reber nos. 1, 2, 3 = Barr nos. 3, 4, 5).

26 Margaret Scolari Barr, 'Alfred H. Barr Jr and the Museum of Modern Art: A Biographical Chronicle of the Years 1930-1944,' in: *The New Criterion*, special issue, 1987, p. 29.

27 A comparison between Barr no. 1 (see fig. 5, p. 83 and Reber no. 11) also shows two different moments during the installation.

28 I am grateful to Casimiro Di Crescenzo for helping to identify the names of the galleries from the photographs of the Matisse exhibition (Matisse Archives, Paris).

29 FitzGerald, 1995 (note 4), p. 201.

30 Ibid., p. 202.

31 Michael FitzGerald 'A Question of Identity,' in: *Picasso's Marie-Thérèse*, exh. cat., Acquavella

Galleries, New York 2008, p. 28, no. 27. We know that Picasso had access to *Les Demoiselles*, because Doucet's widow agreed to lend the small *Head of a Harlequin* (1905; no 28) seen standing on the floor in the right-hand corner of Reber no. 11.

32 Richardson, 2009 (note 12), p. 476.

33 It was in this gallery that the banquet for Matisse had been held. See fig. 1

34 FitzGerald, 1995 (note 4), p. 199.

35 Matisse had tried unsuccessfully to obtain some of his works from these collections for his own exhibition. See Flam, 2003 (note 8), p. 151.

36 G. P. nos. 37, 57, 58, 86, 94 and 95.

37 At this time, the *Portrait of Olga*, 1917 bore the formal title *Portrait of Madame Picasso*.

38 Picasso, interview with Tériade in *L'Intransigeant*, 15 June 1932, repr. in *Verve* 5, nos. 19–20, 1948.

39 Richardson, 2009 (note 12), p. 478.

40 Acting as a supplement to the catalogue, this publication contained illustrations of several works not shown in the exhibition. It also featured an anthology of texts on the artist, some of them commissioned specially by Zervos from well-known European and American critics. These included Harold Stanley Ede, who wrote: "If you have a strong conception of life it will not matter whether you are painting a potato or a Baptism, whether you do it in one manner or another, with academic realism or abstract realism, your conception will come through, and Picasso has this all penetrating vision." Zervos's publication highlighted many of Picasso's Marie-Thérèse paintings by reproducing them full page on thicker card.

41 In 1906 Eugeni d'Ors had coined the term 'noucentisme'; it came to denote a movement influential in all areas of cultural activity in Catalonia from 1908 to 1923 that advocated a reversion to a form of classicism.

42 Eugeni d'Ors, *Pablo Picasso*, Paris, 1930, trans. Warre B. Wells, London 1930, pp. 36–7.

43 It was not the first time that a text by d'Ors had exerted significant influence on Picasso's aesthetic ideas. See Richardson, vol. I, 1991, p. 501, no. 2, and 29. "Ors wrote an uninspired monograph on Picasso in 1930 and then rounded on him in print, challenging him (1936) 'to produce a masterpiece'." (McCully, *A Picasso Anthology*, Princeton, 1981, p. 202). Picasso told Roberto Otero that d'Ors was "[r]eally a fool". See Otero, *Forever, Picasso: An Intimate Look at his Last Years*, trans. Elaine Kerrigan, New York, 1974, p. 169.

44 *Thirty Years of Pablo Picasso*, Alex, Reid & Lefevre Ltd., June 1931.

45 Brassaï, *Conversations avec Picasso*, trans. Jane Marie Todd as *Conversations with Picasso*, Chicago and London 1999, pp. 3–4.

INSTALLATION VIEWS
OF THE PICASSO EXHIBITION AT THE
GALERIES GEORGES PETIT 1932

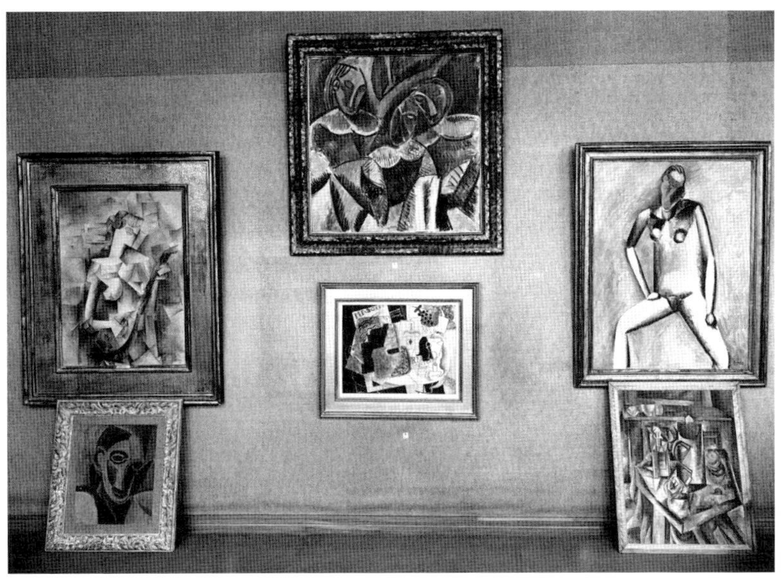

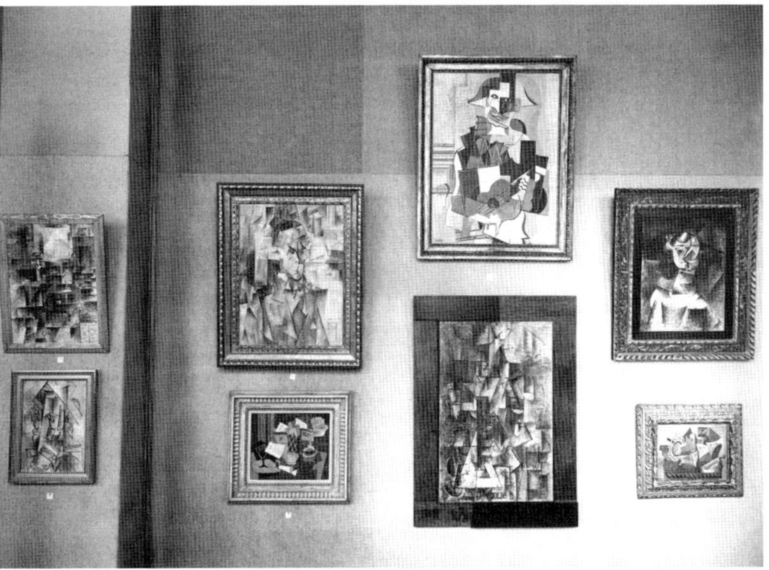

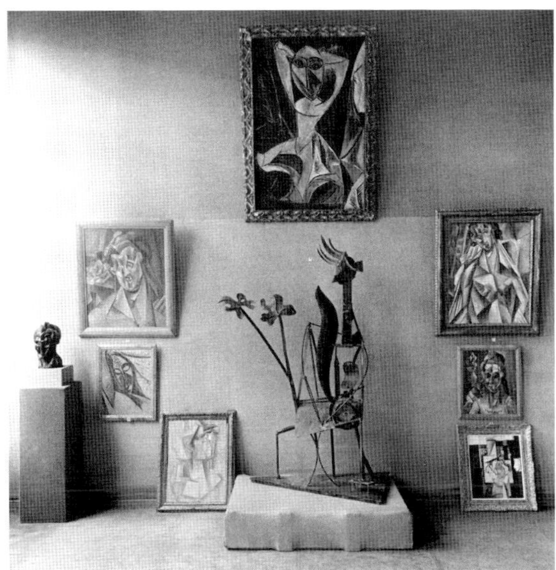

Reber nos. 1–3
Installation views of the
Picasso exhibition at the
Galeries Georges Petit,
Paris 1932

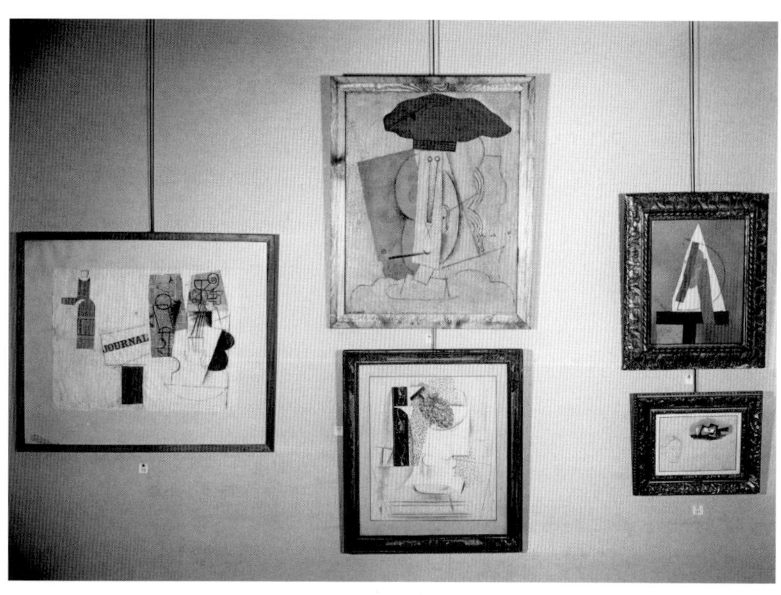

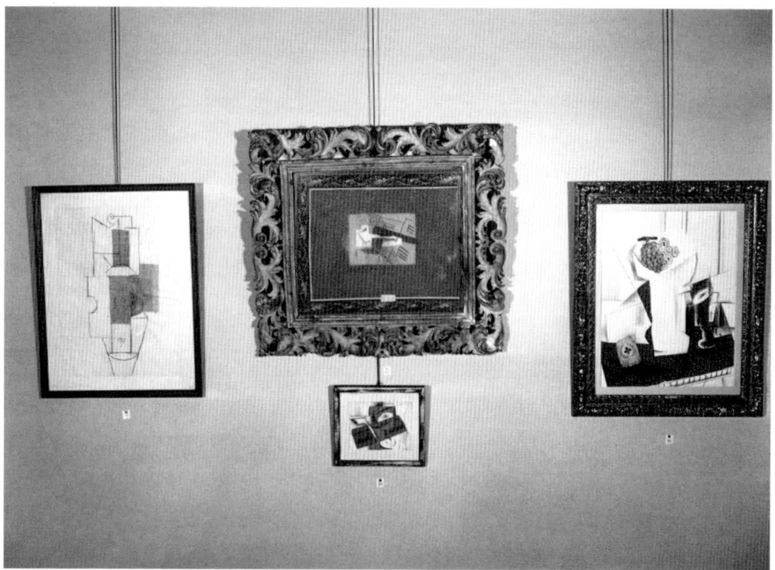

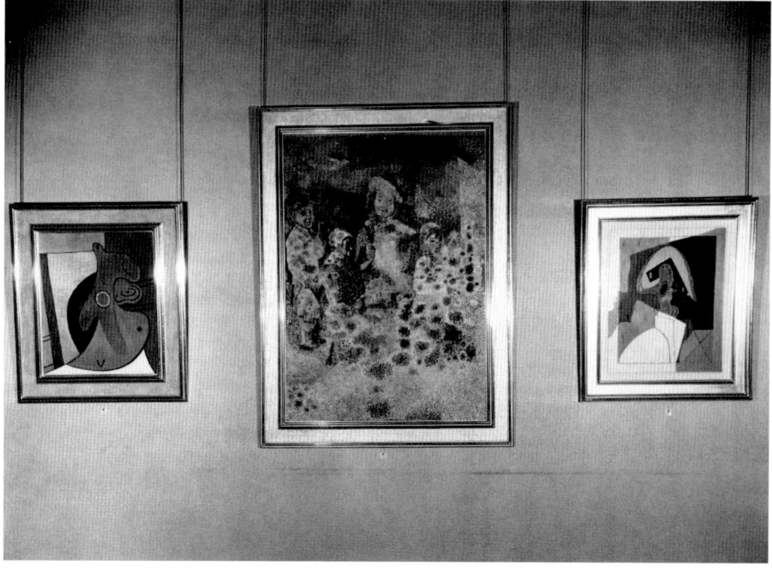

Reber nos. 4–6

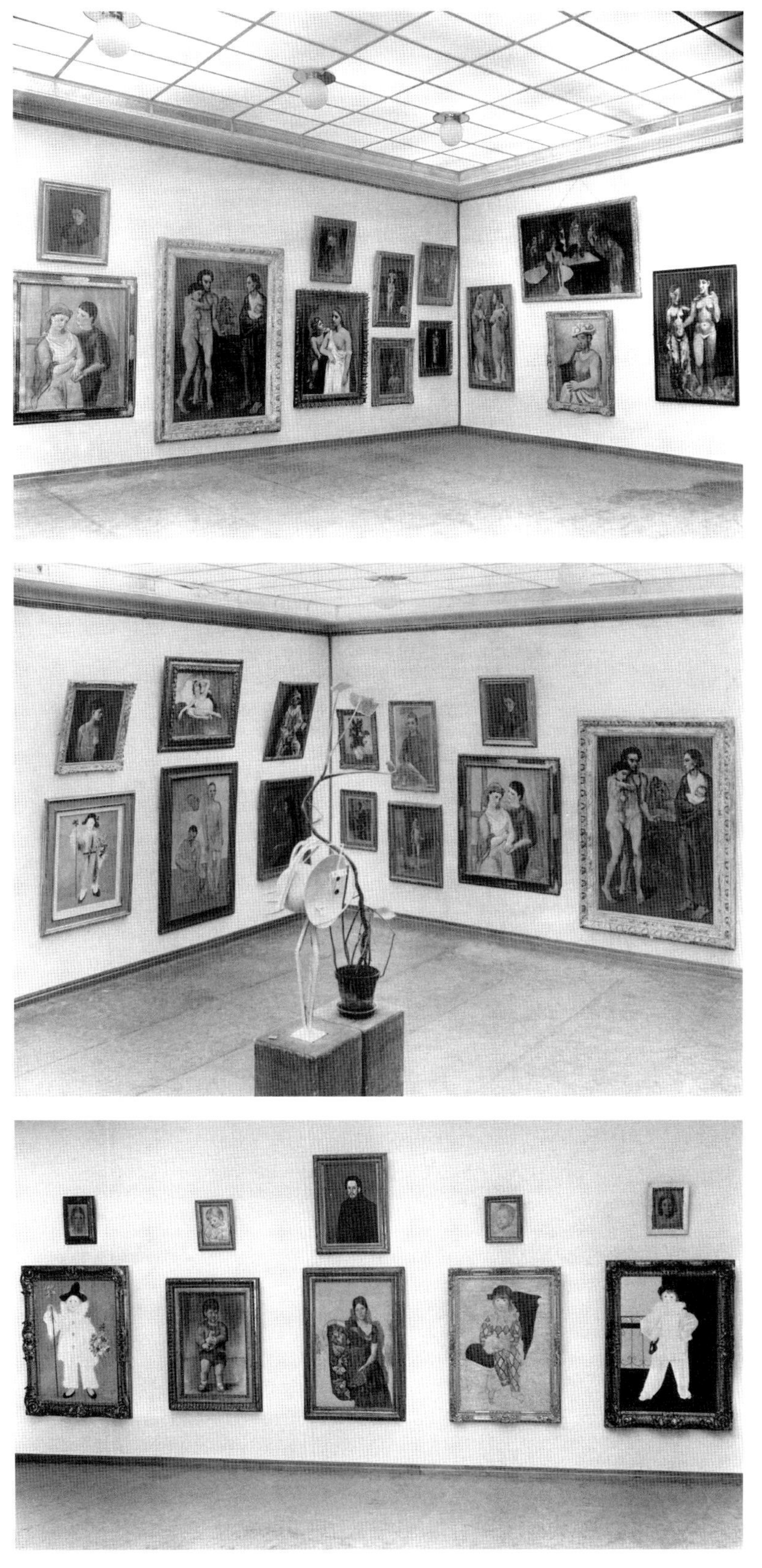

Reber nos. 7–9

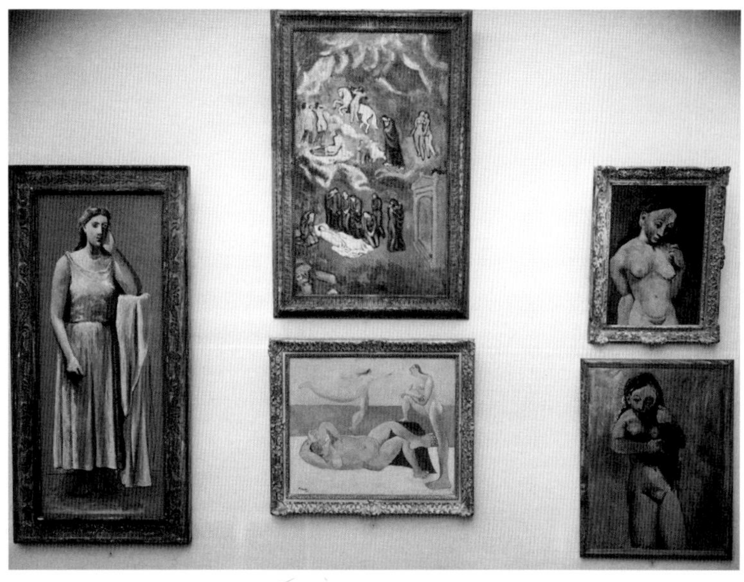

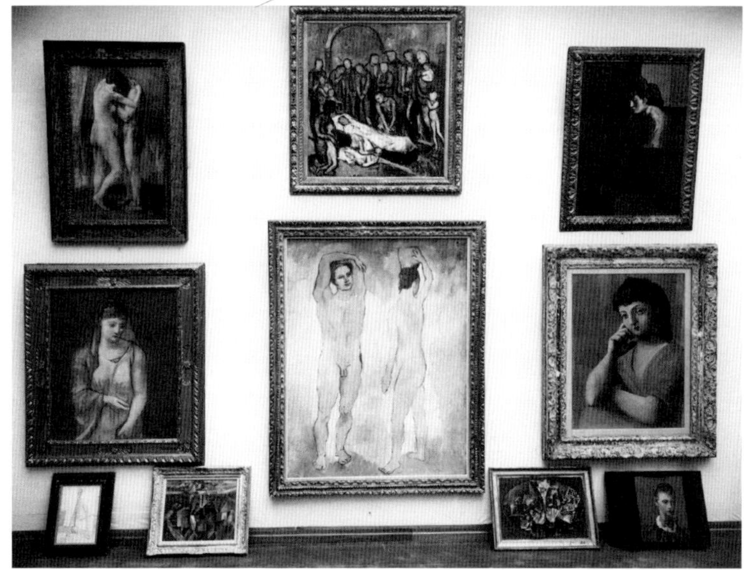

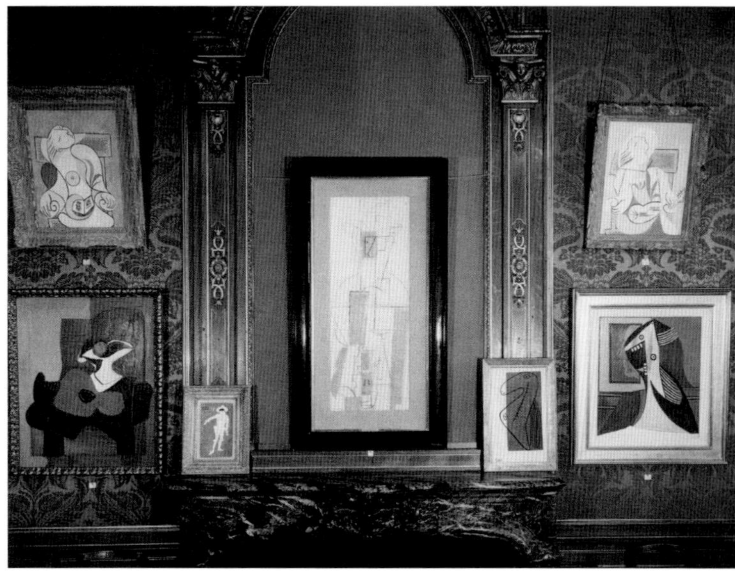

Reber nos. 10–12

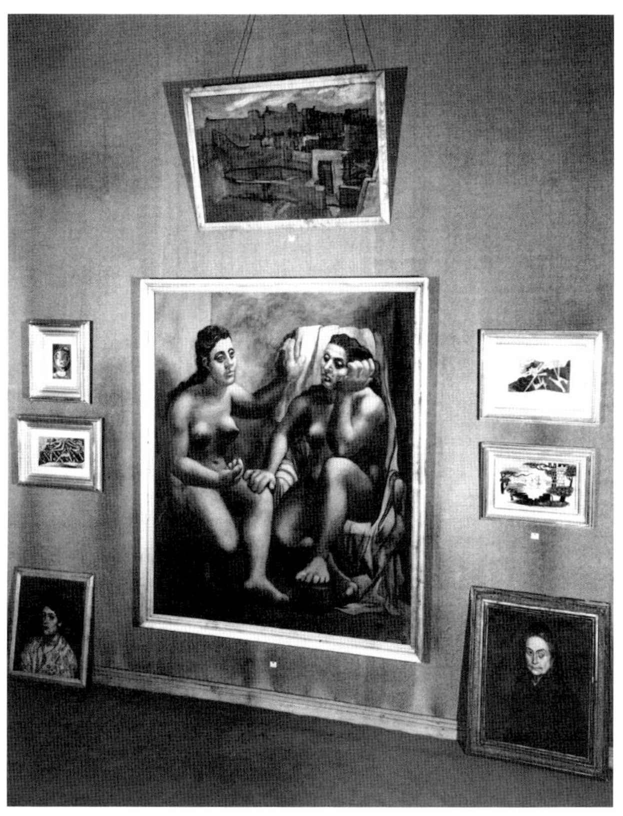
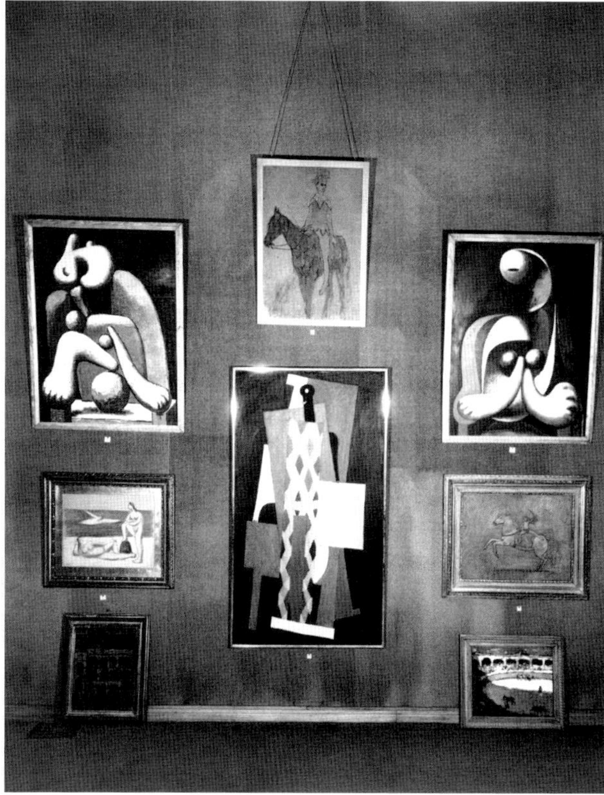

Reber nos. 13-14

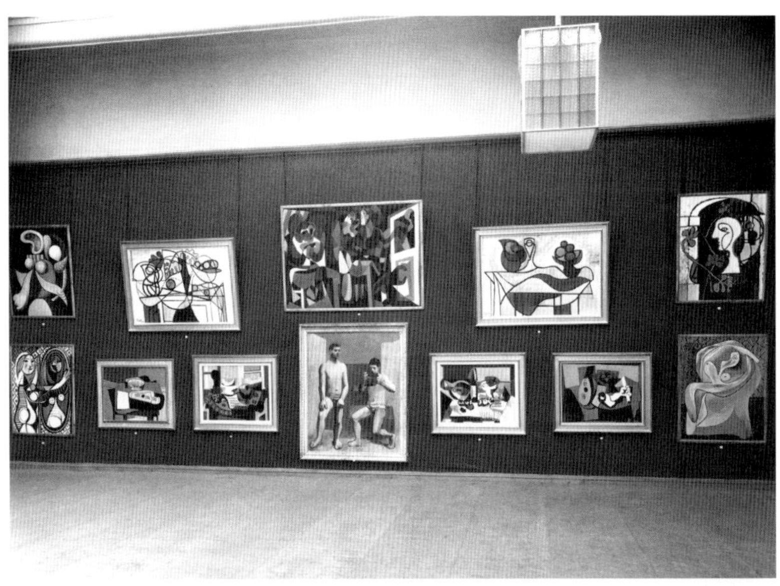

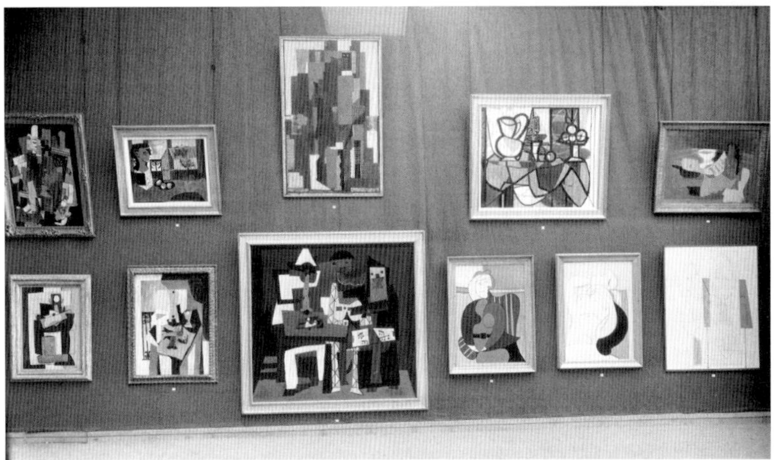

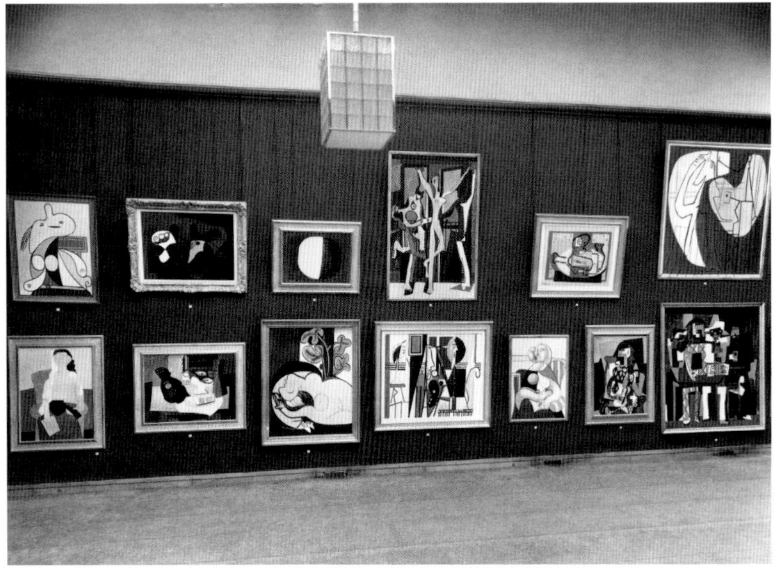

Reber nos. 15–17

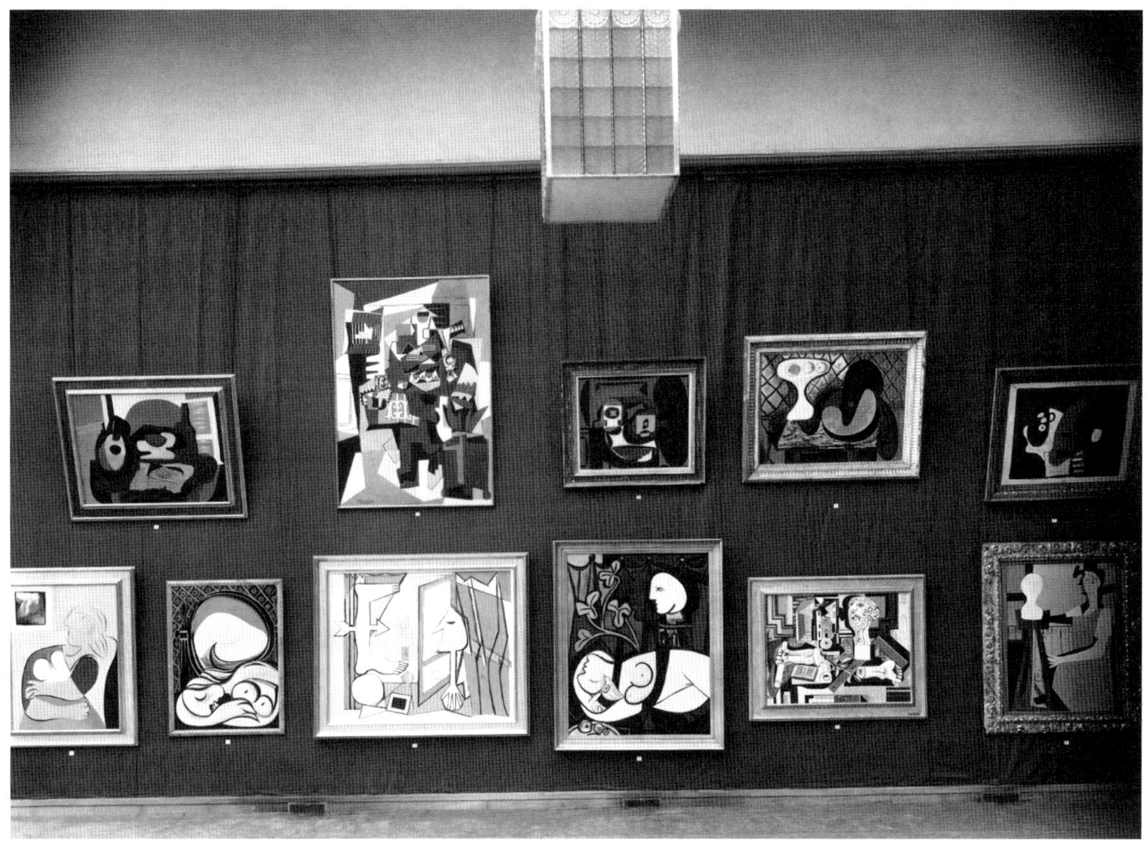

Reber nos. 18

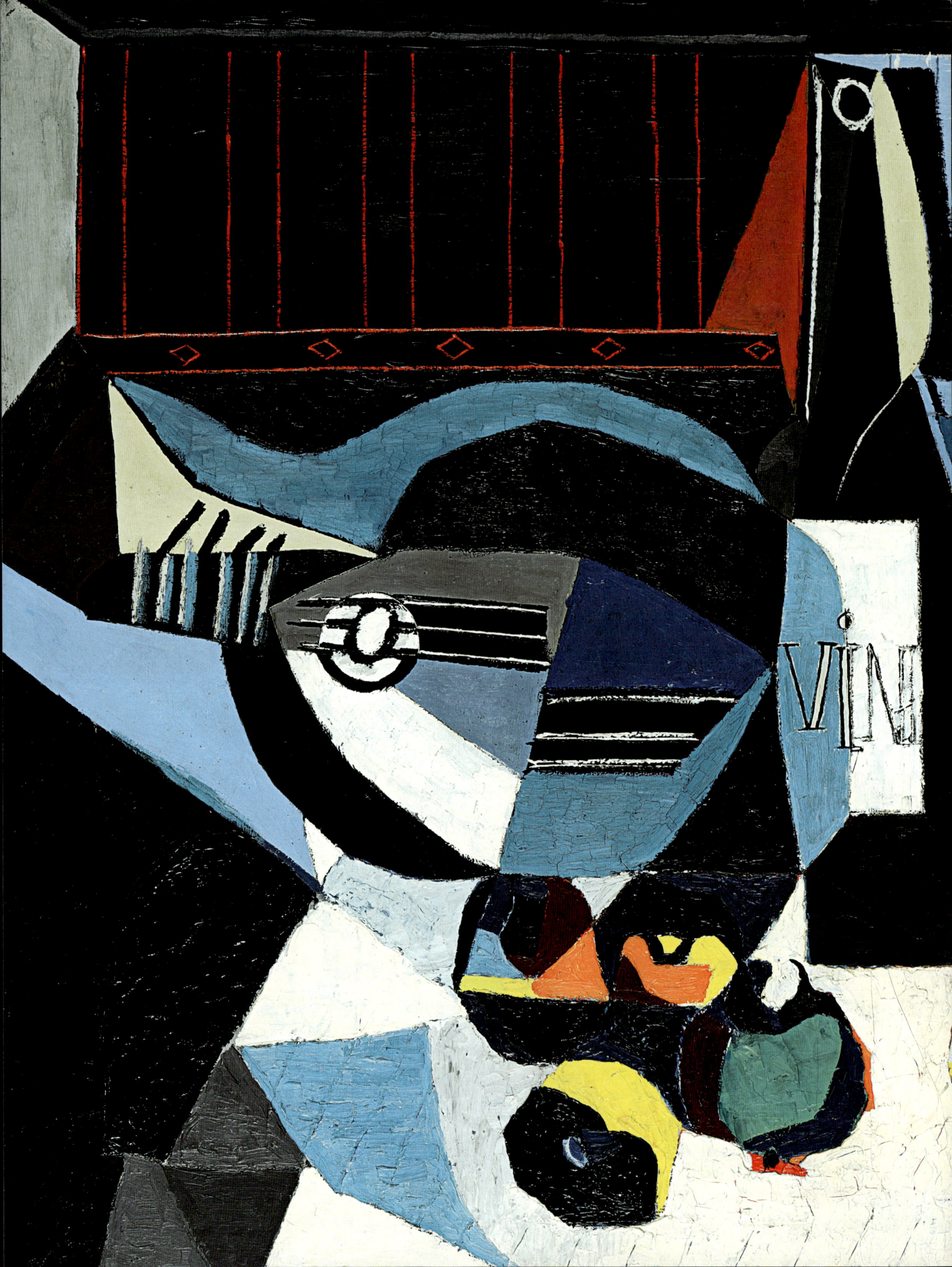
VIN

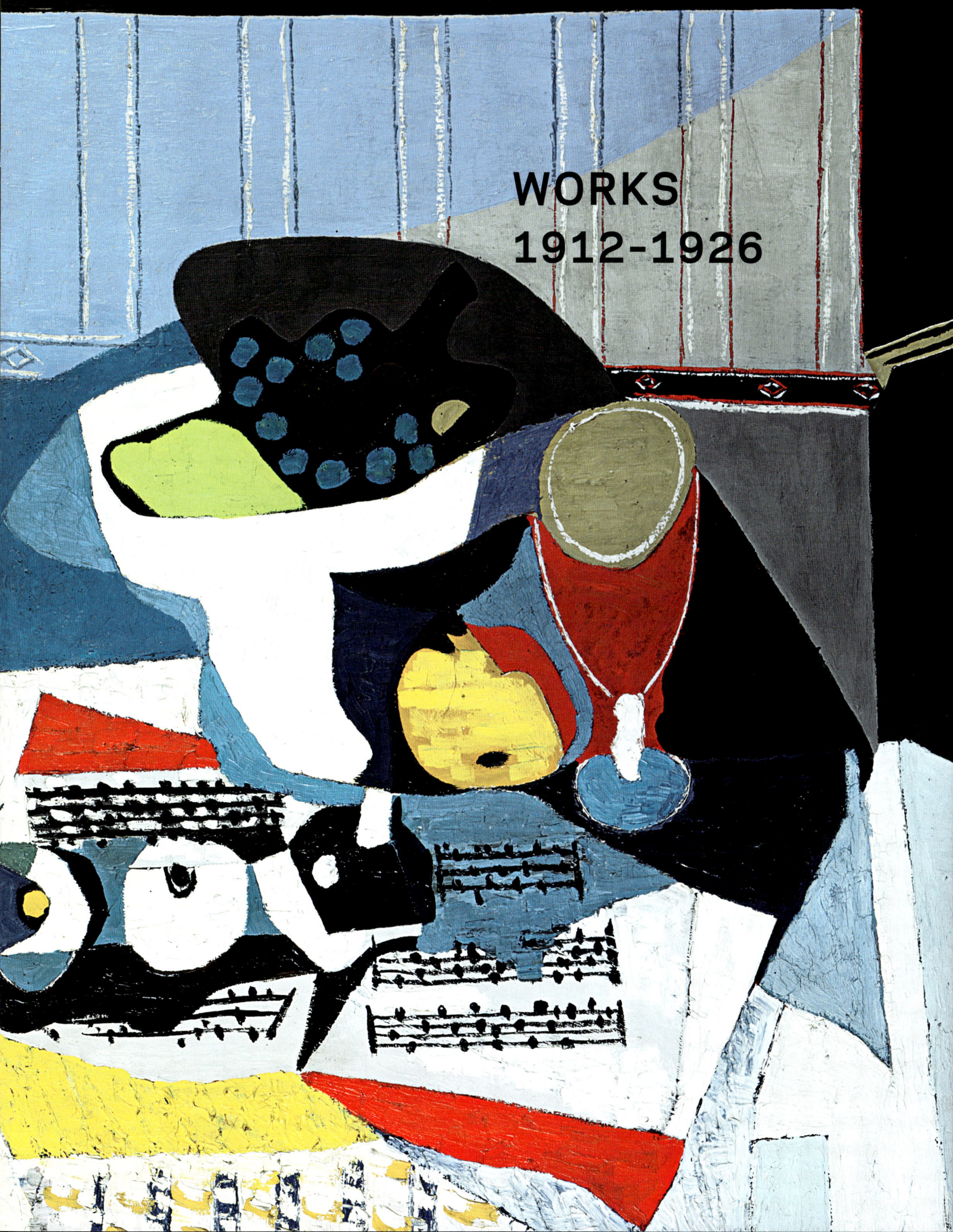

WORKS
1912-1926

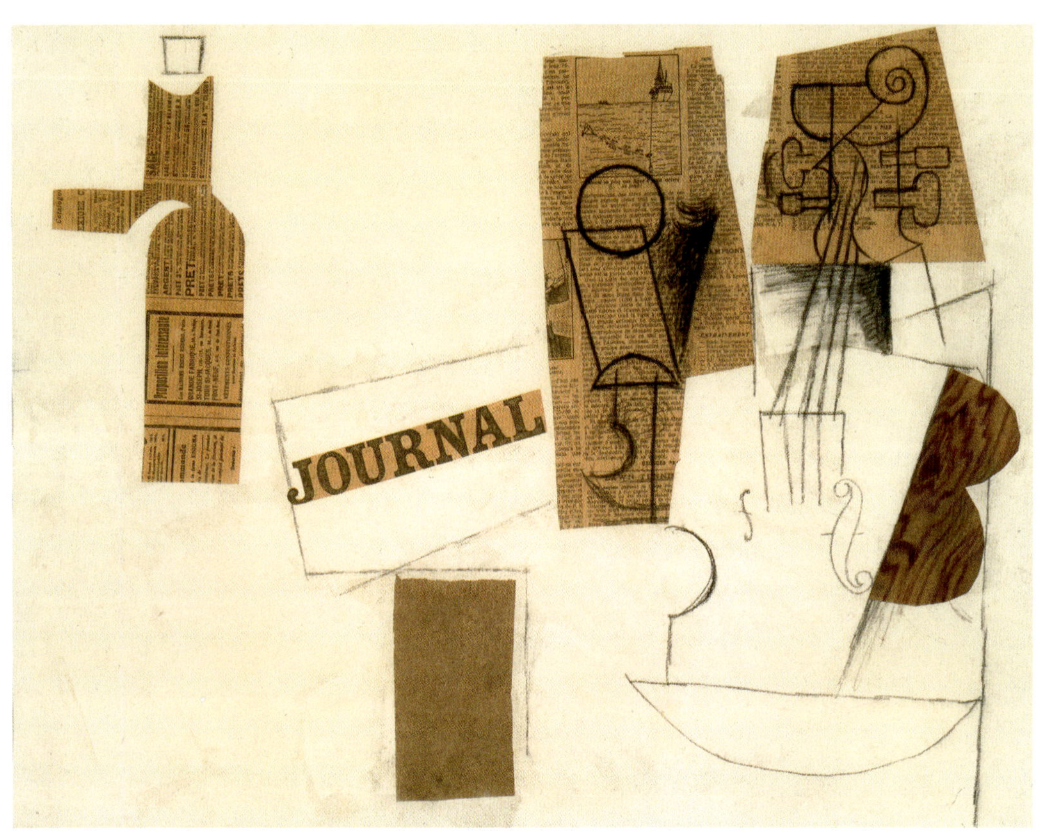

29
Bottle, Glass and Violin, 1912/13
Collage
47 x 62 cm
Moderna Museet, Stockholm

previous double page
Wine Bottle, 1926 (detail)
Oil on canvas
98 x 131.5 cm
Fondation Beyeler, Riehen/Basel

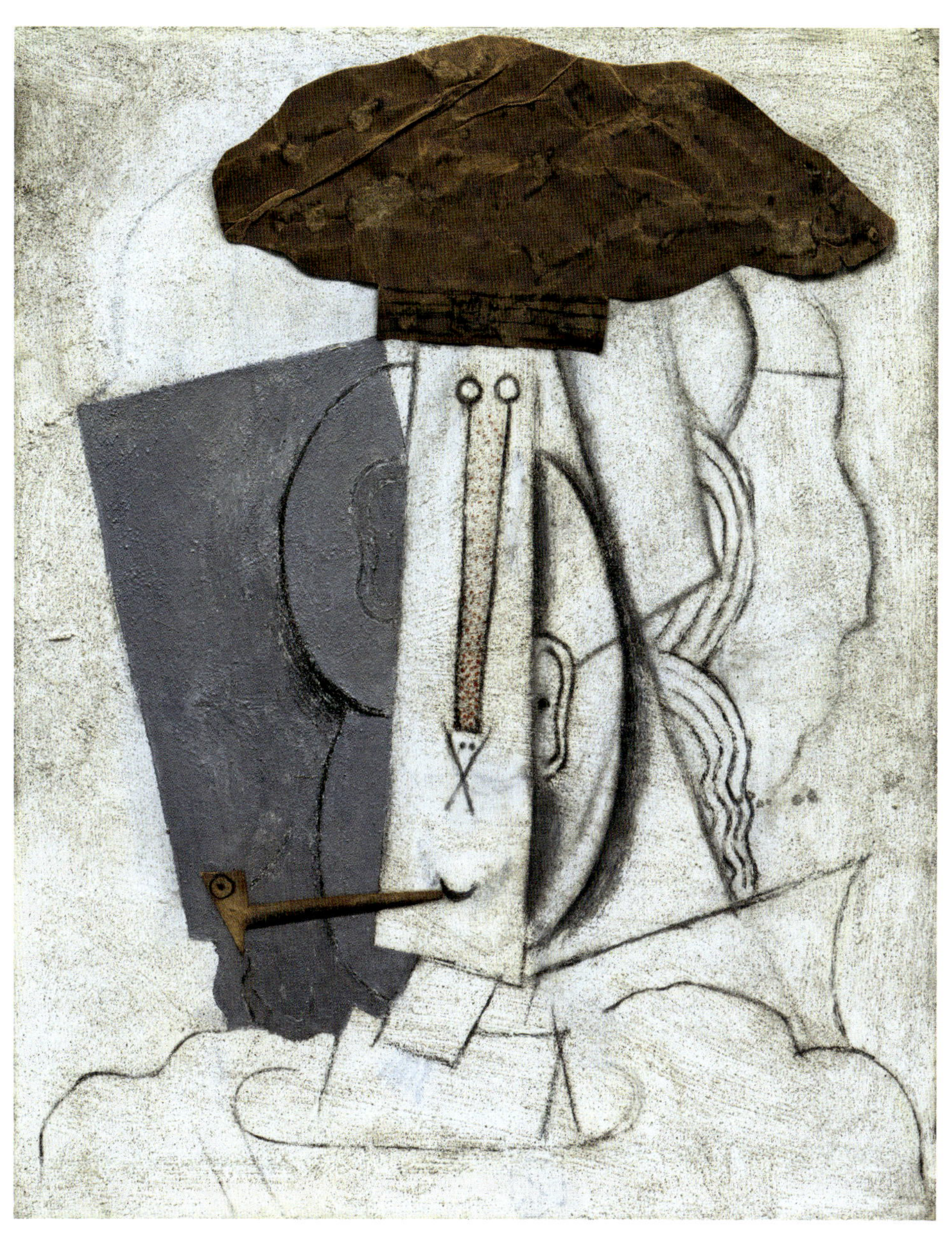

30

Student with a Pipe, 1914
Plaster, sand, pasted paper,
oil and charcoal on canvas
73 x 58.7 cm
The Museum of Modern Art, New York
Nelson A. Rockefeller Bequest, 1979

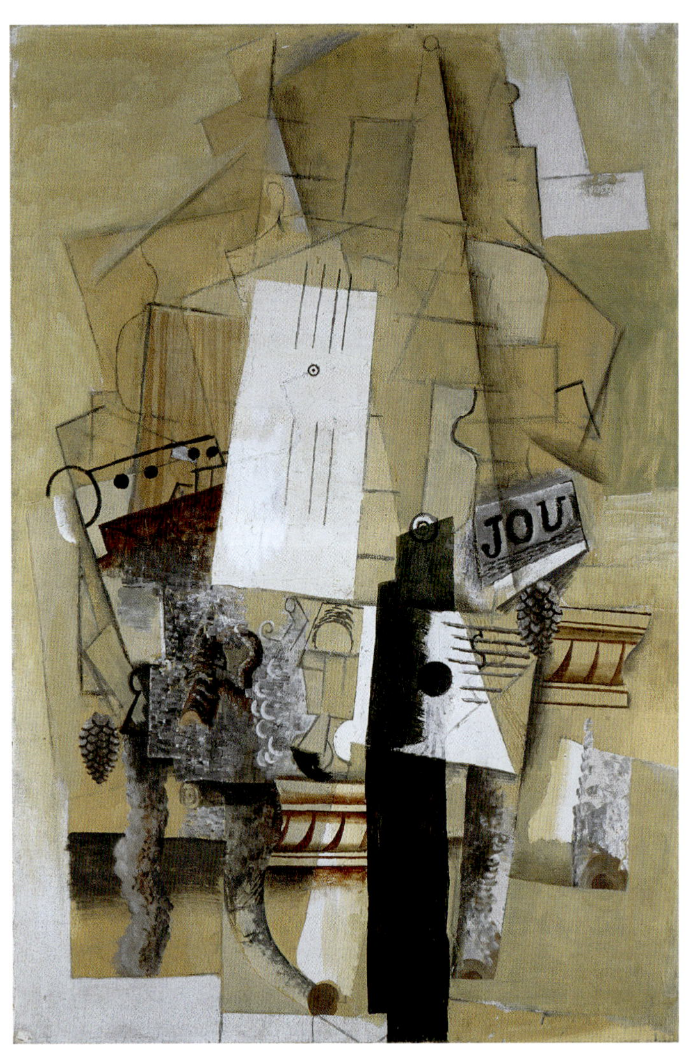

31
The Guéridon, 1913/14
Oil on canvas
130 x 89 cm
Kunstmuseum Basel
Donated by Dr. h.c. Raoul La Roche, 1952

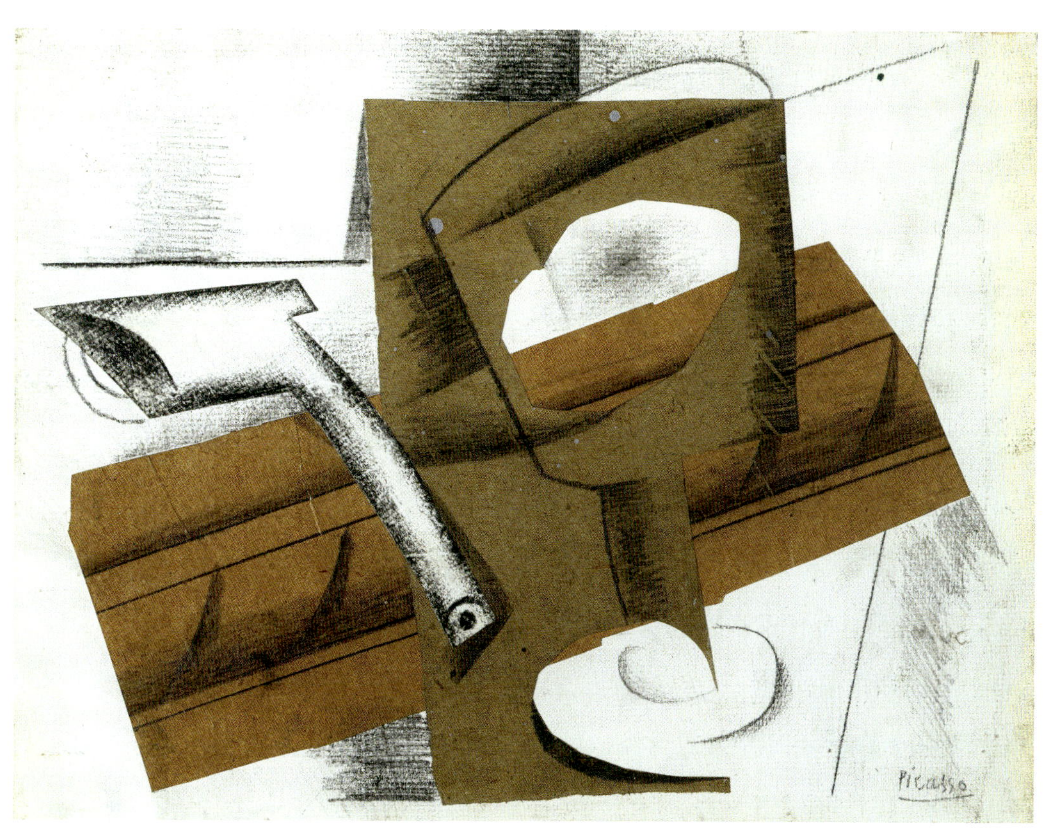

32
Pipe and Wineglass, 1914
Pasted paper and pencil on white,
ribbed paper
17.9 x 24 cm
Thaw Collection, The Pierpont
Morgan Library, New York

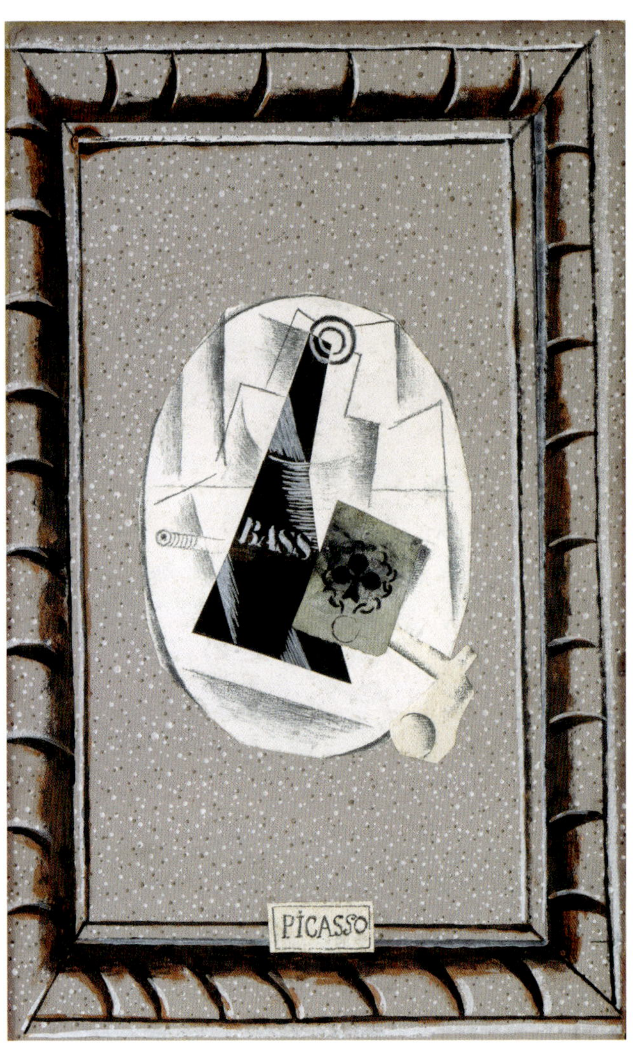

33
Bottle of Bass, Ace of Clubs and Pipe , 1914
Collage (oil, gouache, pencil)
51.5 x 31 cm
Private ownership

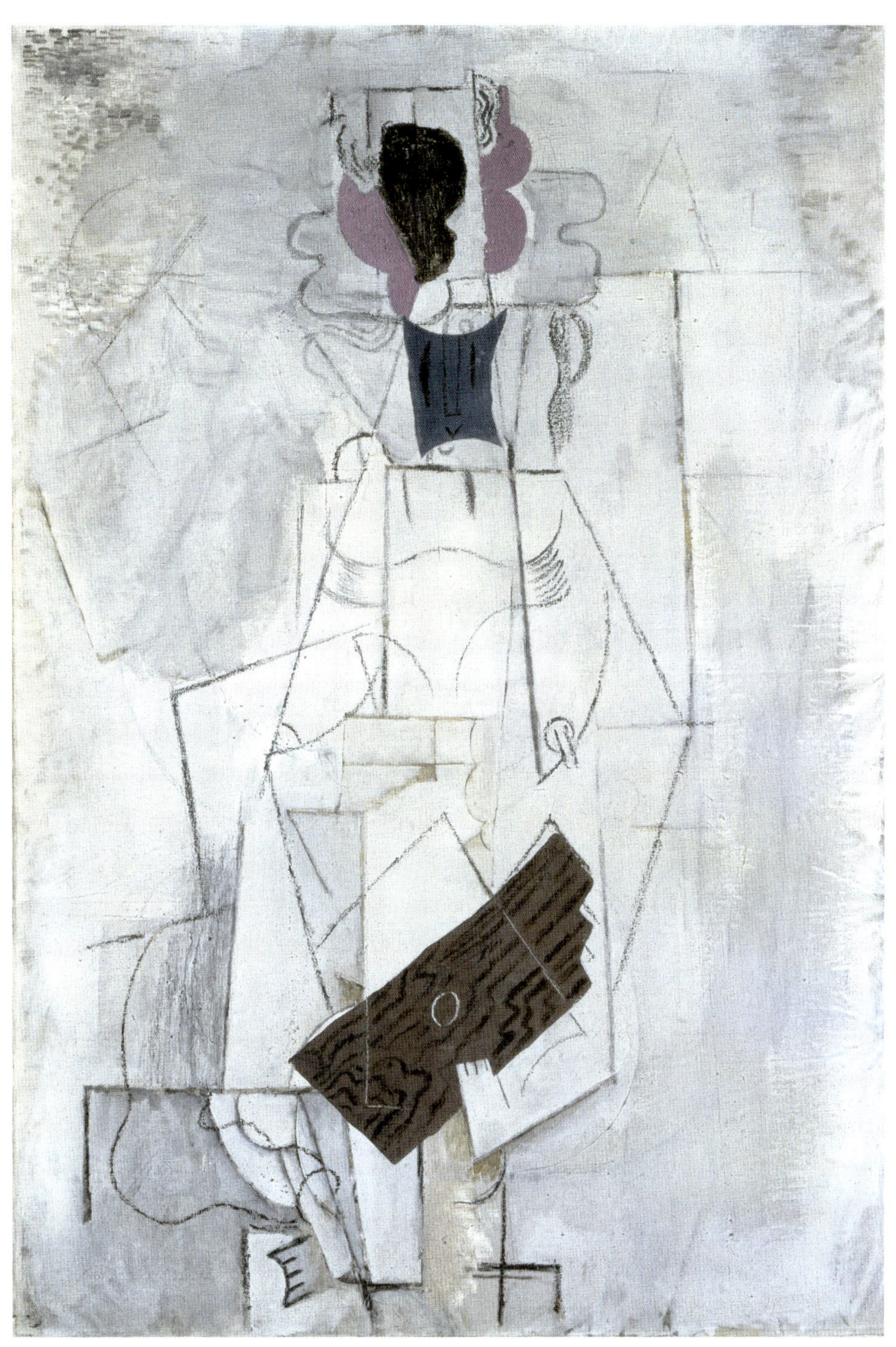

34
Woman with Guitar, 1911/1914
Oil on canvas
130.5 x 90 cm
Kunstmuseum Basel
Donated by Dr. h.c. Raoul La Roche, 1952

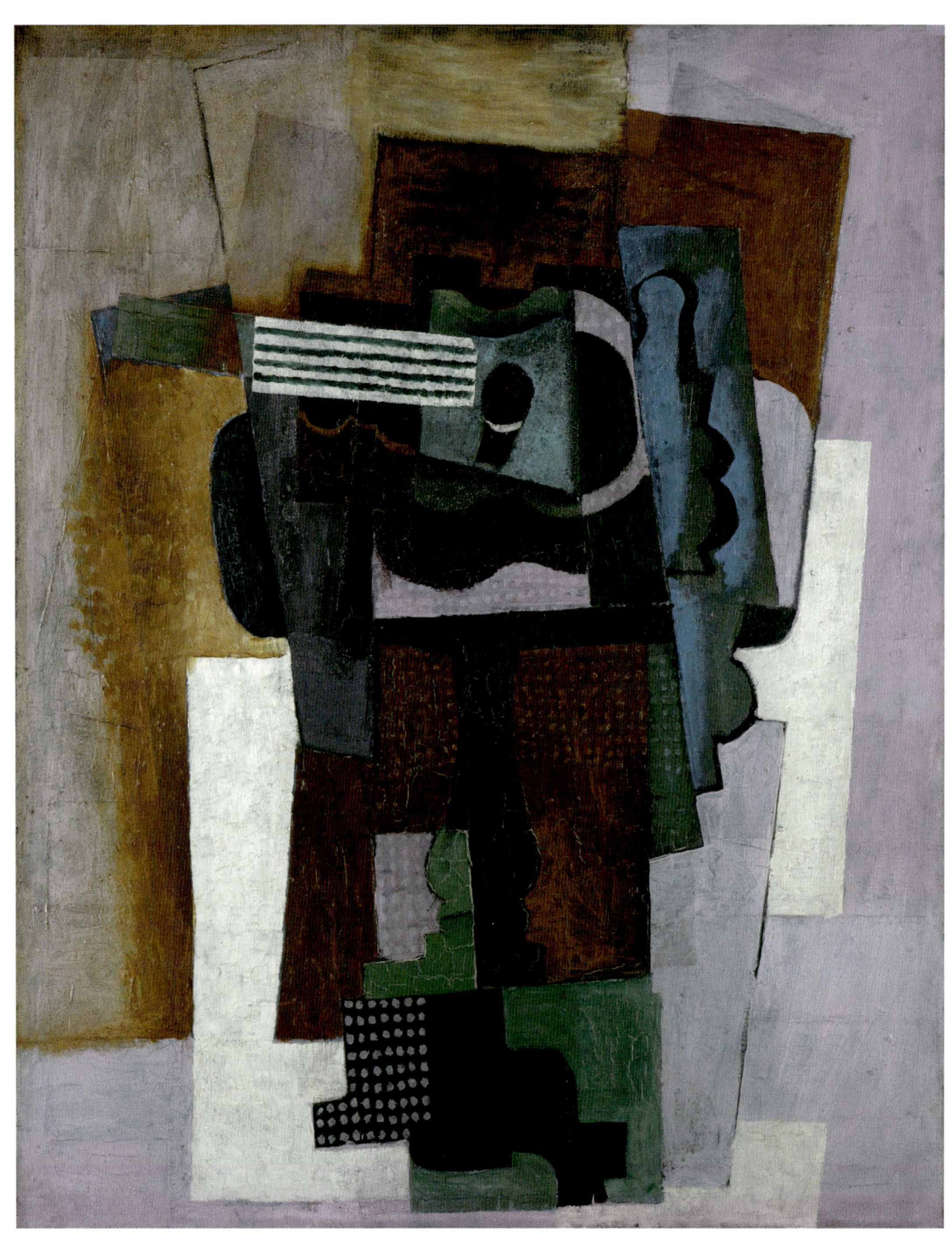

35
Guitar on a Guéridon, 1915
Oil on canvas
133 x 104 cm
Kunsthaus Zürich

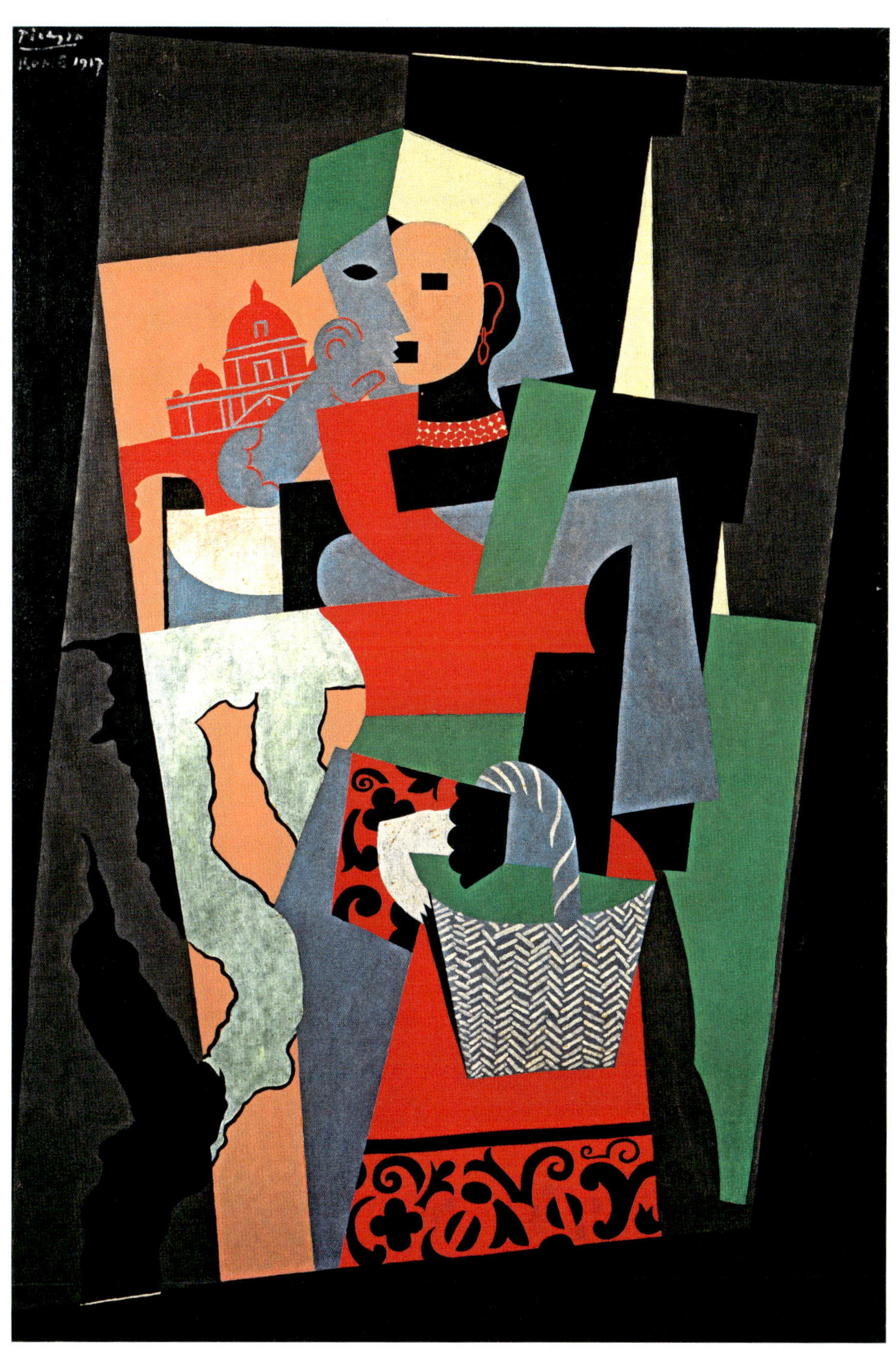

36
The Italian Woman, 1917
Oil on canvas
149.5 × 101.5 cm
Foundation E.G. Bührle Collection, Zurich

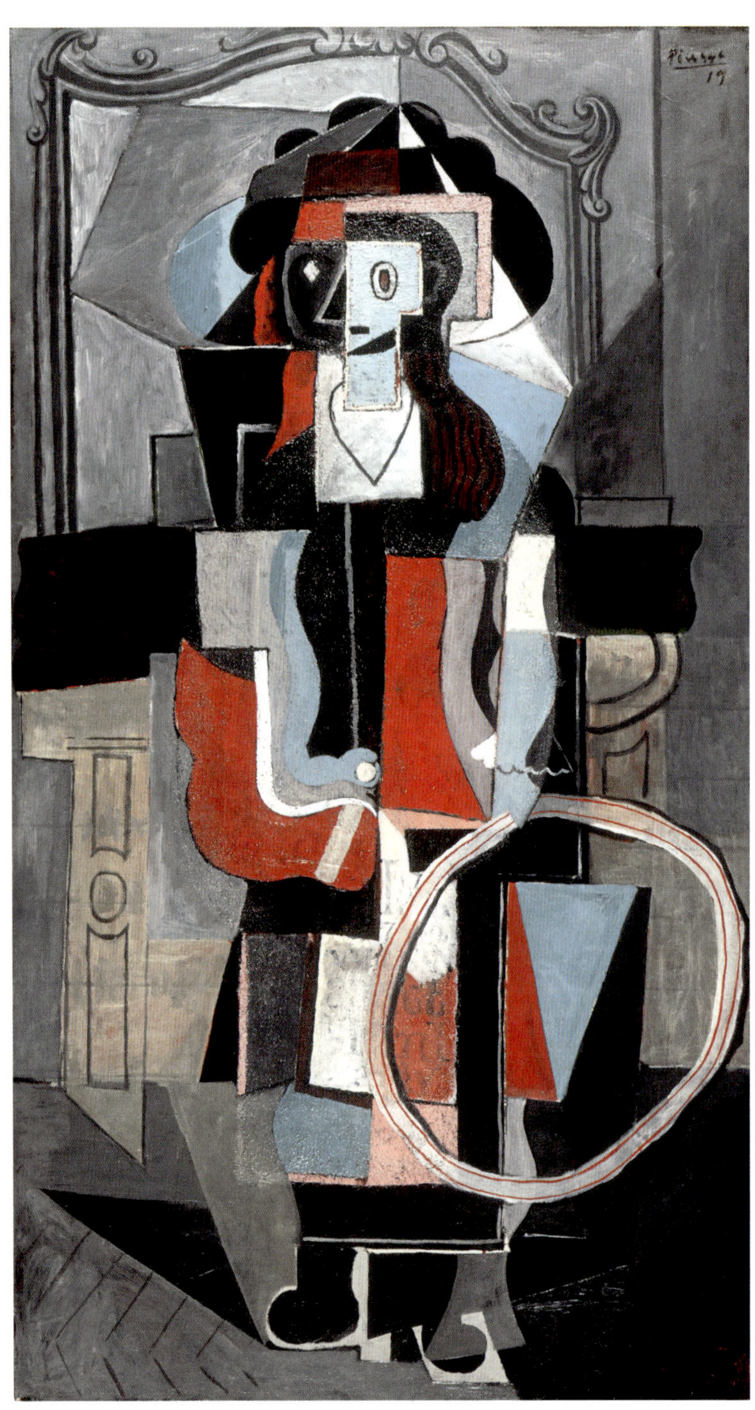

37
Young Girl with Hoop, 1919
Oil and sand on canvas
142.5 x 79 cm
Centre Pompidou, Paris
Musée national d'art moderne/
Centre de création industrielle
Bequest of Baronne Eva Gourgaud, 1965

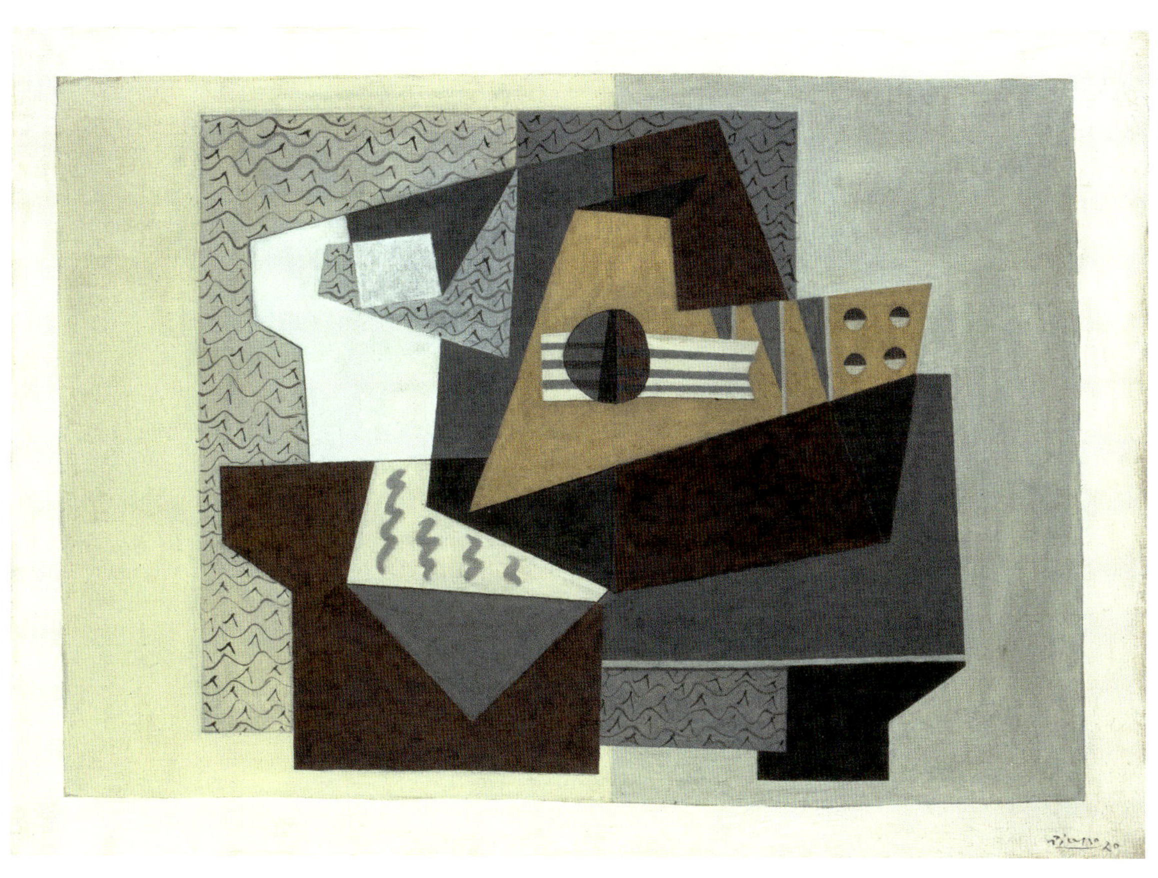

38
The Guitar, 1920
Oil on canvas
65.5 x 92.5 cm
Emanuel Hoffmann-Stiftung
Deposited in the Öffentliche
Kunstsammlung Basel

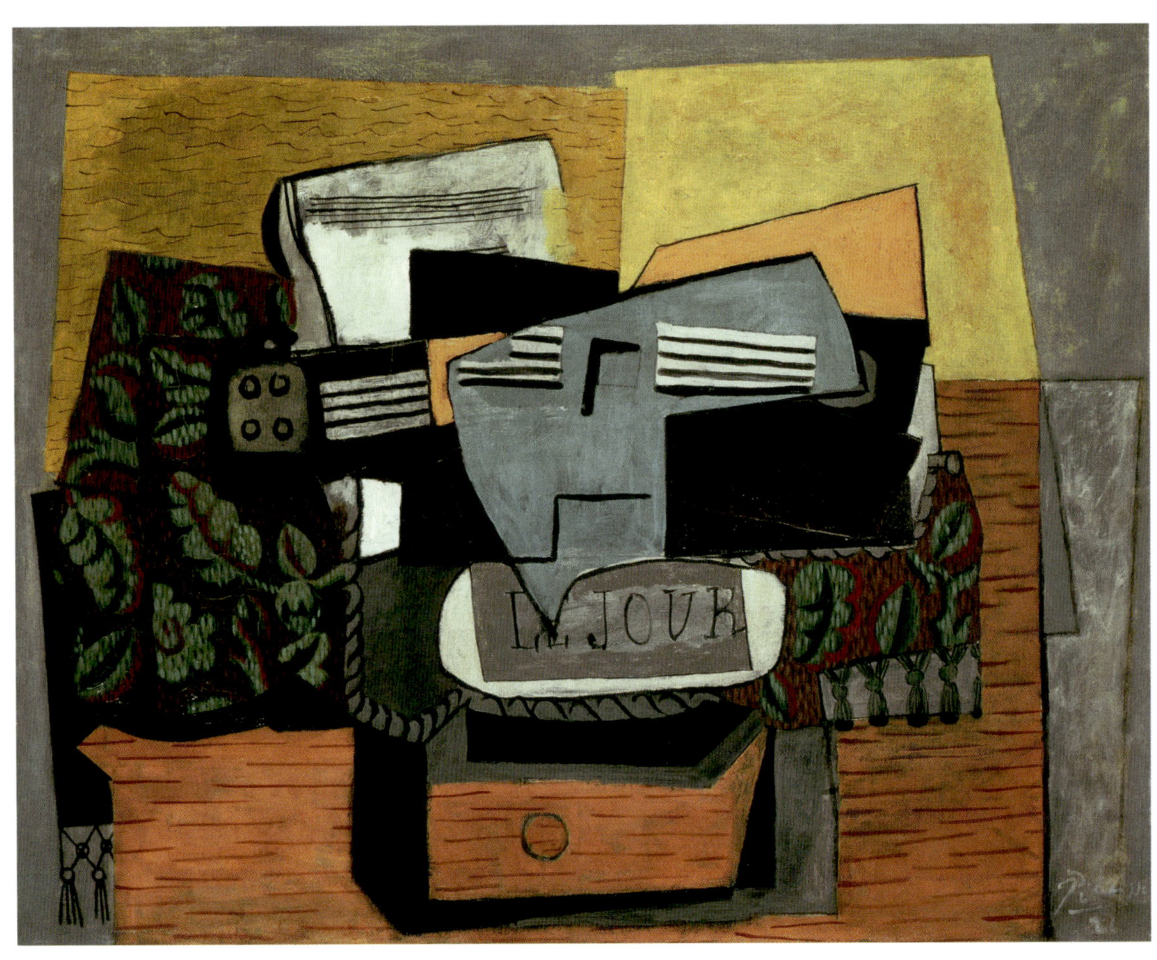

39
**Violin and Journal on a
Green Carpet,** 1921
Oil on canvas
73.3 x 92.1 cm
Courtesy Nahmad Collection, Switzerland

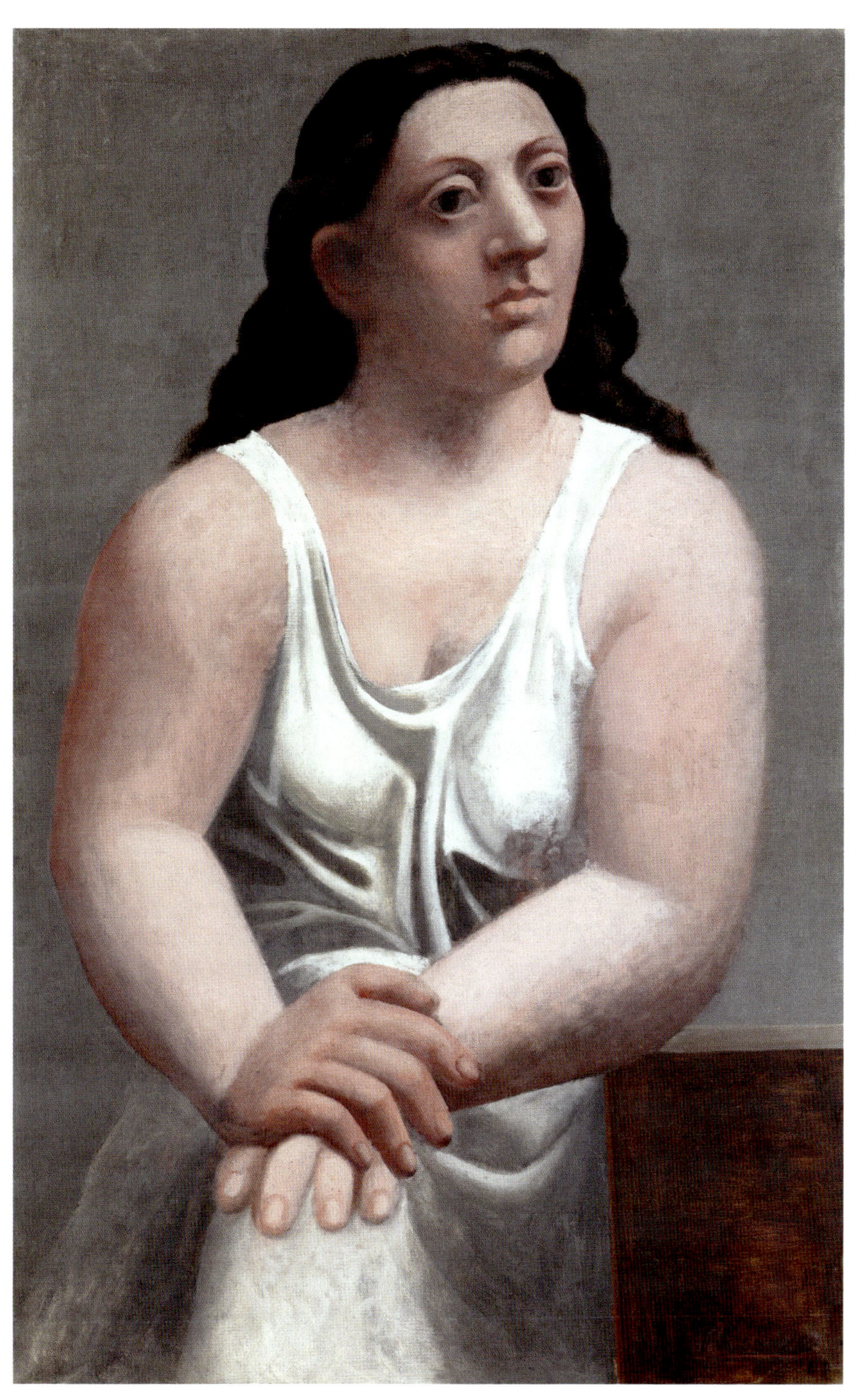

40
**Seated Woman
(Woman with Chemise),** 1921
Oil on canvas
116 x 73 cm
Staatsgalerie Stuttgart

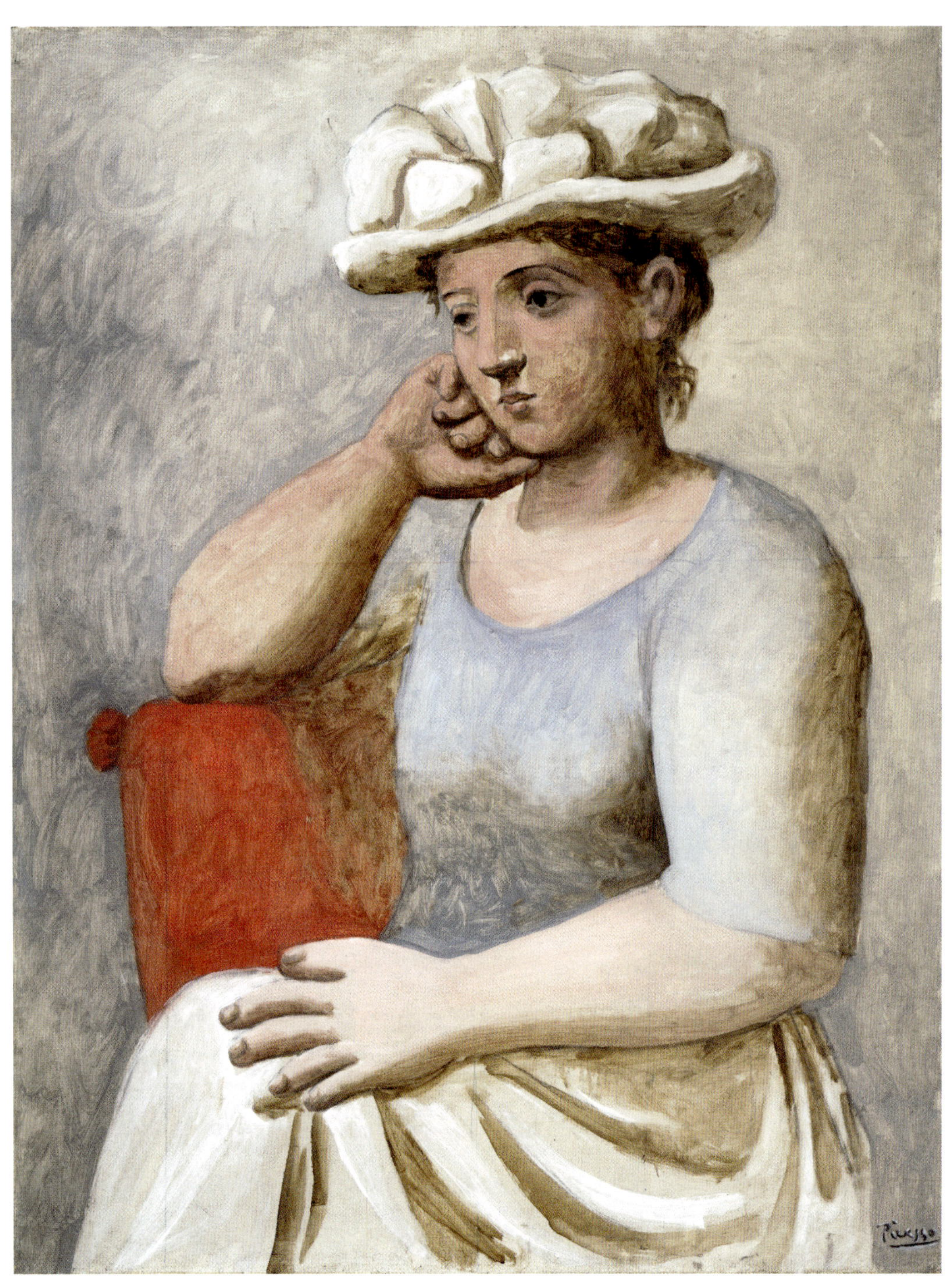

41
Woman with a White Hat, 1921
Oil on canvas
118 x 91 cm
Musée de l'Orangerie, Paris
Collection Jean Walter et Paul Guillaume

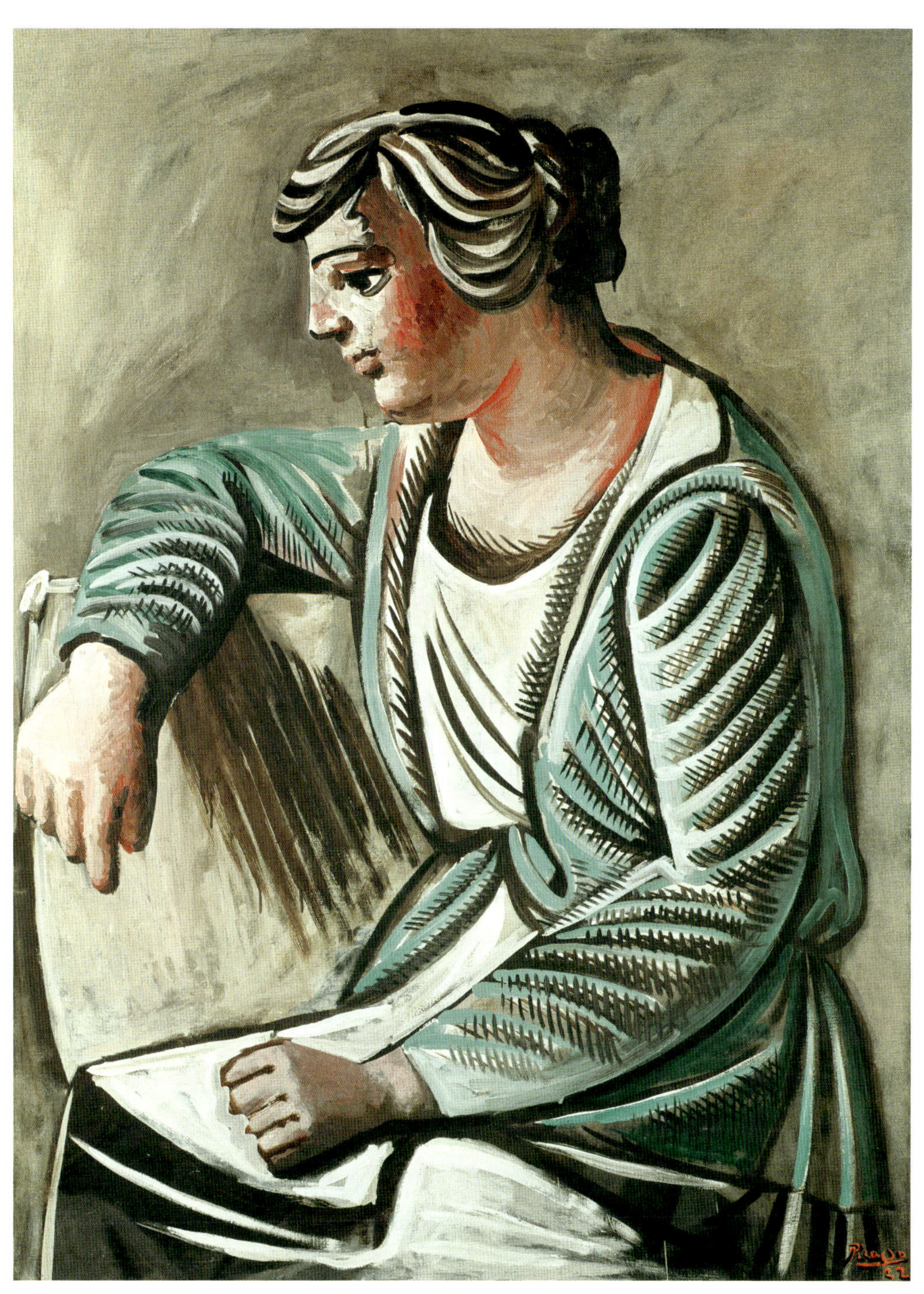

42
Woman in a Green Dressing Gown, 1922
Oil on canvas
130.3 x 96.5 cm
Museum Ludwig Köln

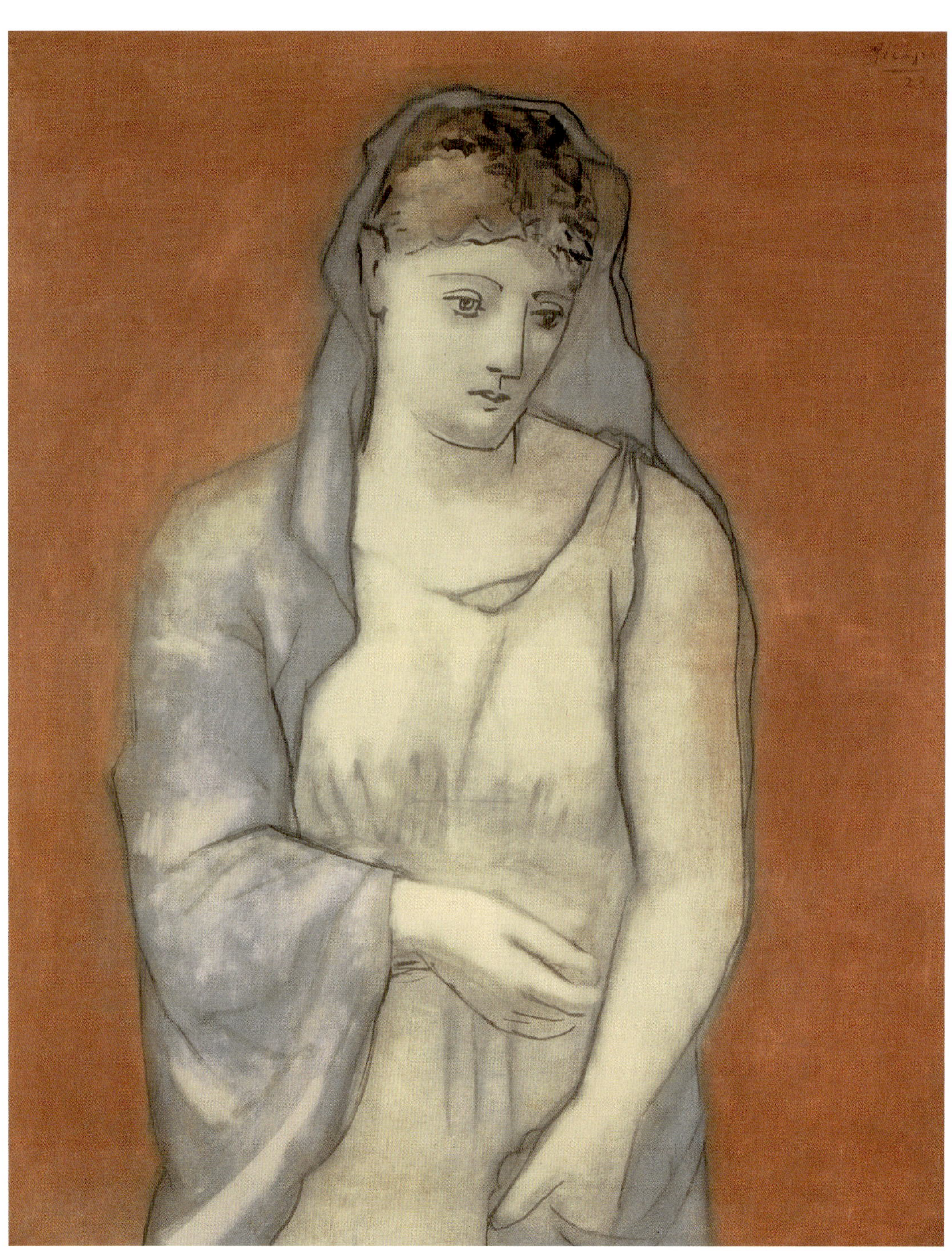

43

Woman with Blue Veil, 1923
Oil on canvas
100.3 x 81.2 cm
Los Angeles County Museum of Art
Mr and Mrs George Gard de Sylva Collection

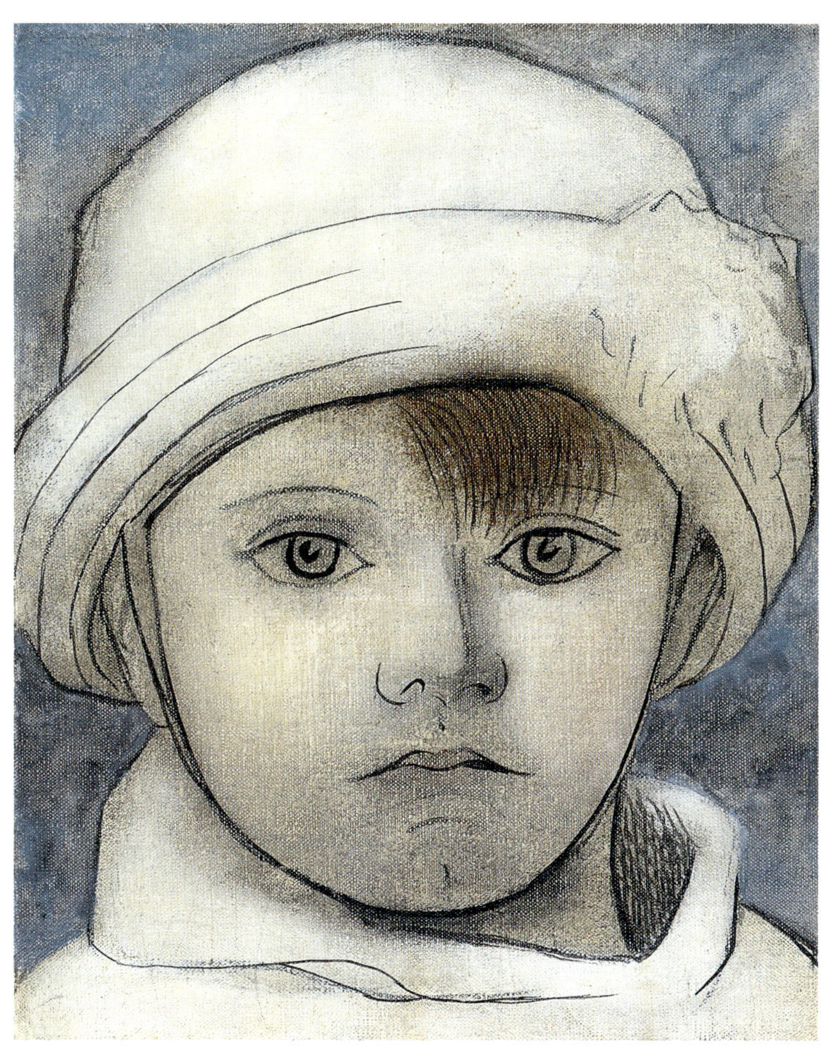

44
Portrait of Paulo in a White Cap, 1923
Oil on canvas
27 x 22 cm
Private collection
Courtesy of Fundación Almine y Bernard
Ruiz-Picasso para el Arte

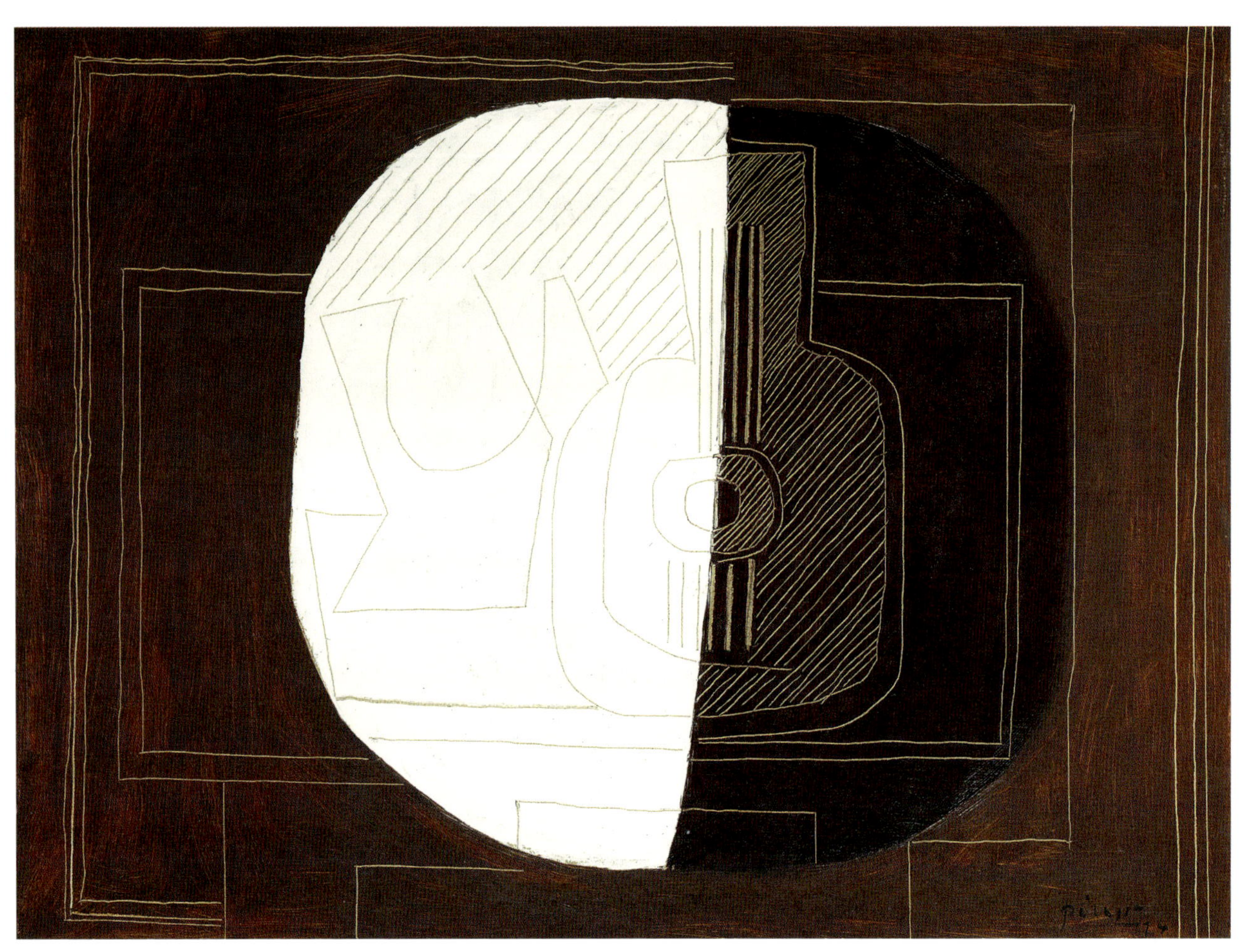

45
Guitar and Fruit Bowl, 1924
Oil on canvas
77 x 106 cm
Courtesy Nahmad Collection, Switzerland

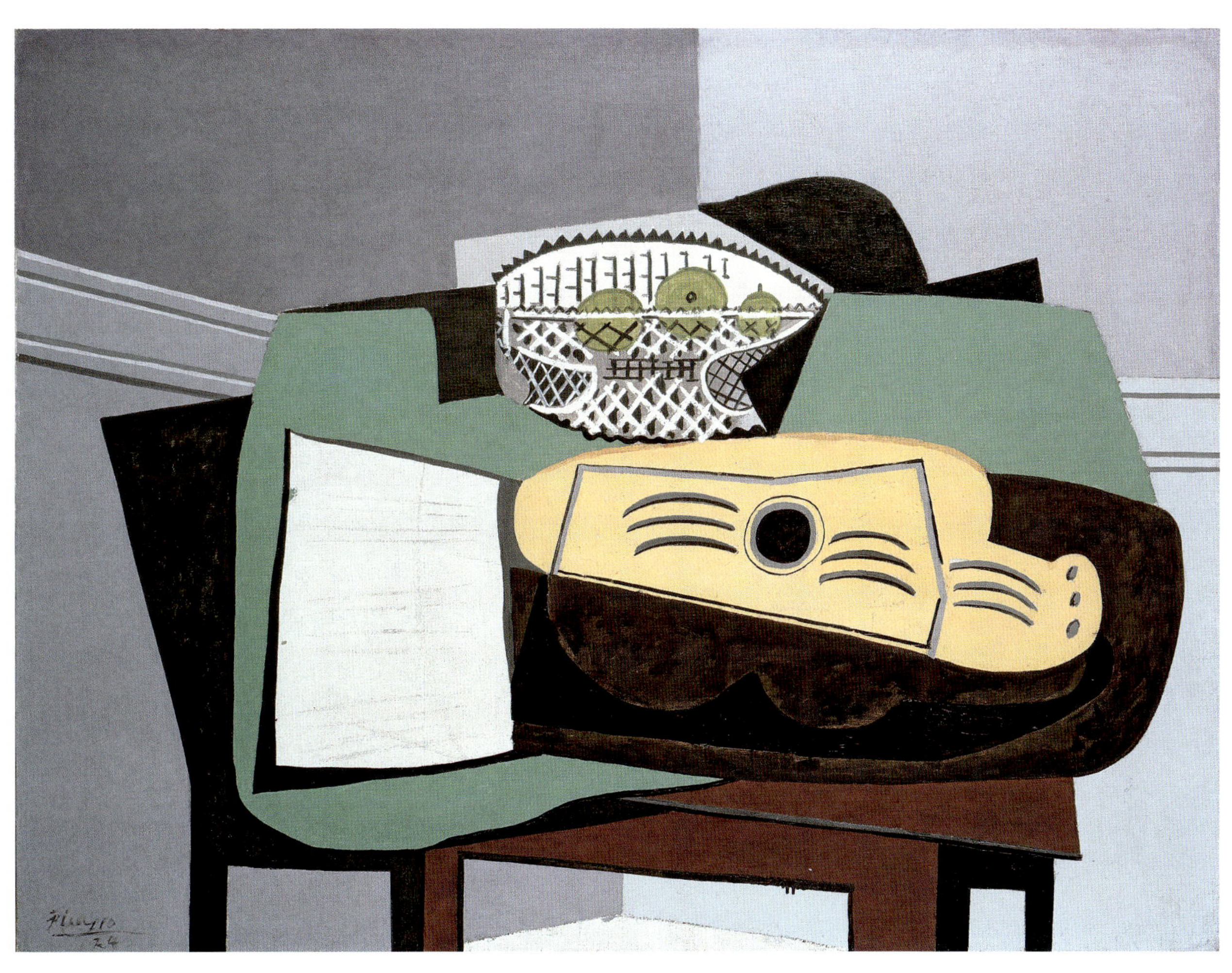

46
Score, Guitar and Fruit Bowl, 1924
Oil on canvas
97.1 x 130.1 cm
Courtesy Nahmad Collection, Switzerland

47
**Guitar, Glass and
Fruit Bowl,** 1924
Oil on canvas
97.5 x 130.5 cm
Kunsthaus Zürich

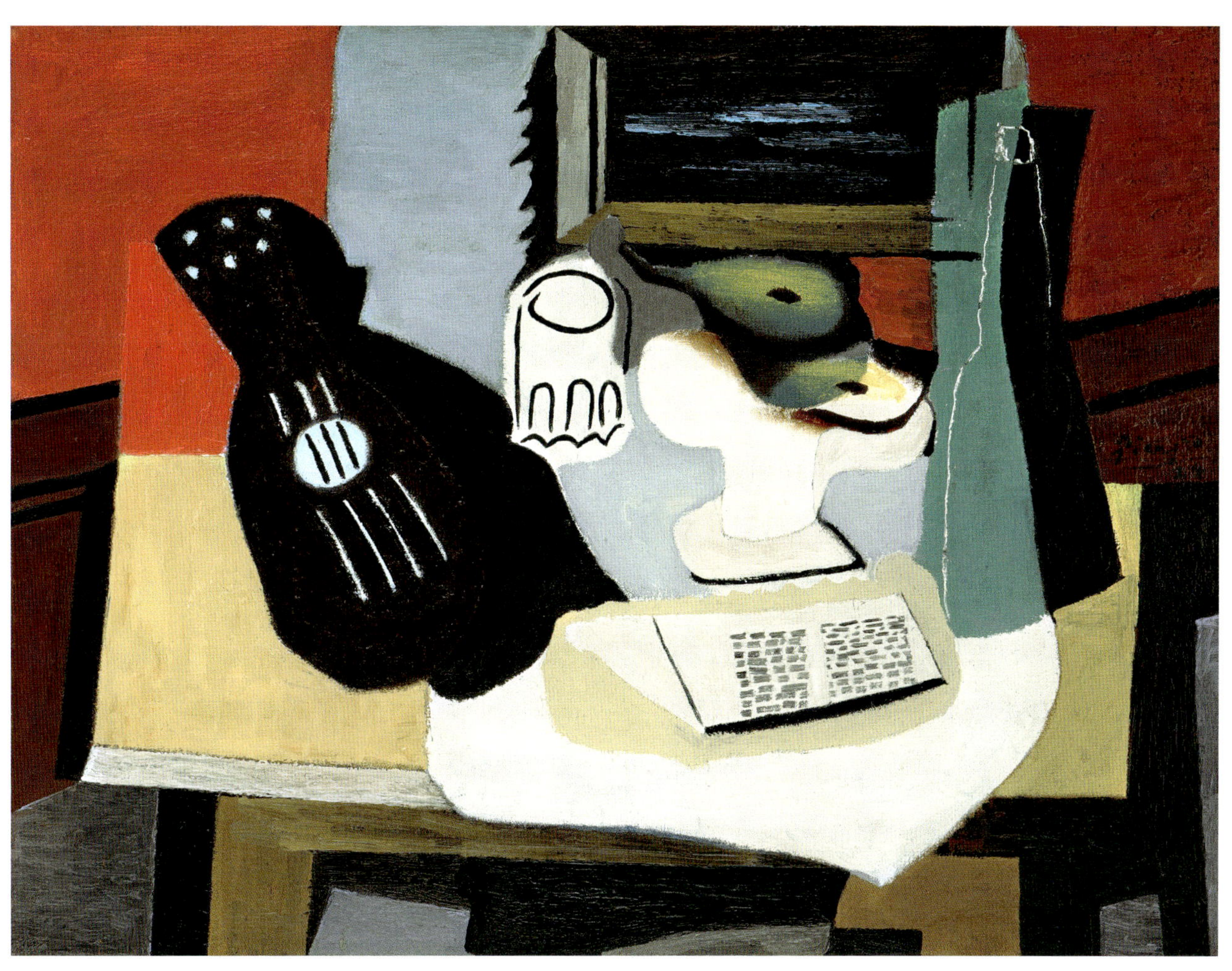

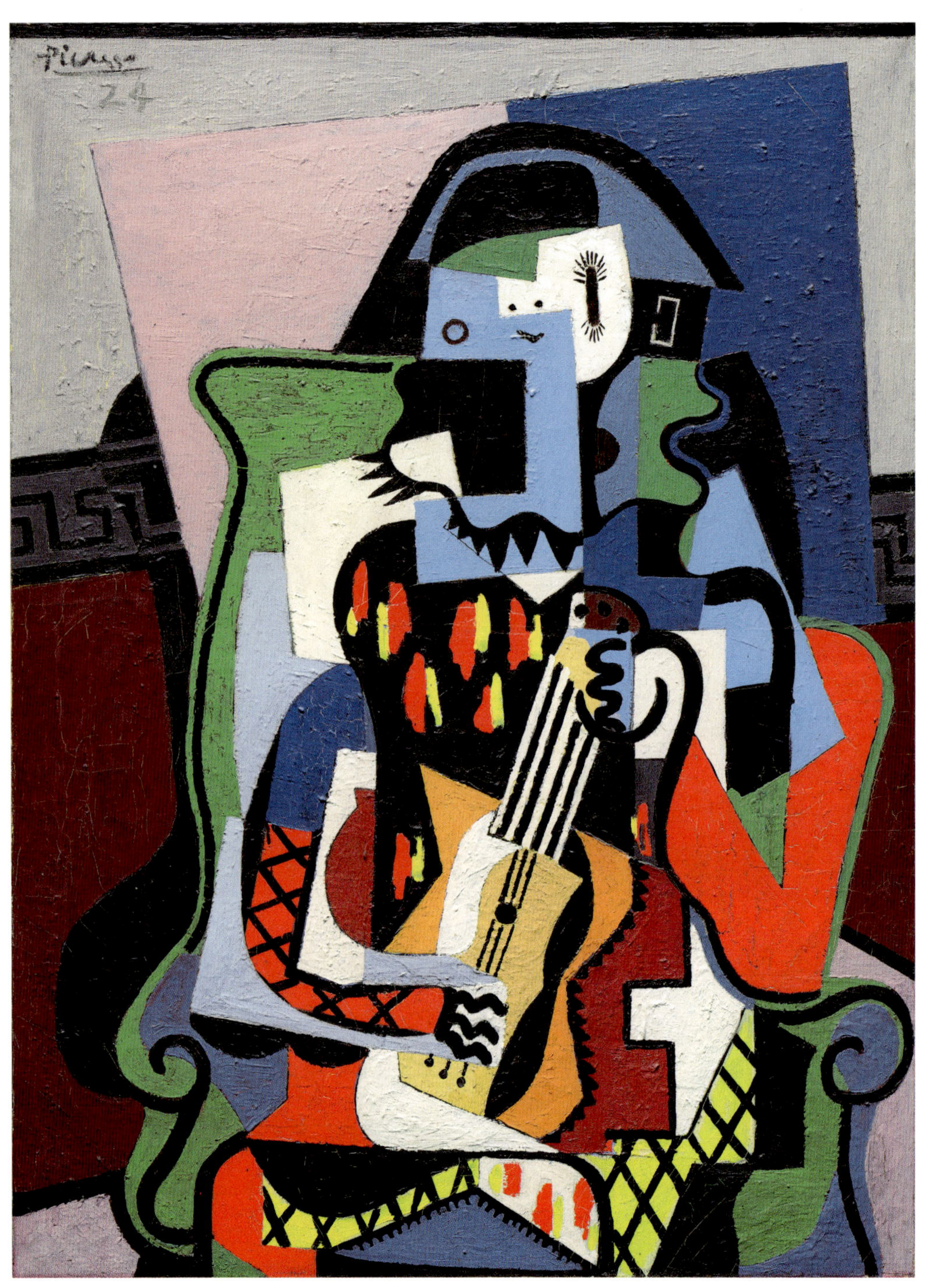

48

Harlequin Musician, 1924
Oil on canvas
113.8 x 97.2 cm
National Gallery of Art,
Washington
Given in loving memory
of her husband, Taft Schreiber, by Rita Schreiber

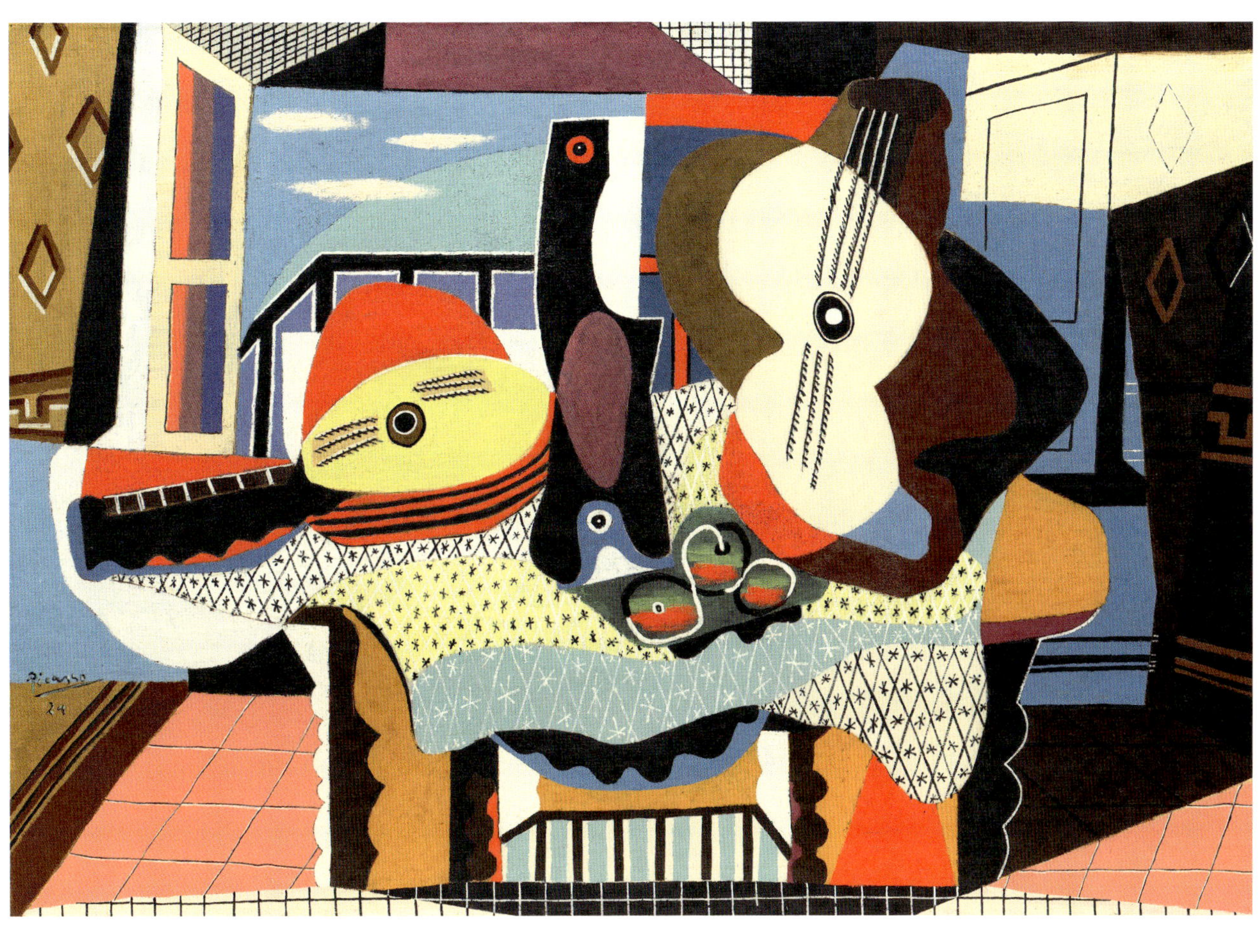

49
Mandolin and Guitar, 1924
Oil with sand on canvas
140.7 x 200.3 cm
Solomon R. Guggenheim
Museum, New York

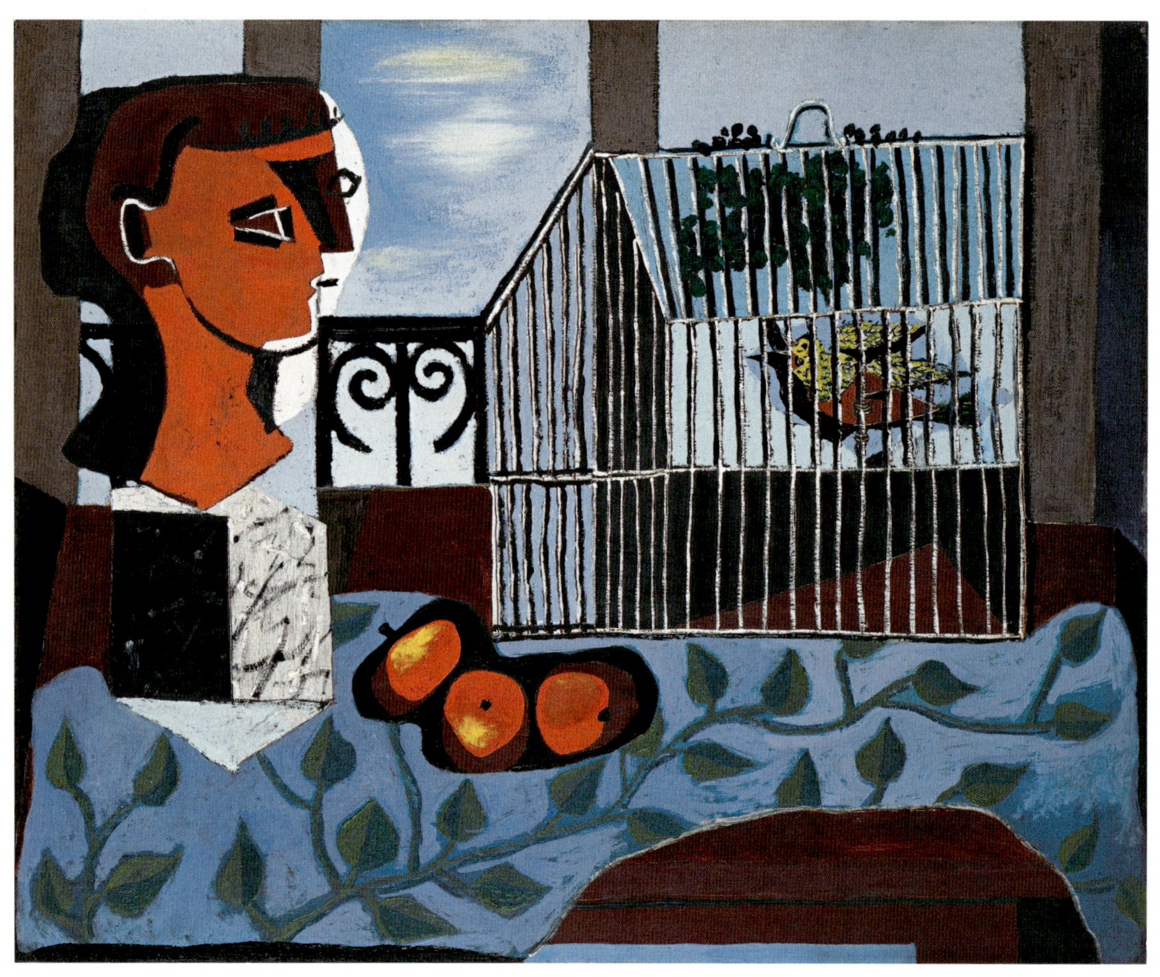

50
The Bird Cage, 1925
Oil on canvas
80.6 x 99.5 cm
Ohara Museum of Art, Japan

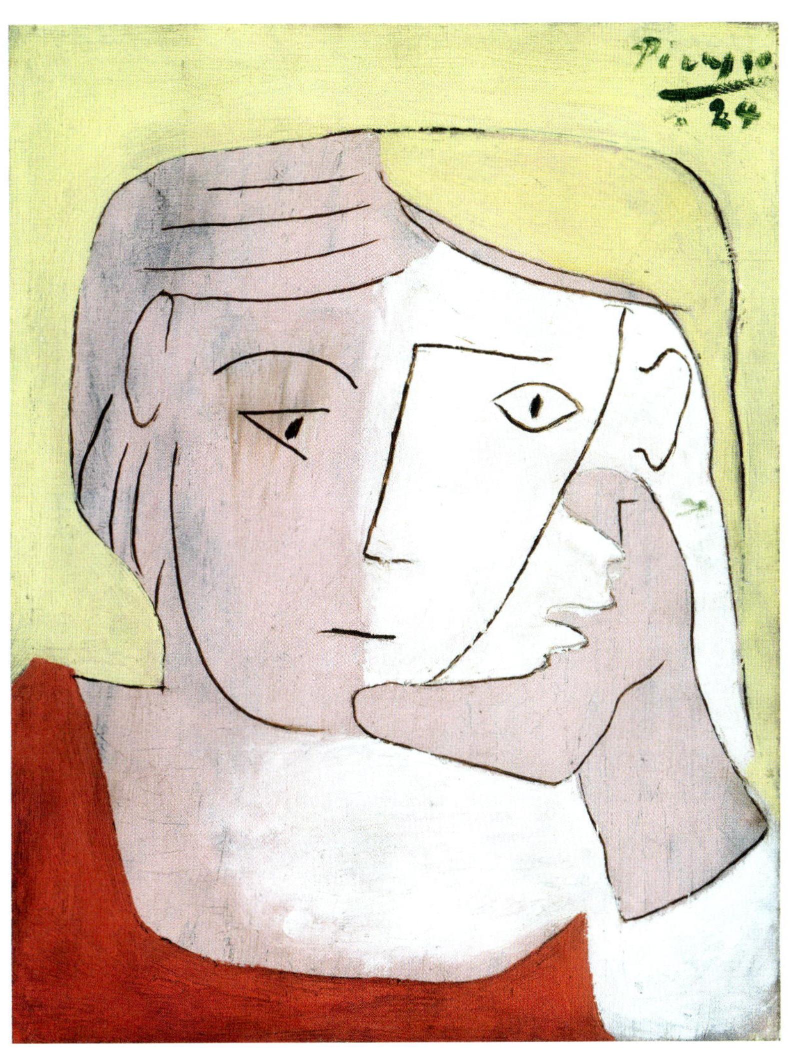

51
Head of a Woman, 1924
Oil on canvas
34.5 x 26.5 cm
Tate, London
Accepted by H. M. Government
in lieu of tax and allocated to the
Tate Gallery, 1995

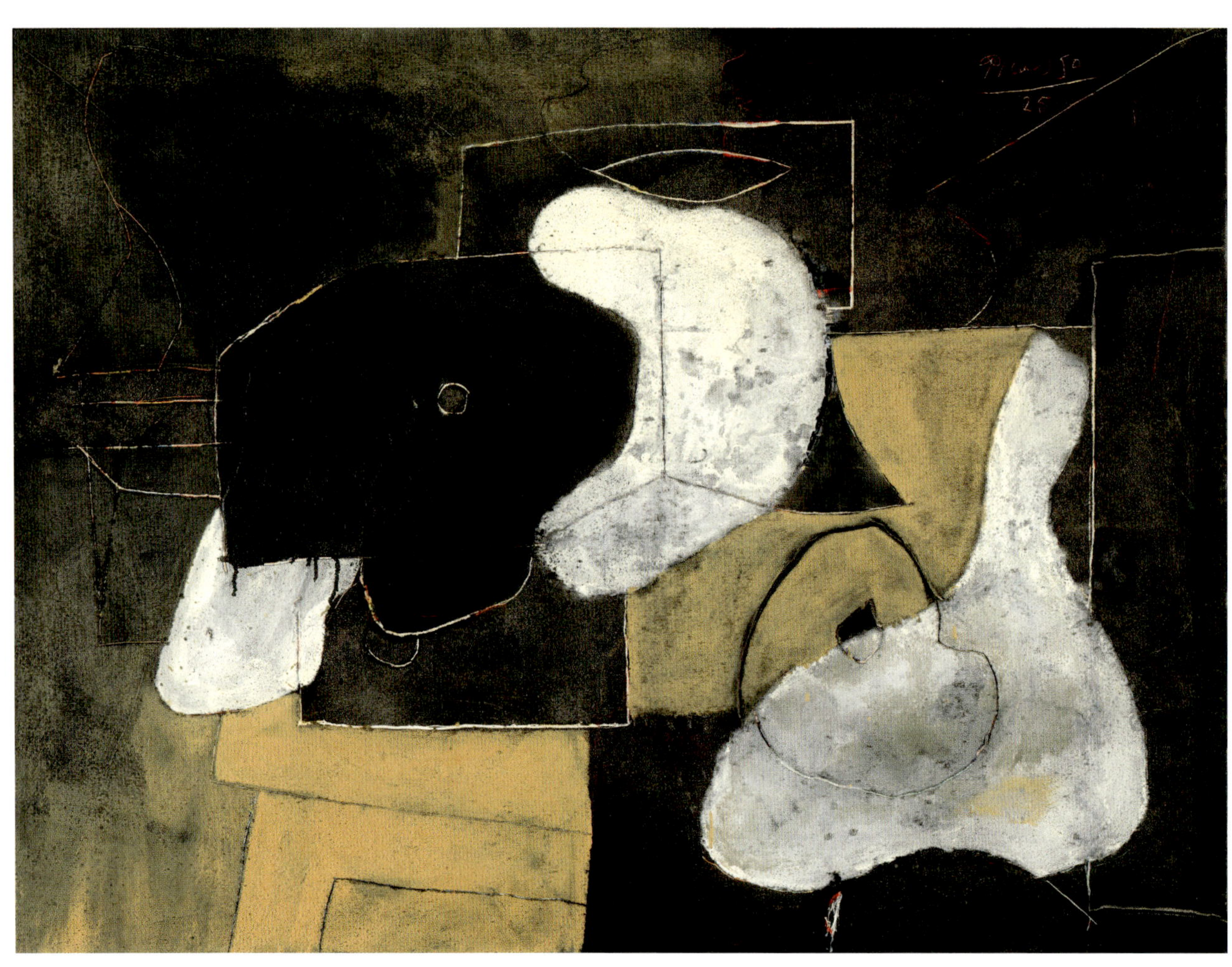

52
Still Life, 1925
Oil and sand on canvas
97.8 x 131.2 cm
Centre Pompidou, Paris
Musée national d'art moderne/
Centre de création industrielle
Donated in 1982

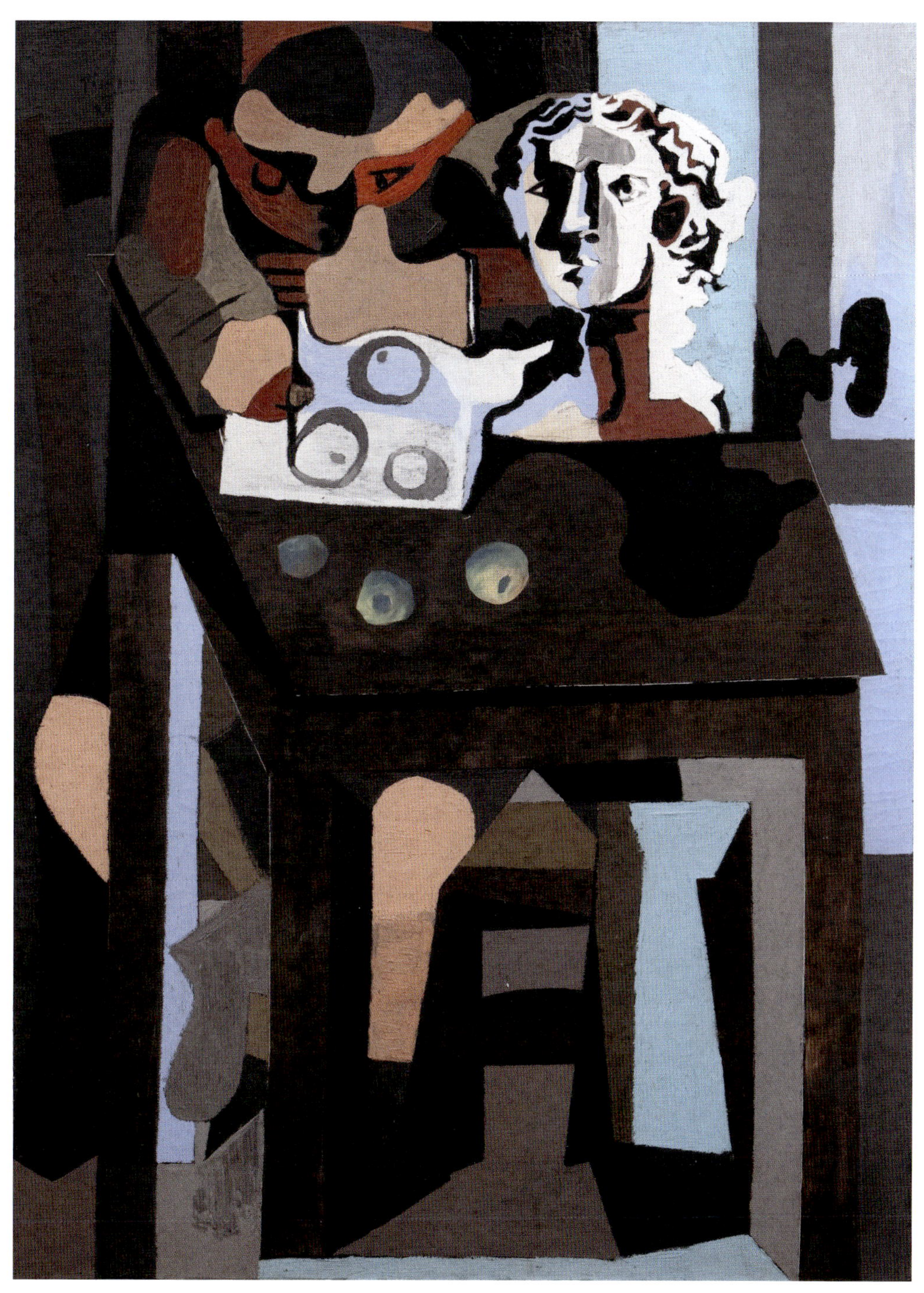

53
The Drawing Lesson, 1925
Oil on canvas
129.5 x 97.2 cm
Private collection

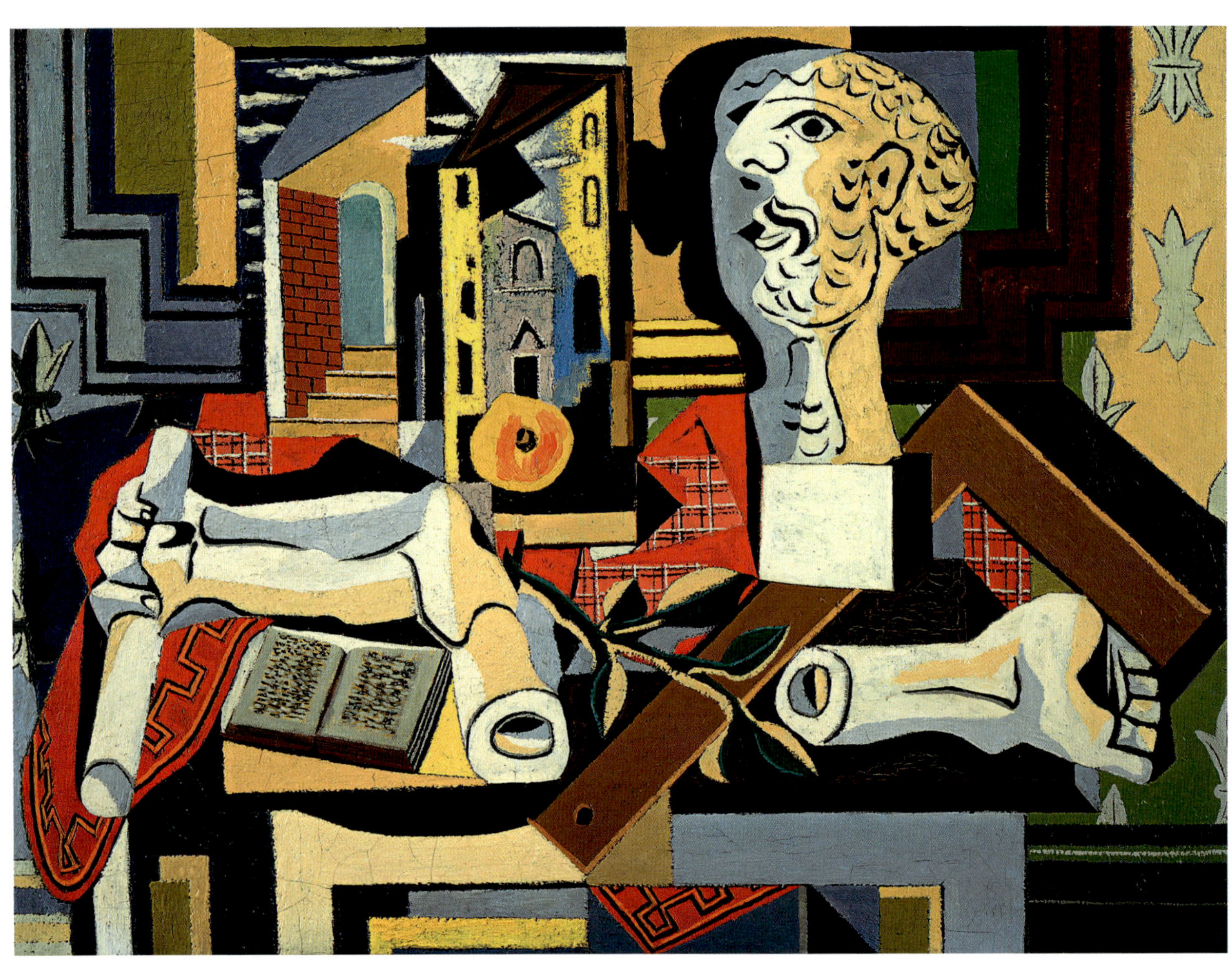

54

Studio with Plaster Head, 1925
Oil on canvas
97.9 x 131.1 cm
The Museum of Modern Art,
New York, Purchase, 1964

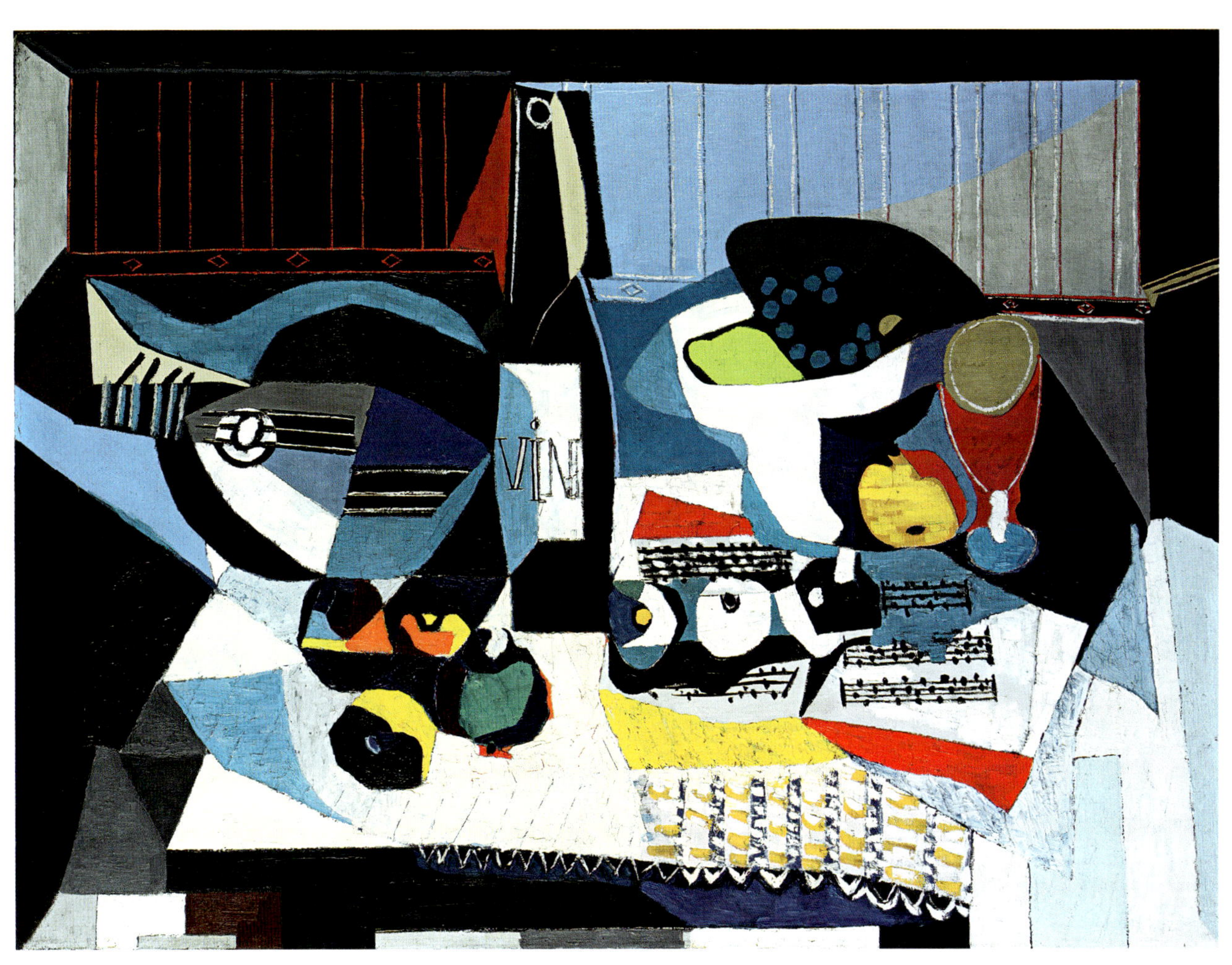

55
Wine Bottle, 1926
Oil on canvas
98 x 131.5 cm
Fondation Beyeler, Riehen/Basel

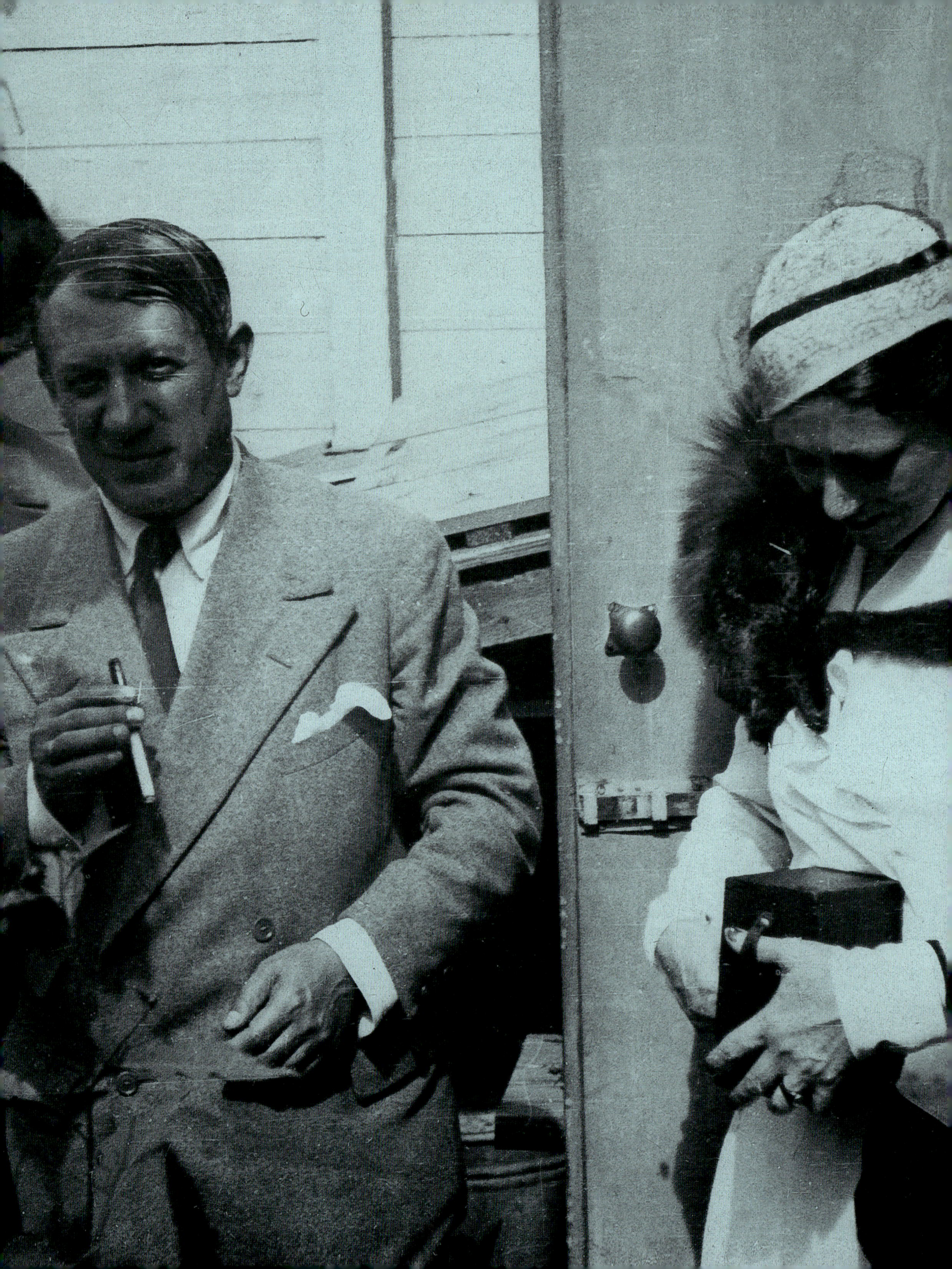

Michael FitzGerald

POST 1932: FROM THE PARIS AND ZURICH RETROSPECTIVES TO 'GUERNICA'

With the Paris and Zurich retrospectives, Picasso achieved a level of recognition that was almost without parallel among contemporary artists, and he enjoyed the rare opportunity of directly crafting the presentation of his more than thirty-year career. The previous year, Matisse's triad of retrospectives at Petit, the Basel Kunsthalle, and New York's Museum of Modern Art had set the standard for retrospectives of twentieth century artists in both galleries and museums, but Picasso had learned from Matisse's detachment from the preparations and the resulting weak representation of his recent accomplishments. At first stunned by Matisse's retrospective at Petit, Picasso jettisoned the chance for a major exhibition at MoMA and threw himself into making a retrospective that would reflect his view of his achievements, painting many new works for the show, selecting among past ones, and arranging the installation in Paris.[1]

Picasso's focus on his latest work and, particularly, the suite of paintings he made from December 1931 through April 1932, created the impact of a "master" — both of the past and of the present. Emphasising painting over his engagement with printmaking, drawing and sculpture (a bias reduced by the Kunsthaus's rebalancing of media), the gathering at Petit showcased his dominance of the grand tradition of figure painting, a mode that enabled him to answer Matisse and slip past him in a dialogue with previous masters. In this cavalcade of great canvases, aesthetics seemed paramount, and references to other types of experience, especially contemporary life, appeared limited to sensual pleasures.

Just as the Kunsthaus exhibition was opening in September, a Peruvian intellectual, Felipe Cossío del Pomar, published a book on leading intellectuals, including Mahatma Gandhi, Miguel de Unamuno and

◄

Picasso with his wife Olga

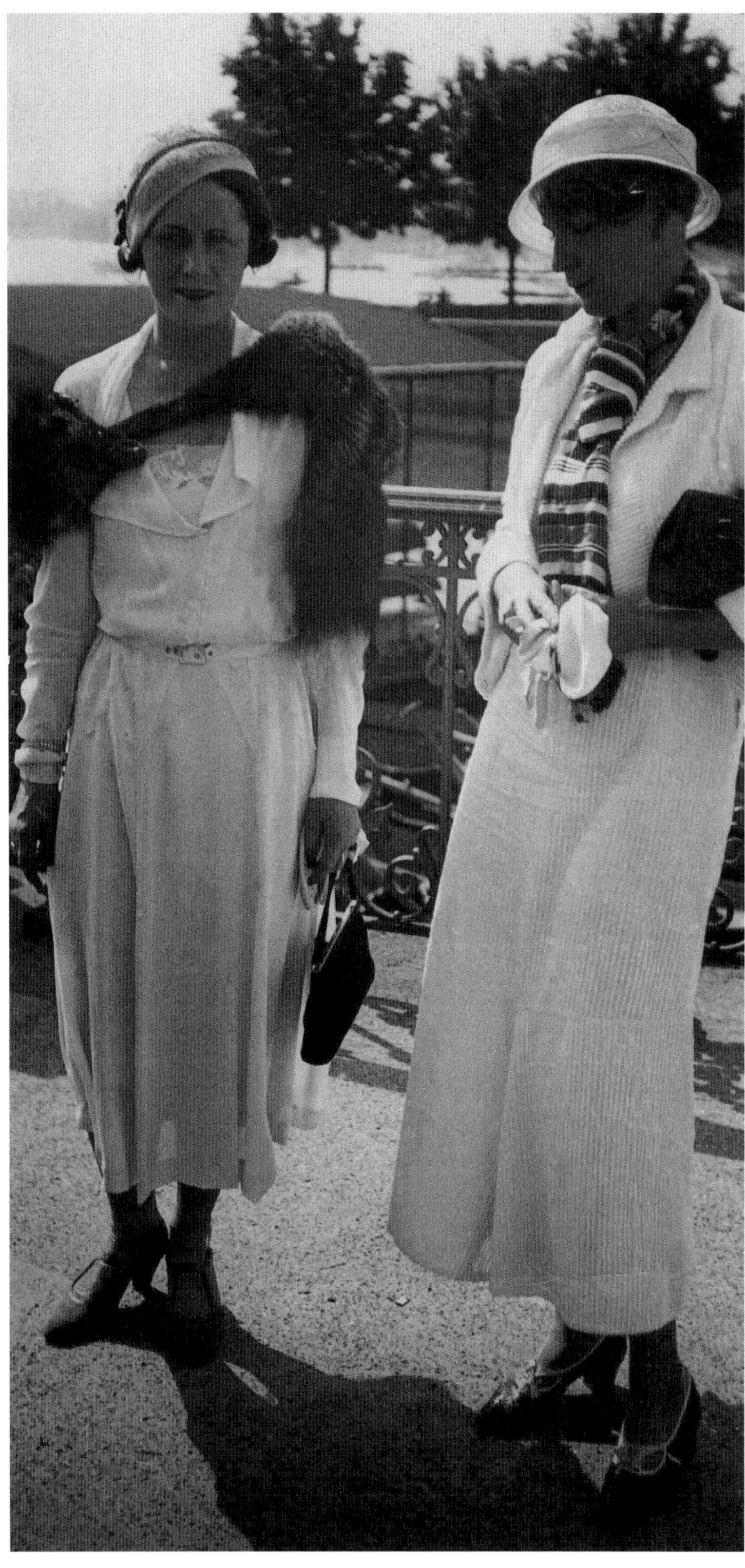

Picasso's wife Olga with
Lucie Turel-Welti on Lake
Zurich 1932

Picasso.[2] Chapters blend biographical summaries with what are apparently excerpts from the author's conversations with the artists and writers profiled. Not surprisingly, Picasso's comments exude self-assurance. He offers no excuses for his idiosyncratic devotion to art without any programmatic goal of relevance to society: "As far as I am concerned, I'll continue to be aesthetic, or, if you prefer, purely cerebral. I'll continue making art without preoccupying myself with the question of its influences, or if it 'humanises' our life, as you put it. If it contains a truth, my work will be useful without my express wish. It if doesn't hold a truth, so much the worse."[3]

As del Pomar's inclusion of Gandhi suggests, he was deeply concerned with questions concerning the relationship of culture to contemporary society. A scholar of pre-Columbian civilisations, del Pomar also engaged in political activities that led to his exile from Peru. He pressed Picasso on political matters, and Picasso responded, "But I will never make art with the preconceived idea of serving the interests of the political, religious or military art of a country."[4] Despite some youthful enthusiasm for anarchism, Picasso had maintained this apolitical stance across his career. His long-standing dealer and friend, Daniel-Henry Kahnweiler, reported[5] that he was the most apolitical of men, and his remarks to del Pomar reflect a deep scepticism of organisations, whether political, religious or artistic. Picasso's subsequent remark that "I will never fit in with the followers of the prophets of Nietzsche's superman" does, however, indicate awareness of the growing authoritarian movements in Europe, whether fascist or communist.[6]

Only five years later, he would create *Guernica*, the first of a series of major works extending through the early 1950s that would not only powerfully embody humanitarian themes but also officially serve the programmes of governments and international political organisations. This transformation is one of the most remarkable of Picasso's career. It is also different from his previous breakthroughs because it does not involve stylistic innovation. Unlike Cubism or even Neoclassicism, Picasso's art of the mid-century draws on the vocabularies he had created in the first three decades of the twentieth century. From the standpoint of Picasso's career, the innovation of *Guernica* and his art of the following fifteen years is institutional: his revival of the subject matter and agency that had driven public art for millennia but which Picasso, in particular, had dismissed in the twentieth century. Of course, style and subject can never be entirely separated, especially in Picasso's art; yet the reorientation in Picasso's case is so substantial and enduring that it cannot be explained as a modest slide along the scale connecting these two core elements of representation.

Writers have frequently ascribed this transformation to Picasso's relationship with Dora Maar, with whom he began an affair in the summer of 1936: the *Weeping Woman* supplanted the *Odalisque*. The common idea is that Picasso changed his art with each lover, and, concomitantly, each woman is captured in his paintings during each liaison. Although far more subtle than this simplistic view, William Rubin's 1996 exhibition and accompanying catalogue for the Museum of Modern Art, *Picasso and Portraiture*, is perhaps the most prominent presentation of this conception, dividing Picasso's career according to his years with Fernande Olivier, Olga Khokhlova, Marie-Thérèse Walter, Dora Maar, Françoise Gilot and Jacqueline Roque. Nonetheless, it is one thing to argue that Picasso's art was largely driven by life and quite another to narrow this autobiographical approach to his relationships with women, or, all too often, his sex life. As the author of two essays in MoMA's catalogue, those on Khokhlova and Gilot, I argued that Picasso's art of these years had at least as much to do with his relationships with dealers, poets and other artists. Recently, I had the opportunity to address this question again in relation to the most potent of the paintings generally characterised as images of a lover — those of Walter, particularly the great series of canvases he painted in 1931–32 in preparation for his retrospective at Petit.[7] My conclusion that these paintings are diminished by seeing them as portraits in any conventional sense, although they pass through her features, and are more fully understood as addressing Picasso's own position as an artist at a crucial time in his career through a complex cluster of issues, including his competition with Henri Matisse and response to Surrealism, stems from the essays of Robert Rosenblum[8] among other scholars and is shared by many who have studied this work, even though the tie to Walter is still exploited to excite popular attention. As Maar said about Picasso's images, "all his portraits of me are lies. They're all Picassos, not one is Dora Maar."[9]

When we look at the great paintings of 1931–32 in this broader if less immediately tangible way, we find there are far more similarities between these paintings and those of the later thirties than the dichotomy of Marie-Thérèse/Dora would suggest.[10] Without minimising the impact of Maar's intelligence and political commitment on Picasso, many of the elements of the art of *Guernica* and after register in the earlier paintings and turn attention to the intervening years between the retrospective in Paris and Zurich and the Spanish Pavilion.

The four years between 1933 and 1936 are unrivalled in their complexity, even in a career as diverse as Picasso's. Moreover, they remain among the least understood. We may hope that the next volume of John Richardson's biography, which will begin with 1933, will clarify many events, but until its publication our primary guide remains the biography written by Pierre Daix.[11] Moreover, Daix is an especially valuable conductor since he grew up in the 1930s, became a friend of Picasso soon after World War II and shared the artist's commitment to the Communist Party.

First of all, the mid-1930s was an extremely turbulent time in French history, as it was in so many other countries worldwide. The depression that began in the U.S. in the autumn of 1929 did not take hold in France until 1932–33, although it led to more substantial political change in France than in the U.S. when the socialist coalition of the Popular Front, led by Léon Blum, won the election in May 1936.[12]

Such recitations of international events rarely find a place in discussions of Picasso's career because before the mid-thirties his art rarely seems to respond to them. Even the First World War does not appear to have had a large impact on his art, and what did register had more to do with his immediate circumstances — the absence of colleagues Georges Braque and Guillaume Apollinaire at the front, the collapse of the art market, and the mortal illness of his lover, Eva Gouel.[13] As was so often the case, Picasso seems not to have responded to world events unless they touched him personally and deeply.

This pattern makes the thirties all the more intriguing as the transition to a very different relationship between his art and world events, one in which Picasso's inspiration came less from his personal situation than from circumstances largely beyond his direct experience.

At the end of 1932, Picasso was certainly isolated from the economic and social losses caused by the Depression. The Petit exhibition had been organised by a consortium of dealers with the unapologetic goal of sales, and the Kunsthaus catalogue forthrightly stated that many of the works in the show were available for purchase. When the works owned by individuals known to have been under financial distress (particularly G. F. Reber) but not listed as "verkäuflich" are added, the considerable majority of works in the exhibition were readily available to any interested buyers. Few acted, and the exhibitions were failures from the standpoint of sales. But this outcome cannot have been a surprise to the organisers or to Picasso, nor is it likely to have posed a problem for the artist. Throughout the 1920s, his dealer, Paul Rosenberg, had guided Picasso's career with great success, establishing a thriving international market for his work, raising prices to phenomenal heights, and buying many works from Picasso at equally strong prices. By the early thirties, Picasso was not only rich but relatively secure, with much of his wealth sheltered in Switzerland. He could easily have withdrawn from the chaos around him and fulfilled his old dream of independence — to live like a poor man but with a lot of money.[14]

And that is the way it started. He avoided the publicity surrounding the exhibition at Petit and the opening in Zurich. He withdrew to Bois-geloup. His paintings through the end of 1932 can be seen as tracking his reclusive life with Walter, even memorialising an illness she contracted while swimming in the river Marne.[15] Yet, the following four years of his life were far from idyllic, and this situation presents the second major factor in studying Picasso's art of the mid-thirties.

If Picasso's wife did not know of his relationship with Walter before the Petit exhibition, the string of paintings bearing the features of a voluptuous young blonde probably convinced her that Picasso was deep into a torrid affair, and the public exhibition of the evidence would have particularly offended her. Perhaps Picasso hoped it would convince Khokhlova that their long-tottering union had ended. Instead it kicked off a period of what was the most intense bickering of their marriage, animosity that was exacerbated by a succession of events. Plans for Fernande Olivier's memoir of her years with Picasso, *Picasso et ses amis*, to appear in book form in 1933 prompted Picasso to attempt to stop publication. If Olivier's recounting of past events angered both Picasso and Olga as a blatant intrusion into private matters, it was nothing in comparison to the birth of Maya, his daughter with Walter, in September 1935.[16] Divorce became a real issue and a tangible threat since it would require the division of the couple's property and Picasso's loss of a substantial number of the artworks he had kept for himself. By November, Picasso and Rosenberg were preparing an inventory, and by

January 1936 Rosenberg warned him that the report was almost ready. Although divorce and the division of the art were avoided, Picasso largely ceased making drawings and paintings from June 1935 through March 1936 in favour of poetry. He later admitted "that was the worst time of my life."[17]

SURREALISM

In the mid-1950s, Picasso publicly accepted that he had been influenced by Surrealism during 1933, specifically in a group of drawings he made while considering divorce. He made this acknowledgement to counter suggestions by the curators of a major post-war retrospective that Surrealism had had a substantial impact on his art since the mid-1920s, an interpretation he directly denied.[18] Since Picasso also asserted that he had not drawn on African art when painting the *Demoiselles d'Avignon*, his statements regarding influence must be suspect, understandably so for an artist constantly subject to the analysis of critics who often sought to diminish his achievements.[19] Nonetheless, the question of Picasso's relationship with Surrealism is at the root of his art during most of the twenties and thirties.[20]

There is no doubt that from the beginning Breton dearly wished to have Picasso's allegiance to his young movement and made great efforts to cultivate him as the most established contemporary artist and the one whom Breton believed most fully anticipated Surrealism. Their relationship developed over the course of 1924, the founding year of Surrealism, as Breton negotiated with Picasso over the sale of the *Demoiselles d'Avignon* to the couturier Jacques Doucet, who employed Breton as his advisor on the development of collections of art and literary manuscripts. If Breton sought to give weight to Surrealism by attaching Picasso, Breton and his band came to Picasso's defence that year by proclaiming him "the eternal personification of youth" when Dadaists called his participation in the ballet *Mercure* decadent.[21] Breton's courtship continued intermittently over the next decade and a half without ever securing Picasso's formal acceptance but Picasso being welcomed in many activities of the Surrealist circles. The issue is not whether Picasso was a card-carrying member — many of those who used Surrealism's ideas most powerfully were not — but whether Surrealism was an important source of his art during these years.

This question is overshadowed both by Picasso's refusal to join and the opinions of scholars devoted to his life and art. As one of the prime promoters of Surrealism in Britain, Roland Penrose walked a fine line as Picasso's first biographer. He was well attuned to the relevance of Surrealism to Picasso's work; yet his relationship with Picasso (which Penrose cherished) and his ongoing biography depended entirely on maintaining the artist's good will.[22] As in the case of other issues, such as Picasso's relationship with his wife Olga, taking a position that differed substantially from Picasso's might be perceived as critical of his stature and could result in banishment from his presence (the regal metaphor is apt).

Moreover, scholars have been all too willing to affirm Picasso's independence. Frequently, writers who focus on a single artist — as has been the case with leading writers on Picasso — become advocates of their subjects, whether intentionally or not. The tremendous respect due to Picasso for his remarkable achievements as an artist may well have led scholars including William Rubin and John Richardson to reinforce his own assertions of autonomy, to portray him as exempt from the patterns of influence observed in the work of other artists. Finally, there is also the belief among many Picasso scholars that he was simply a far greater artist than the Surrealists and so is better understood independently of them, although this judgement is rarely stated in print.

Then there is the question of how to define Surrealism. If it was the formal doctrine of Breton, then Picasso did not conform. But if Surrealism is accepted as a phenomenon beyond Breton's control, then the answer is far less clear. On the one hand, Surrealism perpetuated the anti-military, anti-clerical, and generally anti-establishment assaults of Dada; yet it also re-opened the long-standing issue of creativity by focusing on the mind itself as a source of imagination and particularly the resort to shock as a liberating source of creation. On this basis, it is difficult to conclude that Picasso's art from the mid-twenties onward was not profoundly Surrealist.[23]

The sticking point has generally not been whether the imagery and themes of Picasso's work are Surrealist but whether his methods qualify. In 1930, Michel Leiris, a 'dissident' Surrealist who had rejected Breton's leadership, stated the case: "In most of Picasso's paintings, one remarks that the 'subject' is almost always down to earth, in any case never borrowed from the hazy world of dreams, not susceptible to immediate conversion into symbol — that is to say in no way 'surrealist'."[24]
This distinction is important in affirming that Picasso's art was deeply rooted in experience but it does not address the extent to which Picasso chose certain experiences for his art and interpreted them under the influence of Surrealism.[25]

Picasso's great paintings of 1931–32 are elegant hybrids, ones that draw deeply on the well of Surrealist concerns and yet smoothly, almost seamlessly, incorporate other experiences. This compelling multiplicity of reference is what makes the paintings so significant, but this profusion of ideas also disconcerts those who would like to see Picasso's work as either strictly Surrealist or free of its influence.

When Breton wrote about the Petit exhibition, he did not mention the series of paintings of 1931–32. For all their exposition of the Surrealist themes of sexual liberation and imaginative transformation, they are also deeply rooted in tradition, particularly the figure paintings of Ingres and Matisse. Yet we should keep in mind that the retrospective was not only a gathering of pictures but an installation as well. Compared to conventional displays in galleries or museums at that time (the Zurich venue is a fine example), Picasso's hang was scrambled, chaotic. It was extremely inconsistent, often disregarding chronology but sometimes following it, rarely plotting themes or subjects but sometimes tracking them. As an installation, it was a counterpoint to the tradition of honouring separate works of art. Instead, it was a projection of Picasso's creative process, sweeping across three decades of his career to capture the internal consistency of his work and focusing in the process on that fundamentally Surrealist subject addressed in many of the paintings — the transformations of the imagination.[26] Picasso's installation at Petit seems closer to a Dada happening than an art exhibition and lays out strategies of disruption the Surrealists would employ in years to come.

Dodging the weight of tradition, Breton reserved his praise for a particular group of recent works — Picasso's sculpture. These two versions of *Woman in a Garden* address many of the same themes as the following paintings, but they also shatter the conventions of that medium through their assemblage from disparate objects, shapes and metals so heterogeneous as to make the final sculpture appear without composition in the established sense. They are perfectly suited to Breton's appeal for art that repudiates the conventions of painting and sculpture and his support of diversity of collage.[27]

In 1933, Picasso joined a project that united Breton with many of the dissident Surrealists, including Michel Leiris and Georges Bataille — the newly-founded publication, *Minotaure*.[28] For the first issue, Picasso created an image of the namesake, a collage showing the creature brandishing a dagger and reclining on a bed of refuse (fig. 1). Inside, the issue ran Breton's "Picasso dans son élément", a long essay containing his

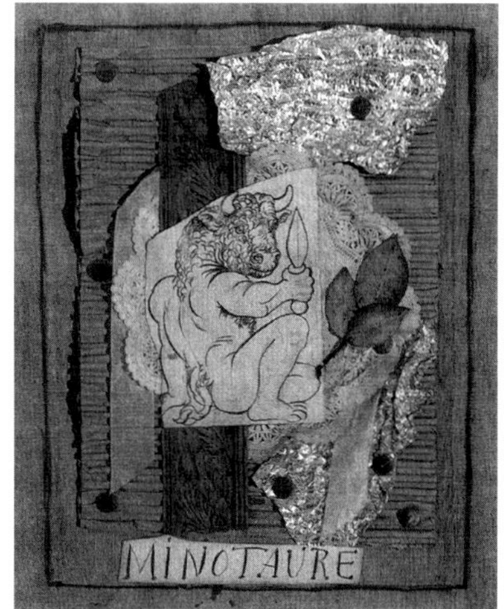

fig. 1
Design for the cover of *Minotaure* magazine, 1933
The Museum of Modern Art, New York
Gift of Mr and Mrs Alexandre P. Rosenberg

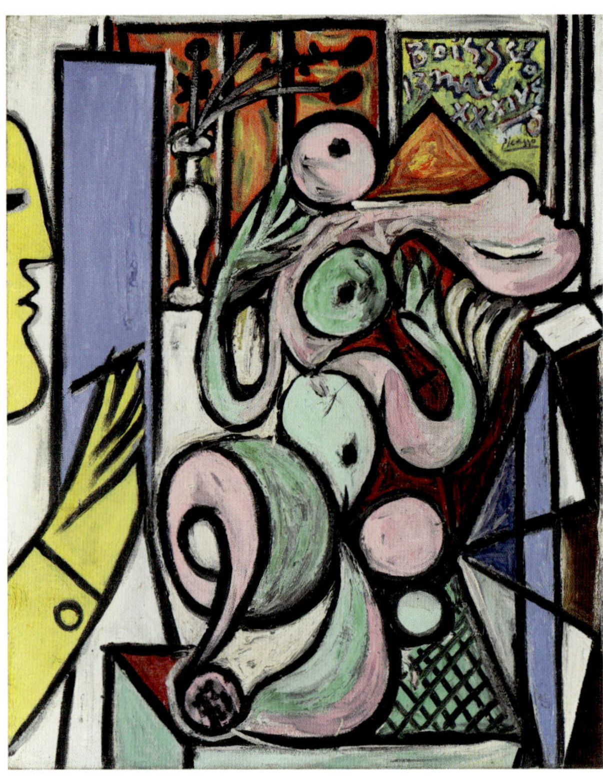

fig. 2
The Painter, 1934
Oil on canvas, 96.5 x 80.1 cm
Wadsworth Atheneum
Museum of Art, Hartford

remarks about the Petit exhibition. The subject was Picasso's creative environment. Breton toured his studio, examining stacks of accumulated paintings and drawings, and accumulated refuse, among other things. He focused on this disparate array of things as if it were itself a work of art, an assemblage that held a key to Picasso's imagination.[29]

During the next few years, Picasso's work is not defined by the monumental paintings of the female figure that had dominated his œuvre during the late twenties and early thirties and would return in 1936 with a procession of compositions linked to his relationship with Maar. Certainly, Picasso painted large figure paintings in the mid-thirties, yet they are not only fewer than before but also less important in his work. These pictures, such as *The Painter* (fig. 2), are largely extensions of his images of the early thirties.[30] The great paintings shown at Petit and the Kunsthaus were made almost entirely without drawn studies. They were developed within the medium of painting, as each canvas evolved and the next sprang from its predecessor. In the mid-thirties, Picasso changed course, returning to drawing as his primary means of exploration. Of course, drawing had been crucial to his early work up to and including the *Demoiselles*, but it had declined in significance during the primary years of Cubism and had played a largely parallel role in his engagement with Neoclassicism. Drawing resurfaced as a driving force in the later twenties, particularly in his designs for metamorphic figures in Cannes during the summer of 1927 and the sketches for metal constructions in 1928. These drawings were closely linked to Picasso's projects for a monument to Guillaume Apollinaire, which not only commemorated the inventor of "surréalisme" but cast his reputation under the sign of Breton and company.

In the mid-thirties, this tendency returned with greater force. The drama of Picasso's work is largely backstage — running through sheaves of sketches, engraved plates, assemblage sculptures and collages, as well as a primary focus on writing in 1935–36. These works of small size and scale, often executed rapidly, burst with transformations as if Picasso was laying down the metamorphosis of ideas as they spun

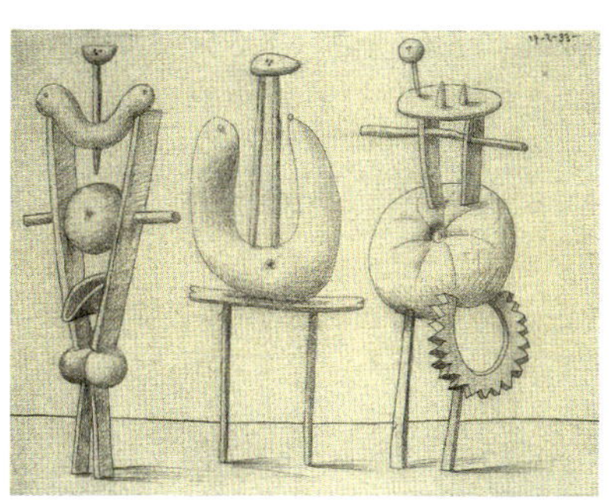

fig. 3
An Anatomy: Three Women,
27 February 1933
Pencil on paper,
20 x 27 cm
Musée Picasso, Paris

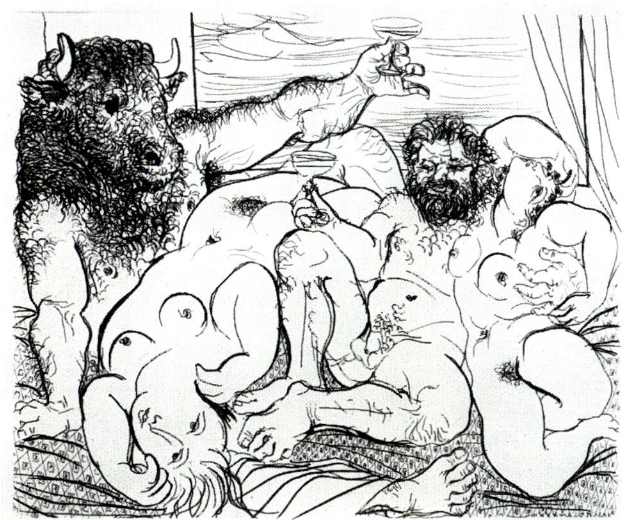

fig. 4
Bacchic Scene with Minotaur,
Paris, 18 May 1933
Copperplate etching,
29.7 cm x 36.6 cm

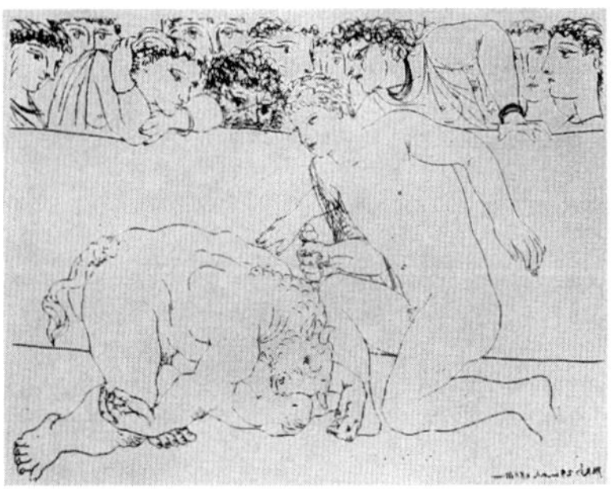

fig. 5
Minotaur Defeated, Paris,
29 May 1933
Copperplate etching,
19.3 cm x 26.9 cm

through his imagination. The *Anatomies* published in the first issue of *Minotaure* both revive his earlier metamorphic figures and suggest seemingly endless permutations (fig. 3). The diversity of this material offers many paths, although no dominant one. Within Picasso's imagery, the minotaur is certainly among the most common, consequent and specific to this period. Picasso's attention to this creature was no doubt fed by the Surrealists' obsession with it as an emblem of the irrationality of the inner mind, yet Picasso certainly did not limit his depictions to their programme and mixed the minotaurs of Breton and Bataille with his immersion in classical myth while illustrating Ovid's *Metamorphoses*.[31]

Among Picasso's many aspects of the minotaur, one of his most evocative is the creature's appearance in images of the artist's studio, reviving a subject that Picasso had addressed in major paintings in the late twenties but much less frequently on canvas in the thirties.[32] Picasso's concentrated return to the subject of the studio in the mid-thirties — this time portrayed in the media of prints and drawings but evident in the explicit assembling of disparate materials in two and three-dimensional collages — parallels and probably responds to Breton's acclaim of his "element" in 1933 and brings to the fore his focus during these years on imaginative transformation as a subject in itself rather than as a means to an expressive end (fig. 4).

In the constantly shifting imagery of these works, man does not merely become minotaur but minotaur becomes beast. Depictions of the minotaur locate him in the bullring as he expires (fig. 5). As the bullring grows in prominence in Picasso's work during the summer of 1934, minotaur and bull merge in some of the most violent scenes of conflict in Picasso's œuvre. On September 8, Picasso made an etching and the following day a painting of a bullfight scene that approach cataclysm (figs. 6 and 7). In both works, bull, horse, picador and toreador clash so

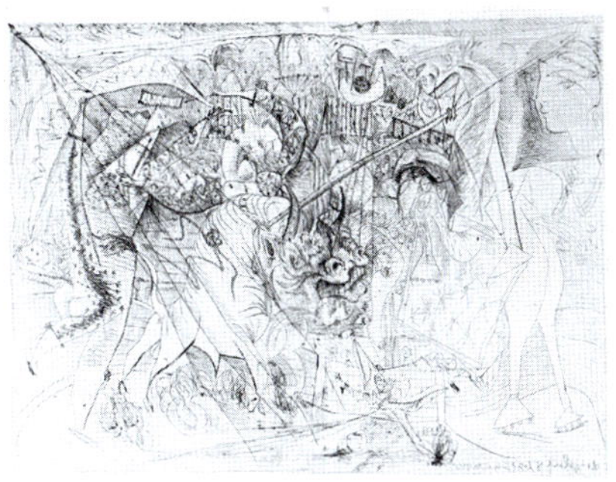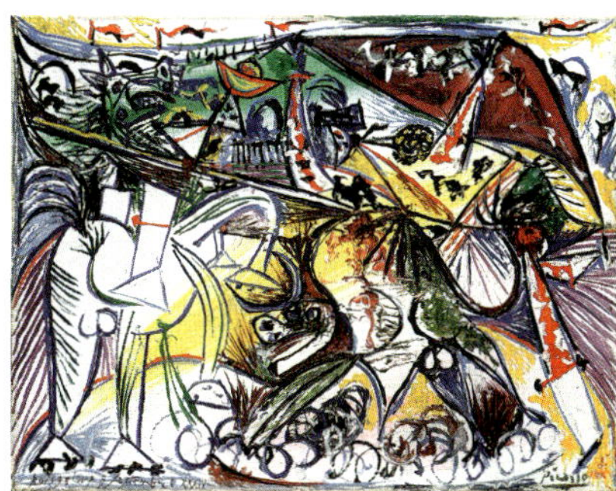

intensely that representation is nearly obliterated by densely cut lines radiating across the plate from the impact of the battling creatures or brilliantly-hued, crude ridges of paint squeezed onto the canvas. The compositions are one step from chaos and strongly evoke his statement one year later that, "In my case a picture is a sum of destructions."[33] His reference to violence as a creative technique cannot help but resonate with the Surrealists' "convulsive beauty," particularly given his comments in the same interview that "The artist is a receptacle for emotions that come from all over the place," and his goal to "discover the path followed by the brain in materialising a dream."[34]

POLITICS

As Pierre Daix has suggested, these images of extreme violence cannot be separated from savage events taking place in Europe. "The times were more and more than ever 'out of joint.' The 'Night of the Long Knives' of 30 June 1934 was the first of Hitler's mass killings to be noticed in the democratic countries. Once again, Picasso's inspiration was coloured by the profound anguish he always felt in the face of inhumanity. That summer, "his painting … carried violence to a paroxysmic intensity in a sequence of corridas."[35]

By 1934, references to destruction, even for creative purposes, resonated beyond the strategies of artists and writers.[36] In his 1935 statement, Picasso ended by placing art in the context of contemporary politics. He remarked that "I can't understand why revolutionary countries should have more prejudice about art than out-of-date countries!," an obvious reference to the programme of socialist realism recently established in Russia and one step in a string of accusations against the institutionalisation of art — "Museums are just a lot of lies, and the people who make art their business are mostly impostors." These comments repeat Picasso's long-standing scepticism of institutions, yet they also expand the context to include governments. More importantly, Picasso specifically adopted the most troubling model of contemporary politics when he claimed "There ought to be an absolute dictatorship ... a dictatorship of painters ... a dictatorship of one painter ... to suppress all those who have betrayed us ...," ending with "The true dictator will always be conquered by the dictatorship of common sense ... and maybe not!"[37] Picasso was obviously being playful, but he was playing provocatively with a term that was tragically reshaping Europe.

Two years after Hitler's assumption of power, dictatorship was not a joke in Picasso's circle. As the French Surrealist Georges Hugnet wrote in 1935, "Picasso knows, we all know, that we shall be among the first victims of Fascism, of French Hitlerism."[38] Published in the issue of *Cahiers d'art* that was devoted to Picasso's poetry, this statement is representative. It grows from the commitment to political action that had been a substantial goal of artists associated with Surrealism.

Beginning only a year after its founding, Surrealism had sought to link its programme of intellectual revolt with real political action through alliances with the French Communist Party and related groups. By the mid-1930s, this history was littered with failures, the predictable result of efforts to unite two groups that strictly controlled their programmes and differently valued intellectual versus political action. Like the question of Picasso's relation to Surrealism, the question of the Surrealists' relation to leftist politics turns not on the official position of Surrealism but the beliefs and activities of the artists and writers associated with the movement, particularly Louis Aragon and Paul Éluard.[39]

In January 1932, Parisian police confiscated copies of the review *Literature of World Revolution* containing Aragon's poem "Front rouge", thereby vaulting the Surrealists into the arena of real politics and, according to Pierre Daix, prompting Picasso to sign a political petition for the first time in his life.[40] Beginning with "Shoot Léon Blum," Aragon's text was more political tract than art. Its call to violence against specific politicians prompted the confiscation and threatened legal action against the author, a challenge that his fellow Surrealists answered with rather illogical claims that literature could not be subject to practical laws. Despite this dissembling, Breton and his colleagues managed to recruit the support of many leading artists and writers, including Bertolt Brecht, García Lorca, Thomas Mann, Le Corbusier and Georges Braque.

Picasso's signature on the petition was not given casually. As Éluard wrote to his wife, Gala, "Picasso is asking to consult a lawyer before signing. He's afraid of being deported."[41] At least since he was interrogated about the theft of sculptures from the Louvre in 1911, Picasso had feared the police might initiate his deportation to Spain. In 1932, he not only risked losing his seat in Paris but transference to Spain at a time of increasing instability. His concerns were real, and his decision to sign was a serious commitment to his friend Aragon and intellectual freedom. It was an acknowledgement that art and politics were intertwined no matter how much he denied to del Pomar that he would ever subordinate his art to a political programme.

Éluard's following comments to Gala that "If he [Picasso] doesn't sign, we'll denounce him, attack him," demonstrates both the not infrequent absurdity of the Surrealists' political campaigns and, more importantly, Picasso's previous detachment from politics. Éluard's conniving is all the more surprising because over the next few years he would become one of Picasso's closest friends and his frequent collaborator on artistic and political projects until Éluard's death in 1952.

Picasso's involvement in *Minotaure* the next year brought them together, and as the mid-thirties passed their growing friendship strengthened over issues of art and politics, particularly regarding Spain. In April 1931, Picasso celebrated the belated proclamation of the Spanish Republic in Catalonia with many gatherings among Spanish friends and found this event provided a great opportunity for art as well. The year before, the regional government of Catalonia had purchased the collection of Luis Plandiura, one of the first buyers of Picasso's work, and these twenty drawings, pastels and paintings were intended for a museum in Barcelona. This was the first group of Picasso's work to enter a public collection in Spain and an event of such importance that Picasso would enlarge the collection with the gift of his series after *Las Meninas* in the 1968. In the summer of 1933, Picasso travelled to Barcelona to see the installation in the Barcelona museum, an event that Pierre Daix suggests profoundly moved Picasso and inspired his hopes that Spain would escape the long-standing dominance of "Black Spain" — fanatical clergy and aristocracy.[42]

He returned the following summer, visiting San Sebastián, Madrid and Toledo before ending the trip in Barcelona. Despite a brief flirtation with the Right during the visit, which John Richardson has recently brought to light and plausibly explained as Picasso's unrealistic desire for sponsorship of a major retrospective in his homeland,[43] this trip must have reinforced Picasso's hope that Spanish society was becoming more liberated and that his own work stood in the vanguard of this process.

This growing sense of solidarity between political developments and the appreciation of Picasso's work in Spain — a remarkable trend in itself — was reinforced by the increasingly urgent need for political action felt by many French intellectuals as violent Fascist actions swept Germany and Italy (commented upon by Hugnet in 1935, see p. 144). Working to achieve an alliance between the Surrealists and the Communist Party, Éluard began to shift from a stance that honoured intellectual freedom above all to a belief that literature and art should engage political causes, a commitment that led to his first explicitly political poem *November 1936*.[44]

The project that sealed Picasso's and Éluard's friendship was another exhibition in Spain, one that was specifically intended to link Picasso with the liberalising initiatives sweeping the country. Organised by ADLAN (Amigos de las Artes Nuevas) under the primary direction of Josep Lluís Sert, it included twenty-five works Picasso had made in the decades since leaving Spain and opened in Barcelona in January 1936. The opening activities included lectures or broadcasts by Dalí and Miró, among others. The primary speaker, however, was Éluard. Although Picasso did not attend, Éluard came as his ambassador and a figure who represented the latest ideas linking France with a revitalised Spain. As a sign of their camaraderie, Picasso drew Éluard's portrait just before the poet left for Spain (fig. 8).[45]

The beginning of Franco's assault on the Republic in July shattered this deepening exchange between intellectuals in the two countries. That Picasso would have been disturbed by the attack is not surprising, but many French writers and artists quickly took up the cause of the Spanish Republic. The bombings of Madrid compelled Éluard to put aside qualms about subordinating literature to politics and write *November 1936*. In January 1937, Éluard began collaborating with José Bengamin, the Republic's cultural attaché in Paris and a person with direct experience of the civil war to create a special issue of *Cahiers d'art* called *At the Weight of Blood*.[46] Apparently, Picasso trusted Bengamin's political judgements and probably had great faith in his

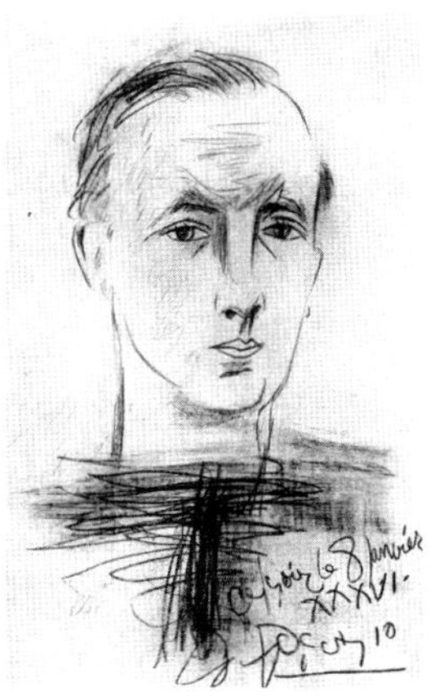

fig. 8
Portrait of Paul Éluard,
8 January 1936
Pencil on paper
Whereabouts unknown

accounts.[47] In January, Picasso, too, placed his art at the service of politics. The previous May, he probably made a watercolour as a design for a stage curtain for Romain Rolland's *The Fourteenth of July*, a play that was chosen by the newly-elected Popular Front.[48] In September he had agreed to the Republican government's designation of him as director of the Prado, although he did not accept repeated invitations to return to the country.

In January, he took action. He began the eighteen-panel print *The Dream and Lie of Franco* (figs. 9A and 9B), which he would complete in June and would be sold to benefit the Republic. This span of six months marks the final phase of Picasso's accommodation to placing his art at the service of politics, even if his commitment would fluctuate substantially during the following decade. The last frames of the *Dream and Lie* depict the victimised women and children of Guernica, yet its initial frames are perhaps more significant. An absurd, tuberous knight travels to a monumental bust of a woman and raises a pick to strike it. This statue returns us to the beginning of this essay and to the great figure paintings Picasso made in 1931–32. The statue bears similar features, yet there is no suggestion it portrays Walter. Here, the woman must embody culture, both classical and modern. In contrast to the grotesque attacker, the statue's pristine beauty seems free of politics, as Picasso had asserted art should be when he made his paintings and sculptures of the early thirties. By recalling this image five years later he not only evoked a previous conception to stand as a poignant image of an innocent culture at risk but also insinuated how radically his position had changed with the violence that had swept across Spain and threatened all of Europe. Art could no longer be isolated. The leap to the *Guernica* mural was huge in terms of scale, visibility and the engagement with the history of public art that these entailed, but, like Éluard, Picasso had already accepted art as a political weapon.

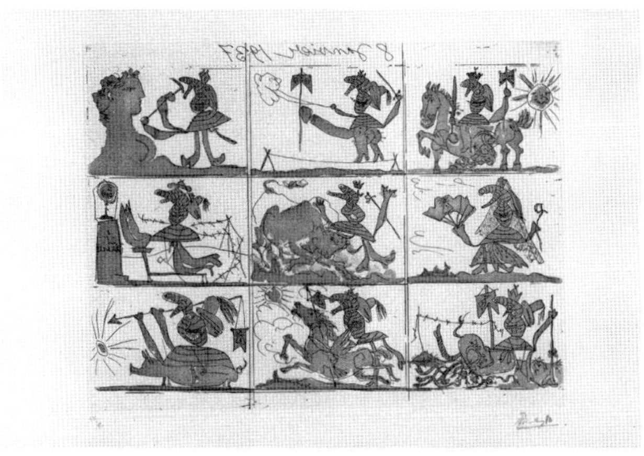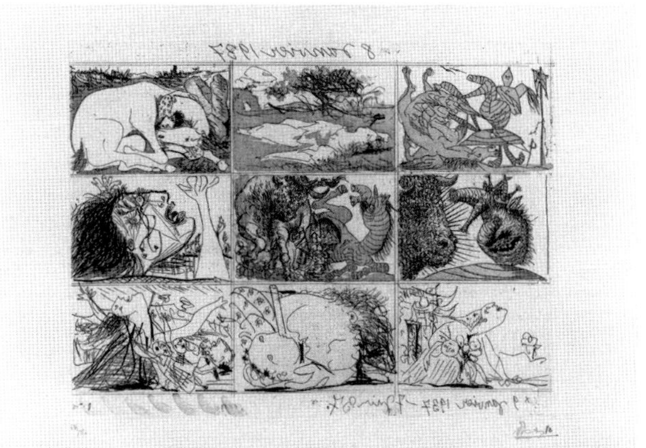

Of course, by January 1937, Dora Maar had been a part of Picasso's life for some months and her longstanding involvement in Surrealist politics and Spanish culture are additional factors in this tremendously complicated period of Picasso's career. Even more than his friendship with Éluard, Picasso's life with Maar bound together the many strands that had threaded through the five years following the exhibitions at Petit and the Kunsthaus. The conundrum this essay has attempted to explore without presuming to solve is how these disparate strands of Picasso's life and art had, by the first months of 1937, shaped an artist so different from the one of 1932.

fig. 9A + 9B
The Dream and Lie of Franco,
1937
Etching, aquatint, scraping,
each 31.7 x 42.2 cm

1 For further discussion of these events see the essays in this volume by Simonetta Fraquelli and Tobia Bezzola and my previous book, *Making Modernism: Picasso and the Creation of the Market for Twentieth-Century Art*, New York 1995, pp. 190–215. In 1932, the first volume of Christian Zervos's multi-volume catalogue raisonné of Picasso's paintings, sculpture and drawings appeared.

2 Felipe Cossío del Pomar, *Con los buscadores del camino*, Madrid 1932.

3 Ibid., pp. 131–2. English translation published in Dore Ashton (ed.), *Picasso On Art: A Selection of Views*, New York 1972, p. 148.

4 Ibid.

5 Gertje Utley, *Picasso: The Communist Years*, Yale, 2000, p. 13.

6 Felipe Cossío del Pomar (note 2).

7 Michael FitzGerald, 'A Question of Identity', in: *Picasso's Marie-Thérèse*, exh. cat., Acquavella Galleries, New York 2008, pp. 8–29.

8 Robert Rosenblum, *Picasso's Blond Muse: The Reign of Marie-Thérèse Walter*, in: William Rubin (ed.), *Picasso and Portraiture*, exh. cat., The Museum of Modern Art, New York 1996, p. 354.

9 James Lord, *Picasso and Dora*, New York 1993, p. 123.

10 In general, I prefer not to refer to these women by their given names. In my opinion, this practice creates a false sense of intimacy and diminishes their stature in relation to Picasso, who is not called "Pablo" in publications, except by some authors who knew him personally.

11 Pierre Daix, *Picasso: Life and Art*, New York 1987.

12 For one important study of this period, see Eugen Weber, *The Hollow Years: France in the 1930s*, New York 1994.

13 For a discussion of Picasso's response to the First World War, see *Making Modernism* (note 1), pp. 47–79.

14 For a discussion of Picasso's career in the 1920s, see ibid, pp. 80–189.

15 See John Richardson, *A Life of Picasso: The Triumphant Years, 1917–32*, vol. III, New York 2007, p. 487.

16 See Daix, *Picasso: Life and Art* (note 11), p. 231 and Marilyn McCully, 'Foreword: The Mirror of the Cubist Acropolis' in: Fernande Olivier, *Loving Picasso*, New York 2001, pp. 10–11.

17 Picasso to David Douglas Duncan cited in Daix, *Picasso Life and Art* (note 11), p. 231.

18 See Musée des Arts Décoratifs, *Picasso: Peintures 1900–55*, Paris, 1955, entry number 40, n.p.

19 Picasso's denial of African influence on the *Demoiselles d'Avignon* was reported by Pierre Daix in an article in 1970 and later amended, see Daix, *Picasso: Life and Art* (note 11), p. 76.

20 Alfred H. Barr, Jr. (ed.), *Picasso: Forty Years of his Art*, exh. cat., The Museum of Modern Art, New York 1939, p. 21.

21 FitzGerald, *Making Modernism* (note 1), p. 141.

22 Elizabeth Cowling, *Visiting Picasso: The Notebooks and Letters of Roland Penrose*, London 2006.

23 John Golding's essay, 'Picasso and Surrealism' in: Roland Penrose and John Golding (eds.), *Picasso in Retrospect*, New York 1973, pp. 76–121, is an exemplary early study.

24 Michel Leiris, 'Toiles récentes de Picasso,' originally published in: *Documents*, no. 2, Paris, 1930 and reprinted in: Leiris, *Un Génie sans piédestal*, Paris 1992, p. 27.

25 Françoise Gilot reported a conversation Picasso had with Henri Matisse in the early 1950s in which Picasso spoke of the use of Surrealist methods without fully accepting their principles, see *Life with Picasso*, 1964, p. 270.

26 At the time of the Petit exhibition, Picasso commented to the journalist Tériade, "for an exhibition is like a picture, whether it is well or badly 'arranged,' all comes down to the same thing. What counts is the element of continuity in [an artist's] ideas. When that element is seen to exist, everything ends up falling into place, just as it does in the worst household," quoted in Richardson, *A Life of Picasso*, vol. III, p. 477.

27 Breton described Picasso's sculpture of this period as "the most incongruous medley of objects conceivable." 'Picasso dans son element,' in: *Minotaure*, no. 1, 1933; reprinted in English translation in: *Surrealism and Painting*, New York 1965, p. 110.

28 See Dawn Ades, *Dada and Surrealism Reviewed*, London 1978, pp. 278–89.

29 For example, Breton suggested during his survey of Picasso's studio that the juxtaposition of bottles of varnish with several of Picasso's wire constructions on a shelf revealed that the sculptures were not abstract designs but containers of a sentient void he called "the philter of life" — an interpretation that tied the works to Picasso's plans for a monument to Guillaume Apollinaire based on Apollinaire's book *Le poète assassiné*. For discussion of this project, see FitzGerald, *Making Modernism* (note 1), p. 178.

30 This shift in Picasso's work was not evident in the public presentation of his work during the mid-1930s. The primary venue, the Galerie Paul Rosenberg, continued to feature his figure and still-life paintings, particularly in the solo exhibition it held of Picasso's art in March 1936.

31 For Picasso's images of the minotaur, especially in prints, see Lisa Florman, *Myth and Metamorphosis: Picasso's Classical Prints of the 1930s*, Cambridge 2000, pp. 140–94.

32 For a treatment of the subject of the artist's studio across Picasso's career, see Michael FitzGerald, *Picasso: The Artist's Studio*, exh. cat. Wadsworth Atheneum, Hartford/The Cleveland Museum of Art, New Haven/London 2001.

33 Picasso's statement appeared in *Cahiers d'art*, 1935, vol. 10, no. 10, pp. 173–8 and was reprinted in English translation in Barr, *Picasso: Forty Years of his Art* (note 20), pp. 13–20.

34 Ibid.

35 Daix, *Picasso: Life and Art* (note 11), p. 230.

36 I would like to express my thanks to Gertje Utley for discussing with me the context of Picasso's work during the mid-thirties. This essay is greatly indebted to her book, *Picasso: The Communist Years*, Yale 2000, as well as the exhibition and catalogue organised by Steven Nash, *Picasso and the War Years, 1937–45*, London 1998.

37 Picasso's statement of 1935 reprinted in Barr, *Picasso: Forty Years of his Art* (note 20), p. 20.

38 Quoted in Daix, *Picasso: Life and Art* (note 11), p. 236. The special issue of *Cahiers d'art* devoted to Picasso's poetry was no. 10, 1935.

39 For the Surrealists' involvement in political action, see Helena Lewis, *The Politics of Surrealism*, New York 1988. For Éluard's relations with Picasso, see particularly Jean-Charles Gateau, *Éluard, Picasso et la peinture*, Geneva 1983.

40 Daix, *Picasso: Life and Art* (note 11), p. 236.

41 Paul Éluard, *Letters to Gala*, New York 1989, p. 122.

42 Daix, *Picasso: Life and Art* (note 11), p. 228. ·

43 Richardson, *A Life of Picasso* (note 15), vol. III, pp. 491–9.

44 Éluard's poem was published in *L'Humanité* on December 17, 1936.

45   Picasso's portrait of Éluard is
dated January 8, 1936. For
ADLAN and the context of French
artists and the writer's involvement
with Spain in the mid 1930s, see
Emmanuel Guigon, "ADLAN", and
Brigitte Léal, "Petite aube de plein
été sur Barcelone," in: Léal and
Ocaña (eds.), *Paris-Barcelone: de
Gaudí à Miró*, Paris 2001,
pp. 557–67 and 577–98.
46   Daix, *Picasso: Life and Art*
(note 11), p. 247; Utley, *Picasso:
The Communist Years* (note 36),
p. 20. For a history of the Spanish
Civil War, see Hugh Thomas,
The Spanish Civil War, New York
1977.
47   Utley, *Picasso: The Communist Years* (note 36), p. 20.
48   Ibid, pp. 14–15. Utley con-
vincingly links Picasso's drawing
with Rolland's text in proposing
that Picasso made the drawing
specifically for the performance of
the play. For Dalí's response to the
war, particularly in his painting *Soft
Construction with Boiled Beans
(Premonition of Civil War)*, 1936,
see entry in Dawn Ades and
Michael Taylor (eds.), *Dalí*,
New York 2005, pp. 262–5.

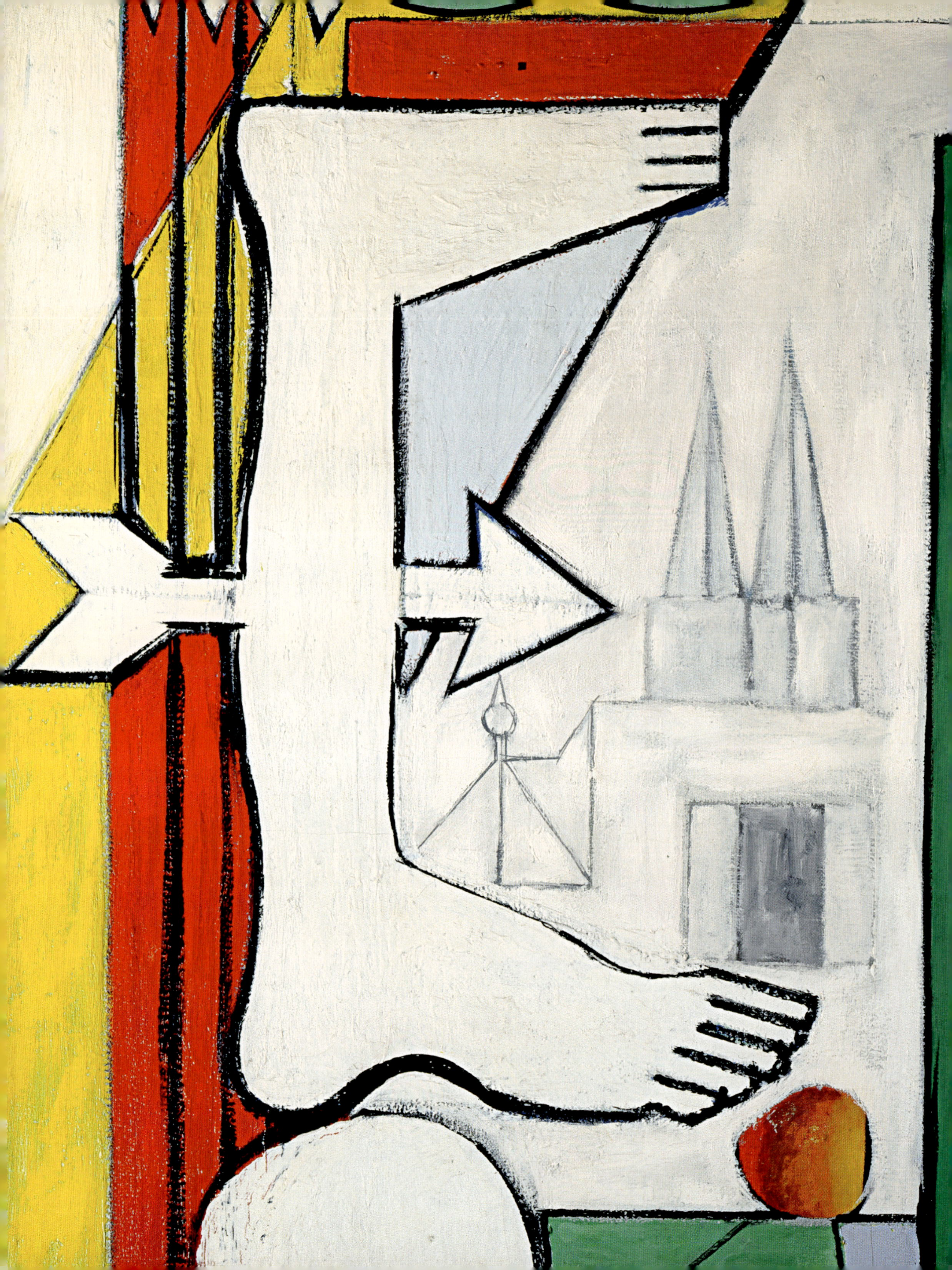

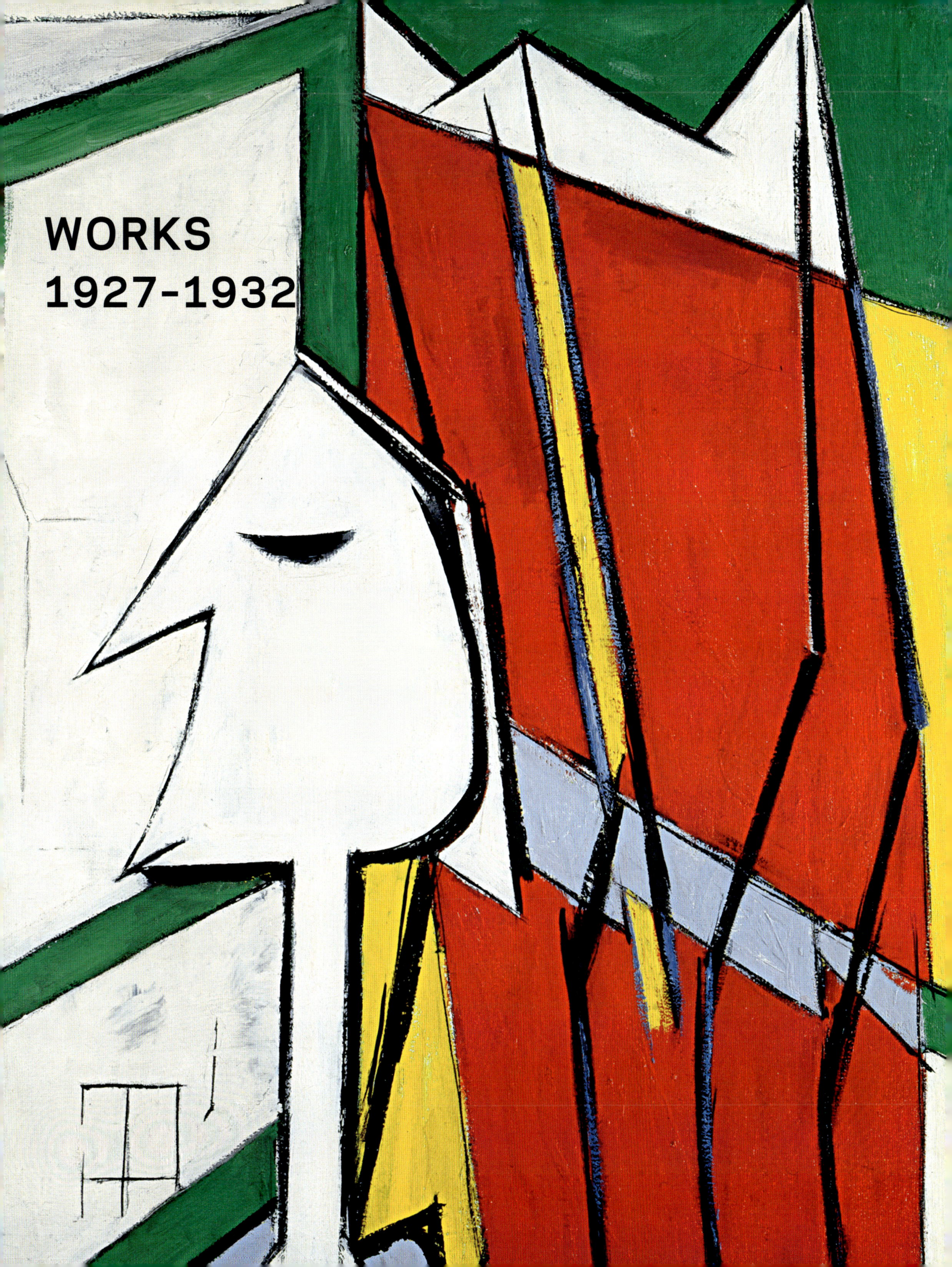
WORKS
1927-1932

56
The Painter and his Model, 1927
Oil on canvas
214 x 200 cm
Tehran Museum of Contemporary Art

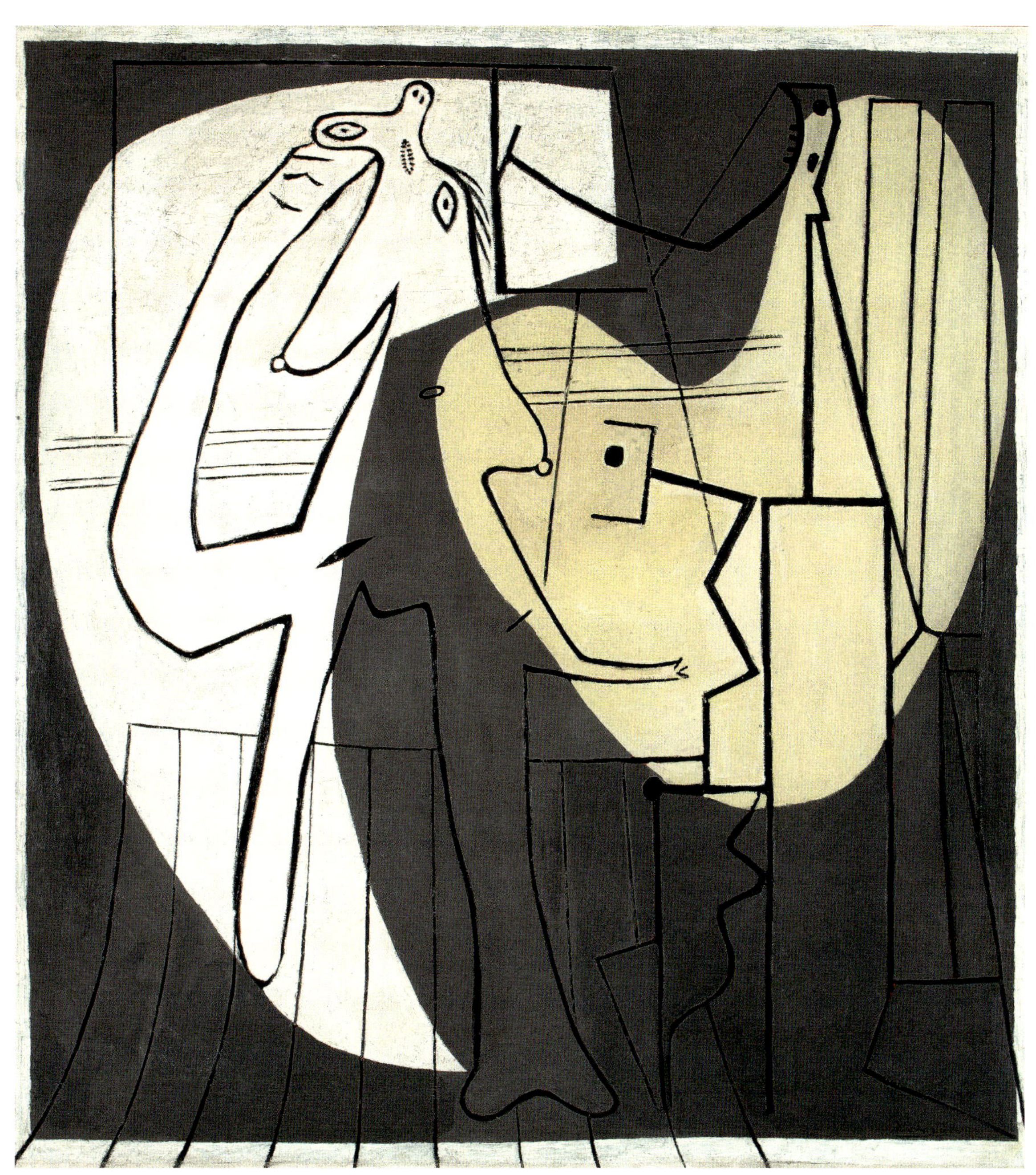

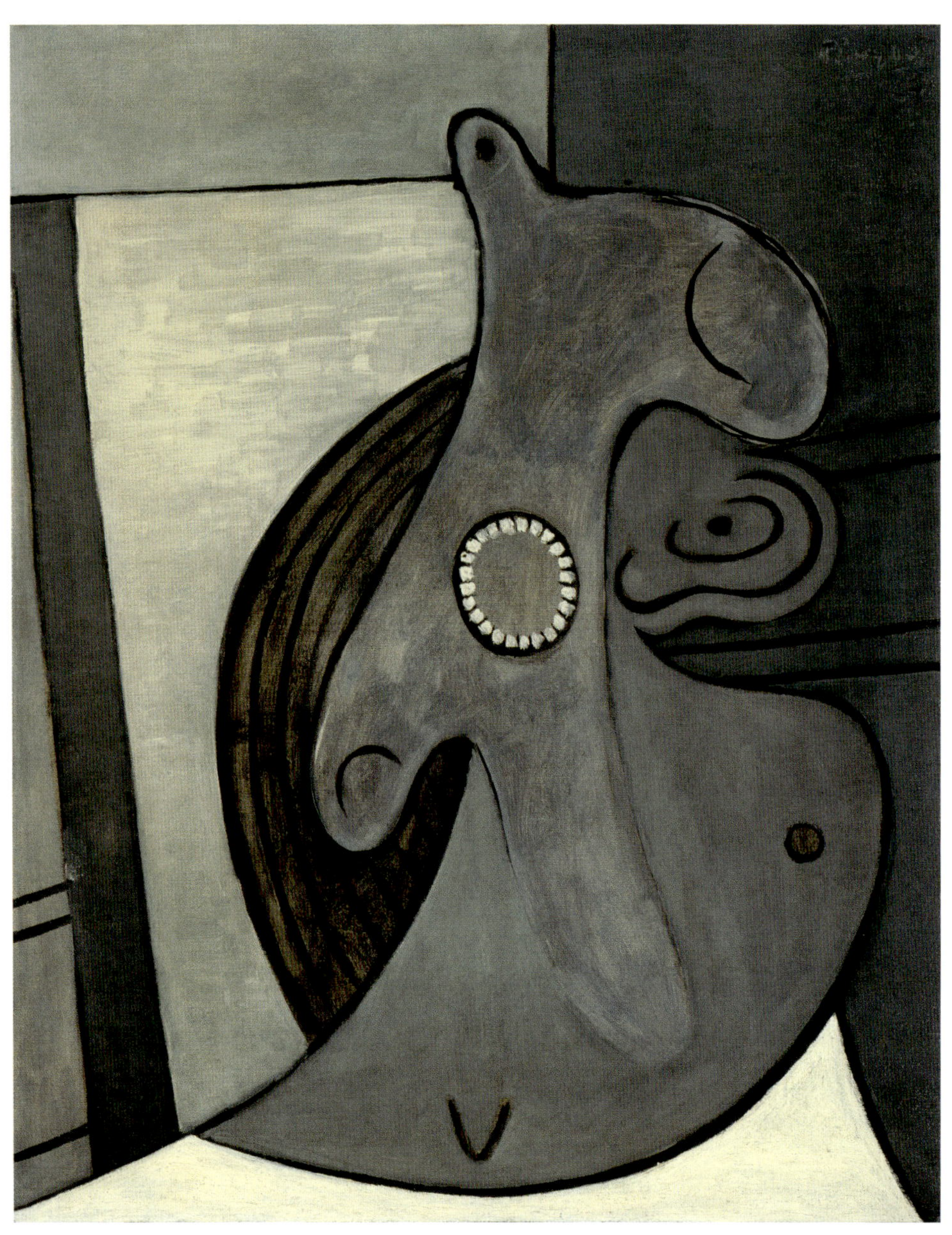

57
Woman in an Armchair, 1927
Oil on canvas
81 x 65 cm
Kawamura Memorial Museum of Art, Japan

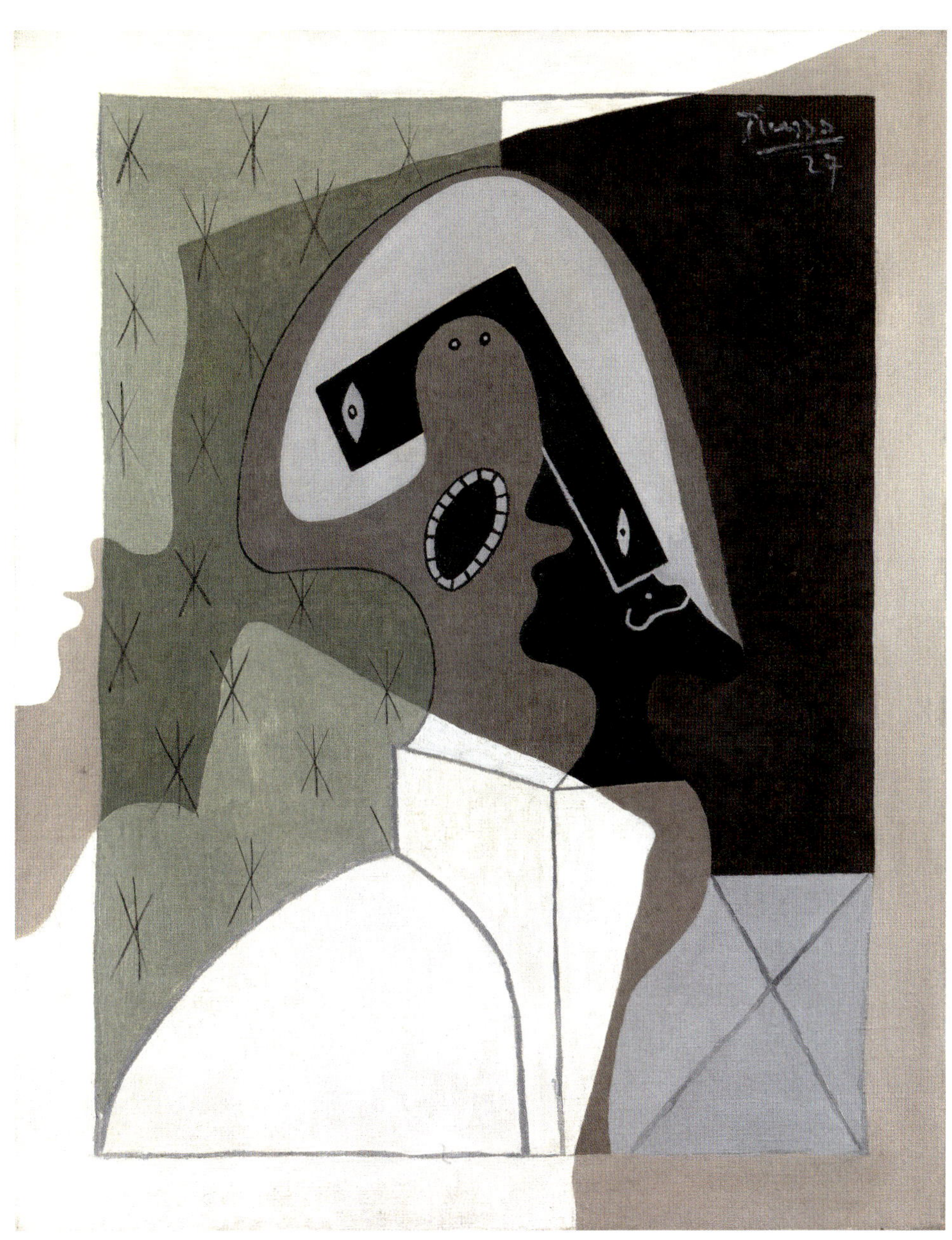

58
Harlequin, 1927
Oil on canvas
81.3 x 65.1 cm
The Metropolitan Museum of Art,
New York
The Mr and Mrs Klaus G. Perls Collection, 1997

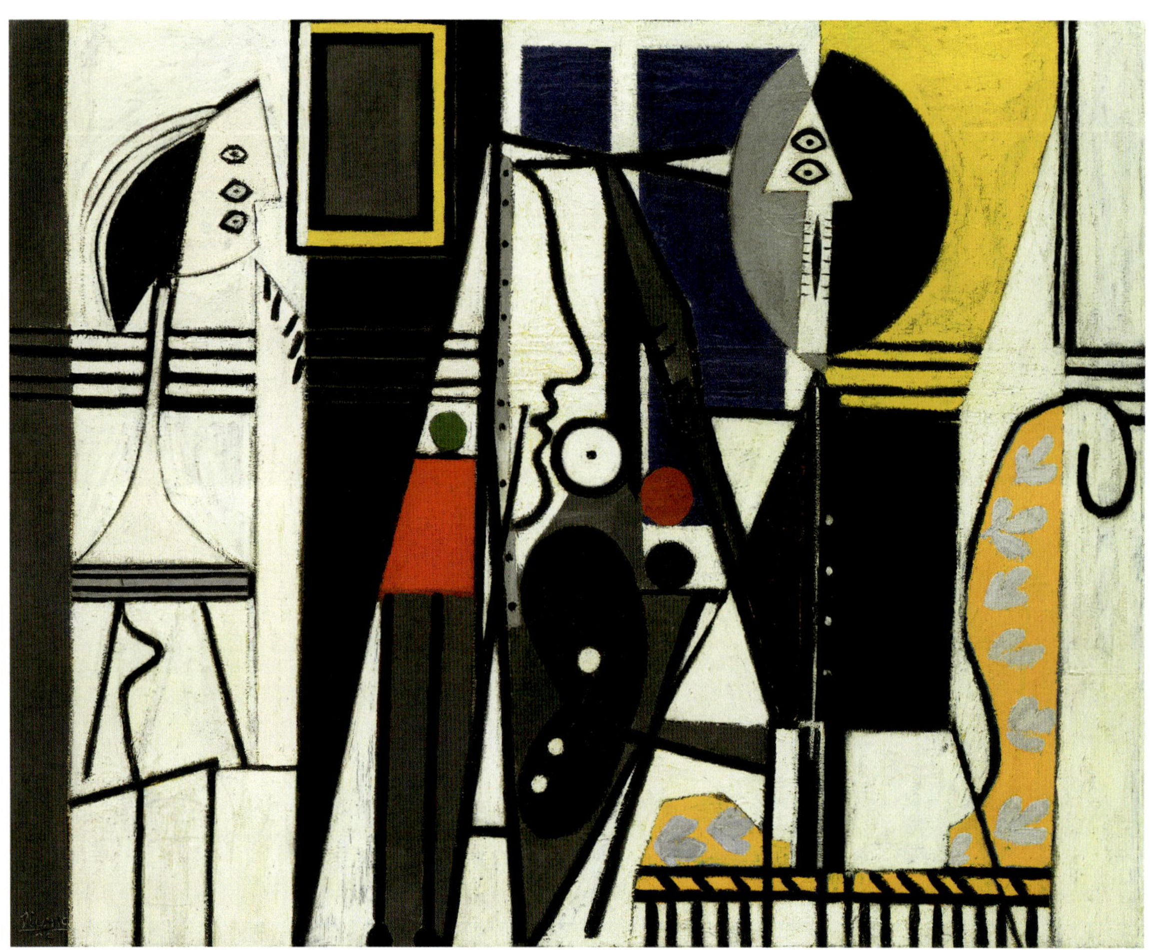

59
Painter and Model, 1928
Oil on canvas
129.8 x 163 cm
The Museum of Modern Art,
New York
The Sidney and Harriet Janis Collection

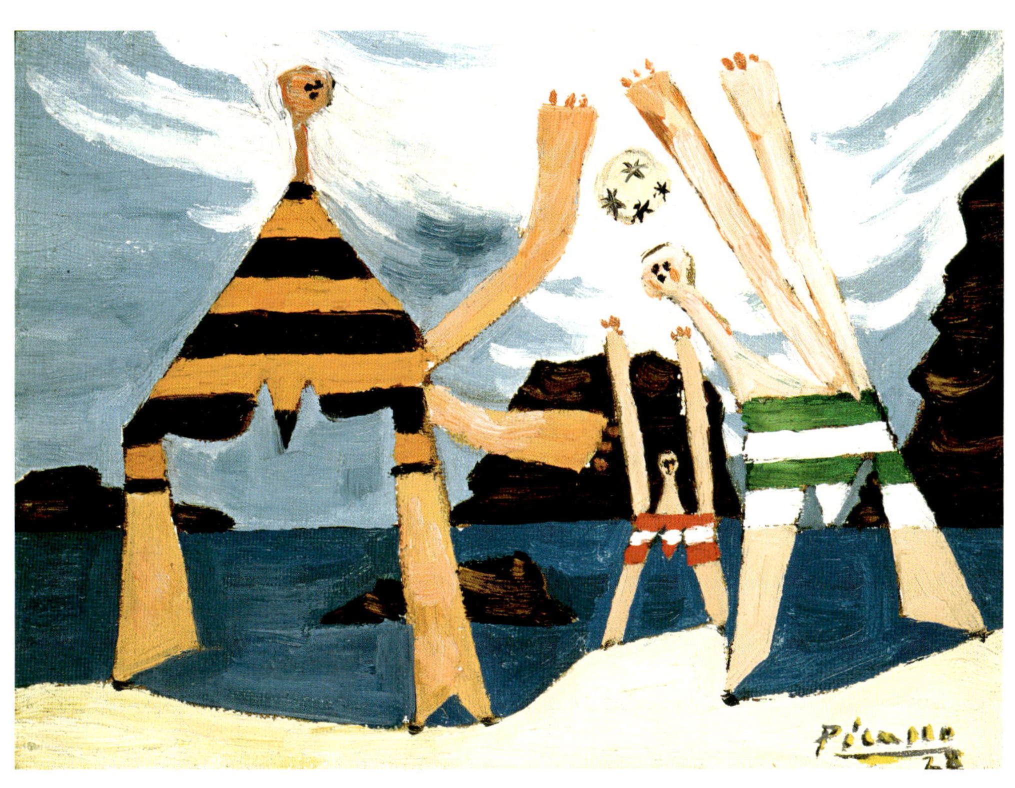

60
Bathers with Beach Ball, 1928
Oil on canvas
15.9 x 21.9 cm
Private collection

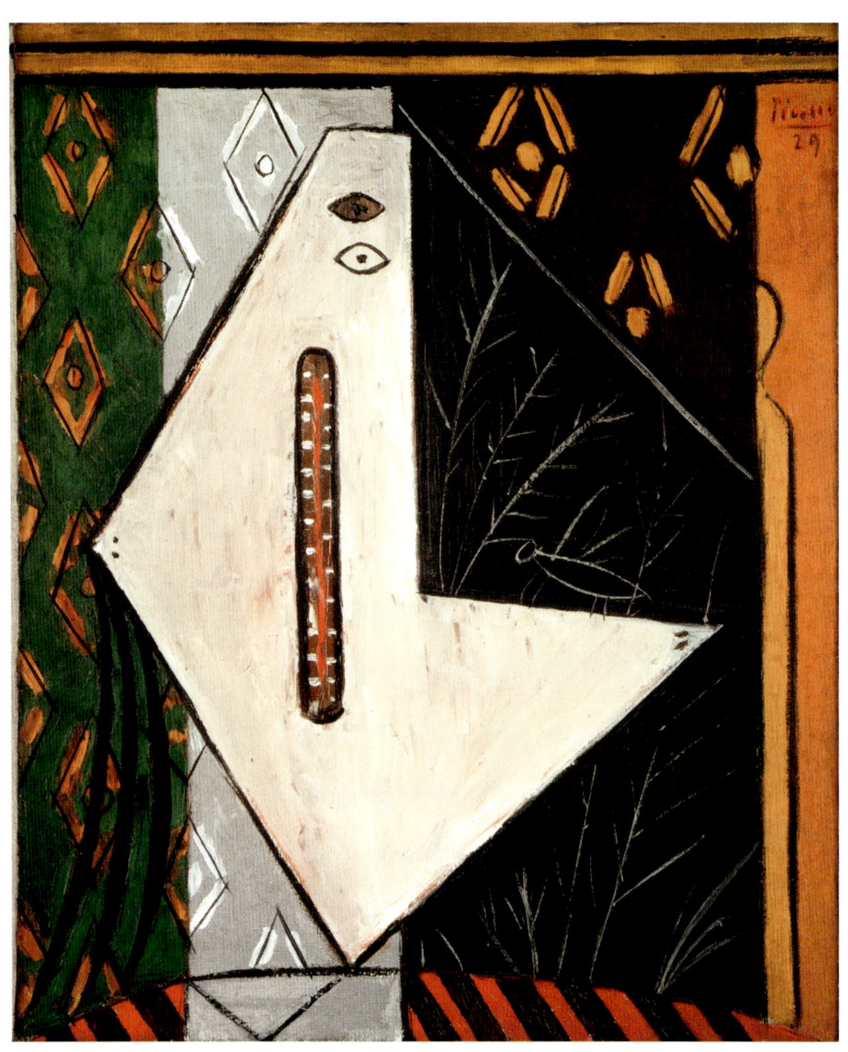

61
Young Girl, 1929
Oil on canvas
54 x 45.5 cm
Moderna Museet, Stockholm

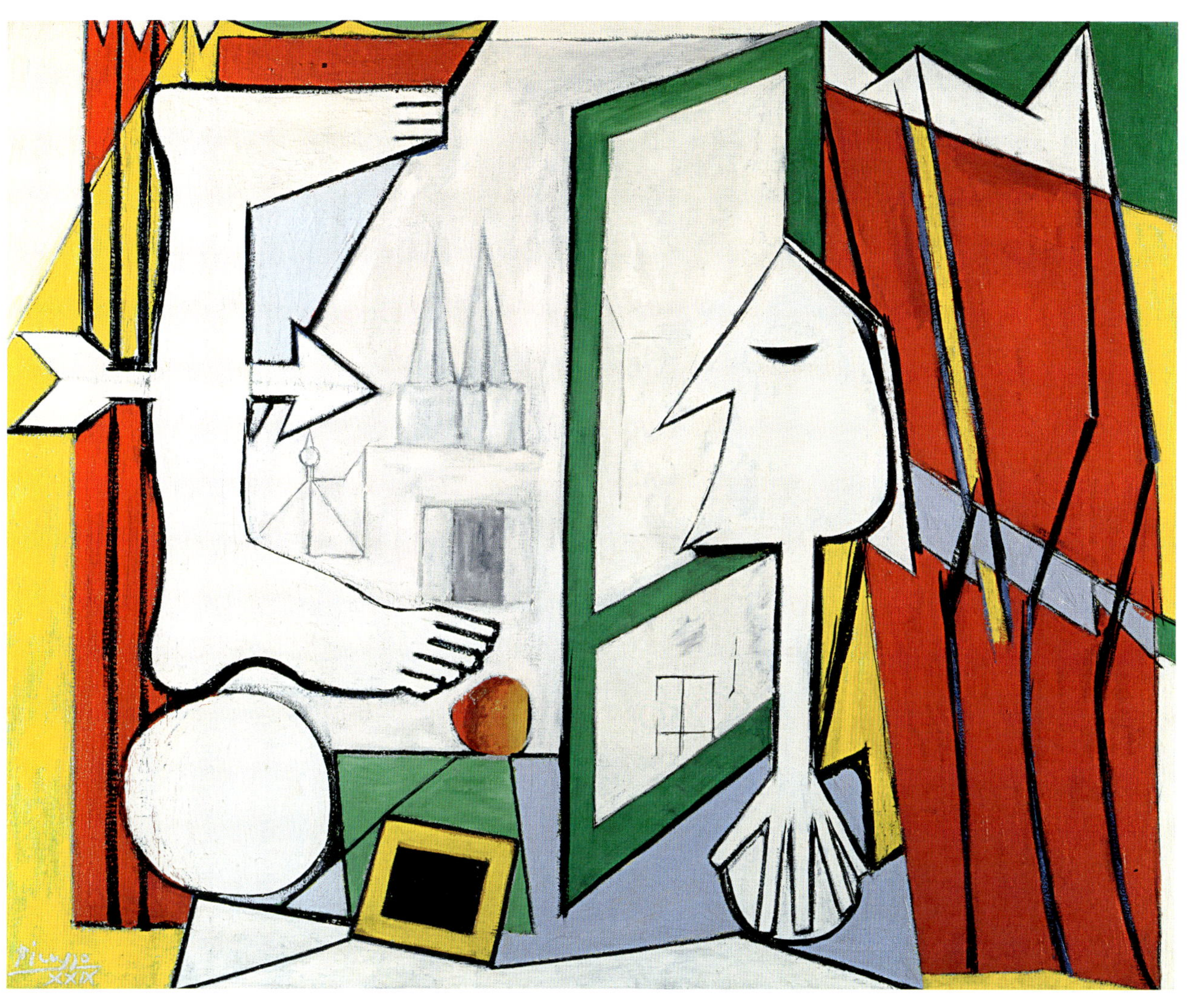

62

The Open Window, 1929
Oil on canvas
130 x 162 cm
Staatsgalerie Stuttgart
Steegmann Collection

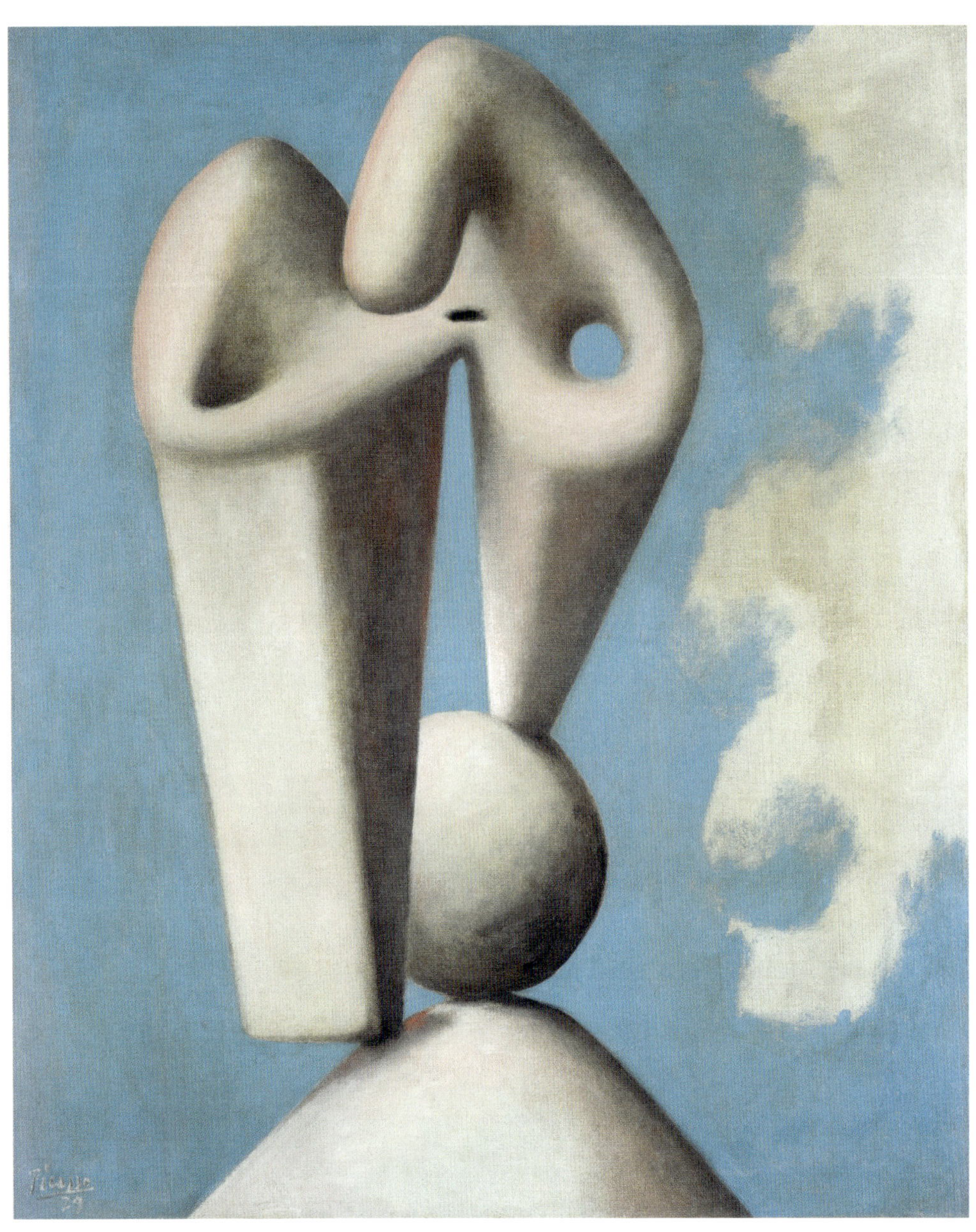

63
**Head: Study for
a Monument,** 1929
Oil on canvas
73 x 59.7 cm
The Baltimore Museum of Art
The Dexter M. Ferry, Jr. Trustee
Corporation Fund

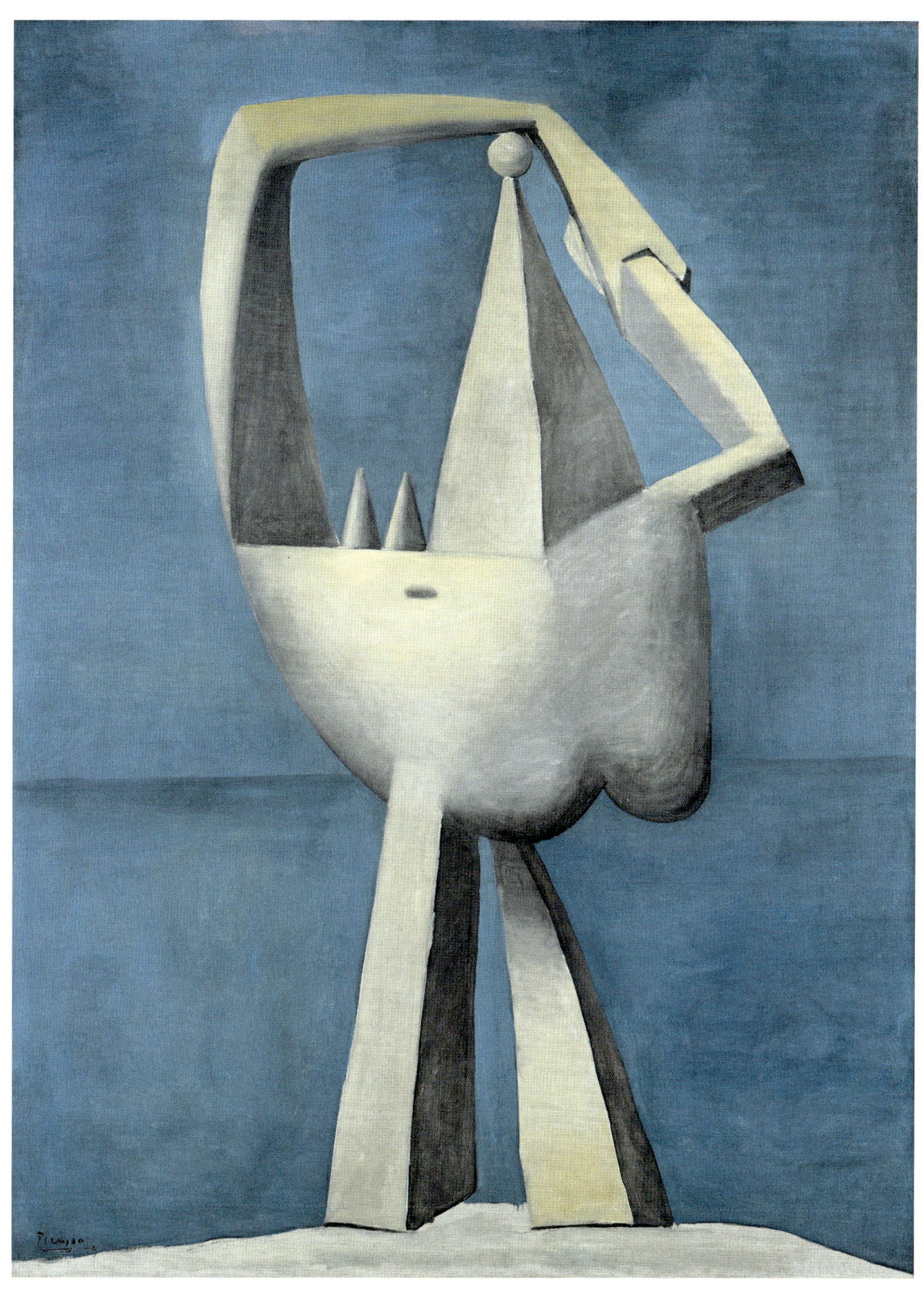

64
Nude Standing by the Sea, 1929
Oil on canvas
129.9 x 96.8 cm
The Metropolitan Museum of Art,
New York
Bequest of Florene M. Schoenborn, 1995

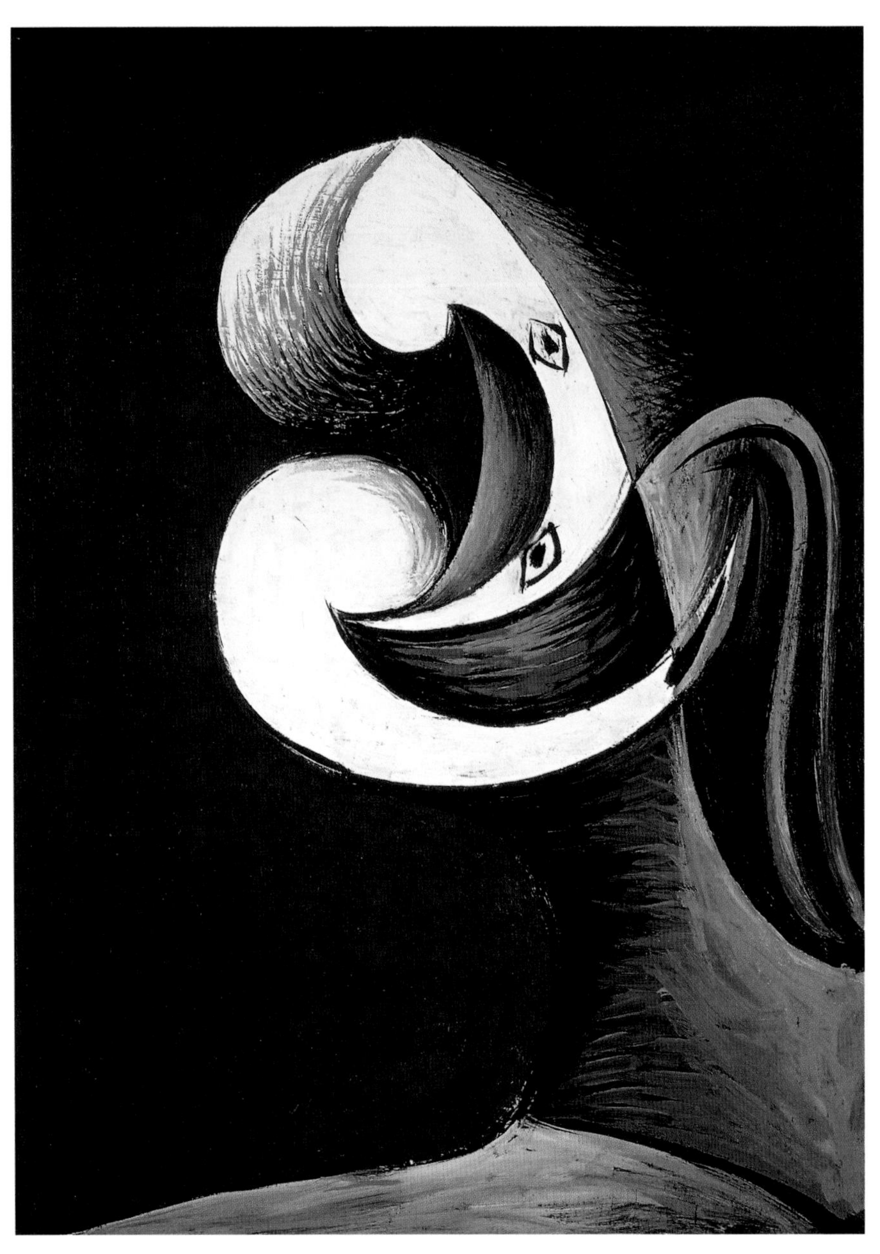

65

Abstraction (Head), 1930
Oil on wood
62.2 x 46.4 cm
Cincinnati Art Museum
Gift of Thomas C. and Emily F. Adler

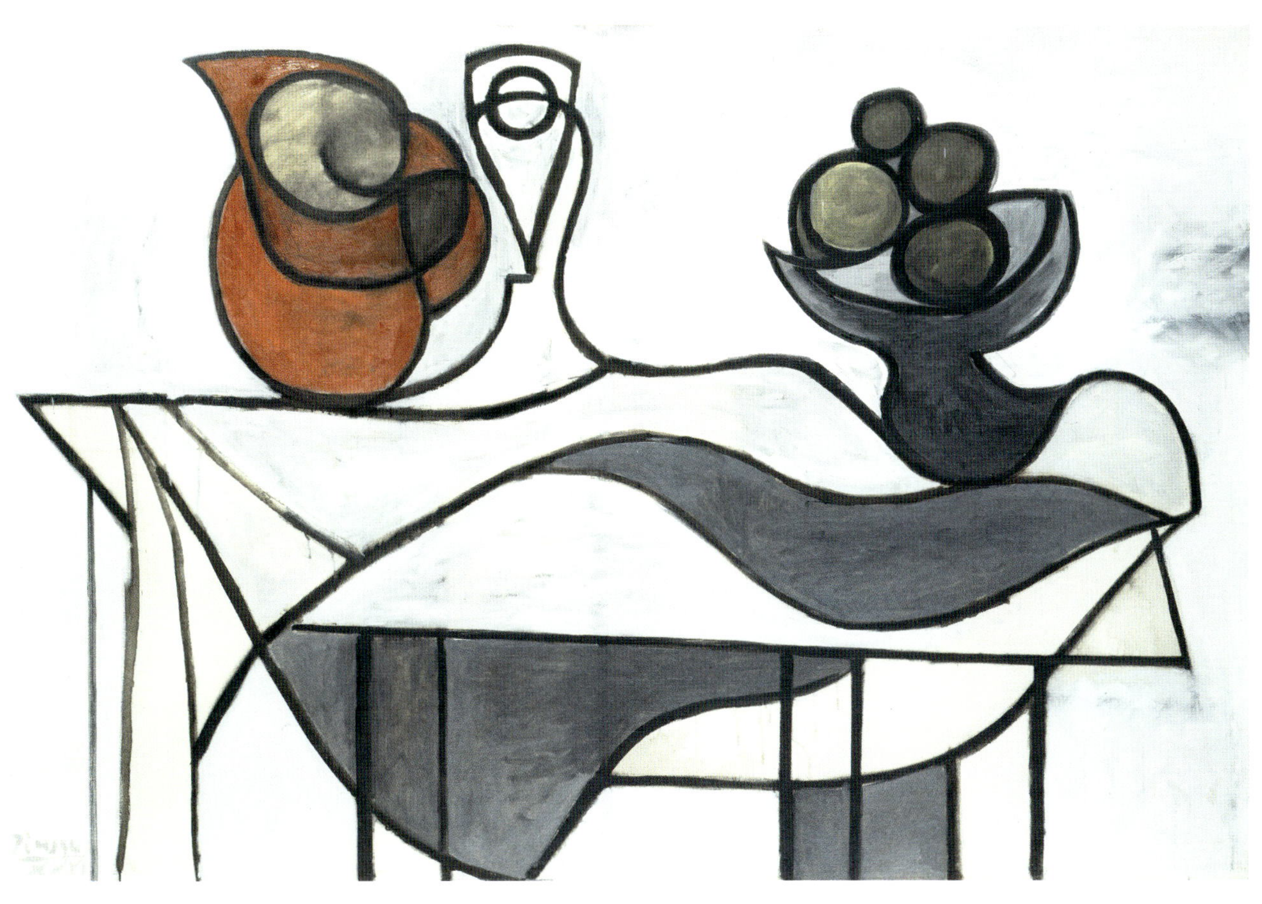

66
Jug and Bowl of Fruit, 1931
Oil on canvas
131 x 196 cm
Courtesy Nahmad Collection,
Switzerland

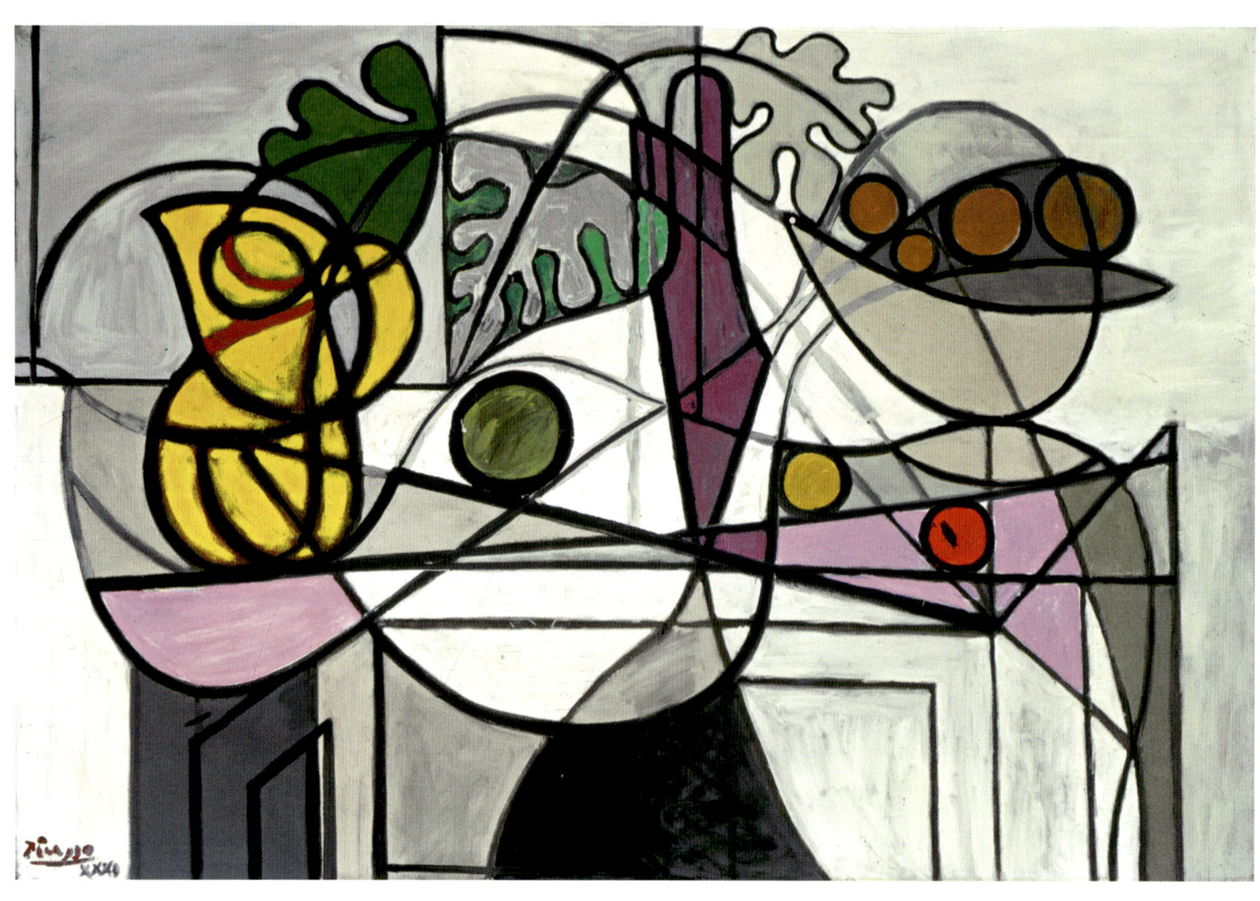

67
Pitcher and Fruit Bowl, 1931
Oil on canvas
130.2 x 194.9 cm
Saint Louis Art Museum
Bequest of Morton D. May

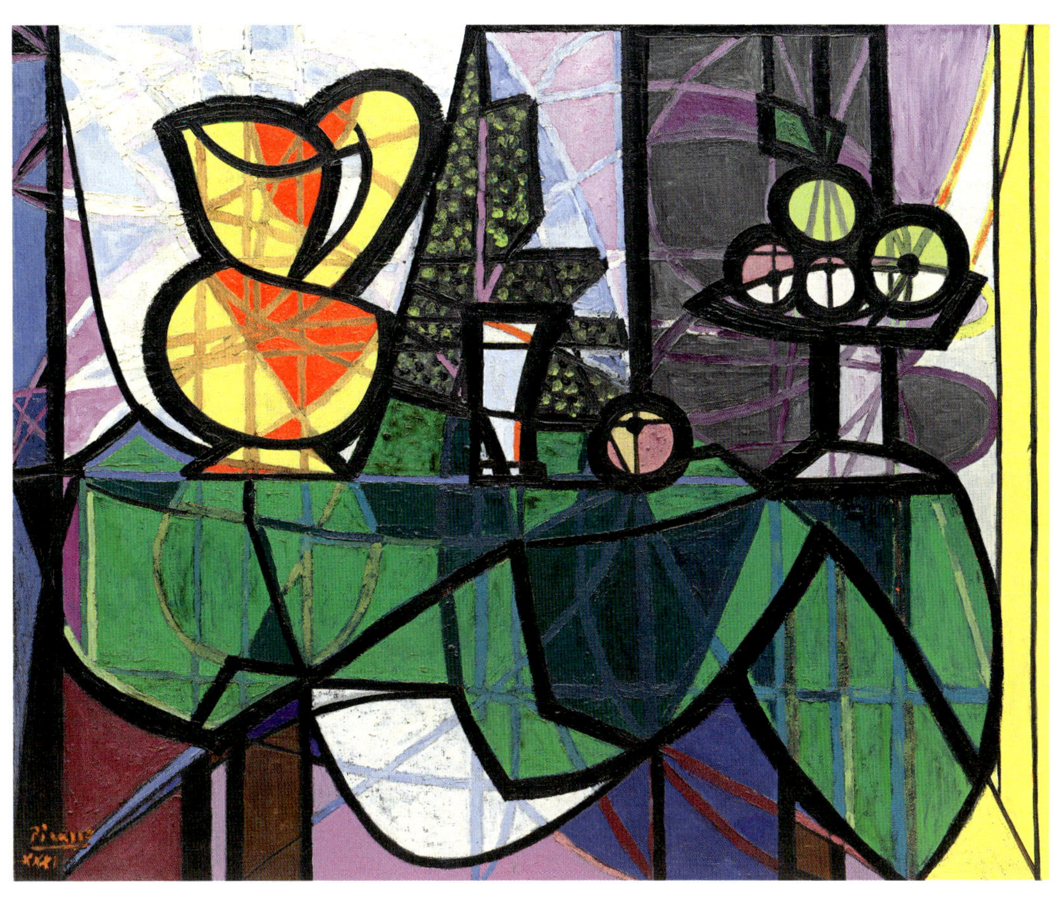

68
Pitcher and Bowl of Fruit, 1931
Oil on canvas
130.8 x 162.6 cm
Solomon R. Guggenheim
Museum, New York
By exchange, 1982

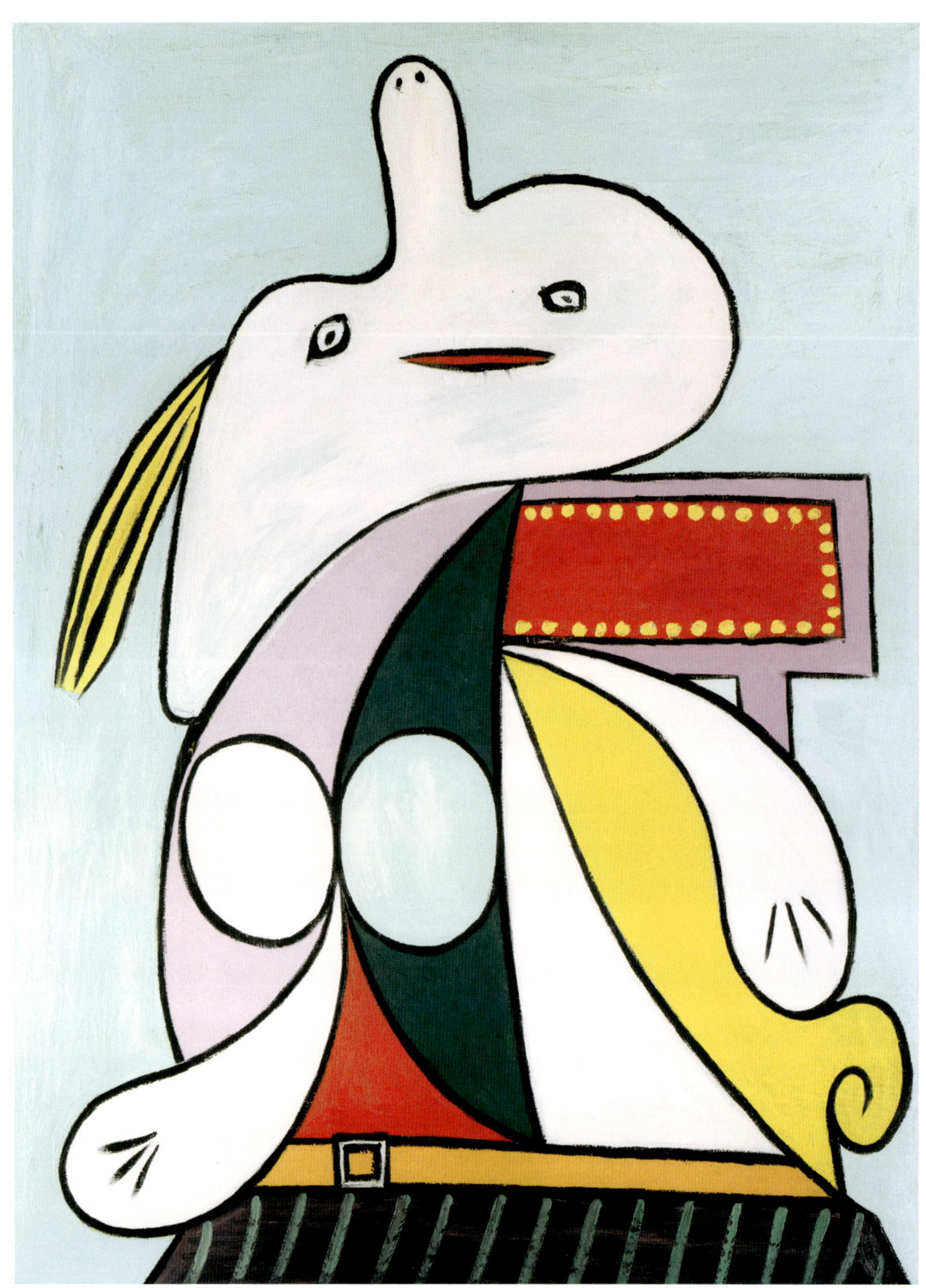

69
The Yellow Belt:
Marie-Thérèse Walter, 1932
Oil on canvas
130 x 97 cm
Courtesy Nahmad Collection, Switzerland

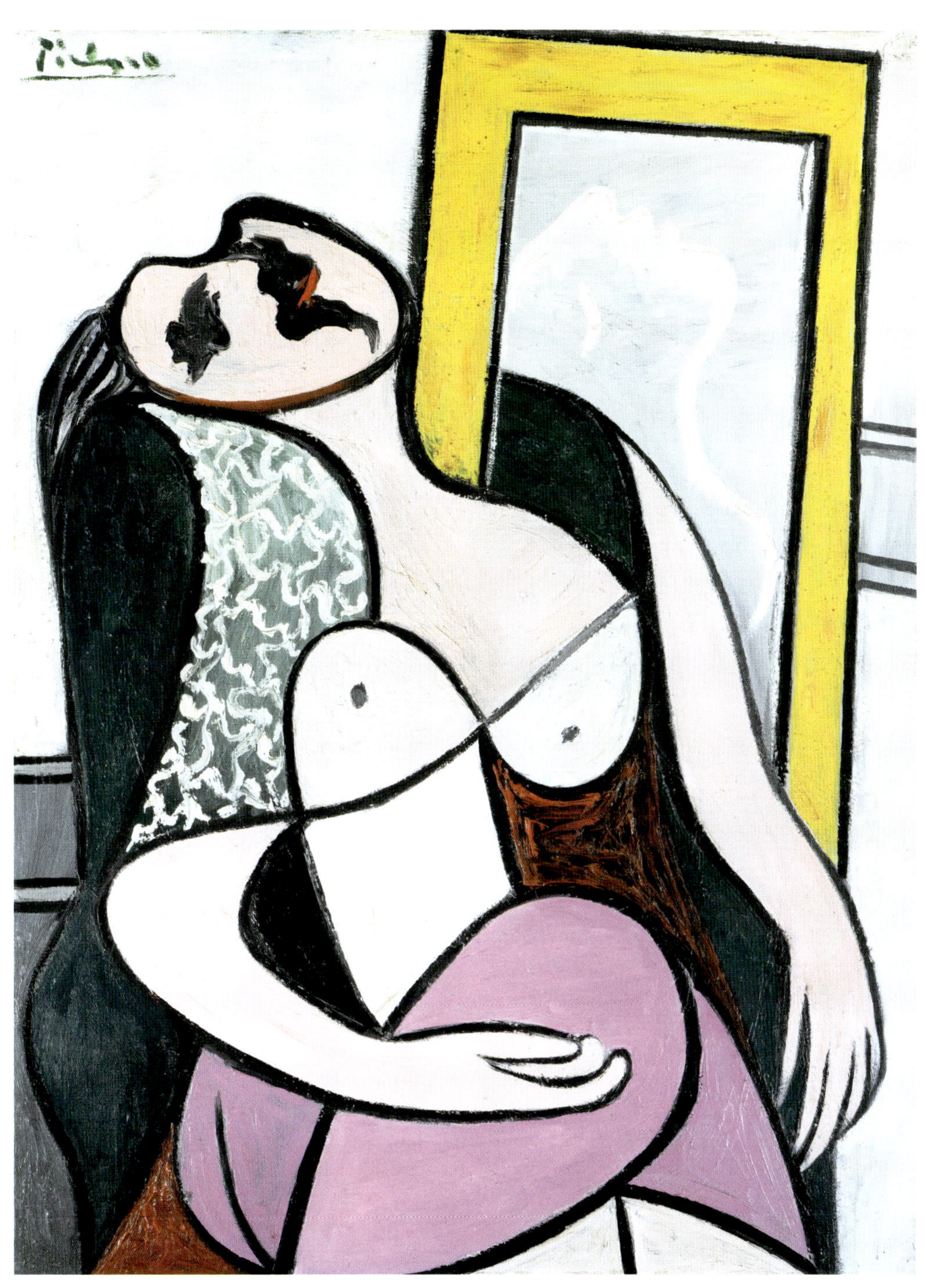

70
Sleeping Woman in a Mirror, 1932
Oil on wood
130 x 97 cm
Courtesy Nahmad Collection, Switzerland

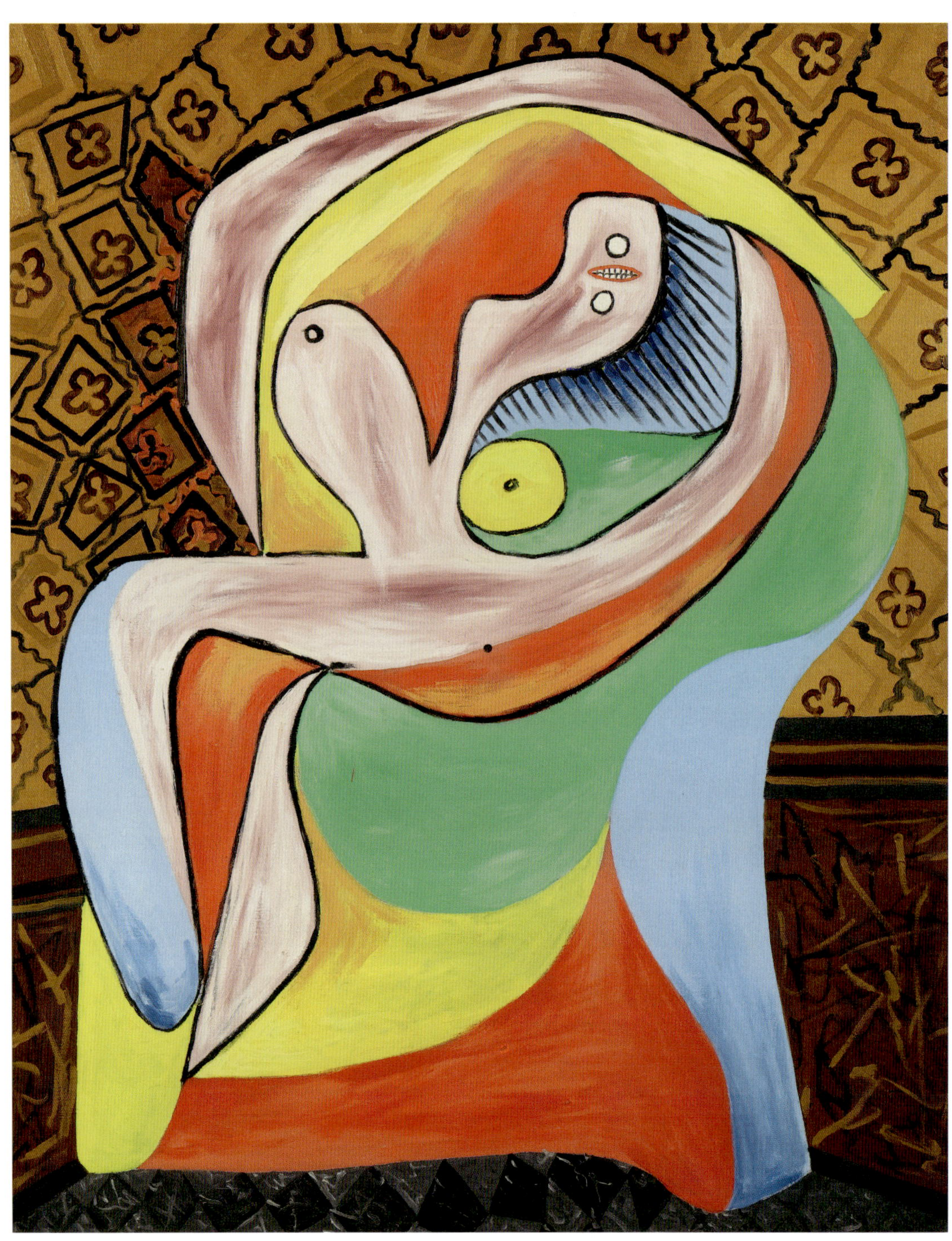

71
Repose, 1932
Oil on canvas
161.9 x 130.2 cm
The Steven and Alexandra Cohen Collection

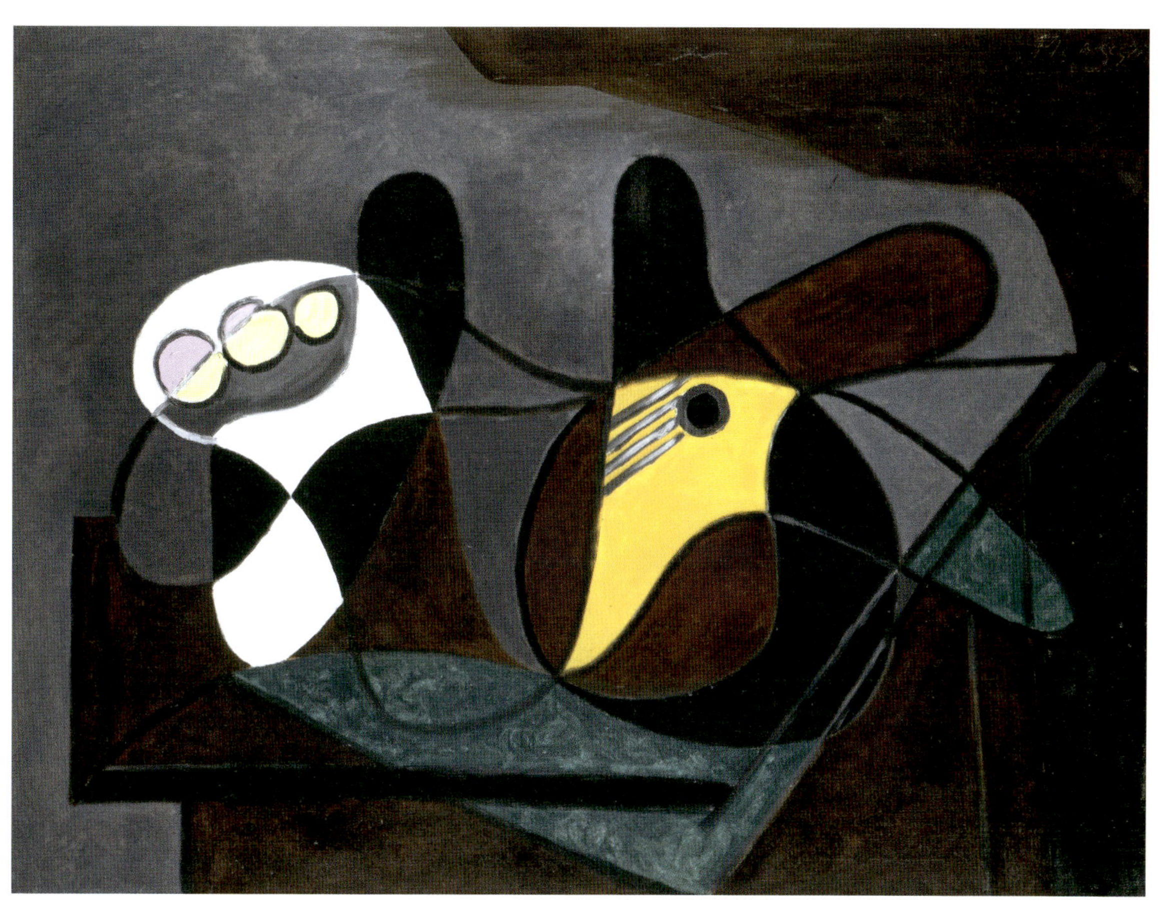

72
Fruit Bowl and Guitar, 1932
Oil on canvas
97 x 130 cm
Courtesy Nahmad Collection,
Switzerland

73
Young Woman with Mandolin, 1932
Oil on wood
64.2 x 46.9 cm
The University of Michigan Museum of Art
Gift of the Carey Walker Foundation

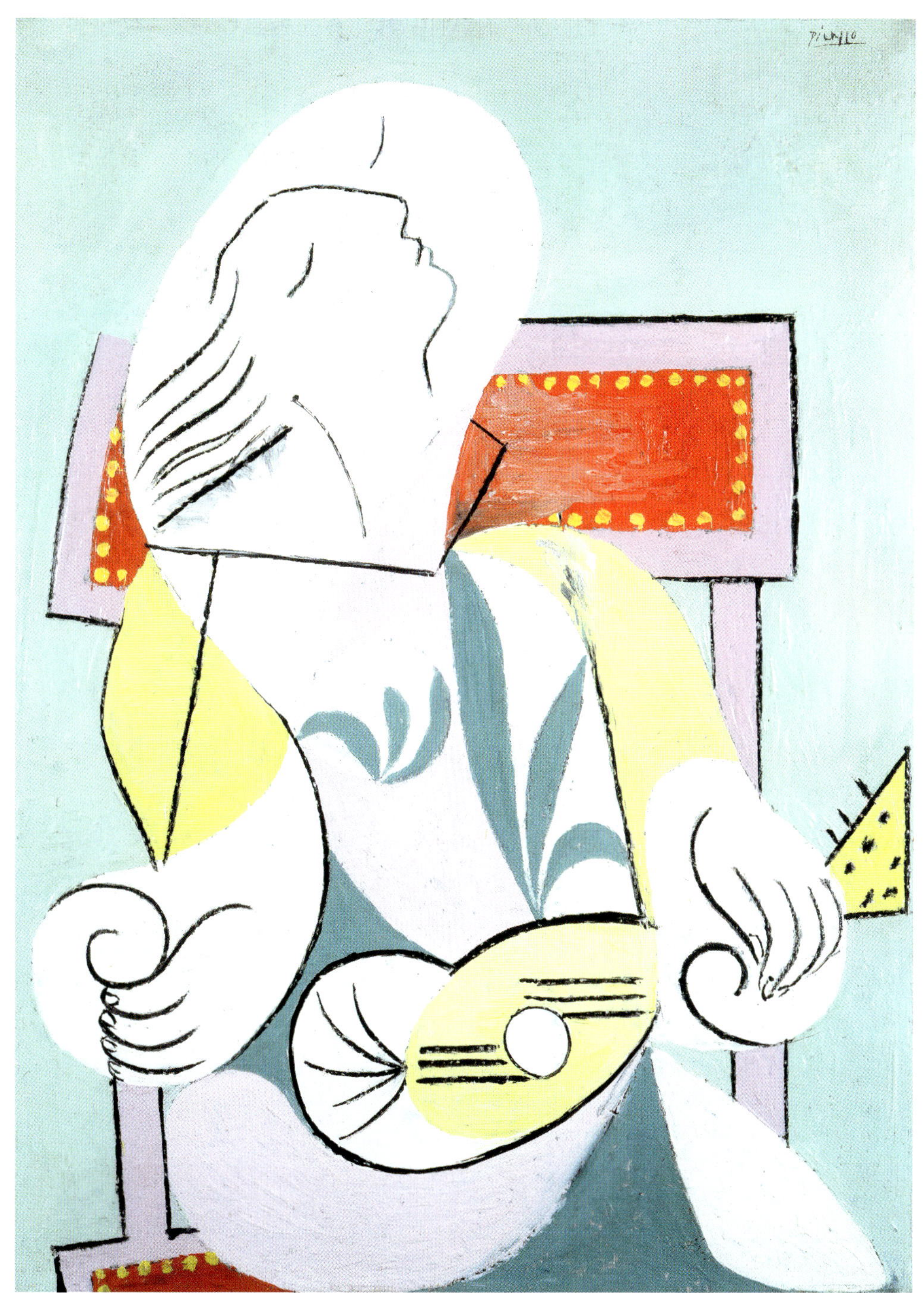

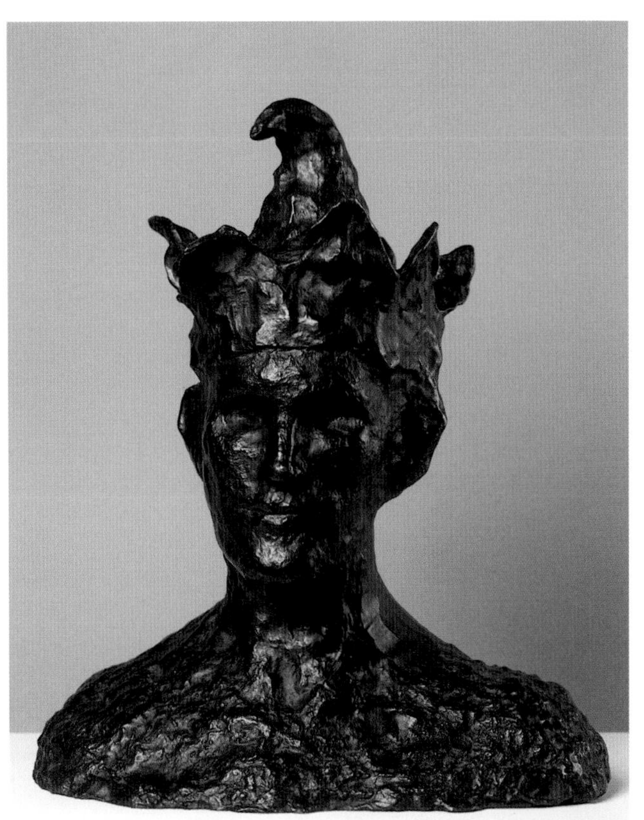

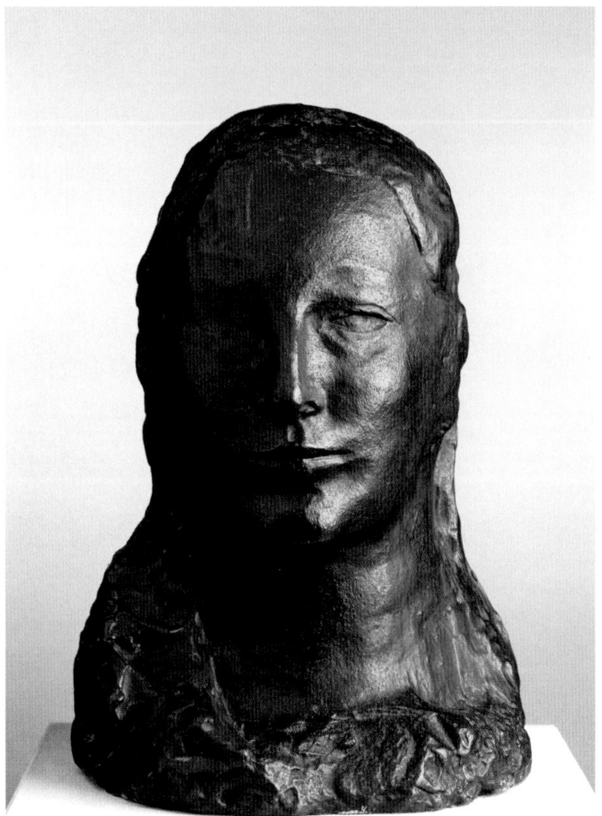

74
Jester, 1905
Bronze
41 x 37 x 21 cm
Kunstmuseum Winterthur
Purchased with a jubilee
donation from Werner Graf
& Co., Winterthur, 1949

75
Head of a Woman (Fernande), 1906
Bronze
41 x 24.5 x 25.5 cm
Kunsthaus Zürich
Werner and Nelly Bär Collection

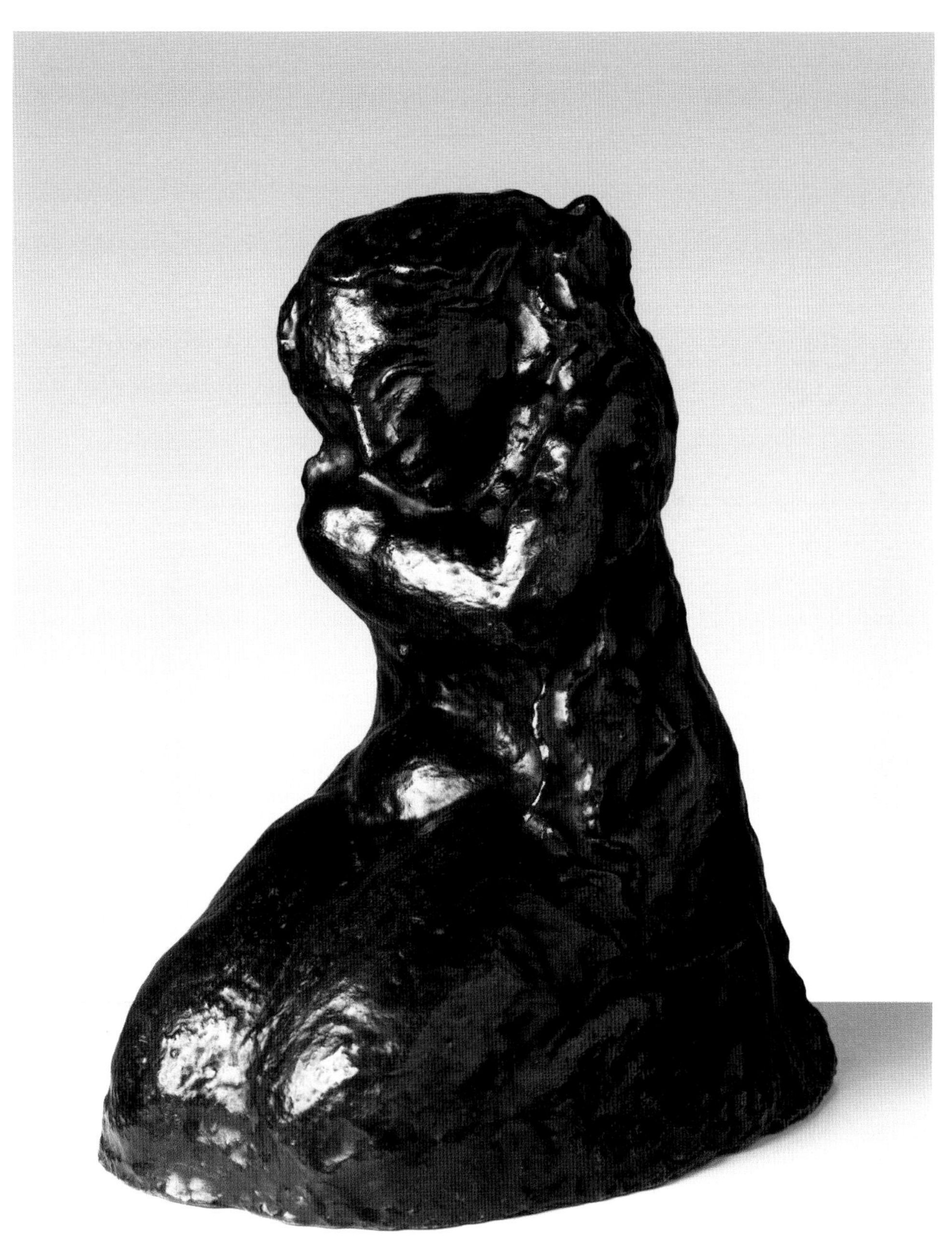

76
Woman Combing Her Hair, 1906
Bronze, patinated
42 x 31.2 x 29.2 cm
Museum Ludwig Köln
Schenkung Ludwig 1994

FACSIMILE OF THE EXHIBITION CATALOGUE OF
THE KUNSTHAUS ZÜRICH, 1932
(EXCERPT)

KUNSTHAUS ZÜRICH

PICASSO

11. SEPTEMBER BIS 30. OKTOBER 1932
VERLÄNGERT BIS 13. NOVEMBER

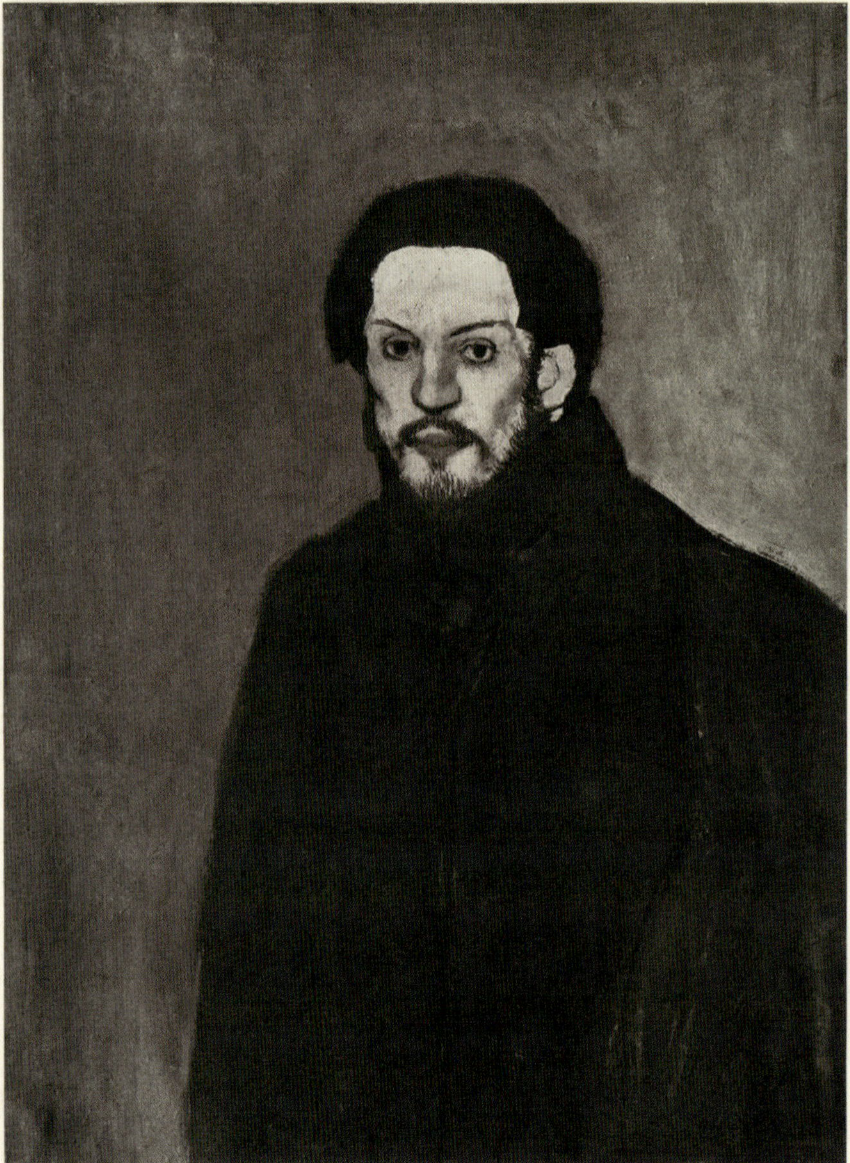

1903   KATALOG NR. 19

KUNSTHAUS ZÜRICH

PICASSO

11. SEPTEMBER BIS 30. OKTOBER 1932

AUSFÜHRLICHES VERZEICHNIS
MIT 32 TAFELN

kunsthaus zürich

Für die Ermöglichung der Picasso-Ausstellung in Zürich
dankt die Zürcher Kunstgesellschaft in erster Linie dem Meister, der mit der Zusage zur Ausstellung bei Georges Petit
in Paris auch den Plan einer Zürcher Ausstellung gutgeheißen
und aus seinem persönlichen Besitz gegen fünfzig Gemälde
zur Verfügung gestellt hat. Von Zürich aus führte erste entscheidende Unterhandlungen mit Pariser Freunden des Meisters Herr Dr. E. Friedrich-Jezler; in Paris vertrat Herr Carl
Montag als altbewährter Freund während Wochen das Zürcher Kunsthaus und sicherte für Zürich vor allem die Beteili-
gung des großen Sammlers Dr. G. F. Reber und der Kunst-
handlung Paul Rosenberg. Die übrigen Eigentümer bedeu-
tender Werke ließen sich für die Mitwirkung gewinnen durch
Fürsprache von Picasso und Herrn Carl Montag, der Galerie
Georges Petit und – vor allem für die in Paris fehlende Abteilung der Zeichnungen, wie Herr Dr. F. B. Geiser Bern für die
systematische Ergänzung der Druckgraphik – auf direkte Ein-
ladung durch das Zürcher Kunsthaus. Ihnen allen danken wir
im Namen von Picasso und der Zürcher Kunstgesellschaft.

DER PRÄSIDENT DER

ZÜRCHER KUNSTGESELLSCHAFT:

JOHR

DER DIREKTOR:

DR. W. WARTMANN

VERZEICHNIS DER LEIHGEBER UND MITGLIEDER DES EHRENKOMITE

Herr Clive Bell . . . . London

Bernheim Jeune & Cie. . . . . Paris

Herr Etienne Bignou . . . . Paris

G. & L. Bollag . . . . Zürich

Herr André Breton . . . . Paris

Herr Paul Chadourne . . . . Paris

Frau Mauricia Coquiot . . . . Paris

Herr Valentine Dudensing . . . . New York

Fräulein Ingeborg Eichmann . . . . Arnau

Herr Paul Eluard . . . . Paris

Frau E. H. Errazuriz . . . . Paris

Herr Alfred Flechtheim . . . . Berlin

Herr Marcel Fleischmann . . . . Zürich

Herr Dr. E. Friedrich . . . . Zürich

Fräulein Irmgard H. Fritsch . . . . Lausanne

Baron G. . . . . Berlin

Herr René Gaffé . . . . Brüssel

Herr Dr. Bernhard Geiser . . . . Bern

Herr Dr. Alfred Gold . . . . Paris

Baron Napoléon Gourgaud . . . . Paris

III

Herr Paul Guillaume . . . .   Paris
Herr Dr. A. Hahnloser . . . .   Winterthur
Herr Dr. E. Hoffmann-Stehlin . . . .   Basel
Herr und Fräulein Rees Jeffries . . . . . .   London
Herr Henry Kahnweiler . . . .   Paris
Knoedler & Co. . . . .   New York
Herr Hermann Lange . . . .   Krefeld
Herr Raoul La Roche . . . .   Paris
Herr Pierre Matisse . . . .   New York
Herr Henri-Louis Mermod . . . .   Lausanne
Herr Bernhard Mayer . . . .   Zürich
Herr Darius Milhaud . . . .   Paris
Herr Carl Montag . . . .   Paris
Herr Joseph Müller . . . .   Solothurn
Herr Luis Neumann . . . .   Zürich
Galerie Neupert . . . .   Zürich
Vicomte de Noailles . . . .   Paris
Galerie Percier . . . .   Paris
Galeries Georges Petit . . . .   Paris
Herr Pablo Picasso . . . .   Paris
Galerie Pierre . . . .   Paris
Herr Dr. G. F. Reber . . . .   Lausanne
Alex Reid & Lefèvre Ltd. . . . .   London
Herr Geo Reinhart . . . .   Winterthur
Herr Paul Rosenberg . . . .   Paris
Herzogin von Roxburghe . . . .   London

IV

Herr H. Rupf-Wirz . . . .   Bern

Herr Albert Skira . . . .   Lausanne

Herr Prof. A. Speiser . . . .   Zürich

Frau E. Staub-Terlinden . . . .   Männedorf

Fräulein Gertrud Stein . . . .   Paris

Herr C. Frank Stoop . . . .   London

Herr Willi Strecker . . . .   Wiesbaden

Galerie Thannhauser . . . .   Luzern

Herr Tristan Tzara . . . .   Paris

Herr Antoine Villard . . . .   Paris

Herr Ambroise Vollard . . . .   Paris

Herr Alexander Vömel . . . .   Düsseldorf

Herr Georges Wildenstein . . . .   Paris

Herr Hugh Willoughby . . . .   Paris

———————

V

Picasso ist außerhalb seines unmittelbaren Umkreises während der letzten zwei Jahrzehnte für Europa mehr kunsttheoretischer Begriff geworden als sinnliches Erlebnis. Seine Freunde, die, um ihn zu preisen und zu beschützen in Büchern und Zeitschriften oder als nachschaffende Jünger für ihn eintraten, traten auch vor ihn hin, so daß der Kunstfreund zunächst sich eben so sehr mit ihnen wie mit dem schwer erreichbaren Meister auseinanderzusetzen hatten. An Ausstellungen erschienen seine Werke vereinzelt oder wirkten doch meist so; in aufreizendem Gegensatz zu den anerkannten Größen der Zeit. Er wurde nicht so sehr gewürdigt und hingenommen als ein Mensch und Künstler wie verherrlicht und bekämpft als ein Programm; bekämpft als eine Kraft von ausgesprochen negativ gerichteter, in Auflösung und Zersetzung mündender Vielfältigkeit. So leidenschaftlich war die Anteilnahme, daß über dem Wohin kaum je nach dem Woher und Was-überhaupt gefragt wurde, und über den immer wieder überraschenden Einzelergebnissen und in scheinbaren Gegensätzen sich abrollenden Phasen es zu ruhiger Betrachtung des Gesamtbildes und Ablaufs der Bewegung aus größerem Abstand nicht kam.

Wenn er als Fünfzigjähriger mit einem kurzen Aufblick von der Arbeit einmal vom unablässig werdenden dem schon geschaffenen Werk sich zuwandte und es in Auswahl für eine große Ausstellung sammelte und sammeln ließ, so wurde dies auch für seine Freunde, die sonst an seiner Seite nur vorwärtsstürmend ihn begleiteten, Anlaß und Möglichkeit zum Atemholen und zur Prüfung, wie weit vom festen Standpunkt aus sich Werk und Mensch umspannen und erfassen lassen. Christian Zervos unternimmt es als erster, das Leben des Meisters als Kette von Tatsachen, auf denen das Werk ruht, ausführlich zu erzählen, und mit dem Streben nach Vollständigkeit und Genauigkeit in der zeitlichen Folge den illustrierten Katalog des Werkes aufzustellen.

Der Künstler wird 1881 am 25. Oktober in Malaga geboren. Seine Eltern sind José Ruiz Blasco und Maria Picasso. Der Vater ist nacheinander Zeichenlehrer oder -professor an den Kunstschulen von Malaga, Corunna und, seit 1891, Barcelona. Unter seiner Leitung oder doch in seiner Atmo-

VII

sphäre zeichnet der Sohn schon in der frühesten Jugend, mit vierzehn und fünfzehn Jahren malt er. 1896 verläßt er das Gymnasium von Barcelona und besteht glanzvoll die Aufnahmeprüfung an der städtischen Kunstschule, im gleichen Jahr auch an der Kunstakademie in Madrid. Wenn auch noch nicht sechzehnjährig, fühlt er sich nach den Lehrjahren bei seinem Vater und im Bewußtsein seiner eigenen Kraft der Schule entwachsen. Nach einigen Monaten kehrt er nach Barcelona zurück und sucht als freier Künstler seinen Weg. Im Spätherbst 1900 kommt er zum erstenmal nach Paris. Im Winter 1901 arbeitet er in Madrid. Im Frühling fährt er zum zweitenmal nach Paris und hat im Juni bei Vollard die erste Ausstellung. Seine Arbeit ist Auseinandersetzung mit den Impressionisten, mit Van Gogh, Toulouse-Lautrec, Gauguin. Er malt von Glut verzehrt und angetrieben Tag und Nacht, während der Ausstellung bei Vollard hat er in seinem Zimmer noch ganze Stapel von Bildern. Weihnacht 1901 verbringt er in Spanien, er bleibt acht Monate und erscheint erst im Herbst 1902 zum drittenmal in Paris. Von Anfang 1903 an ist er wieder in Barcelona. Bei der vierten Rückkehr nach Paris, nach mehr als einem Jahr, im Frühling 1904, bezieht er hier zum erstenmal ein ständiges Atelier. Den Kreis seiner Pariser Freunde vom literarischen linken Flügel, Max Jacob, André Salmon, Gustave Coquiot, verläßt er im Sommer 1905 für einen kurzen Aufenthalt in Holland und im Winter 1905/06 für arbeitsreiche Monate im spanischen Gosol.

Mit dem Jahr 1906 schließt der bisher allein fertiggestellte erste Band von Zervos. Von dieser Zeit an ist einstweilen die Zürcher Ausstellung das vollständigste und schönste Buch über Picasso. Von den 384 Nummern bei Zervos enthält sie 29 Gemälde und 16 Zeichnungen, dazu aber aus dem gleichen Abschnitt 1900 bis 1906 sieben Bilder und fünfzehn Zeichnungen, die Zervos noch nicht kennt. Die ununterbrochenen Annalen, die bei Zervos für die Frühzeit vorliegen, ersetzt die Ausstellung von 1906 an einigermaßen durch die häufigen Datierungen und gelegentlichen Ortsangaben, die auf den Bildern sich finden. Der äußere Lebenslauf des Meisters ist nach der letzten Rückkehr aus Spanien wenig bewegt, er arbeitet in Paris und seiner weiteren Umgebung, in Südfrankreich,

VIII

---

an der spanischen Grenze und an südlichen und nördlichen französischen Küsten, einmal, 1917, während des Krieges, in Rom. Früh schon hat er als Künstler den Geschlechtsnamen seiner Mutter, das spanisch voll tönende Picásso, angenommen. Paris formt mehr den Namen als den Menschen, wenn es ihn leichter und etwas spitz umprägt in Pícasso.

Die nach kurzem Aufenthalt in Paris so oft wiederholte Rückkehr nach Spanien zu längerem Verbleiben mag ihre ganz einfachen materiellen Gründe haben, an sich wirkt sie wie die Flucht eines Tieres mit immer neuem Raub in seine Höhle. Die Bemühung geht aber nicht um Einverleibung, sondern um Überwindung von Paris, der Jüngling entsagt dem bunten Farbenglanz und wendet sich in weltschmerzlicher Lyrik zu mild blauer Eintönigkeit. Aus seinem Lande, das für Frankreich hinter den Bergen liegt, und aus dem Atem seines Volkes, das anders lebt und fühlt als Mitteleuropa, antwortet er mit Bildern, in denen Trauer und Kümmernis der Seele, Pathos der Armut und des Leides, nicht malerisches Leben der Oberfläche, als Stärkstes sprechen. Die zarte Lyrik auch der auf die blauen folgenden rötlichen Bilder verdichtet sich nach der holländischen Reise und dem letzten längern Aufenthalt in Spanien zu größerer Sicherheit und Spannung. Aus Dulden wird Handeln. Der Jüngling träumt, der Mann faßt zu und gestaltet. Die Körper werden plastisch fest und voll, die milden rötlichen und gelben Töne erhitzen sich zu dunkler Kraft in Braunrot und Schwärzlich, hält dem mit dem Menschenschicksal der in das Bild genommenen Gestalten hereingetragene Geist, sondern der Eigengeist von Formen, Farben und Bewegung im Bild hält dieses nun lebendig. Die massigen Figuren von 1906 und die wild und zackig aufgewühlten Flächen der „Neger“-Zeit bereiten die kubistischen Bilder vor. Wenn die farbige Oberfläche der Welt als optische Verführung und ablenkender Überzug der unter der Oberfläche lebenden Wirklichkeit der Dinge empfunden wird, so ist es denkbar, gleich übertreibend wie ein nur den farbigen Schein aufnehmender Impressionismus, das vom Farbenprisma unabhängige räumliche Sein bloßzulegen, die der schmeichlerischen Epidermis entkleidete, eine enthäutete Welt. So wird

IX

„ohne Farbe“ gemalt, mit „Neutral“-Ton, mit Grau, und werden wie im extremen Impressionismus die farbbildenden Töne, hier die raum-, das heißt formbildenden Flächen in gleichartige Elemente zerlegt und diese ohne angleichende Verschmelzung nur wieder aneinander gefügt.

Wie aber für bildende Kunst Gedachtes nicht anders als in sinnlicher Erscheinung Wirklichkeit werden kann, so werden auch diese nur auf Räumlichkeit bedachten Bilder aus grauen Scherben und Splittern doch wieder Malereien in einer neuen, vielleicht vorerst nicht leicht erkannten Farbigkeit. Die das Bild aufbauenden Flächenteile müssen, damit sie überhaupt nebeneinander deutlich werden, im Helligkeitswert voneinander abgestuft, damit sie als in bestimmten Richtungen und Ebenen liegend raumbildend, plastisch, wirken können, auch in der eigenen Umgrenzung mit auf- und abschwellender Helligkeit ausgestattet sein. Und wie das reinste Quellwasser von Beimischungen nicht frei ist, die ihm seinen besonderen Geschmack und Würze geben, und es von andern Fassungen unterscheiden, so kann, solange Künstler diese Bilder schaffen und menschliche Augen in ihnen lesen, das Mitschwingen von Farbklängen in diesen theoretisch farblosen, nur hell und dunkel abgestuften Gebilden nicht ausgeschlossen werden. Mit leichten Schwebungen von wärmerem oder kälterem Grau durch Einsprengung von Gelblich, Bräunlich, Bläulich, Grün, mit dichterem oder loserem Aneinanderfügen von Tief und Hell scheiden sich die scheinbar gleichartigen kubistischen Gebilde, die von außen her in einer und derselben kühlen Sphäre liegen, in Einzelwerke, von denen jedes mit anderer Intensität und in bestimmter, eigener Art anspricht. Vielleicht ist es die Versuchung zu einer neuen, reinen Malerei, vielleicht das Streben, noch weiter von der äußeren Natur, dem „Fertigfabrikat“ sich frei zu machen, was den Kubismus bald sich selbst vergessen läßt.

Picasso abstrahiert schon im Jahr 1910 nicht nur von der natürlichen Farbe der Dinge, sondern immer stärker auch von ihrer plastischen Eigenform. Eine Arlésenin oder ein „Dichter“ besitzen wenig mehr von den Kuben, in die ihre körperliche Erscheinung hineingesehen oder die aus ihr herausgesehen werden könnten. Das Bild stellt sich dar als eine aufgerissene Fläche, über der Flächenfragmente von verschiedener Form

X

---

und Richtung sich durcheinander schieben, es hat das auf die Fläche gebundene kleinplastische Leben einer verwitterten Felswand oder einer Baumrinde, ohne daß aber Fels oder Rinde damit gegeben sein sollen.

Ein Schritt, und diese Flächensplitter, Striche, Töne schwimmen frei von Bedeutung und Gewicht im absoluten Raum; oder, da wir anders als sinnlich nun einmal kaum sehen können, wie Zeichnungen des Zufalls auf einer Wand. Sie sollen keine Beziehungen mehr haben als ihre eigenen untereinander und zur Fläche, auf der sie liegen — das in sich selber ruhende, sich selbst genügende Kunstwerk — und doch springen, durch bestimmte Zeichen, oft auch durch trügerische Bildbenennungen ausgelöst, aus manchen Teilen Teil-Assoziationen wie Raketen ins Reich der Vorstellungen von einer außerhalb bestehenden, greifbaren Welt. Wenn wir aber die Titel dieser Bilder ganz als ihren Inhalt nehmen, vom Bilde aus das Urbild suchen, so kreuzen wir zu ewigem Mißverstehen den Weg des Malers, der vom Urbild zum Bild geht. Wenn wir erst einmal erkennen wollen, was der Künstler sucht, mit allem Vorbehalt, ob sein Ziel unsern Beifall finde, so müssen wir uns mit dem Rücken gegen die „Natur“ neben ihn stellen und vorwärts sehen; rückwärts blicken ist hier so gefährlich wie für Orpheus und für Lots Weib. Gelöst aus aller Abhängigkeit von vorgeformten, nicht vom Künstler geschaffenen Erscheinungen brauchen die Bilder auch nicht mehr die für die nachahmende Malerei gegebenen Mittel. Wenn Papierschnitzeln im neuen Bild ebenso rein zu Form und Farbe werden wie die bisher im Atelier geübte Malerei, so ist ein aus ihnen geklebtes Bild nicht weniger wert als ein Gemälde. Entscheidend ist der Grad der Entstofflichung, daß im Bilde Papier nicht Papier bleibt, sondern Zeichen und Farbe wird.

Picasso leistet sich und uns den Beweis, daß er Papier, Erde, Glasperlen und andere profane Dinge in reinen Farbenklang innerhalb einer höhern künstlerischen Ordnung verwandeln kann. So darf er, nachdem er sich zum Meister über jeden Stoff gemacht hat, auch die alte Technik der Malerei wieder verwenden mit der Gewißheit, daß sie immer nur ihm, niemals er ihr je dienstbar wird. Er darf auch, was er soeben noch ins Bild geklebt hat um zu malen, nun wirklich malen, wie wenn es nur geklebt wäre.

XI

Und auch die mit Entsagung und Einkehr im Suchen nach der neuen Form
gemiedenen vollen Farben braucht er, da er die neue Form besitzt, nicht
mehr zu fürchten.

Nach behutsamem Übergang mit lichten Tönen, die oft erst nur in
Punkten über den hellen Grund verspritzt sind, und durchscheinendem
Goldblond, füllt sich das Bildviereck mit kompakt aufgestrichenen stark-
farbigen Feldern; und das Bild, anfänglich, wenn auch farbig schon belebt,
in vielfältiger Spaltung und Aufrichtung der Ebene noch plastisch reich
gegliedert, wird ruhiger und schwer. Das farbige Mosaik aus breiten, weniger stark geteilten Flächen, dem freilich ein verhaltenes räumliches Leben
immer eigen bleibt, so daß es nie in Dekoration verläuft, wirkt in der derben
Ölmalerei sinnlich näher; auch die Bildform, die bis um 1914 noch beim
aufgelockerten Kubismus bleibt, wird gröber. Sie nähert sich in verschie-
denen Graden massiver Gegenständlichkeit, wenn auch die Bilder noch
„abstrakt" genannt werden. Die Konsequenz und Disziplin der „Neger"-
und der grauen Zeit scheint mehr empirischen, aus Stimmungsantrieb wäh-
lenden und frei schaltenden Kräften Platz zu machen. Dazu erscheinen im
einzelnen Bild gelegentlich neben einander verschieden weit verarbeitete,
mehr „abstrakte" und mehr naturalistische Bestandteile, und im Gesamt-
werk aus bunten Flächen und Schnitzeln aufgebaute „abstrakte" Kompositionen neben unverletzten vollrunden menschlichen Gestalten. Dies erklärt ohne Zwang die Annahme oder Erkenntnis, daß in diesen Jahren,
während und nach dem Kriege, die Bildform für Picasso nicht mehr Ziel
ist, sondern [wieder] Mittel; Mittel für Ausdruck und Mitteilung eines
gefühlten, seelischen Zustandes. Jedes dieser Bilder steht vor uns in seinem
ganz bestimmten Klang, es wirkt, bevor es irgend etwas anderes sagt,
einmal ernst oder heiter, leicht oder schwer, ruhig oder heftig; und wer
bei der Begegnung mit ihnen, vor der interpretierenden Betrachtung, sich
dieses Grundgefühl, die erste, tiefste Resonanz erhält, kann finden, daß
ein in schweren Tönen mit an sich unkörperlichen Ebenen aufgebauter
„Kamin" wenig anders anspricht als eine ernste Frauenfigur. Ein Gedanke
wird vom gleichen Meister als schlichtes Lied oder als streng geführte
„abstrakte" Fuge musikalisch gestaltet, wir nehmen von ihm ohne Unter-

XII

schied Lieder mit Worten und ohne Worte. Picasso bedingt von 1915 etwa
bis 1925 im ganzen Bereich seiner Malerei sich ähnliche Freiheit aus. Die
Bildnisse seiner Gattin und seines Söhnchens wieder schafft er nur im
Gedanken an sie, Sinfonia domestica.

Mit diesen nach dem Krieg entstehenden Werken bleibt Picasso im
allgemeinen in einer immer lichter und zuversichtlicher sich entfaltenden
Farbigkeit. Bunt wie die Bilder oft in sich selber, wirkt ihre Reihe als Ganzes.
Man wird bei ihrer Betrachtung in der genauen zeitlichen Folge kaum eine
Stufe finden, die nicht durch eine vorausgegangene erkennbar vorbereitet
und erklärt und eine nächste teilweise noch bestätigt würde. Die weniger
auffallende schrittweise Wandlung führt aber im ganzen Ablauf zu überraschenden Wendungen; von gewichtiger, farbiger und plastischer Gehal-
tenheit und Fülle zu stark aufgelichteten, fast schwebenden flächigen Kompositionen und Figuren, zu greller Lustigkeit und Pracht in schmetterndem
und glitzerndem Neben- und Übereinander, bis schließlich jene Abstrak-
tionen und Metamorphosen erscheinen, die vom Künstler plastisch in einer
räumlichen Welt geschaffen dieser angehören, von ihm nun aber einfach
auf die Leinwand herüber gemalt werden, oder die Linienspiele, die er so
oder ähnlich als Zeichnungen und Radierungen erfunden und einmal reali-
siert hat und nun als anmutiges oder beklemmendes Netzwerk über die Mal-
fläche und ihren schwer grau und weißlich oder glanzvoll farbig gefüllten
Raum legt.

Plastiker ist Picasso von Zeit zu Zeit. Die vier Bronzen der Ausstellung
aus den Jahren 1905/08 eröffnen eine Reihe von gegen hundert Arbeiten,
mit denen er manche entscheidende Wendung in seiner Malerei begleitet.
Wie in der Malerei gelangt er auch hier zu technischen Verfahren, Mate-
rialien und Formen, die dem Jahrtausende alten Atelier kaum mehr ver-
pflichtet sind. Doch will er diesen Teil seines Werkes vorerst nicht aus
den Händen geben.

Zeichner ist Picasso von Anfang an und immer. Bei der Beschäftigung
mit den Bildern hat diese Erkenntnis von bloßer Ahnung sich zu zwingender
Gewalt gesteigert. Paris hatte nur Druckgraphik gezeigt. So wurde für

XIII

die Zürcher Ausstellung nach eigenem Plan in letzter Stunde noch eine Abteilung von hundert Zeichnungen aufgebaut, die zeitlich gleich weit ausgreifend wie die Bilder, in ihrer größeren inneren Beweglichkeit noch weitere Bezirke von Picassos künstlerischem Wirkungsbereich erschließen und erhellen konnte. Im Anfang übt er sich in allen denkbaren Verfahren. Er „malt" mit Kreide, Stift und Pinsel Studien für Bilder und ganze Bildentwürfe. Die Feder, das beste Instrument für präzises Umreißen, Zeichnen, der Dinge und Figuren und für freies Spiel von Phantasie und Laune, erhält erst wenig Platz. Die Dienerin wird zur Herrin, die Feder und der fein gespitzte Stift geleiten Picasso zu jener Meisterschaft, die mit dünnen Umrißlinien auf weißem Papier körperliche Rundung und Schwere, leicht atmendes Leben, Licht, Fläche und Tiefe erweckt.

Die Druckgraphik, in Paris nur durch einige Vollardsche Editionen und die Metamorphosen des Ovid vertreten, ist in Zürich erweitert durch eine Sammlung von 30 Einzelblättern, in denen anschließend an die Radierungen „Zirkus und Seiltänzer" von 1904/05 die Formen der Radierung und Lithographie in den zwei Jahrzehnten von 1909 bis 1930 in knapper Auswahl lebendig werden. An sie wieder schließen sich die vollständigen Folgen des „Chef d'oeuvre inconnu" und des Ovid von 1931, licht- und schattenlose Linienspiele, deren Schönheit und Kraft im stillen Schwingen und Gleiten der unkörperlichen Kompositionen sich erwahrt; und die ganze Reihe der Vorzeichnungen zum Ovid, wie sie in sparsamsten, gewichtlosen Bleistiftlinien von reinstem Fluß als wild durchwühlte Kämpfe, ausdruckschwere Köpfe, ruhige Unterhaltung fertig und unabänderlich geprägt dem Haupt des Meisters und seiner Hand entsprungen sind.

In einem Augenblick, da Schwierigkeiten eine Verschiebung der Ausstellung zu gebieten schienen, erklärte Picasso, Zürich müßte dabei nicht verlieren, es würden später ja nur um so mehr und neue, wieder andere Bilder als gegenwärtig zur Verfügung stehen. Er bekennt sich lächelnd zu dem, was ihm die öffentliche Meinung am wenigsten verzeiht, die rasche Wandlung im Aussehen seiner Bilder. Vor der einstweilen letzten Phase von 1931/32 mit den sitzenden und liegenden weiblichen Halbfiguren und

XIV

den plastisch gefaßten Kompositionen überläßt der staunende Betrachter es gern dem Künstler den Weg zu finden zu einer neuen fruchtbaren Wendung. Inzwischen erweisen sich die Zeichnungen zu Ovid als aufschlußreich. Auf kleinster Fläche und mit schlichtesten Mitteln erhält Picasso in der gleichen Handschrift die Größe und das Pathos einer fernen Götter- und Heldenwelt wie in den Bildern das Pathos eines scheinbar ganz neuen künstlerischen Willens. Wo man ihn für entfesselt und hemmungslos halten möchte, ist er geläutert, erfüllt er sein Gesetz. Die Farben klingen, die Linien kreisen und schwingen, die Flächen, die mit ihren Umrissen und Tönen zusammen- und wieder auseinanderstreben, sich suchen und meiden, überdecken und durchdringen, ruhen schließlich fest gebettet in organischem Verband. Jedes dieser Bilder geht klar und unverlierbar in uns ein. Wenn wir aber glauben, sie nur Hand in Hand mit einer zugehörigen Vorstellung aus der „natürlichen" Welt einlassen zu dürfen, so verlieren wir uns selber auf der Suche nach solchen Gefährten und in der Auseinandersetzung mit den ungleichen Paaren.

Gilt dies nicht gleich schon für die Bilder der „Neger"-Zeit, die kubistischen und alle seitherigen in so verschiedenem Grad „abstrakten"? Zwischen Geist und Stoff ist Abgrund, das Kunstwerk ist die Brücke, Picasso baut unzählige und will immer neu und besser bauen. Uneinig sind wir vor der Frage: was ist Natur? Stoff oder Geist? Mensch oder Welt? Wenn sie das ist, was wir mit Sinnen und Verstand zu fassen trachten, das Andere, zu dem wir manchmal vor uns selber flüchten, das, was draußen liegt, so tut die Kunst Picassos ihr Gewalt an und ist unnatürlich; wenn wir als Mensch sie fühlend in uns tragen, sie selber sind, so folgt er ihr.

W. WARTMANN.

XV

Das nachfolgende Verzeichnis gibt mit den Titeln die Sig-
naturen und Datierungen auf der Vorder- und Rückseite der
Werke; die Bezeichnungen „G. P." und „Zervos" verweisen
auf die Nummern des Kataloges der Picasso-Ausstellung vom
Sommer 1932 bei Georges Petit Paris und des Verzeichnisses
in „Pablo Picasso par Christian Zervos vol. I Edition Cahiers
d'Art Paris (1931)"; die Hinweise „TAFEL . . ." beziehen sich
auf den Bilderanhang nach Seite 25 dieses Kataloges zur
Zürcher Picasso-Ausstellung.

GEMÄLDE

1 **Der Springbrunnen**
P. Ruiz Picasso
56×61
Zervos 5
A. Pkira, Lausanne   1898
verkäuflich

2 **Im Restaurant Duval**
Picasso
81×45
Gal. Neupert, Zürich   1901
verkäuflich

3 **Stierkampf**
Picasso
56×47
G. P. 2;
Zervos 88
1901
M. Ambroise Vollard, Paris

4 **Akt im Atelier**
Picasso
36,5×50,5
Zervos 50
Kruel / Flechtheim, Düsseldorf   1901
verkäuflich

5 **Begräbnis**
Picasso
90×100
G. P. 6;
Zervos 52
Gal. Pierre, Paris   1901
verkäuflich

6 **Evocation**
Picasso
91,5×150
G. P. 7;
Zervos 55
TAFEL II   1901
M. Ambroise Vollard, Paris

7 **Bildnis Gustave Coquiot**
Picasso
80,5×100
G. P. 5;
Zervos 84
1901
verkäuflich

8 siehe unten S. 2 nach Nr. 17

9 **Liegender Akt**
Picasso
90×70,5
G. P. 13;
Zervos 106
1901
Baron Napoléon Gourgaud,
Paris

10 **Frau mit verschränkten Armen**
Picasso
58,5×81
Zervos 105
1901
Baron G, Berlin

11 **Mutter und Kind**
Picasso
31×46,5
Zervos 110
1901/02
Herr Geo Reinhart, Winterthur

12 **Mutter und Kind**
Picasso
60×92
G. P. 4;
Zervos 109
Bernheim jeune, & C.ie Paris   1901/02
verkäuflich

13 **Trauer**
69×100
G. P. 25;
Zervos 133
P. Guillaume, Paris   1902
verkäuflich

1

14	Das blaue Haus Picasso	40,5×50 G. P. 9	Mlle Gertrud Stein, Paris	1902
15	Bildnis Corinna Pere Ro- meu Picasso	50×60 G. P. 10; Zervos 130	M. Picasso, Paris	1902
16	Männliches Bildnis Picasso	78×90 G. P. 12; Zervos 142	M. Picasso, Paris	1902
17	Weibliches Brustbild Picasso	52,5×63 G. P. 11; Zervos 155	M. Picasso, Paris	1902
8	Kopf eines jungen Mäd- chens 1903	32×40	*A. Flechtheim, Berlin* verkäuflich	1903
18	Das Leben Picasso	129,5×196 G. P. 17; Zervos 179	*gal. Thannhauser, Luzern* *k. Bignou, Paris* TAFEL IIII verkäuflich	1903
19	Selbstbildnis	60×81 G. P. 3; Zervos 91	TAFEL I M. Picasso, Paris	1903
20	Landschaft Barcelona	115×71 G. P. 14; Zervos 207	M. Picasso, Paris	1903
21	Celestina Picasso Rücks. Mz 1904 auf Blindrahmen: Carlota Valdivia Calle Conde Asalto 12- 4⁰ 1ª Esca- lera interior	56×70 G. P. 23; Zervos 183	M. Picasso, Paris	1904
22	Frau mit Krähe Picasso 1904	48,5×65 G. P. 24; Zervos 240	*P. Guillaume, Paris* TAFEL IV verkäuflich	1904
23	Blumen in Vase Picasso	46,5×65,5 G. P. 22; Zervos 242	Herzogin von Roxburghe, London	1904
224	Ein Menschenpaar Picasso	80,5×100 Zervos 224	Herr B. Mayer, Zürich	1904
24	Kopf eines Harlekin Picasso	26,5×35,5 Zervos 252	Herr A. Vömel, Düsseldorf	1905

2

25	**Harlekin und Frau** Picasso	54 × 69		1905 Herr Marcel Fleischmann, Zürich

25 **Harlekin und Frau**
Picasso
54 × 69
1905
Herr Marcel Fleischmann, Zürich

26 **Mädchen mit Blumenkorb**
Picasso
Rücks. Picasso 13 Rue Ravignan
1905
66,5 × 156,5
G. P. 37;
Zervos 256
1905
Mlle Gertrud Stein, Paris

27 **Junge Kunstreiterin**
79 × 60
G. P. 26;
1905
M. Picasso, Paris

28 **Die jungen Akrobaten**
60 × 81
G. P. 27;
1905
M. Picasso, Paris

29 **Frauenkopf im Profil**
Rücks. Blindrahmen: Picasso
38 × 46
G. P. 38
1905
Herr Joseph Müller, Solothurn

30 **Frau beim Frisieren**
Picasso
65 × 81
G. P. 34;
Zervos 309
P. Rosenberg, Paris
verkäuflich
1905

31 **Frau im Hemd**
Picasso 05
60 × 73
G. P. 31;
Zervos 307
1905
Mr. C. Frank Stoop, London

32 **Mädchen mit offenem Haar**
Picasso
54 × 81
G. P. 30;
Zervos 328
P. Guillaume, Paris
verkäuflich
1905/06

33 **Jüngling und Mädchen**
Picasso
118 × 158
G. P. 42;
Zervos 324
P. Guillaume, Paris
verkäuflich
1906

34 **Mädchen beim Haar-
flechten**
Picasso
81 × 106
G. P. 39;
Zervos 344
1906
M. Ambroise Vollard, Paris

35 **Zwei Mädchenakte**
Picasso
100 × 150,5
G. P. 40;
Zervos 360
TAFEL V   1906
Herr Joseph Müller, Solothurn

36 **Zwei weibliche Akte**
Picasso
93 × 151,5
G. P. 41;
Zervos 366
P. Rosenberg, Paris
verkäuflich
1906

37 **Negerkopf**
Picasso
43 × 62
G. P. 44
Gal. Pierre, Paris
verkäuflich
1907

3

38 **Kopf, braun** Picasso	46×54,5 G. P. 43		1907 M. Paul Chadourne, Paris
39 **Kopf, blau** Rücks. Picasso	60×73 G. P. 47		1907 M. Alfred Gold, Paris
40 **Weiblicher Kopf**	46,5×61 G. P. 46		1907 Mlle Gertrud Stein, Paris
41 **Die drei Masken** Picasso	99,5×99,5 G. P. 51		1908 Herr Dr. G. F. Reber, Lausanne
42 **Negertänzerin** Picasso	43,5×63 G. P. 45		1908 M. René Gaffé, Brüssel
43 **Tänzerin** Picasso	99,5×151 G. P. 69	*P. Guillaume,* TAFEL VI *verkäuflich Paris*	1908
44 **Stilleben, zwei Töpfe und Zitrone** Rücks. Blindrahmen: Picasso	46×54,5 G. P. 48		1908 Mr. Clive Bell, London
45 **Männliche Halbfigur** Picasso	73×92 G. P. 49	*Gal. Percier, Paris* *verkäuflich*	1908
46 **Sitzender Frauenakt** Picasso	89×115,5 G. P. 52		1908 Galerie Percier, Paris
47 **Frau mit Mandoline** Picasso	81×100 G. P. 62	*gal. Pierre,* *verkäuflich*	1909
48 **Spanische Landschaft** Picasso	65×54 G. P. 56		1909 M. Ambroise Vollard, Paris
49 **Stilleben, Wasserflasche Fruchtschale, Kerzenstock** Picasso	73,5×54,5 G. P. 54		1909 M. Ambroise Vollard, Paris
50 **Spanische Landschaft**	50×60 G. P. 57		1909 Mlle Gertrud Stein, Paris
51 **Spanische Landschaft**	81×65,5 G. P. 58		1909 Mlle Gertrud Stein, Paris
52 **Frau mit Birnen** Rücks. Picasso	73×92 G. P. 50		1909 Herr Alfred Flechtheim, Berlin
53 **Akt im Lehnstuhl**	73×92,5 G. P. 59	TAFEL VII Herr Dr. G. F. Reber, Lausanne	1909
54 **Sitzende Frau** Picasso 9	73×92 G. P. 61	*gal. Pierre, Paris* *verkäuflich*	1909

4

55	**Frau mit Mandoline** Picasso 10 Rücks. Picasso	73×100 G. P. 67	M. René Gaffé, Brüssel	1910
56	**Bildnis Uhde**	60×81 G. P. 66	M. René Gaffé, Brüssel	1910
57	**Arlésienne** Rücks. Picasso	54×73 G. P. 73	TAFEL VIII Herr A. Flechtheim, Berlin	1910
58	**Mlle Léonie** Picasso 10 Rücks. Picasso	49,5×65 G. P. 65	Herr Dr. E. Hoffmann-Stehlin, Basel	1910
67	**Der Dichter** Picasso 10 Rücks. Picasso Céret	89×131	TAFEL IX Galerie A. Flechtheim, Berlin	1910
59	**Stilleben** Picasso Rücks. Picasso	46×61 G. P. 64	M. Ambroise Vollard, Paris	1910
60	**Die Studentin** Rücks. Picasso	33×45,5	Herr Dr. E. Friedrich, Zürich	1910
61	**Essig- und Ölgestell** Rücks. Picasso j. 1911	19×24 G. P. 70	M. Antoine Villard, Paris	1911
62	**Erinnerung an Le Havre** Rücks. Picasso	53,5×80 G. P. 72	M. Raoul La Roche, Paris	1911
63	**Die toten Vögel** Rücks. Picasso. Sorgues 1912	65×45,5 G. P. 77	Herr A. Flechtheim, Berlin	1912
64	**Die Jakobsmuscheln oder „Notre avenir est dans l'air"** Rücks. Picasso	55×38 G. P. 76	Herr Joseph Müller, Solothurn	1912
65	**Herrenbildnis** Rücks. Picasso	48×60 G. P. 78	Herr Dr. E. Hoffmann-Stehlin, Basel	1912
66	**Frau mit Gitarre** Rücks. Picasso	65×100 G. P. 79	Herr Marcel Fleischmann, Zürich	1912
67	siehe oben S. 5 nach Nr. 58			
68	**Mann mit Klarinette** Rücks. Picasso	69,5×105 G. P. 80	Herr Dr. G. F. Reber, Lausanne	1912
69	**Buffalo Bill** Rücks. Picasso	33×46 G. P. 71	Herr Joseph Müller, Solothurn	1912

5

70 **Mädchen und Soldat**
Picasso
Rücks. Picasso

83,5 × 120,5
G. P. 81

gal. Pierre, Paris
verkäuflich 1912

71 **Figur**
Rücks. Picasso

47 × 125
G. P. 74

1912
M. René Gaffé, Brüssel

72 **Stilleben**

46 × 62
G. P. 82

1912/13
M. Tristan Tzara, Paris

73 **Stilleben**
Rücks. Picasso

62 × 57
G. P. 83

1912/13
M. Tristan Tzara, Paris

74 **Kopf**

33 × 43
G. P. 84

1913
M. André Breton, Paris

75 **Der Student**

59 × 73
G. P. 86

1913
Mlle Gertrud Stein, Paris

76 **Stilleben mit Zeitung**
Rücks. Picasso

60 × 73

1913
M. Raoul La Roche, Paris

77 **Stilleben mit Zeitung**
Picasso CÉRET

89 × 130

1913
M. Raoul La Roche, Paris

78 **Geige an der Wand**
Rücks. Un violon accroché au mur
1913 Picasso

45,5 × 65

1913
Herr H. Rupf-Wirz, Bern

79 **Frau in Lehnstuhl**
Rücks. Picasso PARIS 1913

100 × 150
G. P. 89

1913
Fräulein Ingeborg Eichmann,
Arnau

80 **Stilleben mit Pfeife**
Picasso

24 × 18
G. P. 90

gal. Georges Geht, Paris
verkäuflich 1914

81 **Flasche, Pfeife und Karte**
PICASSO

31 × 52

1914
Herr Alfred Flechtheim, Berlin

82 **Die Traube**

43 × 48
G. P. 91

1914
M. Darius Milhaud, Paris

83 **Stilleben**

80,5 × 75
G. P. 97

1914
M. Raoul La Roche, Paris

84 **Cheminée**
Picasso 1914

66,5 × 52

1914
Herr Alfred Flechtheim, Berlin

85 **Mann mit Gitarre**
Rücks. Picasso CÉRET PARIS 1914

89 × 130

TAFEL X 1914
M. Raoul La Roche, Paris

6

86	„Ma Jolie" Stilleben mit Flasche, Spiel- karten, Zeitungen, Pfeife Rücks. Picasso	67,5 × 51,5 G. P. 96	TAFEL XXII verkäuflich *Paul Rosenberg, Paris*	1914
87	Stilleben mit Zeitung Picasso 1914	41 × 33 G. P. 94	Mlle Gertrud Stein, Paris	1914
88	Flasche mit Strohhülle Picasso 1914	46 × 38 G. P. 95	Mlle Gertrud Stein, Paris	1914
89	Bildnis auf Grün Rücks. Picasso	97 × 130 G. P. 98	Mme Errazuriz, Paris	1914
90	Komposition Picasso	15 × 21	M. Paul Eluard, Paris	1914
91	Das Lesepult	104 × 133 G. P. 100	*P. Picasso, Paris* verkäuflich	1915 *Ankauf Sammlung*
92	Cheminée mit Gitarre Picasso 15	96 × 130	TAFEL XI M. Georges Wildenstein, Paris	1915 *verkäuflich*
93	Aufrechte Gestalt Picasso 1915—16	134 × 199 G. P. 101	Mme Errazuriz, Paris	1915/16
94	Zwei Harlekine Picasso Rome 1917	200 × 200,5 G. P. 106	Baron Napoléon Gourgaud, Paris	1917
95	Die Italienerin Picasso ROME 1917	101 × 149	*Wildenstein, Paris* TAFEL XII verkäuflich	1917
96	Die Mahlzeit der Bauern Nach Le Nain	117,5 × 164 G. P. 107	M. Picasso, Paris	1917
97	Bildnis der Gattin des Künstlers	88 × 130 G. P. 105	M. Picasso, Paris	1917
98	Bildnis Mme Picasso, Kopf Rücks. PORTRAIT DE Olga PI- CASSO NÉE KOKLOVA, FAIT A MONTROUGE LE 27 JANVIER DE 1918	28 × 35	M. Picasso, Paris	1918
99	Musizierender Harlekin Picasso 1918	27 × 35	G. und L. Bollag, Zürich	1918

7

100	**Stilleben, Früchte und Konfekt** Picasso 1918	35 × 27		1918 G. und L. Bollag, Zürich
101	**Harlekin mit Gitarre** Picasso	77 × 98 G. P. 109		1918 Herr Dr. G. F. Reber, Lausanne
102	**Kind mit Reif** Picasso 19	78,5 × 142,5 G. P. 111		1919 Baron Napoléon Gourgaud, Paris
103	**Die Staffelei des Malers** Picasso 1920	110 × 165 G. P. 112	*J. Rosenberg* verkäuflich *Paris*	TAFEL XIII 1920
104	**Die Gitarre** Picasso 20	92 × 64,5 G. P. 114	verkäuflich *do.*	1920
105	**Zwei Frauenakte** Picasso 20	162,5 × 194,5 G. P. 115		1920 Herr Dr. G. F. Reber, Lausanne
106	**Knabenkopf**	27,5 × 32		1920 M. Picasso, Paris
107	**Die drei Musikanten** Picasso Fontainebleau 1921	188,5 × 204 G. P. 119		1921 Herr Dr. G. F. Reber, Lausanne
108	**Sitzende Frau von vorn** Picasso 21	73 × 116		TAFEL XIV 1921 Fräulein Ingeborg Eichmann, Arnau
109	**Mutter und Kind** Picasso	71 × 98 G. P. 117	*A. Flechtheim, Berlin* verkäuflich	1921
110	**Cheminée** Picasso	74 × 105 G. P. 116		1921 Galeries Georges Petit, Paris
111	**Frau mit Hut** Picasso	89 × 117,5 G. P. 118	*P. Guillaume, Paris* verkäuflich	1921
112	**Die drei Musikanten** Picasso Fontainebleau 1921	204 × 226 G. P. 120		TAFEL XXIII 1921 M. Paul Rosenberg, Paris
172	**Stilleben mit Zeitung** Picasso 21	92 × 73	*J. Wildenstein, Paris* verkäuflich	1921
113	**Stilleben im Fenster** Picasso	140 × 200 G. P. 121	*J. Rosenberg* verkäuflich	1921/22
114	**Kind beim Essen**	31 × 37		1921/22 M. Picasso, Paris

8

115 **Kind mit weißer Mütze**   24×33   1922
Rücks. Blindrahmen: M. Picasso, Paris
    Dinard Septembre 1922

116 **Kleiner Knabe, Brustbild**   33×46   1922
Rücks. Dinard Septembre 1922   M. Picasso, Paris

117 **Stilleben mit Gitarre**   103×83   *Knoedler & C⁰ New York* 1922
Picasso 22   G. P. 122   verkäuflich

118 **Komposition**   100×82   *Alex Reid, Lefèvre, London* 1922
Picasso   G. P. 123   verkäuflich

119 **Die grüne Bluse**   97×130   1922
Picasso 22   G. P. 124   Herr Willy Strecker, Wiesbaden

120 **Fische auf einem Tisch**   96×130   1922/23
Picasso 22—23   G. P. 125   Herr Dr. G. F. Reber, Lausanne
Rücks. Blindrahmen:
    Dinard 1922— PARIS 1923

121 **Kind mit Spielzeug**   73×103   1923
    G. P. 126   M. Picasso, Paris

122 **Die Griechin**   77×186   *Alex Reid, Lefèvre, London* 1923
Picasso   G. P. 137   verkäuflich

123 **Frauenkopf**   23×33   1923
Rücks. Blindrahmen: 10-11-23   M. Picasso, Paris

124 **Figuren am Strand**   100×81   1923
Picasso 23   G. P. 129   M. Valentine Dudensing,
    New York

125 **Der blaue Schleier**   81×100   1923
Picasso 23   G. P. 131   Herr Dr. G. F. Reber, Lausanne
Rücks. Blindrahmen: 13 Avril 1923

126 **Ausruhender Akrobat**   97×130   TAFEL XV   1923
Picasso 23   G. P. 134   Herr Dr. G. F. Reber, Lausanne

127 **Tisch vor dem Fenster**   96,5×130,5   1923
Picasso 23   G. P. 135   Herr Dr. G. F. Reber, Lausanne

128 **Frau und Kind**   97×130   1923
Picasso   G. P. 136   M. Pierre Matisse, New York

129 **Die Pansflöte**   174×205   1923
    G. P. 138   verkäuflich *P. Picasso*

130 **La petite cuisine**   55×45,5   1923
Picasso 23   G. P. 127   Herr Dr. G. F. Reber, Lausanne

9

131	**Äpfel** Picasso 23	33 × 24	*Gal. Thannhauser* verkäuflich		1923
132	**Kind mit weißem Hut** Rücks. Blindrahmen: Paris — 14 Avril 1923	22 × 27	M. Picasso, Paris		1923
133	**Harlekin von vorn** Picasso 23	97 × 130	*A. Flechtheim* verkäuflich *Berlin*	TAFEL XVI	1923
134	**Stilleben** Picasso	72 × 97,5 G. P. 128	Herr Dr. E. Hoffmann-Stehlin, Basel		1923
135	**Kinderbildnis**	19 × 24	M. Picasso, Paris		1923
136	**Frau mit Kind**	10 × 15	M. Picasso, Paris		1923
137	**Kinderkopf, Harlekin** Rücks. Blindrahmen: 4 mars 24	27 × 34	M. Picasso, Paris		1924
138	**Der kleine Harlekin**	97,5 × 130,5 G. P. 148	M. Picasso, Paris		1924
139	**Juan-les-Pins** Picasso 24	41 × 24 G. P. 139	Frau E. Staub-Terlinden, Männedorf		1924
140	**Weinkrug, Fruchtschale, Gitarre, Sterne** Picasso 24	130 × 97 G. P. 153	*P. Rosenberg* verkäuflich *Paris*	TAFEL XXIV	1924
141	**Badende Frauen** 24 Picasso	41 × 33 G. P. 141	Herr Dr. G. F. Reber, Lausanne		1924
142	**Stilleben auf Sand** Picasso 24	100 × 80 G. P. 143	Herr Dr. G. F. Reber, Lausanne		1924
143	**Komposition in braun und weiß** Picasso 24	105 × 77 G. P. 144	Herr Dr. G. F. Reber, Lausanne		1924
144	**Stilleben mit Fruchtkorb** Picasso 24	130 × 97 G. P. 149	Herr Dr. G. F. Reber, Lausanne		1924
145	**Gitarre, Trinkglas und Fruchtschale** Picasso 24	130 × 97 G. P. 147	Frau E. Staub-Terlinden, Männedorf		1924
146	**Der Tisch des Musikers** Picasso 24	109 × 88 G. P. 145	Herr Hermann Lange, Krefeld		1924

10

147	**Musizierender Harlekin** Picasso 24	97 × 131 G. P. 152	Herr Dr. G. F. Reber, Lausanne	1924
148	**Imbiß** Picasso 24	101 × 82,5 G. P. 130	M. Paul Rosenberg, Paris	1924
149	**Stilleben vor dem Fenster** Picasso 24	202,5 × 142 G. P. 156	Herr Dr. G. F. Reber, Lausanne	1924
150	**Der rote Teppich** Picasso 24 Rücks. Blindrahmen: Décembre 1924	130 × 97 G. P. 154	M. Paul Rosenberg, Paris	1924
151	**Der Vogelkäfig** Picasso 25 Rücks. Blindrahmen: 13-1-25-	101 × 81,5 G. P. 163	*P. Rosenberg, Paris* verkäuflich	1925
152	**Kleiner Pierrot mit Maske** Rücks. XXVIII-II-XXV-	97 × 130,5 G. P. 166	TAFEL XVII M. Picasso, Paris	1925
153	**Frauenkopf** Picasso 24 Rücks. Blindrahmen: Février 1925	27 × 35 G. P. 140	*X. Villoughby, Paris* verkäuflich	1925
154	**Sitzende Frau mit Gitarre und Notenblatt** Picasso 25	97,5 × 130 G. P. 151	TAFEL XVIII M. Paul Rosenberg, Paris	1925
155	**Stilleben** Picasso 25 Rücks. Blindrahmen: Juan les Pins 1925	131 × 98 G. P. 158	TAFEL XXV Vicomte de Noailles, Paris	1925
156	**Liegende Tänzerin mit Tamburin** Picasso 25	130,5 × 98 G. P. 167	*P. Guillaume, Paris* verkäuflich	1925
157	**Stilleben mit Fischernetz** Picasso 25 Rücks. Blindrahmen: Juan les Pins 1925	82 × 101 G. P. 161	M. Paul Rosenberg, Paris	1925
158	**Das Atelier** Picasso 25 Rücks. Blindrahmen: Juan les Pins 1925	131 × 98 G. P. 160	Herr Dr. G. F. Reber, Lausanne	1925
159	**Der Tisch des Bildhauers** Picasso 25 Rücks. Blindrahmen: 1er Juin 1925	130 × 97,5 G. P. 164	M. Paul Rosenberg, Paris	1925

11

186 **Metamorphose**
Picasso 29
60 × 73
G. P. 184   verkäuflich *Rosenberg*   1929

187 **Figur am Strand**
Picasso 29
97 × 129,5
G. P. 187   verkäuflich *A. Reid y Lefèvre, London*   1929

188 **Badende**
130 × 162
G. P. 190   verkäuflich *Picasso*   TAFEL XIX   1929

189 **Kleiner Pierrot mit Blumen, Sohn des Künstlers**
Picasso 29
Rücks. PARIS le 12 Juillet 1929
97 × 130,5
G. P. 188   M. Picasso, Paris   1929

190 **Das Atelier des Künstlers**
Picasso XXIX
Rücks. Blindrahmen:
     Paris 22 Novembre XXIX
173 × 130,5
G. P. 189   verkäuflich *P. Rosenberg*   TAFEL XXVIII   1929

191 **Abstraktion**
Picasso 4-I-XXX
49 × 66
G. P. 192   verkäuflich *Rees Jeffreys, London / galerie Georges Petit, Jigноn*   1930

192 **Abstraktion**
Picasso 25-I-XXX
48 × 65
G. P. 194   verkäuflich *do.*   1930

193 **Abstraktion**
Picasso 26-I-XXX
49 × 66
G. P. 191   verkäuflich *do.*   1930

194 **Abstraktion**
Picasso - 27-I-XXX
49 × 66
G. P. 193   verkäuflich *do.*   1930

195 **Metamorphose**
Picasso I-II-XXX
49 × 66,5
G. P. 195   verkäuflich *do.*   1930

196 **Kreuzigung**
Rücks. 7-II-XXX-
66,5 × 51
G. P. 196   M. Picasso, Paris   1930

197 **Figuren am Strand**
Rücks. Blindrahmen: 12-I-XXXI-
195,5 × 130,5
G. P. 203   verkäuflich *P. Picasso*   TAFEL XXIX   1931

198 **Krug und Fruchtschale**
Picasso XXXI
Rücks. Blindrahmen: 11-II-XXXI
195 × 131
G. P. 204   verkäuflich *P. Rosenberg*   1931

199 **Cheminée**
Picasso XXXI
Rücks. Blindrahmen: 14-II-XXXI
195,5 × 131
G. P. 205   verkäuflich *do.*   TAFEL XXX   1931

200 **Krug und Fruchtschale**
Picasso XXXI
Rücks. Blindrahmen: 22-II-XXXI-
162 × 130
G. P. 202   verkäuflich *do.*   TAFEL XXXI   1931

14

201	**Die Lampe**	131 × 163,5			*Picasso*	1931
	Rücks. Blindrahmen: 8-VI-XXXI-	G. P. 201	verkäuflich		
202	**Der Bildhauer**	98 × 130		TAFEL XX	1931
	Rücks. 7 - Décembre M. CM. XXXI.	G. P. 198	verkäuflich	*do.*	
202a	**Die eingeschlafene Leserin**	50,5 × 65,5			1931
	Rücks.11 Décembre M.CM.XXXII.[sic]	G. P. 197	verkäuflich	*do.*	
203	**Frau in rotem Lehnstuhl**	98 × 130			1931
	Rücks. 16 Décembre M. CM. XXXI.	G. P. 199	verkäuflich	*do.*	
204	**Die Leserin**	97 × 130			1932
	Rücks. Blindrahmen:	G. P. 207	verkäuflich	*do.*	
	2 Janvier M. CM. XXXII.				
205	**Der gelbe Gürtel**	96,5 × 132			1932
	Rücks. Blindrahmen:	G. P. 208	verkäuflich	*do.*	
	6 Janvier M. CM. XXXII				
206	**Mädchen mit Gitarre**	49 × 66			1932
	Rücks. 10 Janvier M.CM. XXXII.	G. P. 206	verkäuflich	*do.*	
207	**Schläferin vor dem Spiegel**	97 × 130			1932
	Rücks. 14 - Janvier M. CM. XXXII.	G. P. 210	verkäuflich	*do.*	
208	**Stilleben am Fenster**	162 × 130		TAFEL XXXII	1932
	Rücks. Blindrahmen: 18-I-XXXII-	G. P. 219	verkäuflich	*do.*	
209	**Ruhende**	130 × 162			1932
	Rücks. Blindrahmen: 22-I-XXXII-	G. P. 220	verkäuflich	*do.*	
210	**Schlummernde**	97 × 130			1932
	Rücks. Blindrahmen: De 3 H. à 6 H-	G. P. 209	verkäuflich	*do.*	
	23 - Janvier M. CM. XXXII.				
211	**Der Traum**	97 × 130			1932
	Rücks. Blindrahmen:	G. P. 211	verkäuflich	*do.*	
	Fait dans l'après midi du				
	dimanche 24 Janvier				
	M. CM. XXXII.				
212	**Figur vor schwarzem Grund**	97 × 130			1932
	Rücks. 27-Janvier-XXXII.	G. P. 212	verkäuflich	*do.*	
213	**Fruchtschale und Gitarre**	130 × 97,5			1932
	vor grauem Grund	G. P. 214	verkäuflich	*do.*	
	Rücks. 11 Février XXXII				
	fait entre 2 Hs et 4 Hs				

214	Fruchtschale und Gitarre Rücks. 13-2-32-	130×97 G. P. 213	verkäuflich	*Picasso*	1932
215	siehe unten nach Nr. 221				
216	Stilleben mit Tulpen Rücks. 2 Mars XXXII De 9 Hs. à 11½ Hs	97×130 G. P. 216	verkäuflich	*do*	1932
217	Akt vor blauem Vorhang Rücks. Blindrahmen: 6 Mars XXXII	131×161 G. P. 223	verkäuflich	*do.*	1932
218	Akt in schwarzem Lehnstuhl Rücks. Blindrahmen: 9 Mars XXXII	131×162 G. P. 221	verkäuflich	*di.*	1932
219	Der Spiegel Rücks. Blindrahmen: 12 Mars XXXII	97×130 G. P. 217	verkäuflich	*do.*	1932
220	Mädchen vor dem Spiegel Rücks. Blindrahmen: 14 mars XXXII	130×162 G. P. 200	verkäuflich	TAFEL XXI *di.*	1932
221	Frau mit Blumen Rücks. Blindrahmen: 10 - AVRIL - XXXII-	130,5×162 G. P. 222	verkäuflich	*do.*	1932
215	Frau in gelbem Lehnstuhl Rücks. Blindrahmen: Avril XXXII	97×130 G. P. 218	verkäuflich	*do.*	1932
223	Figur in rotem Lehnstuhl	97×130 G. P. 215	verkäuflich	*do.*	1932
224	siehe oben S. 2 nach Nr. 23				

PLASTIK

227	Harlekin	Bronze	G. P. 225	Zervos 322	verkäuflich	um 1905/6
228	Frauenbüste	Bronze	G. P. 224	Zervos 323	verkäuflich	um 1905/6
229	Figur	Bronze	G. P. 227	Zervos 329	verkäuflich	um 1905/6
230	Männerbüste	Bronze	G. P. 226		verkäuflich	um 1908

a. Vollard

16

LIST OF WORKS
WORKS EXHIBITED AT THE KUNSTHAUS ZÜRICH, 1932

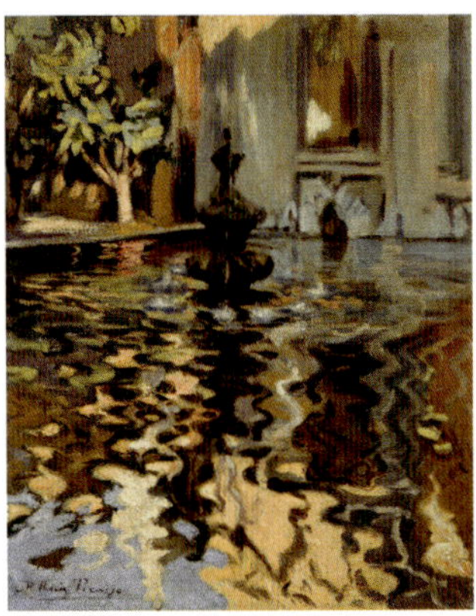

1

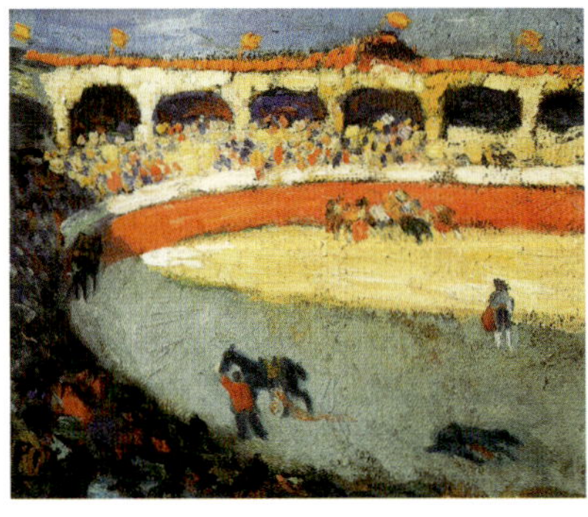

3

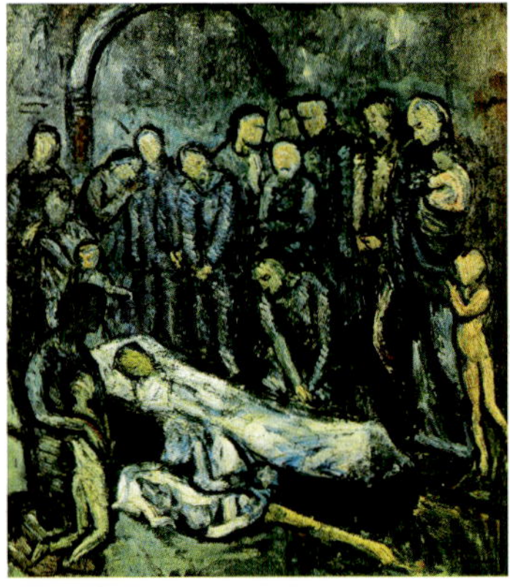

5

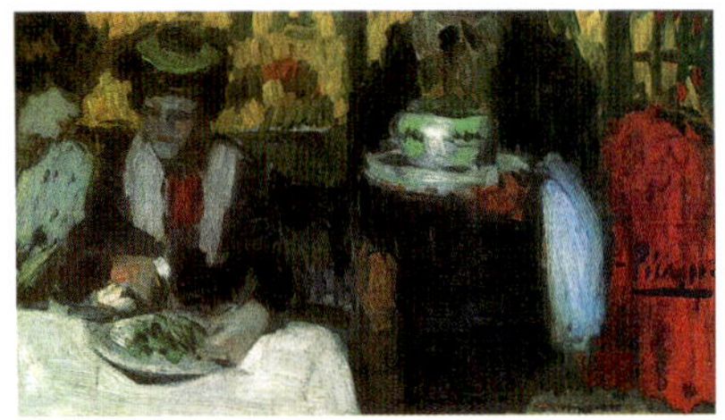

2

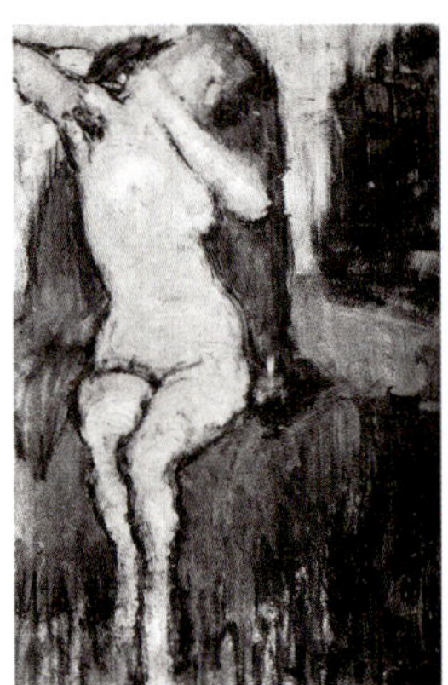

4

6

Cat. Zurich 1
Der Springbrunnen
La fontaine dans le cloître de la
cathédrale de Barcelone, 1899
The Fountain
Oil on canvas, 61 x 50.8 cm
Musée Jenisch, Vevey
Bequest of Alain Ollivier
Zervos: I, no. 5
Plate 1

Cat. Zurich 2
Im Restaurant Duval
Au café de la Rotonde
(L'hippodrome), 1901
At the Café de la Rotonde
(L'Hippodrome)
Oil on canvas, 46 x 81.3 cm
The Kreeger Museum, Washington, D.C.
Zervos: VI, no. 1466

Cat. Zurich 3
Stierkampf
Course de taureaux (Corrida), 1901
The Bullfight (Corrida)
Oil on canvas, 47 x 55.5 cm
Private collection
Zervos: I, no. 88

Cat. Zurich 4
Akt im Atelier
Nu assis, 1901
Seated Nude
Oil on wood, 50.5 x 36.5 cm
Private collection
Zervos: I, no. 50

Cat. Zurich 5
Begräbnis
Le mort, 1901
Death
Oil on canvas, 100 x 90 cm
Private collection
Zervos: I, no. 52

Cat. Zurich 6
Evocation
Évocation (L'enterrement de
Casagemas), 1901
Evocation (The Funeral of Casagemas)
Oil on canvas, 150.5 x 90.5 cm
Musée d'Art Moderne de la Ville de Paris
Zervos: I, no. 55

The chronology and numbering of the exhibition catalogue of 1932 are often not consistent due to editorial oversights. ■ With the exception of the printed graphic works, the more than 200 works on paper which were subsequently added to the 1932 exhibition can no longer be identified because of the lack of documentation. ■ Of the four sculptures exhibited in 1932, one can no longer be identified, probably due to erroneous details in the catalogue.

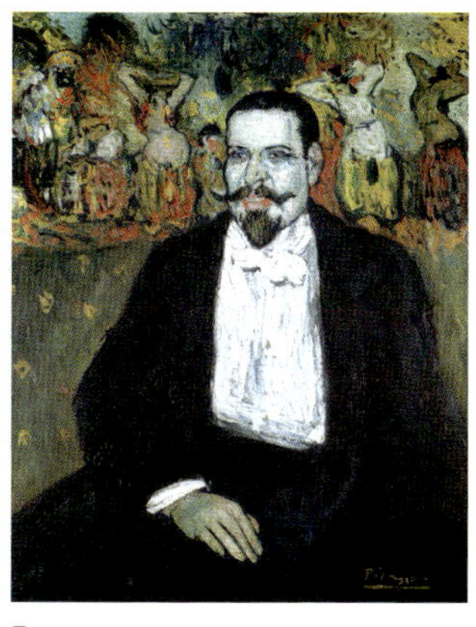

7

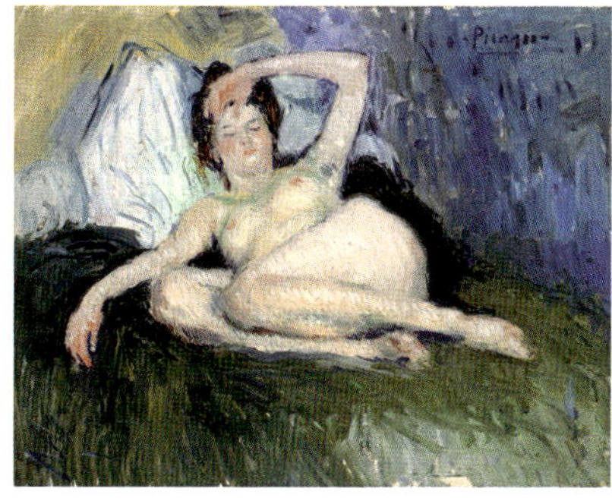

9

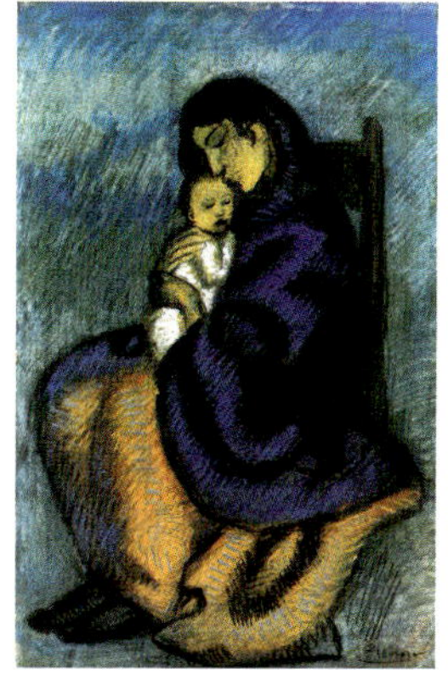

11

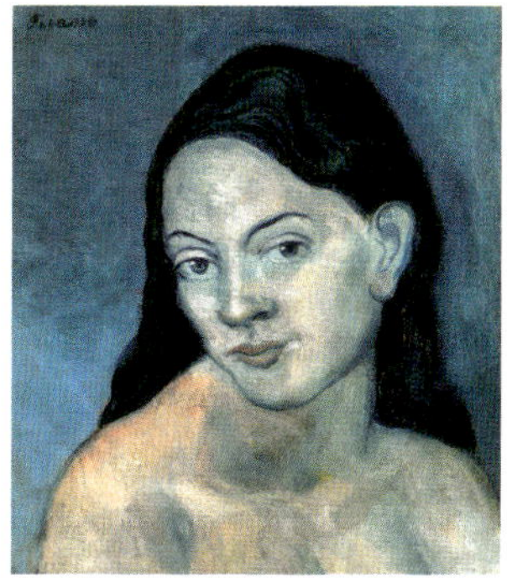

8

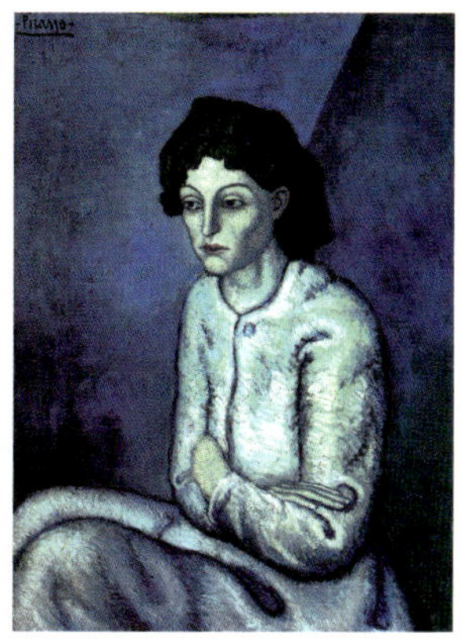

10

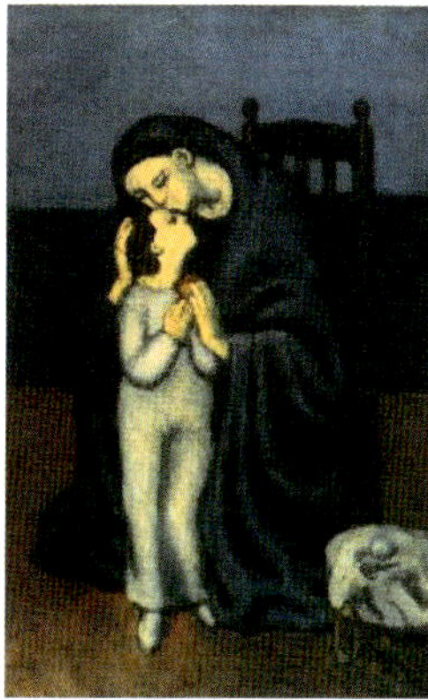

12

Cat. Zurich 7
Bildnis Gustave Coquiot
Gustave Coquiot, 1901
Portrait of Gustave Coquiot
Oil on canvas, 100 x 81 cm
Centre Pompidou, Paris, Musée national d'art moderne/Centre de création industrielle
Donated by Mme Gustave Coquiot, 1933
Zervos: I, no. 84
Plate 2

Cat. Zurich 8
Kopf eines jungen Mädchens
Tête de femme, 1903
Head of a Woman
Oil on canvas, 40.3 x 35.6 cm
The Metropolitan Museum of Art, New York
Bequest of Miss Adelaide Milton de Groot (1876–1967), 1967 (67.187.91)
Zervos: VI, no. 548

Cat. Zurich 9
Liegender Akt
Jeanne, 1901
Jeanne
Oil on canvas, 70.5 x 90 cm
Centre Pompidou, Paris, Musée national d'art moderne/Centre de création industrielle
Bequest of Baronne Eva Gourgaud, 1965
Zervos: I, no. 106
Plate 3

Cat. Zurich 10
Frau mit verschränkten Armen
Femme aux bras croisés, 1901/02
Woman with Arms Crossed
Oil on canvas, 81.3 x 58.4 cm
Private collection
Zervos: I, no. 105
Zervos: VI, no. 543

Cat. Zurich 11
Mutter und Kind
Mère et enfant, 1901
Mother and Child
Pastel chalk on canvas, 46.5 x 31 cm
Private collection
Zervos: I, no. 110

Cat. Zurich 12
Mutter und Kind
Maternité/Mère et enfant, 1901/02
Mother and Child
Oil on canvas, 91.5 x 60 cm
Private collection
Zervos: I, no. 109

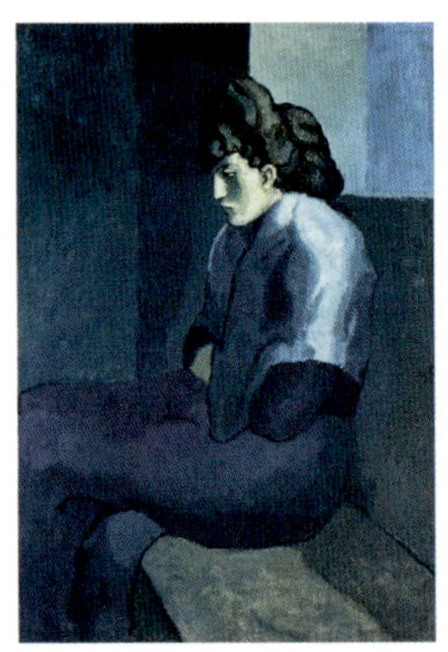

13

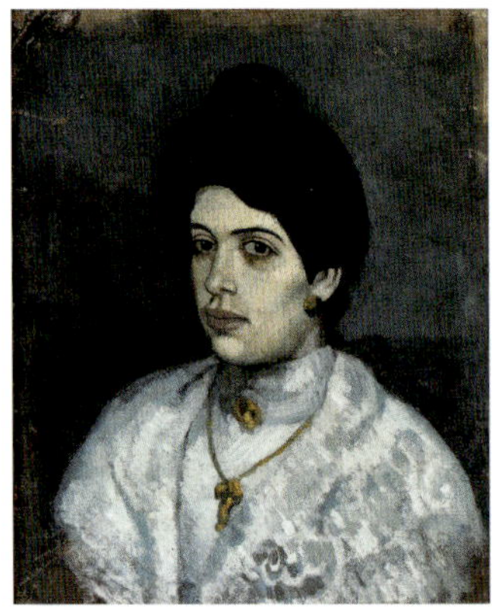

15

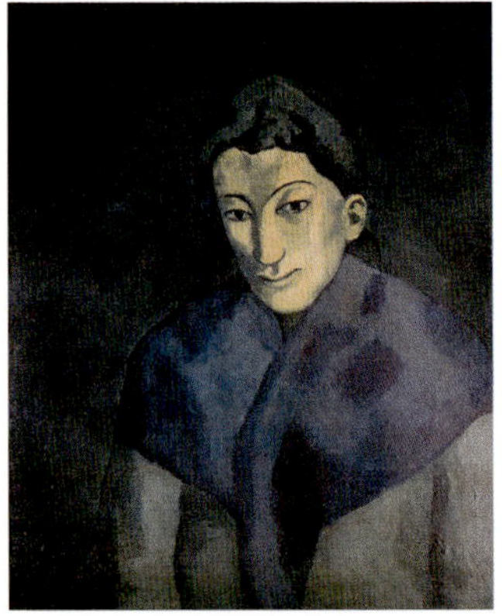

17

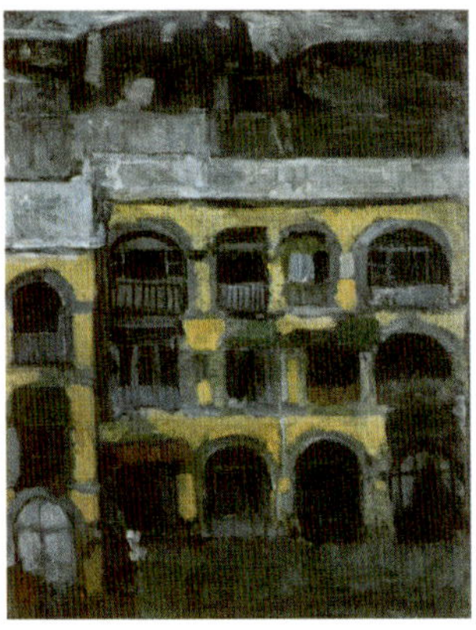

14

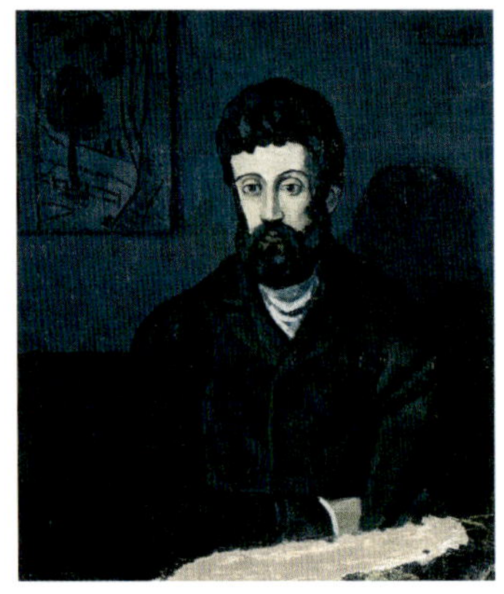

16

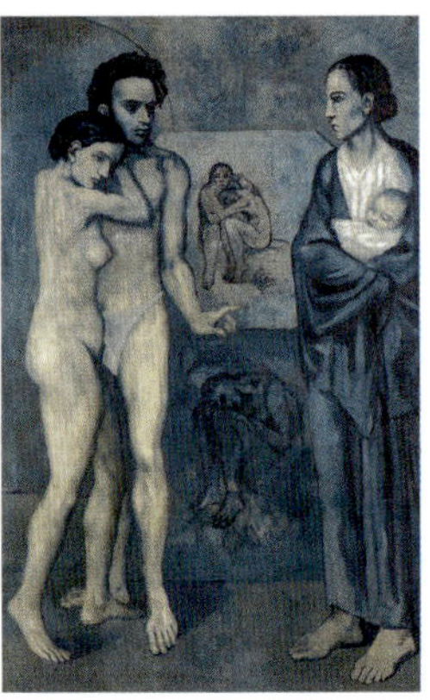

18

Cat. Zurich 13
Trauer
La mélancolie, 1902
Melancholy Woman
Oil on canvas, 100 x 69.2 cm
Detroit Institute of Arts
Bequest of Robert H. Tannahill
Zervos: I, no. 133
Plate 4

Cat. Zurich 14
Das blaue Haus
La maison bleue, 1902
Blue House
Oil on canvas, 50.5 x 40.5 cm
Private collection
Zervos: XXI, no. 280

Cat. Zurich 15
Bildnis Corinna Pere Romeu
Portrait de Corina Pere Romeu, 1902
Portrait of a Man
Oil on canvas, 61 x 50 cm
Collection Musée National Picasso,
Paris
En dépôt au Musée d'art moderne
de Céret
Zervos: I, no. 130

Cat. Zurich 16
Männliches Bildnis
Portrait d'homme, 1902/03
Portrait of a Man
Oil on canvas, 93 x 78 cm
Musée Picasso, Paris
Dation en 1979
Zervos: I, no. 142

Cat. Zurich 17
Weibliches Brustbild
Femme au fichu bleu, 1902
Woman in a Blue Shawl
Oil on canvas, 60.3 x 52.4 cm
Aichi Prefectural Museum of Art, Japan
Zervos: I, no. 155
Plate 5

Cat. Zurich 18
Das Leben
La Vie, 1903
Life
Oil on canvas, 196.5 x 129.2 cm
The Cleveland Museum of Art
Gift of the Hanna Fund
Zervos: I, no. 179

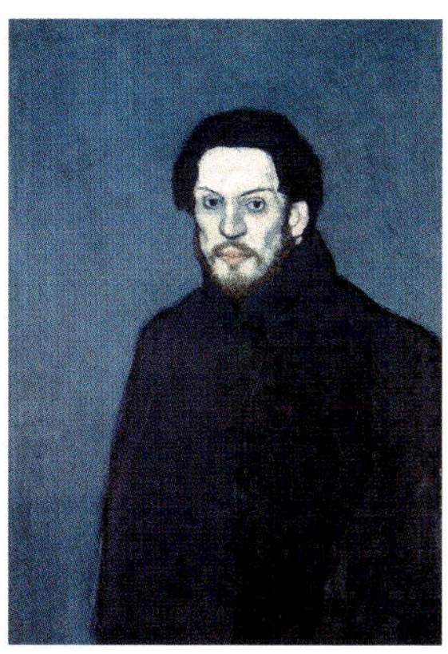

19

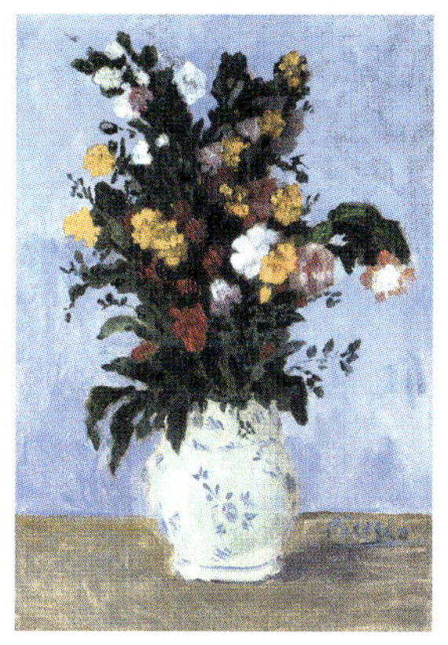

21

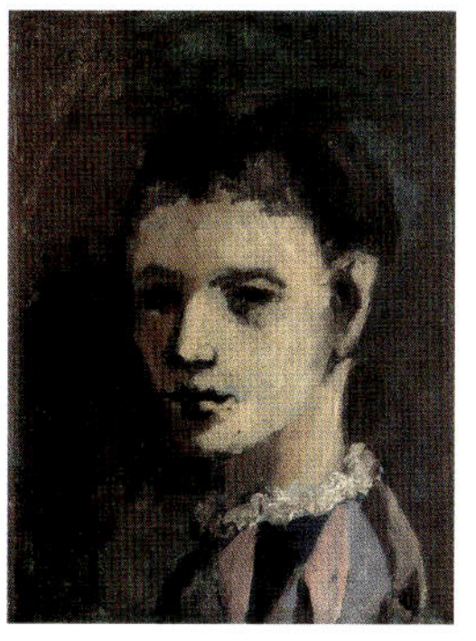

23

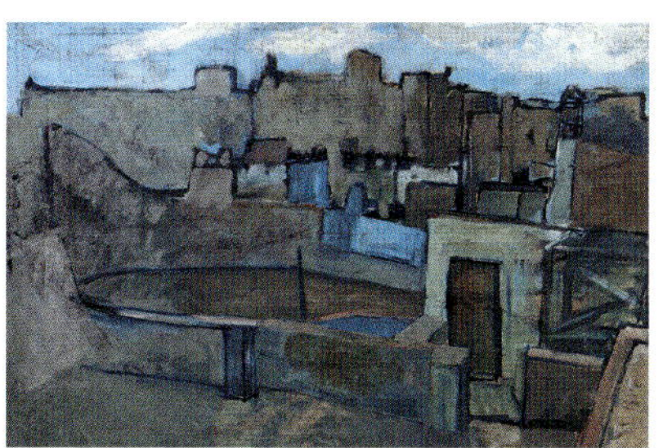

20

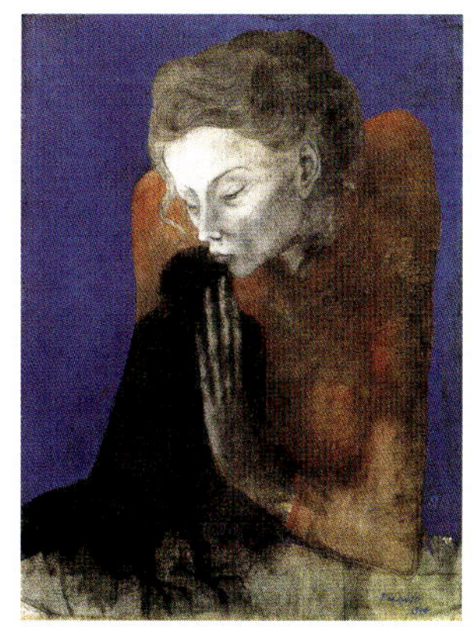

22

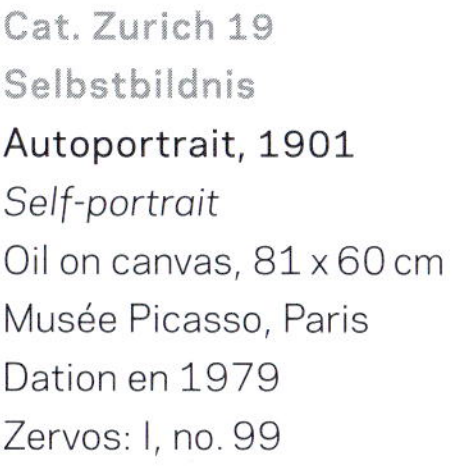

24

Cat. Zurich 19
Selbstbildnis
Autoportrait, 1901
Self-portrait
Oil on canvas, 81 x 60 cm
Musée Picasso, Paris
Dation en 1979
Zervos: I, no. 99

Cat. Zurich 20
Landschaft Barcelona
Les toits de Barcelone, 1902/03
Barcelona Rooftops
Oil on canvas, 71 x 111 cm
Museu Picasso, Barcelona
Ceded by the Ministry of Culture to the
Barcelona City Council, 1991
Zervos: I, no. 207
Plate 8

Cat. Zurich 21
Celestina
La Célestine (La Femme à la taie), 1904
Celestina (The Woman with One Eye)
Oil on canvas, 74.5 x 58.5 cm
Musée Picasso, Paris
Don en 1989
Zervos: I, no. 183

Cat. Zurich 22
Frau mit Krähe
Femme à la corneille, 1904
Woman with a Crow
Charcoal, pastel and watercolour on
paper, 64.6 x 49.5 cm
The Toledo Museum of Art, Toledo, OH
Purchased with funds form the Libbey
Endowment, Gift of Edward Drummond
Libbey, 1936.4
Zervos: I, no. 240

Cat. Zurich 23
Blumen mit Vase
Vase de fleurs, 1901/04
Vase of Flowers
Oil on canvas, 66 x 46.5 cm
Courtesy Nahmad Collection,
Switzerland
Zervos: I, no. 242
Plate 9

Cat. Zurich 24
Kopf eines Harlekin
Tête d'arlequin, 1905
Head of a Harlequin
Oil on bevelled and cradled panel,
35 x 26.5 cm
Private collection
Zervos: I, no. 252

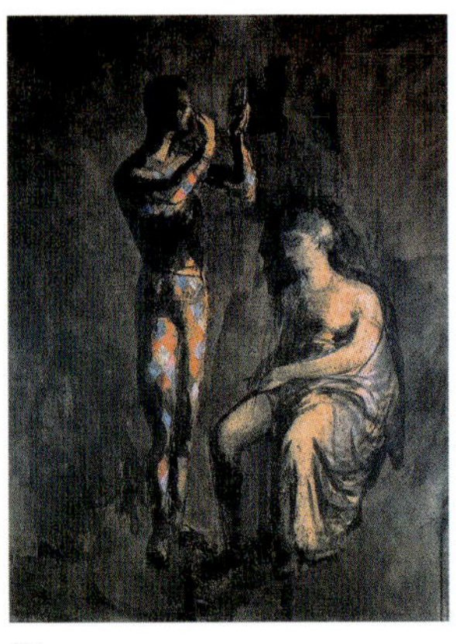

25

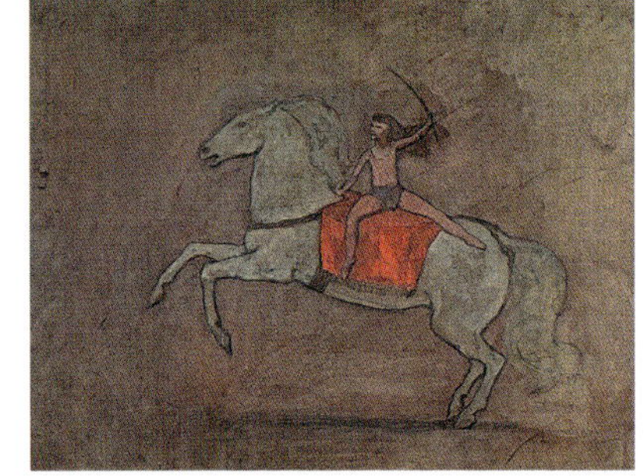

27

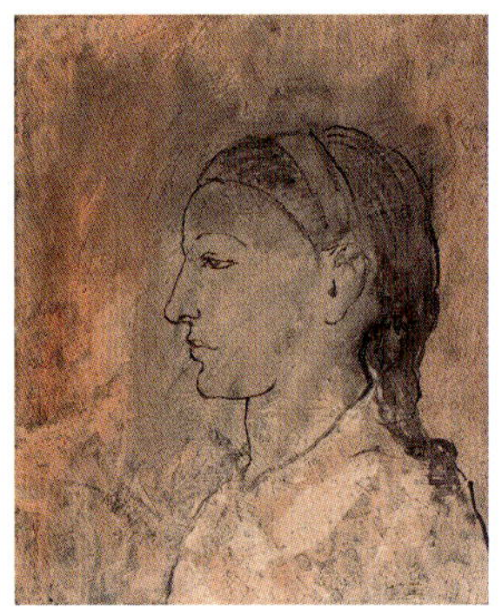

29

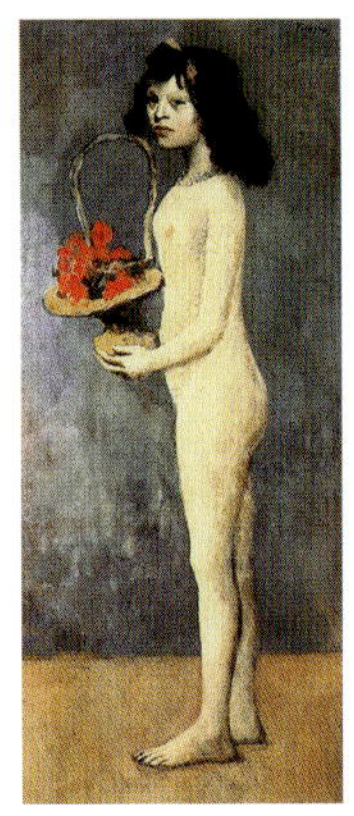

26

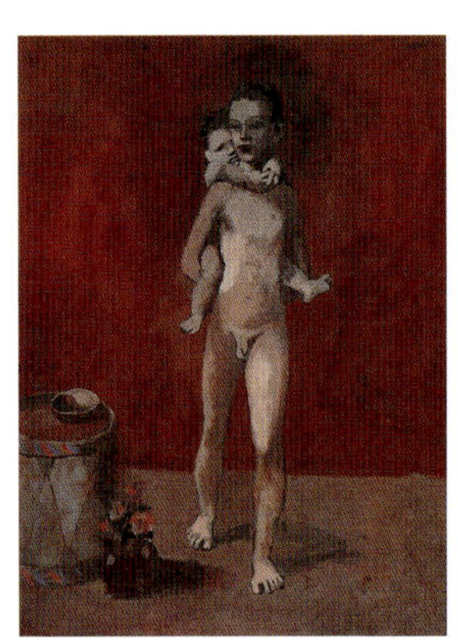

28

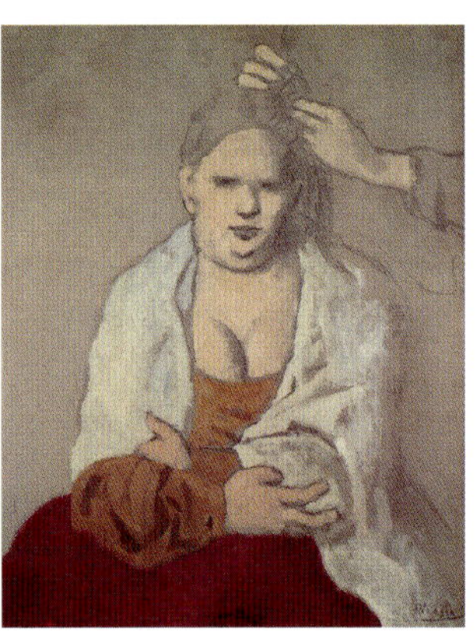

30

Cat. Zurich 25
Harlequin und Frau
Harlequin se maquillant, 1905
Harlequin
Gouache on cardboard, 69 x 54 cm
Private collection
Zervos: I, no. 252

Cat. Zurich 26
Mädchen mit Blumenkorb
**Jeune fille à la corbeille
de fleurs, 1905**
Girl with a Basket of Flowers
Oil on canvas, 155 x 66 cm
Private collection
Zervos: I, no. 256

Cat. Zurich 27
Junge Kunstreiterin
Equestrienne à cheval, 1905
Horse and Rider
Gouache on cardboard, 60 x 79 cm
Private collection
Zervos: XXII, no. 268

Cat. Zurich 28
Die jungen Akrobaten
Les deux frères, 1906
The Two Brothers
Gouache on cardboard, 80 x 59 cm
Musée Picasso, Paris
Dation en 1989
Zervos: VI, no. 720

Cat. Zurich 29
Frauenkopf im Profil
Portrait de Fernande Olivier, 1906
Portrait of Fernande Olivier
Oil on canvas, 46 x 38 cm
Private collection
Zervos: VI, no. 467
Plate 10

Cat. Zurich 30
Frau beim Frisieren
La coiffure, 1905
Woman at the Hairdresser
Oil and charcoal on canvas,
81 x 65.1 cm
The Baltimore Museum of Art
The Cone Collection, formed by
Dr. Claribel Cone and Miss Etta Cone
of Baltimore, Maryland, BMA 1950.269
Zervos: I, no. 309

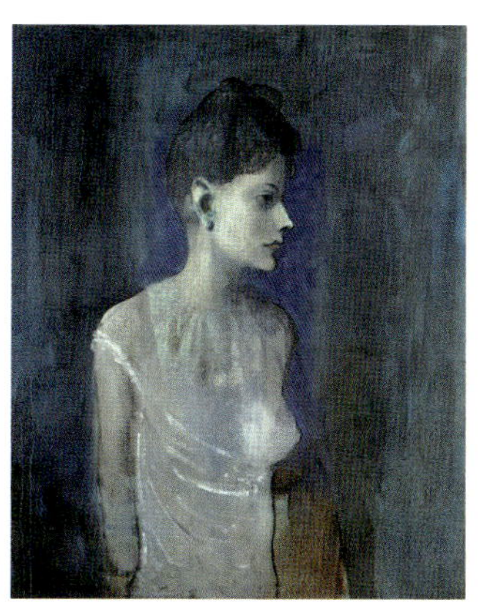

31

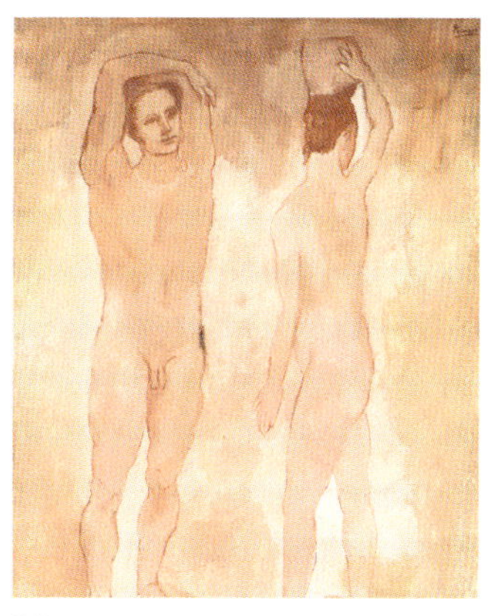

33

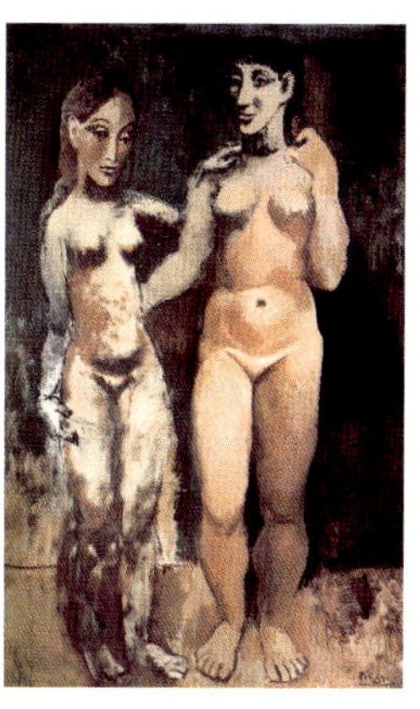

35

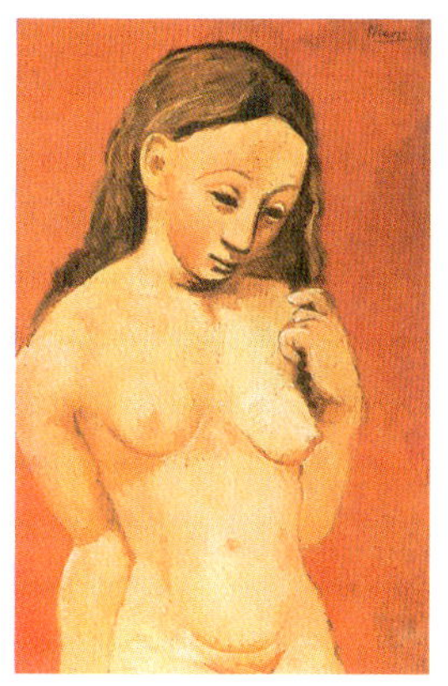

32

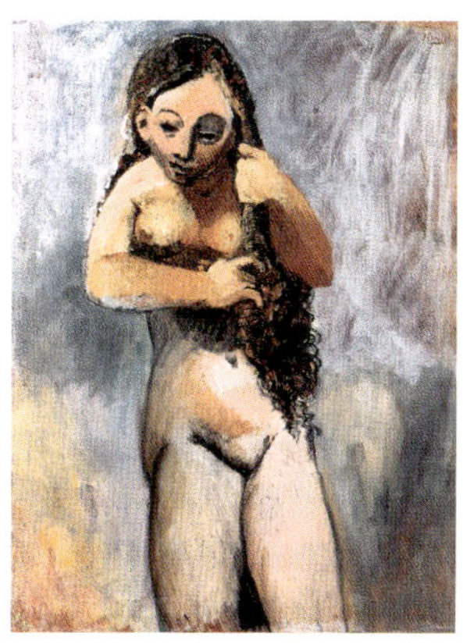

34

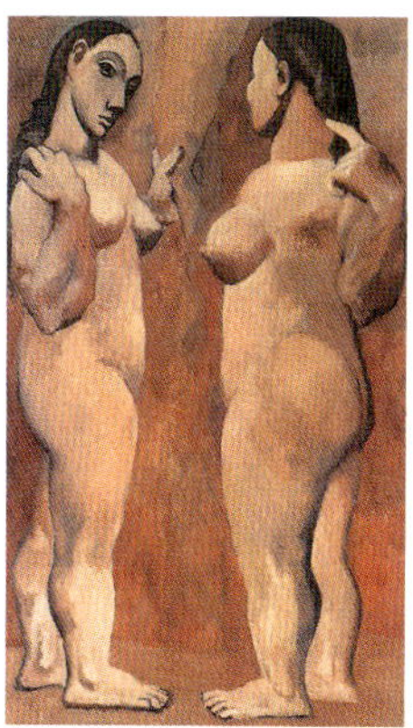

36

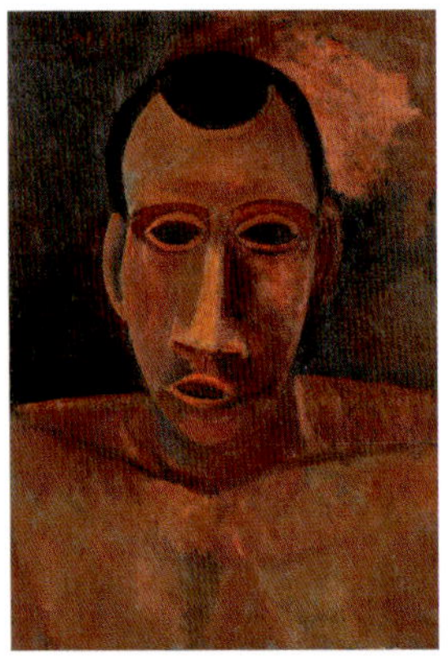

37

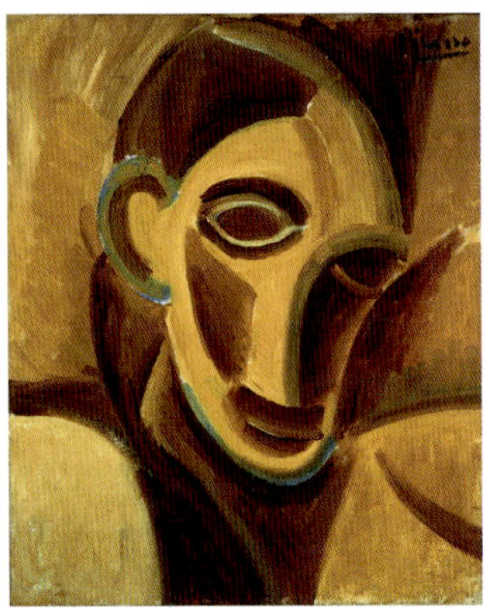

38

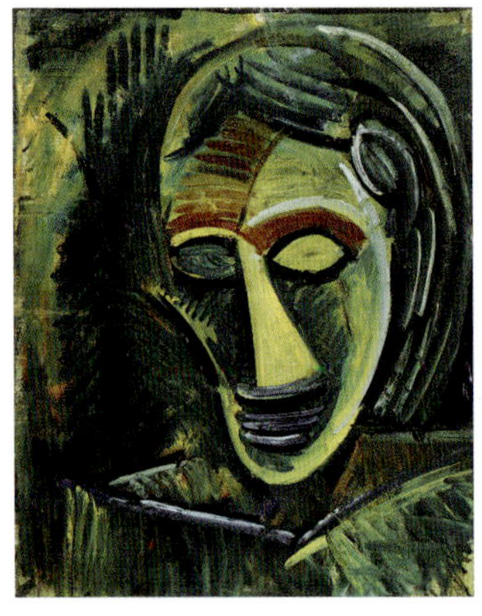

39

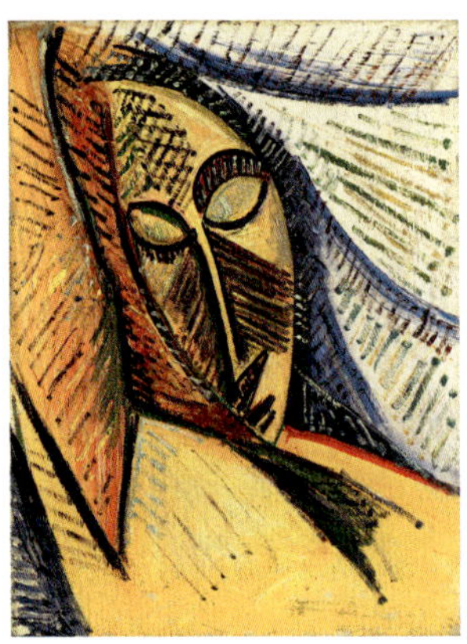

40

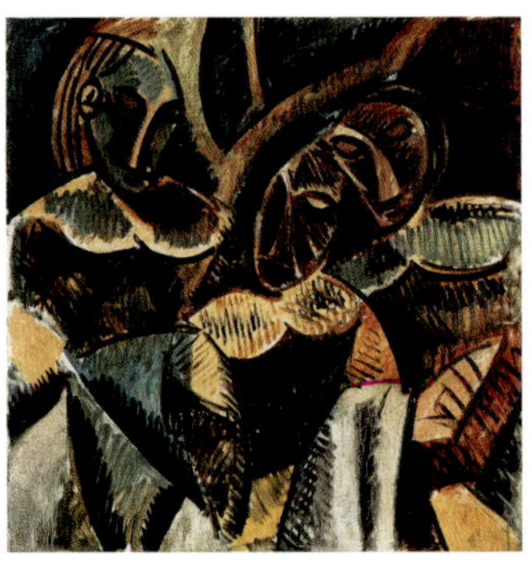

41

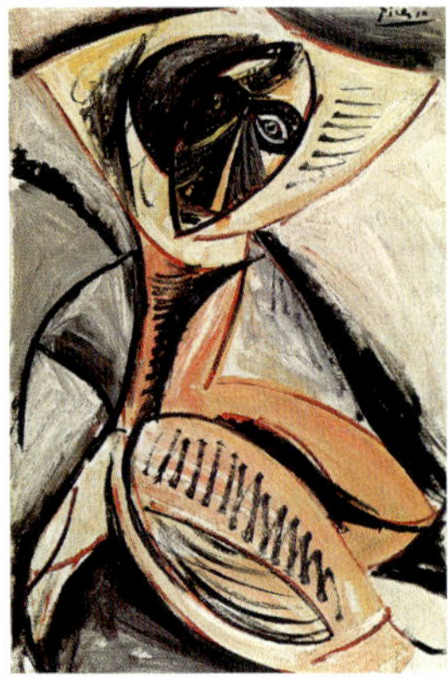

42

Cat. Zurich 37
Negerkopf
Buste d'homme, 1908
Bust of a Man
Oil on canvas, 62.2 x 43.5 cm
The Metropolitan Museum of Art,
New York
Bequest of Florene M. Schoenborn,
1995 (1996.403.5)
Zervos: IIa, no. 76
Plate 13

Cat. Zurich 38
Kopf, braun
Tête de femme, 1907
Woman's Head
Oil on canvas, 54.5 x 46 cm
Private collection
Zervos: IIa, no. 51
Plate 14

Cat. Zurich 39
Kopf, blau
Tête de femme, 1908
Woman's Head
Oil on canvas, 73.6 x 60.6 cm
The Museum of Modern Art, New York
Florene May Schoenborn Bequest, 1996
Zervos: IIa, no. 52
Plate 15

Cat. Zurich 40
Weiblicher Kopf
**Tête de femme (Nu à la draperie
[Étude]), 1907**
*Head of a Sleeping Woman
(Study for Nude with Drapery)*
Oil on canvas, 61.4 x 47.6 cm
The Museum of Modern Art, New York
Estate of John Hay Whitney, 1983
Zervos: IIa, no. 44
Plate 16

Cat. Zurich 41
Die drei Masken
Trois figures sous un arbre, 1907/08
Three Figures under a Tree
Oil on canvas, 99 x 99 cm
Musée Picasso, Paris
Don en 1986
Zervos: IIa, no. 53

Cat. Zurich 42
Negertänzerin
Femme nue aux bras levés, 1907
Nude with Raised Arms
Oil on canvas, 63 x 42.5 cm
Private collection
Zervos: IIa, no. 36

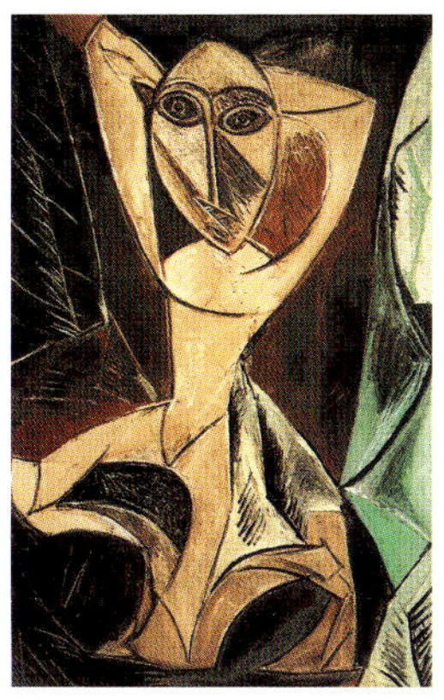

43

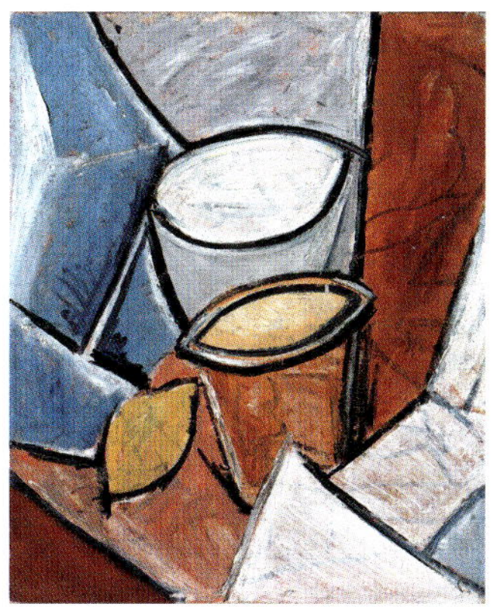

44

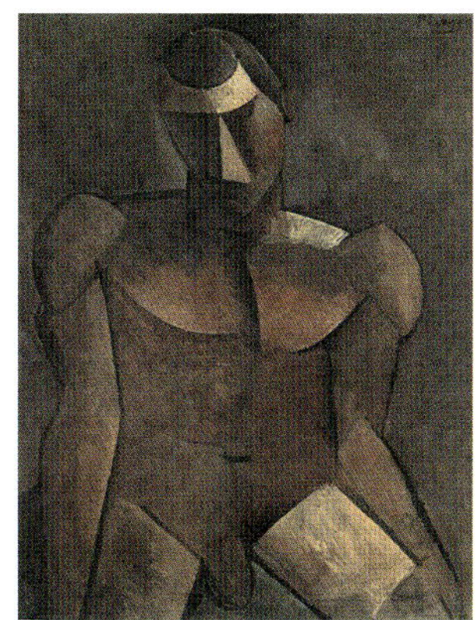

45

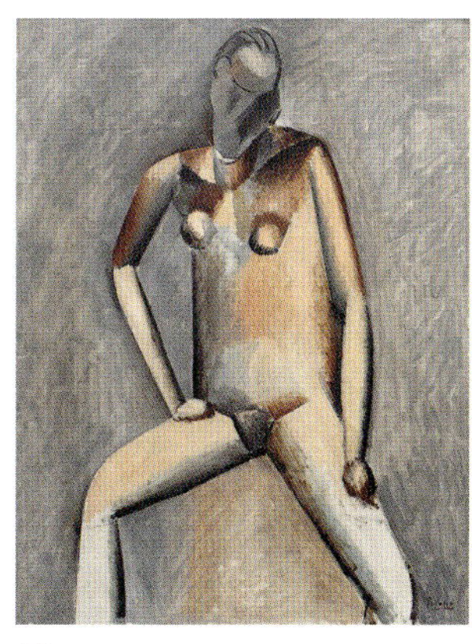

46

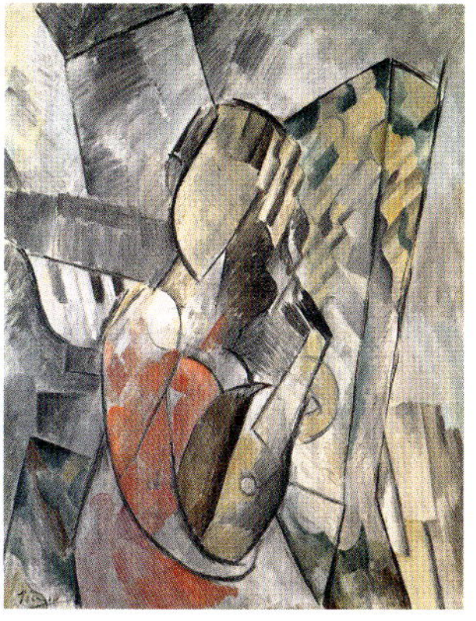

47

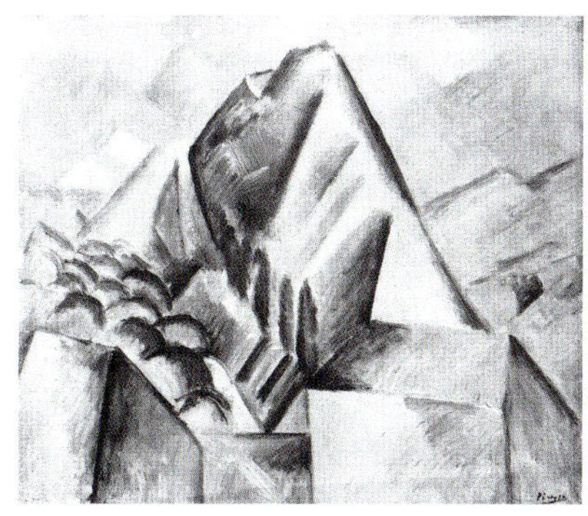

48

Cat. Zurich 43
Tänzerin
Femme nue aux bras levés, 1907
Nude with Raised Arms
Oil on canvas, 150 x 100 cm
Private collection
Zervos: IIa, no. 35

Cat. Zurich 44
Stilleben, zwei Töpfe und Zitrone
Pots et citron, 1907
Jugs with lemon
Oil on canvas, 55 x 46 cm
Albertina, Wien
Batliner Collection
Zervos: IIa, no. 32
Plate 17

Cat. Zurich 45
Männliche Halbfigur
Homme nu assis, 1908/09
Seated Male Nude
Oil on canvas, 96 x 76 cm
Musée d'art moderne de Lille Métropole
Villeneuve d'Ascq
Donation Geneviève et Jean Masurel
en 1979
Zervos: IIa, no. 117

Cat. Zurich 46
Sitzender Frauenakt
Femme nue assise, 1908/09
Seated Female Nude
Oil on canvas, 116.5 x 89.4 cm
Philadelphia Museum of Art
The Louise and Walter Arensberg
Collection, 1950
Zervos: IIa, no. 114
Plate 18

Cat. Zurich 47
Frau mit Mandoline
Femme à la mandoline, 1908
Woman with Mandolin
Oil on canvas, 100 x 80 cm
Kunstsammlung Nordrhein-Westfalen,
Düsseldorf
Zervos: IIa, no. 115
Plate 27

Cat. Zurich 48
Spanische Landschaft
Paysage, Horta de Ebro, 1909
Landscape, Horta de Ebro
Oil on canvas, 54 x 65 cm
Denver Art Museum
Gift of Charles Francis Hendrie
Memorial
Zervos: IIa, no. 151

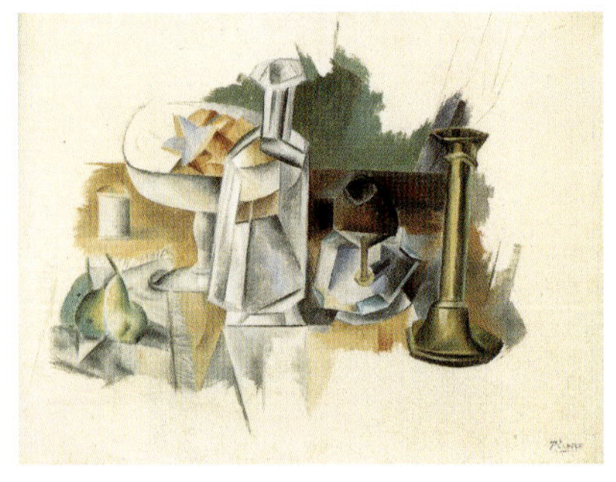

49

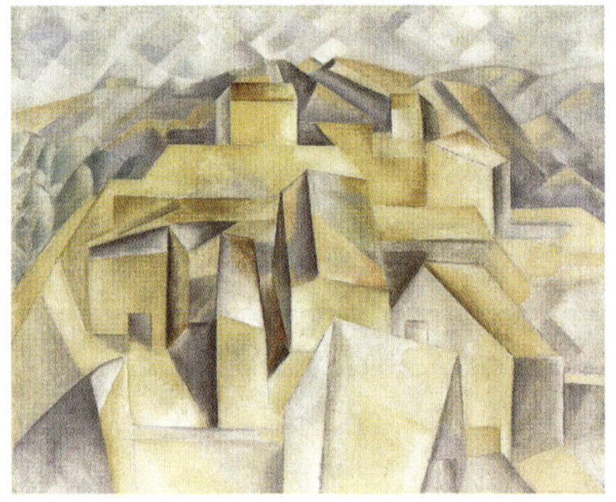

51

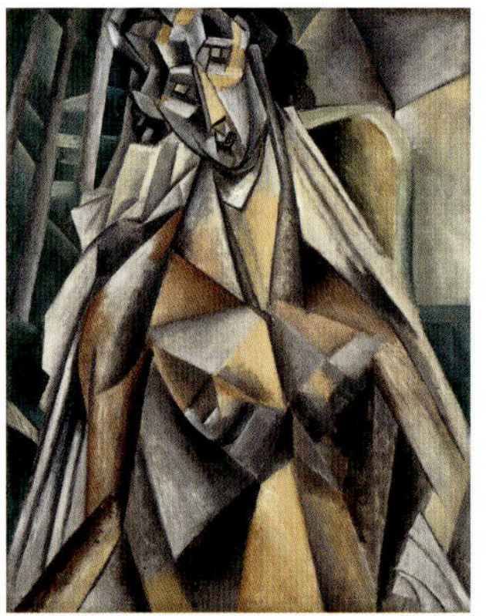

53

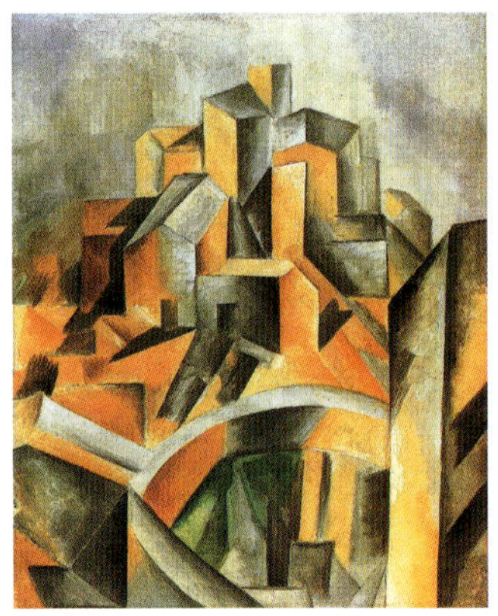

50

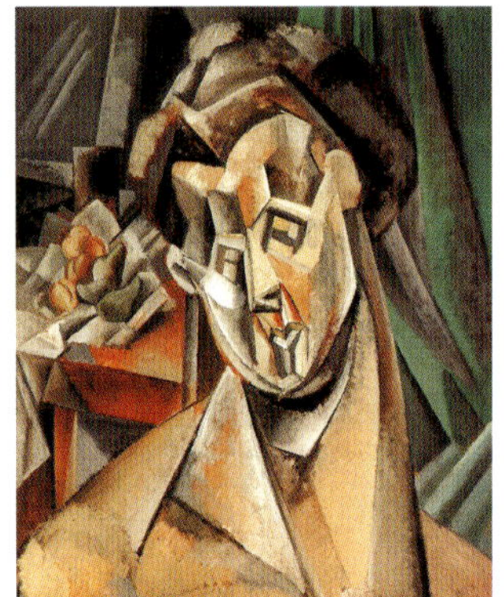

52

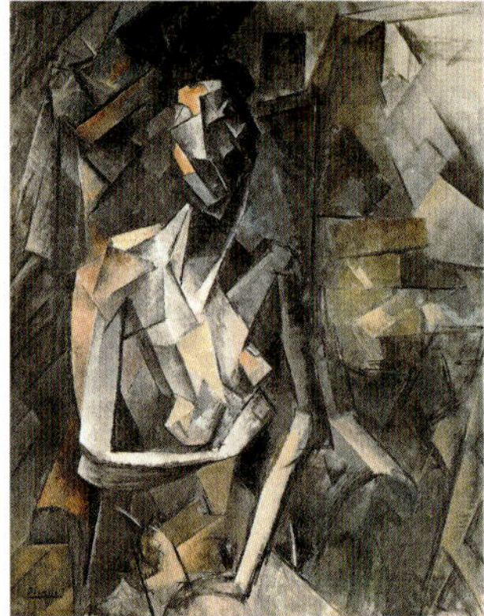

54

Cat. Zurich 49
Stilleben, Wasserflasche,
Fruchtschale, Kerzenstock
Carafe, compote et chandelier, 1909
Carafe, Compote and Candlestick
Oil on canvas, 54.4 x 75 cm
Private collection
Zervos: IIa, no. 187

Cat. Zurich 50
Spanische Landschaft
Le réservoir (Horta de Ebro), 1909
The Reservoir (Horta de Ebro)
Oil on canvas, 60.3 x 50.1 cm
Private collection
Zervos: IIa, no. 157

Cat. Zurich 51
Spanische Landschaft
**Maisons sur la colline,
Horta de Ebro, 1909**
Houses on the Hill, Horta de Ebro
Oil on canvas, 65 x 81 cm
Staatliche Museen zu Berlin, National-
galerie. Museum Berggruen
Zervos: IIa, no. 161

Cat. Zurich 52
Frau mit Birnen
Femme aux poires (Fernande), 1909
Woman with Pears (Fernande)
Oil on canvas, 92.1 x 70.8 cm
The Museum of Modern Art, New York
Florene May Schoenborn Bequest
Zervos: IIa, no. 170

Cat. Zurich 53
Akt im Lehnstuhl
Femme nue dans un fauteuil, 1909
Nude Woman in an Armchair
Oil on canvas, 93.5 x 75 cm
Private collection
Zervos: IIa, no. 174
Plate 19

Cat. Zurich 54
Sitzende Frau
Femme nue assise, 1909/10
Seated Nude
Oil on canvas, 92.1 x 73 cm
Tate, London, Purchased 1949
Zervos: IIa, no. 201
Plate 20

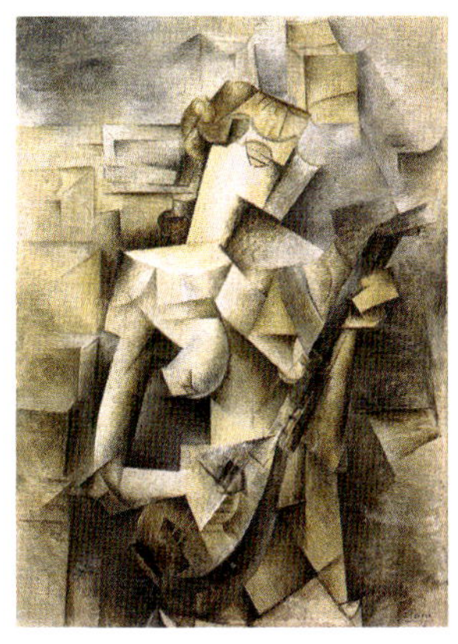

55

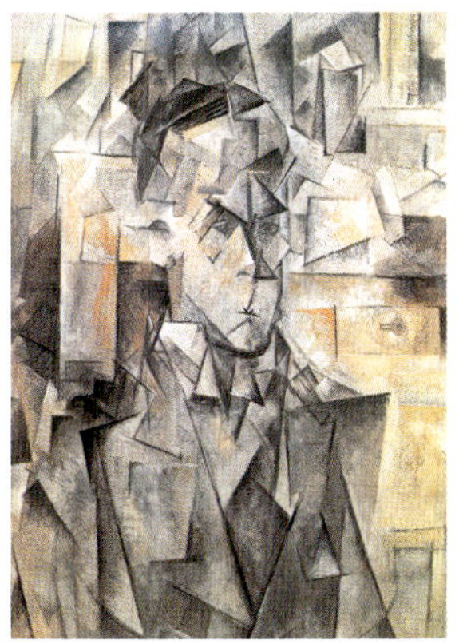

56

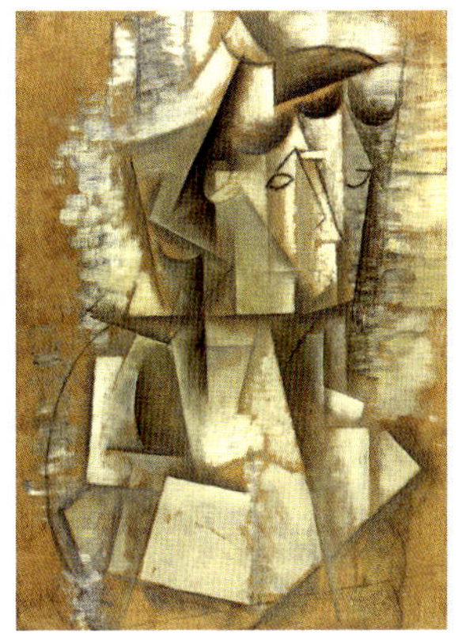

57

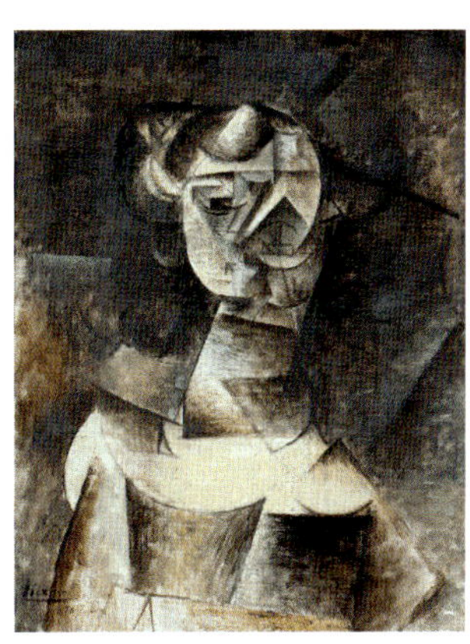

58

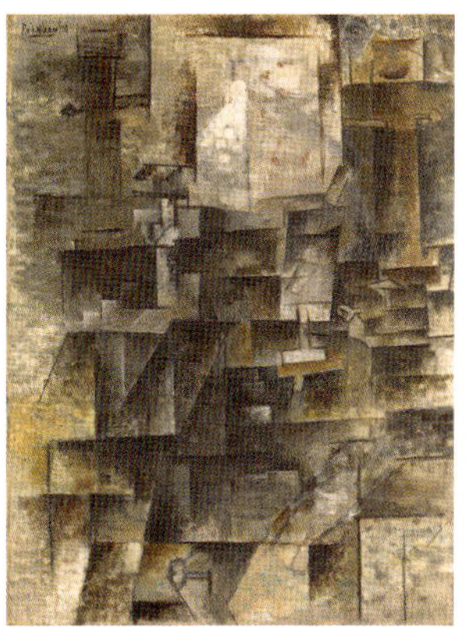

59

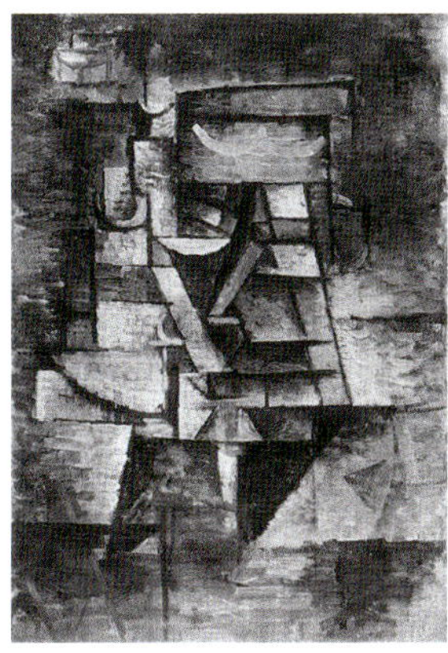

60

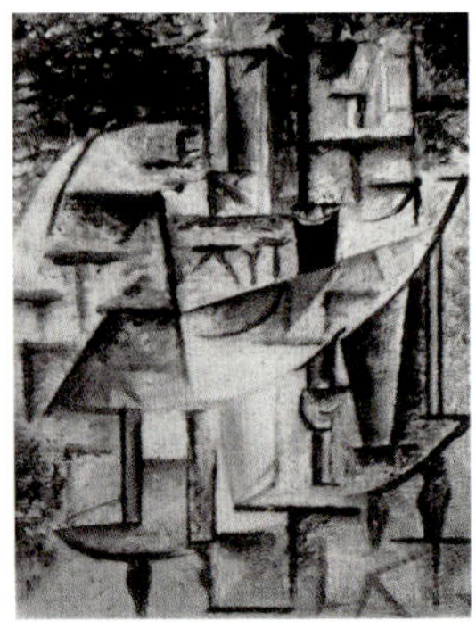

61

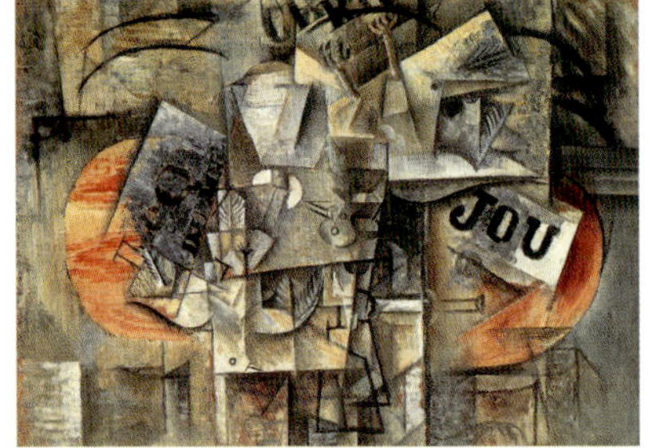

63

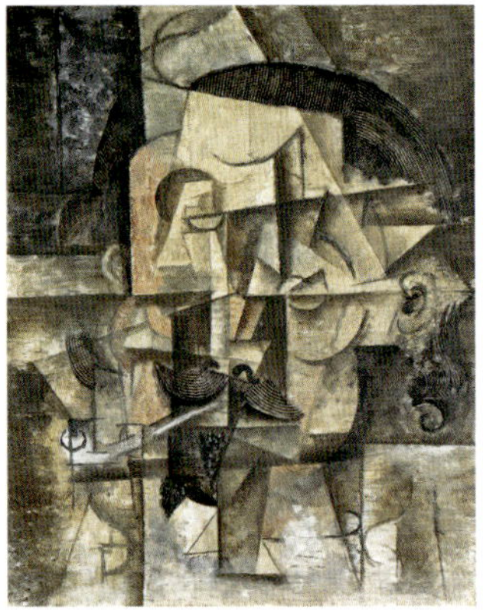

65

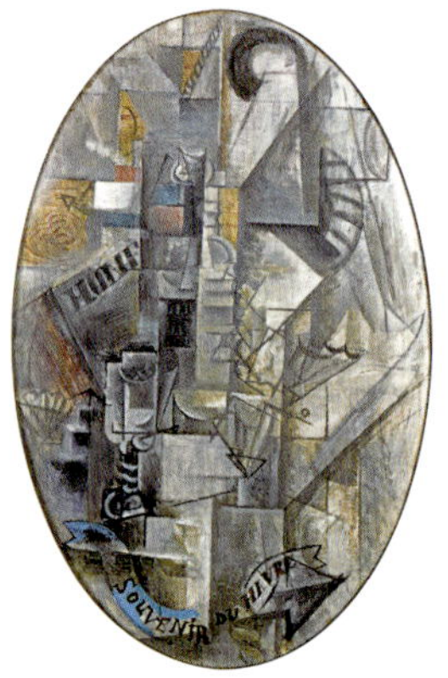

62

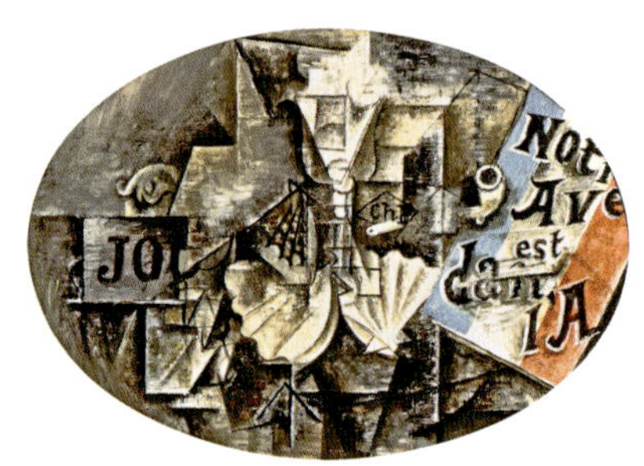

64

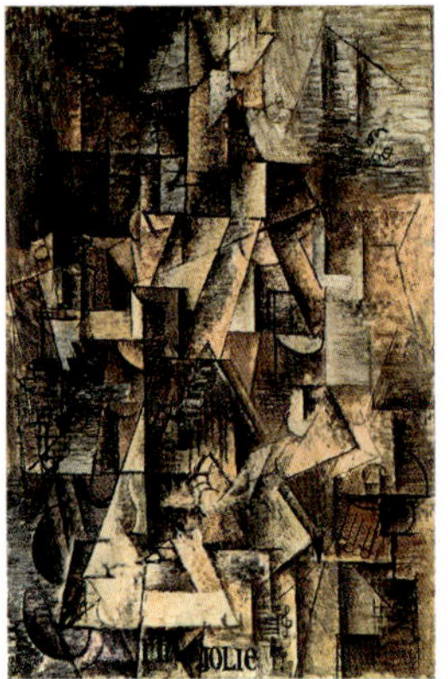

66

Cat. Zurich 61
Essig- und Ölgestell
L'huilier, 1911
The Cruet of Oil
Oil on canvas, 24 x 19 cm
Private collection
Zervos: IIa, no. 249

Cat. Zurich 62
Erinnerung an Le Havre
Souvenir du Havre, 1912
Souvenir du Havre
Oil on canvas, 81 x 54 cm
Private collection, Courtesy Thomas
Ammann Fine Art AG Zurich
Zervos: IIb, no. 367
Plate 23

Cat. Zurich 63
Die toten Vögel
Nature morte (Les oiseaux morts),
1912
Still-Life (Dead Birds)
Oil on canvas, 65 x 46 cm
Museo Nacional Centro de Arte Reina
Sofía, Madrid
Zervos: IIa, no. 339

Cat. Zurich 64
Die Jakobsmuscheln oder
"Notre avenir est dans l'air"
The Scallop Shell.
"Notre avenir est dans l'air"
Oil on canvas, 38 x 55 cm
Private collection
Zervos: IIa, no. 311
Plate 24

Cat. Zurich 65
Herrenbildnis
Le poète, 1912
The Poet
Oil on canvas, 60 x 48 cm
Kunstmuseum Basel
Gift of Maja Sacher-Stehlin, deposited
by the commune of inhabitants of the
canton Basel-Stadt 1967
Zervos: IIa, no. 313
Plate 26

Cat. Zurich 66
Frau mit Gitarre
'Ma Jolie', 1911/12
"Ma Jolie"
Oil on canvas, 100 x 65.4 cm
The Museum of Modern Art, New York
Acquired through the Lillie P. Bliss
Bequest
Zervos: IIa, no. 244

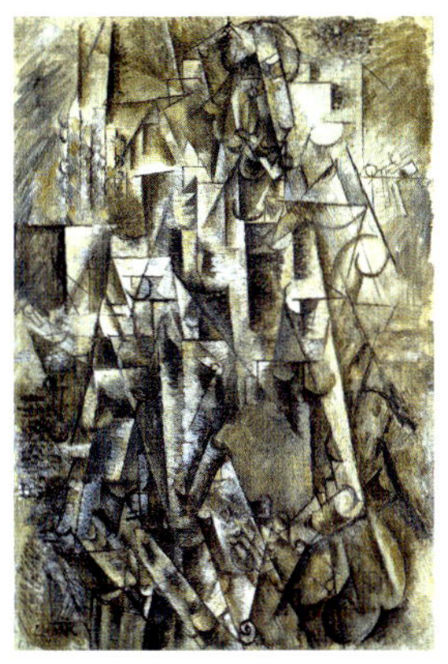

67

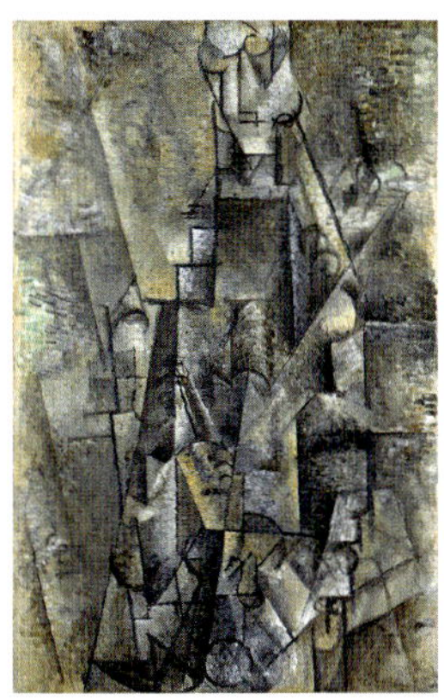

68

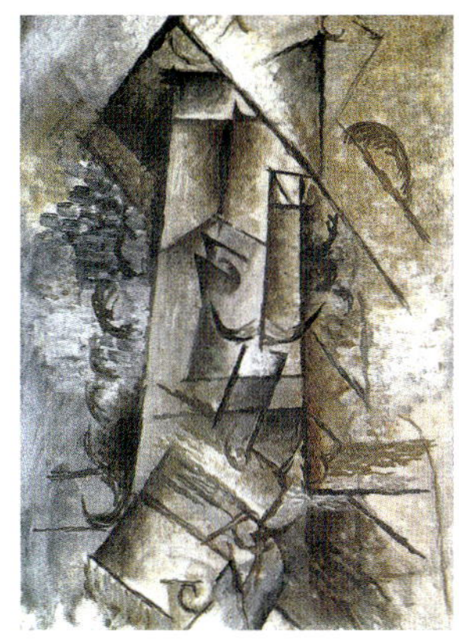

69

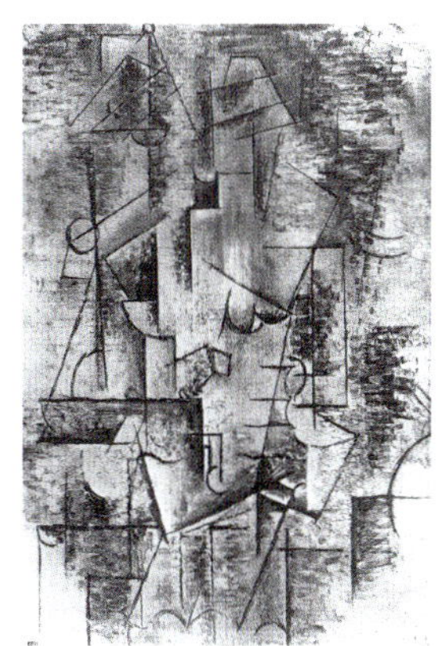

70

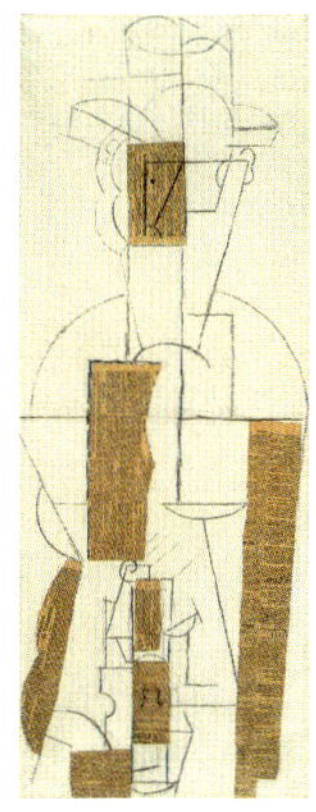

71

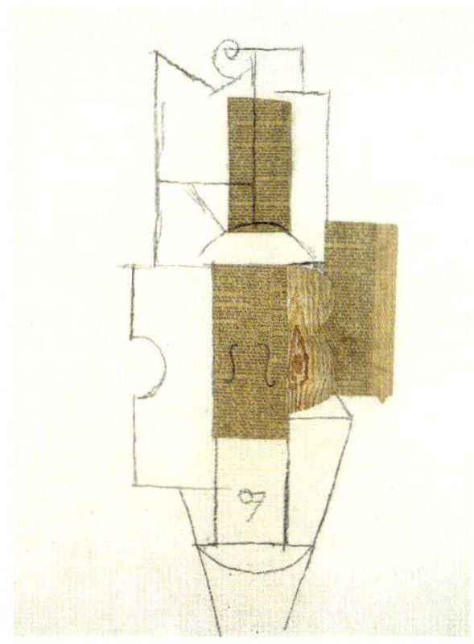

72

Cat. Zurich 67
Der Dichter
Le poète, 1911
The Poet
Oil on canvas, 131 x 89.5 cm
The Solomon R. Guggenheim Foundation
Peggy Guggenheim Collection, Venice,
1976
Zervos: IIa, no. 285

Cat. Zurich 68
Mann mit Klarinette
Homme à la clarinette, 1911/12
Man with a Clarinet
Oil on canvas, 106 x 69 cm
Museo Thyssen-Bornemisza, Madrid
Zervos: IIa, no. 288
Plate 28

Cat. Zurich 69
Buffalo Bill
Buffalo Bill, 1911
Buffalo Bill
Oil on canvas, 46 x 33 cm
Private collection
Zervos: IIa, no. 255

Cat. Zurich 70
Mädchen und Soldat
Soldat et fille, 1910/11
Soldier and Girl
Oil on canvas, 116 x 81 cm
Private collection
Zervos: IIa, no. 254

Cat. Zurich 71
Figur
Homme au violon, 1912
Man with Hat and a Violin
Cut-and-pasted newspaper, with char-
coal, on two sheets of cut-and-pasted
paper, 122.2 x 47.3 cm
The Metropolitan Museum of Art,
New York
Jacques and Natasha Gelman
Collection, 1998
Zervos: IIb, no. 399

Cat. Zurich 72
Stilleben
Violine, 1912
Violin
Pasted paper, watercolour and charcoal,
62.5 x 48 cm
Private collection
Zervos: IIb, no. 409

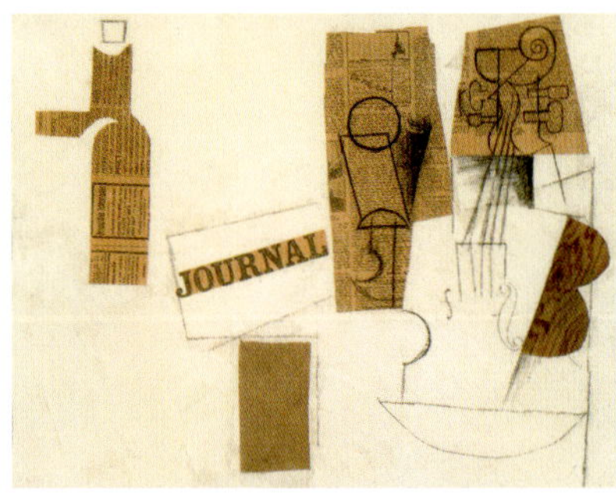

73

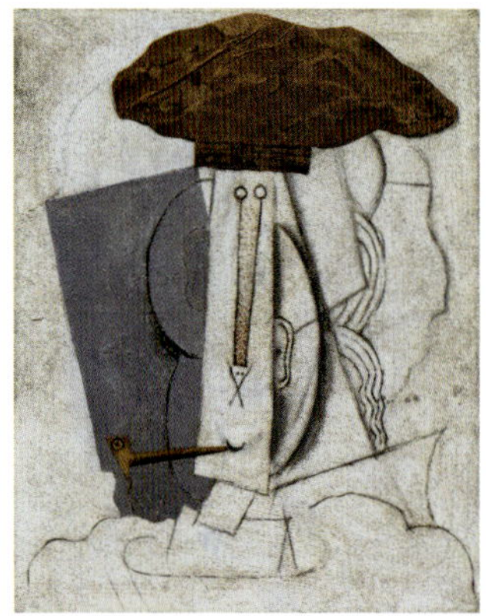

75

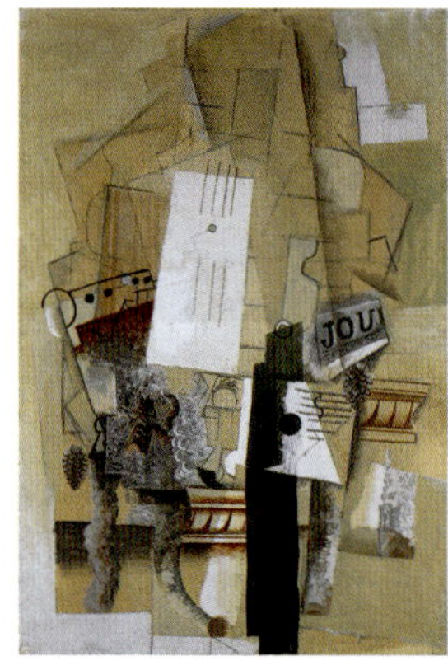

77

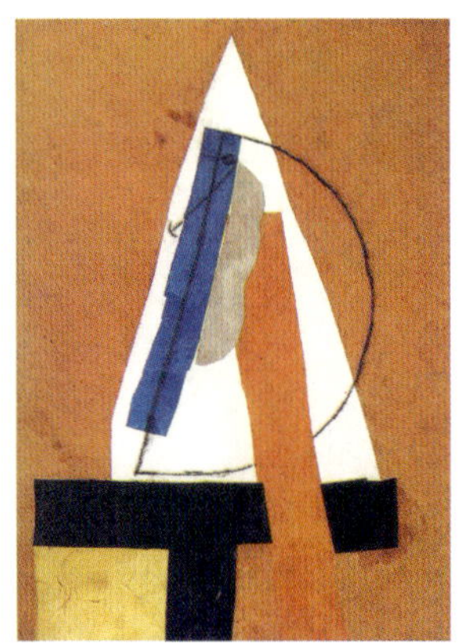

74

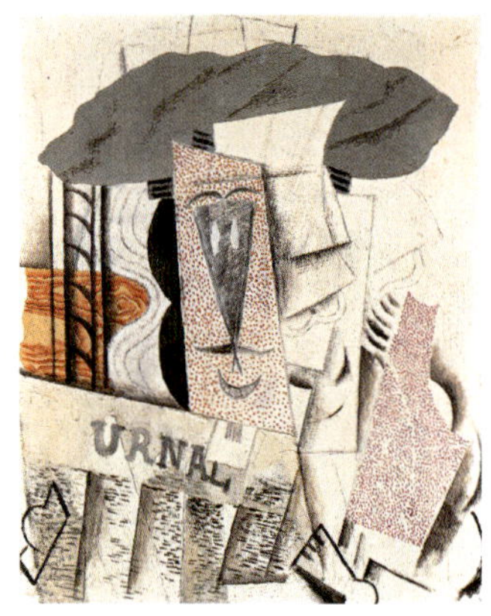

76

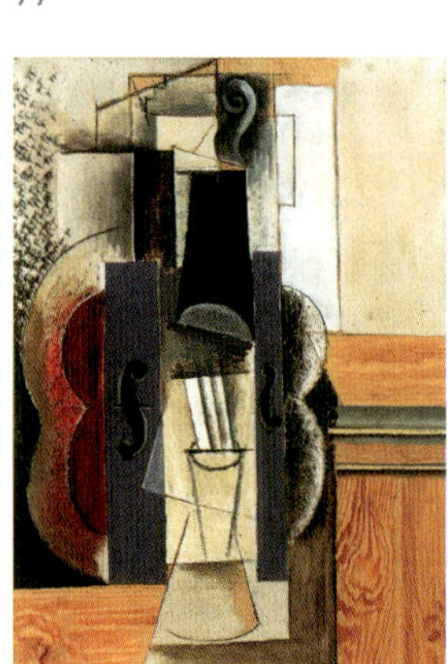

78

Cat. Zurich 73
Stilleben
Bouteille, verre et violon, 1912/13
Bottle, Glass and Violin
Collage, 47 x 62 cm
Moderna Museet, Stockholm
Zervos: IIb, no. 405
Plate 29

Cat. Zurich 74
Kopf
Tête, 1913
Head
Pasted paper, charcoal and pencil on
cardboard , 43.5 x 33 cm
National Galleries of Scotland
Purchased with assistance from the
Heritage Lottery Fund and The Art Fund,
1995
Zervos: IIb, no. 414

Cat. Zurich 75
Der Student
Étudiant à la pipe, 1914
Student with a Pipe
Plaster, sand, pasted paper, oil and
charcoal on canvas, 73 x 58.7 cm
The Museum of Modern Art, New York
Nelson A. Rockefeller Bequest, 1979
Zervos: IIb, no. 444
Plate 30

Cat. Zurich 76
Stilleben mit Zeitung
Étudiant au journal, 1913
Student with Newspaper
Oil and sand on canvas, 73 x 59.5 cm
Private collection
Zervos: IIb, no. 443

Cat. Zurich 77
Stilleben mit Zeitung
Le guéridon, 1913/14
The Guéridon
Oil on canvas, 130 x 89 cm
Kunstmuseum Basel
Donated by Dr. h.c. Raoul La Roche,
1952
Zervos: XXIX, no. 48
Plate 31

Cat. Zurich 78
Geige an der Wand
Violon accroché au mur, 1913
Hanging Violin
Oil on canvas, 65 x 46 cm
Kunstmuseum Bern
Stiftung Hermann und Margrit Rupf
Zervos: IIb, no. 371

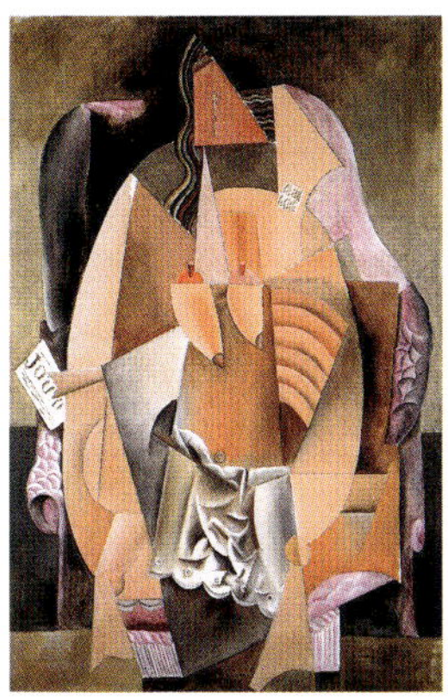

79

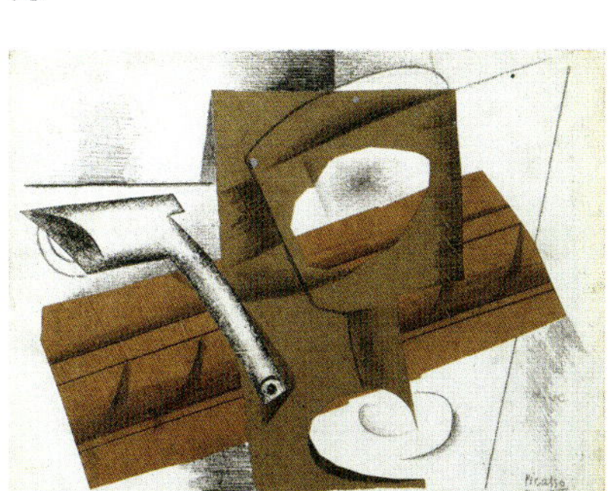

80

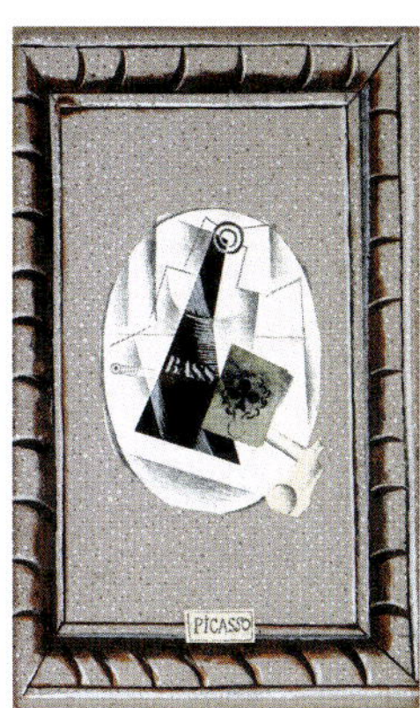

81

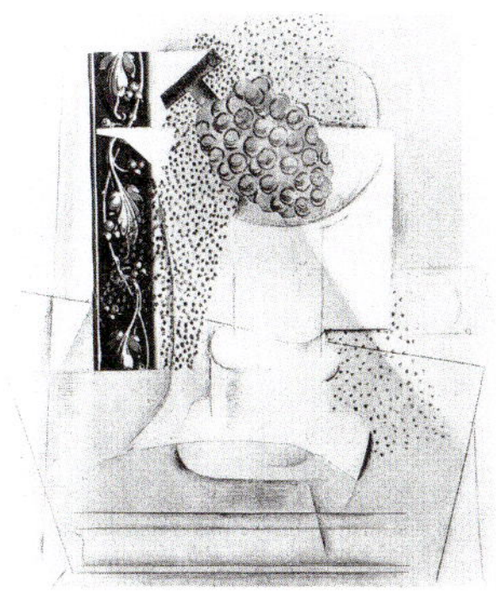

82

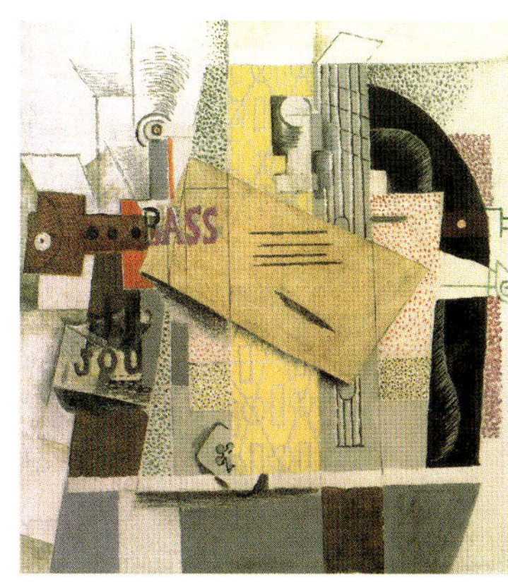

83

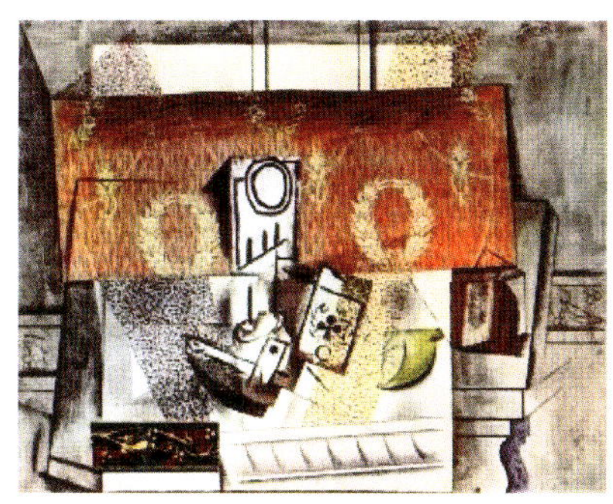

84

Cat. Zurich 79
Frau in Lehnstuhl
Femme assise dans un fauteuil, 1913
Woman in an Armchair
Oil on canvas, 149.9 × 99.5 cm
Private collection
Zervos: IIb, no. 522

Cat. Zurich 80
Stilleben mit Pfeife
Pipe et verre, 1914
Pipe and Wineglass
Pasted paper and pencil on white,
ribbed paper, 17.9 × 24 cm
Thaw Collection, The Pierpont Morgan
Library, New York
Zervos: IIb, no. 455
Plate 32

Cat. Zurich 81
Flasche, Pfeife und Karte
**Bouteille de Bass, as de trèfle,
pipe, 1914**
Bottle of Bass, Ace of Clubs and Pipe
Collage (oil, gouache, pencil),
51.5 × 31 cm
Private ownership
Zervos: IIb, no. 500
Plate 33

Cat. Zurich 82
Die Traube
**Compotier avec grappe de raisin,
1914**
Fruit Bowl with Grapes
Pasted paper, gouache and pencil on
paper, 48 × 43 cm
Private collection
Zervos: IIb, no. 476

Cat. Zurich 83
Stilleben
**Le violon (Titre attribué:
Nature morte), 1914**
The Violin
Oil on canvas, 81 × 75 cm
Centre Pompidou, Paris
Musée national d'art moderne/
Centre de création industrielle
Don de Raoul La Roche, 1952
Zervos: IIb, no. 487

Cat. Zurich 84
Cheminée
**Verre, pipe, citron, as de trèfle,
paquet de tabac, 1914**
*Glass, Pipe, Lemon, Ace of Clubs and
Tobacco*
Pasted paper, oil, charcoal and pencil,
54 × 65 cm
Private collection
Zervos: IIb, no. 482

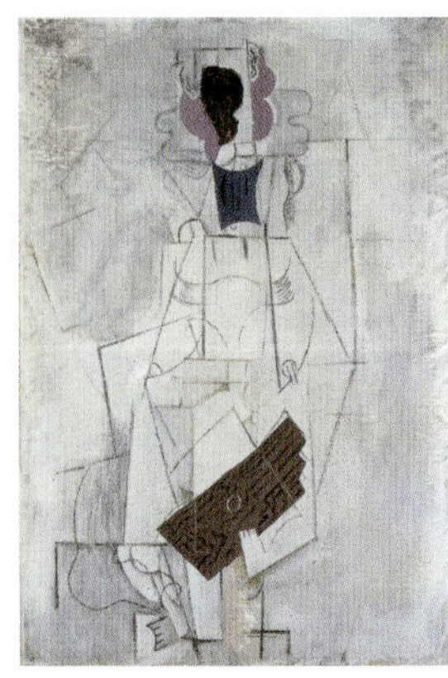

85

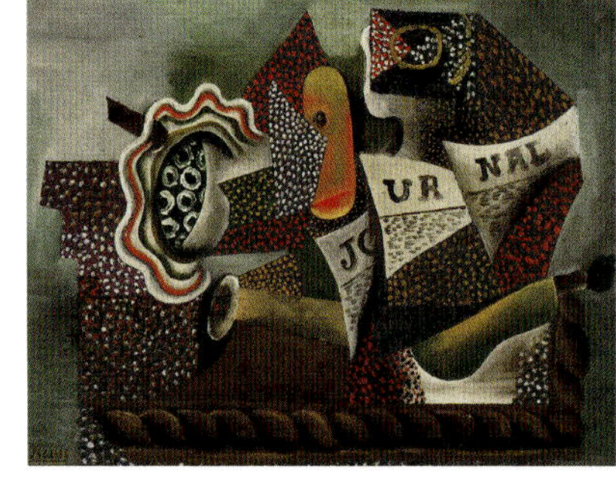

87

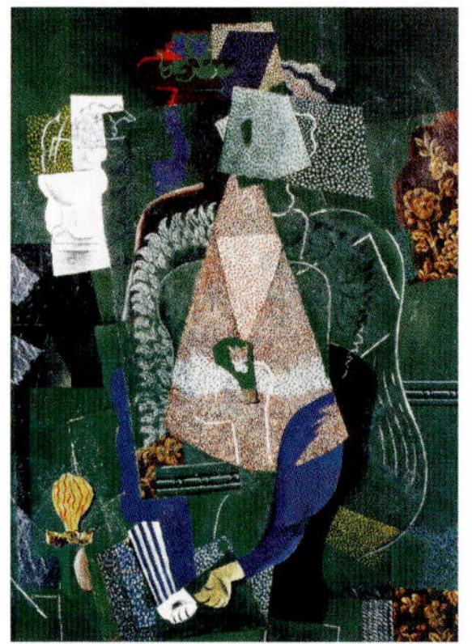

89

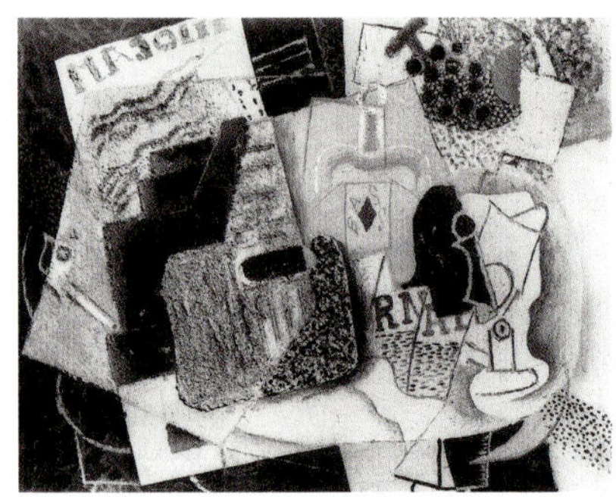

86

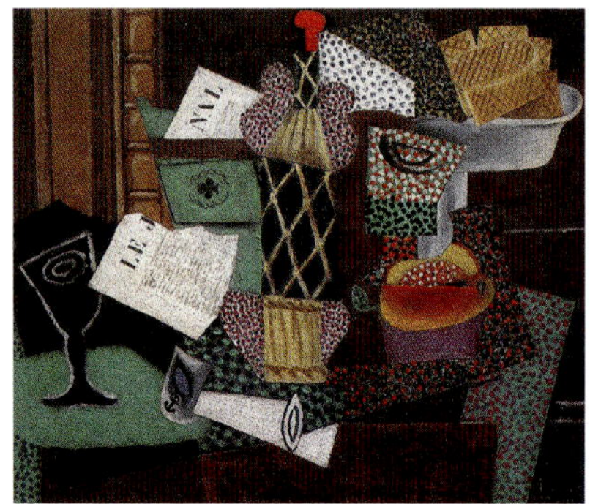

88

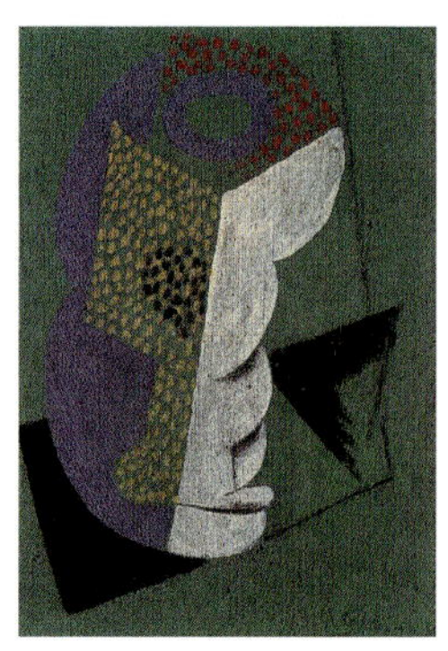

90

Cat. Zurich 85
Mann mit Gitarre
Femme à la guitare, 1911/14
Woman with Guitar
Oil on canvas, 130.5 x 90 cm
Kunstmuseum Basel
Donated by Dr. h.c. Raoul La Roche, 1952
Zervos: IIb, no. 447
Plate 34

Cat. Zurich 86
»Ma Jolie«
Stilleben mit Flasche, Spielkarten,
Zeitungen, Pfeife
**Guitare, bouteille de Bass,
grappe de raisin, pipe et verre
(›Ma Jolie‹), 1914**
*Guitar, Bottle of Bass, Grapes, Pipe and
Glass (Ma Jolie)*
Oil, sand and sawdust on cardboard,
51.5 x 67.5 cm
Private collection
Zervos: IIb, no. 526

Cat. Zurich 87
Stilleben mit Zeitung
**Nature morte avec fruit, verre,
couteau et journal, 1914**
*Still Life with Fruit, Glass, Knife and
Newspaper*
Oil and sand on canvas, 33.5 x 41 cm
The Kreeger Museum, Washington, D.C.
Zervos: IIb, no. 530

Cat. Zurich 88
Flasche mit Strohhülle
**Nature morte à la bouteille
de rhum, 1914**
Still Life with Bottle of Rum
Oil and sand on canvas mounted on
Masonite, 38.1 x 46.3 cm
Private collection
Zervos: IIb, no. 535

Cat. Zurich 89
Bildnis auf Grün
Portrait de jeune fille, 1914
Young Girl
Oil on canvas, 130 x 96.5 cm
Centre Pompidou, Paris
Musée national d'art moderne/
Centre de création industrielle
Legs de Georges Salles 1967
Zervos: IIb, no. 528

Cat. Zurich 90
Komposition
Verre, 1914
The Glass
Oil on canvas, 21 x 15 cm
Private collection
not in Zervos

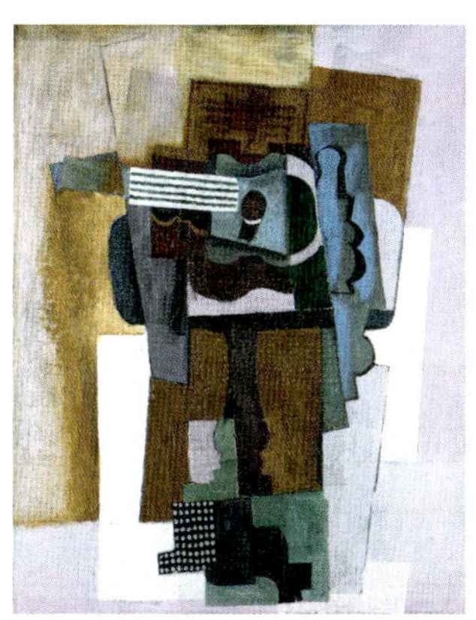

91

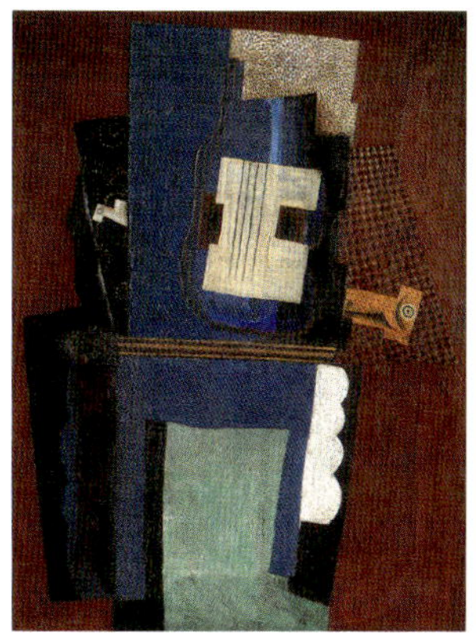

92

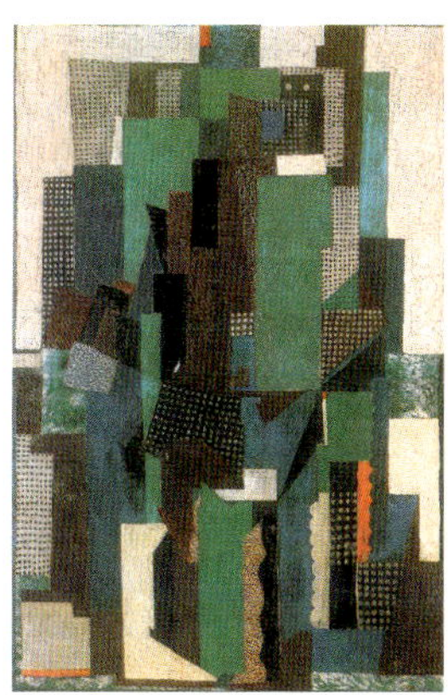

93

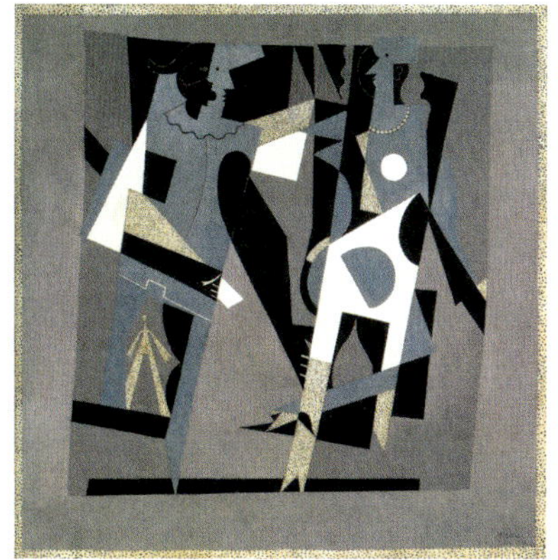

94

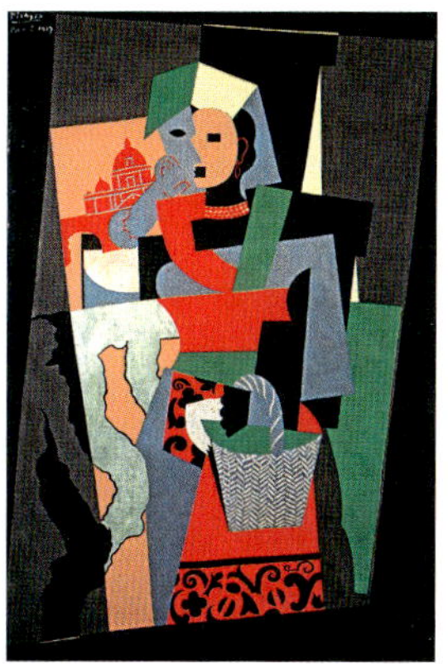

95

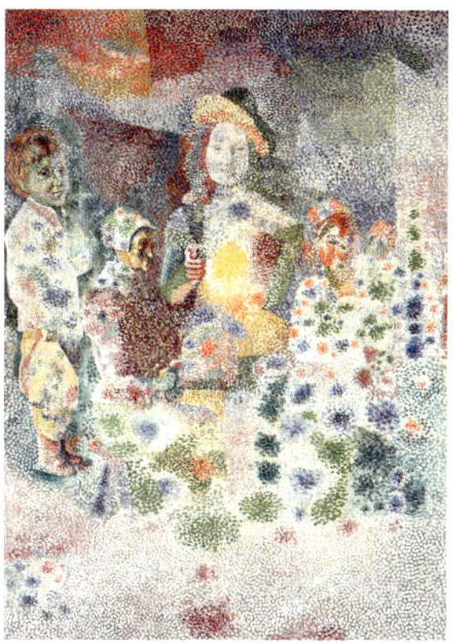

96

Cat. Zurich 91
Das Lesepult
Guitare sur un guéridon, 1915
Guitar on a Guéridon
Oil on canvas, 133 × 104 cm
Kunsthaus Zürich
Zervos: IIb, no. 536
Plate 35

Cat. Zurich 92
Cheminée mit Gitarre
**Guitare et clarinette sur
une cheminée, 1915**
Guitar on a Guéridon
Oil, sand and paper on canvas ,
130.2 × 97.2 cm
The Metropolitan Museum of Art
Bequest of Florene M. Schoenborn,
1995
Zervos: IIb, no. 540

Cat. Zurich 93
Aufrechte Gestalt
**Homme appuyé sur une table,
1915/16**
Man Leaning on a Table
Oil on canvas, 200 × 132 cm
Fondazione Pinacoteca Giovanni e
Marella Agnelli, Turin
Zervos: IIb, no. 550

Cat. Zurich 94
Zwei Harlekine
Arlequin et femme au collier, 1917
Harlequin and Woman with Necklace
Oil on canvas, 200 × 200 cm
Centre Pompidou, Paris
Musée national d'art moderne/
Centre de création industrielle
Bequest of Baronne Eva Gourgaud,
1965
Zervos: III, no. 23

Cat. Zurich 95
Die Italienerin
L'Italienne, 1917
The Italian Woman
Oil on canvas, 149.5 × 101.5 cm
Foundation E.G. Bührle Collection,
Zurich
Zervos: III, no. 18
Plate 36

Cat. Zurich 96
Die Mahlzeit der Bauern,
nach Le Nain
**Le retour du baptême,
d'après Le Nain, 1917**
Return from the Baptisme, after Le Nain
Oil on canvas, 162 × 118 cm
Musée Picasso, Paris
Dation en 1979
Zervos: III, no. 96

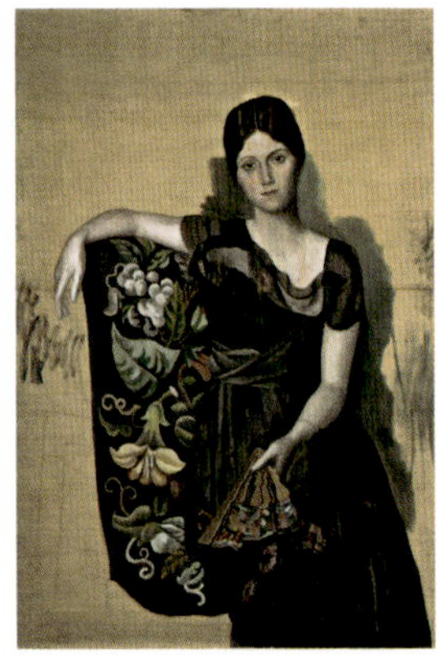

97

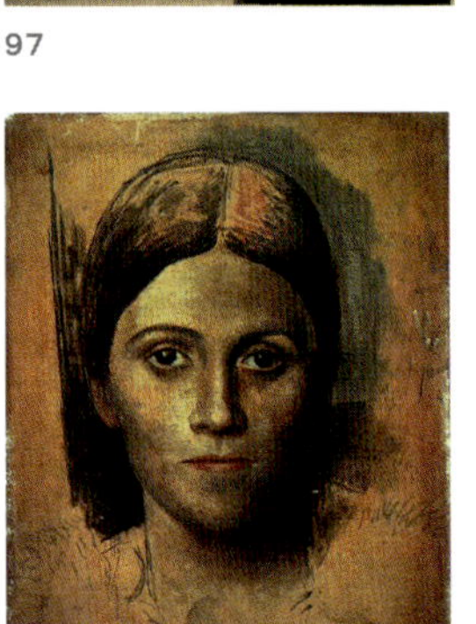

98

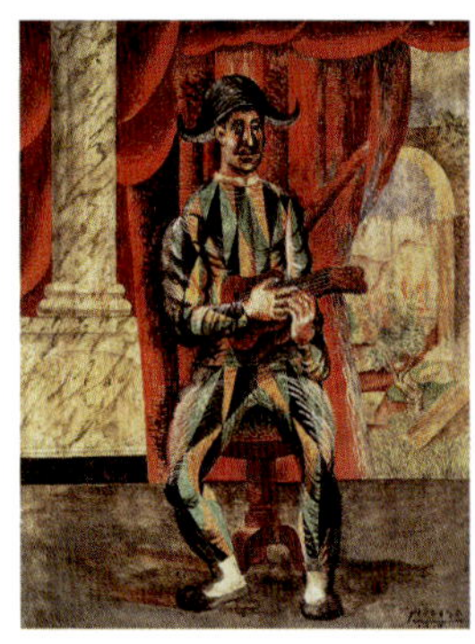

99

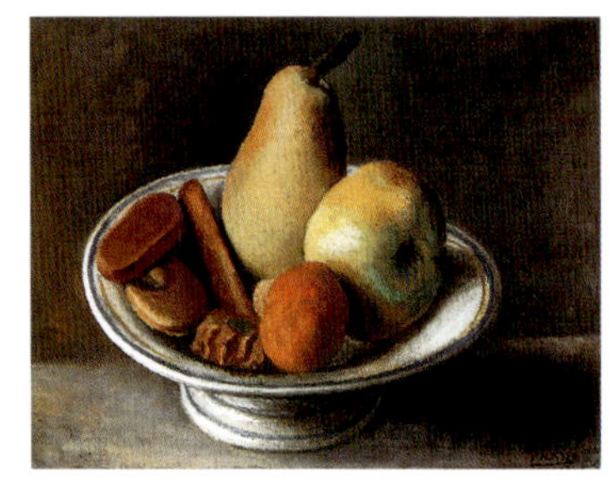

100

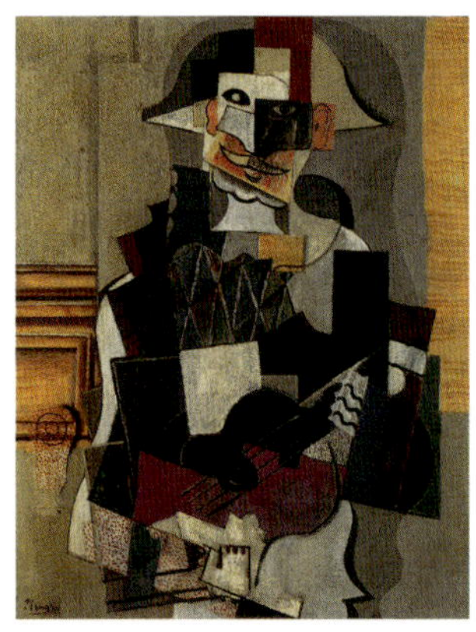

101

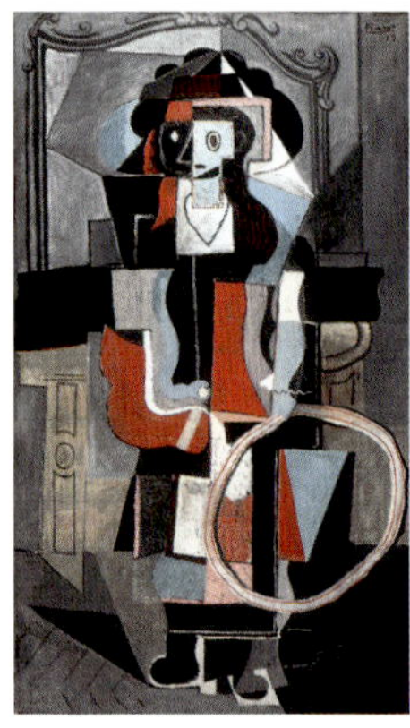

102

Cat. Zurich 97
Bildnis der Gattin des Künstlers
Portrait d'Olga dans un fauteuil, 1917
Portrait of Olga in an Armchair
Oil on canvas, 130 x 88.8 cm
Musée Picasso, Paris
Dation en 1979
Zervos: III, no. 83

Cat. Zurich 98
Bildnis Mme Picasso, Kopf
Portrait de Olga Picasso, 1918
Portrait of Olga Picasso
Oil on canvas, 35.2 x 27.3 cm
Menard Art Museum, Komaki City, Japan
Zervos: III, no. 125

Cat. Zurich 99
Musizierender Harlekin
Harlequin avec guitare, 1918
Harlequin Playing a Guitar
Oil on wood, 35 x 27
Staatliche Museen zu Berlin,
Nationalgalerie
Museum Berggruen
Zervos: III, no. 158

Cat. Zurich 100
Stillleben, Früchte und Konfekt
Compotier avec fruits, 1918
Fruit Bowl
Oil on canvas, 27 x 35 cm
Private collection
Zervos: III, no. 154

Cat. Zurich 101
Harlekin mit Gitarre
Arlequin jouant de la guitare, 1918
Harlequin Playing a Guitar
Oil on canvas, 97 x 76 cm
Private collection
Zervos: IIb, no. 518

Cat. Zurich 102
Kind mit Reif
Fillette au cerceau, 1919
Young Girl with Hoop
Oil and sand on canvas, 142.5 x 79 cm
Centre Pompidou, Paris
Musée national d'art moderne/
Centre de création industrielle
Bequest of Baronne Eva Gourgaud, 1965
Zervos: III, no. 289
Plate 37

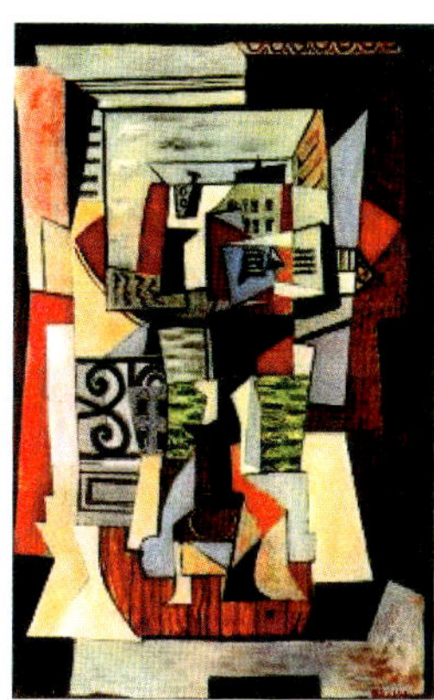

103

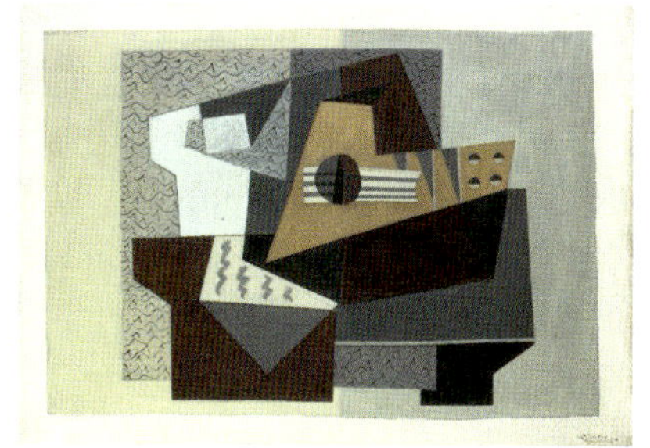

104

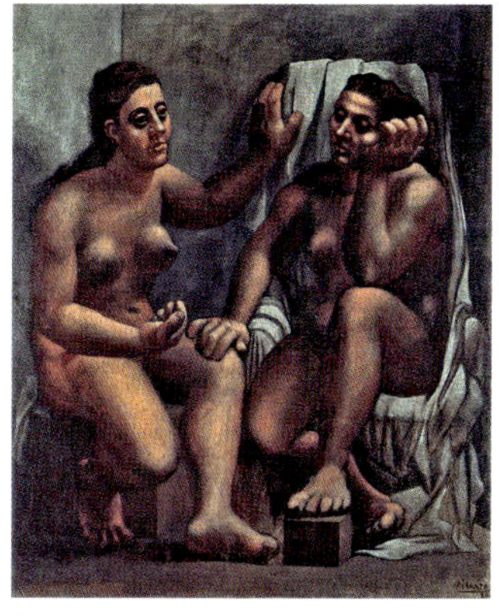

105

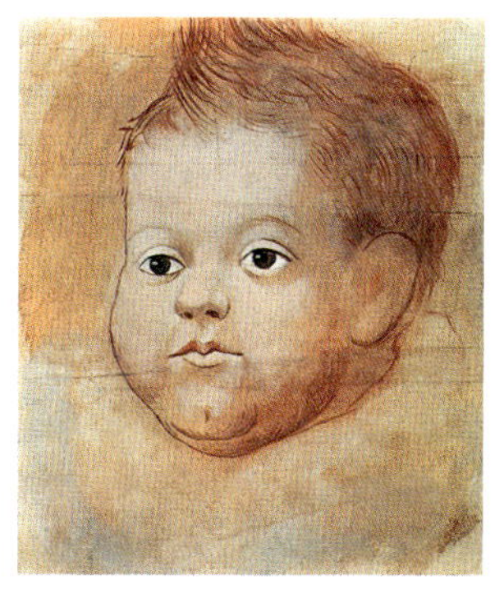

106

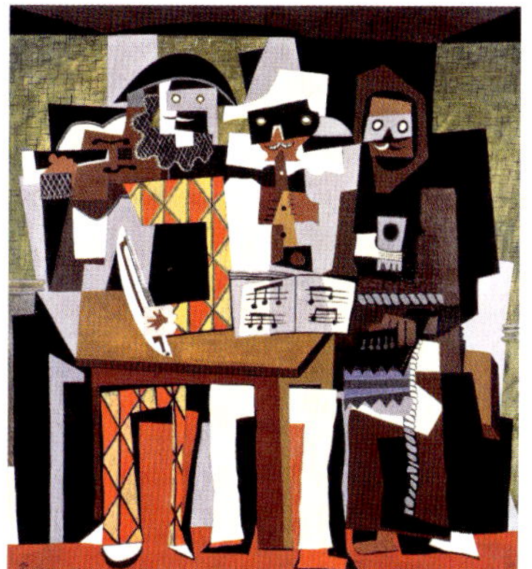

107

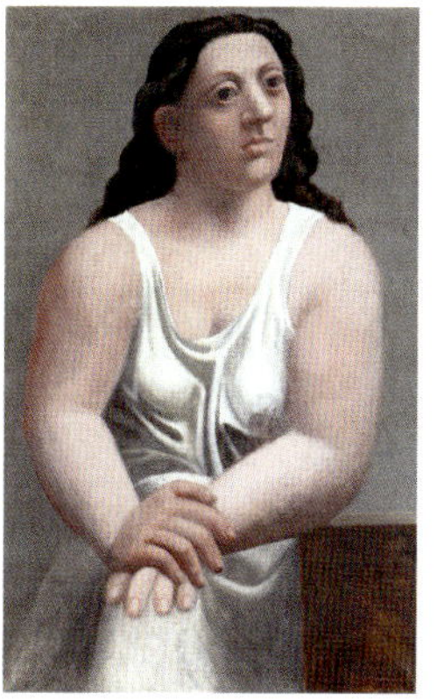

108

Cat. Zurich 103
Die Staffelei des Malers
**Fenêtre ouverte sur la rue
de Penthièvre, 1920**
*Window Opening on the
Rue de Penthièvre*
Oil on canvas, 165 x 110 cm
Tehran Museum of Contemporary Art
Zervos: IV, no. 74

Cat. Zurich 104
Die Gitarre
La Guitare, 1920
The Guitar
Oil on canvas, 65.5 x 92.5 cm
Emanuel Hoffmann-Stiftung
Deposited in the Öffentliche Kunst-
sammlung Basel
Zervos: IV, no. 190
Plate 38

Cat. Zurich 105
Zwei Frauenakte
Deux femmes nues assises, 1920
Two Seated Female Nudes
Oil on canvas, 195 x 163 cm
Kunstsammlung Nordrhein-Westfalen,
Düsseldorf
Zervos: IV, no. 217

Cat. Zurich 106
Knabenkopf
Le fils de l'artiste, 1922
The Artist's Son
Oil on canvas, 33.5 x 27 cm
Private collection
Zervos: IV, no. 434

Cat. Zurich 107
Die drei Musikanten
Trois musiciens, 1921
Three Musicians
Oil on canvas, 204.5 x 188.3 cm
Philadelphia Museum of Art
A. E. Gallatin Collection, 1952,
1952-61-96
Zervos: IV, no. 332

Cat. Zurich 108
Sitzende Frau von vorn
**Femme assise (Femme à
la chemise), 1921**
Seated Woman (Woman with Chemise)
Oil on canvas, 116 x 73 cm
Staatsgalerie Stuttgart
Zervos: IV, no. 328
Plate 40

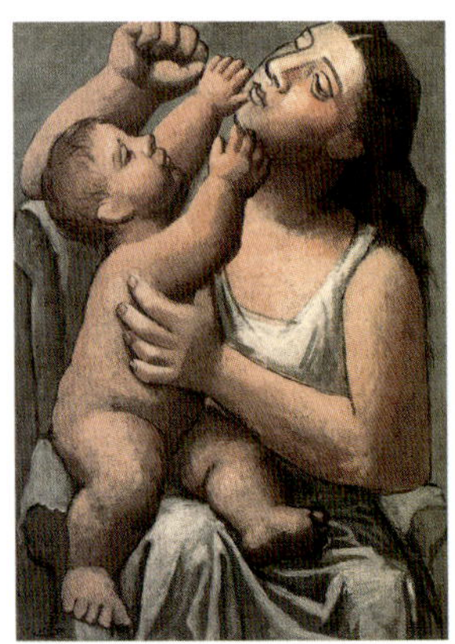

109

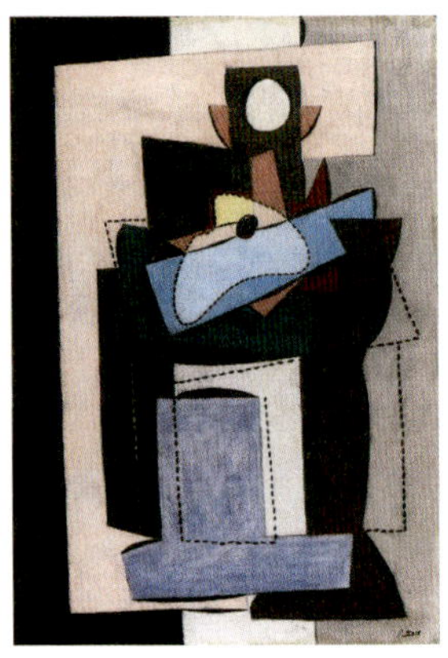

110

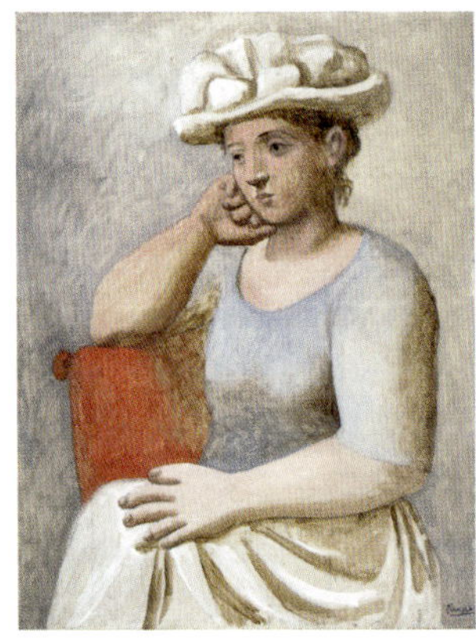

111

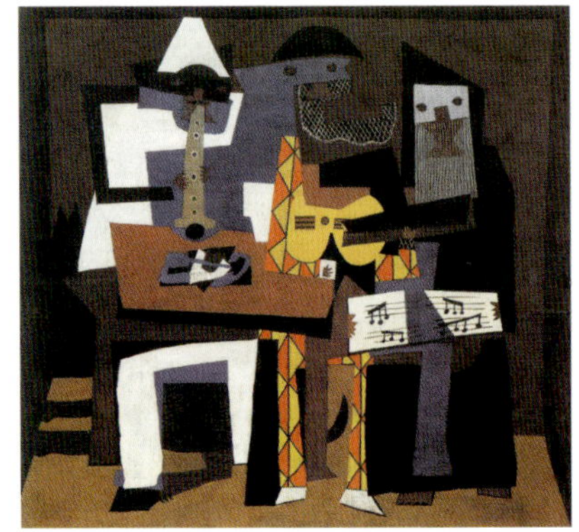

112

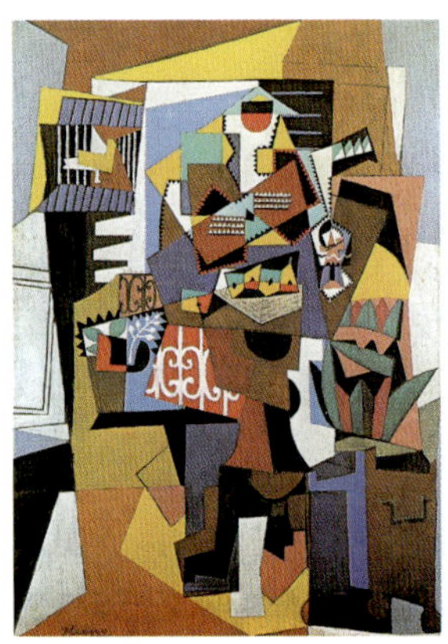

113

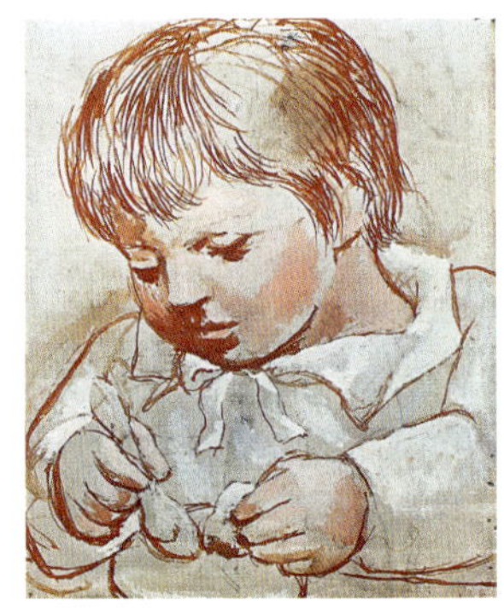

114

Cat. Zurich 109
Mutter und Kind
Mère et enfant, 1921
Mother and Child
Oil on canvas, 97 x 71 cm
Private collection
Zervos: IV, no. 289

Cat. Zurich 110
Cheminée
La Cheminée, 1920/21
The Mantlepiece
Distemper on paper, 105 x 74 cm
Centre Pompidou, Paris
Musée national d'art moderne/
Centre de création industrielle
Donation M. et Mme André Lefèvre,
1952
Zervos: IV, no. 209

Cat. Zurich 111
Frau mit Hut
Femme au chapeau blanc, 1921
Woman with a White Hat
Oil on canvas, 118 x 91 cm
Musée de l'Orangerie, Paris
Collection Jean Walter et Paul Guillaume
Zervos: IV, no. 352
Plate 41

Cat. Zurich 112
Die drei Musikanten
Musiciens aux masques, 1921
Three Musicians
Oil on canvas, 200.7 x 222.9 cm
The Museum of Modern Art, New York
Mrs Simon Guggenheim Fund
Zervos: IV, no. 331

Cat. Zurich 113
Stilleben mit Fenster
La cage d'oiseaux, 1923
The Birdcage
Oil on canvas, 200 x 140 cm
Private collection
Zervos: V, no. 84

Cat. Zurich 114
Kind beim Essen
Le fils de l'artiste, 1922
The Artist's Son
Oil on canvas, 35 x 31 cm
Private collection
Zervos: IV, no. 435

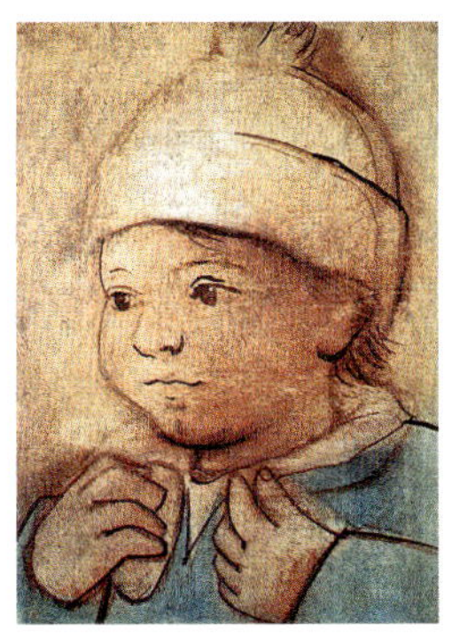

115

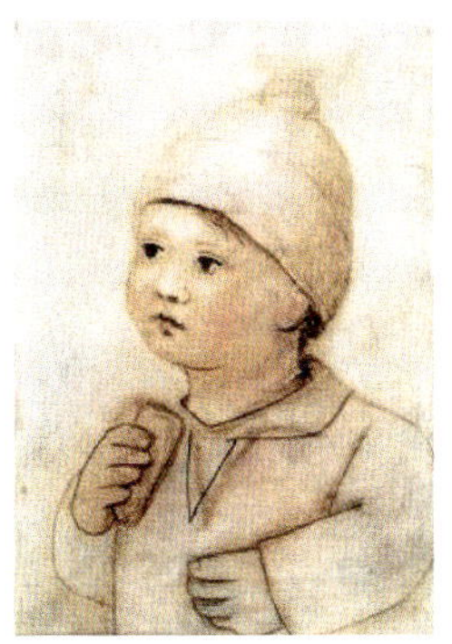

116

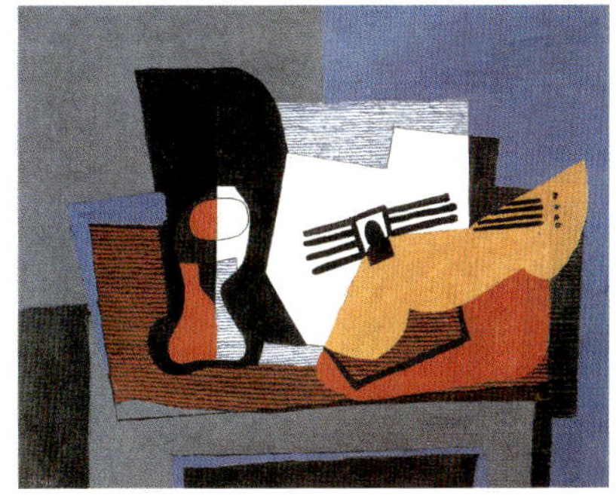

117

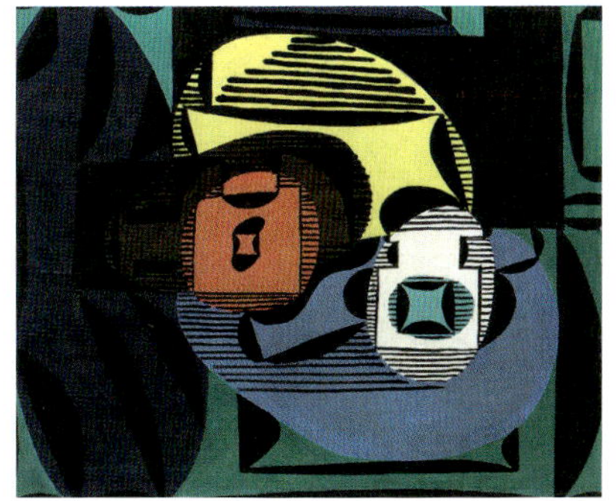

118

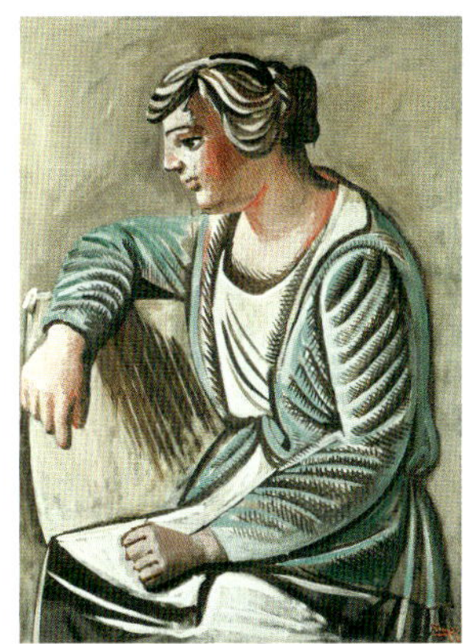

119

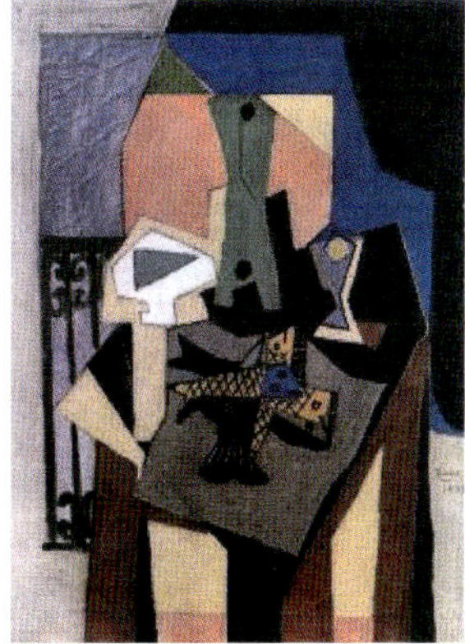

120

Cat. Zurich 115
Kind mit weißer Mütze
Le fils de l'artiste, 1922
The Artist's Son
Oil and bistre on canvas,
32.5 x 24 cm
Private collection
Zervos: IV, no. 437

Cat. Zurich 116
Kleiner Knabe, Brustbild
Le fils de l'artiste, 1922
The Artist's Son
Oil on canvas, 33 x 46 cm
Private collection
Zervos: IV, no. 436

Cat. Zurich 117
Stilleben mit Gitarre
Nature morte à la guitare, 1922
Still Life with Guitar
Oil on canvas, 83 x 102.5 cm
Sammlung Rosengart, Luzern
Zervos: IV, no. 418

Cat. Zurich 118
Komposition
Mandoline sur une table, 1922
Mandolin on a Table
Oil on canvas, 81.6 x 100.1 cm
Private collection
Zervos: IV, no. 422

Cat. Zurich 119
Die grüne Bluse
Femme au peignoir vert, 1922
Woman in a Green Dressing Gown
Oil on canvas, 130.3 x 96.5 cm
Museum Ludwig Köln
Zervos: IV, no. 388
Plate 42

Cat. Zurich 120
Fische auf einem Tisch
**Poissons, bouteille et verre
sur une table, 1923**
Fish, Bottle and Glass on a table
Oil on canvas, 130 x 97 cm
Private collection
Zervos: IV, no. 448

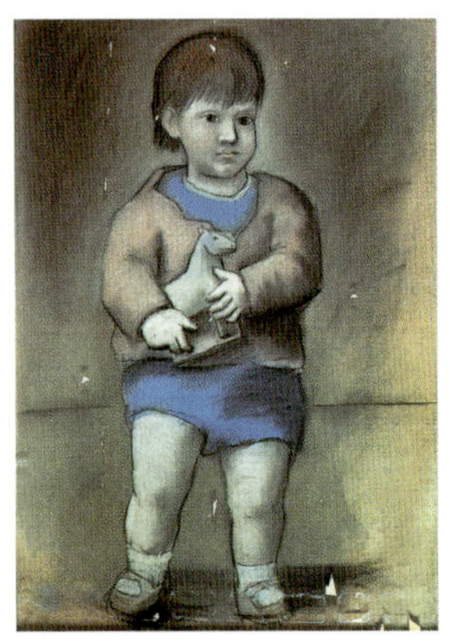

121

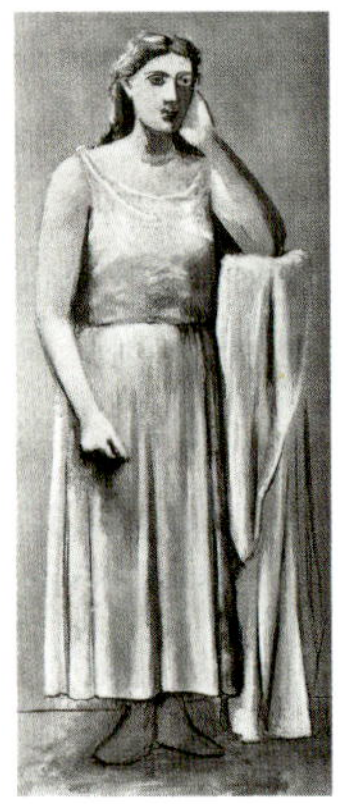

122

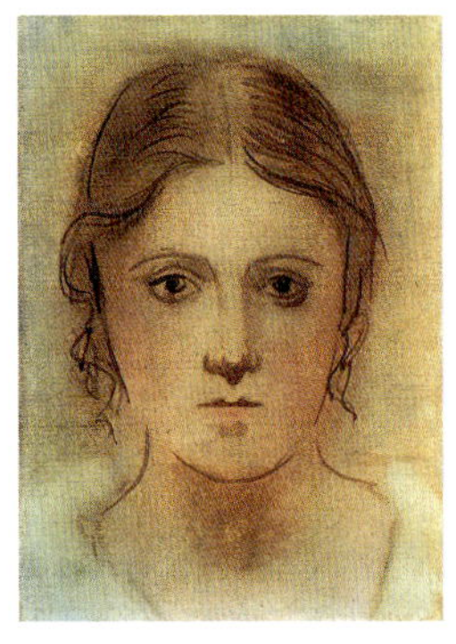

123

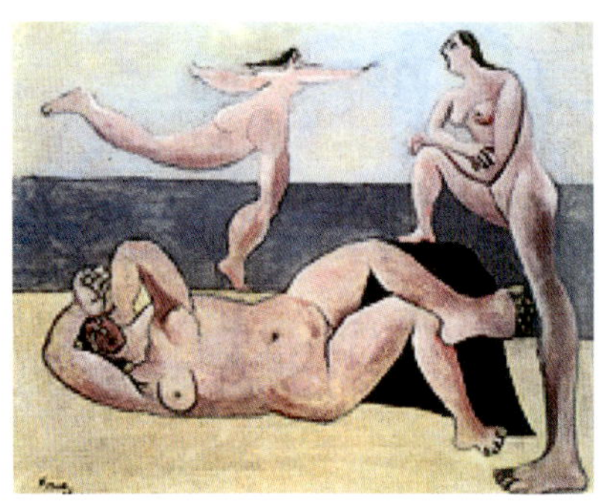

124

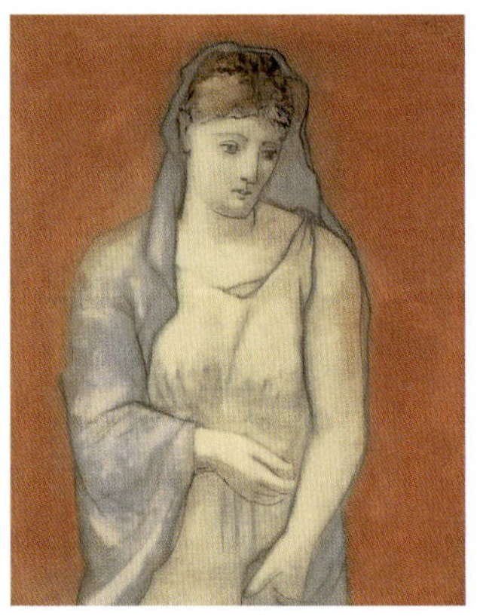

125

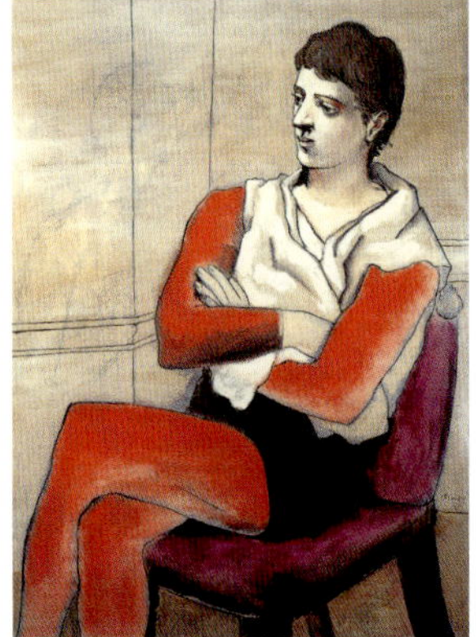

126

Cat. Zurich 121
Kind mit Spielzeug
L'enfant au jouet, 1923
Child with a Toy
Charcoal, pastel and gouache on paper,
103.5 x 73.5 cm
Private collection
Courtesy Fundación Almine y
Bernard Ruiz-Picasso para el Arte
Zervos: V, no. 52

Cat. Zurich 122
Die Griechin
La Grecque, 1923
Grecian Figure
Oil on canvas, 186 x 77 cm
Private collection
Zervos: V, no. 249

Cat. Zurich 123
Frauenkopf
Portrait d'Olga, 1923
Portrait of Olga
Oil and turpentine on canvas,
33 x 24.1 cm
Private collection
Zervos: IV, no. 438

Cat. Zurich 124
Figuren am Strand
Trois baigneuses, 1920
Three Bathers
Oil on canvas, 81 x 100 cm
Private collection
Zervos: IV, no. 169

Cat. Zurich 125
Der blaue Schleier
Femme au voile bleu, 1923
Woman with Blue Veil
Oil on canvas, 100.3 x 81.2 cm
Los Angeles County Museum of Art
Mr and Mrs George Gard de Sylva
Collection (M.46.8.1)
Zervos: V, no. 16
Plate 43

Cat. Zurich 126
Ausruhender Akrobat
Saltimbanque aux bras croisés, 1923
*Saltimbanque Seated with
Arms Crossed*
Oil on canvas, 130.6 x 97.7 cm
Bridgestone Museum of Art, Tokio
Zervos: V, no. 15

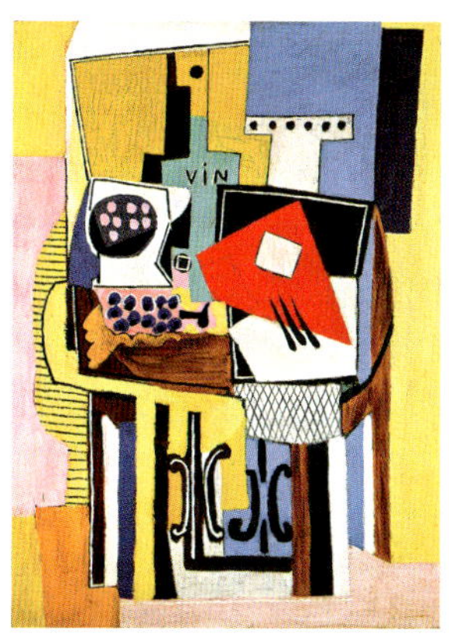

127

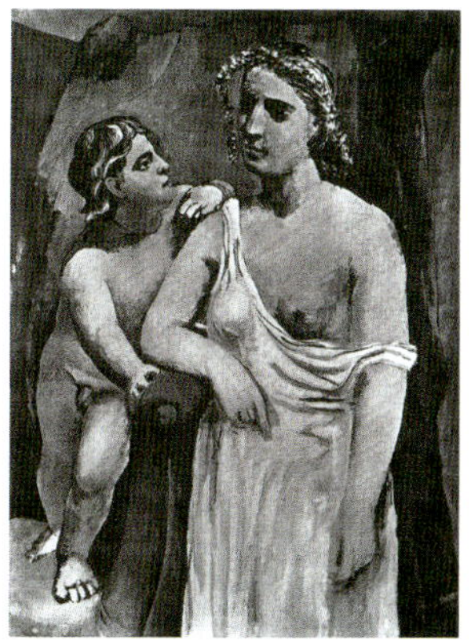

128

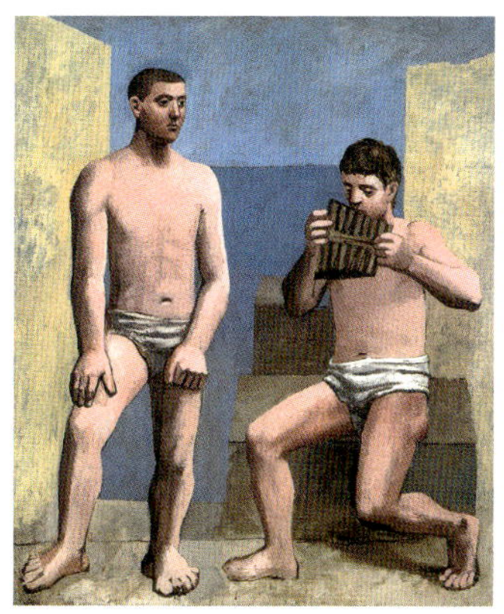

129

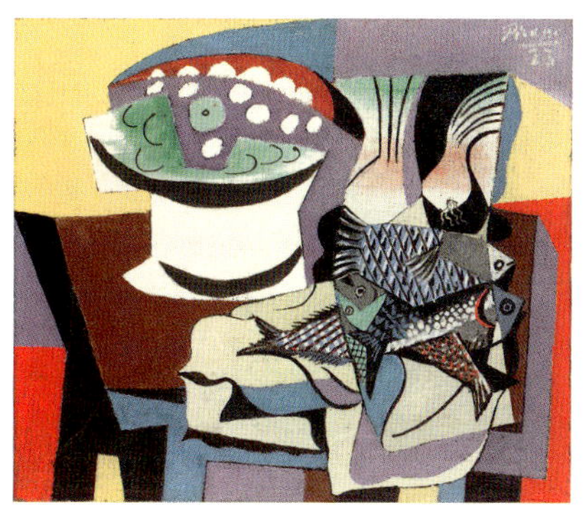

130

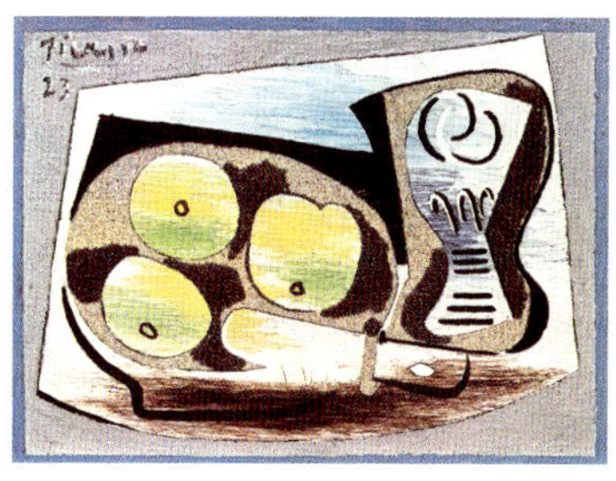

131

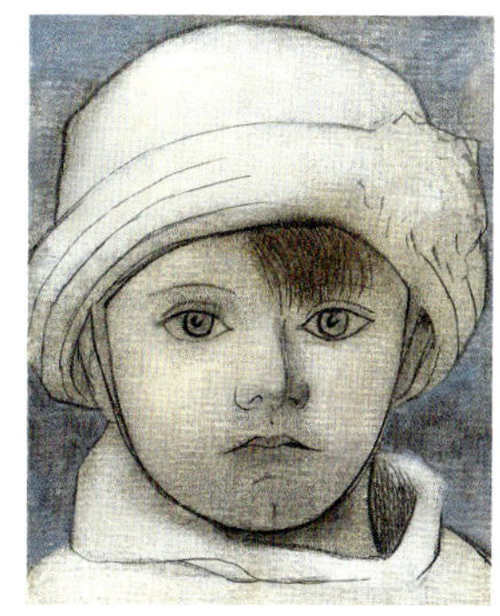

132

Cat. Zurich 127
Tisch vor dem Fenster
Compotier, bouteille et guitare,
1922/23
Fruit Dish, Bottle and Guitar
Oil on canvas, 131 x 97 cm
Private collection
Zervos: IV, no. 441

Cat. Zurich 128
Frau und Kind
Femme et enfant, 1923
Mother and Child
Oil on canvas, 130 x 97 cm
Private collection
Zervos: IV, no. 455

Cat. Zurich 129
Die Pansflöte (sic)
La flûte de Pan, 1923
The Pipes of Pan
Oil on canvas, 205 x 174 cm
Musée Picasso, Paris
Dation en 1979
Zervos: V, no. 141

Cat. Zurich 130
La petite cuisine
La petite cuisine, 1923
Still Life with Fish
Oil on canvas, 46 x 54 cm
Wadsworth Atheneum Museum of Art,
Hartford, CT
The Collection of Philip L. Goodwin
through James L. Goodwin and
Henry Sage Goodwin
Zervos: V, no. 69

Cat. Zurich 131
Äpfel
Nature morte aux pommes, 1923
Still Life with Apples
Oil and sand on canvas, 24.1 x 33 cm
Private collection
Zervos: V, no. 64

Cat. Zurich 132
Kind mit weissem Hut
Portrait de Paulo en bonnet blanc,
1923
Portrait of Paulo in a White Cap
Oil on canvas, 27 x 22 cm
Private collection
Courtesy Fundación Almine y Bernard
Ruiz-Picasso para el Arte
Zervos: V, no. 180
Plate 44

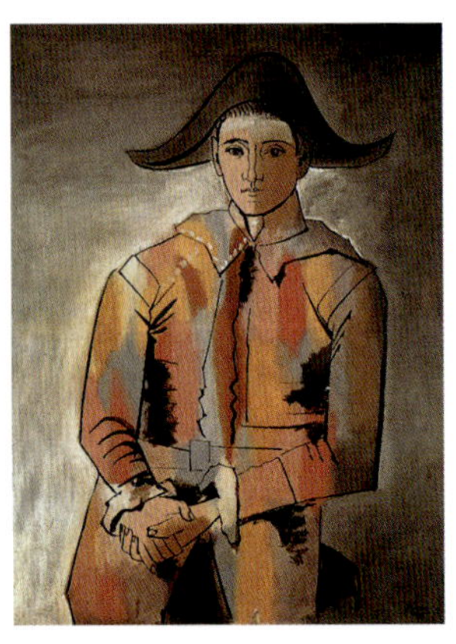

133

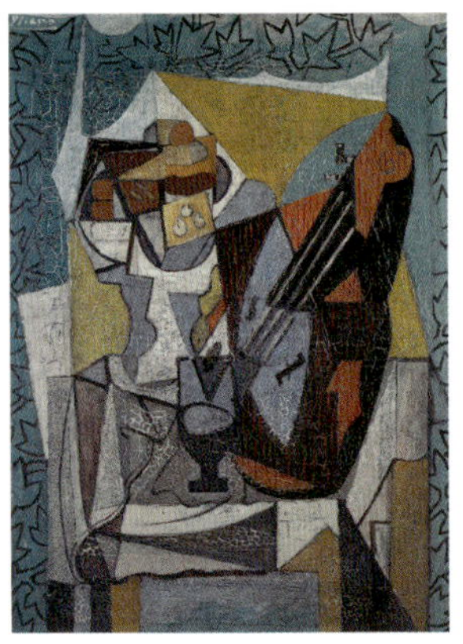

134

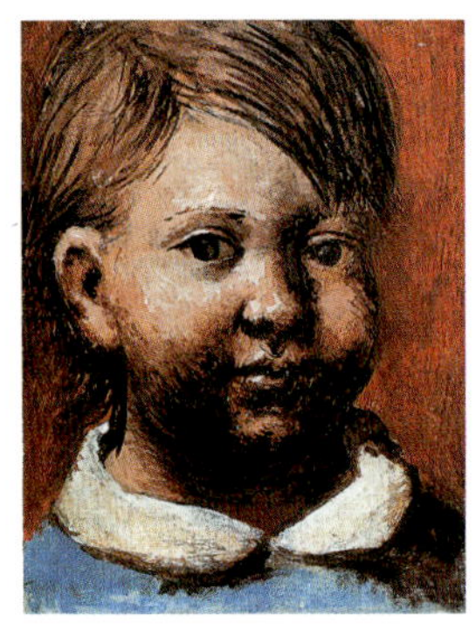

135

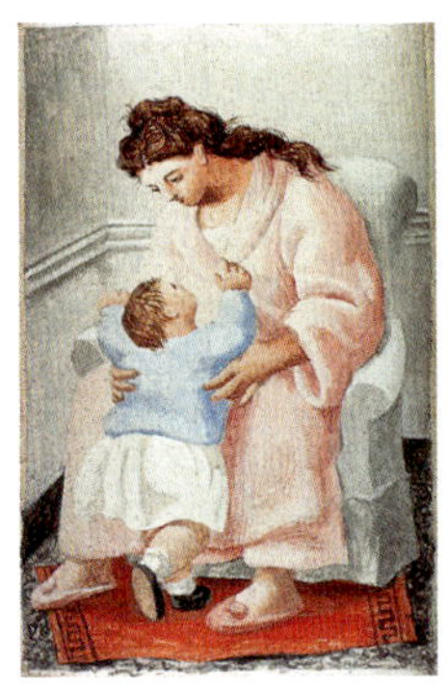

136

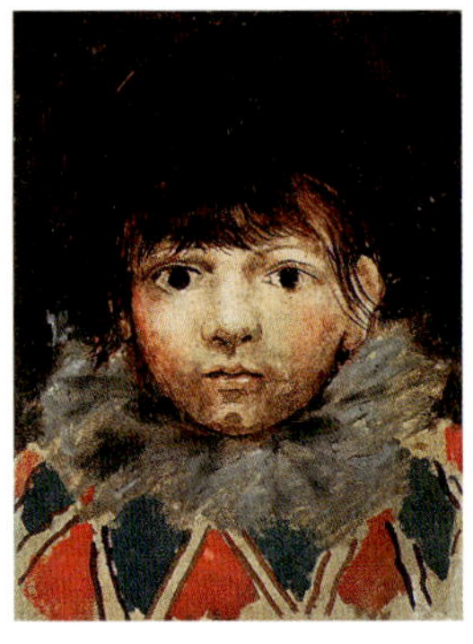

137

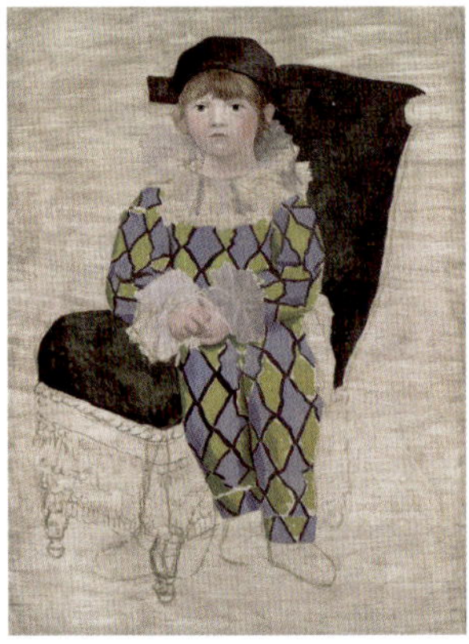

138

Cat. Zurich 133
Harlekin von vorn
Arlequin, les mains croisées, 1923
Harlequin with Clasped Hands
Oil on canvas, 129 x 96 cm
Museum Ludwig Köln
The Ludwig Bequest 1994
Zervos: V, no. 135

Cat. Zurich 134
Stilleben
Les gâteaux, 1917
Still Life
Oil on canvas, 99 x 71 cm
Private collection
Zervos: III, no. 97

Cat. Zurich 135
Kinderbildnis
Tête de Paulo, 1923
Head of Paulo
Oil and sepia on canvas, 24 x 19 cm
Private collection
not in Zervos

Cat. Zurich 136
Frau mit Kind
Mère et enfant, 1922/23
Mother and Child
Gouache and turpentine on wood,
15 x 10 cm
Private collection

Cat. Zurich 137
Kinderkopf, Harlekin
**Le fils de l'artiste en arlequin
(Portrait de Paulo), 1924**
*The Son of the Artist as Harlequin
(Portrait of Paulo)*
Oil on canvas, 34.9 x 27 cm
Private collection
Zervos: V, no. 179

Cat. Zurich 138
Der kleine Harlekin
Paulo en arlequin, 1924
Paulo as a Harlequin
Oil on canvas, 130 x 97.5 cm
Musée Picasso, Paris
Dation en 1979
Zervos: V, no. 178

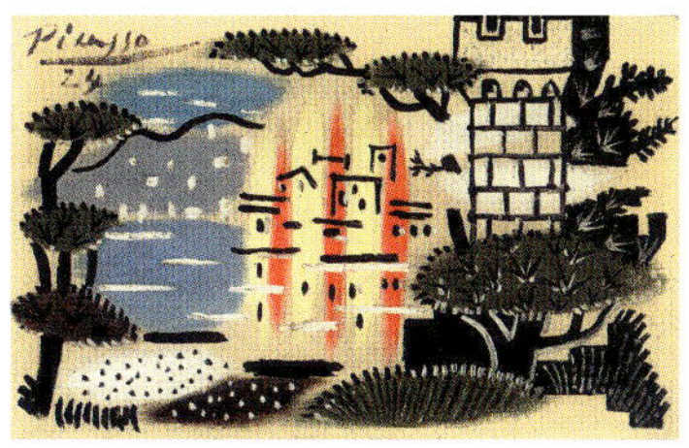

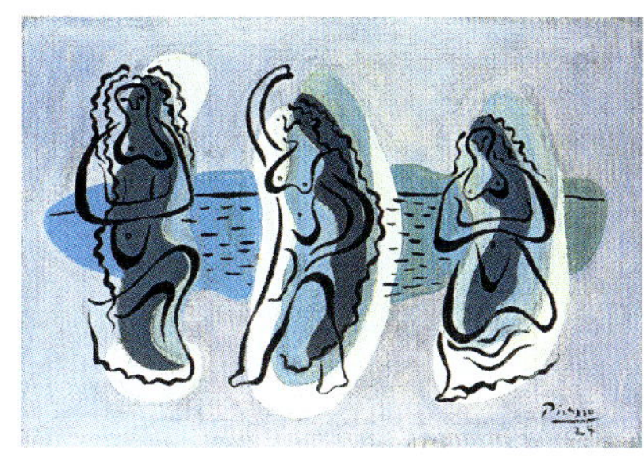

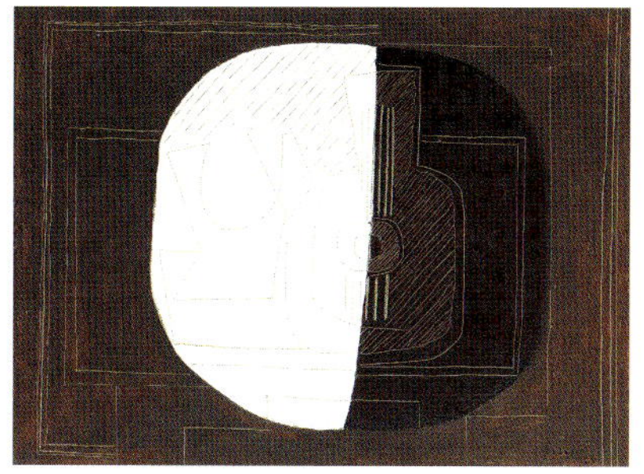

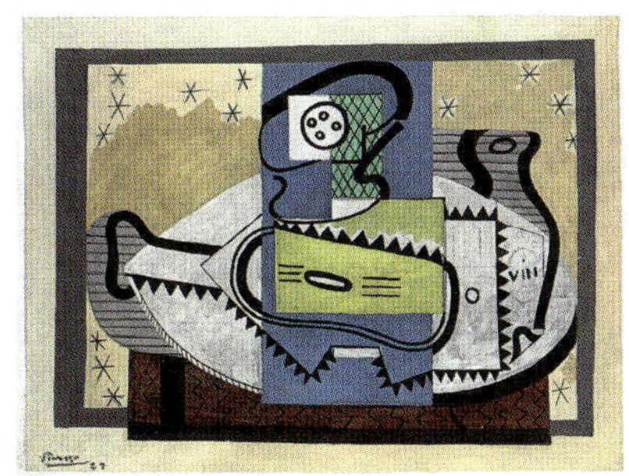

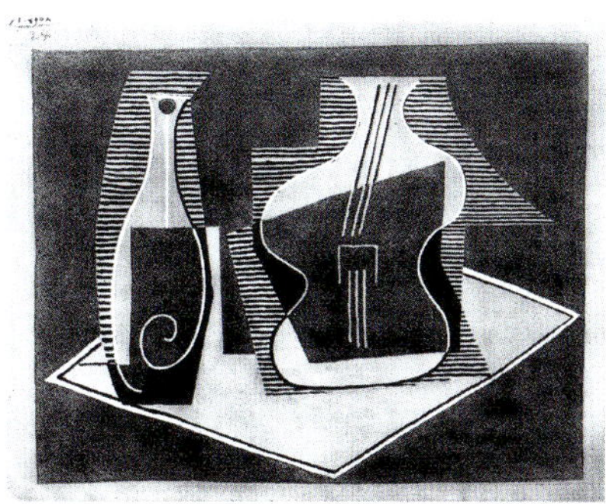

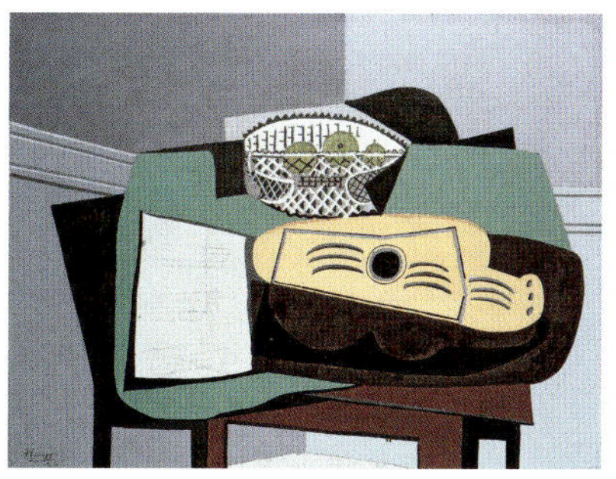

Cat. Zurich 139
Juan-les-Pins
Paysage à Juan-les-Pins, 1924
Landscape at Juan-les-Pins
Oil on canvas, 22.2 x 35.7 cm
Private collection
Zervos: V, no. 330

Cat. Zurich 140
Weinkrug, Fruchtschale,
Gitarre, Sterne
Compotier et guitare, 1924
Fruit Bowl and Guitar
Oil on canvas, 97.1 x 130.8 cm
Private collection
Zervos: V, no. 225

Cat. Zurich 141
Badende Frauen
Trois femmes au bord d'une plage, 1924
Three Women on the Beach
Oil on canvas, 46.1 x 68.3 cm
Private collection
not in Zervos

Cat. Zurich 142
Stilleben auf Sand
Bouteille et guitare, 1924
Bottle and Guitar
Oil on canvas, 81 x 100 cm
Private collection
Zervos: V, no. 365

Cat. Zurich 143
Komposition in braun und weiss
Guitare et compotier, 1924
Guitar and Fruit Bowl
Oil on canvas, 77 x 106 cm
Courtesy Nahmad Collection,
Switzerland
Zervos: V, no. 378
Plate 45

Cat. Zurich 144
Stilleben mit Fruchtkorb
Partition, guitare et compotier, 1924
Score, Guitar and Fruit Bowl
Oil on canvas, 97.1 x 130.1 cm
Courtesy Nahmad Collection,
Switzerland
Zervos: V, no. 221
Plate 46

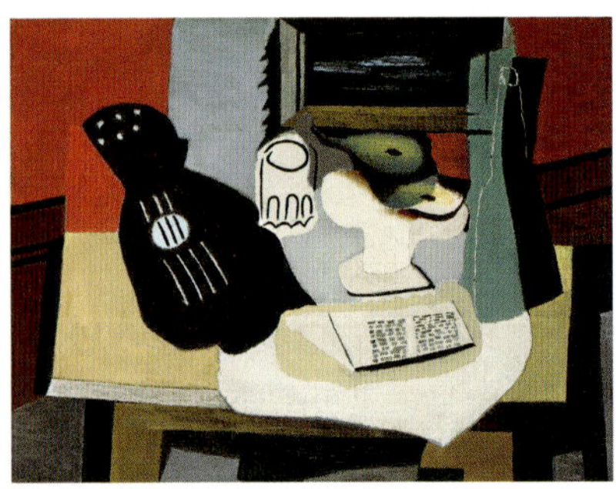

145

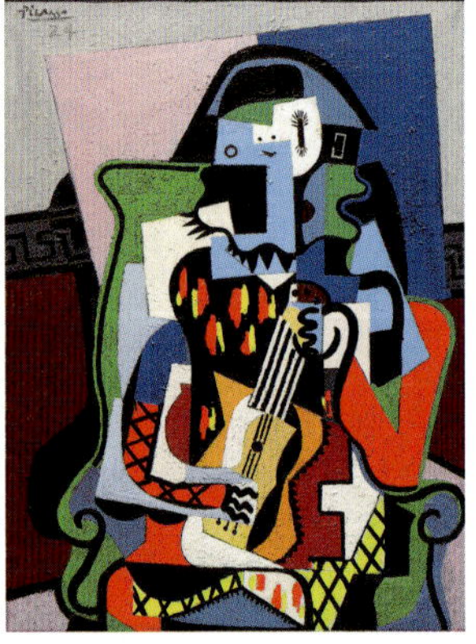

147

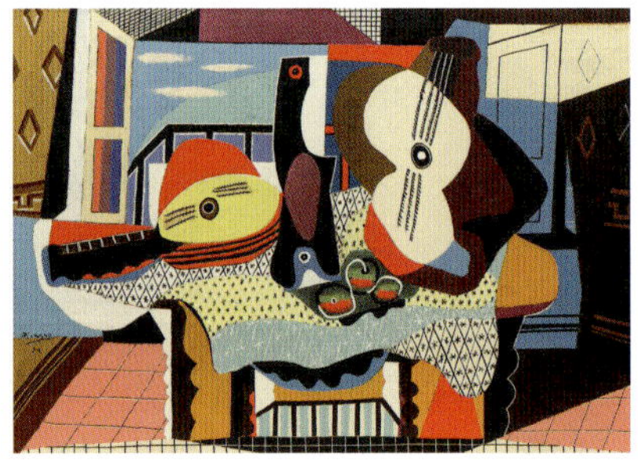

149

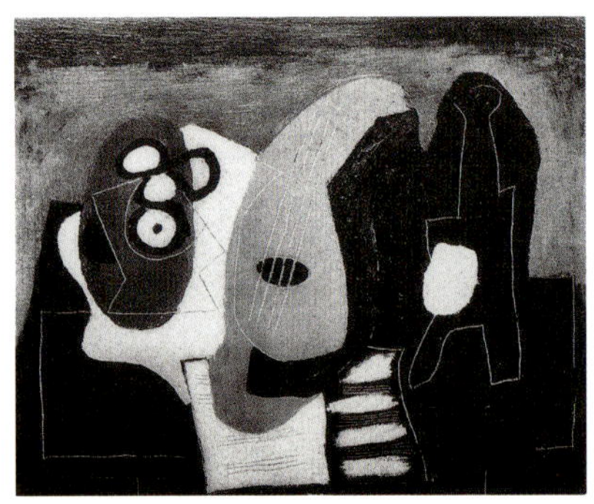

146

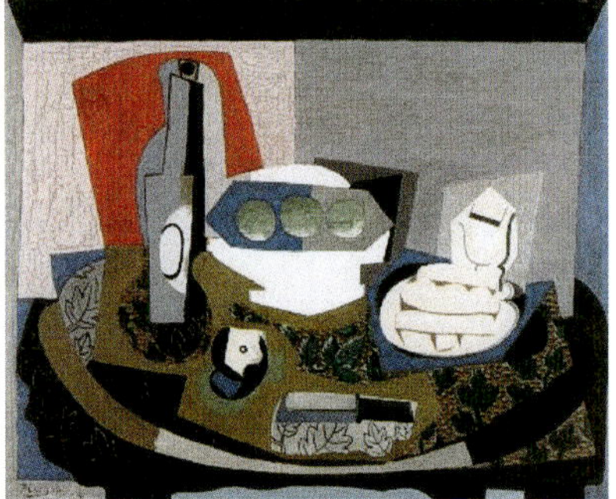

148

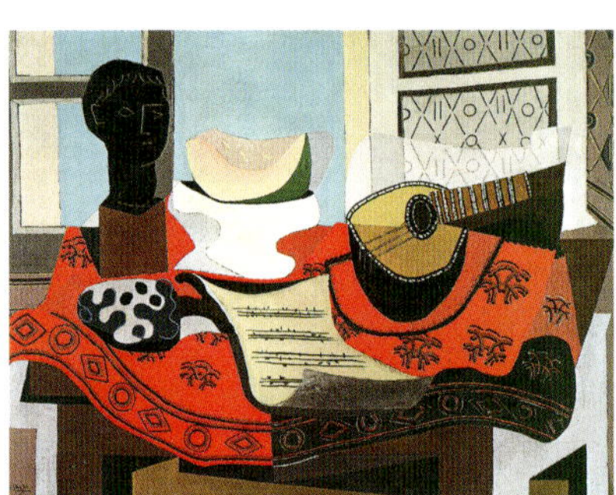

150

Cat. Zurich 145
Gitarre, Trinkglas und Fruchtschale
**Guitare, verre et compotier
avec fruits, 1924**
Guitar, Glass and Fruit Bowl
Oil on canvas, 97.5 x 130.5 cm
Kunsthaus Zürich
Zervos: V, no. 252
Plate 47

Cat. Zurich 146
Der Tisch des Musikers
**Compotier, mandoline,
bouteille, 1924**
Fruit Bowl, Mandolin, Bottle
Oil on canvas
Private collection
Zervos: V, no. 186

Cat. Zurich 147
Musizierender Harlekin
Arlequin musicien, 1924
Harlequin Musician
Oil on canvas, 113.8 x 97.2 cm
National Gallery of Art, Washington
Given in loving memory of her husband,
Taft Schreiber, by Rita Schreiber
(1989.31.2)
Zervos: V, no. 328
Plate 48

Cat. Zurich 148
Imbiss
**Bouteille, compotier, assiette
de biscuits, 1924**
Still Life with Biscuits
Oil (and sand) on canvas,
80.8 x 100.4 cm
The Cleveland Museum of Art
Leonard C. Hanna Jr. Fund
Zervos: V, no. 242

Cat. Zurich 149
Stilleben vor dem Fenster
Mandoline et guitare, 1924
Mandolin and Guitar
Oil with sand on canvas,
140.7 x 200.3 cm
Solomon R. Guggenheim Museum,
New York (53.1358)
Zervos: V, no. 220
Plate 49

Cat. Zurich 150
Der rote Teppich
Le tapis rouge, 1924
The Red Tablecloth
Oil on canvas, 98.5 x 131.5 cm
Private collection
Zervos: V, no. 364

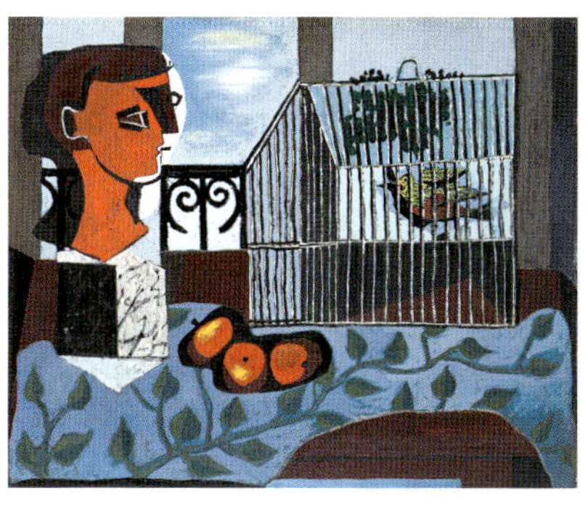

151

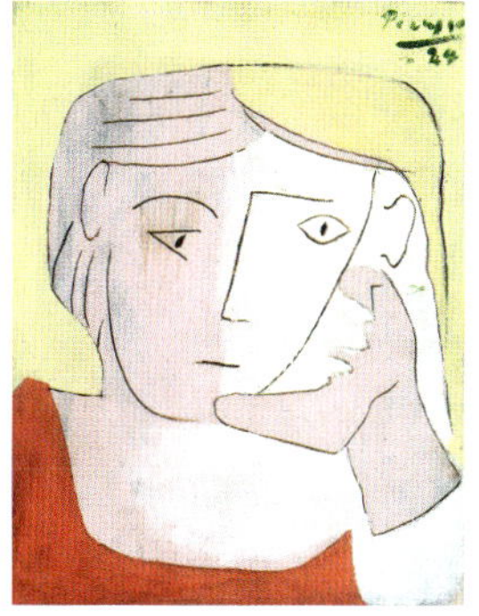

153

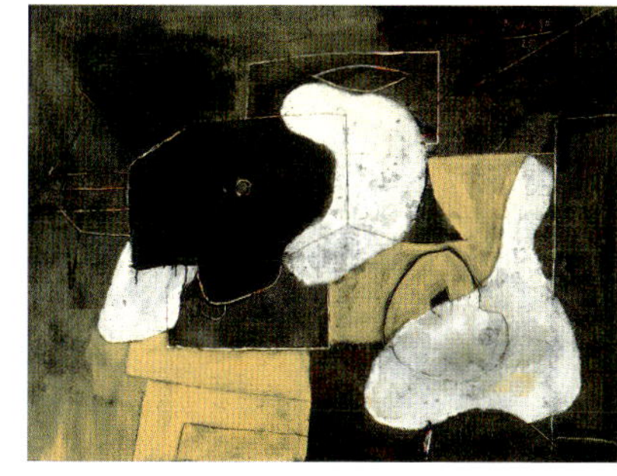

155

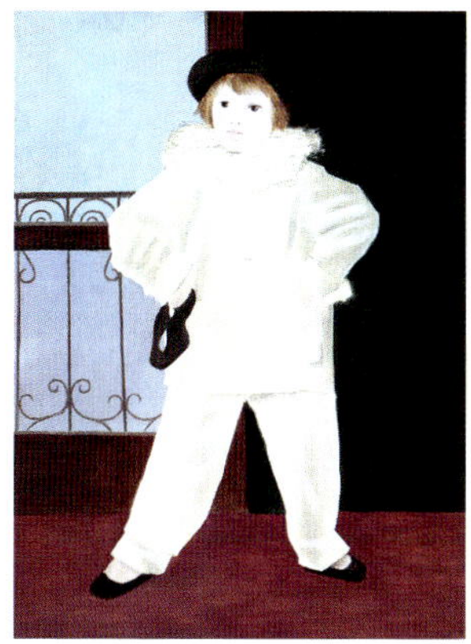

152

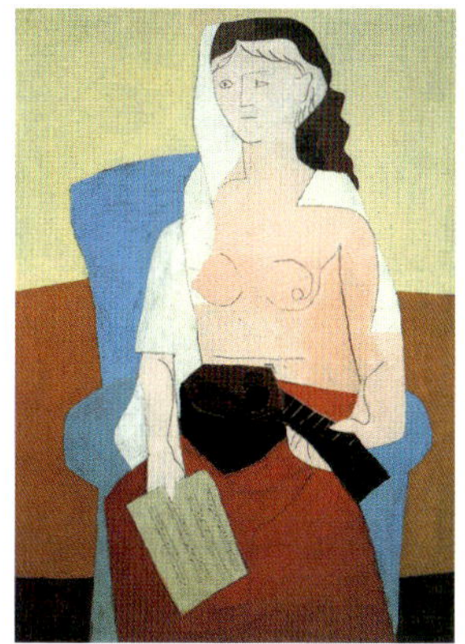

154

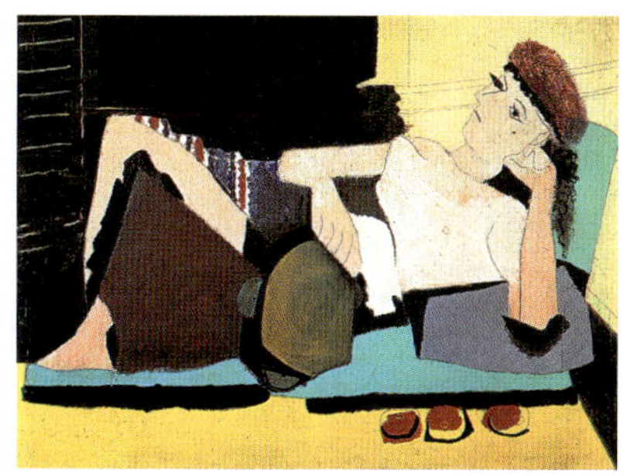

156

Cat. Zurich 151
Der Vogelkäfig
La cage, 1925
The Bird Cage
Oil on canvas, 80.6 x 99.5 cm
Ohara Museum of Art, Japan
Zervos: V, no. 456
Plate 50

Cat. Zurich 152
Kleiner Pierrot mit Maske
Paulo en pierrot, 1925
Paulo as Pierrot
Oil on canvas, 130 x 97 cm
Musée Picasso, Paris
Dation en 1979
Zervos: V, no. 374

Cat. Zurich 153
Frauenkopf
Tête de femme, 1924
Head of a Woman
Oil on canvas, 34.5 x 26.5 cm
Tate, London
Accepted by H. M. Government in lieu
of tax and allocated to the Tate Gallery,
1995
Zervos: V, no. 357
Plate 51

Cat. Zurich 154
Sitzende Frau mit Gitarre
und Notenblatt
Femme à la mandoline, 1925
Woman with Mandolin
Oil on canvas, 130.5 x 97.8 cm
Norton Simon Museum
Purchase (P.1984.2)
Zervos: V, no. 442

Cat. Zurich 155
Stilleben
Nature morte, 1925
Still Life
Oil and sand on canvas, 97.8 x 131.2 cm
Centre Pompidou, Paris
Musée national d'art moderne/
Centre de création industrielle
Donated in 1982
Zervos: V, no. 462
Plate 52

Cat. Zurich 156
Liegende Tänzerin mit Tamburin
Femme au tambourin, 1925
Woman with Tambourine
Oil on canvas, 97 x 130 cm
Musée de l'Orangerie, Paris
Collection Jean Walter et Paul Guillaume
Zervos: V, no. 415

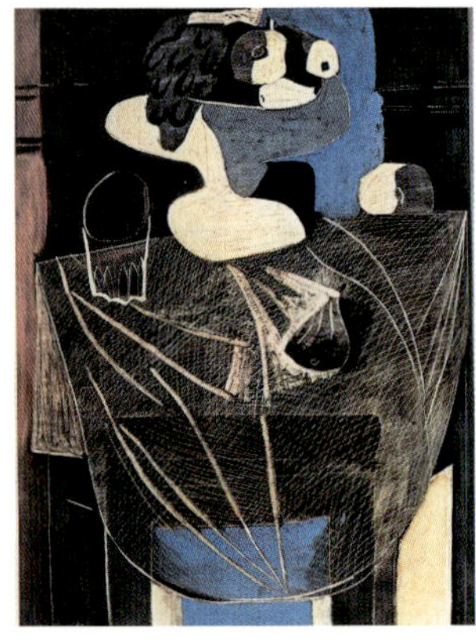

157

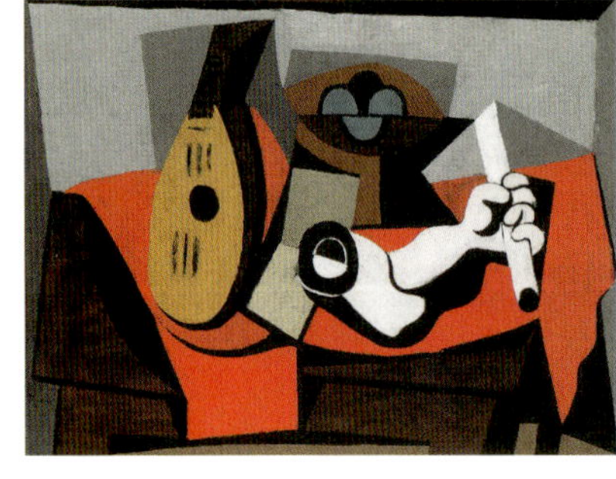

159

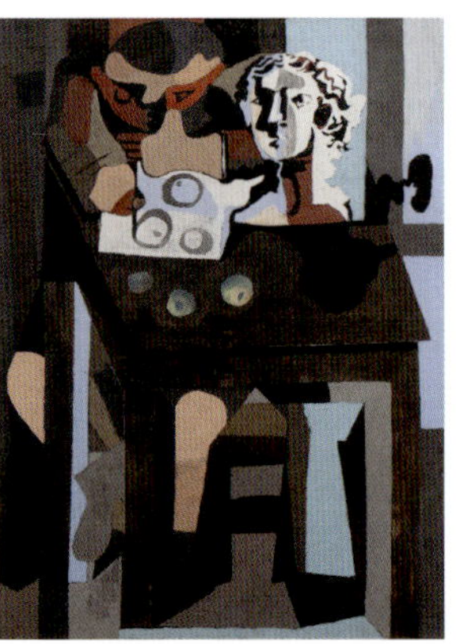

161

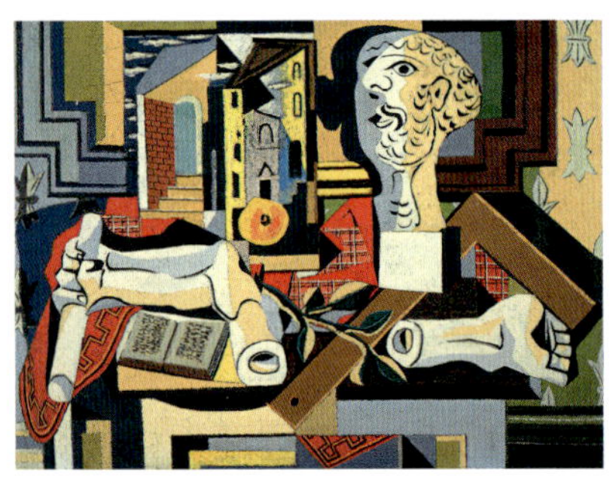

158

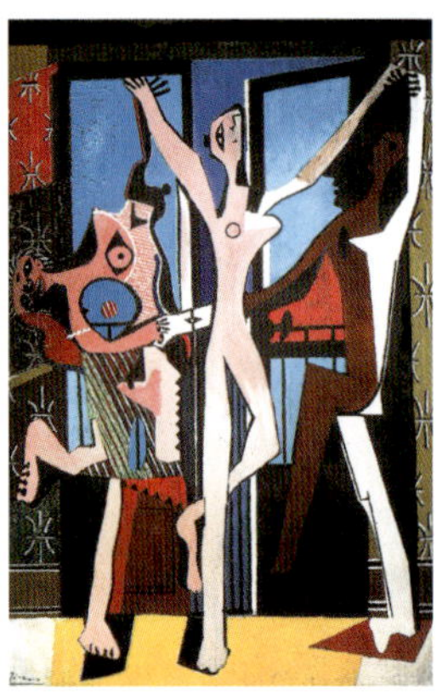

160

162

Cat. Zurich 157
Stilleben mit Fischernetz
Nature morte au filet de pêche, 1925
Still Life with Fisherman's Net
Oil on canvas, 101.6 x 82.5 cm
Private collection
Zervos: V, no. 459

Cat. Zurich 158
Das Atelier
**Atelier avec tête et bras
de plâtre, 1925**
Studio with Plaster Head
Oil on canvas, 97.9 x 131.1 cm
The Museum of Modern Art, New York
Purchase, 1964
Zervos: V, no. 445
Plate 54

Cat. Zurich 159
Der Tisch des Bildhauers
**Mandoline, compotier,
bras de plâtre, 1925**
Mandolin, Fruit Bowl, and Plaster Arm
Oil on canvas, 97.8 x 130.2 cm
The Metropolitan Museum of Art,
New York
Bequest of Florene M. Schoenborn,
1995 (1996.403.2)
Zervos: V, no. 444

Cat. Zurich 160
Stilleben mit Widderkopf
Tête de bélier, 1925
The Ram's Head
Oil on canvas, 80 x 99.1 cm
Norton Simon Museum
Gift of Mr Alexandre P. Rosenberg
(P.1978.6)
Zervos: V, no. 443

Cat. Zurich 161
Die Zeichenstunde
La leçon de dessin, 1925
The Drawing Lesson
Oil on canvas, 129.5 x 97.2 cm
Private collection
Zervos: V, no. 421
Plate 53

Cat. Zurich 162
Der Tanz
Les trois danseuses, 1925
The Three Dancers
Oil on canvas, 215.3 x 142.2 cm
Tate, London
Purchased with a special Grant-in-Aid
and the Florence Fox Bequest with
assistance from the Friends of the
Tate Gallery and the Contemporary
Art Society 1965
Zervos: V, no. 426

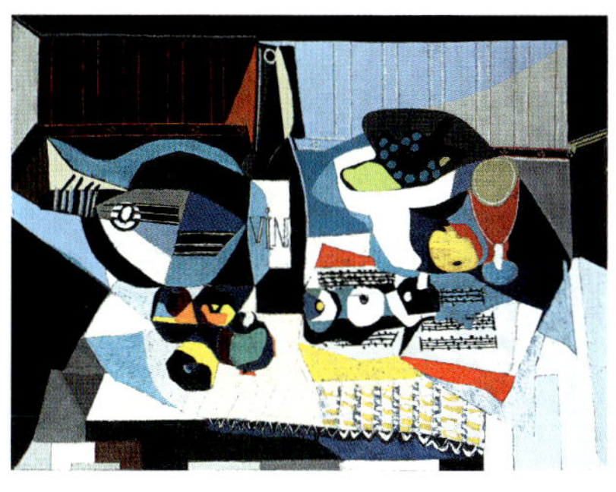

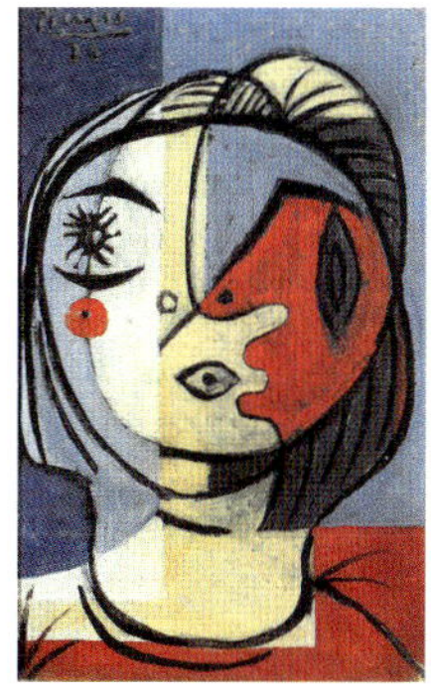

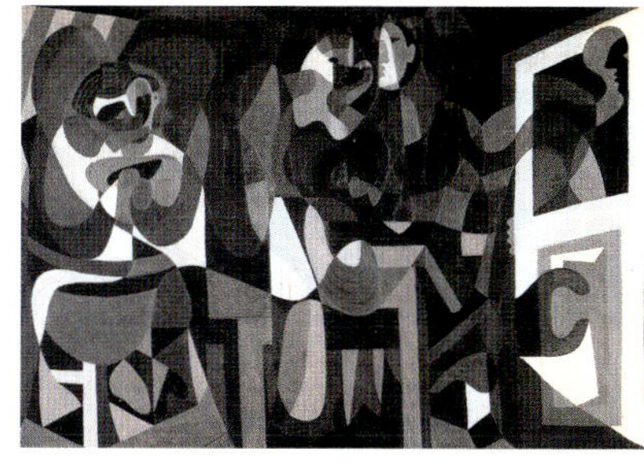

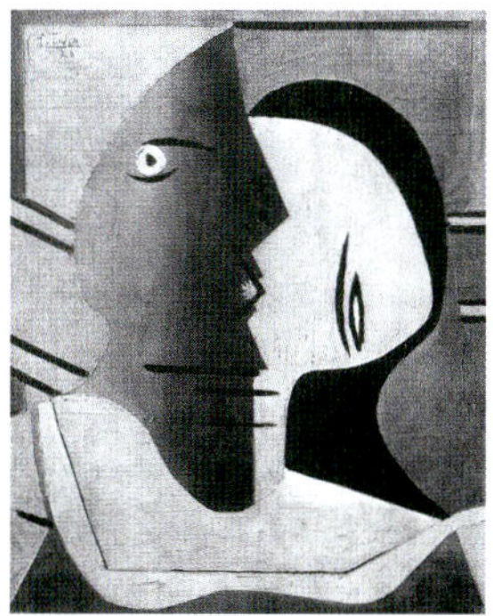

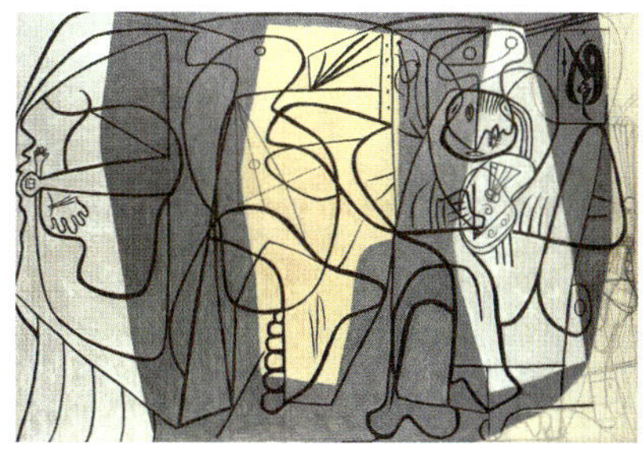

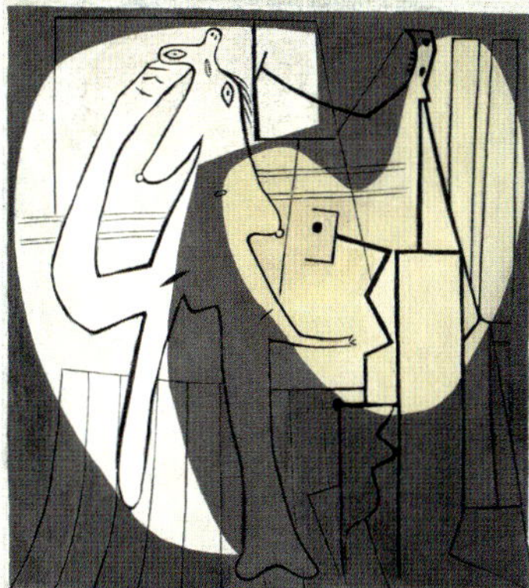

Cat. Zurich 163
Stilleben mit Weinflasche
La bouteille de vin, 1926
Wine Bottle
Oil on canvas, 98 x 131.5 cm
Fondation Beyeler, Riehen/Basel
Zervos: VI, no. 1444
Plate 55

Cat. Zurich 164
Zwei Köpfe
Tête, 1926
Head
Oil on canvas, 41 x 33 cm
Private collection
Zervos: VII, no. 11

Cat. Zurich 165
Kleiner Kopf
Tête, 1926
Head
Oil on canvas, 21.5 x 14 cm
Private collection
Zervos: VII, no. 41

Cat. Zurich 166
Atelier der Modistin
Les modistes (L'atelier de la modiste), 1926
At The Milliner
Oil on canvas, 172 x 265 cm
Centre Pompidou, Paris
Musée national d'art moderne/
Centre de création industrielle
Don de l'artiste 1947
Zervos: VII, no. 2

Cat. Zurich 167
Atelier des Malers
Le peintre et son modèle, 1926
The Painter and his Model
Oil on canvas, 172 x 256 cm
Musée Picasso, Paris
Dation en 1979
Zervos: VII, no. 30

Cat. Zurich 168
Der Maler und sein Modell
Le peintre et son modèle, 1927
The Painter and his Model
Oil on canvas, 214 x 200 cm
Tehran Museum of Contemporary Art
Zervos: VII, no. 59
Plate 56

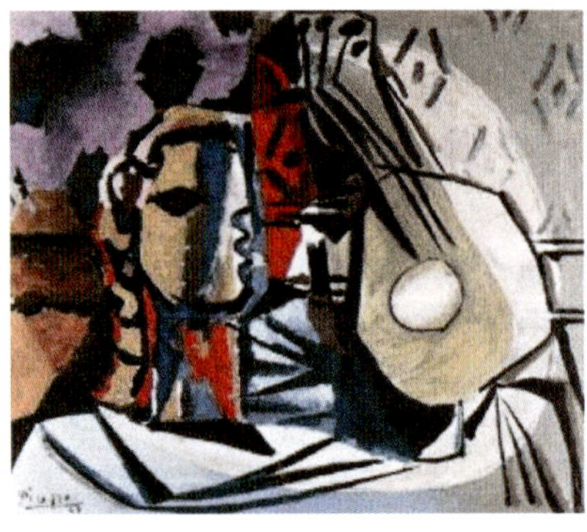

169

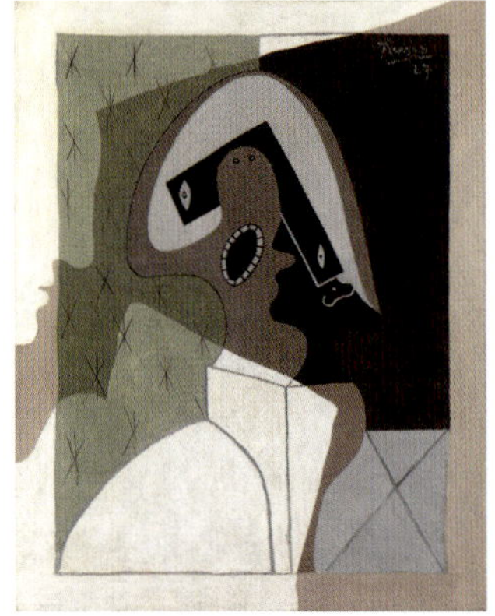

171

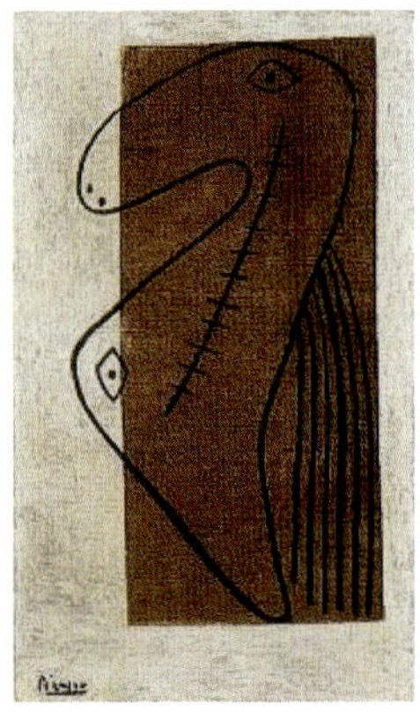

173

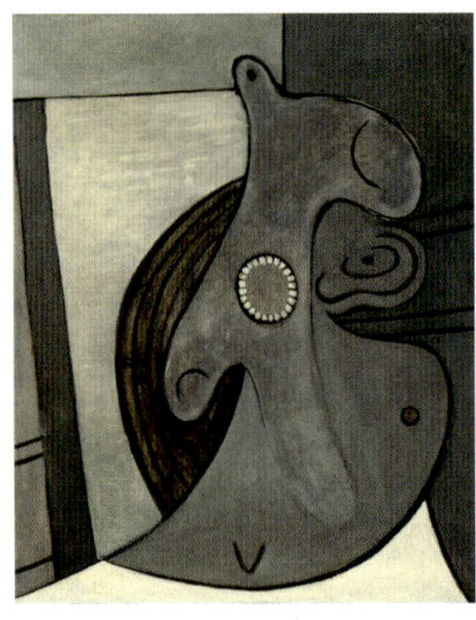

170

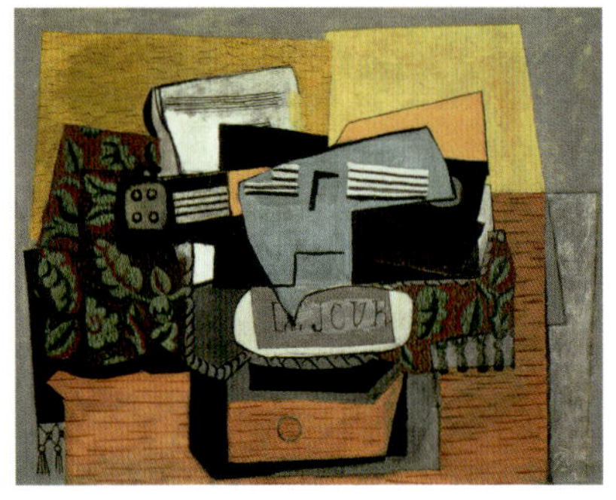

172

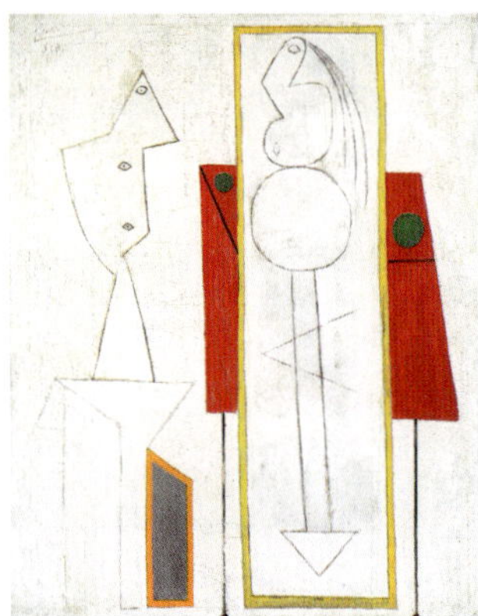

174

Cat. Zurich 169
Der Gipskopf
Tête et guitare, 1927
Head and Guitar
Oil on canvas, 60 x 72 cm
Private collection
Zervos: VII, no. 66

Cat. Zurich 170
Frau im Lehnstuhl
Femme dans un fauteuil, 1927
Woman in an Armchair
Oil on canvas, 81 x 65 cm
Kawamura Memorial Museum of Art,
Japan
Zervos: VII, no. 71
Plate 57

Cat. Zurich 171
Kopf eines Harlekin
L'Arlequin, 1927
Harlequin
Oil on canvas, 81.3 x 65.1 cm
The Metropolitan Museum of Art,
New York
The Mr and Mrs Klaus G. Perls
Collection, 1997 (1997.149.5)
Zervos: VII, no. 80
Plate 58

Cat. Zurich 172
Stilleben mit Zeitung
**Violon et journal sur
un tapis vert, 1921**
Violin and Journal on a Green Carpet
Oil on canvas, 73.3 x 92.1 cm
Courtesy Nahmad Collection,
Switzerland
Zervos: IV, no. 430
Plate 39

Cat. Zurich 173
Kopf
Figure, c. 1927
Head of a Woman
Oil on canvas, 54.9 x 33.3 cm
Norton Simon Museum
The Blue Four Galka Scheyer Collection
(P. 1953.074)
Zervos: VII, no. 122

Cat. Zurich 174
Das Atelier
L'Atelier, 1928
The Studio
Oil and black crayon on canvas ,
161.6 x 129.9 cm
The Solomon R. Guggenheim Foundation
Peggy Guggenheim Collection,
Venice (76.2553.3)
Zervos: VII, no. 136

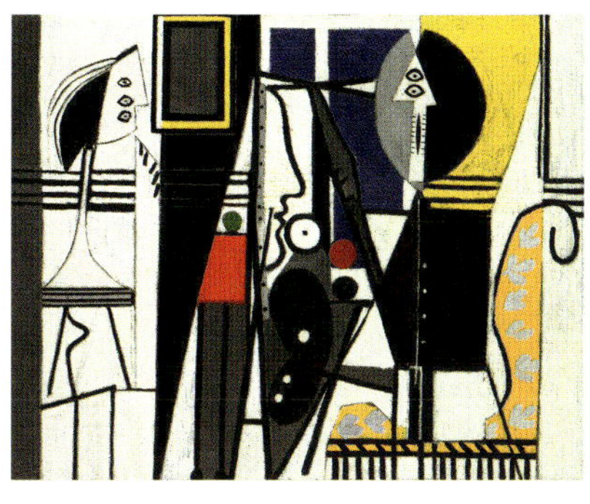

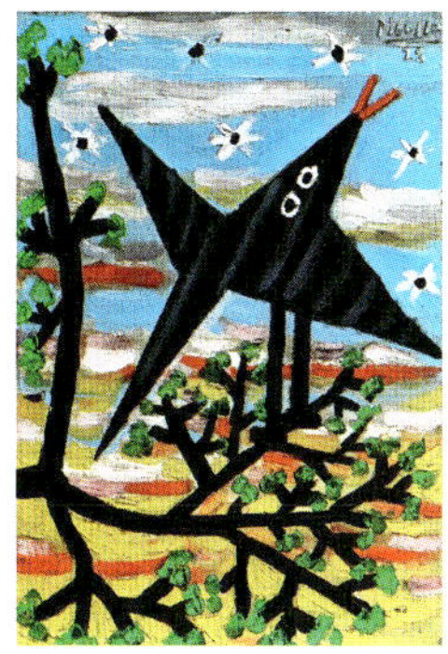

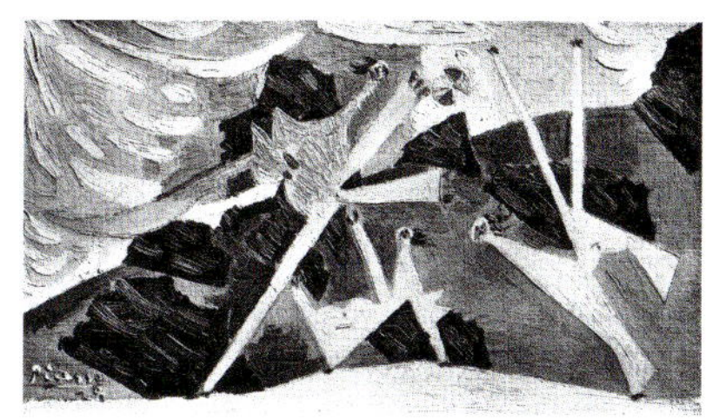

175

177

179

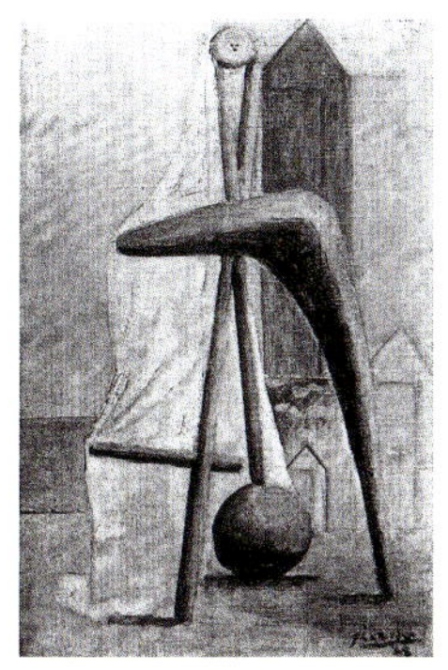

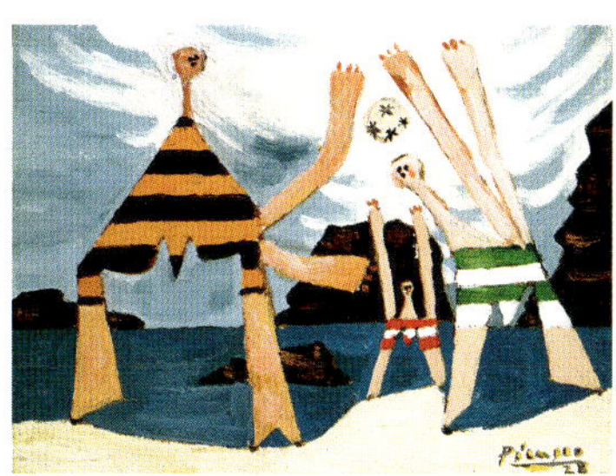

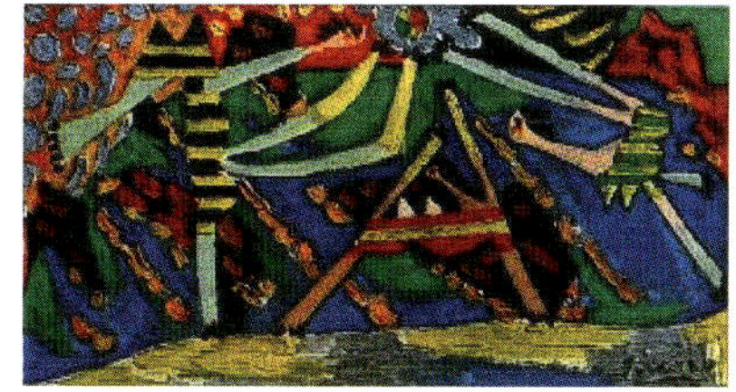

176

178

180

Cat. Zurich 175
Der Künstler und seine Modelle
L'artiste et le modèle, 1928
Painter and Model
Oil on canvas, 129.8 x 163 cm
The Museum of Modern Art, New York
The Sidney and Harriet Janis Collection
Zervos: VII, no. 143
Plate 59

Cat. Zurich 176
Am Strand
Sur la plage, 1928
On the Beach
Oil on canvas, 33 x 22 cm
Private collection
Zervos: VII, no. 235

Cat. Zurich 177
Vogel auf Zweig
L'oiseau, 1928
Bird on a Tree
Oil on canvas, 34.9 x 24.1 cm
Solomon R. Guggenheim Museum,
New York
Thannhauser Collection, Gift,
Justin K. Thannhauser, 1978
Zervos: VII, no. 217

Cat. Zurich 178
Badende, Ballspiel
Baigneuses au ballon, 1928
Bathers with Beach Ball
Oil on canvas, 15.9 x 21.9 cm
Private collection
Zervos: VII, no. 226
Plate 60

Cat. Zurich 179
Badende in Dinard
Baigneuses au ballon, 1928
Bathers with Beach Ball
Oil on canvas, 19 x 32 cm
Private collection
Zervos: VII, no. 218

Cat. Zurich 180
Badende in Dinard
Baigneuses au ballon, 1928
Bathers with Beach Ball
Oil on canvas, 19.6 x 35.8 cm
Private collection
Zervos: VII, no. 236

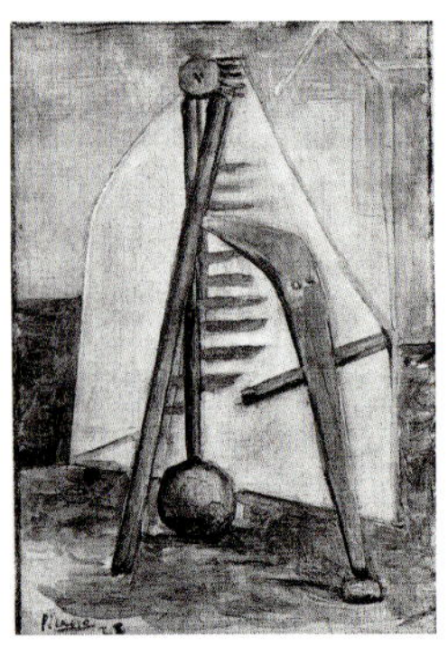

181

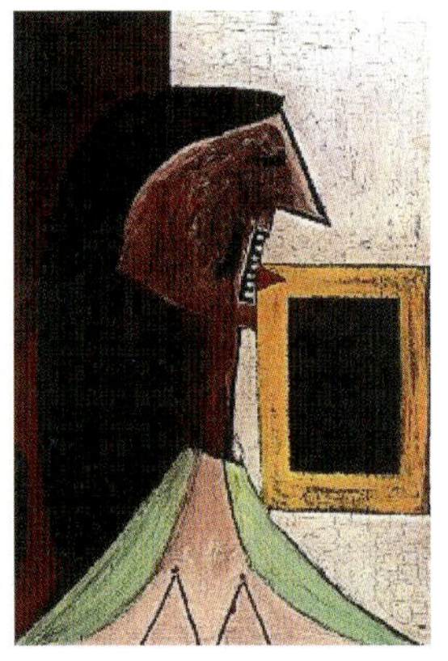

183

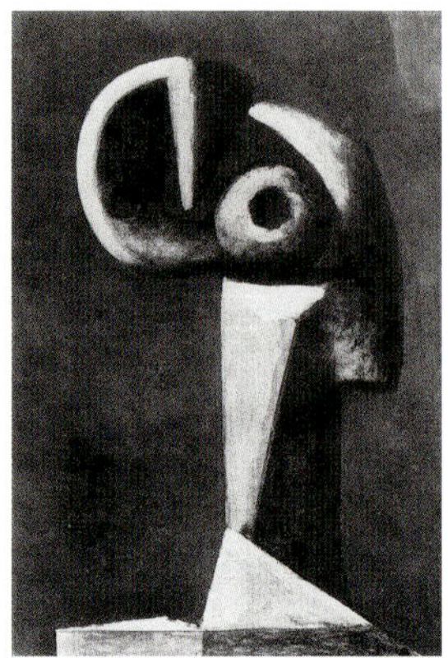

185

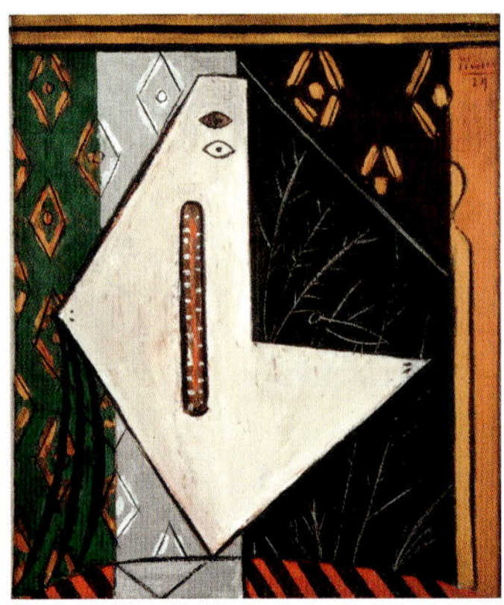

182

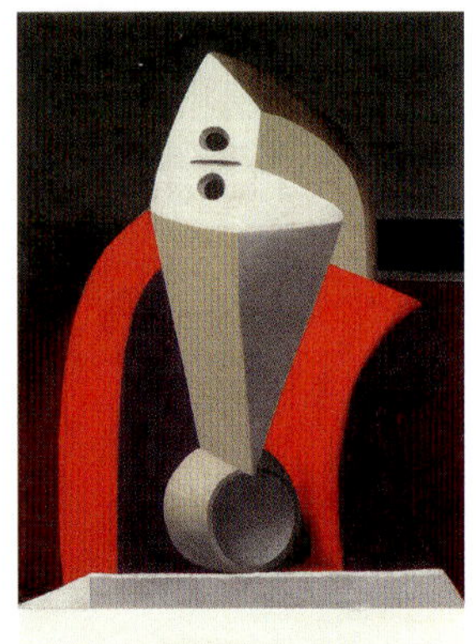

184

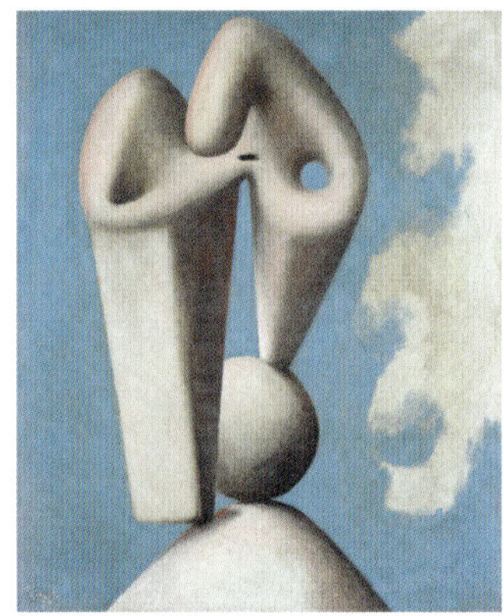

186

Cat. Zurich 181
Am Strand
Baigneuses, 1928
Bathers
Oil on canvas, 35 x 24 cm
Private collection
Zervos: VII, no. 213

Cat. Zurich 182
Das Thermometer
La demoiselle, 1929
Young Girl
Oil on canvas, 54 x 45.5 cm
Moderna Museet, Stockholm
Zervos: VII, no. 289
Plate 61

Cat. Zurich 183
Frau im Profil
Buste de femme, 1929
Bust of a Woman
Oil on canvas, 73 x 60 cm
Private collection
Zervos: VII, no. 247

Cat. Zurich 184
Metamorphose
Femme dans un fauteuil, 1929
Woman in an Armchair
Oil on canvas, 91.6 x 72.4 cm
Museu Colecção Berardo
Zervos: VII, no. 275

Cat. Zurich 185
Metamorphose
Figure, 1929
Figure
Oil on canvas, 92 x 73 cm
Private collection
Zervos: VII, no. 274

Cat. Zurich 186
Metamorphose
Tête: Étude pour un monument, 1929
Head: Study for a Monument
Oil on canvas, 73 x 59.7 cm
The Baltimore Museum of Art
The Dexter M. Ferry, Jr. Trustee
Corporation Fund (BMA.1966.4)
Zervos: VII, no. 273
Plate 63

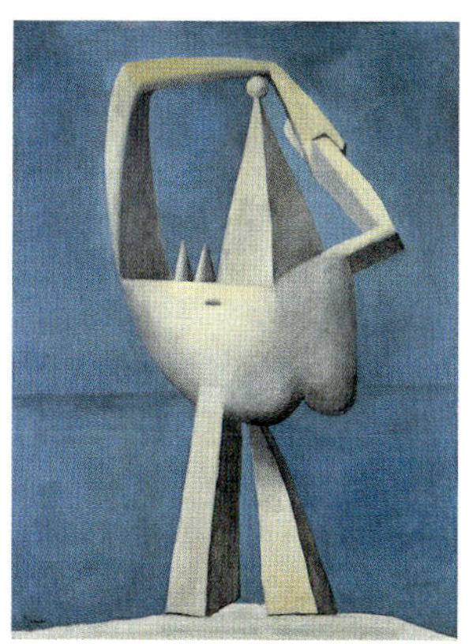

187

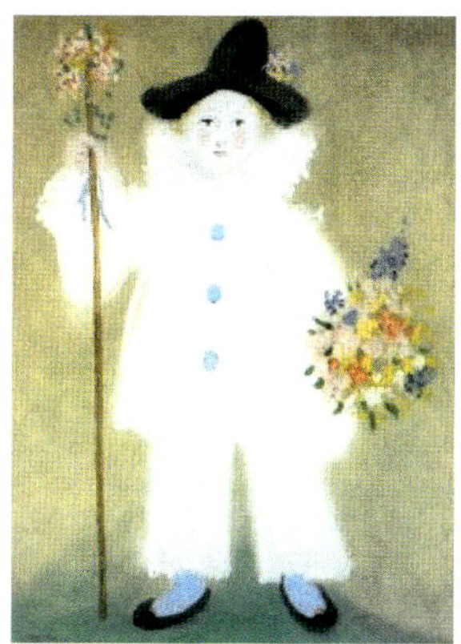

189

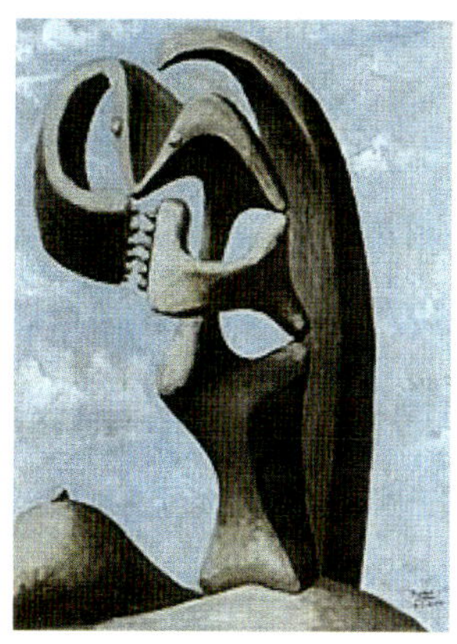

191

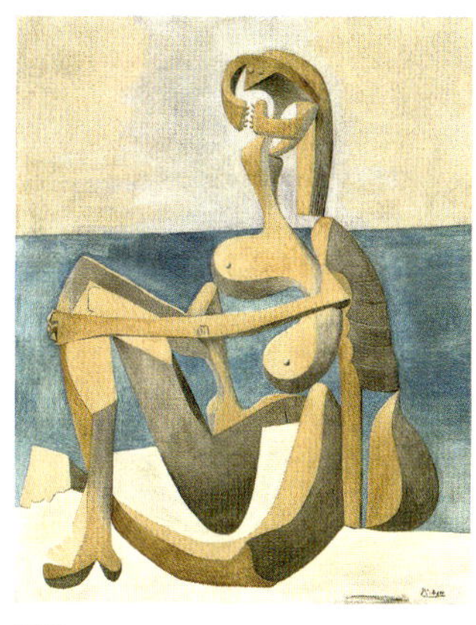

188

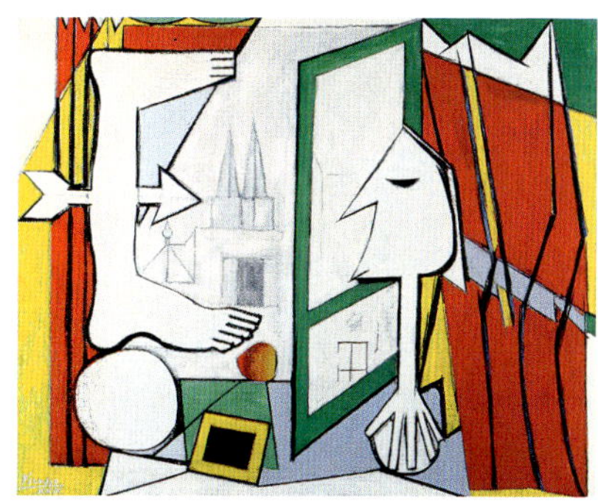

190

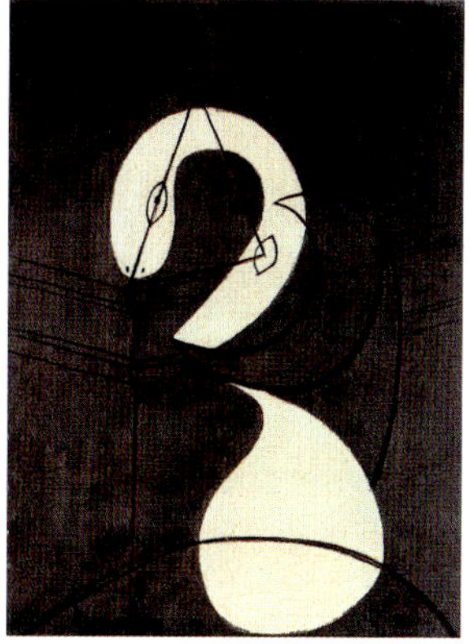

192

Cat. Zurich 187
Figur am Strand
Nu debout au bord de la mer, 1929
Nude Standing by the Sea
Oil on canvas, 129.9 x 96.8 cm
The Metropolitan Museum of Art,
New York
Bequest of Florene M. Schoenborn,
1995 (1996.403.4)
Zervos: VII, no. 252
Plate 64

Cat. Zurich 188
Badende
La Baigneuse, 1930
Seated Bather
Oil on canvas, 163.2 x 129.5 cm
The Museum of Modern Art, New York
Mrs Simon Guggenheim Fund
Zervos: VII, no. 306

Cat. Zurich 189
Kleiner Pierrot mit Blumen,
Sohn des Künstler
Portrait de Paulo en pierrot, 1929
Portrait of Paulo as Pierrot
Oil on canvas, 130.4 x 97.3 cm
Pola Museum of Art, Japan
Zervos: VII, no. 278

Cat. Zurich 190
Das Atelier des Künstlers
La fenêtre ouverte, 1929
The Open Window
Oil on canvas, 130 x 162 cm
Staatsgalerie Stuttgart
Steegmann Collection
Zervos: VII, no. 288
Plate 62

Cat. Zurich 191
Abstraktion
Abstraction: Fond avec ciel couvert
de nuages, 1930
*Abstraction: Background with
Blue Cloudy Sky*
Oil on wood, 66 x 49.2 cm
The Art Institute of Chicago
Gift of Florene May Schoenborn and
Samuel A. Marx; Wilson L. Mead Fund,
1955.748
Zervos: VII, no. 304

Cat. Zurich 192
Abstraktion
Figure (Tête de femme), 1930
Figure
Oil on wood, 64.4 x 47.3 cm
Los Angeles County Museum of Art
Partial, fractional and promised gift
of Janice and Henri Lazarof
(M.2005.70.103)
Zervos: VII, no. 299

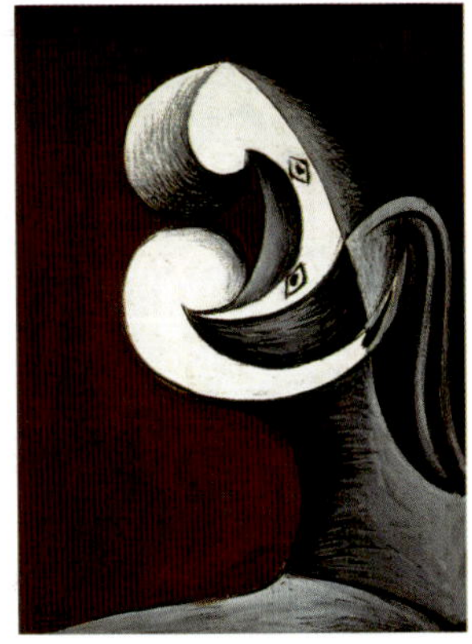

193

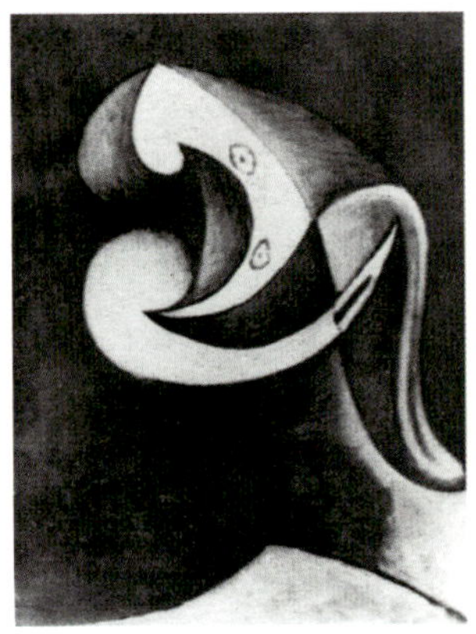

194

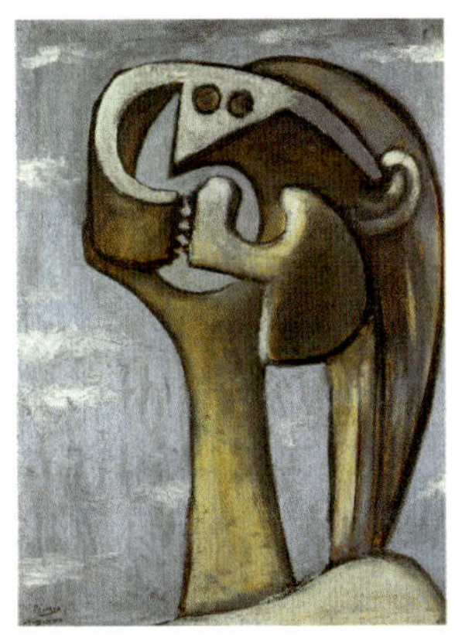

195

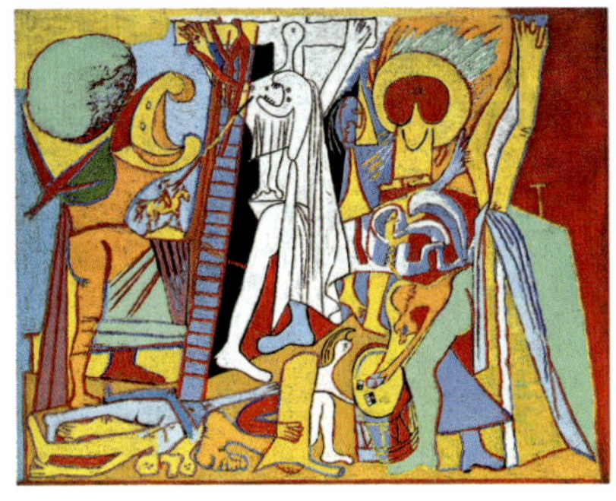

196

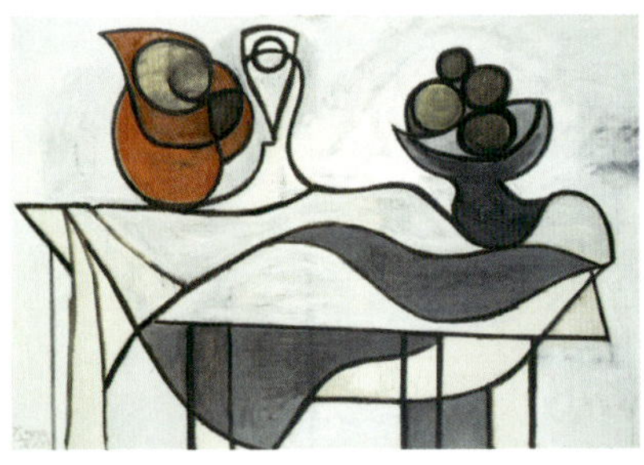

197

198

Cat. Zurich 193
Abstraktion
Abstraction (Tête), 1930
Abstraction (Head)
Oil on wood, 62.2 x 46.4 cm
Cincinnati Art Museum
Gift of Thomas C. and Emily F. Adler
(1991.312)
Zervos: VII, no. 298
Plate 65

Cat. Zurich 194
Abstraktion
Profil, 1930
Profile
Oil on wood, 64 x 47 cm
Private collection
Zervos: VII, no. 303

Cat. Zurich 195
Metamorphose
Figure, 1930
Figure
Oil on wood, 64 x 47 cm
Private collection
Zervos: VII, no. 300

Cat. Zurich 196
Kreuzigung
La crucifixion, 1930
The Crucifixion
Oil on plywood, 51.5 x 66.5 cm
Musée Picasso, Paris
Dation en 1979
Zervos: VII, no. 287

Cat. Zurich 197
Figuren am Strand
Figures au bord de la mer, 1931
Figures on the Seashore
Oil on canvas, 130 x 195 cm
Musée Picasso, Paris
Dation en 1979
Zervos: VII, no. 328

Cat. Zurich 198
Krug und Fruchtschale
Pichet et coupe de fruits, 1931
Jug and Bowl of Fruit
Oil on canvas, 131 x 196 cm
Courtesy Nahmad Collection,
Switzerland
Zervos: VII, no. 327
Plate 66

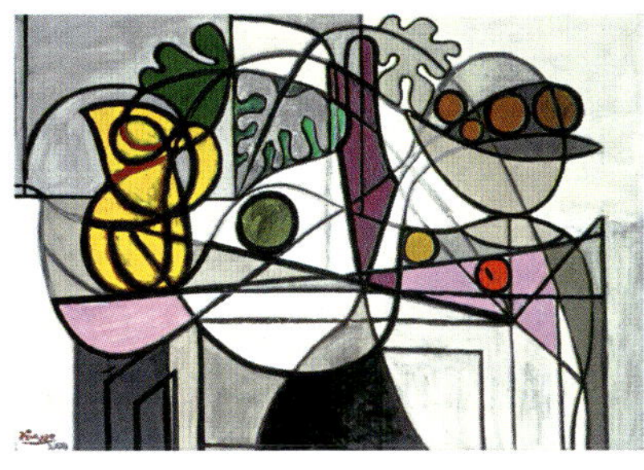

199

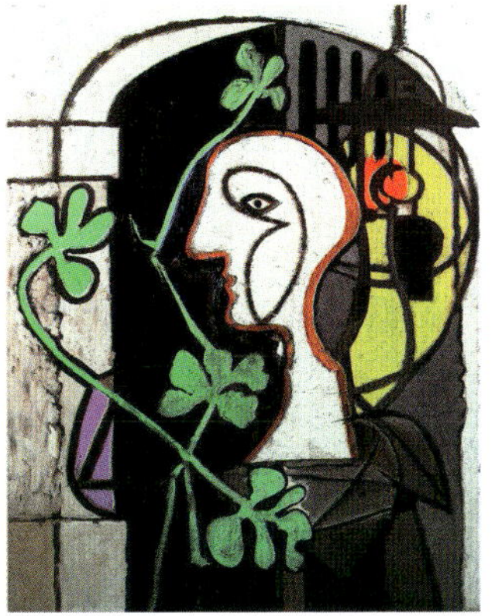

201

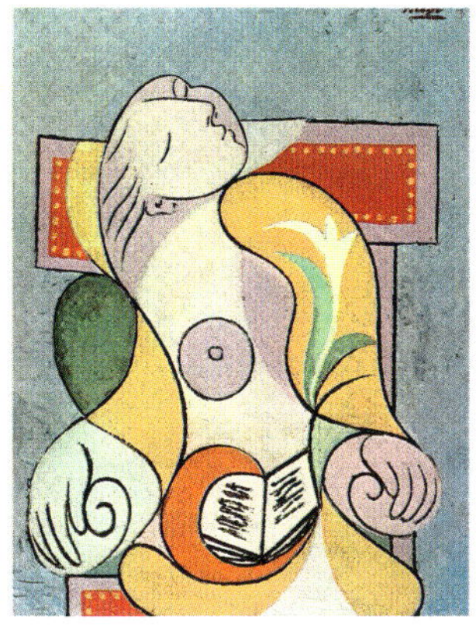

202a

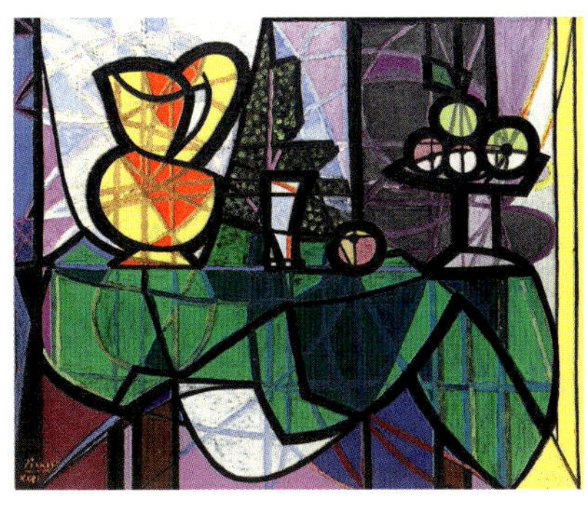

200

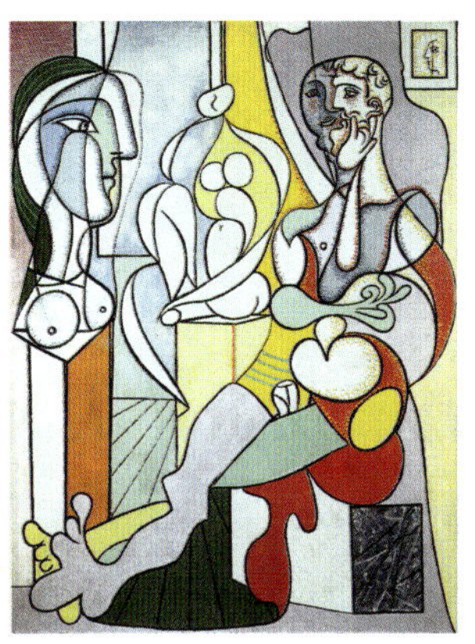

202

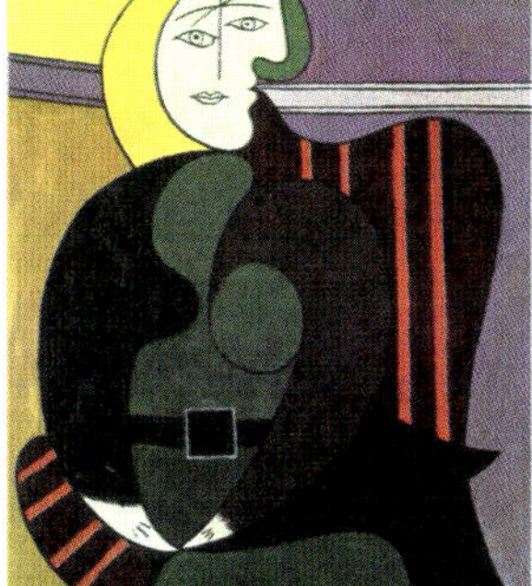

203

Cat. Zurich 199
Cheminée
Pichet et coupe de fruits, 1931
Pitcher and Fruit Bowl
Oil on canvas, 130.2 x 194.9 cm
Saint Louis Art Museum
Bequest of Morton D. May (932:1983)
Zervos: VII, no. 326
Plate 67

Cat. Zurich 200
Krug und Fruchtschale
Pichet et coupe de fruits, 1931
Pitcher and Bowl of Fruit
Oil on canvas, 130.8 x 162.6 cm
Solomon R. Guggenheim Museum,
New York
By exchange, 1982 (82.2947)
Zervos: VII, no. 322
Plate 68

Cat. Zurich 201
Die Lampe
La lampe, 1931
The Lamp
Oil on canvas, 162 x 130 cm
Private collection
Zervos: VII, no. 347

Cat. Zurich 202
Der Bildhauer
Le sculpteur, 1931
The Sculptor
Oil on plywood, 128.5 x 96 cm
Musée Picasso, Paris
Dation en 1979
Zervos: VII, no. 346

Cat. Zurich 202a
Die eingeschlafene Leserin
La lecture interrompue, 1932
The Reading Interrupted
Oil on wood, 65.7 x 49.5 cm
Private collection
Zervos: VII, no. 363

Cat. Zurich 203
Frau in rotem Lehnstuhl
Le fauteuil rouge, 1931
The Red Armchair
Oil and Ripolin on wood,
131.1 x 98.7 cm
The Art Institute of Chicago
Gift of Mr and Mrs Daniel Saidenberg,
1957.72
Zervos: VII, no. 334

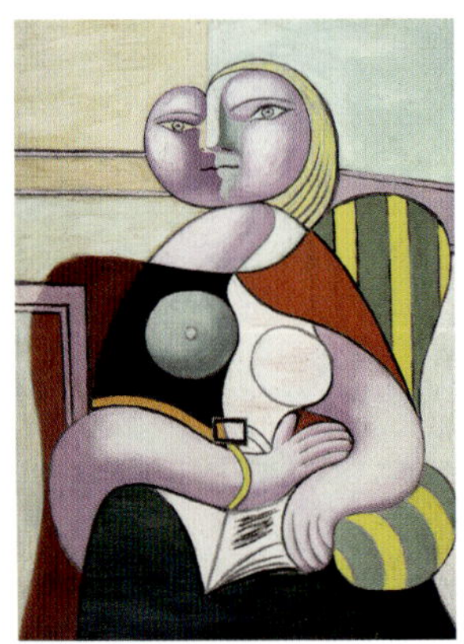

204

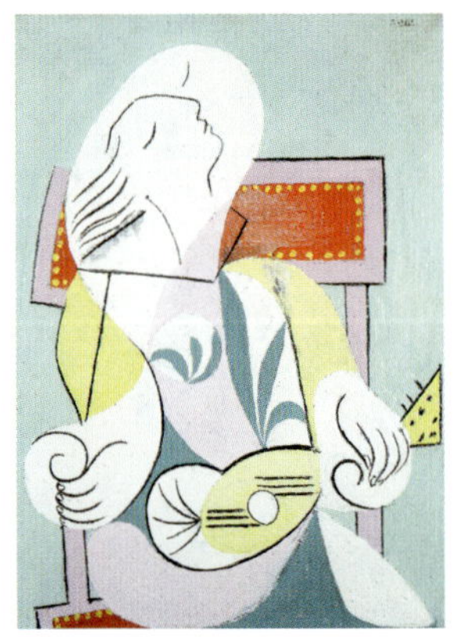

206

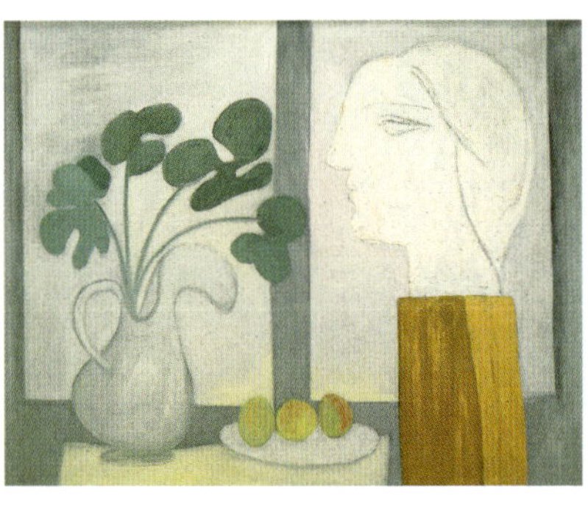

208

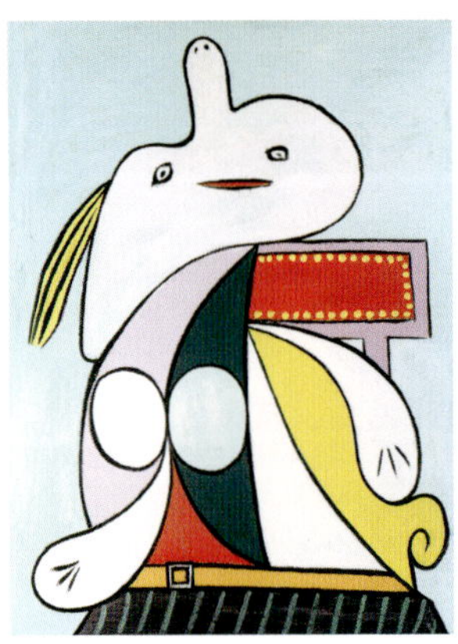

205

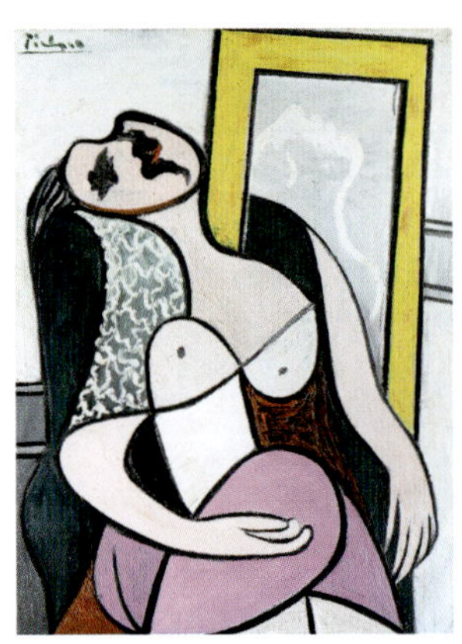

207

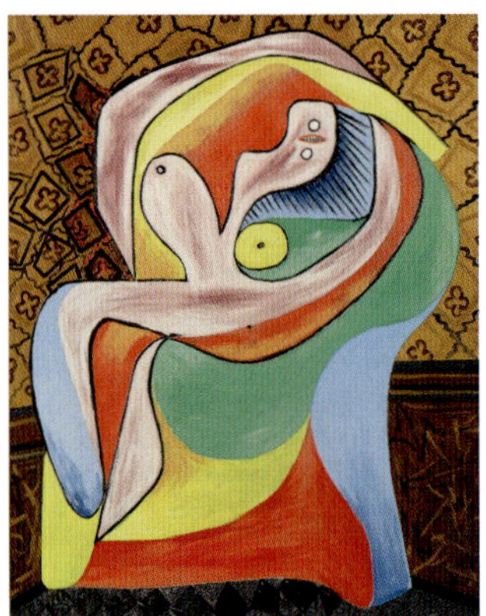

209

Cat. Zurich 204
Die Leserin
La lecture, 1932
Reading
Oil on canvas, 130 x 97 cm
Musée Picasso, Paris
Dation en 1979
Zervos: VII, no. 358

Cat. Zurich 205
Der gelbe Gürtel
La ceinture jaune:
Marie-Thérèse Walter, 1932
The Yellow Belt: Marie-Thérèse Walter
Oil on canvas, 130 x 97 cm
Courtesy Nahmad Collection,
Switzerland
Zervos: VII, no. 357
Plate 69

Cat. Zurich 206
Mädchen mit Gitarre
Jeune fille à la mandoline, 1932
Young Woman with Mandolin
Oil on wood, 64.2 x 46.9 cm
The University of Michigan Museum
of Art
Gift of The Carey Walker Foundation
Zervos: VII, no. 359
Plate 73

Cat. Zurich 207
Schläferin vor dem Spiegel
La dormeuse au miroir, 1932
Sleeping Woman in a Mirror
Oil on wood, 130 x 97 cm
Courtesy Nahmad Collection,
Switzerland
Zervos: VII, no. 360
Plate 67

Cat. Zurich 208
Stilleben am Fenster
Nature morte à la fenêtre, 1932
Still Life at the Window
Oil on canvas, 130 x 162 cm
Private collection
Zervos: VII, no. 374

Cat. Zurich 209
Ruhende
Le repos, 1932
Repose
Oil on canvas, 161.9 x 130.2 cm
The Steven and Alexandra Cohen
Collection
Zervos: VII, no. 361
Plate 71

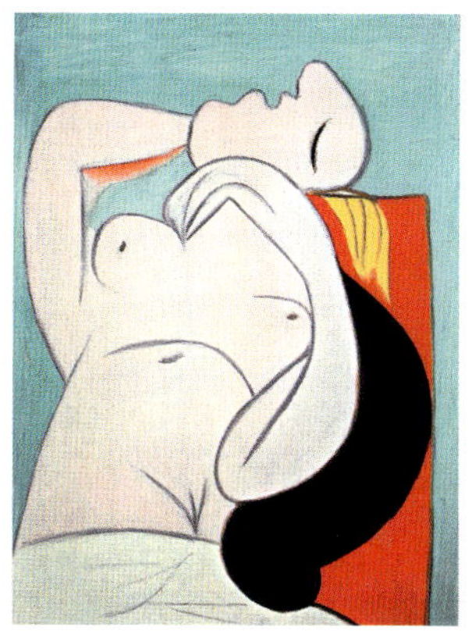

210

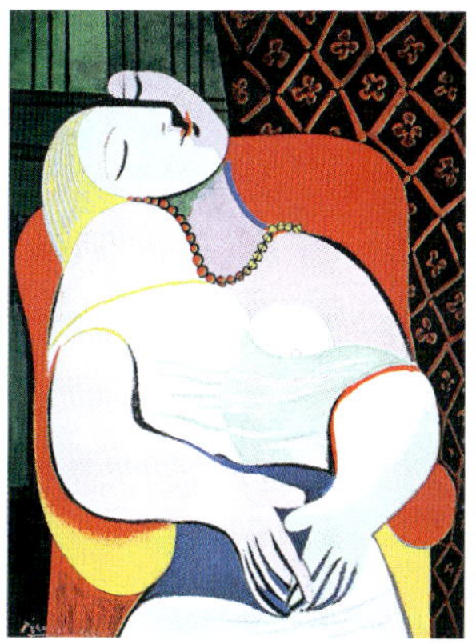

211

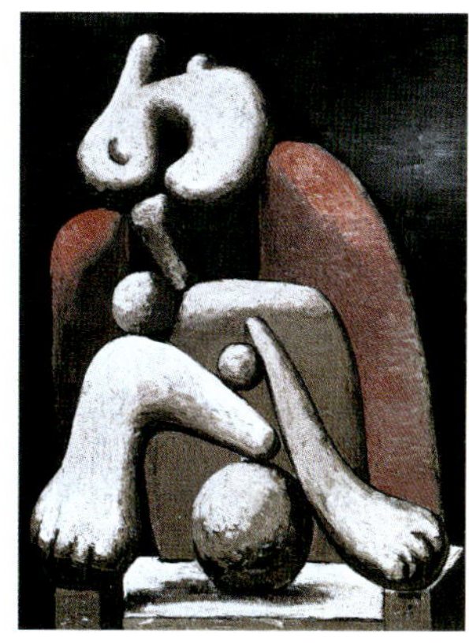

212

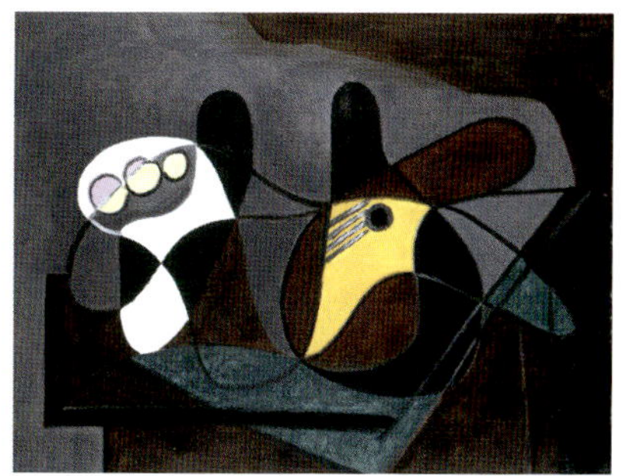

213

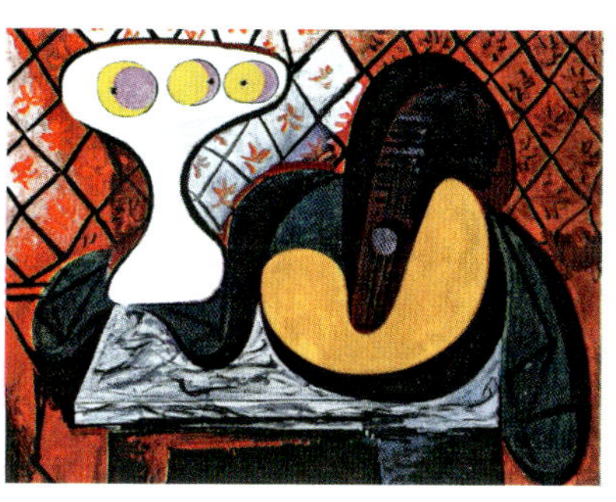

214

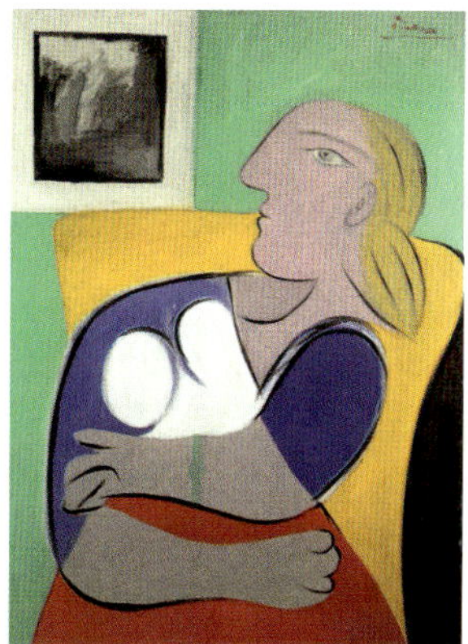

215

Cat. Zurich 210
Schlummernde
Le sommeil, 1932
Slumber
Oil on canvas, 130.2 x 97.2 cm
Private collection
Zervos: VII, no. 362

Cat. Zurich 211
Der Traum
Le rêve, 1932
The Dream
Oil on canvas, 130 x 97 cm
Private collection
Zervos: VII, no. 364

Cat. Zurich 212
Figur vor schwarzem Grund
Femme au fauteuil rouge, 1932
Woman in a Red Armchair
Oil on canvas, 130.2 x 97 cm
Musée Picasso, Paris
Dation en 1979
Zervos: VII, no. 330

Cat. Zurich 213
Fruchtschale und Gitarre
vor grauem Grund
Compotier et guitare, 1932
Fruit Bowl and Guitar
Oil on canvas, 97 x 130 cm
Courtesy Nahmad Collection,
Switzerland
Zervos: VII, no. 354
Plate 72

Cat. Zurich 214
Fruchtschale und Gitarre
Compotier et mandoline, 1932
Still Life with Fruit Bowl and Mandolin
Oil on canvas, 96.8 x 129.9 cm
Private collection
Zervos: VII, no. 375

Cat. Zurich 215
Frau in gelbem Lehnstuhl
Femme au fauteuil jaune, 1932
Woman in Yellow Armchair
Oil on canvas, 130 x 97 cm
Private collection
Zervos: VII, no. 380

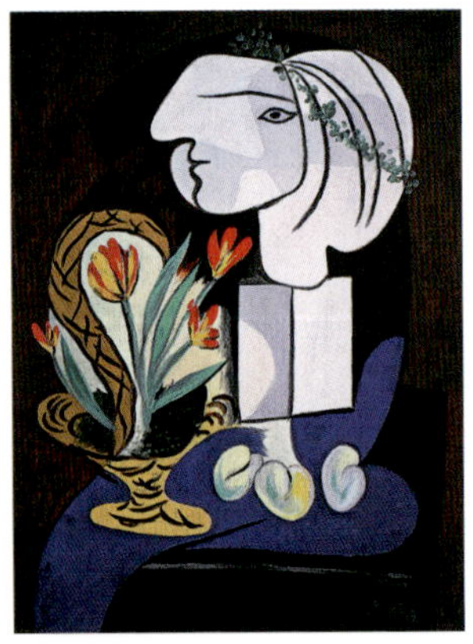

216

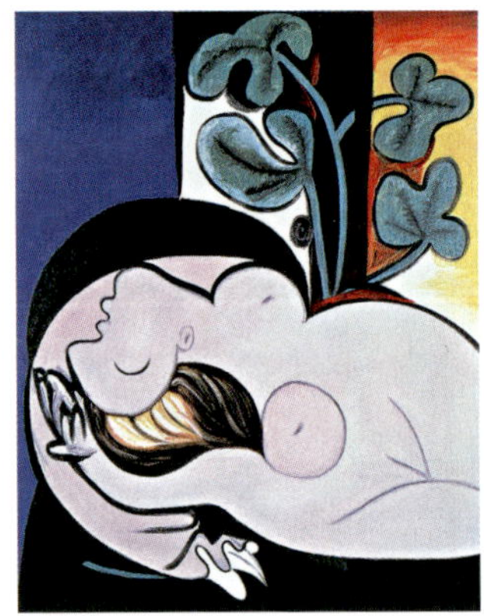

218

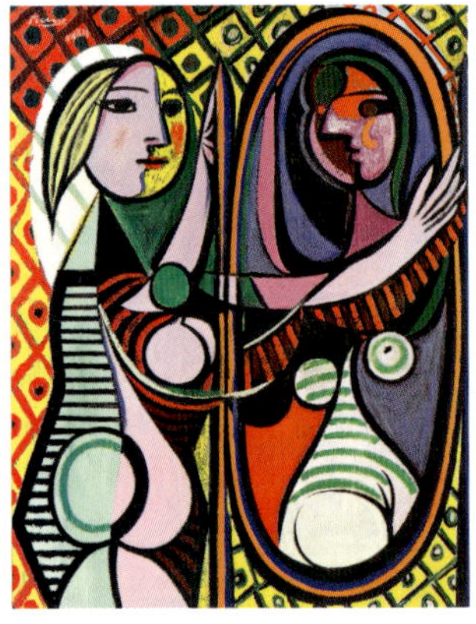

220

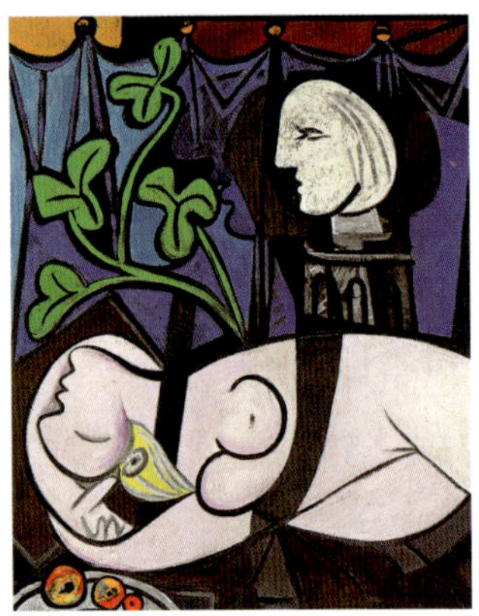

217

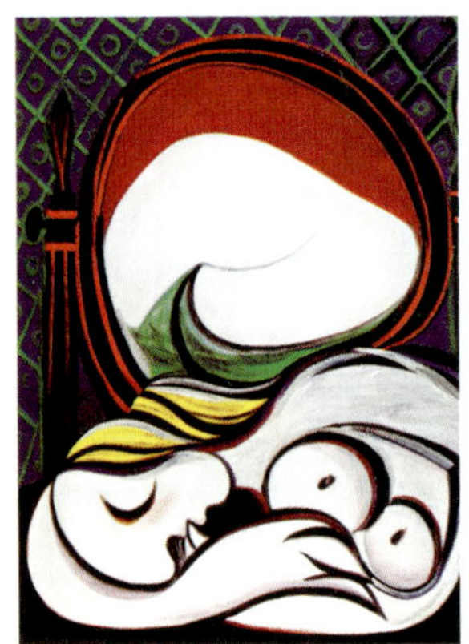

219

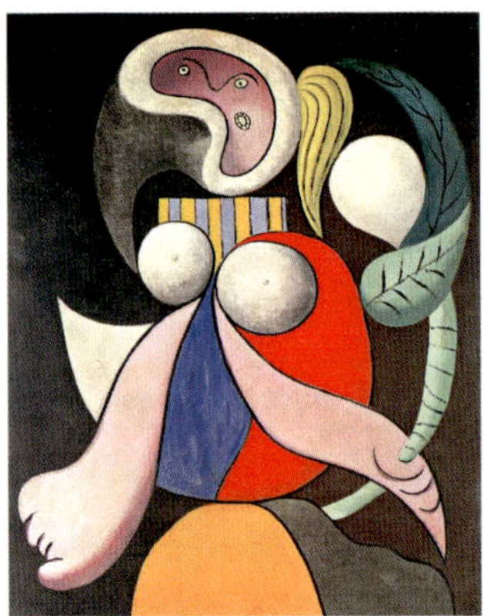

221

Cat. Zurich 216
Stilleben mit Tulpen
Nature morte aux tulipes, 1932
Still Life with Tulips
Oil on canvas, 130 x 97 cm
Private collection
Zervos: VII, no. 376

Cat. Zurich 217
Akt vor blauem Vorhang
Femme nue, feuilles et buste, 1932
Nude, Green Leaves and Bust
Oil on canvas, 162 x 130 cm
Private collection
not in Zervos

Cat. Zurich 218
Akt in schwarzem Lehnstuhl
Nu au fauteuil noir, 1932
Nude on a Black Armchair
Oil on canvas, 161 x 130 cm
Private collection
Courtesy Richard Gray Gallery
Zervos: VII, no. 377

Cat. Zurich 219
Der Spiegel
Le miroir (Marie-Thérèse), 1932
The Mirror (Marie-Thérèse)
Oil on canvas, 63 x 52.4 cm
Private collection
Zervos: VII, no. 378

Cat. Zurich 220
Mädchen vor dem Spiegel
Jeune fille devant un miroir, 1932
Girl before a Mirror
Oil on canvas, 162.3 x 130.2 cm
The Museum of Modern Art, New York
Gift of Mrs Simon Guggenheim
Zervos: VII, no. 379

Cat. Zurich 221
Frau mit Blumen
Femme à la fleur, 1932
Woman with a Flower
Oil on canvas, 162 x 130 cm
Private collection
Zervos: VII, no. 381

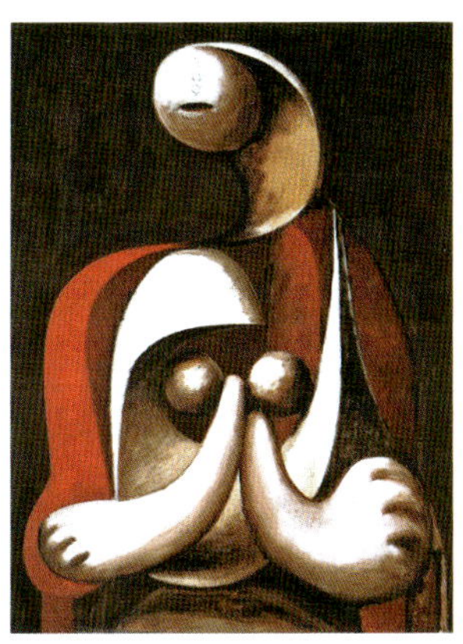

223

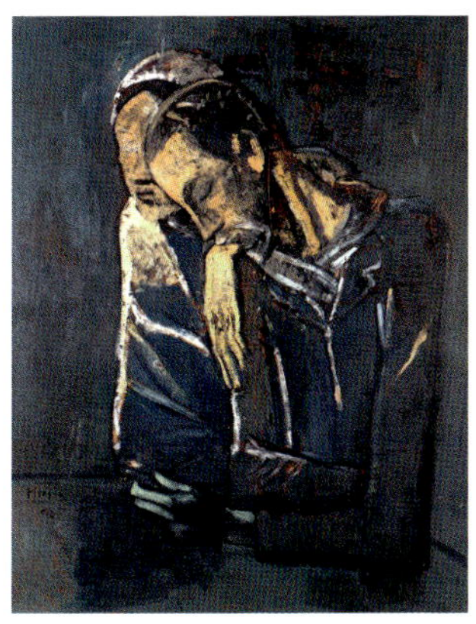

224

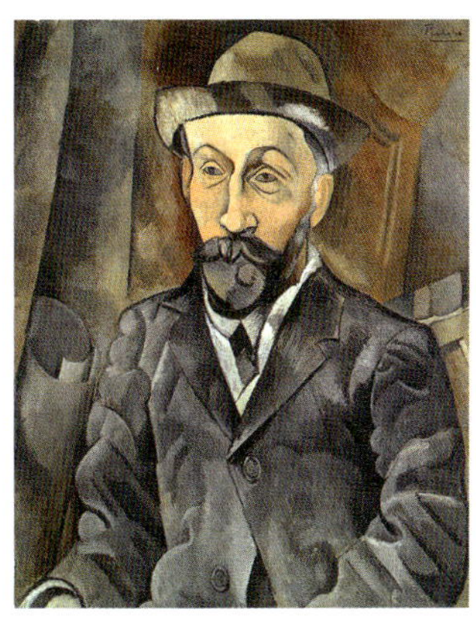

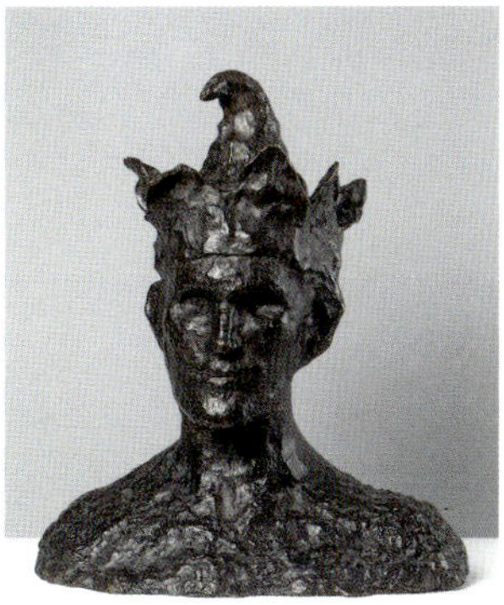

227

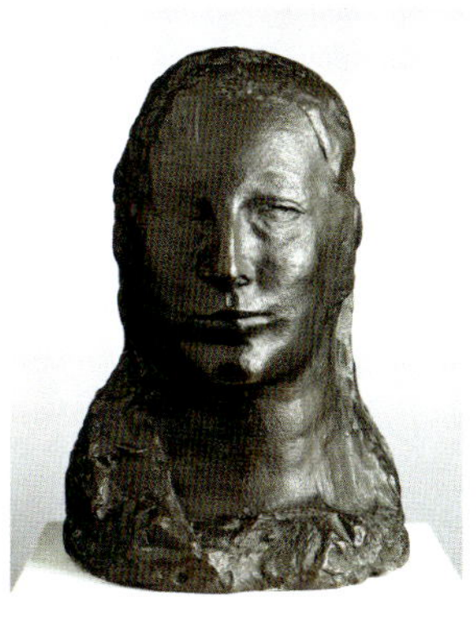

228

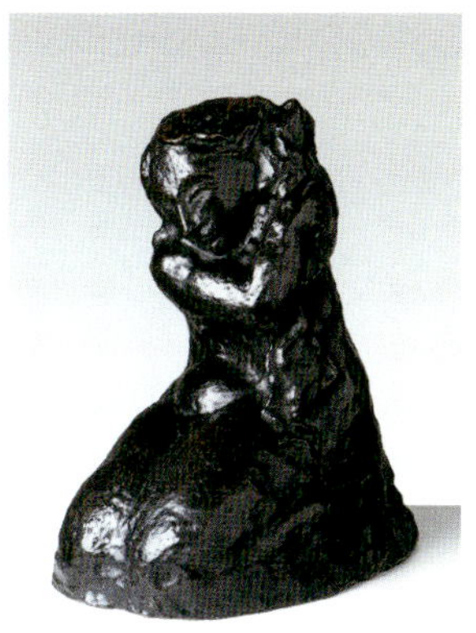

229

Cat. Zurich 223
Frau in rotem Lehnstuhl
Femme assise dans un fauteuil rouge, 1932
Woman in a Red Armchair
Oil on canvas, 130 x 97.5 cm
Musée Picasso, Paris
Donated in 1979
not in Zervos

Cat. Zurich 224
Ein Menschenpaar
Le couple (Les Misérables), 1904
The Couple (The Wretched Ones)
Oil on canvas, 100.5 x 81.5 cm
Merzbacher Kunststiftung
Zervos: I, no. 224
Plate 7

Cat. Zurich ausser Kat.
Der Kunsthändler Clovis Sagot
Portrait de Clovis Sagot, 1909
Portrait of Clovis Sagot
Oil on canvas, 82 x 66 cm
Hamburger Kunsthalle
Zervos: IIa, no. 129

Sculptures

Cat. Zurich 227
Harlekin
Tête de fou oder L'arlequin, 1905
Jester
Bronze, 41 x 37 x 21 cm
Kunstmuseum Winterthur
Purchased with a jubilee donation
from Werner Graf & Co., Winterthur,
1949
Zervos: I, no. 322
Plate 74

Cat. Zurich 228
Frauenbüste
Tête de femme (Fernande), 1906
Head of a Woman (Fernande)
Bronze, 41 x 24.5 x 25.5 cm
Kunsthaus Zürich
Werner and Nelly Bär Collection
Zervos: I, no. 323
Plate 75

Cat. Zurich 229
Figur
Femme se coiffant, 1906
Woman Combing Her Hair
Bronze, patinated, 42 x 31.2 x 29.2 cm
Museum Ludwig Köln
Ludwig Donation 1994
Zervos: I, no. 329
Plate 76

BIOGRAPHY

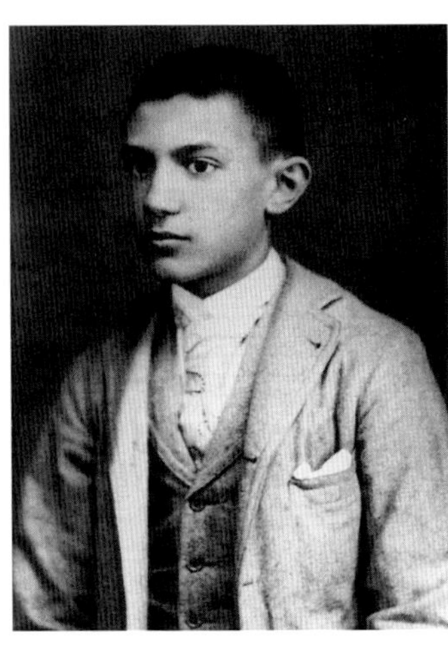

Fig. 1
Picasso at the age of 15

1881	Birth of Pablo Ruiz Picasso in Málaga (Andalusia) on 25 October. His father Don José Ruiz Blasco (1838-1913) is a painter and teacher of drawing at the San Telmo School of Fine Art and conservator of the Municipal Museum in Málaga.
1892	Start of Picasso's training as an artist at the Instituto da Guarda art school in La Coruña (Galicia), where his father now teaches.
1895	Move to Barcelona, as Picasso's father transfers to the art school La Lonja. Picasso attends this school but skips the classes in the lower years thanks to his gifts as an artist.
1897	Enrolment at the San Fernando Royal Academy of Fine Arts in Madrid, which he leaves again after just a few months. Study of the Old Masters in the Prado.
1898	Catches scarlet fever; while convalescing, Picasso spends a considerable period with his friend Manuel Pallarès in Horta de Ebro, a mountain village in the province of Tarragona. Makes studies of nature and landscape and breaks with the academic painting of his father.
1899	Picasso goes to Barcelona and joins the avant-garde movement there. The cabaret café El Quatre Gats is the rendezvous of artists and intellectuals.
1900	Picasso occupies a studio in Barcelona with Carlos Casagemas (1881-1901). First exhibition of his drawings in El Quatre Gats. Picasso takes the name of his mother, Maria Picasso López, and from now on signs his works "Picasso". Travels to Paris with Casagemas; during his first stay there mainly moves in artists' circles around Montmartre. Study of Impressionist and Post-Impressionist painting.
1901	Casagemas, disappointed in love, takes his own life in Paris. This suicide affects Picasso strongly. From autumn start of the Blue Period (1901-1904), during which he principally paints in blues and greys. The motifs of these works, which are characterised by great melancholy, revolve around the subjects of poverty, old age and loneliness. First exhibition in Paris in the gallery of Ambroise Vollard (1865-1939). Financial success thanks to the

sale of several paintings. Meets the French poet and art critic Max Jacob (1876-1944).

1902-04   Picasso returns to Spain, where he mainly lives in Barcelona. Productive phase of work, interspersed with stays of several months in Paris.

1904   Picasso now settles permanently in Paris and like many young artists rents a studio in Bateau-Lavoir, where he works until 1909. In addition to numerous French poets, artists and theatre people, he also makes the acquaintance of Guillaume Apollinaire (1880-1918). Fernande Olivier (1881-1966), who acts as model for him and other artists, becomes his partner for the next seven years.

1905   Picasso develops the style of painting that Gustave Coquiot later names the Rose Period (1904-1906). In these works he paints impressions from the world of the circus. His preferred motifs are clowns, harlequins and acrobats, whom he depicts in shades of pink and ochre.

1906   Meets the American writer Gertrude Stein (1874-1946) and her brother Leo (1872-1947), who become great supporters and collectors of his work. Meets Henri Matisse (1869-1954) and André Derain (1880-1954) as well as the art dealers Wilhelm Uhde (1874-1947) and Daniel-Henry Kahnweiler (1884-1979).

1907   Influenced by African and Iberian sculptures. Friendship with Georges Braque (1882-1963), with whom he is to work closely to develop Cubism. Starts work on his revolutionary painting *Les Demoiselles d'Avignon*. Daniel-Henry Kahnweiler becomes his official agent.

1909   Works closely with Braque; start of Analytical Cubism.

1911   His relationship with Fernande cools off. Picasso meets Eva Gouel (real name Marcelle Humbert, 1885-1915) and falls in love with her. First Picasso exhibition in the USA. Increasing number of international exhibitions.

1912   In autumn Picasso adopts the technique of *papiers collés* (pasted paper; early form of collage) developed by Braque.

1913   *Papiers collés* provide the starting point for Picasso to develop Synthetic Cubism.

1915   Eva Gouel dies of tuberculosis.

1916   *Les Demoiselles d'Avignon* is shown in public for the first time.

1917   Designs costumes and decorations for the ballet *Parade*. Falls in love with the Russian solo dancer Olga Khokhlova (1891-1955).

1918   12 July: marries Olga in the Russian church in Paris. The witnesses are Jean Cocteau (1889-1963), Max Jacob and Guillaume Apolli-

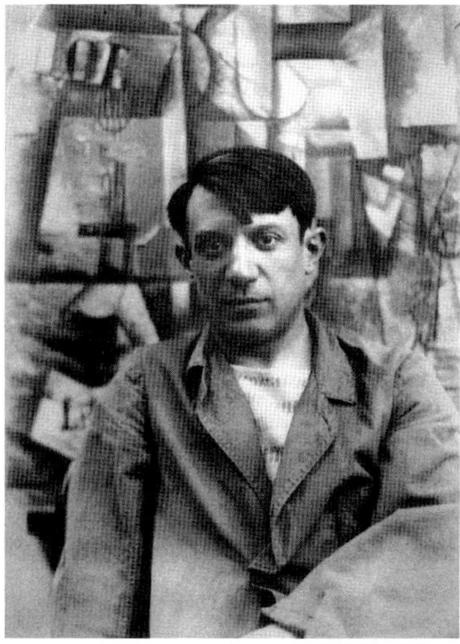

Fig. 2
Picasso in front of *L'aficionado*, 1912

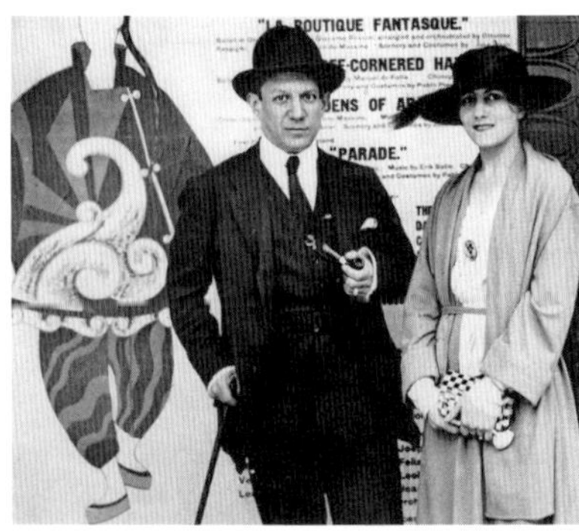

Fig. 3
Picasso and Olga with a
poster for the Ballets Russes
showing Picasso's design for
the costume of a Chinese
conspirator from the per-
formance of *Parade*, Alham-
bra Theatre, London, 1919

naire. Moves into a luxurious apartment in the centre of Paris. Paul Rosenberg (1882–1955) becomes his new dealer.

1919 Start of Picasso's Neoclassical phase. First exhibitions at Paul Rosenberg's.

1921 4 February: birth of son Paulo.

1922 Makes the acquaintance of the Dadaist, later Surrealist poets André Breton (1896–1966), Louis Aragon (1897–1982) and Tristan Tzara (1896–1963).

1923 Simultaneously produces works in the Cubist and Neoclassical styles.

1925 Takes part in the first Surrealist group exhibition in the Galerie Pierre in Paris.

1926 The art historian Christian Zervos founds the *Cahiers d'Art*, a magazine for contemporary art. Zervos devotes several issues to Picasso and from 1932 produces with Picasso a catalogue raisonné on Picasso's paintings and drawings (twenty-two volumes are published up to 1972, eleven further volumes after the death of Zervos).

1927 Meets Marie-Thérèse Walter (1909–1977), who becomes his model and mistress.

1932 Early in the year Picasso paints a series of portraits of Marie-Thérèse.

On 16 June Picasso's major retrospective is opened at the Galeries Georges Petit in Paris (until 30 July); the catalogue lists 225 paintings, seven sculptures and six illustrated books. The scale of the exhibition and the fact that the artist himself curated it are innovations. A special issue of the *Cahiers d'Art* is published on the occasion of this exhibition.

1932 7 September: Picasso travels to Switzerland with his wife Olga and Paulo to make final preparations for the exhibition in the Kunsthaus Zürich; boat trip on Lake Zurich and reception in Belvoir Park.

1932 On 11 September Picasso's first museum exhibition opens in the Kunsthaus Zürich (until 30 October, extended until 13 November). In addition to many guests, representatives of the cantonal government and the city council are present. Picasso travels to the Engadin valley with his family and is not present at the opening.

A total of 225 works are on display, 43 of which were not exhibited in Paris. Many works are in the possession of Picasso himself and are available for purchase.

1935   Olga leaves Picasso when it becomes known that Marie-Thérèse is
        pregnant.
        5 October: birth of Maya, daughter of Picasso and Marie-Thérèse.
        Olga's attempts to get a divorce continue for years and fail due to
        the question of division of assets.

1936   Outbreak of the Spanish Civil War on 18 July. The Republican gov-
        ernment appoints Picasso as director of the Prado in Madrid.
        Picasso meets the photographer and painter Dora Maar (1907–
        1997), who becomes his mistress.

1937   He is commissioned by the Republican government to paint a mural
        for the Spanish Pavilion at the Paris World Fair. The subject of his
        painting *Guernica* is the German bombing raid on the Basque town
        of Guernica.

1943   Picasso meets the young painter Françoise Gilot (*1921), who
        becomes his favourite model.

1947   15 May: birth of Claude, son of Picasso and Françoise Gilot.

1948   Picasso settles on the Côte d'Azur and moves into the Villa La Gal-
        loise in Vallauris. He produces many ceramic works there.

1949   19 April: birth of Paloma, daughter of Picasso and Françoise Gilot.
        Paloma is named after his lithograph *The Dove*, made for the World
        Peace Congress in Paris.

1953   Françoise Gilot leaves Picasso and moves to Paris with their chil-
        dren; he meets Jacqueline Roque (1926–1986), who becomes his
        new partner.

1955   Death of Olga Khokhlova.

1961   Picasso marries Jacqueline Roque and moves to Mougins.

1963   Picasso Museum in Barcelona opens.

1971   On the occasion of his ninetieth birthday the Musée du Louvre
        devotes an exhibition in the Grande Galerie to Picasso. He is the
        first living artist to be honoured in this way.

1973   On 8 April Picasso dies in Mougins and is buried on his estate at
        Vauvenargues.

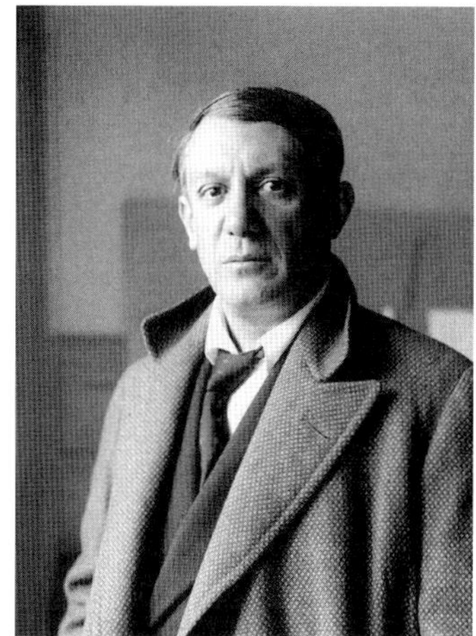

Fig. 4
Picasso in Paris,
c. 1928
Private collection

LIST OF WORKS

EXHIBITED WORKS

The catalogues raisonnés and works overviews highlighted and listed here in abbreviated form are listed in full in the bibliography on page 283.

1

The Fountain, 1899

Oil on canvas
61 x 50.8 cm
Signed bottom left: *P Ruiz Picasso*
Musée Jenisch, Vevey
Bequest of Alain Ollivier, 1994

Cat. Zurich 1
Der Springbrunnen

Provenance: Collection of Albert Skira, Geneva ■ Dugardin Collection, Paris ■ Collection of Alain Ollivier

Exhibitions (selected): 2001 Bern, Kunstmuseum: *Picasso und die Schweiz. Meisterwerke aus Schweizer Sammlungen*, cat. 1 ■ 2002/03 La Coruña, Fundación Pedro Barrié de la Maza Conde de Fenosa: *Picasso Joven*, cat. 80 ■ 2007 Saint-Tropez, L'Annonciade, Musée de Saint-Tropez: *Picasso en Méditerranée*, cat. 4

Selected literature: Zervos: I, no. 5 (Le Bassin, dated 1898) ■ Ocaña, María Teresa (ed.), *Picasso: La formación de un genio/The Development of a Genius 1890–1904*, Barcelona 1997, p. 184

2

Portrait of Gustave Coquiot, 1901

Oil on canvas
100 x 81 cm
Signed bottom right: *Picasso*
Centre Pompidou, Paris
Musée national d'art moderne/Centre de création industrielle
Donated by Mme Gustave Coquiot, 1933

Cat. Zurich 7
Bildnis Gustave Coquiot

Provenance: 1901 Gustave Coquiot, Paris ■ 1933 donated by Mme Gustave Coquiot ■ Musée du Jeu de Paume, Paris ■ Palais de Tokyo, Paris ■ Centre Pompidou, Musée National d'Art Moderne, Paris

Exhibitions (selected): 1932 Paris, Galeries Georges Petit: *Exposition Picasso*, cat. 5 (Portrait de Gustave Coquiot) ■ 1953 Lyon, Musée de Lyon: *Picasso*, cat. 5 ■ 1959 Mar-
seille, Musée Cantini: *Picasso*, cat. 3 ■ 1969 London, The Arts Council of Great Britain/Tate Gallery: *Picasso*, cat. 12 ■ 1975/76 Paris, Musée Jacquemart André: *Le Bâteau-Lavoir*, cat. 51 ■ 1980 New York, The Museum of Modern Art: *Pablo Picasso. A Retrospective*, p. 37 ■ 1984 Bern, Kunstmuseum: *Der junge Picasso. Frühwerk und blaue Periode*, cat. 126 ■ 1994/95 Quimper, Musée des Beaux-Arts: *Max Jacob et Picasso*/Paris, Musée Picasso, cat. 3 ■ 1997/98 Washington, National Gallery of Art: *Picasso. The Early Years, 1892–1906*/Boston, Museum of Fine Arts, p. 145 ■ 1999 London, The Barbican Centre: *The Dark Mirror. Picasso and Photography* ■ 2005/06 Berlin, Neue Nationalgalerie: *Pablo — der private Picasso: Le Musée Picasso à Berlin*, cat. 4 ■ 2006/07 New York, The Metropolitan Museum of Art: *Cézanne to Picasso. Ambroise Vollard, Patron of the Avant-Garde*/Chicago, Art Institute/Paris, Musée d'Orsay, cat. 139, p. 384 (English edition), cat. 89, p. 115 (French edition) ■ 2009 London, National Gallery: *Picasso. Challenging the Past*, cat. 4 and p. 34

Selected literature: Zervos: I, no. 84 (Gustave Coquiot) ■ Daix/Boudaille: V. 64 (Portrait de Gustave Coquiot) ■ Palau i Fabre: vol. 1881–1907, no. 605 (Porträt Gustave Coquiot) ■ Richardson: I, pp. 198, 200, 215 ■ Frank Elgar, Robert Maillard, *Picasso*, Paris 1955, p. 263 ■ Carsten-Peter Warncke, *Picasso 1881–1973*, ed. Ingo F. Walther, Cologne 1991, vol. I, p. 67 ■ Christian Geelhaar, *Picasso. Wegbereiter und Förderer seines Aufstiegs 1899–1939*, Zurich 1993, no. 3 and p. 15 ■ Norman Mailer, *Portrait of Picasso as a Young Man*, New York 1995, p. 56 ■ Brigitte Léal, Christine Pilot, Marie-Laure Bernadac, *The Ultimate Picasso*, New York 2000, no. 69 ■ Elizabeth Cowling, *Picasso. Style and Meaning*, London/New York 2002, pp. 15, 23 ■ *Picasso et les maîtres*, exh. cat., Galeries Nationales du Grand Palais, Paris 2008/09, p. 343f.

3

Jeanne, 1901

Oil on canvas
70.5 x 90 cm
Signed top right: *Picasso*
Centre Pompidou, Paris
Musée national d'art moderne/Centre de création industrielle
Bequest of Baronne Eva Gourgaud, 1965

Cat. Zurich 9
Liegender Akt

Provenance: Ambroise Vollard, Paris ■ 1923 John Quinn, New York ■ 1924–1926 Quinn Estate ■ Paul Rosenberg,

Paris ■ Baron Napoléon Gourgaud, Paris ■ Until 1959
Baronne Eva Gourgaud, Paris ■ Gourgaud Estate

Exhibitions (selected): 1932 Paris, Galeries Georges Petit:
Exposition Picasso, cat. 13 ■ 1984 Bern, Kunstmuseum:
Der junge Picasso. Frühwerk und blaue Periode, cat. 124 ■
2002/03 La Coruña, Fundación Pedro Barrié de la Maza
Conde de Fenosa, *Picasso Joven*

Selected literature: Zervos: I, no. 106 (Nu couché) ■
Daix/Boudaille: V. 52 (Nu couché (Jeanne)) ■ Palau i Fabre:
vol. 1881–1907, no. 606 (Weiblicher Akt) ■ Richardson: I,
p. 194 (Nude on a bed (Jeanne)) ■ *Cahiers d'art*, year 7, 1932,
p. 90 ■ Jean Cassou, *Picasso*, Paris 1940, p. 38 ■ Alexandre
Cirici-Pellicer, *Picasso avant Picasso*, Geneva 1950, no. 67
■ Carsten-Peter Warncke, *Picasso 1881–1973*, ed. Ingo
F. Walther, Cologne 1991, vol. I, p. 82 ■ Christian Geelhaar,
*Picasso. Wegbereiter und Förderer seines Aufstiegs 1899–
1939*, Zurich 1993, no. 68 and p. 82 ■ Norman Mailer,
Portrait of Picasso as a Young Man, New York 1995, p. 67

4
Melancholy Woman, 1902

Oil on canvas
100 x 69.2 cm
Signed top left: *Picasso*
Detroit Institute of Arts
Bequest of Robert H. Tannahill

Cat. Zurich 13
Trauer

Provenance: c. 1905 Pablo Picasso ■ Michael and Sarah
Stein, Paris ■ Daniel-Henry Kahnweiler (?), Paris ■ Paul Guil-
laume, Paris ■ F. Valentine Dudensing, New York ■ 1934
Robert H. Tannahill, Grosse Pointe Farms ■ 1970 Detroit
Institute of Arts

Exhibitions (selected): 1932 Paris, Galeries Georges Petit:
Exposition Picasso, cat. 25 ■ 1936 New York, Jacques Selig-
mann & Co: *Picasso. Blue and Rose Periods*, 1901–1906,
cat. 13 ■ 1997/98 Washington, National Gallery of Art:
Picasso: The Early Years, 1892–1906/Boston, Museum of
Fine Arts, cat. 74 and p. 300 ■ 2000/01 Washington, The
Phillips Collection: *Degas to Matisse. Impressionist and Mod-
ernist Masterworks from the Detroit Institute of Arts*, p. 107

Selected literature: Zervos: I, no. 155 (Femme au fichu
assise) ■ Daix/Boudaille: VII.6 (Femme au fichu assise) ■

Palau i Fabre: vol. 1881–1907, no. 734 (Sitzende Frau mit
Schal) ■ Richardson: I, p. 217 (Saint-Lazare Woman by Moon-
light, dated 1901) ■ Maurice Raynal, *Picasso, Munich 1921*,
plate 10 ■ George Waldemar, *La grande peinture contempo-
raine à la Collection Paul Guillaume*, Paris, 1929, p. 115, fig.
p. 117 ■ Alexandre Cirici-Pellicer, *Picasso avant Picasso*,
Geneva 1950, no. 166 ■ Alberto Moravia, Paolo Lecaldano,
L'opera completa di Picasso blu e rosa, Milan 1968 (Classici
dell'arte 22), no. 28

5
Woman in a Blue Shawl, 1902

Oil on canvas
60.3 x 52.4 cm
Signed top left: *Picasso*
Aichi Prefectural Museum of Art, Japan

Cat. Zurich 17
Weibliches Brustbild

Provenance: Marina Picasso Foundation

Exhibitions (selected): 1932 Paris, Galeries Georges Petit:
Exposition Picasso, cat. 11 ■ 1966/67 Paris, Grand Palais:
Hommage à Pablo Picasso, cat. 12 ■ 1981 Venice, Centro di
Cultura di Palazzo Grassi: *Picasso. Opere dal 1895 al 1971
dalla Collezione Marina Picasso*, cat. 32 ■ 1981/82 Munich,
Haus der Kunst: *Pablo Picasso. Eine Ausstellung zum hunderts-
ten Geburtstag. Werke aus der Sammlung Marina Picasso*/
Cologne, Josef-Haubrich Kunsthalle/Frankfurt, Städtische
Galerie im Städelschen Kunstinstitut/Zurich, Kunsthaus, cat.
17 ■ 1983 Tokyo, National Museum of Modern Art: *Picasso.
Masterpieces from the Marina Picasso Collection and Muse-
ums in U. S. A and U. S. S. R.*/Kyoto, Municipal Museum, cat. 13
■ 1984 Melbourne, National Gallery of Victoria: *Picasso.
Marina Picasso Collection*/Sydney Art Gallery of South Wales,
cat. 43 ■ 1985 Lausanne, Fondation de l'Hermitage: *De
Cézanne à Picasso dans les collections romandes*, cat. 123
■ 1998 Tokyo, The Bunkamura Museum of Art: *Pablo
Picasso*/Nagoya, City Art Museum, cat. 10 ■ 2000/01 Liège,
Salle Saint-Georges, *Pablo Picasso*, cat. 12

Selected literature: Zervos: I, no. 155 (Portrait de femme) ■
Daix/Boudaille: VII.9 (Femme au fichu bleu) ■ Palau i Fabre:
vol. 1881–1907, no. 733 (Die Frau mit dem Schal) ■ Jean
Cassou, *Picasso*, Paris 1940, p. 120 ■ André Fermigier,
Picasso, Paris 1967, p. 150 f. ■ Alberto Moravia, Paolo Lecal-
dano, *L'opera completa di Picasso blu e rosa*, Milan 1968

(Classici dell'arte 22), no. 33 ■ *Pablo Picasso. A Retro-spective*, ed. William Rubin, exh. cat., The Museum of Modern Art, New York 1980, p. 46, 48 ■ Brigitte Léal, Christine Pilot, Marie-Laure Bernadac, *The Ultimate Picasso*, New York 2000, no. 98 ■ Hirotoshi Furuta, Shuji Takahashi (ed.), *Aichi Prefectural Museum of Art: Handbook of the Collections*, Nagoya 2002, no. 1

6
Crouching Woman, 1903

Gouache and watercolour on grounded paper
55 x 38 cm
Signed top right: Picasso
Bollag Galleries

Cat. Zurich 274
Sitzender Akt

Provenance: Pablo Picasso ■ G. and L. Bollag, Zurich ■ Collection of Max G. Bollag, Zurich

Exhibitions (selected): 1964 Lausanne, Palais de Beaulieu: *Chefs-d'œuvre des Collections suisses*, cat. 226

Selected literature: Zervos VI, no. 476 ■ Daix/Boudaille: IX.10

7
The Couple (The Wretched Ones), 1904

Oil on canvas
100.5 x 81.5 cm
Signed bottom left: *Picasso*
Merzbacher Kunststiftung

Cat. Zurich 224
Ein Menschenpaar

Provenance: Thannhauser Collection, Munich ■ Oscar Miller ■ Galerie Bollag, Zurich ■ Bernhard Mayer, Zurich

Exhibitions (selected): 1909 Munich, Galerie Thannhauser: *Picasso* ■ 1953 Milan, Palazzo Reale: *Picasso*, cat. 4 ■ 1964 Lausanne, Palais de Beaulieu: *Chefs-d'œuvre des Collections Suisses de Manet à Picasso (Exposition Nationale Suisse)*, cat. 228 ■ 1967 Paris, Orangerie des Tuileries: *Chefs-d'œuvre des Collections Suisses de Manet à Picasso*, cat. 239 ■ 1981 Basel, Galerie Beyeler: *Picasso 1881–1981*, cat. 1 ■ 1992 Barcelona, Museu Picasso: *Picasso*

1905-1906. Rosa Periode und Gósol/Bern, Kunstmuseum, cat. 13 ■ 1997/98 Washington, National Gallery of Art: *Picasso: The Early Years 1892-1906*/Boston, Museum of Fine Arts, cat. 103 ■ 2001 Bern, Kunstmuseum: *Picasso und die Schweiz. Meisterwerke aus Schweizer Sammlungen*, cat. 15

Selected literature: Zervos: I, no. 224 (Le couple) ■ Daix/Boudaille: XI.5 ■ Palau i Fabre: vol. 1881-1907, no. 985 (Das Paar) ■ André Level, *Picasso*, Paris 1928, plate 8 ■ Jean Cassou, *Picasso*, Paris 1940, p. 48 ■ Maurice Raynal, *Histoire de la peinture moderne, de Picasso au surréalisme*, Geneva 1950, p. 21 ■ Frank Elgar, Robert Maillard, *Picasso*, Paris 1955, p. 365 ■ Jean Leymarie, *Picasso: Métamorphoses et unité*, Geneva 1971, p. 6 ■ Alberto Moravia, Paolo Lecaldano, *L'opera completa di Picasso blu e rosa*, Milan 1968 (Classici dell'arte 22), no. 119 ■ Pierre Daix, *Picasso créateur. La vie intime et l'œuvre*, Paris 1987, p. 54 ■ Carsten-Peter Warncke, *Picasso 1881-1973*, ed. Ingo F. Walther, Cologne 1991, vol. I, p. 109 ■ Christian Geelhaar, *Picasso, Wegbereiter und Förderer seines Aufstiegs, 1899-1939*, Zurich 1993, no. 76

8
Barcelona Rooftops, 1902/03

Oil on canvas
71 x 111 cm
Unsigned
Museu Picasso, Barcelona
Ceded by the Ministry of Culture to the Barcelona City Council, 1991

Cat. Zurich 20
Landschaft Barcelona

Provenance: Collection of the artist ■ 1987 Collection of Jacqueline Picasso ■ 1990 French state ■ 1991 Gift to the Spanish state

Exhibitions (selected): 1932 Paris, Galeries Georges Petit: *Exposition Picasso*, cat. 14 (Paysage à Barcelone, dated 1902/03) ■ 1966/67 Paris, Grand Palais: *Hommage à Pablo Picasso*, cat. 14 ■ 1994/95 Barcelona, Museu Picasso: *Picasso. Paisajes, 1890-1912 de la Academia a la vanguardia* ■ 2001/02 Paris: Galeries Nationales du Grand Palais: *Paris — Barcelone. De Gaudí à Miró*/Barcelona, Museu Picasso, p. 231

Selected literature: Zervos: I, no. 207 ■ Daix/Boudaille: IX.2 (Toits de Barcelone) ■ André Level, *Picasso*, Paris 1928, plate 5 ■ Alexandre Cirici-Pellicer, *Picasso avant Picasso*, Geneva 1950, no. 145 ■ Alberto Moravia, Paolo Lecaldano, *L'opera completa di Picasso blu e rosa*, Milan 1968 (Classici dell'arte 22), no. 58 ■ Brigitte Léal, Christine Pilot, Marie-Laure Bernadac, *The Ultimate Picasso*, New York 2000, no. 135

9

Vase of Flowers, 1901/04

Oil on canvas
66 x 46.5 cm
Signed bottom right: *Picasso*
Courtesy Nahmad Collection, Switzerland

Cat. Zurich 23
Blumen in Vase

Provenance: J. D. Barlow ■ Lefevre Gallery, London ■ 1932 acquired by May, Duchess of Roxburghe ■ The Duke of Roxburghe

Exhibitions (selected): 1927 London, Knoedler Gallery ■ 1932 Paris, Galeries Georges Petit: *Exposition Picasso*, cat. 22. ■ 1998 London, Helly Nahmad Gallery: *Picasso. Artist of the Century*, cat. 6 ■ 1999 Rotterdam, Kunsthal: *Picasso. Artist of the Century*, cat. 6

Selected literature: Zervos: I, no. 242 (Les fleurs, dated 1904) ■ Daix/Boudaille: V.26 (Fleurs (Fleurs dans un vase))

10

Portrait of Fernande Olivier, 1906

Oil on canvas
46 x 38 cm
Signed on canvas stretcher: *Picasso*
Private collection

Cat. Zurich 29
Frauenkopf im Profil

Provenance: c. 1907/08 Collection of Oscar Miller ■ Before 1914 Josef Müller, Solothurn (acquired from Oscar Miller)

Exhibitions (selected): 1932 Paris, Galeries Georges Petit: *Exposition Picasso*, cat. 38 ■ 1992 Barcelona, Museu Picasso: *Picasso 1905-1906. Rosa Periode und Gósol*/Bern, Kunstmuseum, cat. 90 ■ 1999 Munich, Haus der Kunst:

Kunst über Grenzen. Die Klassische Moderne von Cézanne bis Tinguely und die Weltkunst — aus der Schweiz gesehen, cat. 123 ■ 2001 Bern, Kunstmuseum: *Picasso und die Schweiz. Meisterwerke aus Schweizer Sammlungen*, cat. 18

Selected literature: Zervos: VI, no. 467 (dated 1902 or 1903) ■ Daix/Boudaille: X.10 (Tête de femme de profil, dated 1903 (?)) ■ Palau i Fabre: vol. 1881-1907, no. 1275 (Frauenkopf im Profil) ■ Alberto Moravia, Paolo Lecaldano, *L'opera completa di Picasso blu e rosa*, Milan 1968 (Classici dell'arte 22), no. 54 ■ Christian Geelhaar, *Picasso. Wegbereiter und Förderer seines Aufstiegs 1899-1939*, Zurich 1993, no. 75 and p. 92, 125

11

Girl in a Chemise, c. 1905

Oil on canvas
72.7 x 60 cm
Signed and dated bottom left: *Picasso/05*
Tate, London
Bequeathed by C. Frank Stoop, 1933

Cat. Zurich 31
Frau im Hemd

Provenance: 1909 Galerie Kahnweiler, Paris (acquired from the artist) ■ Alfred Flechtheim, Berlin ■ c. 1911/12 C. Frank Stoop, London

Exhibitions (selected): 1921 London, Leicester Galleries: *Works by Pablo Picasso*, cat. 8 ■ 1931 London, Lefevre Gallery: *Thirty Years of Pablo Picasso*, cat. 7 ■ 1932 Paris, Galeries Georges Petit: *Exposition Picasso*, cat. 31 (Portrait de jeune femme) ■ 1960 London, The Arts Council of Great Britain/Tate Gallery: *Picasso*, cat. 22 ■ 1966/67 Paris, Grand Palais: *Hommage à Pablo Picasso*, cat. 22 ■ 1967 Amsterdam, Stedelijk Museum: *Picasso*, cat. 7 ■ 1992 Barcelona, Museu Picasso: *Picasso 1905-1906. Rosa Periode und Gósol*/Bern, Kunstmuseum, cat. 31 ■ 1996 New York, The Museum of Modern Art: *Picasso and Portraiture. Representation and Transformation*/Paris, Grand Palais, p. 244, 246 ■ 1997/98 Washington, National Gallery: *Picasso. The Early Years, 1892-1906*/Boston, Museum of Fine Arts, cat. 112 ■ 2006 Madrid, Museo Nacional del Prado/Museo Nacional Centro de Arte Reina Sofía: *Picasso. Tradición y vanguardia*, cat. 3 ■ 2009 London, National Gallery: *Picasso: Challenging the Past*, cat. 8

Selected literature: Zervos: I, no. 307 (Femme à la chemise)
■ Daix/Boudaille: XII.5 (Femme à la chemise) ■ Palau i Fabre:
vol. 1881-1907, no. 1050 ■ Richardson: I, p. 304 ■ Frank
Elgar, Robert Maillard, Picasso, Paris 1955, p. 265 ■ Alberto
Moravia, Paolo Lecaldano, *L'opera completa di Picasso blu e
rosa*, Milan 1968 (Classici dell'arte 22), no. 157 ■ Ronald
Alley, *Catalogue of the Tate Gallery's Collection of Modern Art
other than Works by British Artists*, London 1981, p. 592 f.
■ Carsten-Peter Warncke, *Picasso 1881-1973*, ed. Ingo
F. Walther, Cologne 1991, vol. I, p. 122 ■ Christian Geelhaar,
*Picasso. Wegbereiter und Förderer seines Aufstiegs 1899-
1939*, Zurich 1993, no. 66 and p. 80 ■ Norman Mailer,
Portrait of Picasso as a Young Man, New York 1995, p. 107 ■
Brigitte Léal, Christine Pilot, Marie-Laure Bernadac, *The Ulti-
mate Picasso*, New York 2000, no. 153 ■ *Picasso. Tradición y
vanguardia*, exh. cat., Museo Nacional del Prado/Museo
Nacional Centro de Arte Reina Sofía, Madrid 2006, pp. 90-94

La vie intime et l'œuvre, Paris 1987, p. 70 ■ *Picasso 1905-
1906, Rosa Periode und Gósol*, exh. cat., Museu Picasso,
Barcelona/Kunstmuseum Bern, 1992, p. 79 ff. ■ Pierre Daix,
'Die Revision des Klassizismus in der modernen Kunst', in:
*Canto d'Amore. Klassizistische Moderne in Musik und bildender
Kunst 1914-1935*, exh. cat., Kunstmuseum Basel, 1996,
p. 74 f. ■ *Picasso. The Early Years, 1892-1906*, exh. cat.,
National Gallery of Art Washington/Museum of Fine Arts
Boston, Washington 1997, p. 271 f. ■ Anne Baldassari,
Picasso and Photography: The Dark Mirror, exh. cat., Museum
of Fine Arts Houston, Paris/New York 1997, fig. 42 ■ Brigitte
Léal, Christine Pilot, Marie-Laure Bernadac, *The Ultimate
Picasso*, New York 2000, no. 188 ■ Gary Tinterow, Susan
Alison Stein (eds.), *Picasso in the Metropolitan Museum of Art*,
exh. cat., The Metropolitan Museum of Art New York, New
Haven/London 2010, p. 92

12
Adolescents, 1906

Oil on canvas
157 x 117 cm
Signed top right: *Picasso*
Musée de l'Orangerie, Paris
Collection Jean Walter et Paul Guillaume

Cat. Zurich 33
Jüngling und Mädchen

Provenance: Ambroise Vollard ■ 1930 Paul Guillaume ■
Mme Vve Jean Walter ■ 1957 Musée de l'Orangerie

Exhibitions (selected): 1932 Paris, Galeries Georges Petit:
Exposition Picasso, cat. 42 ■ 1936 New York, Jacques Selig-
mann: *Picasso. Blue and Rose Periods*, cat. 30 ■ 1966 Paris,
Musée de l'Orangerie des Tuileries: *Collection Jean Walter Paul
Guillaume*, cat. 93 ■ 1997 Paris, Musée Picasso: *Le miroir
noir. Picasso, sources photographiques 1900-1928*/Houston,
Museum of Fine Arts, cat. 53, pp. 63-66 ■ 2008/09 Paris,
Galeries Nationales du Grand Palais/Musée du Louvre/Musée
d'Orsay: *Picasso et les maîtres*/London, National Gallery, p. 139

Selected literature: Zervos: I, no. 324 (dated 1905) ■
Daix/Boudaille: XV.11 ■ Palau i Fabre: vol. 1881-1907,
no. 1239 (Junges Paar) ■ Josep Palau i Fabre, *Picasso en
Cataluña*, Barcelona 1966, no. 112 ■ Alberto Moravia, Paolo
Lecaldano, *L'opera completa di Picasso blu e rosa*, Milan 1968
(Classici dell'arte 22), no. 259 ■ Pierre Daix, *Picasso créateur.*

13
Bust of a Man, 1908

Oil on canvas
62.2 x 43.5 cm
Signed top left: *Picasso*
The Metropolitan Museum of Art, New York
Bequest of Florene M. Schoenborn, 1995 (1996.403.5)

Cat. Zurich 37
Negerkopf, dated 1907

Provenance: c. 1912/13 Gertrude Stein, Paris (?) ■ 1914-
1921 Galerie Kahnweiler, Paris ■ 1921 Henri-Pierre Roché,
Paris (acquired at the auction held by Galerie Kahnweiler, 21
November 1921) ■ 1925 Galerie Vavin-Raspail, Paris ■
1926 Galerie Pierre Loeb, Paris ■ 1936 Walter P. Chrysler
Jr., New York ■ 1954 Gimpel Fils, London ■ 1955 Mr and
Mrs Samuel A. Marx, Chicago, then Florene May Schoenborn
(widow of Samuel A. Marx, later Mrs Wolfgang Schoenborn,
New York) ■ 1971 permanent loan in The Museum of Modern
Art, New York ■ 1985 permanent loan in The Metropolitan
Museum of Art, New York

Exhibitions (selected): 1932 Paris, Galeries Georges Petit:
Exposition Picasso, cat. 44 (Tête d'homme, dated 1907) ■
1936 Barcelona, Sala Esteva: *Picasso* /Bilbao, Galeria
Arte/Madrid, Centro de la Construcción, cat. 2 ■ 1936 New
York, Valentine Gallery: *Picasso 1901-1934. Retrospective
Exhibition*, cat. 29 ■ 1937 New York, Jacques Seligmann &
Co.: *20 Years in the Evolution of Picasso, 1903-1923*, cat. 6
■ 1938 Boston, Museum of Modern Art: *Picasso — Matisse,*

cat. 8 ■ 1939/40 New York, The Museum of Modern Art: *Picasso: Forty Years of His Art*/Chicago, Art Institute/St. Louis, City Art Museum/Boston, Museum of Fine Arts, cat. 78 ■ 1972 New York, The Museum of Modern Art: *Picasso in the Collection of The Museum of Modern Art*, p. 6, 52 f., 201 ■ 1980 New York, The Museum of Modern Art: *Pablo Picasso. A Retrospective*, list of additional works no. 5 ■ 1998/99 Paris, Musée Picasso: *Picasso 1901–1909, Chefs-d'œuvre du Metropolitan Museum of Art*, New York, cat. 17 ■ 2000 New York, The Metropolitan Museum of Art: *Painters in Paris 1895–1950*, p. 66, 125 ■ 2010 New York, The Metropolitan Museum of Art: *Picasso in the Metropolitan Museum of Art*, cat. 46

Selected literature: Zervos: IIa, no. 76 ■ Daix/Rosselet: no. 143 ■ Palau i Fabre: vol. 1907–1917, no. 276 (Negroides Brustbild) ■ Jean Cassou, Picasso, Paris 1940, p. 59 ■ Alfred H. Barr Jr., *Picasso: Fifty Years of His Art*, New York 1946, p. 62 f., 65 ■ Roland Penrose, *Picasso. His Life and Work*, London 1958, plate V/3 ■ Franco Russoli, Fiorella Minervino, *L'opera completa di Picasso cubista*, Milan 1972 (Classici dell'arte 64), no. 177 ■ Scarlett and Philippe Reliquet, *Henri-Pierre Roché: l'enchanteur collectionneur*, Paris 1999, p. 200 ■ Ruben Charles Cordova, *Primitivism and Picasso's Early Cubism*, diss. at University of California, Berkeley 1998, p. 137, 409, fig. 1.77 ■ Brigitte Léal, Christine Pilot, Marie-Laure Bernadac, *The Ultimate Picasso*, New York 2000, no. 290 ■ Michael FitzGerald, *Picasso and American Art*, exh. cat., Whitney Museum of American Art, New York 2007, p. 339 passim

14
Woman's Head, 1907

Oil on canvas
54.5 x 46 cm
Signed top right: *Picasso*
Private collection

Cat. Zurich 38
Kopf, braun

Provenance: Galerie Marlborough ■ 1989 Private collection ■ 1990–1996 Private collection, deposited in the Collecció March, Palma de Mallorca ■ 1996–2009 Private collection, deposited in the Museu d'Art Espanyol Contemporani, Fundación Juan March, Palma de Mallorca ■ 2010 return to the Private collection

Exhibitions (selected): 1932 Paris, Galeries Georges Petit: *Exposition Picasso*, cat. 43 (Tête, dated 1906–1908) ■ 1977 Madrid, Fundación Juan March: *Picasso*, cat. 5 ■ 1977/78 Barcelona, Palacio Meca: *Picasso*, cat. 7 ■ 1996 Albi, Musée de Toulouse-Lautrec: *De Picasso à Barceló*

Selected literature: Zervos: IIa, no. 51 ■ Daix/Rosselet: no. 97 (Etude de tête pour Nu à la serviette) ■ Palau i Fabre: vol. 1907–1917, no. 125 (Frauenkopf, rechtes Halbprofil) ■ Pierre Daix, *Picasso créateur. La vie intime et l'œuvre*, Paris 1987 ■ Franco Russoli, Fiorella Minervino, *L'opera completa di Picasso cubista*, Milan 1972 (Classici dell'arte 64), no. 109

15
Woman's Head, 1908

Oil on canvas
73.6 x 60.6 cm
Signed on the back: *Picasso*
The Museum of Modern Art, New York
Florene May Schoenborn Bequest, 1996

Cat. Zurich 39
Kopf, blau, dated 1907

Provenance: 1908 Maurice de Vlaminck, Paris (?) ■ 1912–1917 Galerie Flechtheim Gallery, Berlin and Düsseldorf (acquired from Kahnweiler ?) ■ 1917 Sally Falk, Mannheim (acquired at the auction held by the Galerie Flechtheim, 5 June) ■ 1932–1942 (?) Alfred Gold, Paris and Berlin ■ 1946 (?) Justin K. Thannhauser, New York (?) ■ 1951–1996 Mr and Mrs Samuel A. Marx, Chicago, then Florene May Schoenborn (widow of Samuel A. Marx, later Mrs Wolfgang Schoenborn, New York

Exhibitions (selected): 1932 Paris, Galeries Georges Petit: *Exposition Picasso*, cat. 47 (Tête, dated 1907) ■ 1980 New York, The Museum of Modern Art: *Pablo Picasso. A Retrospective*, list of additional works no. 3

Selected literature: Zervos: IIa, no. 52 ■ Daix/Rosselet: no. 105 (dated 1907/08) ■ Palau i Fabre: vol. 1907–1917, no. 123 (Frauenkopf, linkes Halbprofil, dated 1907/08) ■ Maurice Gieure, *Initiation à l'œuvre de Picasso*, Paris 1951, no. 17 ■ Franco Russoli, Fiorella Minervino, *L'opera completa di Picasso cubista*, Milan 1972 (Classici dell'arte 64), no. 108 ■ Christian Geelhaar, Picasso. *Wegbereiter und Förderer seines Aufstiegs 1899–1939*, Zurich 1993, no. 36 and p. 47 ■ Brigitte Léal, Christine Pilot, Marie-Laure Bernadac, *The Ultimate Picasso*, New York 2000, no. 272

16

Head of a Sleeping Woman
(Study for Nude with Drapery), 1907

Oil on canvas
61.4 x 47.6 cm
Unsigned
The Museum of Modern Art, New York
Estate of John Hay Whitney, 1983

Provenance: Leo and Gertrude Stein, Paris ■ 1913-1946
Gertrude Stein, Paris and San Francisco ■ 1946-1967
Estate of Gertrude Stein (Alice B. Toklas, Paris) ■ 1968
The Museum of Modern Art syndicate, New York ■ 1968
Mr and Mrs John Hay Whitney, New York

Exhibitions (selected): 1932 Paris, Galeries Georges Petit:
Exposition Picasso, cat. 46 (Tête de femme) ■ 1954 Paris,
Maison de la Pensée Française: *Picasso, œuvres des musées
de Leningrad et de Moscou, 1900-1914*, cat. 4 ■ 1970/71
New York, The Museum of Modern Art: *Four Americans in Paris:
The Collection of Gertrude Stein and Her Family*, cat. 41 ■
1983 Washington, National Gallery of Art: *The John Hay Whitney Collection*, cat. 55 ■ 2010 Bern, Zentrum Paul Klee: *Klee
trifft Picasso*, p. 86 f., 274

Selected literature: Zervos: IIa, no. 44 (Etude pour Nu à la
draperie) ■ Daix/Rosselet: no. 93 (Etude pour la tête du Nu à
la draperie) ■ Palau i Fabre: vol. 1907-1917, no. 72 (Skizze
zum Kopf von Akt mit Kleidungsstück) ■ Maurice Raynal,
Picasso, Munich 1921, plate 28 ■ Gertrude Stein, *Picasso*,
Paris 1938, between p. 72 and 75 ■ Maurice Gieure, *Initiation
à l'œuvre de Picasso*, Paris 1951, no. 18 ■ Franco Russoli,
Fiorella Minervino, *L'opera completa di Picasso cubista*, Milan
1972 (Classici dell'arte 64), no. 103 ■ Pierre Daix, *Picasso
créateur. La vie intime et l'œuvre*, Paris 1987, passim

17

Jugs with lemon, 1907

Oil on canvas
55 x 46 cm
Unsigned
Albertina, Vienna
Batliner Collection

Provenance: Clive Bell, Sussex ■ Mrs David Garnett/Quentin
Bell ■ Charles Kearley, England ■ Galerie Beyeler, Basel

Exhibitions (selected): 1932 Paris, Galeries Georges Petit:
Exposition Picasso, cat. 48 (Nature morte, dated 1908) ■
1960 London, The Arts Council of Great Britain/Tate Gallery:
Picasso, cat. 35 ■ 1989/90 New York, The Museum of Modern Art: *Picasso and Braque. Pioneering Cubism*/Basel, Kunstmuseum, p. 74 (English edition), cat. 3 (German edition) ■
1998 Vienna, Kunstforum: *Monet bis Picasso*, cat. 87 ■
2007/08 Vienna, Albertina: *Monet bis Picasso — Die Sammlung Batliner*, cat. 76

Selected literature: Zervos: IIa, no. 32 ■ Daix/Rosselet: 65
■ Palau i Fabre: vol. 1907-1917, no. 93 (Gefäße und Zitro-
nen) ■ Richardson: II, p. 310 (Jars with lemon) ■ Franco Russoli, Fiorella Minervino, *L'opera completa di Picasso cubista*,
Milan 1972 (Classici dell'arte 64), no. 54 ■ William Rubin,
'The Genesis of 'Les Demoiselles d'Avignon', in: *Les Demoiselles
d'Avignon*, exh. cat., The Museum of Modern Art, New York
1994, p. 47 ■ Rudolf Koella, Felix Billeter, *Verborgene Meisterwerke. R. & H. Batliner Art Foundation, Vaduz 2005, no.
159

18

Seated Female Nude, 1908/09

Oil on canvas
116.5 x 89.4 cm
Signed bottom right: *Picasso*
Philadelphia Museum of Art
The Louise and Walter Arensberg Collection, 1950

Provenance: 1932 Galerie Percier, Paris ■ 1932-1950
Louise and Walter C. Arensberg, Los Angeles (acquired through
Marcel Duchamp)

Exhibitions (selected): 1932 Paris, Galeries Georges Petit:
Exposition Picasso, cat. 52 (Femme nue, dated 1908) ■ 1962
New York, Cooperating New York Galleries: *Picasso: An Ameri-
can Tribute*, cat. 39 (Knoedler & Co.) ■ 1964 Tokyo, National
Museum of Modern Art: *Pablo Picasso Exhibition*/Kyoto,
National Museum of Modern Art/Nagoya, Prefectural Museum
of Art, cat. 12

Selected literature: Zervos: IIa, no. 114 ■ Daix/Rosselet: no. 243 ■ Palau i Fabre: vol. 1907–1917, no. 349 (Nackte Frau, mit gespreizten Beinen) ■ Richardson: II, p. 108 f. (Standing Female Nude, dated 1909) ■ Franco Russoli, Fiorella Minervino, *L'opera completa di Picasso cubista*, Milan 1972 (Classici dell'arte 64), no. 200 ■ John Golding, *Cubism: a history and an analysis, 1907–1914*, London 1959, plate 4 a ■ Pierre Daix, *Picasso créateur. La vie intime et l'œuvre*, Paris 1987, p. 99, 110, 232 ■ Anne Baldassari, *Picasso and Photography: The Dark Mirror*, exh. cat., Museum of Fine Arts Houston, Paris/New York 1997

Russoli, Fiorella Minervino, *L'opera completa di Picasso
cubista*, Milan 1972 (Classici dell'arte 64), no. 323 ■ Ronald
Alley, *Catalogue of the Tate Gallery's Collection of Modern Art
other than Works by British Artists*, London 1981, p. 595 ■
Carsten-Peter Warncke, *Picasso 1881–1973*, ed. Ingo
F. Walther, Cologne 1991, vol. I, p. 190 ■ Christian Geelhaar,
*Picasso. Wegbereiter und Förderer seines Aufstiegs 1899–
1939*, Zurich 1993, no. 109 and p. 117 ■ Brigitte Léal, Christine Pilot, Marie-Laure Bernadac, *The Ultimate Picasso*, New
York 2000 ' no. 323 ■ Pepe Karmel, *Picasso and the Invention
of Cubism*, Yale 2003, no. 85

21
Mademoiselle Léonie, 1910

Oil on canvas
65 x 50 cm
Signed and dated bottom left: *Picasso/10*
Private collection

Provenance: Until 1921 Wilhelm Uhde ■ 1921–1925
Christian Tetzen-Lund, Copenhagen ■ Paul Rosenberg (?) ■
André Breton (?) ■ Galerie Le Centaure, Brüssel

Exhibitions (selected): 1932 Paris, Galeries Georges Petit:
Exposition Picasso, cat. 65 ■ 1939 Bern, Kunsthalle:
Picasso, Braque, Léger, Gris, Bores, Beaudin, Vines, cat. 8 ■
1950 Knokke Le Zoute, Casino Communale: *Picasso*, cat. 15
■ 1989/90 New York, The Museum of Modern Art: *Picasso
and Braque. Pioneering Cubism*/Basel, Kunstmuseum, p. 158
(English edition), cat. 114 (German edition)

Selected literature: Zervos: IIa, no. 226 ■ Daix/Rosselet:
no. 340 ■ Palau i Fabre: vol. 1907-1917, no. 489 ■ *Documents* no. 3, 1930, p. 180 ■ Christian Zervos, *Histoire de l'art
contemporain*, Paris 1938, p. 210 ■ Franco Russoli, Fiorella
Minervino, *L'opera completa di Picasso cubista*, Milan 1972
(Classici dell'arte 64), no. 361 ■ Pierre Daix, *Picasso créateur.
La vie intime et l'œuvre*, Paris 1987, p. 108, 409 ■ Christian
Geelhaar, *Picasso. Wegbereiter und Förderer seines Aufstiegs
1899-1939*, Zurich 1993, no. 124 and p. 117, 127f. ■ Anne
Baldassari, *Picasso and Photography: The Dark Mirror*, exh.
cat., Museum of Fine Arts Houston, Paris/New York 1997,
p. 102

22
Dressing Table, 1910

Oil on canvas
61 x 46 cm
Signed top left and on the back: *Picasso*
Private collection

Provenance: Ambroise Vollard, Paris ■ After 1932 Galerie
Pierre, Paris ■ Walter P. Chrysler Jr., New York ■ Valentine
Gallery ■ 1946 Mr and Mrs Ralph F. Colin, New York
(acquired at the Valentine Gallery) ■ Private collection

Exhibitions (selected): 1932 Paris, Galeries Georges Petit:
Exposition Picasso, cat. 64 (Nature morte) ■ 1936 Barcelona, Sala Esteva: Picasso/Bilbao/Malaga/Madrid, cat. 3 ■
1936 New York, Valentine Gallery: Picasso. *Retrospective
Exhibition 1901–1934* ■ 1962 New York, Cooperating New
York Galleries: *Picasso: An American Tribute*, cat. 12 (Saidenberg Gallery) ■ 1971 New York, Saidenberg Gallery, Marlborough Gallery: *Homage to Picasso for his 90th Birthday*, cat. 12
■ 1989/90 New York, The Museum of Modern Art: *Picasso
and Braque. Pioneering Cubism*/Basel, Kunstmuseum, p. 179
(English edition), cat. 149 (German edition)

Selected literature: Zervos: IIa, no. 220 ■ Daix/Rosselet: no.
356 ■ Palau i Fabre: vol. 1907-1917, no. 521 ■ Richardson: II, p. 160, 162 ■ Jean Cassou, *Picasso*, Paris 1940, p. 75
■ Robert Rosenblum, *Cubism and Twentieth-Century Art*,
New York 1960, no. 74 ■ Franco Russoli, Fiorella Minervino,
L'opera completa di Picasso cubista, Milan 1972 (Classici
dell'arte 64), no. 347 ■ Pierre Daix, *Picasso créateur. La vie
intime et l'œuvre*, Paris 1987, p. 111 ■ Elizabeth Cowling,
Picasso. Style and Meaning, London/New York 2002, p. 214,
221

23
Souvenir du Havre, 1912

Oil and gloss paint on canvas
81 x 54 cm
Signed on the back: *Picasso*
Private collection, Courtesy Thomas Ammann Fine Art AG
Zurich

Provenance: Galerie Kahnweiler, Paris ▪ Raoul La Roche, Paris ▪ Private collection, Basel ▪ Galerie Beyeler, Basel ▪ Private collection USA ▪ Thomas Ammann Fine Art AG Zurich

Exhibitions (selected): 1932 Paris, Galeries Georges Petit: *Exposition Picasso*, cat. 72 (dated 1911) ▪ 1953 Lyon, Musée de Lyon: *Picasso*, cat. 24 ▪ 1953 Milan, Palazzo Reale: *Pablo Picasso*, cat. 24 ▪ 1955/56 Paris, Musée des Arts Décoratifs: *Picasso. Peintures. 1900-1955*/Munich, Haus der Kunst/Cologne, Rheinisches Museum/Hamburg, Kunsthalle, cat. 31 ▪ 1962 Basel, Galerie Beyeler: *Le Cubisme. Braque, Gris, Léger, Picasso*/Paris, Galerie Knoedler, cat. 6 ▪ 1966/67 Basel, Galerie Beyeler: *Picasso*, cat. 19 ▪ 1968 Vienna, Österreichisches Museum für angewandte Kunst: *Pablo Picasso*, cat. 25 ▪ 1976 Basel, Kunstmuseum: *Picasso. Aus dem Museum of Modern Art New York und Schweizer Sammlungen*, cat. 25 ▪ 1981 Basel, Galerie Beyeler: *Picasso 1881-1981*, cat. 12 ▪ 1981/82 Vienna, Rathaus: *Pablo Picasso 1881-1973. Bilder, Zeichnungen, Plastiken*, cat. 17 ▪ 1989/90 New York, The Museum of Modern Art: *Picasso and Braque: Pioneering Cubism*/Basel, Kunstmuseum, p. 219 (English edition), cat. 215 (German edition)

Selected literature: Zervos: IIa, Nr. 367 ▪ Daix/Rosselet: Nr. 458 ▪ Palau i Fabre: Bd. 1907-1917, Nr. 879 (Souvenir du Havre) ▪ *Cahiers d'art*, year 7, 1932, p. 25 ▪ Jean Cassou, *Picasso*, Paris 1940, p. 166 ▪ Wilhelm Boeck, *Pablo Picasso*, Stuttgart/Paris 1955, no. 62 ▪ José Camon Aznar, *Picasso y el cubismo*, Madrid 1956, no. 291 ▪ Franco Russoli, Fiorella Minervino, *L'opera completa di Picasso cubista*, Milan 1972 (Classici dell'arte 64), no. 527 ▪ Marilyn McCully, *A Picasso Anthology: Documents, Criticism, Reminiscences*, p. 73 ▪ Douglas Cooper, Gary Tinterow, *The Essential Cubism*, exh. cat. Tate Gallery, London 1983, p. 276 ▪ Christian Geelhaar, *Picasso. Wegbereiter und Förderer seines Aufstiegs 1899-1939*, Zurich 1993, no. 117 ▪ Elizabeth Cowling, *Picasso. Style and Meaning*, London/New York 2002, p. 230f., 235 ▪ Pepe Karmel, *Picasso and the Invention of Cubism*, Yale 2003, p. 186

24

**The Scallop Shell.
"Notre avenir est dans l'air", 1912**

Oil on canvas
38 x 55 cm
Signed on the back: Picasso
Private collection

Cat. Zurich 64
Die Jakobsmuscheln oder "Notre avenir est dans l'air"

Provenance: Galerie Kahnweiler, Paris ▪ 1921 Auction of Kahnweiler Collection, Hôtel Drouot, Paris (13/14 June, lot 77) ▪ Josef Müller, Solothurn ▪ E. and A. Silberman Galleries, New York ▪ 1962 Sotheby's auction, London (7 November, lot 74) ▪ Mr and Mrs Leigh B. Block, Chicago ▪ Eugene V. Thaw & Co., New York ▪ Private collection

Exhibitions (selected): 1932 Paris, Galeries Georges Petit: *Exposition Picasso*, cat. 76 ▪ 1962 New York, Cooperating New York Galleries: *Picasso: An American Tribute*, cat. 7 (Saidenberg Gallery) ▪ 1967 Washington, National Gallery of Art: *100 European Paintings and Drawings from the Collection of Mr and Mrs Leigh B. Block*, cat. 37 ▪ 1971 New York, Saidenberg Gallery, Marlborough Gallery: *Homage to Picasso for his 90th Birthday*, cat. 15 ▪ 1980 New York, The Museum of Modern Art, *Pablo Picasso. A Retrospective*, p. 157 ▪ 1983 London, Tate Gallery: *The essential cubism. Braque, Picasso and their friends, 1907-1920*, cat. 133 ▪ 1989/90 New York, The Museum of Modern Art: *Picasso and Braque: Pioneering Cubism*/Basel, Kunstmuseum, p. 229 (English edition), cat. 235 (German edition)

Selected literature: Zervos: IIa, no. 311 (La coquille Saint-Jacques) ▪ Daix/Rosselet: no. 464 (La coquille Saint-Jacques (Notre avenir est dans l'air)) ▪ Palau i Fabre: vol. 1907-1917, no. 680 (Notre avenir est dans l'aire [sic] or Die Sankt-Jakobs-Muschel) ▪ Richardson: II, p. 226ff. ▪ Maurice Gieure, *Initiation à l'œuvre de Picasso*, Paris 1951, no. 29 ▪ Franco Russoli, Fiorella Minervino, *L'opera completa di Picasso cubista*, Milan 1972 (Classici dell'arte 64), no. 464 ▪ Jean Sutherland Boggs et al. (ed.), *Picasso and Things*, exh. cat., The Cleveland Museum of Art/The Philadelphia Museum of Art/Galeries Nationales du Grand Palais Paris, Cleveland 1992, p. 100f. ▪ Christian Geelhaar, *Picasso. Wegbereiter und Förderer seines Aufstiegs 1899-1939*, Zurich 1993, no. 121 and p. 125 ▪ Brigitte Léal, Christine Pilot, Marie-Laure Bernadac, *The Ultimate Picasso*, New York 2000, no. 353 ▪ Anne Baldassari, *Picasso and Photography: The Dark Mirror*, exh. cat., Museum of Fine Arts Houston, Paris/New York 1997, p. 106 ▪ Elizabeth Cowling, *Picasso. Style and Meaning*, London/New York 2002, p. 231

25

Girl from Arles, 1912

Oil on canvas
73 x 54 cm
Signed on the back: *Picasso*
Private collection, Courtesy Thomas Ammann Fine Art AG Zurich

Cat. Zurich 57
Arlésienne, dated 1910

Provenance: Galerie Kahnweiler, Paris ■ Collection of Alfred
Flechtheim, Berlin ■ Mrs Mendelssohn-Bartholdy, London ■
Buchholz Gallery, New York ■ Walter P. Chrysler Jr., New York
■ Donald Strahlem, New York ■ Private collection Germany ■
Thomas Ammann Fine Art AG Zurich

Exhibitions (selected): 1932 Paris, Galeries Georges Petit:
Exposition Picasso, cat. 73 (L'Arlésienne, dated 1911/12) ■
1939/40 New York, The Museum of Modern Art: *Picasso:
Forty Years of His Art*/Chicago, Art Institute/St. Louis, City Art
Museum/Boston, Museum of Fine Arts, cat. 100 ■ 1941
Richmond, The Virginia Museum of fine Arts: Collection of
Walter P. Chrysler Jr./Philadelphia, Museum of Art, cat. 167

Selected literature: Zervos: II, Nr. 356 (L'Arlésienne) ■
Daix/Rosselet: Nr. 497 ■ Ivan Alexandrovitch Aksenov,
Picasso i okrestnosti, Moscow 1917, p. 39 ■ Carl Einstein,
*Die Kunst des 20. Jahrhunderts, Propyläen Kunstgeschichte
XVI*, Berlin 1926, fig. p. 313 ■ Eugenio d'Ors, *Pablo Picasso*,
Paris/New York 1930, plate 17 ■ Alfred Barr, *Cubism and
Abstract Art*, New York 1936, no. 22 ■ Jean Cassou, *Picasso*,
Paris 1940, p. 76 ■ Alfred H. Barr Jr., *Picasso: Fifty Years of
his Art*, New York 1946, p. 77 ■ José Camon Aznar, *Picasso y
el cubismo*, Madrid 1956, no. 292 ■ Pierre Daix, *Picasso
créateur. La vie intime et l'œuvre*, Paris 1987, p. 124 f. and passim. ■ Pablo Picasso. Portraits d'Arlésiennes 1912/1958, exh.
cat. Fondation Vincent Van Gogh, Arles 2005, pp. 32–35, 54

26
The Poet, 1912

Oil on canvas
60 x 48 cm
Signed on the back: *Picasso*
Kunstmuseum Basel
Gift of Maja Sacher-Stehlin, deposited by the commune of
inhabitants of the canton Basel-Stadt, 1967

Cat. Zurich 65
Herrenbildnis

Provenance: 1913 Moderne Galerie, Heinrich Thannhauser,
Munich ■ Until 1917 Kluxen Collection, Munich ■ 1917
Muche Collection (acquired from the Kluxen Collection) ■
Galerie Kahnweiler, Paris ■ 1931 Galerie Rosengart, previ-
ously Thannhauser, Lucerne ■ 1931–1967 Collection of
Maja Sacher-Stehlin

Exhibitions (selected): 1913 Munich, Moderne Galerie, Heinrich Thannhauser: *Picasso*, cat. 76 ■ 1932 Paris, Galeries
Georges Petit: *Exposition Picasso*, cat. 78 (Portrait d'homme) ■
1950 Knokke-le-Zoute, Casino Communale: *Picasso*, cat. 20 ■
1976 Basel, Kunstmuseum: *Picasso. Aus dem Museum of Modern Art New York und Schweizer Sammlungen*, cat. 23 ■ 1980
New York, Museum of Modern Art: *Pablo Picasso. A Retrospective*, p. 160 ■ 1988 Lucerne, Kunstmuseum: *Von Matisse
bis Picasso. Hommage an Siegfried Rosengart*, cat. 59 ■
1989/90 New York, The Museum of Modern Art: *Picasso and
Braque: Pioneering Cubism*/Basel, Kunstmuseum, p. 236, 404
(English edition), cat. 247 (German edition) ■ 1990 Leningrad,
The State Hermitage Museum: *Pablo Picasso*, cat. 7, pp. 27–30
■ 2001 Bern, Kunstmuseum, *Picasso und die Schweiz.
Meisterwerke aus Schweizer Sammlungen*, cat. 52 ■ 2005
Riehen/Basel, Fondation Beyeler: *Picasso surreal*, not in cat.

Selected literature: Zervos: IIa, no. 313 ■ Daix/Rosselet:
no. 499 ■ Palau i Fabre: vol. 1907–1917, no. 766 ■ Roland
Penrose, *Picasso, His Life and Work*, London 1958, p. 171 ■
Josep Palau i Fabre, *Picasso en Cataluña*, Barcelona 1966,
no. 128 ■ Franco Russoli, Fiorella Minervino, *L'opera completa di Picasso cubista*, Milan 1972 (Classici dell'arte 64),
no. 455 ■ Franz Mosele, *Die kubistische Bildsprache von
Georges Braque, Pablo Picasso und Juan Gris unter besonderer
Berücksichtigung der Entwicklung der Farbe*, Zurich 1973,
no. 180, p. 193, 285 ■ Ivan A. Aksenov: 'Picasso et autour de
Picasso (1917)', in: *Cahiers du Musée national d'art moderne*,
vol. 4, 1980, p. 321 f. ■ Pierre Daix, *Picasso créateur. La vie
intime et l'œuvre*, Paris 1987, p. 128, 133, 412 ■ Carsten-
Peter Warncke, *Picasso 1881–1973*, ed. Ingo F. Walther,
Cologne 1991, vol. I, p. 200 ■ Christian Geelhaar, *Picasso.
Wegbereiter und Förderer seines Aufstiegs 1899–1939*,
Zurich 1993, p. 55, 128, 253 ■ Katharina Schmidt, Hartwig
Fischer (ed.), *Ein Haus für den Kubismus. Die Sammlung Raoul
La Roche: Picasso, Braque, Léger, Gris, Le Corbusier und Ozen-
fant*, exh. cat., Kunstmuseum Basel, 1998, p. 47 f. ■ Elizabeth
Cowling, *Picasso. Style and Meaning*, London/New York 2002,
p. 230 ■ *Picasso cubiste*, exh. cat., Musée National Picasso,
Paris 2007, p. 45 ff.

27
Woman with Mandolin, 1908

Oil on canvas
100 x 80 cm
Signed bottom left: *Picasso*
Kunstsammlung Nordrhein-Westfalen, Düsseldorf

Cat. Zurich 47
Frau mit Mandoline, datiert 1909

Provenance: Pierre Loeb, Paris ■ G. David Thompson, Pittsburgh ■ 1974 Auction Christie's, London (2. April) ■ Kunsthandelsgesellschaft Modarco, Geneva ■ M. Knoedler & Co., Inc., New York ■ 1979 Kunstsammlung Nordrhein-Westfalen, Düsseldorf

Exhibitions (selected): 1932 Paris, Galeries Georges Petit: *Exposition Picasso*, cat. 62 (dated 1909) ■ 1960/61 Zürich, Kunsthaus: *Thompson Pittsburgh. Aus einer amerikanischen Privatsammlung*/Düsseldorf, Kunstmuseum/Den Haag, Gemeentemuseum, cat. 166 ■ 1962 Basel, Galerie Beyeler: *Le Cubisme. Braque, Gris, Léger, Picasso*/Paris, Galerie Knoedler, cat. 2 ■ 2007/08 Riehen/Basel, Fondation Beyeler: *Die andere Sammlung. Hommage an Ernst und Hildy Beyeler*, p. 75

Selected literature: Zervos: II, Nr. 115 ■ Daix/Rosselet: Nr. 271 (dated 1909) ■ Palau i Fabre: Bd. 1907–1917, Nr. 367 (Die Frau mit der Mandoline, dated 1909) ■ Jaime Sabartés, *Picasso*, Paris 1946, Nr. 4 ■ Franco Russoli, Fiorella Minervino, *L'opera completa di Picasso cubista*, Milan 1972 (Classici dell'arte 64), Nr. 204 ■ Domenico Porzio, Marco Valsecchi, *Understanding Picasso*, New York 1974, no. 33 ■ Werner Spies, *Kontinent Picasso. Ausgewählte Aufsätze aus zwei Jahrzehnten*, Munich 1988, fig. 7 ■ Carsten-Peter Warncke, *Pablo Picasso, 1881–1973*, ed. Ingo F. Walther, Cologne 1991, vol. I, p. 182

28
Man with a Clarinet, 1911/12

Oil on canvas
106 x 69 cm
Signed on the back: *Picasso*
Museo Thyssen-Bornemisza, Madrid

Cat. Zurich 68
Mann mit Klarinette, dated 1912

Provenance: Galerie Kahnweiler, Paris ■ 1912 Wilhelm Uhde, Paris ■ 1914 confiscated by the French state ■ 1921 unknown collector (acquired at the auction of the Uhde Collection, Hôtel Drouot, Paris (30 May, lot 25) ■ From 1930 Dr. G. F. Reber, Lausanne ■ 1937 Douglas Cooper, Monte Carlo ■ 1980 Daniel Malingue, Paris ■ 1982 Thyssen-Bornemisza Collection, Lugano ■ 1992 loan to the Museo Thyssen-Bornemisza, Madrid ■ 1993 presented to the Museo Thyssen-Bornemisza, Madrid

Exhibitions (selection): 1932 Paris, Galeries Georges Petit: *Exposition Picasso*, cat. 80 (L'homme à la clarinette, dated 1912) ■ 1959 Marseille, Musée Cantini: *Picasso*, cat. 18 ■ 1970/71 Los Angeles, County Museum of Art: *The Cubist Epoch*/New York, The Metropolitan Museum of Art, cat. 240 ■ 1990 Houston, Museum of Fine Arts: *Picasso, Braque, Gris, Léger. Douglas Cooper Collecting Cubism*, cat. 28 ■ 2000/01 Segovia, Museo de Arte Contemporáneo Esteban Vicente: *Picasso en las colecciones españolas*, cat. 27 ■ 2007/08 Paris, Musée National *Picasso: Picasso cubiste*, p. 243

Selected literature: Zervos: IIa, no. 288 ■ Daix/Rosselet: no. 426, dated 1911 ■ Palau i Fabre: vol. 1907–1917, no. 644 (Der Klarinettenspieler, dated 1912) ■ Richardson: II, p. 104 (Man with Tenora, dated 1911) ■ Maurice Raynal, *Picasso*, Munich 1921, plate 41 ■ André Breton, "Le Surréalisme et la peinture", in: *La Révolution Surréaliste*, Paris, year 1, no. 4, 15 July 1925, p. 28 ■ Pierre Daix, *Picasso créateur. La vie intime et l'œuvre*, Paris 1987, p. 118 f. ■ Dorothy M. Kosinski, 'G. F. Reber: Collector of Cubism', in: *Burlington Magazine*, vol. 133, 1991, p. 527 ■ José Alvarez Lopera, *Maestros modernos del Museo Thyssen-Bornemisza*, Madrid 1992, no. 710, p. 272 f., 611 ■ Robert Rosenblum, 'The Spanishness of Picasso's Still Lifes', in: Jonathan Brown (ed.), *Picasso and the Spanish Tradition*, New Haven/London 1996, p. 61–94, plate 70 ■ Pepe Karmel, *Picasso and the Invention of Cubism*, Yale 2003, p. 141 f. ■ *El espejo y la máscara: el retrato en el siglo de Picasso*, exh. cat., Museo Thyssen-Bornemisza Madrid/Kimbell Art Museum Fort Worth, 2007, p. 144 f. ■ Paloma Alarcó, *Museo Thyssen-Bornemisza. Pintura moderna*, Madrid 2009, p. 23, 25, 204 f.

29
Bottle, Glass and Violin, 1912/13

Collage
47 x 62 cm
Signed on the back: *Picasso*
Moderna Museet, Stockholm

Cat. Zurich 73
Stilleben

Provenance: Tristan Tzara, Paris ■ Until 1967 Mme Claude Sarraut-Tzara, Paris ■ 1967 Moderna Museet, Stockholm

Exhibitions (selected): 1932 Paris, Galeries Georges Petit: *Exposition Picasso*, cat. 83 (Nature morte) ■ 1955/56 Paris, Musée des Arts Décoratifs: *Picasso. Peintures. 1900–1955/*

Munich, Haus der Kunst/Cologne, Rheinisches Museum/Hamburg, Kunsthalle, cat. 35 ■ 1957 Arles, Musée Réattu: *Picasso. Dessins, gouaches, aquarelles*, cat. 31 ■ 1960 London, The Arts Council of Great Britain/Tate Gallery: *Picasso*, cat. 65 ■ 1965 Kiruna: *Picasso i Kiruna*, cat. 4 ■ 1966/67 Paris, Grand Palais: *Hommage à Pablo Picasso*, cat. 86 ■ 1966 Tel Aviv, Tel-Aviv Museum: *Picasso*, cat. 15 ■ 1967 Amsterdam, Stedelijk Museum: *Picasso*, cat. 35 ■ 1968 Vienna, Österreichisches Museum für Angewandte Kunst: *Pablo Picasso* ■ 1968 Humlebæk, Louisiana Museum: *Pablo Picasso*, cat. 28 ■ 1983 London, Tate Gallery: *The essential cubism. Braque, Picasso and their friends, 1907-1920*, cat. 138 ■ 1988/89 Stockholm, Moderna Museet: *Pablo Picasso*, cat. 168 ■ 1989/90 New York, The Museum of Modern Art: *Picasso and Braque. Pioneering Cubism*/Basel, Kunstmuseum, p. 262 (English edition), cat. 305 (German edition) ■ 1993 Copenhagen, Statens Museum for Kunst: *Picasso & Braque. Kubisme 1907-1914*, cat. 38 ■ 1997 New York, The Museum of Modern Art: *Objects of Desire. The Modern Still Life*, cat. 23 ■ 2007 New York, PaceWildenstein: *Picasso, Braque and early film in cubism*, p. 111

Selected literature: Zervos: IIb, no. 405 (Bouteille, verre, violon) ■ Daix/Rosselet: no. 528 (Siphon, verre journal, violon, dated 1912) ■ Palau i Fabre: vol. 1907-1917, no. 851 (Siphon, Zeitung, Glas und Geige, 1912) ■ Louis Aragon, *La peinture au défi*, Paris 1930, plate II ■ Wilhelm Boeck, *Pablo Picasso*, Stuttgart/Paris 1955, no. 65 ■ Frank Elgar, Robert Maillard, *Picasso*, Paris 1955, fig. p. 65 ■ Roland Penrose, *Picasso. His Life and Work*, London 1958, plate VII/7 ■ Robert Rosenblum, *Cubism and Twentieth-Century Art*, New York 1960, no. 38 ■ Hans Ludwig C. Jaffé, *Pablo Picasso*, New York 1964, p. 94 f. ■ Franco Russoli, Fiorella Minervino, *L'opera completa di Picasso cubista*, Milan 1972 (Classici dell' arte 64), no. 567 ■ William Rubin (ed.), *Picasso and Braque. Pioneering Cubism*, exh. cat., The Museum of Modern Art, New York 1989/Basel, Kunstmuseum, p. 262 (English edition), cat. 305 (German edition) ■ Pepe Karmel, *Picasso and the Invention of Cubism*, Yale 2003, no. 132 ■ *Picasso cubiste*, exh. cat., Musée National Picasso, Paris 2007, pp. 165-175

30
Student with a Pipe, 1914
Plaster, sand, pasted paper, oil and charcoal on canvas
73 x 58.7 cm
Unsigned
The Museum of Modern Art, New York
Nelson A. Rockefeller Bequest, 1979

Provenance: 1914-1946 Gertrude Stein, Paris ■ 1946-1967 Estate of Gertrude Stein (Alice B. Toklas) ■ 1968 The Museum of Modern Art syndicate, New York ■ 1968-1979 Nelson A. Rockefeller, New York

Exhibitions (selected): 1932 Paris, Galeries Georges Petit: *Exposition Picasso*, cat. 86 (L'Étudiant, dated 1913) ■ 1954 Paris, Maison de la Pensée Française: *Picasso. Deux périodes: 1900-1914 & 1950-1954* ■ 1955/56 Paris, Musée des Arts Décoratifs: *Picasso. Peintures. 1900-1955*/Munich, Haus der Kunst/Cologne, Rheinisches Museum/Hamburg, Kunsthalle, cat. 42 ■ 1960 London, The Arts Council of Great Britain/Tate Gallery: *Picasso*, cat. 73 ■ 1970/71 New York, Museum of Modern Art: *Four Americans in Paris: The Collections of Gertrude Stein and Her Family*/Baltimore, Museum of Art/Ottawa, National Gallery of Canada/San Francisco, Museum of Art ■ 1980 New York The Museum of Modern Art: *Pablo Picasso. A Retrospective*, p. 174 ■ 1989/90 New York, The Museum of Modern Art: *Picasso and Braque: Pioneering Cubism*/Basel, Kunstmuseum, p. 302 (English edition), cat. 370 (German edition) ■ 2008 Bergen, Kunstmuseum: *Picasso. Figure and Image*

Selected literature: Zervos: IIb, no. 444, dated 1913 ■ Daix/Rosselet: no. 620 ■ Palau i Fabre: vol. 1907-1917, no. 1017 (Der Student mit der Pfeife, dated 1913/14) ■ Richardson: II, p. 291 ■ Henri Mahaut, *Picasso*, Paris 1930, fig. 21 ■ Carl Einstein, *Die Kunst des 20. Jahrhunderts, Propyläen Kunstgeschichte XVI*, Berlin 1926, fig. p. 275, 3rd edition 1931, fig. p. 315 ■ Tristan Tzara, 'Le papier collé ou le proverbe en peinture', in: *Cahiers d'art*, year 6, 1931, no. 6, p. 66 ■ Guillaume Apollinaire, 'Picasso et les papiers collés', in: *Cahiers d'art*, year 7, 1932, p. 119 ■ Jean Cassou, *Picasso*, Paris 1940, p. 87 ■ Alfred H. Barr Jr., *Picasso: Fifty Years of His Art*, New York 1946, p. 85 ■ Maurice Gieure, *Initiation à l'œuvre de Picasso*, Paris 1951, no. 33 ■ Frank Elgar, Robert Maillard, *Picasso*, Paris 1955, fig. p. 73 ■ Wilhelm Boeck, *Pablo Picasso*, Stuttgart/Paris 1955, p. 379 ■ John Golding, *Cubism: a history and an analysis, 1907-1914*, London 1959, plate 19b ■ Franco Russoli, Fiorella Minervino, *L'opera completa di Picasso cubista*, Milan 1972 (Classici dell'arte 64), no. 646 ■ William Rubin, *Picasso in the Collection of The Museum of Modern Art*, New York 1972, p. 88 f., 212 ■ Pierre Daix, *Picasso créateur. La vie intime et l'œuvre*, Paris 1987, p. 143 f., 150, 413 ■ Brigitte Léal, Christine Pilot, Marie-Laure Bernadac, *The Ultimate Picasso*, New York

2000, no. 362 ■ Pepe Karmel, *Picasso and the Invention of Cubism*, Yale 2003, no. 279 ■ *Picasso cubiste*, exh. cat., Musée National Picasso, Paris 2007, p. 45

31
The Guéridon, 1913/14

Oil on canvas
130 x 89 cm
Signed and dated on the back: *Picasso Céret/1914*
Kunstmuseum Basel
Donated by Dr. h.c. Raoul La Roche, 1952

Provenance: Galerie Kahnweiler, Paris ■ 1921 Amédée Ozenfant (acquired at the auction at Hôtel Drouot, Paris, 17/18 November) ■ Raoul La Roche, Paris

Exhibitions (selected): 1955/56 Munich, Haus der Kunst: *Picasso 1900–1955* /Cologne, Rheinisches Museum/Hamburg, Kunsthalle, cat. 38 ■ 1963 Basel, Kunstmuseum: *Die Schenkungen Raoul La Roche*, p. 12 ■ 1976 Basel, Kunstmuseum: *Picasso. Aus dem Museum of Modern Art New York und Schweizer Sammlungen*, cat. 33 ■ 1989/90 New York, The Museum of Modern Art: *Picasso and Braque: Pioneering Cubism*/Basel, Kunstmuseum, p. 329 (English edition), cat. 416 (German edition) ■ 1990 Leningrad, State Hermitage Museum: *Pablo Picasso*, cat. 11 and p. 35f., 79 ■ 1998 Basel, Kunstmuseum: *Ein Haus für den Kubismus. Die Sammlung Raoul La Roche: Picasso, Braque, Léger, Gris, Le Corbusier und Ozenfant*, cat. 95 and p. 30, 39, 54f., 303 ■ 2007/08 Paris, Musée National Picasso, *Picasso cubiste*, p. 283

Selected literature: Zervos: XXIX, no. 48, dated 1914 ■ Daix/Rosselet: no. 764 ■ Palau i Fabre: vol. 1907–1917, no. 1237 (Das Beistelltischchen) ■ Frank Elgar, Robert Maillard, *Picasso*, Paris 1955, p. 84, fig. p. 87 ■ Franco Russoli, Fiorella Minervino, *L'opera completa di Picasso cubista*, Milan 1972 (Classici dell'arte 64), no. 716 ■ Franz Mosele, *Die kubistische Bildsprache von Georges Braque, Pablo Picasso und Juan Gris unter besonderer Berücksichtigung der Entwicklung der Farbe*, Zurich 1973, no. 231, p. 243, 289 ■ Christian Geelhaar, *Picasso. Wegbereiter und Förderer seines Aufstiegs 1899–1939*, Zurich 1993, p. 123

32
Pipe and Wineglass, 1914

Pasted paper and pencil on white ribbed paper
17.9 x 24 cm
Signed bottom right: *Picasso*
Thaw Collection, The Pierpont Morgan Library, New York

Provenance: Galerie Kahnweiler, Paris ■ 1921 Auction at Hôtel Drouot, Paris (17/18 November, lot 165) ■ Galerie Georges Petit, Paris (?) ■ Marcel C. Coard, Paris ■ Martin M. Janis, Buffalo, New York ■ Sidney Janis Gallery, New York ■ Heinz Berggruen, Paris ■ Eugene V. and Clare E. Thaw, New York

Exhibitions (selected): 1932 Paris, Galeries Georges Petit: *Exposition Picasso*, cat. 90 (Nature morte à la pipe) ■ 1986 New York, Pierpont Morgan Library: *Drawings from the Collection of Mr & Mrs Eugene Victor Thaw*/Virginia, Museum of Fine Arts, cat. 62 ■ 1989/90 New York, The Museum of Modern Art: *Picasso and Braque: Pioneering Cubism*/Basel, Kunstmuseum, p. 310 (English edition), cat. 381 (German edition)

Selected literature: Zervos: IIb, no. 455 ■ Daix/Rosselet: no. 665

33
Bottle of Bass, Ace of Clubs and Pipe, 1914
Collage (oil, gouache, pencil)
51.5 x 31 cm
Signed at bottom centre: *Picasso*
Private ownership

Provenance: Galerie Kahnweiler, Paris (?) ■ Alfred Flechtheim, Berlin (?) ■ Private ownership ■ 1978–2005 loan in Bayerische Staatsgemäldesammlungen, Munich

Exhibitions (selected): 2004/05 Ferrara, Palazzo dei diamanti: *Il cubismo — rivoluzione e tradizione*, cat. 50

Selected literature: Zervos: IIb, no. 500 (Bouteille de Bass, carte à jouer, pipe) ■ Daix/Rosselet: no. 685 ■ Palau i Fabre: vol. 1907–1917, no. 1070 (Bass-Flasche, Kreuz-Ass, Pfeife) ■ Franco Russoli, Fiorella Minervino, *L'opera completa di*

Picasso cubista, Milan 1972 (Classici dell'arte 64), no. 752 ■
Jean Sutherland Boggs et al. (ed.), *Picasso and Things*, exh.
cat., The Cleveland Museum of Art/The Philadelphia Museum of
Art/Galeries Nationales du Grand Palais Paris, Cleveland 1992,
p. 160, fig. 57a

34
Woman with Guitar, 1911/14

Oil on canvas
130.5 x 90 cm
Signed on the back: *Picasso*
Kunstmuseum Basel
Donated by Dr. h.c. Raoul La Roche, 1952

Cat. Zurich 85
Mann mit Gitarre, dated 1914

Provenance: Galerie Kahnweiler, Paris ■ 1923 Kahnweiler
auction, Hôtel Drouot, Paris (7/8 May, lot 364) ■ Raoul La
Roche, Paris

Exhibitions (selected): 1963 Basel, Kunstmuseum: *Die
Schenkungen Raoul La Roche*, cat. 85 ■ 1976 Basel, Kunst-
museum: *Picasso. Aus dem Museum of Modern Art New York
und Schweizer Sammlungen*, cat. 32 ■ 1989/90 New York,
The Museum of Modern Art: *Picasso and Braque. Pioneering
Cubism*/Basel, Kunstmuseum, p. 307 (English edition), cat. 377
(German edition) ■ 1990 Leningrad, State Hermitage
Museum: *Pablo Picasso*, cat. 10 and p. 33f. ■ 1998 Basel,
Kunstmuseum: *Ein Haus für den Kubismus. Die Sammlung
Raoul La Roche: Picasso, Braque, Léger, Gris, Le Corbusier und
Ozenfant*, no. 94 and p. 51ff., 303 ■ 2007/08 Paris, Musée
National Picasso: *Picasso cubiste*, p. 277

Selected literature: Zervos: IIb, no. 447 (Homme à la guitare,
dated 1914) ■ Daix/Rosselet: no. 647 ■ Palau i Fabre: vol.
1907-1917, no. 1043 (Die Frau mit der Gitarre) ■ Franz
Mosele, *Die kubistische Bildsprache von Georges Braque,
Pablo Picasso und Juan Gris unter besonderer Berücksichtigung der Entwicklung der Farbe*, Zurich 1973, no. P. 235,
p. 246, 289 ■ Christian Geelhaar, *Picasso. Wegbereiter und
Förderer seines Aufstiegs 1899-1939*, Zurich 1993, p. 123,
149

35
Guitar on a Guéridon, 1915

Oil on canvas
133 x 104 cm
Unsigned
Kunsthaus Zürich

Cat. Zurich 91
Das Lesepult

Provenance: 1915-1932 Collection of Pablo Picasso ■
1932 acquired from the artist

Exhibitions (selected): 1932 Paris, Galeries Georges Petit:
Exposition Picasso, cat. 100 (Le guéridon) ■ 1967 Amsterdam, Stedelijk Museum: *Picasso*, cat. 43

Selected literature: Zervos: IIb, no. 811 ■ Daix/Rosselet:
no. 811 ■ Palau i Fabre: vol. 1907-1917, no. 1270 (Gitarre
auf einem Beistelltisch) ■ Franco Russoli, Fiorelle Minervino,
L'opera completa di Picasso cubista, Milan 1972 (Classici
dell'arte 64), no. 823 ■ *Picasso und die Schweiz. Meisterwerke aus Schweizer Sammlungen*, exh. cat., Kunstmuseum
Bern, ed. Marc Fehlmann and Toni Stooss, Bern 2001, no. 60
■ Kunsthaus Zürich. *Gesamtkatalog der Gemälde und Skulpturen*, Zurich 2007, p. 622 ■ Kunsthaus Zürich. *Die Meisterwerke*, Zurich 2007, p. 221ff.

36
The Italian Woman, 1917

Oil on canvas
149.5 x 101.5 cm
Signed and dated top left: Picasso/Rome 1917
Foundation E. G. Bührle Collection, Zurich

Cat. Zurich 95
Die Italienierin

Provenance: 1917/18 until at least 1934 Mme George
Wildenstein, Paris ■ 1954 Gustave Kahnweiler, Cambridge ■
1954 Emil G. Bührle, Zurich (November) ■ Heirs of Emil
G. Bührle ■ 1960 Foundation E. G. Bührle Collection, Zurich

Exhibitions (selected): 1934 Hartford, Wadsworth Atheneum:
Pablo Picasso ■ 1958 Zurich, Kunsthaus: *Sammlung Emil
G. Bührle*, cat. 306 ■ 1960 London, The Arts Council of Great
Britain/Tate Gallery: *Picasso*, cat. 85 ■ 1966/67 Paris, Grand
Palais: *Hommage à Pablo Picasso*, cat. 102 ■ 1968 Vienna,
Österreichisches Museum für angewandte Kunst: *Pablo

Picasso, cat. 30 ■ 1990/91 Washington, National Gallery of Art: *Master Paintings from the Collection of Emil G. Bührle*, Zurich/Montreal, Museum of Fine Arts/Yokohama, Museum of Art/London, Royal Academy of Arts, cat. 82 ■ 1998 Venice, Palazzo Grassi: *Picasso, 1917–1924. Le voyage d'Italie*, cat. 47 ■ 2001 Bern, Kunstmuseum: *Picasso und die Schweiz. Meisterwerke aus Schweizer Sammlungen*, cat. 65 ■ 2005 Riehen/Basel, Fondation Beyeler: *Picasso surreal*, cat. 3 ■ 2008/09 Rome, Complesso del Vittoriano: *Picasso Harlequin 1917–1937*, cat. 1 ■ 2010 Zurich, Kunsthaus: *Van Gogh, Cézanne, Monet. Die Sammlung Bührle zu Gast im Kunsthaus Zürich* (no cat.)

Selected literature: Zervos: III, no. 18 (Italienne) ■ Palau i Fabre: vol. 1917–1926, no. 83 ■ Richardson: III, p. 12 f. ■ *Cahiers d'art*, year 7, 1932, p. 127 ■ Wilhelm Boeck, *Pablo Picasso*, Stuttgart/Paris 1955, p. 171–174 ■ R. H. Wilenski, R. Penrose, *Picasso, die frühen Jahre*, Berlin 1961, p. 14 ■ Franco Russoli, Fiorella Minervino, *L'opera completa di Picasso cubista*, Milan 1972 (Classici dell'arte 64), no. 896 ■ Pierre Daix, *Picasso créateur. La vie intime et l'œuvre*, Paris 1987, p. 163, 416 ■ Michael C. FitzGerald, *Making Modernism. Picasso and the Creation of the Market for Twentieth-Century Art*, Berkeley et al. 1996, p. 115, 225 ■ Gottfried Boehm, 'Pablo Picasso: Die römischen Bilder', in: *Canto d'Amore. Klassizistische Moderne in Musik und bildender Kunst 1914–1935*, exh. cat., Kunstmuseum Basel, 1996, pp. 134–138 ■ *Le miroir noir. Picasso, sources photographiques 1900–1928*, exh. cat., Musée Picasso Paris/Museum of Fine Arts Houston, 1997, cat. 224, p. 223 ff. ■ Elizabeth Cowling, *Picasso. Style and Meaning*, London/New York 2002, pp. 308–311 ■ Brigitte Léal, Christine Pilot, Marie-Laure Bernadac, *The Ultimate Picasso*, New York 2000, no. 424 ■ Valentina Moncada, *Picasso in Rome*, Milan 2007, p. 7, pp. 13 ff., fig. p. 42 ■ *Picasso: Challenging the Past*, exh. cat., National Gallery, London 2009, p. 61

37
Young Girl with Hoop, 1919

Oil and sand on canvas
142.5 x 79 cm
Signed and dated top right: *Picasso/19*
Centre Pompidou, Paris
Musée national d'art moderne/Centre de création industrielle
Bequest of Baronne Eva Gourgaud, 1965

Cat. Zurich 102
Kind mit Reif

Provenance: 1919–1920 Paul Rosenberg, Paris ■ 1920–1924 John Quinn, New York ■ 1924–1926 Quinn Estate ■ 1926 Paul Rosenberg & Cie., Paris ■ 1926–1944 Baron Napoléon Gourgaud, Paris ■ 1944–1959 Baronne Eva Gourgaud, Yerre ■ 1959–1965 Gourgaud Estate

Exhibitions (selected): 1932 Paris, Galeries Georges Petit: *Exposition Picasso*, cat. 111 (La fillette au cerceau) ■ 1983 London, Tate Gallery: *The essential cubism. Braque, Picasso and their friends, 1907–1920*, cat. 152 ■ 1991 Madrid, Museo Nacional Centro de Arte Reina Sofía: *André Breton y el surrealismo* ■ 1990/91 Leningrad, State Hermitage Museum: *Pablo Picasso. 25 chefs-d'œuvre des musées de New York, Bâle et Paris/Moscow*, The Pushkin State Museum of Fine Arts ■ 1995/96 Düsseldorf, Kunstsammlung Nordrhein-Westfalen: *Picassos Welt der Kinder*/Stuttgart, Staatsgalerie, cat. 53 ■ 1999 Villeneuve-d'Ascq, Musée d'art moderne Lille Métropole: *Les années cubistes: Collections du Centre Georges Pompidou, Musée national d'art moderne et du Musée d'art moderne de Lille Métropole*, p. 123 ■ 2000 Tokyo, National Museum of Western Art: *Picasso's World of Children*, cat. 48 ■ 2007/08 Paris, Musée National Picasso: *Picasso cubiste*

Selected literature: Zervos: III, no. 289 ■ Palau i Fabre: vol. 1917–1926, no. 349 ■ Richardson: III, p. 106 ■ Jean Leymarie, *Picasso: Métamorphoses et unité*, Geneva 1971, p. 45 ■ Franco Russoli, Fiorella Minervino, *L'opera completa di Picasso cubista*, Milan 1972 (Classici dell'arte 64), no. 922 ■ Carsten-Peter Warncke, *Picasso 1881–1973*, ed. Ingo F. Walther, Cologne 1991, vol. I, p. 272 ■ Ulrich Weisner (ed.), *Picassos Surrealismus. Werke 1925–1937*, exh. cat., Kunsthalle Bielefeld, 1991, p. 198 ■ Brigitte Léal, Christine Pilot, Marie-Laure Bernadac, *The Ultimate Picasso*, New York 2000, no. 452

38
The Guitar, 1920

Oil on canvas
65.5 x 92.5 cm
Signed and dated bottom right: *Picasso/20*
Emanuel Hoffmann-Stiftung
Deposited in the Öffentliche Kunstsammlung Basel

Cat. Zurich 104
Die Gitarre

Provenance: 1944 Emanuel Hoffmann-Stiftung ■ Galerie Rosengart, Lucerne ■ Dr. G. F. Reber, Lausanne ■ Paul Rosenberg, Paris ■ Léonce Rosenberg, Paris

Exhibitions (selected): 1921 Galerie Paul Rosenberg, Paris ■ 1922 Moderne Galerie Thannhauser, Munich ■ 1932 Paris, Galeries Georges Petit: *Exposition Picasso*, cat. 114 ■ 1943 Buenos Aires, Galeria Muller: *Exposition Picasso* ■ 1953 Basel, Kunstmuseum: *Schenkungen, Stiftungen und eigene Ankäufe Moderner Kunst im Kunstmuseum Basel 1928/1953. Zwanzig Jahre Emanuel Hoffmann-Stiftung 1933–1953* ■ 1955/56 Munich: Haus der Kunst: *Picasso*/Cologne, Rheinisches Museum/Hamburg, Kunstverein, p. 44 ■ 1970/71 Basel, Kunstmuseum: *Die Sammlung der Emanuel Hoffmann-Stiftung*, p. 23, no. 4 ■ 1976 Basel, Kunstmuseum: *Picasso. Aus dem Museum of Modern Art New York und Schweizer Sammlungen*, cat. 41 ■ 1980 Basel, Museum für Gegenwartskunst: *Die Sammlung der Emanuel Hoffmann-Stiftung, opening exhibition of the Museum für Gegenwartskunst* ■ 1990 Leningrad, State Hermitage Museum: *Pablo Picasso*

Selected literature: Zervos: IV, no. 190 (Guitare) ■ Palau i Fabre: vol. 1917–1926, no. 941 (Gitarre und Tisch) ■ Maurice Raynal, 'Exposition Picasso', in: *L'Esprit nouveau*, no. 9, 1921, fig. p. 56 ■ Carl Einstein, *Die Kunst des 20. Jahrhunderts, Propyläen Kunstgeschichte XVI*, Berlin 1926, fig. p. 286, 3rd edition 1931, fig. p. 322 ■ Frank Elgar, Robert Maillard, *Picasso*, Paris 1955, p. 103 ■ Pierre Daix, *La vie de peintre de Pablo Picasso*, Paris 1977, p. 179 ■ Erika Billeter, *Leben mit Zeitgenossen. Die Sammlung der Emanuel Hoffmann-Stiftung*, Basel 1980, p. 97 f., 339, fig. p. 181 ■ Christian Geelhaar, *Picasso: Wegbereiter und Förderer seines Aufstiegs 1899–1939*, Zurich 1993, no. 106 and p. 113 ■ *Picasso und die Schweiz. Meisterwerke aus Schweizer Sammlungen*, exh. cat., Kunstmuseum Bern, ed. Marc Fehlmann and Toni Stooss, Bern 2001, no. 68 and p. 30, 51 f.

39
Violin and Journal on a Green Carpet, 1921

Oil on canvas
73.3 x 92.1 cm
Signed and dated bottom right: *Picasso 21*
Courtesy Nahmad Collection, Switzerland

Cat. Zurich 172
Stilleben mit Zeitung

Provenance: Mrs Charles Suydham Cutting ■ Justin K. Thannhauser, New York ■ Joseph H. Hazen

Exhibitions (selected): 1955 New York, Paul Rosenberg & Co.: *Loan Exhibition of Paintings by Picasso*, cat. 3 ■ 1962 New York, Cooperating New York Galleries: *Picasso: An American Tribute*, cat. 26 (Paul Rosenberg & Co.) ■ 1975 New York, Acquavella Galleries: *Picasso* ■ 1998 London, Helly Nahmad Gallery: *Picasso: Artist of the Century*, cat. 11 ■ 1999 Rotterdam, Kunsthal: *Picasso: Artist of the Century*, cat. 15 ■ 2001 London, Helly Nahmad Gallery: *Braque, Gris, Léger and Picasso: Cubism and Beyond*, cat. 39 ■ 2009 London, National Gallery: *Picasso. Challenging the Past*, cat. 18

Selected literature: Zervos: IV, no. 430 (Violon et journal sur un tapis vert) ■ Palau i Fabre: vol. 1917–1926, no. 1267 (Partitur, Gitarre und Zeitung)

40
Seated Woman (Woman with Chemise), 1921

Oil on canvas
116 x 73 cm
Signed and dated bottom right: *Picasso/21*
Staatsgalerie Stuttgart

Cat. Zurich 108
Sitzende Frau von vorn

Provenance: Collection of Ingeborg Eichmann, Zurich ■ Ragnar Moltzau Collection, Oslo ■ 1959 acquired by Staatsgalerie Stuttgart

Exhibitions (selected): 1981 Stuttgart, Staatsgalerie: *Pablo Picasso in der Staatsgalerie Stuttgart. Ausstellung zum 100. Geburtstag des Künstlers mit Leihgaben aus Sammlungen in Baden-Württemberg*, cat. 18 ■ 1998 Venice, Palazzo Grassi: *Picasso, 1917–1924. Le voyage d'Italie*, cat. 207 ■ 1996/97 Humlebæk, Louisiana Museum of Modern Art: *Picasso and the Mediterranean*, cat. 6 ■ 1999/2000 Stuttgart, Staatsgalerie: *Picasso und die Moderne. Meisterwerke der Staatsgalerie Stuttgart und der Sammlung Steegmann*, cat. 125

Selected literature: Zervos: IV, no. 328 (Buste de femme) ■ Palau i Fabre: vol. 1917–1926, no. 1110 (Sitzende Matrone) ■ Vauvrecy, 'Picasso et la peinture d'aujourd'hui', in: *L'Esprit nouveau*, no. 13, 1922, p. 1503 ■ Wilhelm Hausenstein, 'Gespräch über Picasso', in: *Ganymed*, 1922, vol. 4, pp. 288–292 ■ Jean Cassou, Picasso, Paris 1940, p. 108 ■ *Léger*

and Purist Paris, exh. cat., The Tate Gallery, London 1970/71,
p. 65 ■ Staatsgalerie Stuttgart. *Malerei und Plastik des
20. Jahrhunderts*, ed. Karin von Maur and Gudrun Inboden,
Stuttgart 1982, p. 259 ■ Carsten-Peter Warncke, *Picasso
1881–1973*, ed. Ingo F. Walther, Cologne 1991, vol. I, p. 278
■ Christian Geelhaar, *Picasso. Wegbereiter und Förderer
seines Aufstiegs 1899–1939*, Zurich 1993, no. 105 ■
Brigitte Léal, Christine Pilot, Marie-Laure Bernadac, *The Ultimate Picasso*, New York 2000, no. 496

41

Woman with a White Hat, 1921

Oil on canvas
118 x 91 cm
Signed bottom right: Picasso
Musée de l'Orangerie, Paris
Collection Jean Walter et Paul Guillaume

Cat. Zurich 111
Frau mit Hut

Provenance: 1929 Paul Guillaume ■ Mme Vve Jean Walter
■ Musée de l'Orangerie, Paris (acquired 1957)

Exhibitions (selected): 1929 Paris, Galerie Bernheim-Jeune:
La grande peinture à la collection Paul Guillaume ■ 1932
Paris, Galeries Georges Petit: *Exposition Picasso*, cat. 118
(Femme au chapeau) ■ 1946 Paris, Galerie Charpentier: *Cent
chefs-d'œuvre des peintres de l'école de Paris*, cat. 67

Selected literature: Zervos: IV, no. 352 (Femme accoudée au
chapeau) ■ Palau i Fabre: vol. 1917–1926, no. 1134
(Sitzende Frau mit Hut)

42

Woman in a Green Dressing Gown, 1922

Oil on canvas
130.3 x 96.5 cm
Signed bottom right: *Picasso/22*
Museum Ludwig Köln

Cat. Zurich 119
Die Grüne Bluse

Provenance: Galerie Alfred Flechtheim, Berlin ■ 1930–1958
Private collection, Wiesbaden ■ 1958–1976 Cologne, Wallraf-Richartz-Museum & Fondation Corboud ■ 1976 transferred to Museum Ludwig Köln

Exhibitions (selected): 1930 Berlin, Galerie Alfred Flechtheim: Matisse, Braque, *Picasso. 60 works in German ownership*, cat. 47 ■ 1932 Paris, Galeries Georges Petit: *Exposition Picasso*, cat. 124 (La blouse verte) ■ 1958/59 Cologne,
Wallraf-Richartz-Museum: *Die Sammlung Wilhelm Strecker im
Wallraf-Richartz-Museum*, cat. 1 ■ 2002/03 Chemnitz,
Kunstsammlungen: *Picasso et les femmes*, p. 157

Selected literature: Zervos: IV, no. 388 (Femme au peignoir
vert) ■ Palau i Fabre: vol. 1917–1926, no. 1222 (Frau mit
grünem Peignoir) ■ *Cahiers d'art*, vol. 7, 1932, p. 143 ■
Maurice Gieure, *Initiation à l'œuvre de Picasso*, Paris 1951,
no. 45 ■ Museum Ludwig Köln, *Gemälde, Skulpturen, Environ-
ments vom Expressionismus bis zur Gegenwart*, Cologne
1986, no. 48 ■ Museum Ludwig Köln, *Kunst des 20. Jahrhunderts*, Cologne 1996, p. 565, 573

43

Woman with Blue Veil, 1923

Oil on canvas
100.3 x 81.2 cm
Signed and dated top right: *Picasso/23*
Los Angeles County Museum of Art
Mr and Mrs George Gard de Sylva Collection (M.46.8.1)

Cat. Zurich 125
Der blaue Schleier

Provenance: Dr. G. F. Reber, Lausanne ■ Mrs Averill W. Harri-
man ■ J. K. Thannhauser ■ 1946 Los Angeles County
Museum of Art (acquired with the support of Mr and Mrs
George Gard de Sylva)

Exhibitions (selected): 1923 New York, Wildenstein Galleries
■ 1932 Paris, Galeries Georges Petit: *Exposition Picasso*,
cat. 131 (Le voile bleu) ■ 1962 New York, Cooperating New
York Galleries: *Picasso: An American Tribute*, cat. 28 (Duveen
Brothers) ■ 2008/09 Paris, Galeries Nationales du Grand
Palais/Musée du Louvre/Musée d'Orsay: *Picasso et les
maîtres*/London, National Gallery, p. 151

Selected literature: Zervos: V, no. 16 (Femme au voile bleu)
■ Palau i Fabre: vol. 1917–1926, no. 1327 (Die Frau mit dem
blauen Haarschleier) ■ Maurice Gieure, *Initiation à l'œuvre de
Picasso*, Paris 1951, no. 50 ■ Carsten-Peter Warncke,
Picasso 1881–1973, ed. Ingo F. Walther, Cologne 1991, vol. I,
p. 291 ■ William Reinhold Valentiner, *The Mr and Mrs George
Gard de Sylva Collection of French Impressionist and Modern
Paintings and Sculpture*, Los Angeles 1950, cat. 12 and p. 11,

34 f. ■ Brigitte Léal, Christine Pilot, Marie-Laure Bernadac, *The Ultimate Picasso*, New York 2000, no. 523

44

Portrait of Paulo in a White Cap, 1923

Oil on canvas
27 x 22 cm
Dated on the back: *Paris – 14. avril 1923*
Private collection
Courtesy of Fundación Almine y Bernard Ruiz-Picasso para el Arte

Provenance: c. 1953/54–1975 Paul Ruiz-Picasso (gift from the artist to his son) ■ 1975 Christine Pauplin de Ruiz-Picasso

Exhibitions (selected): 1955/56 Paris, Musée des Arts Décoratifs: *Picasso. Peintures. 1900–1955*/Munich, Haus der Kunst/Cologne, Rheinisches Museum/Hamburg, Kunsthalle, cat. 59 ■ 1994/95 Málaga, Palacio Episcopal: *Picasso. Primera mirada*/Sevilla, Pabellón Mudéjar/Nîmes, Carré d'Art, Musée d'Art Contemporain, cat. 7 and p. 29, 312 f. ■ 1995/96 Düsseldorf, Kunstsammlung Nordrhein-Westfalen: *Picassos Welt der Kinder*/Stuttgart, Staatsgalerie, cat. 74 ■ 1996/97 New York, The Museum of Modern Art: *Picasso and Portraiture. Representation and Transformation*/Paris, Grand Palais, p. 322

Selected literature: Zervos: V, no. 180 (Le fils de l'artiste) ■ Palau i Fabre: vol. 1917–1926, no. 1308bis (Paulo mit rundem Hut) ■ *Cahiers d'art*, year 7, 1932, p. 151 f. ■ Frank Elgar, Robert Maillard, *Picasso*, Paris 1955, fig. p. 139 ■ Helen Kay, *Picasso's World of Children*, New York 1964, p. 96, 106 ■ Danièle Giraudy, *Picasso. La mémoire du regard*, Paris 1986, p. 86 ■ Carsten-Peter Warncke, *Picasso 1881–1973*, ed. Ingo F. Walther, Cologne 1991, vol. I, p. 286 ■ Carmen Giménez et al., *Colección Museo Picasso*, Málaga 2003, vol. I, no. 11 and p. 32, 91 f., 96

45

Guitar and Fruit Bowl, 1924

Oil on canvas
77 x 106 cm
Signed and dated bottom right: *Picasso/24*
Courtesy Nahmad Collection, Switzerland

Provenance: Collection of the artist ■ Paul Rosenberg, Paris (?) ■ before 1927–1946 Gottlieb Friedrich & Erna Reber-Sander, Wuppertal, Lugano and Lausanne ■ 1946 Galerie H. U. Gasser, Zurich ■ 1946 Collection of Fritz Gygi, Berne ■ Private collection, Switzerland

Exhibitions (selected): 1932 Paris, Galeries Georges Petit: *Exposition Picasso*, cat. 144 (Composition en marron et blanc) ■ 1948 Bern, Kunsthalle: *Braque — Gris — Picasso*, cat. 135 ■ 1955/56 Paris, Musée des Arts Décoratifs: *Picasso. Peintures. 1900–1955*/Munich, Haus der Kunst/Cologne, Rheinisches Museum/Hamburg, Kunsthalle, cat. 55 ■ 1964 Lausanne, Palais de Beaulieu: *Chefs-d'œuvre des collections suisses de Manet à Picasso*, cat. 243 ■ 1976 Basel, Kunstmuseum: *Picasso. Aus dem Museum of Modern Art New York und Schweizer Sammlungen*, cat. 49 ■ 1992 Cleveland, Museum of Art: *Picasso and Things*/Philadelphia, Museum of Art/Paris, Galeries Nationales du Grand Palais, cat. 81, p. 208 f. ■ 2001 Bern, Kunstmuseum: *Picasso und die Schweiz. Meisterwerke aus Schweizer Sammlungen*, cat. 87

Selected literature: Zervos: V, no. 378 (Guitare) ■ Palau i Fabre: vol. 1917–1926, no. 1550 (Obstschale und Gitarre in Beige und Braun) ■ Documents, no. 3, 1930, p. 158 ■ Carl Einstein, *Die Kunst des 20. Jahrhunderts, Propyläen Kunstgeschichte XVI*, Berlin, 3rd edition, 1931, fig. p. 328 ■ Christian Geelhaar, *Picasso, Wegbereiter und Förderer seines Aufstiegs, 1899–1939*, Zurich 1993, p. 160, 163, 192

46

Score, Guitar and Fruit Bowl, 1924

Oil on canvas
97.1 x 130.1 cm
Signed and dated middle left: *Picasso/24*
Courtesy Nahmad Collection, Switzerland

Provenance: Dr. G. F. Reber, Lausanne ■ Otto Gerson, New York ■ Heinz Berggruen, Paris ■ Acquavella Galleries, New York ■ 1988 Auction at Sotheby's, London (29 November, lot 75)

Exhibitions (selected): 1932 Paris, Galeries Georges Petit: *Exposition Picasso*, cat. 149 (Nature morte à la corbeille de

fruits) ■ 1959 Marseille, Musée Cantini: *Picasso*, cat. 34 ■
1970 Saint Paul de Vence, Fondation Maeght: *Hommage à
Pierre Reverdy* ■ 1998 Tokyo, The Bunkamura Museum of Art:
Pablo Picasso/Nagoya, City Art Museum, cat. 64

Selected literature: Zervos: V, no. 221 (Partition, guitare,
compotier) ■ Christian Zervos, *Histoire de l'art contemporain*,
Paris 1938, p. 256 ■ *Cahiers d'art*, year 7, 1932, p. 164 ■
Dorothy M. Kosinski, G. F. Reber: "Collector of Cubism", in:
Burlington Magazine, year 133, 1991, p. 531

47

Guitar, Glass and Fruit Bowl, 1924

Oil on canvas
97.5 x 130.5 cm
Signed and dated in the centre right: *Picasso/24*
Kunsthaus Zürich

Cat. Zurich 145
Gitarre, Trinkglas und Fruchtschale

Provenance: Mrs E. Staub-Terlinden ■ 1952 acquired from
the bequest of Karl Näf

Exhibitions (selected): 1932 Paris, Galeries Georges Petit:
Pablo Picasso, cat. 147 (Guitare, verre et compotier) ■ 1953
Milan, Palazzo Reale: *Picasso*, cat. 49 ■ 1955 Munich, Haus
der Kunst: *Picasso*, cat. 54 ■ 1967 Amsterdam, Stedelijk
Museum: *Picasso*, cat. 63 ■ 1981 Ingelheim, Villa Schneider:
Pablo Picasso, cat. 5 ■ 1981 Martigny, Fondation Pierre
Gianadda: *Pablo Picasso*, cat. 164 ■ 1999 Zurich, Kunst-
haus: *Max Beckmann und Paris*/Saint Louis, Art Museum,
cat. 94

Selected literature: Zervos: V, no. 252 (Guitare, verre, com-
potier avec fruits) ■ Palau i Fabre: vol. 1917-1926, no. 1453
(Mandoline, Glas, Obstschale mit Früchten) ■ Frank Elgar,
Robert Maillard, *Picasso*, Paris 1955, p. 122 (fig.), 126

48

Harlequin Musician, 1924

Oil on canvas
113.8 x 97.2 cm
Signed and dated upper left: *Picasso/24*
National Gallery of Art, Washington
Given in loving memory of her husband, Taft Schreiber,
by Rita Schreiber (1989.31.2)

Cat. Zurich 147
Musizierender Harlekin

Provenance: 1925 Paul Rosenberg & Co., Paris (acquired
from the artist) ■ Dr. G. F. Reber, Lausanne ■ Mary L. and
Leigh B. Block, Chicago ■ 1968 Rita and Taft B. Schreiber,
Beverly Hills

Exhibitions (selected): 1932 Paris, Galeries Georges Petit:
Exposition Picasso, cat. 152 ■ 1953/54 São Paulo, Museu
de Arte Moderna: *Exposiçao Picasso*, cat. 15 ■ 1962 New
York, Cooperating New York Galleries: *Picasso: An American
Tribute*, cat. 41 (Paul Rosenberg & Co.) ■ 1996 Maine, Port-
land Museum of Art: *Picasso, Braque, Léger and the Cubist
Spirit 1919-1939*, cat. 57 ■ 1996/97 Barcelona, Museu
Picasso: *Picasso y el teatro*, cat. 184 ■ 1998 Venice, Palazzo
Grassi: *Picasso, 1917-1924. Le voyage d'Italie*, cat. 224 ■
2000/01 Paris, Musée d'Art Moderne de la Ville de Paris:
L'École de Paris 1904-1929: la part de l'autre, cat. 163 ■
2003 Barcelona, Museu Picasso: *Picasso. De la caricatura a
las metamorfosis de estilo*, cat. 124 ■ 2006/07 Barcelona,
Museu Picasso: *Picasso y el circo*/Martigny, Fondation Pierre
Gianadda, cat. 189 ■ 2008/09 Rome, Complesso del Vittori-
ano, *Picasso Harlequin 1917-1937*, cat. 17

Selected literature: Zervos: V, no. 328 ■ Palau i Fabre: vol.
1917-1926, no. 1481 (Harlekin als Musikant) ■ Franco Russoli, Fiorella Minervino, *L'opera completa di Picasso cubista*,
Milan 1972 (Classici dell'arte 64), no. 928 ■ Elizabeth Cowling, *Picasso. Style and Meaning*, London/New York 2002,
p. 462f.

49

Mandolin and Guitar, 1924

Oil with sand on canvas
140.7 x 200.3 cm
Signed and dated on the bottom left margin: Picasso/24
Solomon R. Guggenheim Museum, New York (53.1358)

Cat. Zurich 149
Stilleben vor dem Fenster

Provenance: 1924 Galerie Paul Rosenberg, Paris (acquired
from the artist) ■ 1926/27 Dr. G. F. Reber, Lausanne ■
1953 Jon Nicholas Streep Gallery, New York

Exhibitions (selected): 1932 Paris, Galeries Georges Petit:
Exposition Picasso, cat. 156 (Nature morte devant la fenêtre)
■ 1955/56 Paris, Musée des Arts Décoratifs: *Picasso. Pein-*

tures. 1900–1955/Munich, Haus der Kunst/Cologne, Rheini-
sches Museum/Hamburg, Kunsthalle, cat. 61 ■ 1962 New
York, Cooperating New York Galleries: *Picasso: An American
Tribute*, cat. 35 (Paul Rosenberg & Co.) ■ 1966/67 Paris,
Grand Palais: *Hommage à Pablo Picasso*, cat. 133 ■ 1967
Amsterdam, Stedelijk Museum: *Picasso*, cat. 62 ■ 1971 New
York, Saidenberg Gallery, Marlborough Gallery: *Homage to
Picasso for his 90th Birthday*, cat. 37 ■ 1980 New York, The
Museum of Modern Art: *Pablo Picasso. A Retrospective*, p. 249
■ 1981/82 Madrid, Museo Español de Arte Contemporaneo:
Pablo Picasso/Barcelona, Museu Picasso, cat. 87 ■ 1992
Cleveland, Museum of Art: *Picasso and Things*/Philadelphia,
Museum of Art/Paris, Galeries Nationales du Grand Palais,
cat. 84, p. 214 f. ■ 2002/03 London, Tate Modern: *Matisse
— Picasso*/Paris, Grand Palais/New York, The Museum of Mod-
ern Art, cat. 76 ■ 2007 Paris, Musée National Picasso:
Picasso cubiste 1906–1925, p. 330 f. ■ 2008/09
Barcelona, Museu Picasso: *Living Things, Figure and Still Life in
Picasso*, p. 139

Selected literature: Zervos: V, no. 220 ■ Palau i Fabre: vol.
1917-1926, no. 1486 ■ Richardson: III, p. 269 f. ■ *Bulletin
de l'effort moderne*, no. 17, Juli 1925, p. 8 f. ■ Frank Elgar,
Robert Maillard, *Picasso*, Paris 1955, p. 279 ■ Wilhelm
Boeck, *Pablo Picasso*, Stuttgart/Paris 1955, no. 115 ■
Ronald Penrose, *Picasso. His Life and Work*, London 1958,
plate XI/4 ■ Herbert E. Read, *A Concise History of Modern
Painting*, New York 1959, no. 78 ■ Hans Ludwig C. Jaffé,
Pablo Picasso, New York 1964, p. 110 f. ■ Pierre Daix,
Picasso, Paris 1964, p. 128 ■ Franco Russoli, Fiorella Miner-
vino, *L'opera completa di Picasso cubista*, Milan 1972 (Classici
dell'arte 64), no. 979 ■ Pierre Daix, *Picasso créateur. La vie
intime et l'œuvre*, Paris 1987, p. 194, 198 ■ Carsten-Peter
Warncke, *Picasso 1881–1973*, ed. Ingo F. Walther, Cologne
1991, vol. I, p. 300 ■ Brigitte Léal, Christine Pilot, Marie-
Laure Bernadac, *The Ultimate Picasso*, New York 2000,
no. 540 ■ *Picasso. Tradición y vanguardia*, exh. cat., Museo
Nacional del Prado/Museo Nacional Centro de Arte Reina Sofía,
Madrid 2006, p. 189, 191 ■ *Picasso. La joie de vivre*, 1945–
1948, exh. cat., Palazzo Grassi, Venice 2006/07, p. 65 f. ■
Elizabeth Cowling, *Picasso. Style and Meaning*, New York
2002, pp. 460–463

50
The Bird Cage, 1925
Oil on canvas
80.6 x 99.5 cm

Unsigned
Ohara Museum of Art, Japan

Cat. Zurich 151
Der Vogelkäfig

Provenance: 1926 Paul Rosenberg, Paris ■ c. 1932 Shige-
taro Fukushima, Tokyo ■ 1951 Ohara Museum of Art, Japan

Exhibitions (selected): 1926 Paris, Galerie Paul Rosenberg:
Exposition d'œuvres récentes de Picasso, cat. 15 ■ 1932
Paris, Galeries Georges Petit: *Exposition Picasso*, cat. 163

Selected literature: Zervos: V, no. 456 ■ Palau i Fabre: vol.
1917-1926, no. 1613 ■ Maurice Gieure, *Initiation à l'œuvre
de Picasso*, Paris 1951, no. 65 ■ Frank Elgar, Robert Maillard,
Picasso, Paris 1955, p. 281 ■ Wilhelm Boeck, *Pablo Picasso*,
Stuttgart/Paris 1955, no. 120 ■ Jean Sutherland Boggs et al.
(ed.), *Picasso and Things*, exh. cat., The Cleveland Museum of
Art/The Philadelphia Museum of Art/Galeries Nationales du
Grand Palais Paris, Cleveland 1992, p. 200

51
Head of a Woman, 1924
Oil on canvas
34.5 x 26.5 cm
Signed and dated top right: *Picasso/24*
Tate, London
Accepted by H. M. Government in lieu of tax and allocated to
the Tate Gallery, 1995

Cat. Zurich 163
Frauenkopf, dated 1925

Provenance: 1920s: Hugh Willoughby ■ Miss Helen Shipway
■ 1995 Estate of Miss Helen Shipway

Exhibitions (selected): 1932 Paris, Galeries Georges Petit:
Exposition Picasso, cat. 140 ■ 1937 Cheltenham, Art
Gallery: *Picasso*

Selected literature: Zervos: V, no. 357 ■ Palau i Fabre: vol.
1917-1926, no. 1557 (Nachdenkliches Frauengesicht) ■
Richardson: III, p. 301 ■ Alfred H. Barr Jr., *Picasso: Fifty Years
of His Art*, New York 1946, p. 132 ■ Christopher Green,
*Cubism and its Enemies: Modern Movements and Reaction in
French Art, 1916–1928*, New Haven/London 1987, pp. 69–
72 ■ Pierre Daix, *Picasso: Life and Art*, New York 1993,
pp. 181–186 ■ Anne Strathie, Sophia Wilson, *Hugh
Willoughby — The Man Who Loved Picassos*, Cheltenham
2009, p. 9 f

52

Still Life, 1925

Oil and sand on canvas

97.8 x 131.2 cm

Signed and dated top right: *Picasso/25*

Centre Pompidou, Paris

Musée national d'art moderne/Centre de création industrielle

Donated in 1982

Cat. Zurich 155

Stilleben

Provenance: 1932 Vicomte Charles de Noailles, Paris ■ 1955 Vicomtesse Nathalie de Noailles, Paris ■ 1982 Donation of Vicomtesse de Noailles

Exhibitions (selected): 1932 Paris, Galeries Georges Petit: *Exposition Picasso*, cat. 158 ■ 1955/56 Paris, Musée des Arts Décoratifs: *Picasso. Peintures. 1900–1955*/Munich, Haus der Kunst/Cologne, Rheinisches Museum/Hamburg, Kunsthalle, cat. 63 ■ 1992 Cleveland, Museum of Art: *Picasso and Things*/Philadelphia, Museum of Art/Paris, Galeries Nationales du Grand Palais, cat. 87, p. 220 f. ■ 2008/09 Barcelona, Museo Picasso Institut de cultura: *Objetos vivos: figura y naturaleza muerta en Picasso*

Selected literature: Zervos: V, no. 462 ■ Palau i Fabre: vol. 1917–1926, no. 1608 (Viszerales Stilleben) ■ Christian Zervos, 'Œuvres récentes de Picasso', in: *Cahiers d'art*, year 1, 1926, no. 5, p. 89 ■ *Documents*, no. 3, 1930, p. 160 ■ *Cahiers d'art*, year 7, 1932, pp. 154/155 ■ *Picasso. La joie de vivre, 1945–1948*, exh. cat., Palazzo Grassi, Venice 2006/07, p. 66 f. (illustrated wrong side up and mirrored) ■ Christian Geelhaar, *Picasso. Wegbereiter und Förderer seines Aufstiegs 1899–1939*, Zurich 1993, no. 136 and p. 142

53

The Drawing Lesson, 1925

Oil on canvas

129.5 x 97.2 cm

Signed top left: *Picasso/25*, dated on the canvas stretcher: *6 Juin 1925*

Private collection

Cat. Zurich 161

Die Zeichenstunde

Provenance: Galerie Berggruen & Cie, Paris ■ Jorge Brito Collection, Lisbon ■ 1984 Galerie Beyeler, Basel

Exhibitions (selected): 1932 Paris, Galeries Georges Petit: *Exposition Picasso*, cat. 165 ■ 1975/76 Minneapolis, Institute of Arts: *Picasso — Braque — Léger. Masterpieces from Swiss Collections*/Houston, The Sarah Campbell Blaffer Gallery/San Francisco, Museum of Modern Art ■ 1981 Basel, Galerie Beyeler: *Picasso 1881–1981*, cat. 17 ■ 1981/82 Vienna, Kulturamt der Stadt Wien, Rathaus: *Picasso in Wien. Bilder, Zeichnungen, Plastiken*, cat. 28

Selected literature: Zervos: V, no. 421 ■ Palau i Fabre: vol. 1917–1926, no. 1581 ■ Carl Einstein, *Die Kunst des 20. Jahrhunderts, Propylaen Kunstgeschichte XVI*, Berlin, 3rd edition, 1931, fig. p. 327 ■ Maurice Gieure, *Initiation à l'œuvre de Picasso*, Paris 1951, no. 67 ■ Frank Elgar, Robert Maillard, *Picasso*, Paris 1955, p. 280 ■ Pierre Cabanne, *Picasso: pour le centenaire de sa naissance*, Neuchâtel 1981, p. 125, no. 45 ■ Pierre Daix, *Picasso créateur. La vie intime et l'œuvre*, Paris 1987, p. 199, 201, 420 ■ Jean Sutherland Boggs et al. (ed.), *Picasso and Things*, exh. cat., The Cleveland Museum of Art/The Philadelphia Museum of Art/Galeries Nationales du Grand Palais Paris, Cleveland 1992, p. 199 ■ Michael FitzGerald, *Picasso. The Artist's Studio*, exh. cat., Wadsworth Atheneum Hartford/The Cleveland Museum of Art, New Haven/London 2001, p. 35 f.

54

Studio with Plaster Head, 1925

Oil on canvas

97.9 x 131.1 cm

Signed and dated bottom right: *Picasso/25*

The Museum of Modern Art, New York

Purchase, 1964

Cat. Zurich 158

Das Atelier

Provenance: 1926 Galerie Paul Rosenberg, Paris (acquired from the artist) ■ 1926–1939 (or earlier) Dr. G. F. Reber, Lausanne (acquired from Galerie Paul Rosenberg (?)) ■ 1937 (?) A. M. Bellanger (?) ■ 1939 (?)–1964 James Johnson Sweeney, Houston (acquired from G. F. Reber (?))

Exhibitions (selected): 1926 Galerie Paul Rosenberg, Paris: *Exposition d'œuvres récentes de Picasso*, cat. 43 ■ 1932 Paris, Galeries Georges Petit: *Exposition Picasso*, cat. 160 (L'Atelier) ■ 1939/40 New York, The Museum of Modern Art: *Picasso. Forty Years of his Art*/Chicago, Art Institute/San Francisco, Museum of Art, cat. 192 (only in cat.) ■ 1972 New York, The Museum of Modern Art: *Picasso in the Collection of*

The Museum of Modern Art, p.120ff., 221f. ■ 1976 Basel,
Kunstmuseum: *Picasso. Aus dem Museum of Modern Art New
York und Schweizer Sammlungen*, cat. 51, p.102ff. ■ 1980
New York, The Museum of Modern Art: *Pablo Picasso. A Retro-
spective*, p.250 ■ 1992 Cleveland, Museum of Art: *Picasso
and Things*/Philadelphia, Museum of Art/Paris, Galeries
Nationales du Grand Palais, cat. 86, p.218f. ■ 1995 Kyoto,
National Museum of Modern Art: *Picasso: The Love and the
Anguish — The Road to Guernica* ■ 1999/2000 Barcelona,
Museu Picasso: *Picasso: Paisaje interior y exterior* ■ 2010
Bern, Zentrum Paul Klee: *Klee trifft Picasso*, p.128, 146f.
(fig.), 275

Selected literature: Zervos: V, no. 445 (Tête et bras de plâtre)
■ Palau i Fabre: vol. 1917–1926, no. 1595 (Komposition mit
Gipskopf) ■ Richardson: III, p.292f., 295f. ■ Carl Einstein,
*Die Kunst des 20. Jahrhunderts, Propyläen Kunstgeschichte
XVI*, Berlin, 3rd edition, 1931, fig. p.323 ■ Christian Zervos,
'Œuvres récentes de Picasso', in: *Cahiers d'art*, year 1, 1926,
no. 5, p. 92 ■ Wilhelm Uhde, *Picasso et la tradition française*,
Paris 1928, between pp.18 and 19 ■ Alfred H. Barr Jr.,
Picasso: Fifty Years of His Art, New York 1946, p.138f. ■
Maurice Gieure, *Initiation à l'œuvre de Picasso*, Paris 1951,
no. 61 ■ Wilhelm Boeck, *Pablo Picasso*, Stuttgart/Paris 1955,
no. 119 ■ Frank Elgar, Robert Maillard, *Picasso*, Paris 1955,
p. 281 ■ Roland Penrose, *Picasso. His Life and Work*, London
1958, p. 226 and plate XI/3 ■ Hans Ludwig C. Jaffé, *Pablo
Picasso*, New York 1964, p.116f. ■ Jean Leymarie, *Picasso:
Métamorphoses et unité*, Geneva 1971, p.169ff. ■ Pierre
Daix, *Picasso créateur. La vie intime et l'œuvre*, Paris 1987,
p.197f. ■ Carsten-Peter Warncke, *Picasso 1881–1973*, ed.
Ingo F. Walther, Cologne 1991, vol. I, p. 315 ■ Christian Geel-
haar, *Picasso. Wegbereiter und Förderer seines Aufstiegs
1899–1939*, Zurich 1993, no. 167 and p.160 ■ Brigitte
Léal, Christine Pilot, Marie-Laure Bernadac, *The Ultimate
Picasso*, New York 2000, no. 546 ■ Elizabeth Cowling,
Picasso. Style and Meaning, London/New York 2002, p. 481f.,
587 ■ *Picasso Tradición y vanguardia*, exh. cat., Museo
Nacional del Prado/Museo Nacional Centro de Arte Reina Sofía,
Madrid 2006, p.189, 191

55
Wine Bottle, 1926
Oil on canvas
98 x 131.5 cm
Signed and dated bottom left: *Picasso/26*
Fondation Beyeler, Riehen/Basel

Cat. Zurich 163
Stilleben mit Weinflasche

Provenance: Galerie Paul Rosenberg, Paris ■ 1927
Dr. G. F. Reber, Lausanne ■ 1930 Galerie Paul Rosenberg,
Paris ■ 1962 Private collection, New York ■ 1979 Beyeler
Collection

Exhibitions (selected): 1926 Paris, Galerie Paul Rosenberg:
Exposition d'œuvres récentes de Picasso, cat. 58 (Compotier
de raisin) ■ 1932 Paris, Galeries Georges Petit: *Exposition
Picasso*, cat. 150 (Nature morte à la bouteille de vin, dated
1924) ■ 1934 Hartford, Wadsworth Atheneum: *Picasso*,
cat.55 ■ 1939/40 New York, The Museum of Modern Art:
Picasso: Forty Years of His Art/Chicago, Art Institute/St. Louis,
City Art Museum/Boston, Museum of Fine Arts, cat. 193 ■
1962 New York, Cooperating New York Galleries: *Picasso: An
American Tribute*, cat. 46 (Paul Rosenberg & Co.) ■ 1981
Basel, Galerie Beyeler: *Picasso 1881–1981*, cat. 18 ■ 1992
Cleveland, Museum of Art: *Picasso and Things*/Philadelphia,
Museum of Art/Paris, Galeries Nationales du Grand Palais,
cat. 89 ■ 1993 Berlin, Nationalgalerie: *Wege der Moderne.
Die Sammlung Beyeler*, cat. 98 ■ 2001 Bern, Kunstmuseum:
*Picasso und die Schweiz. Meisterwerke aus Schweizer Samm-
lungen*, cat. 92

Selected literature: Zervos: VI, no. 1444 ■ Palau i Fabre:
vol. 1917–1926, no. 1660 (Die Weinflasche) ■ Maud Dale,
Modern Art: Picasso, New York 1930, no. 39 ■ *Cahiers d'art*,
year 7, 1932, p.158 ■ Jaime Sabartés, *Picasso*, Paris 1946,
no. 10 ■ Frank Elgar, Robert Maillard, *Picasso*, Paris 1955,
p.280 ■ Wilhelm Boeck, *Picasso*, Stuttgart/Paris 1955,
no. 121 ■ Pierre Cabanne, *Picasso. Pour le centenaire de sa
naissance*, Neuchâtel 1981, p.126f., no. 46 ■ Carsten-Peter
Warncke, *Pablo Picasso, 1881–1973*, ed. Ingo F. Walther,
Cologne 1991, vol. I, p. 311 ■ Angela Schneider, Christian
Langner (ed.), *Wege der Moderne. Die Sammlung Beyeler*, exh.
cat., Staatliche Museen zu Berlin — Preußischer Kulturbesitz,
Nationalgalerie, Berlin 1993, no. 98 ■ Christian Geelhaar,
*Picasso. Wegbereiter und Förderer seines Aufstiegs 1899–
1939*, Zurich 1993, no. 159 and p.153 ■ *Sammlung Beyeler*,
Ostfildern 2007, no. 156

56
The Painter and his Model, 1927
Oil on canvas
214 x 200 cm
Signed bottom right: *Picasso*
Tehran Museum of Contemporary Art

Cat. Zurich 168
Der Maler und sein Modell

Provenance: Christian Zervos, Paris ■ Carlo Frua de Angeli, (Milan?) ■ c. 1974 Alberto Ulrich ■ Galerie Beyeler ■ 1975 Tehran Museum of Contemporary Art

Exhibitions (selected): 1948 Venice Biennale ■ 1955/56 Paris, Musée des Arts Décoratifs: *Picasso. Peintures. 1900–1955*/Munich, Haus der Kunst/Cologne, Rheinisches Museum/ Hamburg, Kunsthalle, cat. 72 ■ 1974 Basel, Galerie Beyeler: *Surréalisme et peinture*, cat. 36 ■ 2005 Riehen/Basel, Fondation Beyeler: *Picasso surreal*, cat. 20

Selected literature: Zervos: VII, no. 59 ■ Frank Elgar, Robert Maillard, *Picasso*, Paris 1955, fig. p. 154 ■ Pierre Daix, *Picasso créateur. La vie intime et l'œuvre*, Paris 1987, p. 218 f., 423 ■ Ulrich Weisner (ed.), *Picassos Surrealismus. Werke 1925–1937*, exh. cat., Kunsthalle Bielefeld, 1991, p. 178

57

Woman in an Armchair, 1927

Oil on canvas
81 x 65 cm
Signed and dated top right: *Picasso/27*
Kawamura Memorial Museum of Art, Japan

Cat. Zurich 170
Frau im Lehnstuhl

Provenance: Minami Art Gallery, Tokyo ■ 1976 Dainichi Can Co., Ltd., Tokyo ■ Since 1990 loan to the Kawamura Memorial Museum of Art

Exhibitions (selected): 1932 Paris, Galeries Georges Petit: *Exposition Picasso*, cat. 174 (Femme au fauteuil) ■ 1971 New York, Saidenberg Gallery, Marlborough Gallery: *Homage to Picasso for his 90th Birthday*, cat. 39 ■ 1995/96 Kyoto, The National Museum of Modern Art: *Picasso: The Love and The Anguish — The Road to Guernica*/Tokyo, Tobu Museum of Art ■ 1998 Tokyo, The Bunkamura Museum of Art: *Picasso. A Retrospective*/Nagoya, City Art Museum, cat. 67

Selected literature: Zervos: VII, no. 71 ■ *Cahiers d'art*, year 7, 1932, p. 160 ■ Wilhelm Boeck, *Pablo Picasso*, Stuttgart/ Paris 1955, no. 261 ■ Makoto Ohoka, *A Portrait of an Art Dealer. Kusuo Shimizu*, in: Mizue, Juni 1975, p. 94 ■ Ulrich Weisner (ed.), *Picassos Surrealismus. Werke 1925–1937*, exh. cat., Kunsthalle Bielefeld, 1991, p. 225

58

Harlequin, 1927

Oil on canvas
81.3 x 65.1 cm
Signed and dated top right: *Picasso/27*
The Metropolitan Museum of Art, New York
The Mr. and Mrs. Klaus G. Perls Collection, 1997 (1997.149.5)

Cat. Zurich 171
Kopf eines Harlekin

Provenance: 1930 Paul Rosenberg and Georges Wildenstein, Paris and New York (acquired jointly from the artist) ■ 1961 Perls Galleries, New York ■ Mr and Mrs Klaus G. Perls, New York

Exhibitions (selected): 1931 New York, Valentine Gallery: *Abstractions of Picasso*, cat. 11 ■ 1932 Paris, Galeries Georges Petit: *Exposition Picasso*, cat. 173 (Tête d'Arlequin) ■ 1938 Boston, Museum of Modern Art: *Picasso — Matisse*, cat. 21 ■ 1942 New York, Valentine Gallery: *Picasso & Miró*, cat. 6 ■ 1962 New York, Cooperating New York Galleries: *Picasso: An American Tribute*, cat. 47 (Paul Rosenberg & Co.) ■ 1964 Toronto, Art Gallery of Toronto: *Picasso and Man*/Montreal, Museum of Fine Arts, cat. 92 ■ 1965 Toulouse, Musée des Augustins: *Picasso et le théâtre*, cat. 102 ■ 1965 New York, Perls Galleries: *Pablo Picasso: Highlights in Retrospect*, cat. 9 ■ 1967 Dallas, Museum of Fine Arts: *Pablo Picasso*, cat. 46 ■ 1977/78 Tokyo, Museum of the City of Tokyo: *Exposition Picasso*/Nagoya, Prefectural Museum of Art/ Fukoaka, Cultural Center/Kyoto, National Museum of Modern Art, cat. 40 ■ 1994 Los Angeles, County Museum of Art: *Picasso and the Weeping Women: The Years of Marie-Thérèse Walter and Dora Maar*/New York, The Metropolitan Museum of Art ■ 2007 Barcelona, Museu Picasso: *Picasso y el circo*/ Martigny, Fondation Pierre Gianadda, cat. 192, p. 222, 339 ■ 2008/09 Rome, Complesso del Vittoriano: *Picasso Harlequin 1917-1937*, cat. 19, p. 18 f., 22, 150 f. ■ 2010 New York, The Metropolitan Museum of Art: *Picasso in the Metropolitan Museum of Art*, cat. 75

Selected literature: Zervos: VII, no. 80 ■ *Documents*, no. 3, 1930, p. 132 ■ Maud Dale, *Modern Art: Picasso*, New York 1930, no. 42 ■ *Cahiers d'art*, year 7, 1932, p. 169 ■ Jean Leymarie, *Picasso: Métamorphoses et unité*, Geneva 1971, p. 25 ■ Carsten-Peter Warncke, *Picasso 1881-1973*, ed. Ingo F. Walther, Cologne 1991, vol. I, p. 79 ■ Kirk Varnedoe, 'Picasso's Self-Portraits', in: William Rubin (ed.), *Picasso and Portraiture. Representation and Transformation*, exh. cat., Museum of Modern Art New York/Grand Palais Paris, New York

1996, p.146 f., 150 ■ Jean Clair (ed.), *Picasso, 1917–1924.
Le voyage d'Italie*, exh. cat., Palazzo Grassi Venice, Milan
1998, p. 91 ■ Elizabeth Cowling, *Picasso: Style and Meaning*,
London 2002, p. 486 ■ Anne Baldassari, *Bacon — Picasso:
La vie des images*, exh. cat., Musée Picasso, Paris 2005, p. 74,
77, 111 f. ■ Olivier Berggruen, Max Hollein, *Picasso und das
Theater*, exh. cat., Schirn Kunsthalle, Frankfurt 2006, p. 246 f.
■ Michael FitzGerald, *Picasso and American Art*, exh. cat.,
Whitney Museum of American Art New York/San Francisco
Museum of Modern Art/Walker Art Center Minneapolis, New
York 2006, p. 337

59
Painter and Model, 1928

Oil on canvas
129.8 x 163 cm
Signed and dated bottom left: *Picasso/28*
The Museum of Modern Art, New York
The Sidney and Harriet Janis Collection

Cat. Zurich 175
Der Künstler und seine Modelle

Provenance: 1928-1933 Paul Rosenberg, Paris (acquired
from the artist) ■ 1933-1967 Sidney and Harriet Janis,
New York (acquired from Paul Rosenberg)

Exhibitions (selected): 1929 Paris, Galerie Paul Rosenberg:
Picasso ■ 1932 Paris: Galeries Georges Petit: *Exposition
Picasso*, cat. 181 (L'artiste et son modèle) ■ 1934 Hartford,
Wadsworth Atheneum: *Picasso* ■ 1939/40 New York, The
Museum of Modern Art: *Picasso: Forty Years of his Art*,
cat. 216 ■ 1941 New York, The Museum of Modern Art:
Masterpieces of Picasso ■ 1949 Toronto, Art Gallery:
Picasso, cat. 19 ■ 1957 New York, The Museum of Modern
Art: *Picasso. 75th Anniversary Exhibition*/Chicago, The Art
Institute, p. 65 ■ 1958 Philadelphia, Museum of Art: *Picasso*
■ 1959 Marseille, Musée Cantini: *Picasso*, cat. 37 ■ 1960
London, The Arts Council of Great Britain/Tate Gallery: *Picasso*,
cat. 117 ■ 1967 Dallas, Museum of Fine Arts: *Picasso* ■
1973 New York, The Museum of Modern Art: *Pablo Picasso
1881-1973* ■ 1975 New York, Acquavella Gallery: *Picasso*
■ 1976 Basel, Kunstmuseum: *Picasso. Aus dem Museum of
Modern Art und aus Schweizer Sammlungen*, cat. 54 ■ 1980
New York, The Museum of Modern Art: *Pablo Picasso. A Retrospective*, p. 269 ■ 1999 Fort Worth, Kimbell Art Museum:
Matisse and Picasso: A Gentle Rivalry, cat. 25 ■ 2002/03
London, Tate Modern: Matisse — *Picasso*/Paris, Grand Palais/
New York, The Museum of Modern Art, cat. 80 ■ 2005

Riehen/Basel, Fondation Beyeler: *Picasso surreal*, cat. 22 ■
2008 Bergen, Kunstmuseum: *Picasso. Figure and Image*

Selected literature: Zervos: VII, no. 143 (Le peintre et son
modèle) ■ Richardson III, p. 353 ■ Eugenio d'Ors, *Pablo
Picasso*, Paris/New York 1930, plate 46 ■ Alfred Barr, *Cubism
and Abstract Art*, New York 1936, no. 228 ■ Alfred H. Barr
Jr., *Picasso: Fifty Years of his Art*, New York 1946, p. 156 ■
Frank Elgar, Robert Maillard, *Picasso*, Paris 1955, p. 282 ■
Roland Penrose, *Picasso. His Life and Work*, London 1958,
p. 234, plate XII/8 ■ Jean Leymarie, *Picasso: Métamorphoses
et unité*, Geneva 1971, p.169 ff. ■ William Rubin, *Picasso in
the Collection of The Museum of Modern Art*, New York 1972,
p.130 f., 224 ■ Pierre Daix, *Picasso créateur. La vie intime et
l'œuvre*, Paris 1987, p. 218 f., 423 ■ Carsten-Peter Warncke,
Picasso 1881–1973, ed. Ingo F. Walther, Cologne 1991, vol. I,
p. 317 ■ Ulrich Weisner (ed.), *Picassos Surrealismus. Werke
1925–1937*, exh. cat., Kunsthalle Bielefeld, 1991, cat. 15 b ■
Christian Geelhaar, *Picasso. Wegbereiter und Förderer seines
Aufstiegs 1899-1939*, Zurich 1993, no. 226 and p. 204 ■
Susan Grace Galassi, *Picasso's Variations on the Masters:
Confrontations With the Past*, New York 1996 ■ Brigitte Léal,
Christine Pilot, Marie-Laure Bernadac, *The Ultimate Picasso*,
New York 2000, no. 580 ■ Elizabeth Cowling, *Picasso. Style
and Meaning*, London/New York 2002, pp. 498–502 and pas-
sim ■ Michael FitzGerald, *Picasso and American Art,* exh. cat.,
Whitney Museum of American Art New York/San Francisco
Museum of Modern Art/Walker Art Center Minneapolis, New
York 2006, p.140 ff.

60
Bathers with Beach Ball, 1928

Oil on canvas
15.9 x 21.9 cm
Signed and dated bottom right: *Picasso/28*
Private collection

Cat. Zurich 178
Badende, Ballspiel

Provenance: Rosenberg and Helft Limited, New York ■ Mr
and Mrs William McKim, Palm Beach ■ Private collection
Switzerland

Exhibitions (selected): 1939/40 New York, The Museum of
Modern Art: *Picasso: Forty Years of His Art*, cat. 221 ■ 1980
New York, The Museum of Modern Art: *Pablo Picasso. A Retro-
spective*, p. 271 ■ 1981 Munich, Haus der Kunst: *Pablo
Picasso: Sammlung Marina Picasso*/Cologne, Josef-Haubrich-

Kunsthalle/Frankfurt, Städtische Galerie, p.152 ■ 1988/89
Stockholm, Moderna Museet: *Pablo Picasso*, cat.38 ■ 1991
Bielefeld, Kunsthalle: *Picassos Surrealismus. Werke 1925–
1937*, cat.21 ■ 2002 Paris, Centre Pompidou: *La Révolution
Surréaliste*, p.172 ■ 2006/07 New York, Whitney Museum:
Picasso and American Art/San Francisco, Museum of Art/
Minneapolis, The Walker Art Center, plate 144 and p.270

Selected literature: Zervos: VII, no.226 (Baigneuse au ballon)
■ Christian Zervos, 'Picasso à Dinard, Eté 1928', in: *Cahiers
d'art*, year 4, 1929, no.1, p.17 ■ Roland Penrose, *Picasso.
His Life and Work*, London 1958, plate XII/2 ■ Werner Spies,
Pablo Picasso. Wege zur Skulptur, Munich/New York 1995,
no.68 ■ Brigitte Léal, Christine Pilot, Marie-Laure Bernadac,
The Ultimate Picasso, New York 2000, no.593 ■ Robert
Hughes, *The Portable Picasso*, New York 2003, p.216

61
Young Girl, 1929

Oil on canvas
54 x 45.5 cm
Signed and dated top right: *Picasso/29*
Moderna Museet, Stockholm

Cat. Zurich 182
Das Thermometer

Provenance: 1964 Moderna Museet, Stockholm (acquired
1964 at an auction at the Palais Galliera)

Exhibitions (selected): 1991 Bielefeld, Kunsthalle: *Picassos
Surrealismus. Werke 1925–1937*, cat.27 ■ 2002/03 Oslo,
Munch Museet: *Picasso, Braque, Léger, Gris* ■ 2005 Paris,
Musée Picasso: *Bacon — Picasso: La vie des images*, cat.107
■ 2005 Riehen/Basel, Fondation Beyeler: *Picasso surreal*,
cat.16 ■ 2006 Göteborg, Göteborgs Konstmuseum: *Pablo
Picasso, akrobater och harlekiner, familj och kvinnor*, cat.51

Selected literature: Zervos: VII, no.289 (Tête)

62
The Open Window, 1929

Oil on canvas
130 x 162 cm
Signed and dated bottom left: *Picasso/XXIX*
Staatsgalerie Stuttgart
Steegmann Collection

Cat. Zurich 190
Das Atelier des Künstlers

Provenance: Collection of Mollie Bostwick, Chicago ■ Galerie
Beyeler, Basel ■ 1974 Collection of Josef Steegmann

Exhibitions (selected): 1932 Paris, Galeries Georges Petit:
Exposition Picasso, cat.189 (L'atelier de l'artiste) ■ 1968
New York, The Museum of Modern Art: *Dada, Surrealism, and
their Heritage*/Los Angeles, County Museum of Art/Chicago,
The Art Institute, cat.181 ■ 1974 Basel, Galerie Beyeler:
Surréalisme et peinture, cat.37 ■ 1976 Basel, Kunst-
museum: *Picasso. Aus dem Museum of Modern Art und aus
Schweizer Sammlungen*, cat.55 ■ 1998/99 Stuttgart,
Staatsgalerie: *Picasso. Klee. Giacometti: Die Sammlung Steeg-
mann*, cat.9 ■ 2002 Düsseldorf, Kunstsammlung Nordrhein-
Westfalen: *La Révolution surréaliste* ■ 2005 Riehen/Basel,
Fondation Beyeler: *Picasso surreal*, cat.21

Selected literature: Zervos: VII, no.288 ■ Michel Leiris,
"Toiles récentes de Picasso", in: *Documents*, no.2, 1930, p.57
■ Pierre Daix, *Picasso créateur. La vie intime et l'œuvre*, Paris
1987, p.225 ■ *Picassos Surrealismus. Werke 1925–1937*,
exh. cat., Kunsthalle Bielefeld, 1991, p.183 ■ Jean Sutherland Boggs et al. (ed.), *Picasso and Things*, exh. cat., The Cleveland Museum of Art/The Philadelphia Museum of Art/Galeries
Nationales du Grand Palais Paris, Cleveland 1992, p.202

63
Head: Study for a Monument, 1929

Oil on canvas
73 x 59.7 cm
Signed and dated bottom left: *Picasso/29*
The Baltimore Museum of Art
The Dexter M. Ferry, Jr. Trustee Corporation Fund
(BMA.1966.41)

Cat. Zurich 186
Metamorphose

Provenance: 1929 Galerie Paul Rosenberg (acquired from the
artist) ■ 1948 Paul Rosenberg & Co, New York ■ G. David
Thompson Collection, Pittsburgh (stolen 1961, recovered by
the FBI) ■ 1966 Parke-Bernet Galleries, New York ■ Galerie
Beyeler, Basel ■ 1966 The Baltimore Museum of Art

Exhibitions (selected): 1932 Paris, Galeries Georges Petit:
Exposition Picasso, cat.184 (Métamorphose) ■ 1934 Hartford, Wadsworth Atheneum: *Picasso*, cat.68 ■ 1948 New

York, Paul Rosenberg & Co.: *Drawings, Gouaches, Paintings from 1913–1947 by Picasso*, cat. 17 ■ 1975 New York, Acquavella Galleries: *Picasso* ■ 1970 Portland Art Museum: *Picasso for Portland*, p. 65 ■ 1994 London, Tate Gallery: *Picasso: Sculptor, Painter*, cat. 92 ■ 1998 Tokyo, The Bunkamura Museum of Art: *Picasso. A Retrospective*/Nagoya, City Art Museum, cat. 72 ■ 2004 Baltimore, The Baltimore Museum of Art: *Pablo Picasso. Surrealism and the War Years* ■ 2004/05 Raleigh, North Carolina Museum of Art: *Matisse, Picasso and the School of Paris* ■ 2005 Baltimore, The Baltimore Museum of Art: *Picasso and Surrealism* ■ 2005 Stuttgart, Staatsgalerie: *Picasso — Badende*, cat. 59 ■ 2008/09 Rome, Complesso del Vittoriano: *Picasso Harlequin 1917–1937*

Selected literature: Zervos: VII, no. 273 (Tête) ■ Christian Zervos, "Les derniers œuvres de Picasso", in: *Cahiers d'art*, year 4, 1929, no. 6, p. 247 ■ *Documents*, no. 3, 1930, p. 166 ■ Carl Einstein, Die *Kunst des 20. Jahrhunderts, Propyläen Kunstgeschichte XVI*, Berlin, 3rd edition, 1931, fig. p. 340 ■ *Cahiers d'art*, year 7, 1932, p. 179 ■ Christian Zervos, *Histoire de l'art contemporain*, Paris 1938, p. 264 ■ Dawn Ades, *Dada and Surrealism Reviewed*, London 1978, p. 245 ■ Carsten-Peter Warncke, *Picasso 1881–1973*, ed. Ingo F. Walther, Cologne 1991, vol. I, p. 327 ■ Elizabeth Cowling, *Picasso. Style and Meaning*, London/New York 2002, p. 517

64

Nude Standing by the Sea, 1929

Oil on canvas
129.9 x 96.8 cm
Signed and dated bottom left: *Picasso/29*
The Metropolitan Museum of Art, New York
Bequest of Florene M. Schoenborn, 1995 (1996.403.4)

Cat. Zurich 187
Figur am Strand

Provenance: 1929 until at least 1934 Alex Reid & Lefevre, London (acquired from the artist, jointly with Etienne Bignou, Paris and New York and M. Knoedler & Co., New York, London, Paris) ■ Until 1952 Aline Barnsdall, Santa Barbara ■ March – Sept. 1952 M. Knoedler & Co. ■ Mr and Mrs Samuel A. Marx, Chicago ■ 1964 Florene May Schoenborn (widow of Samuel A. Marx, later Mrs. Wolfgang Schoenborn, New York) ■ 1971 Permanent loan at The Museum of Modern Art, New York ■ 1980–1995 Permanent loan at The Metropolitan Museum of Art, New York

Exhibitions (selected): 1930 Paris, Galeries Georges Petit: *Cent ans de peinture française*, cat. 56 ■ 1931 New York, Valentine Gallery: *Abstractions of Picasso*, cat. 15 ■ 1931 London, Alex Reid & Lefevre Ltd.: *Thirty Years of Pablo Picasso*, cat. 31 ■ 1932 Paris, Galeries Georges Petit: *Exposition Picasso*, cat. 187 (Figure au bord de la mer) ■ 1957 New York, The Museum of Modern Art: *Picasso. 75th Anniversary Exhibition*/Chicago, The Art Institute, p. 66 ■ 1958 Philadelphia, Museum of Art: *Picasso*, cat. 120, p. 19 ■ 1972 New York, The Museum of Modern Art: *Picasso in the Collection of The Museum of Modern Art*, p. 134, 225 ■ 1994 Los Angeles, County Museum of Art: *Picasso and the Weeping Women: The Years of Marie-Thérèse Walter and Dora Maar*/New York, The Metropolitan Museum of Art ■ 1998 Tokyo, The Bunkamura Museum of Art: *Pablo Picasso*/Nagoya, City Art Museum, cat. 73 ■ 2010 New York, The Metropolitan Museum of Art: *Picasso in the Metropolitan Museum of Art*, cat. 77

Selected literature: Zervos: VII, no. 252 (Femme) ■ Richardson: III, p. 366 f. ■ *Documents*, no. 3, 1930, p. 114 ■ Maurice Gieure, *Initiation à l'œuvre de Picasso*, Paris 1951, no. 87 ■ Maud Dale, *Modern Art: Picasso*, New York 1930, no. 43 ■ Frank Elgar, Robert Maillard, *Picasso*, Paris 1955, p. 282 ■ Felix Andreas Baumann, *Pablo Picasso: Leben und Werk*, Stuttgart 1976, p. 120 ■ Anne Baldassari, *Bacon — Picasso: La vie des images*, exh. cat., Musée Picasso, Paris 2005, p. 81 ■ Michael FitzGerald, *Picasso and American Art*, exh. cat., Whitney Museum of American Art New York/San Francisco Museum of Modern Art/Walker Art Center Minneapolis, New York 2006, p. 127, 337 and passim

65

Abstraction (Head), 1930

Oil on wood
62.2 x 46.4 cm
Signed bottom left: *Picasso/26-I–XXX*
Cincinnati Art Museum
Gift of Thomas C. and Emily F. Adler (1991.312)

Cat. Zurich 193
Abstraktion

Provenance: Until at least 1931 Collection of the artist ■ c. 1941 (?) Galerie Bignou, New York ■ Before 1945 Theodore Schempp, New York ■ 1945–1952 Charles W. Adler, Cincinnati ■ 1952–1991 Mr and Mrs Thomas C. Adler, Cincinnati

Exhibitions (selected): 1931 New York, Valentine Gallery: *Abstractions of Picasso* ■ 1931 London, Alex, Reid & Lefevre Gallery: *Thirty Years of Pablo Picasso*, cat. 35 ■ 1932 Paris, Galeries Georges Petit: *Exposition Picasso*, cat. 194 (Abstraction) ■ 1937 New York, Jacques Seligmann & Co.: *Twenty Years in the Evolution of Picasso* ■ 1941 New York, Bignou Gallery: *Picasso, Early and Late*

Selected literature: Zervos VII, no. 298 (Profil) ■ Michel Leiris, 'Toiles récentes de Picasso', in: *Documents*, no. 2, 1930, p. 58 ■ Carl Einstein, *Die Kunst des 20. Jahrhunderts, Propyläen Kunstgeschichte XVI*, Berlin, 3rd edition, 1931, fig. p. 341

66
Jug and Bowl of Fruit, 1931

Oil on canvas
131 x 196 cm
Signed and dated bottom left: *Picasso/XXXI*
Additional date on the back: *11.II. XXXI*
Courtesy Nahmad Collection, Switzerland

Provenance: Paul Rosenberg, Paris ■ Yvon Helft, Paris ■ Madeleine Helft, Paris ■ Otto Preminger

Exhibitions (selected): 1931 Paris, Galerie Paul Rosenberg: *Pablo Picasso* ■ 1932 Paris, Galeries Georges Petit: *Exposition Picasso*, cat. 204 (Cruche et compotier) ■ 1998 London, Helly Nahmad Gallery: *Picasso: Artist of the Century*, cat. 16 ■ 1999 Rotterdam, Kunsthal: *Picasso: Artist of the Century*, cat. 21 ■ 2001 London, Helly Nahmad Gallery: *Braque, Gris, Léger and Picasso: Cubism and Beyond*, cat. 43 ■ 2008/09 Barcelona, Museu Picasso Institut de cultura: *Objetos vivos: figura y naturaleza muerta en Picasso*, p. 181

Selected literature: Zervos: VII, no. 327 ■ Pierre Guéguen, 'Picasso et le Métapicassisme', in: *Cahiers d'art*, year 6, 1931, no. 7 f., p. 327 ■ *Cahiers d'art*, year 7, 1932, p. 187 ■ Maurice Gieure, *Initiation à l'œuvre de Picasso*, Paris 1951, no. 88 ■ Wilhelm Boeck, *Pablo Picasso*, Stuttgart/Paris 1955, no. 134

67
Pitcher and Fruit Bowl, 1931

Oil on canvas
130.2 x 194.9 cm

Signed and dated bottom left: *Picasso/XXXI*
Saint Louis Art Museum
Bequest of Morton D. May (932:1983)

Provenance: 1931 Paris, Galerie Paul Rosenberg ■ 1938 London, Rosenberg & Helft ■ 1948 New York, Paul Rosenberg & Co. ■ 1948–1983 St. Louis, Morton D. May (acquired from Paul Rosenberg)

Exhibitions (selected): 1931 Paris, Galerie Paul Rosenberg: *Pablo Picasso* ■ 1932 Paris, Galeries Georges Petit: *Exposition Picasso*, cat. 205 (La cheminée) ■ 1934 Hartford, Wadsworth Atheneum: *Picasso* ■ 1938 London, Rosenberg & Helft: *Bonnard, Braque, Henri Matisse, Picasso, Rouault*, cat. 11 ■ 1957 Milwaukee, Art Museum: *An Inaugural Exhibition: El Greco, Rembrandt, Goya, Cézanne, van Gogh, Picasso* ■ 1967 Dallas, Museum of Art: *Pablo Picasso: A Retrospective Exhibition*, cat. 71, p. 73, 96 ■ 1992 Cleveland, Museum of Art: *Picasso and Things*/Philadelphia, Museum of Art/Paris, Galeries Nationales du Grand Palais, cat. 91 ■ 1994 West Palm Beach, The Norton Gallery and School of Art: *Pablo Picasso: A Vision*, cat. 18 ■ 1999 Forth Worth, Kimbell Art Museum: *Matisse and Picasso: A Gentle Rivalry*, cat. 48

Selected literature: Zervos: VII, no. 326 (Pichet, coupe de fruits et feuillage) ■ Pierre Guéguen, 'Picasso et le Métapicassisme', in: *Cahiers d'art*, year 6, 1931, no. 7 f., p. 327 ■ *Cahiers d'art*, year 7, 1932, p. 185 ■ Frank Elgar, Robert Maillard, *Picasso*, Paris 1955, fig. p. 170 ■ Wilhelm Boeck, *Pablo Picasso*, Stuttgart/Paris 1955, no. 133 ■ *Objetos vivos: figura y naturaleza muerta en Picasso*, exh. cat., Museu Picasso Institut de Cultura, Barcelona 2008, p. 171

68
Pitcher and Bowl of Fruit, 1931

Oil on canvas
130.8 x 162.6 cm
Signed and dated bottom left: Picasso/XXXI
Solomon R. Guggenheim Museum, New York
By exchange, 1982 (82.2947)

Provenance: 1932 Galerie Paul Rosenberg, Paris ■ 1934 Henry P. McIlhenny, Philadelphia ■ 1939 Galerie Paul Rosenberg, Paris and New York ■ c. 1944 (?) Henry P. McIlhenny ■ 1950 (?) Buchholz Gallery ■ 1955 Nelson A. Rockefeller, New York ■ 1979 Gift of Nelson A. Rockefeller to the Museum of Modern Art, New York

Exhibitions (selected): 1931 Paris, Galerie Paul Rosenberg: *Pablo Picasso* ■ 1932 Paris, Galeries Georges Petit: *Exposition Picasso*, cat. 202 ■ 1937 London, Rosenberg & Helft: *Recent Works by Picasso*, cat. 2 ■ 1939/40 New York, The Museum of Modern Art: *Picasso: Forty Years of His Art*/ Chicago, Art Institute/St. Louis, City Art Museum/Boston, Museum of Fine Arts, cat. 238 ■ 1957 New York, The Museum of Modern Art: *Picasso. 75th Anniversary Exhibition*/Chicago, The Art Institute, p. 67 ■ 1960 London, The Arts Council of Great Britain/Tate Gallery: *Picasso*, cat. 125 ■ 1962 New York, Cooperating New York Galleries: *Picasso: An American Tribute*, cat. 1 (Perls Galleries) ■ 1966/67 Paris, Grand Palais: *Hommage à Pablo Picasso*, cat. 150 ■ 1970 Portland, Portland Art Museum: *Picasso for Portland*, cat. 29 ■ 1972 New York, The Museum of Modern Art: *Picasso in the Collection of the Museum of Modern Art*, p. 134 f. ■ 1980 New York, The Museum of Modern Art: *Pablo Picasso. A Retrospective*, p. 290 ■ 1992 Cleveland, Museum of Art: *Picasso and Things*/Philadelphia, Museum of Art/Paris, Galeries Nationales du Grand Palais, cat. 92 ■ 1998 Tokyo, The Bunkamura Museum of Art: *Pablo Picasso*/Nagoya, City Art Museum, cat. 74 ■ 2008/09 Rome, Complesso del Vittoriano: *Picasso Harlequin 1917–1937*, cat. 42

Selected literature: Zervos VII, no. 322 ■ Jean Cassou, *Picasso*, Paris 1940, p. 121 (Nature morte au pichet jaune) ■ Alfred H. Barr Jr., Picasso: *Fifty Years of his Art*, New York 1946, p. 168 ■ Frank Elgar, Robert Maillard, *Picasso*, Paris 1955, p. 284 ■ Roland Penrose, *Picasso. His Life and Work*, London 1958, plate XIII/7 ■ Hans L. C. Jaffé, *Pablo Picasso*, New York 1964, p. 124 f.

69
The Yellow Belt: Marie-Thérèse Walter, 1932
Oil on canvas
130 x 97 cm
Dated on the back: *6 Janvier M. CM. XXXII*
Courtesy Nahmad Collection, Switzerland

Cat. Zurich 205
Der gelbe Gürtel

Provenance: Paloma Picasso, Paris ■ Mr and Mrs Thomas Dittmer, Chicago ■ Mr and Mrs Klaus Perls, New York

Exhibitions (selected): 1932 Paris, Galeries Georges Petit: *Exposition Picasso*, cat. 208 (La ceinture jaune) ■ 1966/67 Paris, Grand Palais: *Hommage à Pablo Picasso*, cat. 154 ■ 1967 Amsterdam, Stedelijk Museum: *Picasso*, cat. 73 ■ 1985: Chicago, Richard Gray Gallery: *Picasso's Picassos*, cat. 25 ■ 1998 London, Helly Nahmad Gallery: *Picasso: Artist of the Century*, cat. 24 ■ 1999 Rotterdam, Kunsthal: *Picasso: Artist of the Century*, cat. 34 ■ 2001 London, Helly Nahmad Gallery: *Braque, Gris, Léger and Picasso: Cubism and Beyond*, cat. 44 ■ 2008 New York, Acquavella Galleries: *Picasso's Marie-Thérèse*, cat. 14

Selected literature: Zervos: VII, no. 357 (La ceinture jaune) ■ *Cahiers d'art*, year 7, 1932, p. 116 ■ Ron Kaal, *Respectable Populisme*, Kunsthal Rotterdam, Rotterdam 2003, p. 109

70
Sleeping Woman in a Mirror, 1932
Oil on wood
130 x 97 cm
Signed top left: Picasso
Date and title inscribed on the back: *14 janvier M. CM. XXXII*
Courtesy Nahmad Collection, Switzerland

Cat. Zurich 207
Schläferin vor dem Spiegel

Provenance: Pablo Picasso ■ 1965: Galerie Louise Leiris, Paris ■ Saidenberg Gallery, New York ■ Perls Gallery, New York

Exhibitions (selected): 1932 Paris, Galeries Georges Petit: *Exposition Picasso*, cat. 210 ■ 1998 London, Helly Nahmad Gallery: *Picasso: Artist of the Century*, cat. 25 ■ 1999 Rotterdam, Kunsthal: *Picasso: Artist of the Century*, cat. 33

Selected literature: Zervos: VII, no. 360 ■ *Cahiers d'art*, vol. 7, 1932, p. 98 ■ Maurice Gieure, *Initiation à l'œuvre de Picasso*, Paris 1951, no. 91 ■ Ulrich Weisner (ed.), *Picassos Surrealismus. Werke 1925–1937*, exh. cat., Kunsthalle Bielefeld, 1991, cat. 37 a

71
Repose, 1932
Oil on canvas
161.9 x 130.2 cm

Dated on the back: *22-1-XXXII*
The Steven and Alexandra Cohen Collection

Cat. Zurich 209
Ruhende

Provenance: Artist's estate ■ Private collection, France ■
Steven and Alexandra Cohen Collection, Connecticut

Exhibitions (selected): 1932 Paris, Galeries Georges Petit:
Exposition Picasso, cat. 220 ■ 1953 Rome, Galleria
Nazionale d'Arte Moderna: *Pablo Picasso*, cat. 72 ■ 1953
Milan, Palazzo Reale: *Pablo Picasso*, cat. 62 ■ 1996/97 New
York, Museum of Modern Art: *Picasso and Portraiture. Repre-
sentation and Transformation*/Paris, Grand Palais, p. 345 ff. ■
1999 Forth Worth, Kimbell Art Museum: *Matisse and Picasso:
A Gentle Rivalry*, cat. 61 ■ 2000/02 Vienna, Kunstforum:
*Picasso: Figur und Porträt. Hauptwerke aus der Sammlung
Bernard Picasso*/Tübingen, Kunsthalle, cat. 52 ■ 2004/05:
Malaga, Museo Picasso: *30 obras de Picasso*, cat. 13 ■ 2008
New York, Acquavella Galleries, *Picasso's Marie-Thérèse*,
cat. 13

Selected literature: Zervos: VII, no. 361 ■ Richardson: III,
p. 372, 466 f., 470, 479 ■ Brigitte Léal, Christine Pilot, Marie-
Laure Bernadac, *The Ultimate Picasso*, New York 2000,
no. 644 ■ Elizabeth Cowling, *Picasso. Style and Meaning*,
London/New York 2002, p. 490

72
Fruit Bowl and Guitar, 1932

Oil on canvas
97 x 130 cm
Signed top right: *Picasso*
Dated on the back: 11 Février XXXII
Courtesy Nahmad Collection, Switzerland

Cat. Zurich 213
Fruchtschale und Gitarre vor grauem Grund

Provenance: Galerie Simon, Paris ■ Galerie Louise Leiris,
Paris ■ Collection of Mme Bourdon, Paris

Exhibitions (selected): 1932 Paris, Galeries Georges Petit:
Exposition Picasso, cat. 214 (Compotier et guitare, fonds gris)
■ 1953 Milan, Palazzo Reale: *Picasso*, cat. 60 ■ 1999 Rotterdam, Kunsthal: *Picasso: Artist of the Century*, cat. 22

Selected literature: Zervos: VII, no. 354 ■ *Cahiers d'art*,
year 7, 1932, p. 145

73
Young Woman with Mandoline, 1932

Oil on wood
64.2 x 46.9 cm
Signed top right: *Picasso*
The University of Michigan Museum of Art
Gift of The Carey Walker Foundation

Cat. Zurich 206
Mädchen mit Gitarre

Provenance: Pablo Picasso ■ Herschel Carey Walker ■
1969 The Carey Walker Foundation ■ 1994 The University
of Michigan Museum of Art

Exhibitions (selected): 1932 Paris, Galeries Georges Petit:
Exposition Picasso, cat. 206 (La jeune fille à la guitare) ■
1996 Maine, Portland Museum of Art: *Picasso, Braque, Léger
and the Cubist Spirit 1919–1939*, p. 14 ■ 2008/09: Rom,
Complesso del Vittoriano: Picasso Harlequin 1917–1937,
p. 204 f.

Selected literature: Zervos: VII, Nr. 359 (Jeune fille à la
guitare) ■ Frank Elgar, Robert Maillard, *Picasso*, Paris 1955,
p. 265

74
Jester, 1905

Bronze
41 x 37 x 21 cm
Name on back and bottom centre: *Picasso*
Kunstmuseum Winterthur
Purchased with a jubilee donation from Werner Graf & Co.,
Winterthur, 1949

Cat. Zurich 227
Harlekin (different version)

Provenance: Werner Hiltbrunner, Aarau

Exhibitions (version at the Kunstmuseum Winterthur, selec-
tion): 1932 Paris, Galeries Georges Petit: *Exposition Picasso*,
cat. 225 (Arlequin, different version) ■ 1978 Berlin, National-
galerie: *Picasso und der Zirkus* ■ 1997/98 Washington,
National Gallery of Art: *Picasso. The Early Years, 1892–
1906*/Boston, Museum of Fine Arts, cat. 129 ■ 2001 Bern,
Kunstmuseum: *Picasso und die Schweiz. Meisterwerke aus
Schweizer Sammlungen*, cat. 25 ■ 2006 Baden, Museum
Langmatt: *Renoir, Cézanne, Picasso und ihr Galerist Ambroise
Vollard*, p. 113

Selected literature: Zervos: I, no. 322 (Tête de ›Fou‹) ■ Palau i Fabre: vol. 1881–1907, no. 1061 (Kopf des Narren) ■ Christian Zervos, 'Sculptures des peintres d'aujourd'hui', in: *Cahiers d'art*, year 3, 1928, no. 7, p. 287 ■ André Level, *Picasso*, Paris 1928, plate 54 ■ Alfred Barr Jr. (ed.), *Picasso: Forty Years of his Art*, exh. cat., The Museum of Modern Art New York/The Art Institute of Chicago, New York 1939, no. 32 ■ Carola Giedion-Welcker, *Plastik des XX. Jahrhunderts: Volumen- und Raumgestaltung*, Zurich 1955, p. 40 (version at the Kunstmuseum Winterthur) ■ Roland Penrose, *Picasso. His Life and Work*, London 1958, plate III/4 ■ Werner Spies, *Pablo Picasso. Das plastische Werk*, Teufen 1971, no. 4, p. 17f. ■ Jean Leymarie, *Picasso: Métamorphoses et unité*, Geneva 1971, p. 26 ■ Una E. Johnson, Ambroise Vollard, Éditeur: *Prints, Books, Bronzes*, New York 1977, no. 227 ■ Marilyn McCully (ed.), *Picasso. The Early Years, 1892–1906*, exh. cat., National Gallery of Art Washington/Museum of Fine Arts Boston, Washington 1997, no. 129 ■ *Picasso um 1905*, exh. cat., Kunsthalle Bielefeld, 1999, passim ■ Brigitte Léal, Christine Pilot, Marie-Laure Bernadac, *The Ultimate Picasso*, New York 2000, no. 175 (different version) ■ Werner Spies (ed.), *Picasso sculpteur*, exh. cat., Centre Georges Pompidou, Paris 2000, no. 4 ■ Markus Müller, *Der Künstler als Gaukler*, exh. cat., Graphikmuseum Pablo Picasso, Münster 2006, p. 9f. ■ Diana Widmaier Picasso, 'Vollard and the Sculpture of Picasso', in: *Cézanne to Picasso: Ambroise Vollard, Patron of the Avant-Garde*, exh. cat., The Metropolitan Museum of Art New York/Art Institute of Chicago/Musée d'Orsay Paris, New Haven/London 2006, pp. 182–188

75
Head of a Woman (Fernande), 1906

Bronze
41 x 24.5 x 25.5 cm
Name on rear at bottom: Picasso
Kunsthaus Zürich
Werner and Nelly Bär Collection

Cat. Zurich 228
Frauenbüste (different version)

Provenance: Ambroise Vollard ■ Galerie Flechtheim, Berlin ■ 1933 Werner und Nelly Bär Collection ■ 1968 Donation to Kunsthaus Zürich

Exhibitions (version at the Kunsthaus Zürich, selection): 1981 Ingelheim, Villa Schneider: *Pablo Picasso*, cat. 134 ■ 1981 Martigny, Fondation Pierre Gianadda: *Pablo Picasso*, cat. 138

■ 1992 Barcelona, Museu Picasso: *Picasso 1905–1906. Rosa Periode und Gósol*/Bern, Kunstmuseum, cat. 133 ■ 2006 Baden, Villa Langmatt: *Renoir, Cézanne, Picasso und ihr Galerist Ambroise Vollard*, p. 112

Selected literature: Zervos: I, no. 323 ■ Palau i Fabre: vol. 1881–1907, no. 1205 (Fernande) ■ Werner Spies, *Pablo Picasso. Das plastische Werk*, Teufen 1971, no. 6, p. 18ff. ■ Werner Spies, *Pablo Picasso. Das plastische Werk*, Ostfildern-Ruit 1983, no. 6 (version at the Kunsthaus Zürich) ■ Ursula Merkel, *Das plastische Porträt im 19. und frühen 20. Jahrhundert*, Berlin 1995, p. 284 (version at the Kunsthaus Zürich) ■ Brigitte Léal, Christine Pilot, Marie-Laure Bernadac, *The Ultimate Picasso*, New York 2000, no. 196 (different version) ■ Werner Spies (ed.), *Picasso sculpteur*, exh. cat., Centre Georges Pompidou, Paris 2000, no. 6 and p. 22f.

76
Woman Combing Her Hair, 1906

Bronze, patinated
42 x 31.2 x 29.2 cm
Name at bottom left: *Picasso*
Museum Ludwig Köln
Ludwig Donation 1994

Cat. Zurich 229
Figur

Provenance: Galerie Berggruen, Paris ■ Hanover Gallery, London ■ Galerie Rosengart, Lucerne ■ Until 1994 Peter and Irene Ludwig, Aachen

Exhibitions (version at the Museum Ludwig, selection): 1992/93 Barcelona, Museu Picasso: *Picasso. Colección Ludwig*/Cologne, Museum Ludwig/Nürnberg, Germanisches Nationalmuseum, cat. 9 ■ 2002 Chemnitz, Kunstsammlungen: *Picasso et les femmes*, p. 75 ■ 2005: Stuttgart, Staatsgalerie: *Picasso — Badende*, cat. 3

Selected literature: Zervos: I, no. 329 ■ Palau i Fabre: vol. 1881–1907, no. 1364 (Kniende Frau beim Kämmen) ■ André Level, *Picasso*, Paris 1928, p. 28, plate 55 ■ Werner Spies, *Pablo Picasso. Das plastische Werk*, Teufen 1971, no. 7, p. 18ff. ■ Werner Spies, *Pablo Picasso. Das plastische Werk*, Ostfildern-Ruit 1983, no. 7 ■ Wiliam Rubin (ed.), *Picasso and Portraiture. Representation and Transformation*, exh. cat., Museum of Modern Art New York/Grand Palais Paris, New York 1996, p. 264 ■ Brigitte Léal, Christine Pilot, Marie-Laure Bernadac, *The Ultimate Picasso*, New York 2000, no. 201 (different version)

BIBLIOGRAPHY

Bibliography

Brigitte Baer, *Picasso Peintre-Graveur* (continuation of the catalogues by Bernhard Geiser), vols. III–VIII, Bern 1986–1996

Georges Bloch, *Pablo Picasso. Katalog des graphischen Werkes,* vols. I–IV, Bern 1972–1979

Herschel Chipp and Alan Wofsky (eds.), *The Picasso Project. Picasso's Paintings, Watercolors, Drawings and Sculpture. A Comprehensive Illustrated Catalogue 1885–1973,* vols. I–XVII, San Francisco 1995–2008

[Daix/Boudaille]
Pierre Daix, Georges Boudaille, *Picasso 1900–1906. Catalogue raisonné de l'œuvre peint,* Neuchâtel 1966

[Daix/Rosselet]
Pierre Daix, Joan Rosselet, *Le Cubisme de Picasso. Catalogue raisonné de l'œuvre peint 1907–1916,* Neuchâtel 1979

Bernhard Geiser, *Picasso Peintre-Graveur,* vols. I–IV, Bern 1933 and 1968

Alberto Moravia, Paolo Lecaldano, *L'opera completa di Picasso blu e rosa,* Classici dell'Arte 22, Milan 1968

[Palau i Fabre: vol. 1881–1907]
Josep Palau i Fabre, *Picasso. Kindheit und Jugend eines Genies: 1881–1907,* Munich 1981 (Catalan orig. edit. *Picasso vivent 1881–1907,* Barcelona 1980)

[Palau i Fabre: vol. 1907–1917]
Josep Palau i Fabre, *Picasso. Der Kubismus: 1907–1917,* Cologne 1998 (Catalan orig. edit. *Picasso cubisme 1907–1917,* Barcelona 1990)

[Palau i Fabre: vol. 1917–1926]
Josep Palau i Fabre, *Picasso. Von den Balletts zum Drama: 1917–1926,* Cologne 1999 (Catalan orig. edit. *Picasso, de los ballets al drama 1917–1926,* Barcelona 1999)

Franco Russoli, Minervino Fiorello, *L'opera completa di Picasso cubista,* Classici dell'Arte 64, Milan 1972

[Zervos]
Christian Zervos, *Pablo Picasso,* vols. I–XXXIII., Paris 1932–1978

Literature on the 1932 exhibition at the Kunsthaus Zürich:

Michael FitzGerald, *Making Modernism: Picasso and the Creation of the Market for Twentieth-Century Art,* New York 1995

Christian Geelhaar, *Picasso. Wegbereiter und Förderer seines Aufstiegs 1899–1939,* Zurich 1993

Johannes Nathan, '…für Picasso mindestens 240 Meter…', in: *Picasso und die Schweiz. Meisterwerke aus Schweizer Sammlungen,* ed. by Marc Fehlmann and Toni Stooss, exh. cat. Kunstmuseum Bern, 2001, pp. 65–73

John Richardson, 'Paris and Zurich Retrospective (1932)', in: ibid., *A Life of Picasso. The Triumphant Years, 1917–1932,* vol. III, London 2007, pp. 473–490

Cahiers d'art, vol. 7, 1932

'Exposition d'œuvres de Picasso aux Galeries Georges Petit', in: *Cahiers d'art,* Numéro special, June 1932, p. 49

K. H. David, 'Picasso als Patient?' in: *Neue Zürcher Zeitung,* vol. 153, no. 2145, 18. November 1932, sheet 3

dt. [Georg Schmidt], 'Pablo Picasso. Im Zürcher Kunsthaus', I, in: *National-Zeitung,* vol. 90, no. 486, 18 October, p. 2f.; II, no. 488, 19 October, p. 2f; III, no. 492, 21 October 1932, p. 2

Berthold Fenigstein, 'Picasso im Kunsthaus', I, in: *Tages-Anzeiger,* vol. 40, no. 222, 21 September; II, no. 229, 29 September; III, no. 233, 4 October; IV, no. 241, 13 October 1932

S. Giedion, 'Über Picasso. Ist das Schaffen Picassos typisch bürgerlich-dekadent?', in: *Volksrecht,* vol. 35, no. 246, 19 October 1932

H. Gr. [Hans Graber], 'Picasso im Zürcher Kunsthaus', I, in: *Neue Zürcher Zeitung,* vol. 153, no. 1743, 22 September, sheet 1; II, no. 1811, 2 October, sheet 3; III, no. 1895, 13 October, sheet 6; IV, no 1997, 28 October, sheet 1; V, no. 2055, 5 November, sheet 2; VI, no. 2094, 10 November 1932, sheet 7

Reinhold Hohl, 'Picasso, Zürich und die C. G. Jung-Konservativen', in: *Tages-Anzeiger,* vol. 90, no. 30, 6/7 February 1982, p. 49f.

Gotthard Jedlicka, 'Matisse und Picasso', in: *Neue Zürcher Zeitung,* vol. 153, no. 1811, 2 October 1932, sheet 3

C. G. Jung, 'Picasso', in: *Neue Zürcher Zeitung,* vol. 153, no. 2107, 13 November 1932, sheet 2

H. O., 'Soll die Stadt der Picasso-Ausstellung finanzieren helfen?', in: *Volksrecht,* vol. 35, no. 239, 11 October 1932

r., 'Max Raphael über Picasso', in: *Neue Zürcher Zeitung,* vol. 153, no. 1855, 7 October 1932, sheet 6

r., 'Hans Hildebrandt über Picasso', in: *Neue Zürcher Zeitung,* vol. 153, no. 1905, 14 October 1932, sheet 9

r., 'Strawinsky und Picasso', in: *Neue Zürcher Zeitung,* vol. 153, no. 1952, 21 October 1932, sheet 6

r., 'Gotthard Jedlicka über Picasso', in: *Neue Zürcher Zeitung,* no. 2008, 29 October 1932, sheet 3

H. W., 'Picasso ein Drama', in: *Neue Zürcher Zeitung,* vol. 153, no. 2233, 30 November 1932, sheet 5

Hanns Welti, 'Picasso auf dem Zürichsee', in: *Neue Zürcher Zeitung,* vol. 153, no. 1693, 14 September 1932, sheet 6

Hanns Welti, 'Picasso in Zürich', in: *Sie und Er,* no. 39, 24 September 1932, p. 1021

wti. [Jakob Welti], 'Eröffnung der Picasso-Ausstellung', in: *Neue Zürcher Zeitung*, vol. 153, no. 1675, 12 September 1932, sheet 1

wti. [Jakob Welti], 'Aus dem Zürcher Kunsthaus', in: *Neue Zürcher Zeitung*, vol. 161, no. 468, 30 March 1940, sheet 2

Doris Wild, 'Begegnung mit Picasso', in: *Neue Zürcher Zeitung*, vol. 153, no. 1811, 2 October 1932, sheet 3

'C. G. Jung vergreift sich an Picasso', in: *Information*, Zürich, No. 6, December 1932, pp. 4–7

'C. G. Jung diagnostiziert Picasso', in: *Kunst und Künstler*, vol. 32, no. 1, January 1933, p. 28ff.

'Pablo Picasso in Zürich', in: *Zürcher Illustrierte*, vol. 8, no. 39, 23 September 1932, p. 1230

'Picasso étudié par le Dr Jung', in: *Cahiers d'art*, vol. 7, 1932 , nos. 8–10, p. 352ff.

Selected literature:

Felix A. Baumann, *Pablo Picasso — Leben und Werk*, Stuttgart 1976

Georges Boudaille, Marie-Laure Bernadac, Marie Pierre Gauthier, *Picasso*, Paris 1985

Wilhelm Boeck, *Picasso*, Stuttgart/Paris 1955

Brassaï, *Conversations avec Picasso*, Paris 1964 (German *Gespräche mit Picasso*, Reinbek bei Hamburg 1966)

André Breton, *Le surrealisme et la peinture*, Paris 1928

Pierre Cabanne, *Le siècle de Picasso*, 2 vols., Paris 1975

Pierre Cabanne, *Picasso — Pour le centenaire de sa naissance*, Neuchâtel 1981

Jean Cassou, *Picasso*, Paris 1940

Alexandre Cirici-Pellicer, *Picasso avant Picasso*, Geneva 1950

Elizabeth Cowling, *Picasso. Style and Meaning*, London/New York 2002

Elizabeth Cowling, *Visiting Picasso: The Notebooks and Letters of Roland Penrose*, London 2006

Eugeni d'Ors, *Pablo Picasso*, Paris 1930

Pierre Daix, *Picasso*, Paris 1964 (German *Picasso. Der Mensch und sein Werk*, Gütersloh 1973)

Pierre Daix, *La vie de peintre Pablo Picasso*, Paris 1977

Pierre Daix, *Le cubisme de Picasso*, Neuchâtel 1979

Pierre Daix, *Picasso créateur. La vie intime et l'œuvre*, Paris 1987

Pierre Daix, *Dictionnaire Picasso*, Paris 1995

Pierre Daix, *Pablo Picasso*, Paris 2007

Frank Elgar, Robert Maillard, *Picasso*, Paris 1955

Jack Flam, *Matisse and Picasso: The Story of their Rivalry and Friendship*, Cambridge, Mass., 2003

Lisa Florman, *Myth and Metamorphosis: Picasso's Classical Prints of the 1930s*, Cambridge 2000

Klaus Gallwitz, *Picasso Laureatus. Sein malerisches Werk seit 1954*, Lucerne/Munich 1971 (enlarged and improved edition *Picasso Laureatus. Die späten Jahre 1954–1973*, Zurich 1985)

Jean-Charles Gateau, *Éluard, Picasso et la peinture*, Geneva 1983

Maurice Gieure, *Initiation à l'œuvre de Picasso*, Paris 1951

Danièle Giraudy, *Picasso: la mémoire du regard*, Paris 1986 (German *Pablo Picasso. Die Bilanz eines schöpferischen Lebens*, Stuttgart/Zurich 1986)

László Glozer, *Picasso und der Surrealismus*, Cologne 1974

Hans Ludwig C. Jaffé, *Pablo Picasso*, Paris 1967

Gotthard Jedlicka, *Picasso*, Zurich 1934

Pepe Karmel, *Picasso and the Invention of Cubism*, Yale 2003

Helen Kay, *Picasso's World of Children*, New York 1964

Brigitte Léal, Christine Piot, Marie-Laure Bernadac, *The Ultimate Picasso*, New York 2000

Michel Leiris, *Un génie sans piédestal*, Paris 1992

Jean Leymarie, *Picasso: Métamorphoses et unité*, Geneva 1971

Marylin McCully, *A Picasso Anthology: Documents, Criticism, Reminiscences*, London 1981

María Teresa Ocaña (ed.), *Picasso: La formación de un genio/ The Development of a Genius 1890–1904*, Barcelona 1997

Roland Penrose, *Picasso. His Life and Work*, London 1958 (German *Leben und Werk*, Munich 1961)

Roland Penrose, John Golding (eds.), *Picasso in Retrospect*, New York 1973

Maurice Raynal, *Picasso*, Munich 1921

[Richardson: I]
John Richardson, *A Life of Picasso, 1881–1906*, vol. I, New York 1991 (German *Picasso. Leben und Werk, 1881–1906*, vol. I, Munich 1991)

[Richardson: II]
John Richardson, *A Life of Picasso, 1907–1917*, vol. II, New York 1996 (German *Picasso. Leben und Werk, 1907–1917*, vol. II, Munich 1997)

[Richardson: III]
John Richardson, *A Life of Picasso. The Triumphant Years, 1917–1932*, vol. III, London 2007

Jaime Sabartés, *Picasso. Gespräche und Erinnerungen*, Zurich 1956

Meyer Schapiro, *The Unity of Picasso's Art*, New York 2001

Gerd Schiff (ed.), *Picasso in Perspective*, New Jersey 1976

Gertrude Stein, *Picasso*, New York 1938 (German Zürich 1958)

Wilhelm Uhde, *Picasso et la tradition française*, Paris 1928

Gertje R. Utley, *Picasso: The Communist Years*, Yale 2000

Carsten-Peter Warncke, *Pablo Picasso, 1881–1973*, ed. by Ingo F. Walther, 2 vols., Cologne 1991

Selected exhibition catalogues:

New York/Chicago 1939/40
Picasso: Forty Years of his Art, ed. by Alfred Barr Jr., exh. cat. The Museum of Modern Art New York/The Art Institute of Chicago, New York 1939

New York 1946
Picasso: Fifty Years of his Art, ed. by Alfred Barr Jr., exp. edit. of exh. cat. *Picasso: Forty Years of his Art*, New York 1946

New York 1972
Picasso in the Museum of Modern Art, ed. by William Rubin, exh. cat. The Museum of Modern Art, New York 1972

Basel 1976
Picasso. Aus dem Museum of Modern Art und Schweizer Sammlungen, exh. cat. Kunstmuseum Basel, 1976

New York 1980
Pablo Picasso. A Retrospective, ed. by William Rubin, exh. cat. The Museum of Modern Art, New York 1980

Berlin/Düsseldorf 1983/84
Pablo Picasso. Das plastische Werk. Werkverzeichnis der Skulpturen, ed. by Werner Spies in collaboration with Christine Piot, exh. cat. Nationalgalerie Berlin/ Kunsthalle Düsseldorf, 2nd rev.and exp. edit., Ostfildern-Ruit 2002

Bern 1984/85
Der junge Picasso. Frühwerk und Blaue Periode, ed. by Jürgen Glaesemer, exh. cat. Kunstmuseum Bern, 1984

Bielefeld 1988
Picassos Klassizismus. Werke 1914–1934, ed. by Ulrich Weisner, exh. cat. Kunsthalle Bielefeld, Stuttgart 1988

Paris/Barcelona 1988
Pablo Picasso — Les Demoiselles d'Avignon, ed. by Hélène Seckel, exh. cat. Musée Picasso Paris/ Museu Picasso Barcelona, Paris 1988

New York/Basel 1989/90
Picasso and Braque. Pioneering Cubism, ed. by William Rubin, exh. cat. The Museum of Modern Art New York/Kunstmuseum Basel, New York 1989 (German *Picasso and Braque. Die Geburt des Kubismus*, Munich 1990)

Bielefeld 1991
Picassos Surrealismus. Werke 1925–1937, ed. by Ulrich Weisner, exh. cat. Kunsthalle Bielefeld, Stuttgart 1991

Barcelona/Berne 1992
Picasso 1905–1906. Rosa Periode und Gósol, exh. cat. Museu Picasso Barcelona/Kunstmuseum Bern, Barcelona 1992

Cleveland/Philadelphia/Paris 1992
Picasso & Things: The Still Lifes of Picasso, exh. cat. The Cleveland Museum of Art/The Philadelphia Museum of Art/Galeries Nationales du Grand Palais Paris, Cleveland 1992

London 1994
Picasso. Sculptor / Painter, ed. by Elizabeth Cowling and John Golding, exh. cat. Tate Gallery, London 1994

Los Angeles/New York/Chicago 1994/95
Picasso and the Weeping Women: The Years of Marie-Thérèse Walter and Dora Maar, ed. by Judy Freeman, exh. cat. Los Angeles County Museum of Art/The Metropolitan Museum of Art New York/The Art Institute of Chicago, Los Angeles 1994

Düsseldorf/Stuttgart 1995/96
Picassos Welt der Kinder, ed. by Werner Spies, exh. cat. Kunstsammlung Nordrhein-Westfalen Düsseldorf/Staatsgalerie Stuttgart, Munich 1995

New York/Paris 1996/97
Picasso and Portraiture. Representation and Transformation, ed. by William Rubin, exh. cat. The Museum of Modern Art New York/ Galerie Nationales du Grand Palais Paris, New York 1996 (French *Picasso et le portrait*, Paris 1996)

Paris 1997
Le miroir noir. Picasso, sources photographiques 1900–1928, ed. by Anne Baldassari, exh. cat. Musée Picasso Paris/Museum of Fine Arts Houston, Paris 1997 (engl. *Picasso and Photography: The Dark Mirror*, New York 1997)

Washington/Boston 1997
Picasso. The Early Years, 1892–1906, ed. by Marilyn McCully, exh. cat. National Gallery of Art Washington/Museum of Fine Arts, Boston, Washington 1997

Fort Worth 1999
Matisse and Picasso: A Gentle Rivalry, ed. by Yve-Alain Bois, exh. cat. Kimbell Art Gallery Fort Worth, Paris 1998

Venice 1998
Picasso 1917–1924. Le Voyage d'Italie, ed. by Jean Clair, exh. cat. Palazzo Grassi Venice, Milan 1998

San Francisco/New York 1998/99
Picasso and the War Years, 1937–1945, ed. by Stephen Nash and Robert Rosenblum, exh. cat. Museum of Fine Arts San Francisco/Solomon R. Guggenheim Museum New York, London 1998

Paris 2000
Picasso sculpteur, ed. by Werner Spies, exh. cat. Centre Georges Pompidou, Paris 2000

Hartford/Cleveland 2001
Picasso. The Artist's Studio, ed. by Michael FitzGerald, exh. cat. Wadsworth Atheneum Hartford/ The Cleveland Museum of Art, New Haven/London 2001

Berne 2001/02
Picasso und die Schweiz. Meisterwerke aus Schweizer Sammlungen, ed. by Marc Fehlmann and Toni Stooss, exh. cat. Kunstmuseum Bern, 2001

London/Paris/New York 2002/03
Matisse Picasso, exh. cat. Tate London/Galeries Nationales du Grand Palais Paris/The Museum of Modern Art New York, London 2002

PHOTO CREDITS

Riehen/Basel 2005
Picasso surreal, exh. cat. Fondation Beyeler Riehen/Basel, 2005

Madrid 2006
Picasso. Tradición y vanguardia, exh. cat. Museo Nacional del Prado/Museo Nacional Centro de Arte Reina Sofía, Madrid 2006 (English *Picasso. Tradition and Avant-Garde*, Madrid 2006)

New York/San Francisco/Minneapolis 2007
Picasso and American Art, ed. by Michael FitzGerald, exh. cat. Whitney Museum of American Art New York/San Francisco Museum of Modern Art/Walker Art Center Minneapolis 2007, New York 2006

Paris 2007
Picasso cubiste, exh. cat. Musée National Picasso, Paris 2007

New York 2008
Picasso's Marie-Thérèse, exh. cat. Acquavella Galleries, New York 2008

Paris 2008
Picasso et les maîtres, exh. cat. Galeries Nationales du Grand Palais/Musée du Louvre/Musée d'Orsay Paris/National Gallery London, Paris 2008

London 2009
Picasso: Challenging the Past, ed. by Elizabeth Cowling et al., exh. cat. National Gallery, London 2009

New York 2010
Picasso in the Metropolitan Museum of Art, exh. cat. The Metropolitan Museum of Art New York, New Haven/London 2010

Ann Arbor
© The University of Michigan Museum of Art/Photo: Patrick Young: p.177

Baltimore
The Baltimore Museum of Art: p.166

Barcelona
© Museu Picasso, Barcelona/Photo: Gasull Fotografia: p.55

Basel
Kunstmuseum Basel, Martin P. Bühler: pp.73, 106, 109, 113

Cincinnati
Cincinnati Art Museum: p.168

Cologne
Rheinisches Bildarchiv Köln: pp.117, 179

Detroit
© The Detroit Institute of Arts, USA/Bequest of Robert H. Tannahill/bridgemanart.com: p.51

Düsseldorf
© Kunstsammlung Nordrhein-Westfalen, Düsseldorf/Photo: Walter Klein, Düsseldorf: p.74

Hartford
© 2010. Wadsworth Atheneum Museum of Art/Art Resource, NY/Scala, Florence, fig. 2, p.144

Kurashiki
Ohara Museum of Art: p.126

London
© Tate, London 2010: pp.58, 67, 127

Los Angeles
© 2010. Digital Image Museum Associates/LACMA/Art Resource NY/Scala, Florence: p.118

Madrid
© Museo Thyssen-Bornemisza, Madrid. Photographer: Jose Loren: p.75

Malaga
Museo Picasso Malaga
© Eric Baudouin: p.119

Nagoya
Aichi Prefectural Museum of Art: p.52

New York
Solomon R. Guggenheim Museum, New York: pp.125, 171
© 2010. Digital image, The Museum of Modern Art, New York/Scala, Florence: p.18, pp.62, 63, 83, 86, 87, 105, 130, 162,
© 2010 The Pierpont Morgan Library: p.107
© bpk/The Metropolitan Museum of Art: pp.60, 161, 167

Paris
© Collection Centre Pompidou, Dist. RMN/All rights reserved: p.128/Béatrice Hatala: p.49, 50/Philippe Migeat: p.112
© RMN/Madeleine Coursaget: p.249
© RMN (Musée de l'Orangerie)/Hervé Lewandowski: pp.59, 116
© Roger-Viollet, Paris/bridgemanart.com: p.251

Philadelphia
Philadelphia Museum of Art, Photo by Lynn Rosenthal: p.65

Riehen/Basel
Fondation Beyeler, Riehen/Basel, Foto: Peter Schibli, Basel: p.131

Saint Louis
Saint Louis Art Museum: p.170

Sakura
Kawamura Memorial Museum of Art: p.160

Stockholm
Moderna Museet, Stockholm. pp.104, 164

Stuttgart
Staatsgalerie Stuttgart
© Photo: Staatsgalerie Stuttgart: pp.115, 165

Switzerland
© Courtesy Nahmad Collection, Switzerland: pp.56, 114, 120, 121, 169, 172, 173, 175

Tehran
Tehran Museum of Contemporary Art: p.159

Vevey
© Musée Jenisch Vevey; Photo: Claude Bornand, Lausanne: p.48

Vienna
Albertina, Vienna: p.64

Winterthur
Swiss Institute for Art Research, Zurich: Jean-Pierre Kuhn: p.178 (left)

Washington
Board of Trustees, National Gallery of Art, Washington, D. C.: p.124

Zurich
Estate of Hanny Fries, Zurich. Unknown photographer: p.17
© 2010 Kunsthaus Zürich. All rights reserved: pp.21–25, 95–101
Kunsthaus Zürich: pp.108, 110, 123, 178 (right)
Foundation E. G. Bührle Collection, Zurich: p.111
© Adrian Turel Foundation, Zurich: pp.12, 26, 76, 132, 134, 143

We have endeavoured to trace all copyright holders. Any copyright holders who have not been contacted by us are requested to contact Cécile Brunner at the Kunsthaus Zürich.

IMPRINT

This book is published to accompany the exhibition
PICASSO.
His First Museum Exhibition 1932

Kunsthaus Zürich
15 October 2010 to
30 January 2011

Exhibition
Conception: Tobia Bezzola in collaboration with Simonetta Fraquelli
Organisation, coordination:
Esther Braun-Kalberer
Insurance and transport:
Gerda Kram
Restoration: Hanspeter Marty

Publicity: Björn Quellenberg,
Kristin Steiner
Sponsorship: Monique Spaeti
Documentation: Cécile Brunner
Technical support: Robert Sulzer
and team

Catalogue
Published by: Zürcher Kunstgesellschaft, Kunsthaus Zürich
Editors: Tobia Bezzola, Esther
Braun-Kalberer, Simonetta
Fraquelli, Franziska Lentzsch
Research: Julia Burckhardt Bild,
Florence Isler-Gächter, Franziska
Lentzsch, Linda Schädler
Reproduction: Arthur Faust

© 2010 Kunsthaus Zürich, Prestel
Verlag, Munich · Berlin · London ·
New York
© Succession Picasso/ProLitteris,
Zürich; VG Bild-Kunst, Bonn 2010

Man Ray Pablo Picasso, 1933
(detail)
© Man Ray Trust, Paris/
ProLitteris, Zurich; VG Bild-Kunst,
Bonn 2010

Frontispiece and back cover trade
edition: Original poster
Kunsthaus Zürich – Pablo Picasso –
11. Sept.–30. Okt. 1932 Letterpress, 128 x 90.5 cm
© museum of design zurich, poster
collection/Photograph: Franz Xaver
Jaggy

p. 6 Picasso in Zurich
Photo from the magazine *Sie & Er*,
no. 39, 24 September 1932,
Archive Kunsthaus Zürich
p. 288 Three inseparable friends:
Picasso, his wife and their tenyear-old son make friends with a
dog
Photo from the magazine *Sie & Er*,
no. 39, 24 September 1932,
Archive Kunsthaus Zürich
p. 134 Picasso's wife Olga
with Lucie Turel-Welti on Lake
Zurich 1932
© Adrian Turel Foundation, Zurich

The Deutsche Nationalbibliothek
holds a record of this publication in
the Deutsche Nationalbibliografie;
detailed bibliographical data can
be found under http://dnb.d-nb.de.

Publisher:
Prestel Verlag, Munich
Part of Verlagsgruppe Random
House GmbH

Königinstrasse 9
80539 Munich
Germany
Tel. +49 (0) 89 24 29 08-300
Fax +49 (0) 89 24 29 08-335
www.prestel.de

Editorial direction: Anja Besserer
in collaboration with Stefanie
Eckmann
Project management: Buchwerk |
Victoria Salley, Munich
Translation from the German:
John Sykes, Cologne
Copy editing: Jane Michael,
Munich
Cover draught, layout concept:
SOFAROBOTNIK,
Augsburg & Munich
Design and layout:
Saskia Helena Kruse, Potsdam
Production: Simone Zeeb,
Andrea Cobré
Art direction: Cilly Klotz
Reproduction: Kunsthaus Zürich,
Reproline mediateam
Typesetting: Vornehm Mediengestaltung, Munich
Font: Galaxie Polaris
Paper: 150 g/qm Primaset
Printing and binding: Mohn Media,
Gütersloh

Museum edition:
ISBN 978-3-906574-66-0
(German),
ISBN 978-3-906574-67-7
(French),
ISBN 978-3-906574-68-4
(English)
Book trade edition:
ISBN 978-3-7913-5068-4
(German),
ISBN 978-3-7913-5070-7
(French),
ISBN 978-3-7913-5069-1
(English)

FSC
Mix
Produktgruppe aus vorbildlich
bewirtschafteten Wäldern und
anderen kontrollierten Herkünften
Zert.-Nr. SGS-COC-001425
www.fsc.org
© 1996 Forest Stewardship Council

Printed in Germany

Supported by

CREDIT SUISSE

Partner of the Kunsthaus Zürich

and the Truus and Gerrit
van Riemsdijk Foundation

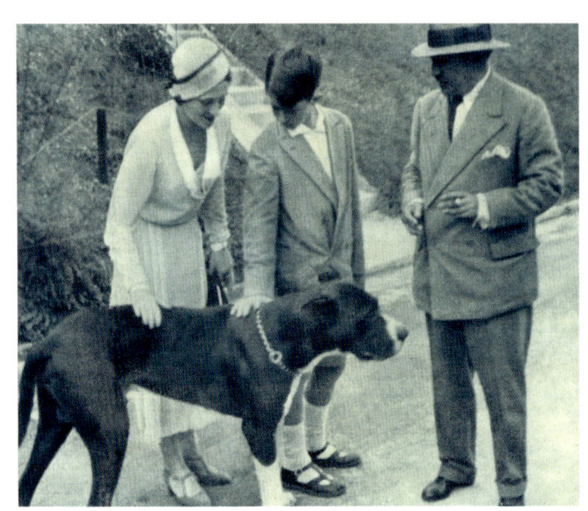